In this table, in which all amounts are in billions of dollars, we see historical data for the various components of nominal GDP. These are given in the first four columns. We then show the rest of the national income accounts going from GDP to NDP to NI to PI to DPI. The last column gives real GDP.

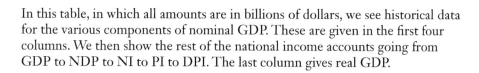

	The Sum of These Expenditures				Equals	Less	Equals	Plus	Less	Equals	Less			Plus	Equals	Less	Equals	
Year	Personal Consumption Expenditures	Gross Private Domestic Investment	Government Purchases of Goods and Services	Net Exports	Gross Domestic Product	Depreciation	Net Domestic Product	Net U.S. Income Earned Abroad	Indirect Business Taxes and Transfers and Other Adjustments	National Income	Undistributed Corporate Profits	Social Security Taxes	Corporate Income Taxes	Transfer Payments and Net Interest Earnings	Personal Income	Personal Income Taxes and Nontax Payments	Disposable Personal Income	Real GDP (2005 Dollars)
1988	3353.6	821.6	1039.0	−110.4	5103.8	611.0	4492.8	23.6	−33.0	4549.4	155.1	361.5	141.6	362.5	4253.7	505.0	3748.7	7607.4
1989	3598.5	874.9	1099.1	−88.2	5484.4	651.5	4832.9	26.2	32.5	4826.6	121.5	385.2	146.1	414.0	4587.8	566.1	4021.7	7879.2
1990	3839.9	861.0	1180.2	−78.0	5803.1	691.2	5111.9	34.8	57.6	5089.1	120.0	410.1	145.4	465.0	4878.6	592.8	4285.8	8027.1
1991	3986.1	802.9	1234.4	−27.5	5995.9	724.4	5271.5	30.4	74.0	5227.9	138.0	430.2	138.6	529.9	5051.0	586.7	4464.3	8008.3
1992	4235.3	864.8	1271.0	−33.2	6337.9	744.4	5593.5	29.7	110.4	5512.8	159.5	455.0	148.7	612.4	5362.0	610.6	4751.4	8280.0
1993	4477.9	953.4	1291.2	−65.0	6657.5	778.0	5879.5	31.9	138.0	5773.4	169.7	477.4	171.0	603.2	5558.5	646.6	4911.9	8516.2
1994	4743.3	1097.1	1325.5	−93.6	7072.3	819.2	6253.1	26.2	157.0	6122.3	199.4	508.2	193.1	620.9	5842.5	690.7	5151.8	8863.1
1995	4975.8	1144.0	1369.2	−91.4	7397.6	869.5	6528.1	35.8	110.0	6453.9	243.9	532.8	217.8	692.9	6152.3	744.1	5408.2	9086.0
1996	5256.8	1240.3	1416.0	−96.2	7816.9	912.5	6904.4	35.0	99.3	6840.1	272.3	555.1	231.5	739.4	6520.6	832.1	5688.5	9425.8
1997	5547.4	1389.8	1468.7	−101.6	8304.3	963.8	7340.5	33.0	81.3	7292.2	308.2	587.2	245.4	763.7	6915.1	926.3	5988.8	9845.9
1998	5879.5	1509.1	1518.3	−159.9	8747.0	1020.5	7726.5	21.3	−5.0	7752.8	212.6	624.7	248.4	755.9	7423.0	1027.1	6395.9	10274.7
1999	6342.8	1641.5	1631.3	−262.1	9353.5	1094.4	8259.1	33.8	−65.1	8358.0	260.1	661.4	258.8	733.1	7910.8	1107.5	6803.3	10770.7
2000	6830.4	1772.2	1731.0	−382.1	9951.5	1184.3	8767.2	39.0	−132.7	8938.9	176.3	705.8	265.1	767.7	8559.4	1232.2	7327.2	11216.4
2001	7148.8	1661.9	1846.4	−371.0	10286.1	1256.2	9029.9	43.6	−111.7	9185.2	210.0	733.2	203.3	844.6	8883.3	1234.8	7648.5	11337.5
2002	7439.2	1647.0	1983.3	−427.2	10642.3	1305.0	9337.3	30.7	−40.5	9408.5	280.6	751.5	192.3	876.0	9060.1	1050.4	8009.7	11543.1
2003	7804.0	1729.7	2112.6	−504.1	11142.2	1354.1	9788.1	68.1	16.0	9840.2	309.2	778.9	243.8	869.8	9378.1	1000.3	8377.8	11836.4
2004	8270.6	1968.6	2232.8	−618.7	11853.3	1432.8	10420.5	53.7	−59.8	10534.0	390.5	827.3	306.1	927.1	9937.2	1047.8	8889.4	12246.9
2005	8803.5	2172.3	2369.9	−722.7	12623.0	1541.4	11081.6	68.5	−123.7	11273.8	486.4	872.7	412.4	983.6	10485.9	1208.6	9277.3	12623.0
2006	9301.0	2327.1	2518.4	−769.3	13377.2	1660.7	11716.5	58.0	−256.7	12031.2	430.3	921.8	473.3	1062.3	11268.1	1352.4	9915.7	12958.5
2007	9772.3	2295.2	2674.2	−713.0	14028.7	1767.5	12261.2	64.4	−122.6	12448.2	270.7	959.5	445.5	1139.8	11912.3	1488.7	10423.6	13206.4
2008	10035.5	2087.6	2878.1	−709.7	14291.5	1854.1	12437.4	141.9	131.1	12448.2	152.5	987.3	309.0	1460.8	12460.2	1107.6	11024.5	13161.9
2009	9866.1	1546.8	2917.5	−391.4	13939.0	1866.2	12072.8	152.3	77.5	12147.6	469.6	964.1	272.4	1488.7	11930.2	1141.4	10788.8	12703.1
2010	10245.5	1795.1	3002.8	−516.9	14526.5	1874.9	12651.6	189.4	0.9	12840.1	651.7	986.8	411.1	1583.0	12373.5	1193.8	11179.7	13088.0
2011ᵃ	10726.0	1916.2	3030.6	−578.7	15094.1	1950.0	13144.1	192.3	−100.9	13437.3	677.2	920.1	453.2	1618.5	13005.3	1449.1	11556.2	13315.1
2012ᵃ	10915.3	1954.0	3439.8	−602.2	15706.9	2029.2	13677.7	198.3	−106.8	13982.8	704.7	957.5	471.6	1684.2	13533.3	1507.9	12025.4	13597.4
2013ᵃ	11211.5	2033.3	3726.6	−626.7	16344.7	2111.6	14233.1	205.6	−111.9	14550.6	733.3	996.3	490.7	1752.6	14082.8	1569.2	12513.6	13858.5

ᵃAuthor's estimates.

*Note: Some notes may not add up due to rounding.

Macroeconomics
for Professor Paul Graf's ECON 202

Fourth Custom Edition for Indiana University

Taken from:
Economics Today: The Macro View, Seventeenth Edition
by Roger LeRoy Miller

Macroeconomics, Fourth Edition
by R. Glenn Hubbard and Anthony Patrick O'Brien

Cover Photo: Courtesy of Photodisc/Getty Images.

Taken from:

Economics Today: The Macro View, Seventeenth Edition
by Roger LeRoy Miller
Copyright © 2014, 2012, 2011, 2010, 2008, 2006 by Pearson Education, Inc.
Published by Addison-Wesley
Boston, Massachusetts 02116

Macroeconomics, Fourth Edition
by R. Glenn Hubbard and Anthony Patrick O'Brien
Copyright © 2013, 2011, 2010, 2009, 2008, 2006 by Pearson Education, Inc.
Published by Prentice Hall
Upper Saddle River, New Jersey 07458

This special edition published in cooperation with Pearson Learning Solutions.

Credits and acknowledgments borrowed from other sources and reproduced, with permission, in this textbook beginning on page xi.

Microsoft and/or its respective suppliers make no representations about the suitability of the information contained in the documents and related graphics published as part of the services for any purpose. All such documents and related graphics are provided "as is" without warranty of any kind. Microsoft and/or its respective suppliers hereby disclaim all warranties and conditions with regard to this information, including all warranties and conditions of merchantability, whether express, implied or statutory, fitness for a particular purpose, title and non-infringement. In no event shall Microsoft and/or its respective suppliers be liable for any special, indirect or consequential damages or any damages whatsoever resulting from loss of use, data or profits, whether in an action of contract, negligence or other tortious action, arising out of or in connection with the use or performance of information available from the services.

The documents and related graphics contained herein could include technical inaccuracies or typographical errors. Changes are periodically added to the information herein. Microsoft and/or its respective suppliers may make improvements and/or changes in the product(s) and/or the program(s) described herein at any time. Partial screen shots may be viewed in full within the software version specified.

Microsoft® and Windows® are registered trademarks of the Microsoft Corporation in the U.S.A. and other countries. This book is not sponsored or endorsed by or affiliated with the Microsoft Corporation.

All trademarks, service marks, registered trademarks, and registered service marks are the property of their respective owners and are used herein for identification purposes only.

Pearson Learning Solutions, 501 Boylston Street, Suite 900, Boston, MA 02116
A Pearson Education Company
www.pearsoned.com

Printed in the United States of America

1 2 3 4 5 6 7 8 9 10 V056 18 17 16 15 14 13

000200010271802156

ML

ISBN 10: 1-269-42066-6
ISBN 13: 978-1-269-42066-2

Brief Contents

---

* Additional Readings taken from: *Macroeconomics*, Fourth Edition by Glenn Hubbard and Anthony Patrick O'Brien.

Contents

MODULE 1 Three Basic Macroeconomic Variables

MODULE 2 Basic Macroeconomic Models

MODULE 5 International Economics

INTERNATIONAL POLICY EXAMPLE
Poland's Floating Exchange Rate Protects It from Euro Ills 299

INTERNATIONAL EXAMPLE
The Most Traded Currencies in Foreign Exchange Markets 295

---

* Additional Readings taken from: *Macroeconomics*, Fourth Edition by Glenn Hubbard and Anthony Patrick O'Brien.

Acknowledgments

I am the most fortunate of economics textbook writers, for I receive the benefit of literally hundreds of suggestions from those of you who use *Economics Today*. Some professors have been asked by my publisher to participate in a more detailed reviewing process of this edition. I list them below. I hope that each one of you so listed accepts my sincere appreciation for the fine work that you have done.

Hamilton Galloway, *College of Western Idaho*
Frank Garland, *TriCounty Technical College*
Reza G. Hamzaee, *Missouri Western State University*
Ricot Jean, *Valencia College*
Richard W. Kreissle, *Landmark College*
James M. Leaman, *Eastern Mennonite University*
Dr. Larry Olanrewaju, *John Tyler Community College*
Benny E. Overton, *Vance/Granville Community College*

Elizabeth Patch, *Broome Community College*
Van Thi Hong Pham, *Salem State University*
Leila Angelica Rodemann, *Trident Technical College*
Lewis Sage, *Baldwin-Wallace College*
Jonathan Silberman, *Oakland University*
Brian Sommer, *Lynn University*
Manjuri Talukdar, *Northern Illinois University*
Ethel C. Weeks, *Nassau Community College*

I also thank the reviewers of previous editions:

Rebecca Abraham
Cinda J. Adams
Esmond Adams
John Adams
Bill Adamson
Carlos Aguilar
John R. Aidem
Mohammed Akacem
Ercument Aksoy
M. C. Alderfer
John Allen
Ann Al-Yasiri
Charles Anderson
Leslie J. Anderson
Fatma W. Antar
Len Anyanwu
Rebecca Arnold
Mohammad Ashraf
Ali A. Ataiifar
Aliakbar Ataiifar
Leonard Atencio
John Atkins
Glen W. Atkinson
Thomas R. Atkinson
James Q. Aylesworth
John Baffoe-Bonnie
Kevin Baird
Maurice B. Ballabon
Charley Ballard
G. Jeffrey Barbour
Robin L. Barlett
Daniel Barszcz
Kari Battaglia
Robert Becker
Charles Beem
Glen Beeson
Bruce W. Bellner
Daniel K. Benjamin
Emil Berendt
Charles Berry
Abraham Bertisch
John Bethune
R. A. Blewett
Scott Bloom
John Bockino
M. L. Bodnar
Mary Bone
Karl Bonnhi

Thomas W.
    Bonsor
John M. Booth
Wesley F. Booth
Thomas
    Borcherding
Melvin Borland
Tom Boston
Barry Boyer
Maryanna
    Boynton
Ronald Brandolini
Fenton L.
    Broadhead
Elba Brown
William Brown
Michael Bull
Maureen Burton
Conrad P.
    Caligaris
Kevin Carey
James Carlson
Robert Carlsson
Dancy R. Carr
Scott Carson
Doris Cash
Thomas H. Cate
Richard J. Cebula
Catherine
    Chambers
K. Merry
    Chambers
Richard Chapman
Ronald Cherry
Young Back Choi
Marc Chopin
Carol Cies
Joy L. Clark
Curtis Clarke
Gary Clayton
Marsha Clayton
Dale O.
    Cloninger
Warren L. Coats
Ed Coen
Pat Conroy
James Cox
Stephen R. Cox

Eleanor D. Craig
Peggy Crane
Jerry Crawford
Patrick M. Crowley
Joanna Cruse
John P. Cullity
Will Cummings
Thomas Curtis
Margaret M.
    Dalton
Andrew J. Dane
Mahmoud Davoudi
Diana Denison
Edward Dennis
Julia G. Derrick
Sowjanya
    Dharmasankar
Carol Dimamro
William Dougherty
Barry Duman
Diane Dumont
Floyd Durham
G. B. Duwaji
James A. Dyal
Ishita Edwards
Robert P. Edwards
Alan E. Ellis
Miuke Ellis
Steffany Ellis
Frank Emerson
Carl Enomoto
Zaki Eusufzai
Sandy Evans
John L. Ewing-
    Smith
Frank Falero
Frank Fato
Abdollah Ferdowsi
Grant Ferguson
Victoria L. Figiel
Mitchell Fisher
David Fletcher
James Foley
John Foreman
Diana Fortier
Ralph G. Fowler
Arthur Friedberg
Peter Frost

Timothy S. Fuerst
Tom Fullerton
E. Gabriel
James Gale
Byron Gangnes
Peter C. Garlick
Steve Garner
Neil Garston
Alexander Garvin
Joe Garwood
Doug Gehrke
Robert Gentenaar
J. P. Gilbert
Otis Gilley
Frank Glesber
Jack Goddard
Michael G. Goode
Allen C. Goodman
Richard J.
    Gosselin
Paul Graf
Anthony J. Greco
Edward
    Greenberg
Gary Greene
Peter A.
    Groothuis
Philip J. Grossman
Nicholas Grunt
William Gunther
Kwabena Gyimah-
    Brempong
Demos Hadjiyanis
Martin D. Haney
Mehdi Haririan
Ray Harvey
Michael J.
    Haupert
E. L. Hazlett
Sanford B.
    Helman
William
    Henderson
Robert Herman
Gus W. Herring
Charles Hill
John M. Hill
Morton Hirsch

Benjamin
    Hitchner
Charles W.
    Hockert
R. Bradley
    Hoppes
James Horner
Grover Howard
Nancy Howe-
    Ford
Yu-Mong Hsiao
Yu Hsing
James Hubert
George Hughes
Joseph W. Hunt
    Jr.
Scott Hunt
John Ifediora
R. Jack Inch
Christopher Inya
Tomotaka
    Ishimine
E. E. Jarvis
Parvis Jenab
Allan Jenkins
John Jensel
Mark Jensen
S. D. Jevremovic
J. Paul Jewell
Nancy
    Jianakoplos
Frederick
    Johnson
David Jones
Lamar B. Jones
Paul A. Joray
Daniel A. Joseph
Craig Justice
M. James Kahiga
Septimus Kai Kai
Devajyoti Kataky
Timothy R. Keely
Ziad Keilany
Norman F. Keiser
Brian Kench
Randall G.
    Kesselring
Alan Kessler

E. D. Key
Saleem Khan
M. Barbara Killen
Bruce Kimzey
Terrence Kinal
Philip G. King
E. R. Kittrell
David Klingman
Charles Knapp
Jerry Knarr
Tori Knight
Faik Koray
Janet Koscianski
Dennis Lee Kovach
Marie Kratochvil
Peter Kressler
Paul J. Kubik
Michael Kupilik
Margaret Landman
Richard LaNear
Larry Landrum
Keith Langford
Theresa Laughlin
Anthony T. Lee
Jim Lee
Loren Lee
Bozena Leven
Donald Lien
George Lieu
Stephen E. Lile
Lawrence W.
    Lovick
Marty Ludlum
Laura Maghoney
G. Dirk Mateer
Robert McAuliffe
James C. McBrearty
Howard J. McBride
Bruce McClung
John McDowell
E. S. McKuskey
James J. McLain
Kevin McWoodson
John L. Madden
Mary Lou Madden
John Marangos
Dan Marburger
Glen Marston

John M. Martin
Paul J. Mascotti
James D. Mason
Paul M. Mason
Tom Mathew
Warren Matthews
Akbar Marvasti
Pete
   Mavrokordatos
Fred May
G. Hartley Mellish
Mike Melvin
Diego Mendez-
   Carbajo
Dan C.
   Messerschmidt
Michael Metzger
Herbert C.
   Milikien
Joel C. Millonzi
Glenn Milner
Daniel Mizak
Khan Mohabbat
Thomas Molloy
William H. Moon
Margaret D. Moore
William E. Morgan
Stephen Morrell
Irving Morrissett
James W. Moser
Thaddeaus
   Mounkurai
Martin F. Murray
Densel L. Myers
George L. Nagy

Solomon Namala
Ronald M. Nate
Jerome Neadly
James E. Needham
Claron Nelson
Douglas Nettleton
William Nook
Gerald T. O'Boyle
Greg Okoro
Richard E. O'Neill
Lucian T. Orlowski
Diane S. Osborne
Joan Osborne
Melissa A Osborne
James O'Toole
Jan Palmer
Zuohong Pan
Gerald Parker
Ginger Parker
Randall E. Parker
Mohammed
   Partapurwala
Kenneth Parzych
Norm Paul
Wesley Payne
Raymond A. Pepin
Martin M. Perline
Timothy Perri
Jerry Petr
Maurice Pfannesteil
James Phillips
Raymond J. Phillips
I. James Pickl
Bruce Pietrykowski
Dennis Placone

Mannie Poen
William L.
   Polvent
Robert Posatko
Greg Pratt
Leila J. Pratt
Steven Pressman
Rick Pretzsch
Reneé Prim
Robert E.
   Pulsinelli
Rod D. Raehsler
Kambriz Raffiee
Sandra Rahman
Jaishankar Raman
John Rapp
Richard Rawlins
Gautam
   Raychaudhuri
Ron Reddall
Mitchell Redlo
Charles Reichhelu
Robert S. Rippey
Charles Roberts
Ray C. Roberts
Richard Romano
Judy Roobian-
   Mohr
Duane Rosa
Richard Rosenberg
Larry Ross
Barbara Ross-
   Pfeiffer
Marina Rosser
Philip Rothman

John Roufagalas
Stephen Rubb
Henry Ryder
Basel Saleh
Patricia Sanderson
Thomas N. Schaap
William A.
   Schaeffer
William Schamoe
David Schauer
A. C. Schlenker
David Schlow
Scott J. Schroeder
William Scott
Dan Segebarth
Paul Seidenstat
Swapan Sen
Augustus
   Shackelford
Richard Sherman
   Jr.
Liang-rong Shiau
Gail Shields
David Shorow
Vishwa Shukla
R. J. Sidwell
David E. Sisk
Alden Smith
Garvin Smith
Howard F. Smith
Lynn A. Smith
Phil Smith
William Doyle
   Smith
Lee Spector

George Spiva
Richard L. Sprinkle
Alan Stafford
Amanda Stallings-Wood
Herbert F. Steeper
Diane L. Stehman
Columbus Stephens
William Stine
Allen D. Stone
Osman Suliman
J. M. Sullivan
Rebecca Summary
Terry Sutton
Joseph L. Swaffar
Thomas Swanke
Frank D. Taylor
Daniel Teferra
Lea Templer
Gary Theige
Dave Thiessen
Robert P. Thomas
Deborah Thorsen
Richard Trieff
George Troxler
William T. Trulove
William N. Trumbull
Arianne K. Turner
Kay Unger
Anthony Uremovic
John Vahaly
Jim Van Beek
David Van Hoose
Lee J. Van Scyoc
Roy Van Til
Sharmila Vishwasrao

Craig Walker
Robert F. Wallace
Henry C. Wallich
Milledge Weathers
Ethel Weeks
Roger E. Wehr
Robert G. Welch
Terence West
James Wetzel
Wylie Whalthall
James H. Wheeler
Everett E. White
Michael D. White
Mark A. Wilkening
Raburn M. Williams
James Willis
George Wilson
Travis Wilson
Mark Wohar
Ken Woodward
Tim Wulf
Peter R. Wyman
Whitney Yamamura
Donald Yankovic
Alex Yguado
Paul Young
Shik Young
Mohammed Zaheer
Ed Zajicek
Charles Zalonka
Sourushe Zandvakili
Paul Zarembka
George K. Zestos
William J. Zimmer
   Jr.

As always, a revision of *Economics Today* requires me to put in the latest data at the last minute. If I did not have such an incredible editorial and production team, I wouldn't be able to do so. I do have a fantastic team both at the publisher—Pearson—and at our production house—Nesbitt (Cenveo Publisher Services), working through them with my long-time Production Manager, John Orr of Orr Book Services. He again did a terrific job. I was fortunate to once more have Kathryn Dinovo, Senior Production Project Manager at Pearson, lead the production team to as perfect a textbook as possible. To be sure, I was pushed hard by my long-time Senior Acquisitions Editor, Noel Seibert, and I was helped greatly by Carolyn Terbush, the Senior Editorial Project Manager on this project. The "pushing" all makes sense now.

I am greatly pleased with the design revision created by Jerilyn Bockorick of Nesbitt Graphics. It is always a challenge to keep the traditional feel of this book, yet make it more exciting for today's students. I think that she succeeded. I am appreciative of the hard work my copy editor, Bonnie Boehme, did. And, of course, the proofreader *par excellence*, Pat Lewis, made sure that everything was perfect. As for the supplements for this edition, I wish to thank the team at Nesbitt for producing them for students and professors. On the marketing side, I appreciate the fine work performed by Lori DeShazo and Kim Lovato.

The online media materials, particularly great improvements in *MyEconLab*, were accomplished by Melissa Honig, Noel Lotz, and Courtney Kamauf.

Jim Lee of Texas A&M University–Corpus Christi, Ercument Aksoy of Los Angeles Valley College, and Fatma Antar of Manchester Community College undertook the vast job of revising and improving the three test banks. David Van Hoose of Baylor University continued to create an accurate *Study Guide*. The *Instructor's Manual* was masterfully revised by Jim Lee of Texas A&M University–Corpus Christi. PowerPoint presentations were updated and improved by Debbie Evercloud of the University of Colorado–Denver. Rick Pretzsch of Lonestar College–Cyfair provided the clicker PowerPoint slides.

As always, my "super reviewer," Professor Dan Benjamin of Clemson University, really kept me honest this time around. And, as always, my long-time assistant, Sue Jasin, did enough typing and retyping to fill a room with paper. I welcome comments and ideas from professors and students alike and hope that you enjoy this latest edition of *Economics Today*.

R. L. M.

Credits

Cover images: Solar power panel array, S.R. Lee Photo Traveller/Shutterstock; Woman riding a bicycle in Vietnam, MJ Prototype/Shutterstock; Eye chart test, Pinkcandy/Shutterstock; Plant sample, Chepko Danil Vitalevich/Shutterstock; Bags in warehouse in shop, Mikhail Zahranichny/Shutterstock; Apple on stack of books and laptop computer, Andreka Photography/Shutterstock; Crowd at a music concert, Alexey Lysenko/Shutterstock; Goalman on the stadium field, Andrey Yurlov/Shutterstock

FRED® is a registered trademark and the FRED® logo and ST. LOUIS FED are trademarks of the Federal Reserve Bank of St Louis, http://research.stlouisfed.org/fred2/

Chapter 1	Rick Bowmer/AP Images	3, 23
Chapter 2	Kin Cheung/AP Images	25, 44
Chapter 3	Filmfoto/Alamy	51, 70
Chapter 4	Shutterstock	85, 98
Chapter 5	Dario Cantatore	104, 120
Chapter 6	Mark Ralston/Newscom	134, 156
Chapter 7	Bloomberg/Getty Images, Everett Collection	168, 174
Chapter 8	Mark Duncan/AP Images	185, 197
Chapter 9	AP Images	206, 220
Chapter 10	David R. Frazier Photolibrary/Alamy	227, 248
Chapter 11	Susan Walsh/AP Images	254, 271
Chapter 12	Fotolia	283, 300

Module 1

Three Basic
Macroeconomic Variables

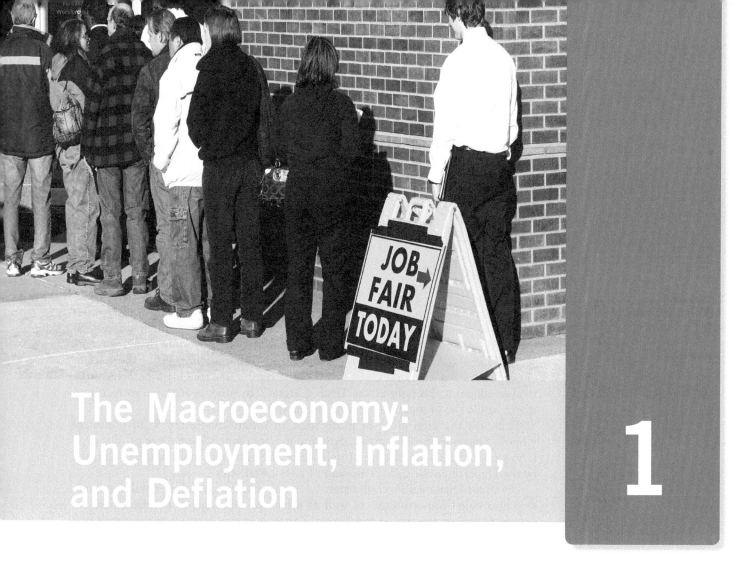

The Macroeconomy: Unemployment, Inflation, and Deflation

1

LEARNING OBJECTIVES

After reading this chapter, you should be able to:

▶ Explain how the U.S. government calculates the official unemployment rate

▶ Discuss the types of unemployment

▶ Describe how price indexes are calculated and define the key types of price indexes

▶ Distinguish between nominal and real interest rates

▶ Evaluate who loses and who gains from inflation

▶ Understand key features of business fluctuations

MyEconLab helps you master each objective and study more efficiently. See end of chapter for details.

At one time, a person who qualified for *unemployment benefits*—monthly payments that are coordinated by a U.S. government insurance program financed by taxes on employers—was eligible to receive benefits for no longer than 26 weeks. Since 2009, however, Congress has used general taxpayer funds to extend the duration of unemployment benefits. Thus, most people who qualify for such benefits are eligible to receive them for as long as 99 weeks. A number of economists have suggested that this policy change has resulted in at least 600,000 and perhaps even more than 4 million additional jobless people at any given time. In this chapter, you will learn how economists define unemployment. In addition, you will study concepts that will help you understand how extending unemployment benefits may have contributed to higher measured unemployment.

between 2008 and 2010, the number of people gainfully employed in the United States declined by nearly 9 million? Since then, more than 2 million of these people have found new jobs. Nevertheless, in excess of 6 million people who had jobs in 2008 were still not employed in 2013. Some of these people have given up looking for work, but most are classified by economists as *unemployed*—looking for positions, but so far unable to obtain jobs.

Trying to understand determinants of unemployment and of the overall performance of the national economy is a central objective of macroeconomics. This branch of economics seeks to explain and predict movements in the average level of prices, unemployment, and the total production of goods and services. This chapter introduces you to these key issues of macroeconomics.

Unemployment

Unemployment
The total number of adults (aged 16 years or older) who are willing and able to work and who are actively looking for work but have not found a job.

Unemployment is normally defined as the number of adults who are actively looking for work but do not have a job. Unemployment is costly in terms of lost output for the entire economy. One estimate indicates that at the end of the first decade of the twenty-first century, when the unemployment rate rose by more than 4 percentage points and firms were operating below 80 percent of their capacity, the amount of output that the economy lost due to idle resources was roughly 5 percent of the total production throughout the United States. (In other words, we were somewhere inside the production possibilities curve.)

That was the equivalent of more than an inflation-adjusted $700 billion of schools, houses, restaurant meals, cars, and movies that *could have been* produced. It is no wonder that policymakers closely watch the unemployment figures published by the Department of Labor's Bureau of Labor Statistics.

On a more personal level, the state of being unemployed often results in hardship and failed opportunities as well as a lack of self-respect. Psychological researchers believe that being fired creates at least as much stress as the death of a close friend. The numbers that we present about unemployment can never fully convey its true cost to the people of this or any other nation.

Historical Unemployment Rates

Labor force
Individuals aged 16 years or older who either have jobs or who are looking and available for jobs; the number of employed plus the number of unemployed.

The unemployment rate, defined as the proportion of the measured **labor force** that is unemployed, hit a low of 1.2 percent of the labor force at the end of World War II, after having reached 25 percent during the Great Depression in the 1930s. You can see in Figure 1-1 on the facing page what has happened to the unemployment rate in the United States since 1890. The highest level ever was reached in the Great Depression, but the unemployment rate was also high during the Panic of 1893.

Employment, Unemployment, and the Labor Force

Figure 1-2 on the facing page presents the population of individuals 16 years of age or older broken into three segments: (1) employed, (2) unemployed, and (3) not in the civilian labor force (a category that includes homemakers, full-time students, military personnel, persons in institutions, and retired persons). The employed and the unemployed, added together, make up the labor force. In 2013, the labor force amounted to 142.1 million + 12.4 million = 154.5 million people. To calculate the unemployment rate, we simply divide the number of unemployed by the number of people in the labor force and multiply by 100: 12.4 million/154.5 million × 100 = 8.0 percent.

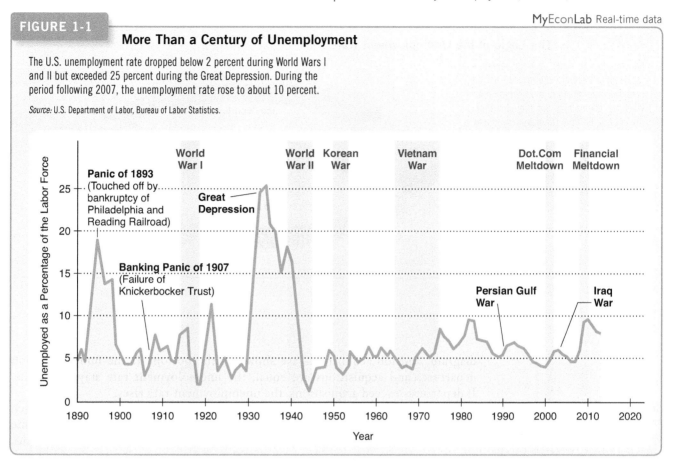

MyEconLab Real-time data

FIGURE 1-1

More Than a Century of Unemployment

The U.S. unemployment rate dropped below 2 percent during World Wars I and II but exceeded 25 percent during the Great Depression. During the period following 2007, the unemployment rate rose to about 10 percent.

Source: U.S. Department of Labor, Bureau of Labor Statistics.

The Arithmetic Determination of Unemployment

Because there is a transition between employment and unemployment at any point in time—people are leaving jobs and others are finding jobs—there is a simple relationship between the employed and the unemployed, as can be seen in Figure 1-3 on the following page. Job departures are shown at the top of the

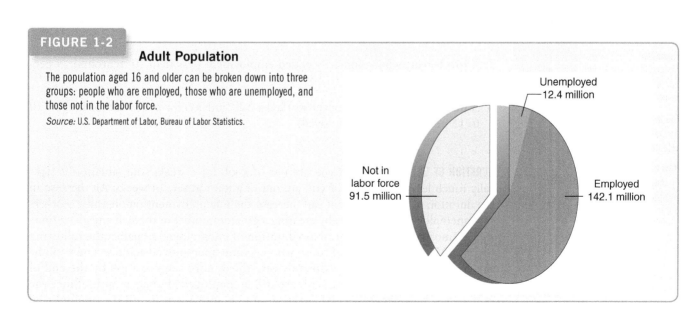

FIGURE 1-2

Adult Population

The population aged 16 and older can be broken down into three groups: people who are employed, those who are unemployed, and those not in the labor force.

Source: U.S. Department of Labor, Bureau of Labor Statistics.

FIGURE 1-3

The Logic of the Unemployment Rate

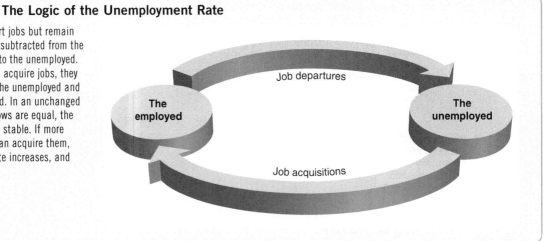

Individuals who depart jobs but remain in the labor force are subtracted from the employed and added to the unemployed. When the unemployed acquire jobs, they are subtracted from the unemployed and added to the employed. In an unchanged labor force, if both flows are equal, the unemployment rate is stable. If more people depart jobs than acquire them, the unemployment rate increases, and vice versa.

Stock
The quantity of something, measured at a given point in time—for example, an inventory of goods or a bank account. Stocks are defined independently of time, although they are assessed at a point in time.

Flow
A quantity measured per unit of time; something that occurs over time, such as the income you make per week or per year or the number of individuals who are fired every month.

Job loser
An individual in the labor force whose employment was involuntarily terminated.

Reentrant
An individual who used to work full-time but left the labor force and has now reentered it looking for a job.

Job leaver
An individual in the labor force who quits voluntarily.

New entrant
An individual who has never held a full-time job lasting two weeks or longer but is now seeking employment.

diagram, and job acquisitions are shown at the bottom. If the numbers of job departures and acquisitions are equal, the unemployment rate stays the same. If departures exceed acquisitions, the unemployment rate rises.

The number of unemployed is some number at any point in time. It is a **stock** of individuals who do not have a job but are actively looking for one. The same is true for the number of employed. The number of people departing jobs, whether voluntarily or involuntarily, is a **flow**, as is the number of people acquiring jobs.

CATEGORIES OF INDIVIDUALS WHO ARE WITHOUT WORK According to the Bureau of Labor Statistics, an unemployed individual will fall into any of four categories:

1. A **job loser,** whose employment was involuntarily terminated or who was laid off (40 to 60 percent of the unemployed)

2. A **reentrant,** who worked a full-time job before but has been out of the labor force (20 to 30 percent of the unemployed)

3. A **job leaver,** who voluntarily ended employment (less than 10 to around 15 percent of the unemployed)

4. A **new entrant,** who has never worked a full-time job for two weeks or longer (10 to 15 percent of the unemployed)

DURATION OF UNEMPLOYMENT If you are out of a job for a week, your situation is typically much less serious than if you are out of a job for, say, 14 weeks. An increase in the duration of unemployment can increase the unemployment rate because workers stay unemployed longer, thereby creating a greater number of them at any given time.

The most recent information on duration of unemployment paints the following picture: More than a third of those who become unemployed acquire a new job by the end of one month, approximately one-third more acquire a job by the end of two months, and only about a sixth are still unemployed after six months. Since the mid-1960s, the average annual duration of unemployment for all the unemployed has varied between 10 and 20 weeks. The overall average duration for the past 25 years has been at least 16 weeks.

When overall business activity goes into a downturn, the duration of unemployment tends to rise, thereby accounting for much of the increase in the estimated unemployment rate. In a sense, then, it is the increase in the *duration* of unemployment during a downturn in national economic activity that generates the bad news that concerns policymakers in Washington, D.C. Furthermore, the individuals who stay unemployed longer than six months are the ones who create pressure on Congress to "do something." What Congress does, typically, is extend and supplement unemployment benefits.

THE DISCOURAGED WORKER PHENOMENON Critics of the published unemployment rate calculated by the federal government believe that it fails to reflect the true numbers of **discouraged workers** and "hidden unemployed." Though there is no agreed-on method to measure discouraged workers, the Department of Labor defines them as people who have dropped out of the labor force and are no longer looking for a job because they believe that the job market has little to offer them. To what extent do we want to include in the measured labor force individuals who voluntarily choose not to look for work or those who take only a few minutes a day to scan the want ads and then decide that there are no jobs?

Some economists argue that people who work part-time but are willing to work full-time should be classified as "semihidden" unemployed. Estimates range as high as 6 million workers at any one time. Offsetting this factor, though, is *overemployment*. An individual working 50 or 60 hours a week is still counted as only one full-time worker. Some people hold two or three jobs but still are counted as just one employed person.

LABOR FORCE PARTICIPATION The way in which we define unemployment and membership in the labor force will affect the **labor force participation rate.** It is defined as the proportion of noninstitutionalized (i.e., not in prisons, mental institutions, etc.) working-age individuals who are employed or seeking employment.

The U.S. labor force participation rate has risen somewhat over time, from 60 percent in 1950 to almost 64 percent today. The gender composition of the U.S. labor force has changed considerably during this time. In 1950, more than 83 percent of men and fewer than 35 percent of women participated in the U.S. labor force. Today, fewer than 70 percent of men and nearly 60 percent of women are U.S. labor force participants.

What do you suppose accounts for a recent decline in the U.S. labor force participation rate?

Discouraged workers
Individuals who have stopped looking for a job because they are convinced that they will not find a suitable one.

Labor force participation rate
The percentage of noninstitutionalized working-age individuals who are employed or seeking employment.

EXAMPLE

Fewer Men Are at Work—or Even Looking for It

Since the beginning of 2008, the overall U.S. labor force participation rate has decreased by nearly 3 percentage points, to less than 64 percent. Three percentage points may not sound like very much. Nevertheless, this reduction in labor force participation represents the steepest decline within a few years' time to have taken place over the past several decades. The nearly 3-percentage-point decrease translates into a labor force reduction of more than 7 million people.

Male workers who have dropped out of the labor force account for the bulk of this reduction. During the 2008–2009 recession, the unemployment rates of both men and women shot up, but occupations dominated by male workers, such as construction and manufacturing, experienced the largest job losses. Consequently, the differential between male and female unemployment rates rose by nearly 3 percentage points. Many of the men who lost jobs did not find new positions, became discouraged workers, and departed from the labor force. Thus, the primary element accounting for the recent drop in U.S. labor force participation is the transformation, since 2008, of millions of male employees into discouraged workers.

FOR CRITICAL THINKING

What would happen to the overall U.S. labor force participation rate if the construction and manufacturing industries were to experience significant upswings?

QUICK QUIZ See page 24 for the answers. Review concepts from this section in MyEconLab.

_____ persons are adults who are willing and able to work and are actively looking for a job but have not found one. The unemployment rate is computed by dividing the number of unemployed by the total _____ _____, which is equal to those who are employed plus those who are unemployed.

The unemployed are classified as _____ _____, _____, _____ _____, and _____ _____ to the labor force. The flow of people departing jobs and people acquiring jobs

determines the stock of the unemployed as well as the stock of the employed.

The duration of unemployment affects the unemployment rate. If the duration of unemployment increases, the measured unemployment rate will _____, even though the number of unemployed workers may remain the same.

Whereas overall labor force participation on net has risen only modestly since World War II, there has been a major increase in _____ labor force participation.

The Major Types of Unemployment

Unemployment has been categorized into four basic types: frictional, structural, cyclical, and seasonal.

Frictional Unemployment

Frictional unemployment
Unemployment due to the fact that workers must search for appropriate job offers. This activity takes time, and so they remain temporarily unemployed.

Of the more than 154 million people in the labor force, more than 50 million will either change jobs or take new jobs during the year. In the process, in excess of 22 million persons will report themselves unemployed at one time or another each year. This continuous flow of individuals from job to job and in and out of employment is called **frictional unemployment.** There will always be some frictional unemployment as resources are redirected in the economy, because job-hunting costs are never zero, and workers never have full information about available jobs. To eliminate frictional unemployment, we would have to prevent workers from leaving their present jobs until they had already lined up other jobs at which they would start working immediately. And we would have to guarantee first-time job seekers a job *before* they started looking.

Structural Unemployment

Structural unemployment
Unemployment of workers over lengthy intervals resulting from skill mismatches with position requirements of employers and from fewer jobs being offered by employers constrained by governmental business regulations and labor market policies.

Structural changes in our economy cause some workers to become unemployed for very long periods of time because they cannot find jobs that use their particular skills. This is called **structural unemployment.** Structural unemployment is not caused by general business fluctuations, although business fluctuations may affect it. And unlike frictional unemployment, structural unemployment is not related to the movement of workers from low-paying to high-paying jobs.

At one time, economists thought about structural unemployment only from the perspective of workers. The concept applied to workers who did not have the ability, training, and skills necessary to obtain available jobs. Today, it still encompasses these workers. In addition, however, economists increasingly look at structural unemployment from the viewpoint of employers, many of whom face government mandates requiring them to take such steps as providing funds for social insurance programs for their employees and announcing plant closings months or even years in advance.

There is now considerable evidence that government labor market policies influence how many job positions businesses wish to create, thereby affecting structural unemployment. In the United States, many businesses appear to have adjusted to these policies by hiring more "temporary workers" or establishing short-term contracts with "private consultants." Such measures may have increased the extent of U.S. structural unemployment in recent years.

How may a federal law be increasing structural unemployment?

POLICY EXAMPLE

Warning: WARN May Boost the Natural Unemployment Rate

In 1989, Congress passed the Worker Adjustment and Retraining Notification (WARN) Act. The law required firms to notify and provide special benefits to employees in advance of what the legislation defines as a "mass layoff" involving fifty or more full-time workers constituting at least one-third of a company's staff. The law rarely applied until the 2008–2009 recession. When their sales plummeted during that recession, a number of companies rapidly laid off large numbers of workers to cut costs in an attempt to remain in business. Job losers alleged violations of WARN and sought extra termination payments and benefits.

As economic activity recovered somewhat but remained dampened in the years following the recession, managers found out that WARN-related caseloads in the courts had tripled. Those managers worried that if they were to hire workers they might later have to lay off, WARN might apply. This concern discouraged managers from hiring back as many workers as they might have otherwise. As a consequence, unemployment remained high even as companies' prospects improved. Thus, the WARN law undoubtedly contributed to greater structural unemployment.

FOR CRITICAL THINKING
How has structural unemployment been affected by the actions of several state governments in requiring firms to grant longer paid "family leaves"?

Cyclical Unemployment

Cyclical unemployment is related to business fluctuations. It is defined as unemployment associated with changes in business conditions—primarily recessions and depressions. The way to lessen cyclical unemployment would be to reduce the intensity, duration, and frequency of downturns of business activity. Economic policymakers attempt, through their policies, to reduce cyclical unemployment by keeping business activity on an even keel.

Cyclical unemployment
Unemployment resulting from business recessions that occur when aggregate (total) demand is insufficient to create full employment.

YOU ARE THERE
To consider how difficulties in finding workers with required skills might contribute to unemployment, take a look at **Struggling to Hire with the Unemployment Rate above 9 Percent** on page 19.

Seasonal Unemployment

Seasonal unemployment comes and goes with seasons of the year in which the demand for particular jobs rises and falls. In northern states, construction workers can often work only during the warmer months. They are seasonally unemployed during the winter. Summer resort workers can usually get jobs in resorts only during the summer season. They, too, sometimes become seasonally unemployed during the winter. The opposite is sometimes true for ski resort workers.

The unemployment rate that the Bureau of Labor Statistics releases each month is "seasonally adjusted." This means that the reported unemployment rate has been adjusted to remove the effects of variations in seasonal unemployment. Thus, the unemployment rate that the media dutifully announce reflects only the sum of frictional unemployment, structural unemployment, and cyclical unemployment.

Seasonal unemployment
Unemployment resulting from the seasonal pattern of work in specific industries. It is usually due to seasonal fluctuations in demand or to changing weather conditions that render work difficult, if not impossible, as in the agriculture, construction, and tourist industries.

Full Employment and the Natural Rate of Unemployment

Does full employment mean that everybody has a job? Certainly not, for not everyone is looking for a job—full-time students and full-time homemakers, for example, are not. Is it always possible for everyone who is looking for a job to find one? No, because transaction costs in the labor market are not zero. Transaction costs are those associated with any activity whose goal is to enter into, carry out, or terminate contracts. In the labor market, these costs involve time spent looking for a job, being interviewed, negotiating the terms of employment, and the like.

Full Employment

Full employment
An arbitrary level of unemployment that corresponds to "normal" friction in the labor market. In 1986, a 6.5 percent rate of unemployment was considered full employment. Today it is somewhat higher.

We will always have some frictional unemployment as individuals move in and out of the labor force, seek higher-paying jobs, and move to different parts of the country. **Full employment** is therefore a concept that implies some sort of balance or equilibrium in an ever-shifting labor market. Of course, this general notion of full employment must somehow be put into numbers so that economists and others can determine whether the economy has reached the full-employment point.

The Natural Rate of Unemployment

Natural rate of unemployment
The rate of unemployment that is estimated to prevail in long-run macroeconomic equilibrium, when all workers and employers have fully adjusted to any changes in the economy.

In trying to assess when a situation of balance has been attained in the labor market, economists estimate the **natural rate of unemployment,** the rate that is expected to prevail in the long run once all workers and employers have fully adjusted to any changes in the economy. If correctly estimated, the natural rate of unemployment should not include cyclical unemployment. When seasonally adjusted, the natural unemployment rate should include only frictional and structural unemployment.

A long-standing difficulty, however, has been a lack of agreement about how to estimate the natural unemployment rate. Until the late 2000s, most economists, including those with the president's Council of Economic Advisers and those at the Federal Reserve, had concluded that the natural unemployment rate was slightly above 5 percent.

Since the 2008–2009 recession, the actual unemployment rate has remained considerably above 5 percent. This fact suggests that perhaps the natural rate of unemployment has increased because of a rise in structural unemployment. Some economists propose that the collapse of the U.S. housing industry precipitated this rise. The housing meltdown, these economists suggest, left people possessing skills that were poorly matched to the requirements of jobs other than those in construction, housing finance, and real estate. In contrast, other economists contend that increases in the scope of government regulations and taxes have raised the costs confronted by firms when they contemplate hiring job applicants. Government policies, these economists argue, are to blame for a higher natural unemployment rate.

Of course, both explanations together could help to account for an upswing in structural unemployment. What has yet to be determined by economists is exactly how much higher than 5 percent the natural unemployment rate now may be. Some estimates indicate that it may be at least 7 percent.

WHAT IF... **city governments passed more laws to benefit all employees?**

Beginning in 2013, a new health care law went into effect that most businesses predict will raise their costs of providing health insurance coverage to employees. In addition, new federal laws and court interpretations of existing laws are increasing the number of days off that firms are obliged to grant employees who are parents of a new child. Many municipalities, such as

Seattle, Washington, have even passed ordinances requiring companies to provide more paid "sick days" each year. These and many other laws reduce the incentive for companies to hire workers and thereby decrease employment. As a result, the proliferation of such laws drives up structural unemployment and boosts the natural rate of unemployment.

QUICK QUIZ See page 24 for the answers. Review concepts from this section in MyEconLab.

_____ **unemployment** occurs because of transaction costs in the labor market. For example, workers do not have full information about vacancies and must search for jobs.

_____ **unemployment** occurs when there is a poor match of workers' skills and abilities with available jobs,

perhaps because workers lack appropriate training or government labor rules reduce firms' willingness to hire.

The levels of frictional and structural unemployment are used in part to determine our (somewhat arbitrary) measurement of the _____ rate of unemployment.

Inflation and Deflation

During World War II, you could buy bread for 8 to 10 cents a loaf and have milk delivered fresh to your door for about 25 cents a half gallon. The average price of a new car was less than $700, and the average house cost less than $3,000. Today, bread, milk, cars, and houses all cost more—a lot more. Prices are about 15 times what they were in 1940. Clearly, this country has experienced quite a bit of *inflation* since then. We define **inflation** as an upward movement in the average level of prices. The opposite of inflation is **deflation,** defined as a downward movement in the average level of prices. Notice that these definitions depend on the *average* level of prices. This means that even during a period of inflation, some prices can be falling if other prices are rising at a faster rate. The prices of electronic equipment have dropped dramatically since the 1960s, even though there has been general inflation.

Inflation
A sustained increase in the average of all prices of goods and services in an economy.

Deflation
A sustained decrease in the average of all prices of goods and services in an economy.

Inflation and the Purchasing Power of Money

By definition, the value of a dollar does not stay constant when there is inflation. The value of money is usually talked about in terms of **purchasing power.** A dollar's purchasing power is the real goods and services that it can buy. Consequently, another way of defining inflation is as a decline in the purchasing power of money. The faster the rate of inflation, the greater the rate of decline in the purchasing power of money.

One way to think about inflation and the purchasing power of money is to discuss dollar values in terms of *nominal* versus *real* values. The nominal value of anything is simply its price expressed in today's dollars. In contrast, the real value of anything is its value expressed in purchasing power, which varies with the overall price level. Let's say that you received a $100 bill from your grandparents this year. One year from now, the nominal value of that bill will still be $100. The real value will depend on what the purchasing power of money is after one year's worth of inflation. Obviously, if there is inflation during the year, the real value of that $100 bill will have diminished. For example, if you keep the $100 bill in your pocket for a year during which the rate of inflation is 3 percent, at the end of the year you will have to come up with $3 more to buy the same amount of goods and services that the $100 bill can purchase today.

To discuss what has happened to prices here and in other countries, we have to know how to measure inflation.

Purchasing power
The value of money for buying goods and services. If your money income stays the same but the price of one good that you are buying goes up, your effective purchasing power falls.

Measuring the Rate of Inflation

How can we measure the rate of inflation? It is easy to determine how much the price of an individual commodity has risen: If last year a light bulb cost 50 cents, and this year it costs 75 cents, there has been a 50 percent rise in the price of that light bulb over a one-year period. We can express the change in the individual light bulb price in one of several ways: The price has gone up 25 cents. The price is one and a half (1.5) times as high. The price has risen by 50 percent. An *index number* of this price rise is simply the second way (1.5) multiplied by 100, meaning that the index today would stand at 150. We multiply by 100 to eliminate decimals because it is easier to think in terms of percentage changes using whole numbers. This is the standard convention adopted for convenience in dealing with index numbers or price levels.

Computing a Price Index

The measurement problem becomes more complicated when it involves a large number of goods, especially if some prices have risen faster than others and some have even fallen. What we have to do is pick a representative bundle, a so-called market basket, of goods and compare the cost of that market basket of goods over time. When we do this, we obtain a **price index,** which is defined as the cost of a market basket of goods today, expressed as a percentage of the cost of that identical market basket of goods in some starting year, known as the **base year.**

Price index
The cost of today's market basket of goods expressed as a percentage of the cost of the same market basket during a base year.

Base year
The year that is chosen as the point of reference for comparison of prices in other years.

$$\text{Price index} = \frac{\text{cost of market basket today}}{\text{cost of market basket in base year}} \times 100$$

TABLE 1-1

Calculating a Price Index for a Two-Good Market Basket

In this simplified example, there are only two goods—corn and digital devices. The quantities and base-year prices are given in columns 2 and 3. The 2005 cost of the market basket, calculated in column 4, comes to $1,400. The 2015 prices are given in column 5. The cost of the market basket in 2015, calculated in column 6, is $1,650. The price index for 2015 compared with 2005 is 117.86.

(1) Commodity	(2) Market Basket Quantity	(3) 2005 Price per Unit	(4) Cost of Market Basket in 2005	(5) 2015 Price per Unit	(6) Cost of Market Basket in 2015
Corn	100 bushels	$ 4	$ 400	$ 8	$ 800
Digital devices	2	500	1,000	425	850
Totals			$1,400		$1,650

$$\text{Price index} = \frac{\text{cost of market basket in 2015}}{\text{cost of market basket in base year 2005}} \times 100 = \frac{\$1,650}{\$1,400} \times 100 = 117.86$$

In the base year, the price index will always be 100, because the year in the numerator and in the denominator of the fraction is the same. Therefore, the fraction equals 1, and when we multiply it by 100, we get 100. A simple numerical example is given in Table 1-1 above. In the table, there are only two goods in the market basket—corn and digital devices. The *quantities* in the basket are the same in the base year, 2005, and the current year, 2015. Only the *prices* change. Such a *fixed-quantity* price index is the easiest to compute because the statistician need only look at prices of goods and services sold every year rather than observing how much of these goods and services consumers actually purchase each year.

REAL-WORLD PRICE INDEXES Government statisticians calculate a number of price indexes. The most often quoted are the **Consumer Price Index (CPI)**, the **Producer Price Index (PPI)**, the **GDP deflator**, and the **Personal Consumption Expenditure (PCE) Index.** The CPI attempts to measure changes only in the level of prices of goods and services purchased by consumers. The PPI attempts to show what has happened to the average price of goods and services produced and sold by a typical firm. (There are also *wholesale price indexes* that track the price level for commodities that firms purchase from other firms.) The GDP deflator is the most general indicator of inflation because it measures changes in the level of prices of all new goods and services produced in the economy. The PCE Index measures average prices using weights from surveys of consumer spending.

THE CPI The Bureau of Labor Statistics (BLS) has the task of identifying a market basket of goods and services of the typical consumer. Today, the BLS uses the time period 1982–1984 as its base of market prices. The BLS has indicated an intention to change the base to 1993–1995 but has yet to do so. It has, though, updated the expenditure weights for its market basket of goods to reflect consumer spending patterns in 2001–2002. All CPI numbers since February 1998 reflect these expenditure weights.

Economists have known for years that there are possible problems in the CPI's market basket. Specifically, the BLS has been unable to account for the way consumers substitute less expensive items for higher-priced items. The reason is that the CPI is a fixed-quantity price index, meaning that the BLS implicitly ignores changes in consumption patterns that occur between years in which it revises the index. Until recently, the BLS has also been unable to take quality changes into account as they occur. Now, though, it is subtracting from certain list prices estimated effects of qualitative improvements and adding to other list prices to account for deteriorations in quality. An additional flaw is that the CPI usually ignores successful new products until long after they have been introduced. Despite these flaws, the CPI is widely followed because its level is calculated and published monthly.

Consumer Price Index (CPI)
A statistical measure of a weighted average of prices of a specified set of goods and services purchased by typical consumers in urban areas.

Producer Price Index (PPI)
A statistical measure of a weighted average of prices of goods and services that firms produce and sell.

GDP deflator
A price index measuring the changes in prices of all new goods and services produced in the economy.

Personal Consumption Expenditure (PCE) Index
A statistical measure of average prices that uses annually updated weights based on surveys of consumer spending.

Within which group of products are prices rising with sufficient speed to account for a significant portion of China's annual rate of consumer price inflation?

INTERNATIONAL EXAMPLE

Why the Value of China's Consumer Price Index Is Rising

In China, food's weight in the CPI is slightly below 35 percent. Food prices have been rising so rapidly, though, that the overall rate of increase in food prices per year has been contributing to 75 percent of China's officially measured annual rate of CPI inflation. Consequently, during a recent 12-month period in which the nation's measured rate of CPI inflation was 6.4 percent, the rate of increase in food prices accounted for 4.8 percentage points of that annual rate of inflation.

FOR CRITICAL THINKING
Food's weight in the U.S. CPI is about 16 percent. If U.S. food prices rose as rapidly as Chinese food prices, would the U.S. CPI increase as much as the CPI in China? Explain.

THE PPI There are a number of Producer Price Indexes, including one for foodstuffs, another for intermediate goods (goods used in the production of other goods), and one for finished goods. Most of the producer prices included are in mining, manufacturing, and agriculture. The PPIs can be considered general-purpose indexes for nonretail markets.

Although in the long run the various PPIs and the CPI generally show the same rate of inflation, that is not the case in the short run. Most often the PPIs increase before the CPI because it takes time for producer price increases to show up in the prices that consumers pay for final products. Changes in the PPIs are watched closely as a hint that CPI inflation is going to increase or decrease.

THE GDP DEFLATOR The broadest price index reported in the United States is the GDP deflator, where GDP stands for gross domestic product, or annual total national income. Unlike the CPI and the PPIs, the GDP deflator is *not* based on a fixed market basket of goods and services. The basket is allowed to change with people's consumption and investment patterns. In this sense, the changes in the GDP deflator reflect both price changes and the public's market responses to those price changes. Why? Because new expenditure patterns are allowed to show up in the GDP deflator as people respond to changing prices.

Go to www.econtoday.com/chap01 to obtain information about inflation and unemployment in other countries from the International Monetary Fund. Click on "World Economic Outlook Databases."

THE PCE INDEX Another price index that takes into account changing expenditure patterns is the Personal Consumption Expenditure (PCE) Index. The Bureau of Economic Analysis, an agency of the U.S. Department of Commerce, uses continuously updated annual surveys of consumer purchases to construct the weights for the PCE Index. Thus, an advantage of the PCE Index is that weights in the index are updated every year. The Federal Reserve has used the rate of change in the PCE Index as its primary inflation indicator because Fed officials believe that the updated weights in the PCE Index make it more accurate than the CPI as a measure of consumer price changes. Nevertheless, the CPI remains the most widely reported price index, and the U.S. government continues to use the CPI to adjust the value of Social Security benefits to account for inflation.

HISTORICAL CHANGES IN THE CPI Between World War II and the early 1980s, the Consumer Price Index showed a fairly dramatic trend upward. Figure 1-4 on the following page shows the annual rate of change in the CPI since 1860. Prior to World War II, there were numerous periods of deflation interspersed with periods of inflation. Persistent year-in and year-out inflation seems to be a post–World War II phenomenon, at least in this country. As far back as before the American Revolution, prices used to rise during war periods but then would fall back toward prewar levels afterward. This occurred after the Revolutionary War, the War of 1812, the Civil War, and to a lesser extent World War I. Consequently, the overall price level in 1940 wasn't much different from 150 years earlier.

MyEconLab Real-time data

FIGURE 1-4

Inflation and Deflation in U.S. History

For 80 years after the Civil War, the United States experienced alternating inflation and deflation. Here we show them as reflected by changes in the Consumer Price Index. Since World War II, the periods of inflation have not been followed by periods of deflation. Even during peacetime, the price index has continued to rise. The shaded areas represent wartime.

Source: U.S. Department of Labor, Bureau of Labor Statistics.

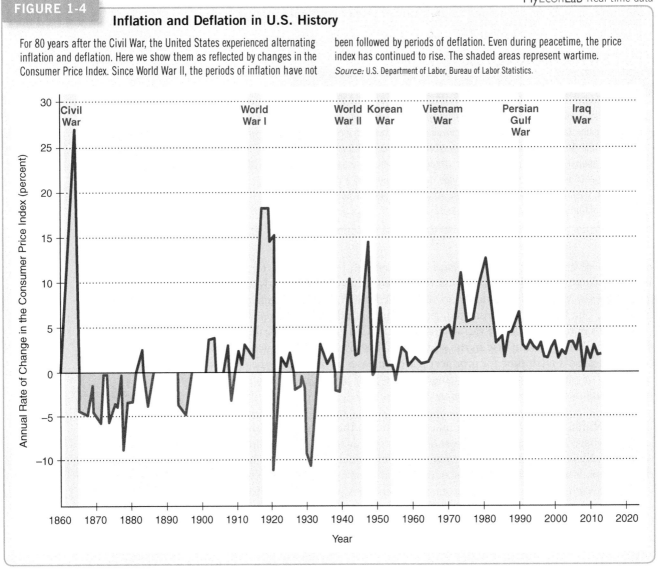

Why is Argentina's government imposing substantial fines on private firms that release their own independent estimates of the nation's inflation rate?

INTERNATIONAL POLICY EXAMPLE

Argentina Penalizes Inflation Estimates That Are "Too High"

Argentina's national statistics agency, Indec, releases official government measures of consumer price inflation. Many observers question the reliability of this agency's tabulations of price indexes and inflation rates. These observers give more credence to inflation estimates tabulated and released by private economic consulting firms in Argentina.

Recently, private firms such as Econviews, Finsoport, and GRA Consultoras have released estimates of annual inflation rates for Argentina that have been more than twice as high as Indec's. Argentina's government has accused these companies of engaging in activities that "lack scientific vigor" and that "undermine confidence in the nation's economy." The government has imposed fines exceeding $120,000 for publicly releasing inflation estimates that differ substantially from those of Indec. Today, most private companies in Argentina that independently tabulate price index and inflation data will provide them only to private customers at a price—and under the condition of confidentiality.

FOR CRITICAL THINKING

Argentina's government offers extra payments based on Indec's inflation tabulations to induce savers to buy its bonds. Could this explain its concern about competing private inflation estimates? Explain.

Once we pick a market basket of goods, we can construct a **price index** that compares the cost of that market basket today with the cost of the same market basket in a _____ year.

The _____ _____ Index is the most often used price index in the United States. The **Producer Price Index (PPI)** is also widely mentioned.

The _____ _____ measures what is happening to the average price level of *all* new, domestically produced final goods and services in our economy.

The _____ _____ _____ Index uses annually updated weights from consumer spending surveys to measure average prices faced by consumers.

Anticipated versus Unanticipated Inflation

To determine who is hurt by inflation and what the effects of inflation are in general, we have to distinguish between anticipated and unanticipated inflation. We will see that the effects on individuals and the economy are vastly different, depending on which type of inflation exists.

Anticipated inflation is the rate of inflation that most individuals believe will occur. If the rate of inflation this year turns out to be 5 percent, and that's about what most people thought it was going to be, we are in a situation of fully anticipated inflation.

Unanticipated inflation is inflation that comes as a surprise to individuals in the economy. For example, if the inflation rate in a particular year turns out to be 10 percent when, on average, people thought it was going to be 3 percent, there was unanticipated inflation—inflation greater than anticipated.

Some of the problems caused by inflation arise when it is unanticipated, because then many people are unable to protect themselves from its ravages. Keeping the distinction between anticipated and unanticipated inflation in mind, we can easily see the relationship between inflation and interest rates.

Anticipated inflation
The inflation rate that we believe will occur. When it does occur, we are in a situation of fully anticipated inflation.

Unanticipated inflation
Inflation at a rate that comes as a surprise, either higher or lower than the rate anticipated.

Inflation and Interest Rates

Let's start in a hypothetical world in which there is no inflation and anticipated inflation is zero. In that world, you may be able to borrow funds—to buy a house or a car, for example—at a **nominal rate of interest** of, say, 6 percent. If you borrow the funds to purchase a house or a car and your anticipation of inflation turns out to be accurate, neither you nor the lender will have been fooled. Each dollar you pay back in the years to come will be just as valuable in terms of purchasing power as the dollar that you borrowed.

What you ordinarily want to know when you borrow is the *real* rate of interest that you will have to pay. The **real rate of interest** is defined as the nominal rate of interest minus the anticipated rate of inflation. In effect, we can say that the nominal rate of interest is equal to the real rate of interest plus an *inflationary premium* to take account of anticipated inflation. That inflationary premium covers depreciation in the purchasing power of the dollars repaid by borrowers. (Whenever there are relatively high rates of anticipated inflation, we must add an additional factor to the inflationary premium—the product of the real rate of interest times the anticipated rate of inflation. Usually, this last term is omitted because the anticipated rate of inflation is not high enough to make much of a difference.)

Nominal rate of interest
The market rate of interest observed in contracts expressed in today's dollars.

Real rate of interest
The nominal rate of interest minus the anticipated rate of inflation.

Does Inflation Necessarily Hurt Everyone?

Most people think that inflation is bad. After all, inflation means higher prices, and when we have to pay higher prices, are we not necessarily worse off? The truth is that inflation affects different people differently. Its effects also depend on whether it is anticipated or unanticipated.

UNANTICIPATED INFLATION: CREDITORS LOSE AND DEBTORS GAIN In most situations, unanticipated inflation benefits borrowers because the nominal interest rate they are being charged does not fully compensate creditors for the inflation that actually occurred. In other words, the lender did not anticipate inflation correctly. Whenever inflation rates are underestimated for the life of a loan, creditors lose and debtors gain. Periods of considerable unanticipated (higher than anticipated) inflation occurred in the late 1960s and all of the 1970s. During those years, creditors lost and debtors gained.

PROTECTING AGAINST INFLATION Lenders attempt to protect themselves against inflation by raising nominal interest rates to reflect anticipated inflation. Adjustable-rate mortgages in fact do just that: The interest rate varies according to what happens to interest rates in the economy. Workers can protect themselves from inflation by obtaining **cost-of-living adjustments (COLAs),** which are automatic increases in wage rates to take account of increases in the price level.

To the extent that you hold non-interest-bearing cash, you will lose because of inflation. If you have put $100 in a mattress and the inflation rate is 5 percent for the year, you will have lost 5 percent of the purchasing power of that $100. If you have your funds in a non-interest-bearing checking account, you will suffer the same fate. Individuals attempt to reduce the cost of holding cash by putting it into interest-bearing accounts, some of which pay nominal rates of interest that reflect anticipated inflation.

THE RESOURCE COST OF INFLATION Some economists believe that the main cost of inflation is the opportunity cost of resources used to protect against distortions that inflation introduces as firms attempt to plan for the long run. Individuals have to spend time and resources to figure out ways to adjust their behavior in case inflation is different from what it has been in the past. That may mean spending a longer time working out more complicated contracts for employment, for purchases of goods in the future, and for purchases of raw materials to be delivered later.

Inflation requires that price lists be changed. This is called the **repricing,** or **menu, cost of inflation.** The higher the rate of inflation, the higher the repricing cost of inflation, because prices must be changed more often within a given period of time.

Cost-of-living adjustments (COLAs)
Clauses in contracts that allow for increases in specified nominal values to take account of changes in the cost of living.

Repricing, or menu, cost of inflation
The cost associated with recalculating prices and printing new price lists when there is inflation.

QUICK QUIZ See page 24 for the answers. Review concepts from this section in MyEconLab.

Whenever inflation is _____ than anticipated, creditors lose and debtors gain. Whenever the rate of inflation is _____ than anticipated, creditors gain and debtors lose.

Holders of cash lose during periods of inflation because the _____ _____ of their cash depreciates at the rate of inflation.

Households and businesses spend resources in attempting to protect themselves against the prospect of inflation, thus imposing a _____ cost on the economy.

Changing Inflation and Unemployment: Business Fluctuations

Business fluctuations
The ups and downs in business activity throughout the economy.

Expansion
A business fluctuation in which the pace of national economic activity is speeding up.

Contraction
A business fluctuation during which the pace of national economic activity is slowing down.

Some years unemployment goes up, and some years it goes down. Some years there is a lot of inflation, and other years there isn't. We have fluctuations in all aspects of our macroeconomy. The ups and downs in economywide economic activity are sometimes called **business fluctuations.** When business fluctuations are positive, they are called **expansions**—speedups in the pace of national economic activity. The opposite of an expansion is a **contraction,** which is a slowdown in the pace of national economic activity. The top of an expansion is usually called its *peak*, and the bottom of a contraction is usually called its *trough*. Business fluctuations used to be called *business cycles*, but that term no longer seems appropriate because *cycle* implies regular or automatic recurrence, and we have never had automatic recurrent fluctuations in general business and

FIGURE 1-5

The Idealized Course of Business Fluctuations

A hypothetical business cycle would go from peak to trough and back again in a regular cycle. Real-world business cycles are not as regular as this hypothetical cycle.

economic activity. What we have had are contractions and expansions that vary greatly in length. For example, the 10 post–World War II expansions have averaged 57 months, but three of those exceeded 90 months, and two lasted less than 25 months.

If the contractionary phase of business fluctuations becomes severe enough, we call it a **recession.** An extremely severe recession is called a **depression.** Typically, at the beginning of a recession, there is a marked increase in the rate of unemployment, and the duration of unemployment increases. In addition, people's incomes start to decline. In times of expansion, the opposite occurs.

In Figure 1-5 above, you see that typical business fluctuations occur around a growth trend in overall national business activity shown as a straight upward-sloping line. Starting out at a peak, the economy goes into a contraction (recession). Then an expansion starts that moves up to its peak, higher than the last one, and the sequence starts over again.

Recession
A period of time during which the rate of growth of business activity is consistently less than its long-term trend or is negative.

Depression
An extremely severe recession.

A Historical Picture of Business Activity in the United States

Figure 1-6 on the following page traces changes in U.S. business activity from 1880 to the present. Note that the long-term trend line is shown as horizontal, so all changes in business activity focus around that trend line. Major changes in business activity in the United States occurred during the Great Depression, World War II, and, most recently, the sharp recession of the late 2000s. Note that none of the actual business fluctuations in Figure 1-6, exactly mirror the idealized course of a business fluctuation shown in Figure 1-5 above.

Go to www.econtoday.com/chap01 to learn how economists at the National Bureau of Economic Research formally determine when a recession started.

Explaining Business Fluctuations: External Shocks

As you might imagine, because changes in national business activity affect everyone, economists for decades have attempted to understand and explain business fluctuations. For years, one of the most obvious explanations has been external events that tend to disrupt the economy. In many of the graphs in this chapter, you have seen that World War II was a critical point in this nation's economic history. A war is certainly an external shock—something that originates outside our economy.

In trying to help account for shocks to economic activity that may induce business fluctuations and thereby make fluctuations easier to predict, the U.S. Department of Commerce and private firms and organizations tabulate indexes (weighted averages) of

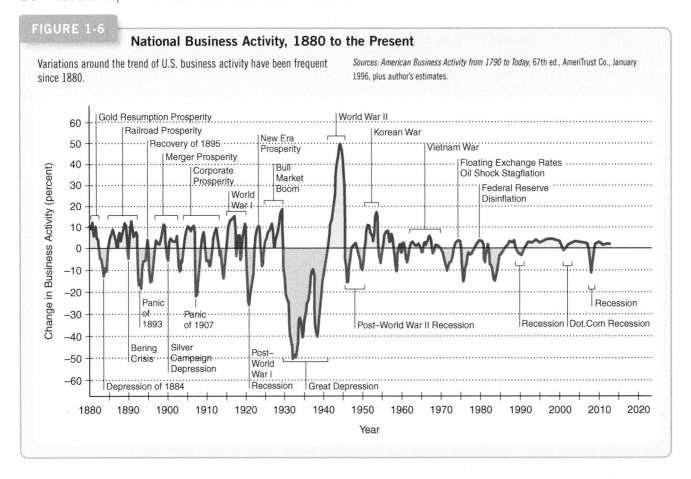

FIGURE 1-6

National Business Activity, 1880 to the Present

Variations around the trend of U.S. business activity have been frequent since 1880.

Sources: *American Business Activity from 1790 to Today*, 67th ed., AmeriTrust Co., January 1996, plus author's estimates.

Leading indicators	**leading indicators.** These are events that economists have noticed typically occur *before* changes in business activity. For example, economic downturns often follow such events as a reduction in the average workweek, an increase in unemployment insurance claims, a decrease in the prices of raw materials, or a drop in the quantity of money in circulation.
Events that have been found to occur before changes in business activity.	

What new measure are economists at the Bank of England thinking of adding to their list of leading economic indicators?

INTERNATIONAL POLICY EXAMPLE

Internet Search Activity as a Leading Indicator

Economists at the Bank of England are studying the volume of Internet searches as a leading indicator of economic activity. The economists have found that Web search activity possesses appealing leading-indicator properties. First, Internet search data are readily available on a daily basis. Second, nearly 60 percent of the United Kingdom's adult population now regularly engages in Web searches every day. Third, evidence is increasing that the volume of online searches is related to key measures of economic activity, such as transactions in housing and labor markets. Thus, the Bank of

England is already employing data on Internet search volumes as leading indicators of activity in each of these sectors of the British economy. Its economists are experimenting with using these data as overall economic indicators.

FOR CRITICAL THINKING

Why are Bank of England economists seeking to determine whether the number of searches is closely related to purchases of goods and services from businesses?

To better understand the role of shocks in influencing business fluctuations, we need a theory of why national economic activity changes. The remainder of the macro chapters in this book develop the models that will help you understand the ups and downs of our business fluctuations.

The ups and downs in economywide business activity are called _____ _____, which consist of **expansions** and **contractions** in overall business activity.

The lowest point of a contraction is called the _____.
The highest point of an expansion is called the _____.

A _____ is a downturn in business activity for some length of time.

One possible explanation for business fluctuations relates to _____ _____, such as wars, dramatic increases in the prices of raw materials, and earthquakes, floods, and droughts.

YOU ARE THERE
Struggling to Hire with the Unemployment Rate above 8 Percent

Jack Kelly, chief executive officer of Hamill Manufacturing, is looking for people to hire, as the company seeks to replace older skilled workers who are choosing to retire. Even though millions of U.S. residents are unemployed and seeking work, Kelly is having trouble filling a handful of open positions. Kelly has received many applications. So far, however, none of the applicants possesses the skills required to operate and repair computer-controlled metal-shaping equipment.

Key skills sought by Kelly are not far beyond those that students can learn in high school courses in trigonometry and science. Kelly's problem is that most students who take such courses in high school go on to college and never consider a career as a skilled manufacturing laborer earning as much as $80,000 per year. Among the non-college-bound high

school graduates who might consider such a position, it is rare to find one who has learned enough math and science even to begin to know how to set up and direct the firm's machinery. Thus, although thousands of people are unemployed in the area near Hamill's manufacturing facilities, Kelly finds it difficult to fill positions that have been open for several months. Amid a sea of unemployment, Kelly cannot find anyone to hire.

Critical Thinking Questions

1. What type of unemployment issue is Kelly confronting?
2. Is Kelly's failure to hire contributing to higher natural unemployment? Explain.

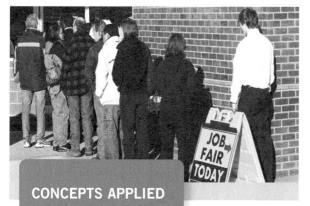

ISSUES & APPLICATIONS

CONCEPTS APPLIED
▶ Unemployment Rate
▶ Cyclical Unemployment
▶ Structural Unemployment

Have Unemployment Benefits Boosted Unemployment?

Between June 2008 and February 2009, the U.S. unemployment rate rose sharply, from 5.6 percent to more than 8 percent. Although the recession officially ended in June 2009, the unemployment rate ultimately reached a peak of 10.1 percent in October 2009. Since then, the unemployment rate has stayed near 8 percent. Thus, the unemployment rate remained above its prior level by at least 2 percentage points for more than three years. Many economists conclude that structural unemployment has risen. One element contributing to this rise, they suggest, was a substantial increase in the length of time the government paid benefits to unemployed workers.

The Significant Extension of Unemployment Benefits

People who lose jobs and are unable to find new positions are eligible for government unemployment benefits. Traditionally, these benefits constitute a form of insurance. Employers have long contributed to a government fund from which benefit payments to unemployed workers can be drawn for intervals up to 26 weeks. Nevertheless, during business contractions, Congress commonly has dipped into taxpayer funds to extend the duration of unemployment benefits. Such extensions typically have lasted for periods of about 15 weeks.

During 2008 and 2009, however, Congress nearly *quadrupled* the duration of unemployment benefits, to 99 weeks. This lengthened stream of government benefits reduced the incentive to find new jobs. As a consequence, many people spent more time searching for jobs that they hoped might be "better" instead of seeking out work that might have been more readily obtainable. So, the unemployment-benefits extension to 99 weeks tended to drive up structural unemployment and increase the measured unemployment rate.

The Benefits Extension's Impact on Structural Unemployment

Economists at the Federal Reserve Bank of San Francisco have estimated that the increase in unemployment benefits was sufficient to boost the U.S. unemployment rate by about 0.4 percentage point. Robert Barro of Harvard University has estimated a much larger effect—in excess of 2.7 percentage points.

Most other estimates of the benefits extension's impact on structural unemployment are about midway between these two extremes. If these "midpoint estimates" are correct, then the government's action to extend the duration of unemployment benefits by a factor of nearly four raised the U.S. unemployment rate by approximately 1.5 percentage points.

For Critical Thinking

1. What else might have accounted for an increase in structural unemployment in recent years? (Hint: Take a look back at the definition of structural unemployment on page 8.)
2. Given that the recession officially ended in June 2009, why might some economists contend that very little of the persistently high unemployment is cyclical unemployment?

Web Resources

1. Learn how economists at the Federal Reserve Bank of San Francisco obtained their estimate of the impact of extended unemployment benefits on structural unemployment at www.econtoday.com/chap01.
2. Read about how Robert Barro arrived at his much larger estimate of the effect of extended unemployment benefits on structural unemployment at www.econtoday.com/chap01.

MyEconLab

For more questions on this chapter's Issues & Applications, go to MyEconLab. In the Study Plan for this chapter, select Section N: News.

MyEconLab

Here is what you should know after reading this chapter. MyEconLab will help you identify what you know, and where to go when you need to practice.

WHAT YOU SHOULD KNOW		WHERE TO GO TO PRACTICE
How the U.S. Government Calculates the Official Unemployment Rate The total number of workers who are officially unemployed consists of noninstitutionalized people aged 16 or older who are willing and able to work and who are actively looking for work but have not found a job. To calculate the unemployment rate, the government determines what percentage this quantity is of the labor force, which consists of all noninstitutionalized people aged 16 years or older who either have jobs or are available for and actively seeking employment.	unemployment, 4 labor force, 4 stock, 6 flow, 6 job loser, 6 reentrant, 6 job leaver, 6 new entrant, 6 discouraged workers, 7 labor force participation rate, 7 **Key Figure** Figure 1-3, 6	• MyEconLab Study Plan 1.1 • Animated Figure 1-3

MyEconLab *continued*

The Types of Unemployment Temporarily unemployed workers who are searching for appropriate job offers are frictionally unemployed. The structurally unemployed lack the skills currently required by prospective employers. People unemployed due to business contractions are cyclically unemployed. Seasonal patterns of occupations within specific industries generate seasonal unemployment.	frictional unemployment, 8 structural unemployment, 8 cyclical unemployment, 9 seasonal unemployment, 9 full employment, 10 natural rate of unemployment, 10	• MyEconLab Study Plans 1.2, 1.3
How Price Indexes Are Calculated and Key Price Indexes To calculate any price index, economists multiply 100 times the ratio of the cost of a market basket of goods and services in the current year to the cost of the same market basket in a base year. The Consumer Price Index (CPI) is computed using a weighted set of goods and services purchased by a typical consumer in urban areas. The Producer Price Index (PPI) is a weighted average of prices of goods sold by a typical firm. The GDP deflator measures changes in the overall level of prices of all goods produced during a given interval. The Personal Consumption Expenditure (PCE) Index is a measure of average prices using weights from surveys of consumer spending.	inflation, 10 deflation, 10 purchasing power, 11 price index, 11 base year, 11 Consumer Price Index (CPI), 12 Producer Price Index (PPI), 12 GDP deflator, 12 Personal Consumption Expenditure (PCE) Index, 12 **Key Figure** Figure 1-4, 14	• MyEconLab Study Plan 1.4 • Animated Figure 1-4
Nominal Interest Rate versus Real Interest Rate The nominal interest rate applies to contracts expressed in current dollars. The real interest rate is net of inflation anticipated to erode the value of nominal interest payments during the period that a loan is repaid. Hence, the real interest rate equals the nominal interest rate minus the expected inflation rate.	anticipated inflation, 15 unanticipated inflation, 15 nominal rate of interest, 15 real rate of interest, 15	• MyEconLab Study Plan 1.5
Losers and Gainers from Inflation Creditors lose as a result of unanticipated inflation, because the real value of the interest payments they receive will turn out to be lower than they had expected. Borrowers gain when unanticipated inflation occurs, because the real value of their interest and principal payments declines. Key costs of inflation include expenses of protecting against inflation, costs of altering business plans because of unexpected changes in prices, and menu costs of repricing goods and services.	cost-of-living adjustments (COLAs), 16 repricing, or menu, cost of inflation, 16	• MyEconLab Study Plan 1.5

MyEconLab *continued*

WHAT YOU SHOULD KNOW ———————————————————————— WHERE TO GO TO PRACTICE ——

Key Features of Business Fluctuations

Business fluctuations are increases and decreases in business activity. A positive fluctuation is an expansion, which is an upward movement in business activity from a trough, or low point, to a peak, or high point. A negative fluctuation is a contraction, which is a drop in the pace of business activity from a previous peak to a new trough.

business fluctuations, 16
expansion, 16
contraction, 16
recession, 17
depression, 17
leading indicators, 18

Key Figure

Figure 1-6, 18

- MyEconLab Study Plan 1.6
- Animated Figure 1-6

Log in to MyEconLab, take a chapter test, and get a personalized Study Plan that tells you which concepts you understand and which ones you need to review. From there, MyEconLab will give you further practice, tutorials, animations, videos, and guided solutions. For more information, visit www.myeconlab.com

PROBLEMS

All problems are assignable in MyEconLab; *exercises that update with real-time data are marked with* 🌐. *Answers to odd-numbered problems appear at the back of the book.*

1-1. Suppose that you are given the following information (see page 4):

Total population	300.0 million
Adult, noninstitutionalized, nonmilitary population	200.0 million
Unemployment	7.5 million

   a. If the labor force participation rate is 70 percent, what is the labor force?

   b. How many workers are employed?

   c. What is the unemployment rate?

1-2. Suppose that you are given the following information (see page 4):

Labor force	206.2 million
Adults in the military	1.5 million
Nonadult population	48.0 million
Employed adults	196.2 million
Institutionalized adults	3.5 million
Nonmilitary, noninstitutionalized adults not in labor force	40.8 million

   a. What is the total population?

   b. How many people are unemployed, and what is the unemployment rate?

   c. What is the labor force participation rate?

1-3. Suppose that the U.S. nonmilitary, noninstitutionalized adult population is 224 million, the number employed is 156 million, and the number unemployed is 8 million. (See page 4.)

   a. What is the unemployment rate?

   b. Suppose that there is a difference of 60 million between the adult population and the combined total of people who are employed and unemployed. How do we classify these 60 million people? Based on these figures, what is the U.S. labor force participation rate?

1-4. During the course of a year, the labor force consists of the same 1,000 people. Employers have chosen not to hire 20 of these people in the face of government regulations making it too costly to employ them. Hence, they remain unemployed throughout the year. At the same time, every month during the year, 30 different people become unemployed, and 30 other different people who were unemployed find jobs. There is no seasonal employment. (See pages 6–8.)

   a. What is the frictional unemployment rate?

   b. What is the unemployment rate?

   c. Suppose that a system of unemployment compensation is established. Each month, 30 new people (not including the 20 that employers have chosen not to employ) continue to become unemployed, but each monthly group of newly unemployed now takes two months to find a job. After this change, what is the frictional unemployment rate?

d. After the change discussed in part (c), what is the unemployment rate?

1-5. Suppose that a nation has a labor force of 100 people. In January, Amy, Barbara, Carine, and Denise are unemployed. In February, those four find jobs, but Evan, Francesco, George, and Horatio become unemployed. Suppose further that every month, the previous four who were unemployed find jobs and four different people become unemployed. Throughout the year, however, three people—Ito, Jack, and Kelley—continually remain unemployed because firms facing government regulations view them as too costly to employ. (See page 8.)

a. What is this nation's frictional unemployment rate?

b. What is its structural unemployment rate?

c. What is its unemployment rate?

1-6. In a country with a labor force of 200, a different group of 10 people becomes unemployed each month, but becomes employed once again a month later. No others outside these groups are unemployed. (See pages 6–8.)

a. What is this country's unemployment rate?

b. What is the average duration of unemployment?

c. Suppose that establishment of a system of unemployment compensation increases to two months the interval that it takes each group of job losers to become employed each month. Nevertheless, a different group of 10 people still becomes unemployed each month. Now what is the average duration of unemployment?

d. Following the change discussed in part (c), what is the country's unemployment rate?

1-7. A nation's frictional unemployment rate is 1 percent. Seasonal unemployment does not exist in this country. Its cyclical rate of unemployment is 3 percent, and its structural unemployment rate is 4 percent. What is this nation's overall rate of unemployment? (See pages 8–9.)

1-8. In 2012, the cost of a market basket of goods was $2,000. In 2014, the cost of the same market basket of goods was $2,100. Use the price index formula to calculate the price index for 2014 if 2012 is the base year. (See pages 11–12.)

1-9. Suppose that in 2013, a typical U.S. student attending a state-supported college bought 10 textbooks at a price of $100 per book and enrolled in 25 credit hours of coursework at a price of $360 per credit hour. In 2014, the typical student continued to purchase 10 textbooks and enroll in 25 credit hours, but the price of a textbook rose to $110 per book, and the tuition price increased to $400 per credit hour. The base year for computing a "student price index" using this information is 2013. What is the value of the student price index in 2013? In 2014? Show your work. (See pages 11–12.)

1-10. Between 2013 and 2014 in a particular nation, the value of the consumer price index—for which the base year is 2010—rose by 9.091 percent, to a value of 120 in 2014. What was the value of the price index in 2013? (See pages 11–12.)

1-11. Consider the following price indexes: 90 in 2013, 100 in 2014, 110 in 2015, 121 in 2016, and 150 in 2017. Answer the following questions. (See pages 11–12.)

a. Which year is likely the base year?

b. What is the inflation rate from 2014 to 2015?

c. What is the inflation rate from 2015 to 2016?

d. If the cost of a market basket in 2014 is $2,000, what is the cost of the same basket of goods and services in 2013? In 2017?

1-12. The real interest rate is 4 percent, and the nominal interest rate is 6 percent. What is the anticipated rate of inflation? (See page 15.)

1-13. Currently, the price index used to calculate the inflation rate is equal to 90. The general expectation throughout the economy is that next year its value will be 99. The current nominal interest rate is 12 percent. What is the real interest rate? (See page 15.)

1-14. At present, the nominal interest rate is 7 percent, and the expected inflation rate is 5 percent. The current year is the base year for the price index used to calculate inflation. (See page 15.)

a. What is the real interest rate?

b. What is the anticipated value of the price index next year?

1-15. Suppose that in 2017 there is a sudden, unanticipated burst of inflation. Consider the situations faced by the following individuals. Who gains and who loses? (See pages 15–16.)

a. A homeowner whose wages will keep pace with inflation in 2017 but whose monthly mortgage payments to a savings bank will remain fixed

b. An apartment landlord who has guaranteed to his tenants that their monthly rent payments during 2017 will be the same as they were during 2016

c. A banker who made an auto loan that the auto buyer will repay at a fixed rate of interest during 2017

d. A retired individual who earns a pension with fixed monthly payments from her past employer during 2017

1-16. Consider the diagram at the right. The line represents the economy's growth trend, and the curve represents the economy's actual course of business fluctuations. For each part below, provide the letter label from the portion of the curve that corresponds to the associated term. (See page 17.)

    a. Contraction

    b. Peak

    c. Trough

    d. Expansion

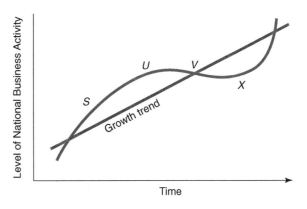

ECONOMICS ON THE NET

Looking at the Unemployment and Inflation Data This chapter reviewed key concepts relating to unemployment and inflation. In this application, you get a chance to examine U.S. unemployment and inflation data on your own.

Title: Bureau of Labor Statistics: Employment and Unemployment

Navigation: Use the link at **www.econtoday.com/chap01** to visit the "Employment" page of the Bureau of Labor Statistics (BLS). Click on "Top Picks" next to *Labor Force Statistics (Current Population Survey–CPS).*

Application Perform the indicated operations, and answer the following questions.

  1. Retrieve data for Civilian Labor Force Level, Employment Level, and Unemployment Level. Can you identify periods of sharp cyclical swings? Do they show up in data for the labor force, employment, or unemployment?

  2. Are cyclical factors important?

For Group Study and Analysis Divide the class into groups, and assign a price index to each group. Ask each group to take a look at the index for All Years at the link to the BLS statistics on inflation at **www.econtoday.com /chap01**. Have each group identify periods during which their index accelerated or decelerated (or even fell). Do the indexes ever provide opposing implications about inflation and deflation?

ANSWERS TO QUICK QUIZZES

p. 7: (i) Unemployed . . . labor force; (ii) job losers . . . reentrants . . . job leavers . . . new entrants; (iii) increase; (iv) female

p. 10: (i) **Frictional;** (ii) **Structural;** (iii) natural

p. 15: (i) base; (ii) Consumer Price; (iii) GDP deflator; (iv) Personal Consumption Expenditure

p. 16: (i) greater . . . less; (ii) purchasing power; (iii) resource

p. 19: (i) business fluctuations; (ii) trough . . . peak; (iii) recession; (iv) external shocks

Measuring the Economy's Performance

2

MyEconLab helps you master each objective and study more efficiently. See end of chapter for details.

LEARNING OBJECTIVES

After reading this chapter, you should be able to:

▶ Describe the circular flow of income and output

▶ Define gross domestic product (GDP)

▶ Understand the limitations of using GDP as a measure of national welfare

▶ Explain the expenditure approach to tabulating GDP

▶ Explain the income approach to computing GDP

▶ Distinguish between nominal GDP and real GDP

Some commentators are already referring to the twenty-first century as the "Asian century." In contrast to the dampened economies of the United States and Europe, economic activity has been booming in China, Hong Kong, Singapore, South Korea, Taiwan, and other Asian countries. Some media reports are suggesting that China's economy will be "larger" than the U.S. economy by 2020. How might we go about trying to measure an economy's "size"? How could we then compare its "size" to the economy of another nation? The starting point for contemplating these questions is the market value of all final goods and services produced within a nation's borders during a given year. Economists refer to this quantity as *gross domestic product*, or *GDP*, which is a key concept covered in this chapter

National income accounting
A measurement system used to estimate national income and its components. One approach to measuring an economy's aggregate performance.

? DID YOU KNOW THAT... the flow of U.S. economic activity since June 2009, when the 2008–2009 recession officially ended, has been more dampened than during any other comparable postrecession period since the Great Depression of the 1930s? To measure the nation's overall economic performance over time, the government utilizes what has become known as **national income accounting**. How this measurement is done is the main focus of this chapter. But first we need to look at the flow of income within an economy, for it is the flow of goods and services from businesses to consumers and of payments from consumers to businesses, that constitutes economic activity.

The Simple Circular Flow

The concept of a circular flow of income (ignoring taxes) involves two principles:

1. In every economic exchange, the seller receives exactly the same amount that the buyer spends.

2. Goods and services flow in one direction and money payments flow in the other.

In the simple economy shown in Figure 2-1 below, there are only businesses and households. It is assumed that businesses sell their *entire* output in the current period to households and that households spend their *entire* income in the current period on consumer products. Households receive their income by selling the use of whatever factors of production they own, such as labor services.

FIGURE 2-1

The Circular Flow of Income and Product

Businesses provide final goods and services to households (upper clockwise loop), who in turn pay for them (upper counterclockwise loop). Payments flow in a counterclockwise direction and can be thought of as a circular flow. The dollar value of output is identical to total income because profits are defined as being equal to total business receipts minus business outlays for wages, rents, and interest. Households provide factor services to businesses and receive income (lower loops).

Product markets

$ value of output = total monetary value of all final goods and services

Final consumer goods and services

Businesses

Households

Factor services: labor, land, capital, entrepreneurial activity

Total income = wages + rents + interest + profits

Factor markets

Profits Explained

We have indicated in Figure 2-1 on the facing page that profit is a cost of production. You might be under the impression that profits are not part of the cost of producing goods and services, but profits are indeed a part of this cost because entrepreneurs must be rewarded for providing their services or they won't provide them. Their reward, if any, is profit. The reward—the profit—is included in the cost of the factors of production. If there were no expectations of profit, entrepreneurs would not incur the risk associated with the organization of productive activities. That is why we consider profits a cost of doing business. Just as workers expect wages, entrepreneurs expect profits.

Total Income or Total Output

The arrow that goes from businesses to households at the bottom of Figure 2-1 is labeled "Total income." What would be a good definition of **total income?** If you answered "the total of all individuals' income," you would be right. But all income is actually a payment for something, whether it be wages paid for labor services, rent paid for the use of land, interest paid for the use of capital, or profits paid to entrepreneurs. It is the amount paid to the resource suppliers. Therefore, total income is also defined as the annual *cost* of producing the entire output of **final goods and services.**

The arrow going from households to businesses at the top of Figure 2-1 represents the dollar value of output in the economy. This is equal to the total monetary value of all final goods and services for this simple economy. In essence, it represents the total business receipts from the sale of all final goods and services produced by businesses and consumed by households. Business receipts are the opposite side of household expenditures. When households purchase goods and services, those payments become a *business receipt.* Every transaction, therefore, simultaneously involves an expenditure and a receipt.

PRODUCT MARKETS Transactions in which households buy goods take place in the product markets—that's where households are the buyers and businesses are the sellers of consumer goods. *Product market* transactions are represented in the upper loops in Figure 2-1 on the facing page. Note that consumer goods and services flow to household demanders, while money flows in the opposite direction to business suppliers.

FACTOR MARKETS *Factor market* transactions are represented by the lower loops in Figure 2-1. In the factor market, households are the sellers. They sell resources such as labor, land, capital, and entrepreneurial ability. Businesses are the buyers in factor markets. Business expenditures represent receipts or, more simply, income for households. Also, in the lower loops of Figure 2-1, factor services flow from households to businesses, while the payments for these services flow in the opposite direction from businesses to households. Observe also the flow of money (counterclockwise) from households to businesses and back again from businesses to households: It is an endless circular flow.

Why the Dollar Value of Total Output Must Equal Total Income

Total income represents the income received by households in payment for the production of goods and services. Why must total income be identical to the dollar value of total output? First, as Figure 2-1 shows, spending by one group is income to another. Second, it is a matter of simple accounting and the economic definition of profit as a cost of production. Profit is defined as what is *left over* from total business receipts after all other costs—wages, rents, interest—have been paid. If the dollar value of total output is $1,000 and the total of wages, rent, and interest for producing that output is $900, profit is $100. Profit is always the *residual* item that makes total income equal to the dollar value of total output.

Total income
The yearly amount earned by the nation's resources (factors of production). Total income therefore includes wages, rent, interest payments, and profits that are received by workers, landowners, capital owners, and entrepreneurs, respectively.

Final goods and services
Goods and services that are at their final stage of production and will not be transformed into yet other goods or services. For example, wheat ordinarily is not considered a final good because it is usually used to make a final good, bread.

QUICK QUIZ See page 50 for the answers. Review concepts from this section in MyEconLab.

In the circular flow model of income and output, households sell _____ services to businesses that pay for those services. The receipt of payments is total _____. Businesses sell goods and services to households that pay for them.

The dollar value of total output is equal to the total monetary value of all _____ goods and services produced.

The dollar value of final output must always equal total income. The variable that adjusts to make this so is known as _____.

National Income Accounting

We have already mentioned that policymakers require information about the state of the national economy. Economists use historical statistical records on the performance of the national economy for testing their theories about how the economy really works. Thus, national income accounting is important. Let's start with the most commonly presented statistic on the national economy.

Gross Domestic Product (GDP)

Gross domestic product (GDP)
The total market value of all final goods and services produced during a year by factors of production located within a nation's borders.

Gross domestic product (GDP) represents the total market value of the nation's annual final product, or output, produced by factors of production located within national borders. We therefore formally define GDP as the total market value of all final goods and services produced in an economy during a year. We are referring here to the value of a *flow of production*. A nation produces at a certain rate, just as you receive income at a certain rate. Your income flow might be at a rate of $20,000 per year or $100,000 per year. Suppose you are told that someone earns $5,000. Would you consider this a good salary? There is no way to answer that question unless you know whether the person is earning $5,000 per month or per week or per day. Thus, you have to specify a time period for all flows. Income received is a flow. You must contrast this with, for example, your total accumulated savings, which are a stock measured at a point in time, not over time. Implicit in just about everything we deal with in this chapter is a time period—usually one year. All the measures of domestic product and income are specified as *rates* measured in dollars per year.

Stress on Final Output

Intermediate goods
Goods used up entirely in the production of final goods.

GDP does not count **intermediate goods** (goods used up entirely in the production of final goods) because to do so would be to count them twice. For example, even though grain that a farmer produces may be that farmer's final product, it is not the final product for the nation. It is sold to make bread. Bread is the final product.

Value added
The dollar value of an industry's sales minus the value of intermediate goods (for example, raw materials and parts) used in production.

We can use a numerical example to clarify this point further. Our example will involve determining the value added at each stage of production. **Value added** is the dollar value contributed to a product at each stage of its production. In Table 2-1 on the facing page, we see the difference between total value of all sales and value added in the production of a donut. We also see that the sum of the values added is equal to the sale price to the final consumer. It is the 45 cents that is used to measure GDP, not the 97 cents. If we used the 97 cents, we would be double counting from stages 2 through 5, for each intermediate good would be counted at least twice—once when it was produced and again when the good it was used in making was sold. Such double counting would greatly exaggerate GDP.

TABLE 2-1

Sales Value and Value Added at Each Stage of Donut Production

(1) Stage of Production	(2) Dollar Value of Sales	(3) Value Added
Stage 1: Fertilizer and seed	$.03	$.03
Stage 2: Growing	.07	.04
Stage 3: Milling	.12	.05
Stage 4: Baking	.30	.18
Stage 5: Retailing	.45	.15

Total dollar value of all sales $.97   Total value added $.45

Stage 1: A farmer purchases 3 cents worth of fertilizer and seed, which are used as factors of production in growing wheat.

Stage 2: The farmer grows the wheat, harvests it, and sells it to a miller for 7 cents. Thus, we see that the farmer has added 4 cents' worth of value. Those 4 cents represent income over and above expenses incurred by the farmer.

Stage 3: The miller purchases the wheat for 7 cents and adds 5 cents as the value added. That is, there is 5 cents for the miller as income. The miller sells the ground wheat flour to a donut-baking company.

Stage 4: The donut-baking company buys the flour for 12 cents and adds 18 cents as the value added. It then sells the donut to the final retailer.

Stage 5: The donut retailer sells donuts at 45 cents apiece, thus creating an additional value of 15 cents.

We see that the total value of the transactions involved in the production of one donut is 97 cents, but the total value added is 45 cents, which is exactly equal to the retail price. The total value added is equal to the sum of all income payments.

Exclusion of Financial Transactions, Transfer Payments, and Secondhand Goods

Remember that GDP is the measure of the dollar value of all final goods and services produced in one year. Many more transactions occur that have nothing to do with final goods and services produced. There are financial transactions, transfers of the ownership of preexisting goods, and other transactions that should not (and do not) get included in our measure of GDP.

FINANCIAL TRANSACTIONS There are three general categories of purely financial transactions: (1) the buying and selling of securities, (2) government transfer payments, and (3) private transfer payments.

Securities When you purchase shares of existing stock in Apple, Inc., someone else has sold it to you. In essence, there was merely a *transfer* of ownership rights. You paid $100 to obtain the stock. Someone else received the $100 and gave up the stock. No producing activity was consummated at that time, unless a broker received a fee for performing the transaction, in which case only the fee is part of GDP. The $100 transaction is not included when we measure GDP.

Government Transfer Payments Transfer payments are payments for which no productive services are concurrently provided in exchange. The most obvious government transfer payments are Social Security benefits and unemployment compensation. The recipients add nothing to current production in return for such transfer

Go to www.econtoday.com/chap02 for the most up-to-date U.S. economic data at the Web site of the Bureau of Economic Analysis.

payments (although they may have contributed in the past to be eligible to receive them). Government transfer payments are not included in GDP.

Private Transfer Payments Are you receiving funds from your parents in order to attend school? Has a wealthy relative ever given you a gift of cash? If so, you have been the recipient of a private transfer payment. This payment is merely a transfer of funds from one individual to another. As such, it does not constitute productive activity and is not included in GDP.

YOU ARE THERE

To consider how much difference it can make if economists broaden the measure of GDP in just a few ways, read on page 44 **Has the Economy Grown More Than Official GDP Data Suggest?**

TRANSFER OF SECONDHAND GOODS If I sell you my two-year-old laptop computer, no current production is involved. I transfer to you the ownership of a computer that was produced years ago. In exchange, you transfer to me $350. The original purchase price of the computer was included in GDP in the year I purchased it. To include the price again when I sell it to you would be counting the value of the computer a second time.

OTHER EXCLUDED TRANSACTIONS Many other transactions are not included in GDP for practical reasons:

* Household production—housecleaning, child care, and other tasks performed by people in their *own* households and for which they receive no payments through the marketplace

* Otherwise legal underground transactions—those that are legal but not reported and hence not taxed, such as paying housekeepers in cash that is not declared as income to the Internal Revenue Service

* Illegal underground activities—these include prostitution, illegal gambling, and the sale of illicit drugs

WHAT IF... **market prices of housecleaning, child care, and lawn care services were valued for inclusion in GDP?**

Even if the prices of household services determined in markets were used to try to place a dollar value on nonmarket household production, national income accountants still would not know annual *volumes* of such nonmarket services. Thus, to attempt to include the total value of nonmarket household production in GDP, the accountants would have to *estimate* the volumes of production performed outside markets. Then they would multiply these volumes times the market prices. The resulting new measure of GDP would be subject to likely estimation mistakes, in addition to the measurement errors that already occur. This would make GDP a less reliable measure of the overall value of final production of goods and services within U.S. borders each year.

Recognizing the Limitations of GDP

Like any statistical measure, gross domestic product is a concept that can be both well used and misused. Economists find it especially valuable as an overall indicator of a nation's economic performance. But it is important to realize that GDP has significant weaknesses. Because it includes only the value of goods and services traded in markets, it excludes *nonmarket* production, such as the household services of homemakers discussed earlier. This can cause some problems in comparing the GDP of an industrialized country with the GDP of a highly agrarian nation in which nonmarket production is relatively more important.

It also causes problems if nations have different definitions of legal versus illegal activities. For instance, a nation with legalized gambling will count the value of gambling services, which has a reported market value as a legal activity. But in a country where gambling is illegal, individuals who provide such services will not report the market value of gambling activities, and so they will not be counted in that country's GDP. This can complicate comparing GDP in the nation where gambling is legal with GDP in the country that prohibits gambling.

Furthermore, although GDP is often used as a benchmark measure for standard-of-living calculations, it is not necessarily a good measure of the well-being of a nation. No measured figure of total national annual income can take account of changes in the degree of labor market discrimination, declines or improvements in personal safety, or the quantity or quality of leisure time. Measured GDP also says little about our environmental quality of life.

As the now-defunct Soviet Union illustrated to the world, the large-scale production of such items as minerals, electricity, and irrigation for farming can have negative effects on the environment: deforestation from strip mining, air and soil pollution from particulate emissions or nuclear accidents at power plants, and erosion of the natural balance between water and salt in bodies of water such as the Aral Sea. Other nations, such as China and India, have also experienced greater pollution problems as their levels of GDP have increased. Hence, it is important to recognize the following point:

> *GDP is a measure of the value of production in terms of market prices and an indicator of economic activity. It is not a measure of a nation's overall welfare.*

Nonetheless, GDP is a relatively accurate and useful measure of the economy's domestic economic activity, measured in current dollars. Understanding GDP is thus an important first step for analyzing changes in economic activity over time.

What new index of a country's broad economic performance has been developed by a large group of developed nations?

POLICY EXAMPLE

Developed Nations Look for a "Happier" Alternative to GDP

The thirty-four member nations of the Organization for Economic Cooperation and Development (OECD) are aiming to supplement or even replace GDP with a new gauge of a country's standard of living and well-being called "Your Better Life Index." This index is geared to measure determinants of human happiness levels. Toward this end, it tabulates a nation's "quality scores" in eleven areas: community, education, environment, governance, health, housing, income, jobs, life satisfaction, safety, and work-life balance. A nation's scores in each of these areas are based on various economic indicators and public opinion polls.

To determine how these scores should be combined to calculate a single value for each nation's Your Better Life Index, the OECD is conducting surveys of large groups of residents in each member country. Each nation's weights for the eleven sets of quality scores will differ, but the OECD plans to rate nations on the basis of their overall index values. The OECD's initial values for the Your Better Life Index yielded rankings in which Denmark, Canada, and Norway rate highest among OECD nations, with Hungary, Portugal, and Estonia rating lowest.

FOR CRITICAL THINKING

How would you determine each person's level of life satisfaction?

QUICK QUIZ See page 50 for the answers. Review concepts from this section in MyEconLab.

_____ _____ _____ is the total market value of final goods and services produced in an economy during a one-year period by factors of production within the nation's borders. It represents the dollar value of the flow of final production over a one-year period.

To avoid double counting, we look only at final goods and services produced or, equivalently, at _____ _____.

In measuring GDP, we must _____ (1) purely financial transactions, such as the buying and selling of securities; (2) government transfer payments and private transfer payments; and (3) the transfer of secondhand goods.

Many other transactions are excluded from measured _____, among them household services rendered by homemakers, underground economy transactions, and illegal economic activities, even though many of these result in the production of final goods and services.

GDP is a useful measure for tracking changes in the _____ _____ of overall economic activity over time, but it is not a measure of the well-being of a nation's residents because it fails to account for nonmarket transactions, the amount and quality of leisure time, environmental or safety issues, labor market discrimination, and other factors that influence general welfare.

Two Main Methods of Measuring GDP

The definition of GDP is the total dollar value of all final goods and services produced during a year. How, exactly, do we go about actually computing this number?

The circular flow diagram presented in Figure 2-1 on page 26 gave us a shortcut method for calculating GDP. We can look at the *flow of expenditures*, which consists of consumption, investment, government purchases of goods and services, and net expenditures in the foreign sector (net exports). In this **expenditure approach** to measuring GDP, we add the dollar value of all final goods and services. We could also use the *flow of income*, looking at the income received by everybody producing goods and services. In this **income approach,** we add the income received by all factors of production.

Deriving GDP by the Expenditure Approach

To derive GDP using the expenditure approach, we must look at each of the separate components of expenditures and then add them together. These components are consumption expenditures, investment, government expenditures, and net exports.

CONSUMPTION EXPENDITURES How do we spend our income? As households or as individuals, we spend our income through consumption expenditure (*C*), which falls into three categories: **durable consumer goods, nondurable consumer goods,** and **services.** Durable goods are *arbitrarily* defined as items that last more than three years. They include automobiles, furniture, and household appliances. Nondurable goods are all the rest, such as food and gasoline. Services are intangible commodities: medical care, education, and the like.

Housing expenditures constitute a major proportion of anybody's annual expenditures. Rental payments on apartments are automatically included in consumption expenditure estimates. People who own their homes, however, do not make rental payments. Consequently, government statisticians estimate what is called the *implicit rental value* of existing owner-occupied homes. It is roughly equal to the amount of rent you would have to pay if you did not own the home but were renting it from someone else.

GROSS PRIVATE DOMESTIC INVESTMENT We now turn our attention to **gross private domestic investment** (*I*) undertaken by businesses. When economists refer to investment, they are referring to additions to productive capacity. **Investment** may be thought of as an activity that uses resources today in such a way that they allow for greater production in the future and hence greater consumption in the future. When a business buys new equipment or puts up a new factory, it is investing. It is increasing its capacity to produce in the future.

In estimating gross private domestic investment, government statisticians also add consumer expenditures on *new* residential structures because new housing represents an addition to our future productive capacity in the sense that a new house can generate housing services in the future.

The layperson's notion of investment often relates to the purchase of stocks and bonds. For our purposes, such transactions simply represent the *transfer of ownership* of assets called stocks and bonds. Thus, you must keep in mind the fact that in economics, investment refers *only* to *additions* to productive capacity, not to transfers of assets.

FIXED VERSUS INVENTORY INVESTMENT In our analysis, we will consider the basic components of investment. We have already mentioned the first one, which involves a firm's purchase of equipment or construction of a new factory. These are called **producer durables,** or **capital goods.** A producer durable, or a capital good, is simply a good that is purchased not to be consumed in its current form but to be used to make other goods and services. The purchase of equipment and factories—capital goods—is called **fixed investment.**

Expenditure approach
Computing GDP by adding up the dollar value at current market prices of all final goods and services.

Income approach
Measuring GDP by adding up all components of national income, including wages, interest, rent, and profits.

Durable consumer goods
Consumer goods that have a life span of more than three years.

Nondurable consumer goods
Consumer goods that are used up within three years.

Services
Mental or physical labor or assistance purchased by consumers. Examples are the assistance of physicians, lawyers, dentists, repair personnel, housecleaners, educators, retailers, and wholesalers; items purchased or used by consumers that do not have physical characteristics.

Gross private domestic investment
The creation of capital goods, such as factories and machines, that can yield production and hence consumption in the future. Also included in this definition are changes in business inventories and repairs made to machines or buildings.

Investment
Any use of today's resources to expand tomorrow's production or consumption.

Producer durables, or **capital goods**
Durable goods having an expected service life of more than three years that are used by businesses to produce other goods and services.

Fixed investment
Purchases by businesses of newly produced producer durables, or capital goods, such as production machinery and office equipment.

The other type of investment has to do with the change in inventories of raw materials and finished goods. Firms do not immediately sell off all their products to consumers. Some of this final product is usually held in inventory waiting to be sold. Firms hold inventories to meet future expected orders for their products. When a firm increases its inventories of finished products, it is engaging in **inventory investment.** Inventories consist of all finished goods on hand, goods in process, and raw materials.

The reason that we can think of a change in inventories as being a type of investment is that an increase in such inventories provides for future increased consumption possibilities. When inventory investment is zero, the firm is neither adding to nor subtracting from the total stock of goods or raw materials on hand. Thus, if the firm keeps the same amount of inventories throughout the year, inventory *investment* has been zero.

Inventory investment
Changes in the stocks of finished goods and goods in process, as well as changes in the raw materials that businesses keep on hand. Whenever inventories are decreasing, inventory investment is negative. Whenever they are increasing, inventory investment is positive.

GOVERNMENT EXPENDITURES In addition to personal consumption expenditures, there are government purchases of goods and services (G). The government buys goods and services from private firms and pays wages and salaries to government employees. Generally, we value goods and services at the prices at which they are sold. But many government goods and services are not sold in the market. Therefore, we cannot use their market value when computing GDP. The value of these goods is considered equal to their *cost.* For example, the value of a newly built road is considered equal to its construction cost and is included in the GDP for the year it was built.

What portion of official U.S. GDP comprises transactions not directly valued in terms of actual market prices?

EXAMPLE
Imputing Part of the Government's Contribution to GDP

A number of items included in U.S. GDP are not explicitly priced in markets. This is particularly true of a significant portion of the government's provision of goods such as public education, fire protection, and national defense. National income accountants have decided that government expenditures on these activities understate the values they would have if private firms provided them in private markets. Thus, the accountants "impute" dollar amounts to these items by valuing them in terms of prices determined in markets for privately produced education, fire protection, and security services.

In recent years, imputed values of such government-provided activities have constituted as much as 15 percent of GDP. As the share of GDP involving activities by federal, state, and local governments continues to rise, this percentage likely will increase as well.

FOR CRITICAL THINKING
If governmental payments for educational services exceed families' valuations of those services, does the imputing process overstate or understate public education's contribution to GDP?

NET EXPORTS (FOREIGN EXPENDITURES) To obtain an accurate representation of GDP, we must include the foreign sector. As U.S. residents, we purchase foreign goods called *imports.* The goods that foreign residents purchase from us are our *exports.* To determine the *net* expenditures from the foreign sector, we subtract the value of imports from the value of exports to get net exports (X) for a year:

Net exports (X) = total exports − total imports

To understand why we subtract imports rather than ignoring them altogether, recall that we want to estimate *domestic* output, so we have to subtract U.S. expenditures on the goods produced in other nations.

Presenting the Expenditure Approach
We have just defined the components of GDP using the expenditure approach. When we add them all together, we get a definition for GDP, which is as follows:

$$GDP = C + I + G + X$$

FIGURE 2-2

GDP and Its Components

Here we see a display of gross domestic product, personal consumption expenditures, government purchases, and gross private domestic investment plus net exports for the years since 1929. (Note that the scale of the vertical axis changes as we move up the axis.) During the Great Depression of the 1930s, gross private domestic investment *plus* net exports was negative because we were investing very little at that time. Since the late 1990s, the sum of gross private domestic investment and net exports has been highly variable.

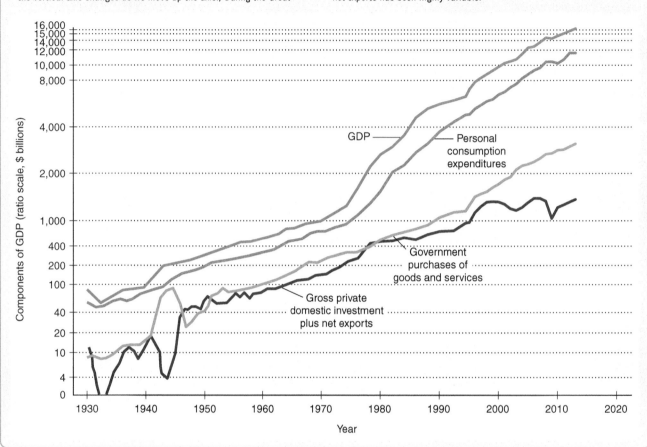

where

C = consumption expenditures
I = investment expenditures
G = government expenditures
X = net exports

THE HISTORICAL PICTURE To get an idea of the relationship among C, I, G, and X, look at Figure 2-2 above, which shows GDP, personal consumption expenditures, government purchases, and gross private domestic investment plus net exports since 1929. When we add up the expenditures of the household, business, government, and foreign sectors, we get GDP.

DEPRECIATION AND NET DOMESTIC PRODUCT We have used the terms *gross domestic product* and *gross private domestic investment* without really indicating what *gross* means. The dictionary defines it as "without deductions," the opposite of *net*. Deductions for what? you might ask. The deductions are for something we call **depreciation.** In the course of a year, machines and structures wear out or are used up in the production of domestic product. For example, houses deteriorate as they are occupied, and machines need repairs or they will fall apart and stop working. Most capital, or durable, goods depreciate.

An estimate of the amount that capital goods have depreciated during the year is subtracted from gross domestic product to arrive at a figure called **net domestic product (NDP),** which we define as follows:

$$NDP = GDP - depreciation$$

Depreciation
Reduction in the value of capital goods over a one-year period due to physical wear and tear and also to obsolescence; also called *capital consumption allowance*.

Net domestic product (NDP)
GDP minus depreciation.

Depreciation is also called **capital consumption allowance** because it is the amount of the capital stock that has been consumed over a one-year period. In essence, it equals the amount a business would have to put aside to repair and replace deteriorating machines. Because we know that

$$GDP = C + I + G + X$$

we know that the formula for NDP is

$$NDP = C + I + G + X - \text{depreciation}$$

Alternatively, because net $I = I - $ depreciation,

$$NDP = C + \text{net } I + G + X$$

Net investment measures *changes* in our capital stock over time and is positive nearly every year. Because depreciation does not vary greatly from year to year as a percentage of GDP, we get a similar picture of what is happening to our national economy by looking at either NDP or GDP data.

Net investment is an important variable to observe over time nonetheless. If everything else remains the same in an economy, changes in net investment can have dramatic consequences for future economic growth (a topic we cover in more detail in Chapter 3). Positive net investment by definition expands the productive capacity of our economy.

This capacity expansion means that there is increased capital, which will generate even more income in the future. When net investment is zero, we are investing just enough to take account of depreciation. Our economy's productive capacity remains unchanged. Finally, when net investment is negative, we can expect negative economic growth prospects in the future. Negative net investment means that our productive capacity is actually declining—we are disinvesting. This actually occurred during the Great Depression.

Capital consumption allowance
Another name for depreciation, the amount that businesses would have to put aside in order to take care of deteriorating machines and other equipment.

Net investment
Gross private domestic investment minus an estimate of the wear and tear on the existing capital stock. Net investment therefore measures the change in the capital stock over a one-year period.

QUICK QUIZ See page 50 for the answers. Review concepts from this section in MyEconLab.

The _____ approach to measuring GDP requires that we add up consumption expenditures, gross private investment, government purchases, and net exports. Consumption expenditures include consumer _____, consumer _____, and _____.

Gross private domestic investment *excludes* transfers of asset ownership. It includes only additions to the productive _____ of a nation, repairs on existing capital goods, and changes in business _____.

We value most government expenditures at their cost because we usually do not have _____ prices at which to value government goods and services.

To obtain **net domestic product (NDP),** we subtract from GDP the year's _____ of the existing capital stock.

Deriving GDP by the Income Approach

If you go back to the circular flow diagram in Figure 2-1 on page 26, you see that product markets are at the top of the diagram and factor markets are at the bottom. We can calculate the value of the circular flow of income and product by looking at expenditures—which we just did—or by looking at total factor payments. Factor payments are called income. We calculate **gross domestic income (GDI),** which we will see is identical to gross domestic product (GDP). Using the income approach, we have four categories of payments to individuals: wages, interest, rent, and profits.

Gross domestic income (GDI)
The sum of all income—wages, interest, rent, and profits—paid to the four factors of production.

1. *Wages.* The most important category is, of course, wages, including salaries and other forms of labor income, such as income in kind and incentive payments.

Go to www.econtoday.com/chap02 to examine recent trends in U.S. GDP and its components.

We also count Social Security taxes (both the employees' and the employers' contributions).

2. *Interest.* Here interest payments do not equal the sum of all payments for the use of funds in a year. Instead, interest is expressed in *net* rather than in gross terms. The interest component of total income is only net interest received by households plus net interest paid to us by foreign residents. Net interest received by households is the difference between the interest they receive (from savings accounts, certificates of deposit, and the like) and the interest they pay (to banks for home mortgages, credit cards, and other loans).

3. *Rent.* Rent is all income earned by individuals for the use of their real (nonmonetary) assets, such as farms, houses, and stores. As stated previously, we have to include here the implicit rental value of owner-occupied houses. Also included in this category are royalties received from copyrights, patents, and assets such as oil wells.

4. *Profits.* Our last category includes total gross corporate profits plus *proprietors' income.* Proprietors' income is income earned from the operation of unincorporated businesses, which include sole proprietorships, partnerships, and producers' cooperatives. It is unincorporated business profit.

All of the payments listed are *actual* factor payments made to owners of the factors of production. When we add them together, though, we do not yet have gross domestic income. We have to take account of two other components: **indirect business taxes,** such as sales and business property taxes, and depreciation, which we have already discussed.

Indirect business taxes
All business taxes except the tax on corporate profits. Indirect business taxes include sales and business property taxes.

INDIRECT BUSINESS TAXES Indirect taxes are the (nonincome) taxes paid by consumers when they buy goods and services. When you buy a book, you pay the price of the book plus any state and local sales tax. The business is actually acting as the government's agent in collecting the sales tax, which it in turn passes on to the government. Such taxes therefore represent a business expense and are included in gross domestic income.

DEPRECIATION Just as we had to deduct depreciation to get from GDP to NDP, so we must *add* depreciation to go from net domestic income to gross domestic income. Depreciation can be thought of as the portion of the current year's GDP that is used to replace physical capital consumed in the process of production. Because somebody has paid for the replacement, depreciation must be added as a component of gross domestic income.

Nonincome expense items
The total of indirect business taxes and depreciation.

The last two components of GDP—indirect business taxes and depreciation—are called **nonincome expense items.**

Figure 2-3 on the facing page shows a comparison between estimated gross domestic product and gross domestic income for 2013. Whether you decide to use the expenditure approach or the income approach, you will come out with the same number. There are sometimes statistical discrepancies, but they are usually relatively small.

QUICK QUIZ   See page 50 for the answers. Review concepts from this section in MyEconLab.

To derive GDP using the income approach, we add up all factor payments, including _____, _____, _____, and _____.	To get an accurate measure of GDP using the income approach, we must also add _____ _____ and _____ to those total factor payments.

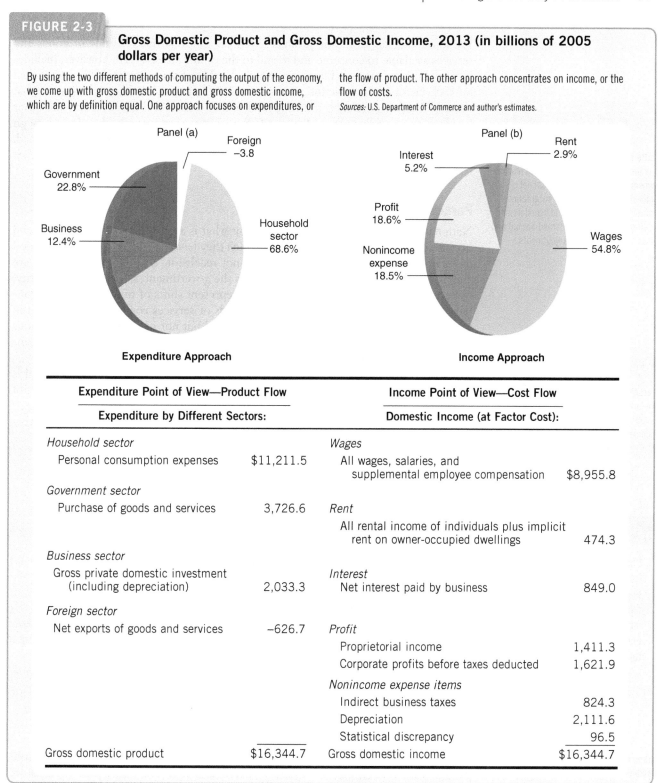

FIGURE 2-3

Gross Domestic Product and Gross Domestic Income, 2013 (in billions of 2005 dollars per year)

By using the two different methods of computing the output of the economy, we come up with gross domestic product and gross domestic income, which are by definition equal. One approach focuses on expenditures, or the flow of product. The other approach concentrates on income, or the flow of costs.

Sources: U.S. Department of Commerce and author's estimates.

Panel (a)

- Foreign −3.8
- Government 22.8%
- Business 12.4%
- Household sector 68.6%

Expenditure Approach

Panel (b)

- Interest 5.2%
- Rent 2.9%
- Profit 18.6%
- Wages 54.8%
- Nonincome expense 18.5%

Income Approach

Expenditure Point of View—Product Flow		Income Point of View—Cost Flow	
Expenditure by Different Sectors:		**Domestic Income (at Factor Cost):**	
Household sector		*Wages*	
Personal consumption expenses	$11,211.5	All wages, salaries, and supplemental employee compensation	$8,955.8
Government sector		*Rent*	
Purchase of goods and services	3,726.6	All rental income of individuals plus implicit rent on owner-occupied dwellings	474.3
Business sector		*Interest*	
Gross private domestic investment (including depreciation)	2,033.3	Net interest paid by business	849.0
Foreign sector		*Profit*	
Net exports of goods and services	−626.7	Proprietorial income	1,411.3
		Corporate profits before taxes deducted	1,621.9
		Nonincome expense items	
		Indirect business taxes	824.3
		Depreciation	2,111.6
		Statistical discrepancy	96.5
Gross domestic product	$16,344.7	Gross domestic income	$16,344.7

Other Components of National Income Accounting

Gross domestic income or product does not really tell us how much income people have access to for spending purposes. To get to those kinds of data, we must make some adjustments, which we now do.

National Income (NI)

We know that net domestic product (NDP) is the total market value of goods and services available to consume and to add to the capital stock. NDP, however, includes indirect business taxes and transfers, which should not count as part of income earned by U.S. factors of production, but does not include various business incomes that should. We therefore subtract from NDP indirect taxes and transfers and add other business income adjustments. Because U.S. residents earn income abroad and foreign residents earn income in the United States, we also add *net* U.S. income earned abroad. The result is what we define as **national income (NI)**—income earned by all U.S. factors of production.

National income (NI)
The total of all factor payments to resource owners. It can be obtained from net domestic product (NDP) by subtracting indirect business taxes and transfers and adding net U.S. income earned abroad and other business income adjustments.

Personal Income (PI)

National income does not actually represent what is available to individuals to spend because some people obtain income for which they have provided no concurrent good or service and others earn income but do not receive it. In the former category are mainly recipients of transfer payments from the government, such as Social Security, welfare, and food stamps. These payments represent shifts of funds within the economy by way of the government, with no goods or services concurrently rendered in exchange. For the other category, income earned but not received, the most obvious examples are corporate retained earnings that are plowed back into the business, contributions to social insurance, and corporate income taxes.

When transfer payments are added and when income earned but not received is subtracted, we end up with **personal income (PI)**—income *received* by the factors of production prior to the payment of personal income taxes.

Why are economists becoming increasingly concerned about trends in the sources of U.S. personal income?

Personal income (PI)
The amount of income that households actually receive before they pay personal income taxes.

EXAMPLE

Sources of U.S. Personal Income Exhibit Unsustainable Trends

During the years since early 2010, the share of personal income derived from private payrolls has dropped to the lowest levels in U.S. history. At the same time, the portion of personal income obtained from government-provided benefits, such as Social Security, food stamps, and unemployment insurance, has risen to the highest level ever. These trends are unsustainable because the government finances its benefit programs by taxing privately generated income sources. In the future, therefore, either the private-payroll share of personal income must increase, or the government-benefit portion must decrease.

FOR CRITICAL THINKING

How could a sustained upswing in economic activity in the private sector of the economy help to reverse both trends in the sources of personal income?

Disposable Personal Income (DPI)

Everybody knows that you do not get to take home all your salary. To obtain **disposable personal income (DPI)**, we subtract all personal income taxes from personal income. This is the income that individuals have left for consumption and saving.

Disposable personal income (DPI)
Personal income after personal income taxes have been paid.

Deriving the Components of GDP

Table 2-2 on the facing page shows how to derive the various components of GDP. It explains how to go from gross domestic product to net domestic product to national income to personal income and then to disposable personal income. On the frontpapers of your book, you can see the historical record for GDP, NDP, NI, PI, and DPI for selected years since 1929.

TABLE 2-2

Going from GDP to Disposable Income, 2013

	Billions of Dollars
Gross domestic product (GDP)	16,344.7
Minus depreciation	−2,111.6
Net domestic product (NDP)	14,233.1
Minus indirect business taxes and transfers	−1,409.6
Plus other business income adjustments	1,521.5
Plus net U.S. income earned abroad	205.6
National income (NI)	14,550.6
Minus corporate taxes, Social Security contributions, corporate retained earnings	−2,220.3
Plus government transfer payments	1,752.5
Personal income (PI)	14,082.8
Minus personal income taxes	−1,569.2
Disposable personal income (DPI)	12,513.6

Sources: U.S. Department of Commerce and author's estimates.

We have completed our rundown of the different ways that GDP can be computed and of the different variants of national income and product. What we have not yet touched on is the difference between national income measured in this year's dollars and national income representing real goods and services.

QUICK QUIZ   See page 50 for the answers. Review concepts from this section in MyEconLab.

To obtain _____ _____, we subtract indirect business taxes and transfers from net domestic product and add other business income adjustments and net U.S. income earned abroad.

To obtain _____ _____, we must add government transfer payments, such as Social Security benefits and food stamps. We must subtract income earned but not received by factor owners, such as corporate retained earnings, Social Security contributions, and corporate income taxes.

To obtain disposable personal income, we subtract all personal _____ _____ from personal income. Disposable personal income is income that individuals actually have for consumption or saving.

Distinguishing between Nominal and Real Values

So far, we have shown how to measure *nominal* income and product. When we say "nominal," we are referring to income and product expressed in the current "face value" of today's dollar. Given the existence of inflation or deflation in the economy, we must also be able to distinguish between the **nominal values** that we will be looking at and the **real values** underlying them. Nominal values are expressed in current dollars. Real income involves our command over goods and services—purchasing power—and therefore depends on money income and a set of prices. Thus, real income refers to nominal income corrected for changes in the weighted average of all prices. In other words, we must make an adjustment for changes in the price level.

Consider an example. Nominal income *per person* in 1960 was only about $2,800 per year. In 2013, nominal income per person was about $50,000. Were people really that badly off in 1960? No, for nominal income in 1960 is expressed in 1960 prices, not in the prices of today. In today's dollars, the per-person income of 1960 would be

Nominal values
The values of variables such as GDP and investment expressed in current dollars, also called *money values;* measurement in terms of the actual market prices at which goods and services are sold.

Real values
Measurement of economic values after adjustments have been made for changes in the average of prices between years.

closer to $14,500, or about 30 percent of today's income per person. This is a meaningful comparison between income in 1960 and income today. Next we will show how we can translate nominal measures of income into real measures by using an appropriate price index, such as the Consumer Price Index or the GDP deflator discussed in Chapter 1.

Correcting GDP for Price Changes

If a tablet device costs $200 this year, 10 tablet devices will have a market value of $2,000. If next year they cost $250 each, the same 10 tablet devices will have a market value of $2,500. In this case, there is no increase in the total quantity of tablet devices, but the market value will have increased by one-fourth. Apply this to every single good and service produced and sold in the United States, and you realize that changes in GDP, measured in *current* dollars, may not be a very useful indication of economic activity.

If we are really interested in variations in the *real* output of the economy, we must correct GDP (and just about everything else we look at) for changes in the average of overall prices from year to year. Basically, we need to generate an index that approximates the average prices and then divide that estimate into the value of output in current dollars to adjust the value of output to what is called **constant dollars,** or dollars corrected for general price level changes. This price-corrected GDP is called *real GDP*.

Constant dollars
Dollars expressed in terms of real purchasing power, using a particular year as the base or standard of comparison, in contrast to current dollars.

How much has correcting for price changes caused real GDP to differ from nominal GDP during the past few years?

EXAMPLE

Correcting GDP for Price Index Changes, 2003–2013

Let's take a numerical example to see how we can adjust GDP for changes in the price index. We must pick an appropriate price index in order to adjust for these price level changes. We mentioned the Consumer Price Index, the Producer Price Index, and the GDP deflator in Chapter 1. Let's use the GDP deflator to adjust our figures. Table 2-3 on the facing page gives 11 years of GDP figures. Nominal GDP figures are shown in column 2. The price index (GDP deflator) is in column 3, with base year of 2005, when the GDP deflator equals 100. Column 4 shows real (inflation-adjusted) GDP in 2005 dollars.

The formula for real GDP is

$$\text{Real GDP} = \frac{\text{nominal GDP}}{\text{price index}} \times 100$$

The step-by-step derivation of real (constant-dollar) GDP is as follows: The base year is 2005, so the price index for that year must equal 100. In 2005, nominal GDP was $12,623.0 billion, and so was real GDP expressed

in 2005 dollars. In 2006, the price index increased to 103.23108. Thus, to correct 2006's nominal GDP for inflation, we divide the price index, 103.23108, into the nominal GDP figure of $13,377.2 billion and then multiply it by 100. The rounded result is $12,958.5 billion, which is 2006 GDP expressed in terms of the purchasing power of dollars in 2005. What about a situation when the price index is lower than in 2005? Look at 2003. Here the price index shown in column 3 is only 94.13504. That means that in 2003, the average of all prices was just above 94 percent of prices in 2005. To obtain 2003 GDP expressed in terms of 2005 purchasing power, we divide nominal GDP, $11,142.2 billion, by 94.13504 and then multiply by 100. The rounded result is a larger number—$11,836.4 billion. Column 4 in Table 2-3 is a better measure of how the economy has performed than column 2, which shows nominal GDP changes.

FOR CRITICAL THINKING
Based on the information in Table 2-3, in what years was the economy in a recession? Explain briefly.

Plotting Nominal and Real GDP

Nominal GDP and real GDP since 1970 are plotted in Figure 2-4 on the facing page. There is quite a big gap between the two GDP figures, reflecting the amount of inflation that has occurred. Note that the choice of a base year is arbitrary. We have chosen 2005 as the base year in our example. This happens to be the base year that is currently used by the government for the GDP deflator.

TABLE 2-3

Correcting GDP for Price Index Changes

To correct GDP for price index changes, we first have to pick a price index (the GDP deflator) with a specific year as its base. In our example, the base year is 2005. The price index for that year is 100. To obtain 2005 constant-dollar GDP, we divide the price index into nominal GDP and multiply by 100. In other words, we divide column 3 into column 2 and multiply by 100. This gives us column 4, which (taking into account rounding of the deflator) is a measure of real GDP expressed in 2005 purchasing power.

(1) Year	(2) Nominal GDP (billions of dollars per year)	(3) Price Index (base year 2005 = 100)	(4) = [(2) ÷ (3)] × 100 Real GDP (billions of dollars per year, in constant 2005 dollars)
2003	11,142.2	94.13504	11,836.4
2004	11,853.3	96.78613	12,246.9
2005	12,623.0	100.00000	12,623.0
2006	13,377.2	103.23108	12,958.5
2007	14,028.7	106.22653	13,206.4
2008	14,291.5	108.58235	13,161.9
2009	13,939.0	109.72912	12,703.1
2010	14,526.5	110.99098	13,088.0
2011	15,094.0	113.36002	13,315.1
2012	15,706.9	115.51386	13,597.4
2013	16,344.7	117.93965	13,858.5

Sources: U.S. Department of Commerce, Bureau of Economic Analysis, and author's estimates.

Per Capita Real GDP

Looking at changes in real GDP as a measure of economic growth may be deceiving, particularly if the population size has changed significantly. If real GDP over a 10-year period went up 100 percent, you might jump to the conclusion that the real income of a typical person in the economy had increased by that amount. But what if during the

FIGURE 2-4

Nominal and Real GDP

Here we plot both nominal and real GDP. Real GDP is expressed in the purchasing power of 2005 dollars. The gap between the two represents price level changes.

Source: U.S. Department of Commerce.

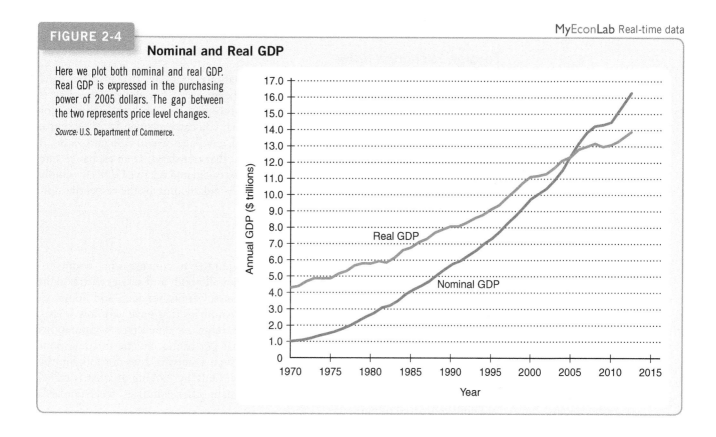

same period the population increased by 200 percent? Then what would you say? Certainly, the amount of real GDP per person, or *per capita real GDP*, would have fallen, even though *total* real GDP had risen. To account not only for price changes but also for population changes, we must first deflate GDP and then divide by the total population, doing this for each year. If we were to look at certain less developed countries, we would find that in many cases, even though real GDP has risen over the past several decades, per capita real GDP has remained constant or fallen because the population has grown just as rapidly or even more rapidly.

QUICK QUIZ   See page 50 for the answers. Review concepts from this section in MyEconLab.

To correct **nominal GDP** for price changes, we first select a base year for our price index and assign it the number _____. Then we construct an index based on how a weighted average of prices has changed relative to that base year. For example, if in the next year a weighted average of the prices indicates that prices have increased by 10

percent, we would assign it the number _____. We then divide each year's price index, so constructed, into its respective nominal GDP figure (and multiply by 100).

We can divide the _____ into real GDP to obtain per capita real GDP.

Comparing GDP throughout the World

It is relatively easy to compare the standard of living of a family in Los Angeles with that of one living in Boston. Both families get paid in dollars and can buy the same goods and services at Wal-Mart, McDonald's, and Costco. It is not so easy, however, to make a similar comparison between a family living in the United States and one in, say, Indonesia. The first problem concerns currency comparisons. Indonesian residents get paid in rupiah, their national currency, and buy goods and services with those rupiah. How do we compare the average standard of living measured in rupiah with that measured in dollars?

Foreign Exchange Rates

Foreign exchange rate
The price of one currency in terms of another.

In earlier chapters, you have encountered international examples that involved local currencies, but the dollar equivalent has always been given. The dollar equivalent is calculated by looking up the **foreign exchange rate** that is published daily in major newspapers throughout the world. If you know that you can exchange $1.25 per euro, the exchange rate is 1.25 to 1 (or otherwise stated, a dollar is worth 0.80 euros). So, if French incomes per capita are, say, 33,936 euros, that translates, at an exchange rate of $1.25 per euro, to $42,420. For years, statisticians calculated relative GDPs by simply adding up each country's GDP in its local currency and dividing by the respective dollar exchange rate.

True Purchasing Power

Purchasing power parity
Adjustment in exchange rate conversions that takes into account differences in the true cost of living across countries.

The problem with simply using foreign exchange rates to convert other countries' GDPs and per capita GDPs into dollars is that not all goods and services are bought and sold in a world market. Restaurant food, housecleaning services, and home repairs do not get exchanged across countries. In countries that have very low wages, those kinds of services are much cheaper than foreign exchange rate computations would imply. Government statistics claiming that per capita income in some poor country is only $300 a year seem shocking. But such a statistic does not tell you the true standard of living of people in that country. Only by looking at what is called **purchasing power parity** can you hope to estimate other countries' true standards of living compared to ours.

Given that nations use different currencies, how can we compare nations' levels of real GDP per capita?

INTERNATIONAL EXAMPLE

Purchasing Power Parity Comparisons of World Incomes

A few years ago, the International Monetary Fund accepted the purchasing power parity approach as the correct one. It started presenting international statistics on each country's GDP relative to every other's based on purchasing power parity relative to the U.S. dollar. The results were surprising. As you can see from Table 2-4 below, China's per capita GDP is higher based on purchasing power parity than when measured at market foreign exchange rates.

FOR CRITICAL THINKING

What is the percentage increase in China's per capita GDP when one switches from foreign exchange rates to purchasing power parity?

TABLE 2-4

Comparing GDP Internationally

Country	Annual GDP Based on Purchasing Power Parity (billions of U.S. dollars)	Per Capita GDP Based on Purchasing Power Parity (U.S. dollars)	Per Capita GDP Based on Foreign Exchange Rates (U.S. dollars)
United States	15,094	48,450	48,450
United Kingdom	2,287	36,511	37,780
Germany	3,221	39,414	43,980
France	2,303	35,194	42,420
Japan	4,381	34,278	45,180
Italy	1,979	32,569	35,330
Russia	3,031	21,358	10,400
Brazil	2,305	11,719	10,720
China	11,347	8,442	4,930
Indonesia	1,131	4,668	2,940

Source: World Bank.

QUICK QUIZ See page 50 for the answers. Review concepts from this section in MyEconLab.

The foreign _____ _____ is the price of one currency in terms of another.

Statisticians often calculate relative GDP by adding up each country's GDP in its local currency and dividing by the dollar _____ _____.

Because not all goods and services are bought and sold in the world market, we must correct exchange rate conversions of other countries' GDP figures to take into account differences in the true _____ of _____ across countries.

YOU ARE THERE
Has the Economy Grown More Than Official GDP Data Suggest?

Economists Bart Hobijn and Charles Steindel of the Federal Reserve Bank of New York are studying how to adjust GDP to take into account three items that the official measure ignores: (1)"intangible investment," including spending on research into new processes or products that currently is not counted within GDP as business fixed investment; (2) real investment in capital goods undertaken by the government but potentially undercounted in official GDP tabulations; and (3) the shift from nonmarket home production not counted as GDP to market production because more women are entering the U.S. labor force.

Hobijn and Steindel find that adding the first two items tends to push up fixed investment measures and consequently increases their broadened GDP measure. Taking into account the third item tends to reduce this broadened measure, because it subtracts an imputed value of home production from the higher official market production of women who have joined the labor force. The net effect of taking all three items into account, Hobijn and Steindel conclude, is that the average official growth rate of inflation-adjusted (real) GDP is nearly 0.5 percentage point per year lower than the rate of growth of their altered GDP measure after adjusting for inflation. Consequently, they conclude that the official U.S. economic growth rate may be significantly understated.

Critical Thinking Questions

1. Why is intangible investment harder to measure than tangible investment?
2. What makes it difficult to assign a dollar value to nonmarket home production?

ISSUES & APPLICATIONS

Asia's "Economic Size" Depends on How It Is Measured

CONCEPTS APPLIED
▶ Real GDP
▶ Purchasing Power Parity
▶ Per Capita Real GDP

The media have reported on the growing economic clout of Asian nations. How large is the combined "economic size" of Asian nations in comparison with other nations, such as the United States? The answer depends on what measure we use when making comparisons between Asia and the world as a whole.

Asian Real GDP as a Percentage of Global Real GDP

Figure 2-5 on the facing page displays the combined real GDP of Asia as a percentage of the combined real GDP of the entire world. The figure displays this percentage according to two different measures. One measure uses prevailing exchange rates in currency markets to adjust all countries' real GDP levels to allow for comparisons. The other measure utilizes purchasing power parity adjustments.

Utilizing market exchange rates indicates that Asian real GDP's share of global real GDP generally rose steadily between 1980 and the mid-1990s from less than one-fifth to slightly more than one-fourth of global GDP. In contrast, purchasing power parity measures of real GDP indicate that Asia's measured share of the world economy has grown to more than 35 percent.

Asian versus Global Per Capita Real GDP

Another measure for comparing the relative "economic sizes" of Asia and the world is per capita real GDP. This measure also can be computed using either foreign exchange rates or purchasing power parities to allow for cross-country comparisons.

When per capita real GDP is computed using foreign exchange rates, Asian per capita real GDP is only 11 percent of global per capita real GDP. When the tabulation uses purchasing power parity adjustments, Asian per capita real GDP is 26 percent of global real GDP per capita. Thus, both measures indicate that although Asia's economic size has risen in relation to the world as a whole, Asia's per capita real GDP remains relatively low. Even though Asian real GDP is relatively high, so is Asia's population, which is why the region's per capita real GDP remains only a fraction of the global level.

FIGURE 2-5

Asia's Share of Global Real GDP

This figure displays two measures of real GDP in Asia as a percentage of worldwide real GDP. The measure that uses foreign exchange rates to adjust real GDP data to comparable amounts across countries indicates a rise in Asia's share until the mid-1990s and a leveling off since then. The measure based on purchasing power parity comparisons shows a larger and longer-lived rise in Asia's share of global real GDP.

Source: International Monetary Fund.

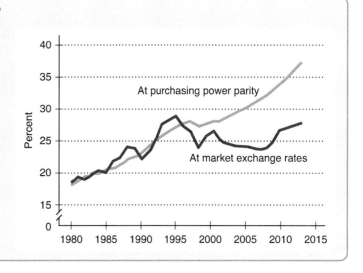

For Critical Thinking

1. Why is there such a difference in Asia's share of global real GDP, depending on whether the computation uses purchasing power parities or exchange rates?

2. Why is Asia's "economic size" so much smaller on a per capita basis than on an absolute basis?

Web Resources

1. For a recent analysis of the growth of Asia's share of global economic activity, go to www.econtoday.com/chap02.

2. To learn about a recent claim that China's economy is already "larger" than the U.S. economy, go to www.econtoday.com/chap02.

MyEconLab

For more questions on this chapter's Issues & Applications, go to MyEconLab. In the Study Plan for this chapter, select Section N: News.

MyEconLab

Here is what you should know after reading this chapter. MyEconLab will help you identify what you know, and where to go when you need to practice.

WHAT YOU SHOULD KNOW

The Circular Flow of Income and Output The circular flow of income and output captures two principles: (1) In every transaction, the seller receives the same amount that the buyer spends; and (2) goods and services flow in one direction, and money payments flow in the other direction. Households ultimately purchase the nation's total output of final goods and services. They make these purchases using income—wages, rents, interest, and profits—earned from selling labor, land, capital, and entrepreneurial services, respectively. Hence, income equals the value of output.

national income accounting, 26
total income, 27
final goods and services, 27

Key Figure
Figure 2-1, 26

WHERE TO GO TO PRACTICE

- MyEconLab Study Plan 2.1
- Animated Figure 2-1

MyEconLab *continued*

WHAT YOU SHOULD KNOW		WHERE TO GO TO PRACTICE
Gross Domestic Product (GDP) A nation's gross domestic product is the total market value of its final output of goods and services produced within a given year using factors of production located within the nation's borders. Because GDP measures the value of a flow of production during a year in terms of market prices, it is not a measure of a nation's wealth.	gross domestic product (GDP), 28 intermediate goods, 28 value added, 28	• MyEconLab Study Plan 2.2
The Limitations of Using GDP as a Measure of National Welfare Gross domestic product is a useful measure for tracking year-to-year changes in the value of a nation's overall economic activity in terms of market prices. But it excludes nonmarket transactions that may add to or detract from general welfare. It also fails to account for factors such as environmental quality and the amount and quality of leisure time.		• MyEconLab Study Plan 2.2
The Expenditure Approach to Tabulating GDP To calculate GDP using the expenditure approach, we sum consumption spending, investment expenditures, government spending, and net export expenditures. Thus, we add up the total amount spent on newly produced goods and services to obtain the dollar value of the output produced and purchased during the year.	expenditure approach, 31 income approach, 31 durable consumer goods, 32 nondurable consumer goods, 32 services, 32 gross private domestic investment, 32 investment, 32 producer durables, or capital goods, 32 fixed investment, 32 inventory investment, 33 depreciation, 34 net domestic product (NDP), 34 capital consumption allowance, 35 net investment, 35 Key Figure Figure 2-2, 34	• MyEconLab Study Plan 2.3 • Animated Figure 2-2
The Income Approach to Computing GDP To tabulate GDP using the income approach, we add total wages and salaries, rental income, interest income, profits, and nonincome expense items—indirect business taxes and depreciation—to obtain gross domestic income, which is equivalent to gross domestic product. Thus, the total value of all income earnings (equivalent to total factor costs) equals GDP.	gross domestic income (GDI), 35 indirect business taxes, 36 nonincome expense items, 36 national income (NI), 38 personal income (PI), 38 disposable personal income (DPI), 38	• MyEconLab Study Plans 2.3, 2.4

WHAT YOU SHOULD KNOW

Distinguishing between Nominal GDP and Real GDP Nominal GDP is the value of newly produced output during the current year measured at current market prices. Real GDP adjusts the value of current output into constant dollars by correcting for changes in the overall level of prices from year to year. To calculate real GDP, we divide nominal GDP by the price index (the GDP deflator) and multiply by 100.

nominal values, 39
real values, 39
constant dollars, 40
foreign exchange rate, 42
purchasing power parity, 42

Key Figure
Figure 2-4, 41

WHERE TO GO TO PRACTICE

- MyEconLab Study Plans 2.5, 2.6
- Animated Figure 2-4

Log in to MyEconLab, take a chapter test, and get a personalized Study Plan that tells you which concepts you understand and which ones you need to review. From there, MyEconLab will give you further practice, tutorials, animations, videos, and guided solutions. For more information, visit www.myeconlab.com

PROBLEMS

All problems are assignable in MyEconLab; exercises that update with real-time data are marked with ◉. Answers to odd-numbered problems appear at the back of the book.

2-1. Explain in your own words why the flow of gross domestic product during a given interval must always be equivalent to the flow of gross domestic income within that same period. (See page 26.)

2-2. In the first stage of manufacturing each final unit of a product, a firm purchases a key input at a price of $4 per unit. The firm then pays a wage rate of $3 for the time that labor is exerted, combining an additional $2 of inputs for each final unit of output produced. The firm sells every unit of the product for $10. What is the contribution of each unit of output to GDP in the current year? (See page 29.)

2-3. Each year after a regular spring cleaning, Maria spruces up her home a little by retexturing and repainting the walls of one room in her house. In a given year, she spends $25 on magazines to get ideas about wall textures and paint shades, $45 on newly produced texturing materials and tools, $35 on new paintbrushes and other painting equipment, and $175 on newly produced paint. Normally, she preps the walls, a service that a professional wall-texturing specialist would charge $200 to do, and applies two coats of paint, a service that a painter would charge $350 to do, on her own. (See pages 28–30.)

  a. When she purchases her usual set of materials and does all the work on her home by herself in a given spring, how much does Maria's annual spring texturing and painting activity contribute to GDP?

  b. Suppose that Maria hurt her back this year and is recovering from surgery. Her surgeon has instructed her not to do any texturing work, but he has given her the go-ahead to paint a room as long as she is cautious. Thus, she buys all the equipment required to both texture and paint a room. She hires someone else to do the texturing work but does the painting herself. How much would her spring painting activity add to GDP?

  c. As a follow-up to part (b), suppose that as soon as Maria bends down to dip her brush into the paint, she realizes that painting will be too hard on her back after all. She decides to hire someone else to do all the work using the materials she has already purchased. In this case, how much will her spring painting activity contribute to GDP?

2-4. Each year, Johan typically does all his own landscaping and yard work. He spends $200 per year on mulch for his flower beds, $225 per year on flowers and plants, $50 on fertilizer for his lawn, and $245 on gasoline and lawn mower maintenance. The lawn and garden store where he obtains his mulch and fertilizer charges other customers $500 for the service of spreading that much mulch in flower beds and $50 for the service of distributing fertilizer over a yard the size of Johan's. Paying a professional yard care service to mow his lawn would require an expenditure of $1,200 per year, but in that case Johan would not have to buy gasoline or maintain his own lawn mower. (See pages 28–30.)

  a. In a normal year, how much does Johan's landscaping and yard work contribute to GDP?

  b. Suppose that Johan has developed allergy problems this year and will have to reduce the amount of his yard work. He can wear a mask while running his lawn mower, so he will keep mowing his yard, but he will pay the lawn and garden center to spread mulch and distribute fertilizer. How much will all the work on Johan's yard contribute to GDP this year?

c. As a follow-up to part (b), at the end of the year, Johan realizes that his allergies are growing worse and that he will have to arrange for all his landscaping and yard work to be done by someone else next year. How much will he contribute to GDP next year?

2-5. Consider the following hypothetical data for the U.S. economy in 2016 (all amounts are in trillions of dollars; see pages 32–35).

Consumption	11.0
Indirect business taxes	.8
Depreciation	1.3
Government spending	2.8
Imports	2.7
Gross private domestic investment	3.0
Exports	2.5

a. Based on the data, what is GDP? NDP? NI?

b. Suppose that in 2017, exports fall to $2.3 trillion, imports rise to $2.85 trillion, and gross private domestic investment falls to $2.25 trillion. What will GDP be in 2017, assuming that other values do not change between 2016 and 2017?

2-6. Look back at Table 2-3 on page 41, which explains how to calculate real GDP in terms of 2005 constant dollars. Change the base year to 2003. Recalculate the price index, and then recalculate real GDP—that is, express column 4 of Table 2-3 in terms of 2003 dollars instead of 2005 dollars. (See page 41.)

2-7. Consider the following hypothetical data for the U.S. economy in 2016 (in trillions of dollars), and assume that there are no statistical discrepancies or other adjustments. (See pages 33–39.)

Profit	2.8
Indirect business taxes and transfers	.8
Rent	.7
Interest	.8
Wages	8.2
Depreciation	1.3
Consumption	11.0
Exports	1.5
Government transfer payments	2.0
Personal income taxes and nontax payments	1.7
Imports	1.7
Corporate taxes and retained earnings	.5
Social Security contributions	2.0
Government spending	1.8

a. What is gross domestic income? GDP?

b. What is gross private domestic investment?

c. What is personal income? Personal disposable income?

2-8. Which of the following are production activities that are included in GDP? Which are not? (See pages 28–30.)

a. Mr. King performs the service of painting his own house instead of paying someone else to do it.

b. Mr. King paints houses for a living.

c. Mrs. King earns income from parents by taking baby photos in her digital photography studio.

d. Mrs. King takes photos of planets and stars as part of her astronomy hobby.

e. E*Trade charges fees to process Internet orders for stock trades.

f. Mr. Ho spends $10,000 on shares of stock via an Internet trade order and pays a $10 brokerage fee.

g. Mrs. Ho receives a Social Security payment.

h. Ms. Hernandez makes a $300 payment for an Internet-based course on stock trading.

i. Mr. Langham sells a used laptop computer to his neighbor.

2-9. Explain what happens to contributions to GDP in each of the following situations. (See page 29.)

a. A woman who makes a living charging for investment advice on her Internet Web site marries one of her clients, to whom she now provides advice at no charge.

b. A man who had washed the windows of his own house every year decides to pay a private company to wash those windows this year.

c. A company that had been selling used firearms illegally finally gets around to obtaining an operating license and performing background checks as specified by law prior to each gun sale.

2-10. Explain what happens to the official measure of GDP in each of the following situations. (See page 29.)

a. Air quality improves significantly throughout the United States, but there are no effects on aggregate production or on market prices of final goods and services.

b. The U.S. government spends considerably less on antipollution efforts this year than it did in recent years.

c. The quality of cancer treatments increases, so patients undergo fewer treatments, which hospitals continue to provide at the same price per treatment as before.

2-11. Which of the following activities of a computer manufacturer during the current year are included in this year's measure of GDP? (See page 29.)

a. The manufacturer produces a chip in June, uses it as a component in a computer in August, and sells the computer to a customer in November.

b. A retail outlet of the firm sells a computer completely built during the current year.

c. A marketing arm of the company receives fee income during the current year when a buyer of one of its computers elects to use the computer manufacturer as her Internet service provider.

2-12. A number of economists contend that official measures of U.S. gross private investment expenditures are understated. Answer parts (a) and (b) below to determine just how understated these economists believe that officially measured investment spending may be. (See page 32.)

a. Household spending on education, such as college tuition expenditures, is counted as consumption spending. Some economists suggest that these expenditures, which amount to 6 percent of GDP, should be counted as investment spending instead. Based on this 6 percent estimate and the GDP computations detailed in Figure 2-3 on page 37, how many billions of dollars would shift from consumption to investment if this suggestion was adopted?

b. Some economists argue that intangible forms of investment—business research spending, educational expenses for employees, and the like—should be included in the official measure of gross private domestic investment. These expenditures, which amount to about 9 percent of GDP, currently are treated as business input expenses and are not included in GDP. Based on this 9 percent estimate and the GDP computations detailed in Figure 2-3 on page 37, how much higher would gross private domestic investment be if intangible investment expenditures were counted as investment spending?

c. Based on your answers to parts (a) and (b), what is the total amount that gross private domestic investment may be understated, according to economists who argue that household education spending and business intangible investments should be added? How much may GDP be understated?

2-13. Consider the table at the top of the next column for the economy of a nation whose residents produce five final goods. (See pages 39–40.)

Good	2013 Price	2013 Quantity	2017 Price	2017 Quantity
Shampoo	$ 2	15	$ 4	20
External hard drives	200	10	250	10
Books	40	5	50	4
Milk	3	10	4	3
Candy	1	40	2	20

Assuming a 2013 base year:

a. What is nominal GDP for 2013 and 2017?

b. What is real GDP for 2013 and 2017?

2-14. Consider the following table for the economy of a nation whose residents produce four final goods. (See pages 39–40.)

Good	2015 Price	2015 Quantity	2016 Price	2016 Quantity
Computers	$1,000	10	$800	15
Bananas	6	3,000	11	1,000
Televisions	100	500	150	300
Cookies	1	10,000	2	10,000

Assuming a 2016 base year:

a. What is nominal GDP for 2015 and 2016?

b. What is real GDP for 2015 and 2016?

2-15. In the table for Problem 2-14, if 2016 is the base year, what is the price index for 2015? (Round decimal fractions to the nearest tenth.)

2-16. Suppose that early in a year, a hurricane hits a town in Florida and destroys a substantial number of homes. A portion of this stock of housing, which had a market value of $100 million (not including the market value of the land), was uninsured. The owners of the residences spent a total of $5 million during the rest of the year to pay salvage companies to help them save remaining belongings. A small percentage of uninsured owners had sufficient resources to spend a total of $15 million during the year to pay construction companies to rebuild their homes. Some were able to devote their own time, the opportunity cost of which was valued at $3 million, to work on rebuilding their homes. The remaining people, however, chose to sell their land at its market value and abandon the remains of their houses. What was the combined effect of these transactions on GDP for this year? (Hint: Which transactions took place in the markets for *final* goods and services?) In what ways, if any, does the effect on GDP reflect a loss in welfare for these individuals? (See page 29.)

2-17. Suppose that in 2015, geologists discover large reserves of oil under the tundra in Alaska. These new reserves have a market value estimated at $50 billion at current oil prices. Oil companies spend $1 billion to hire workers and move and position equipment to begin exploratory pumping during that same year. In the process of loading some of the oil onto tankers at a port, one company accidentally spills some of the oil into a bay and by the end of the year pays $1 billion to other companies to clean it up. The oil spill kills thousands of birds, seals, and other wildlife. What was the combined effect of these events on GDP for this year? (Hint: Which transactions took place in the markets for *final* goods and services?) In what ways, if any, does the effect on GDP reflect a loss in national welfare? (See page 29.)

2-18. Consider the diagram below, and answer the following questions. (See page 41.)
   a. What is the base year? Explain.
   b. Has this country experienced inflation or deflation since the base year? How can you tell?

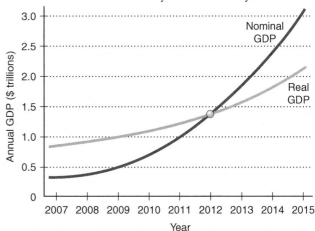

ECONOMICS ON THE NET

Tracking the Components of Gross Domestic Product
One way to keep tabs on the components of GDP is via the FRED database at the Web site of the Federal Reserve Bank of St. Louis.

Title: Gross Domestic Product and Components

Navigation: Use the link at **www.econtoday.com/chap02** to visit the home page of the Federal Reserve Bank of St. Louis. Click on *Gross Domestic Product (GDP) and Components*.

Application

1. Click on *GDP/GNP*, and then click a checkmark next to *GDP (Gross Domestic Product)*. Write down nominal GDP data for the past 10 quarters.

2. Back up to *GDPCA (Real Gross Domestic Product) Dollars.* Write down the amounts for the past 10 quarters. Use the formula on page XXX to calculate the price level for each quarter. Has the price level decreased or increased in recent quarters?

For Group Study and Analysis Divide the class into "consumption," "investment," "government sector," and "foreign sector" groups. Have each group evaluate the contribution of each category of spending to GDP and to its quarter-to-quarter volatility. Reconvene the class, and discuss the factors that appear to create the most variability in GDP.

ANSWERS TO QUICK QUIZZES

p. 28: (i) factor . . . income; (ii) final; (iii) profit

p. 31: (i) Gross domestic product; (ii) value added; (iii) exclude; (iv) GDP; (v) market value

p. 35: (i) expenditure . . . durables . . . nondurables . . . services; (ii) capacity . . . inventories; (iii) market; (iv) depreciation

p. 36: (i) wages . . . interest . . . rent . . . profits; (ii) indirect business taxes . . . depreciation

p. 39: (i) national income; (ii) personal income; (iii) income taxes

p. 42: (i) 100 . . . 110; (ii) population

p. 43: (i) exchange rate; (ii) exchange rate; (iii) cost . . . living

Global Economic Growth and Development

3

LEARNING OBJECTIVES

After reading this chapter, you should be able to:

▶ Define economic growth

▶ Recognize the importance of economic growth rates

▶ Explain why productivity increases are crucial for maintaining economic growth

▶ Describe the fundamental determinants of economic growth

▶ Understand the basis of new growth theory

▶ Discuss the fundamental factors that contribute to a nation's economic development

MyEconLab helps you master each objective and study more efficiently. See end of chapter for details.

From the late 1990s through most of the first decade of the 2000s, media reports bemoaned the sorry state of the U.S. private *saving rate,* or the annual flow of saving per year as a percentage of households' personal disposable income per year. U.S. residents were saving only a little over 2 percent of their annual personal disposable income, so few resources were available to finance the purchase of capital goods. This fact, observers worried, would tend to drag down U.S. economic growth. Since 2007, the average private saving rate has increased significantly, which has led some observers to become more optimistic about U.S. growth prospects. Nevertheless, others point to a sharp drop in the *overall* national saving rate, inclusive of *government* saving, as reason for even greater concern about the prospects for future U.S. economic growth. By the time you have completed this chapter, you will be able to evaluate these alternative perspectives about the U.S. saving rate and economic growth.

since 2009, the U.S. birthrate has been at its lowest level in a century? This development is a striking turnabout from 2007, when more babies were born in the United States than in any prior year in the nation's history. In this chapter, you will learn why this lower U.S. birthrate would tend to boost the near-term measured rate of U.S. *economic growth,* other things being equal. You will also discover why a prolonged drop in the country's birthrate would have a theoretically ambiguous effect on the long-term economic growth rate.

How Do We Define Economic Growth?

We can show economic growth graphically as an outward shift of a production possibilities curve, as is seen in Figure 3-1 below. If there is economic growth between 2015 and 2037, the production possibilities curve will shift outward toward the red curve. The distance that it shifts represents the amount of economic growth, defined as the increase in the productive capacity of a nation. Although it is possible to come up with a measure of a nation's increased productive capacity, it would not be easy. Therefore, we turn to a more readily obtainable definition of economic growth.

Most people have a general idea of what economic growth means. When a nation grows economically, its citizens must be better off in at least some ways, usually in terms of their material well-being. Typically, though, we do not measure the well-being of any nation solely in terms of its total output of real goods and services or in terms of real GDP without making some adjustments. After all, India has a real GDP more than 15 times as large as that of Denmark. The population in India, though, is about 200 times greater than that of Denmark. Consequently, we view India as a relatively poor country and Denmark as a relatively rich country. Thus, when we measure economic growth, we must adjust for population growth. Our formal definition becomes this: **Economic growth** occurs when there are increases in *per capita* real GDP, measured by the rate of change in per capita real GDP per year. Figure 3-2 on page 54 presents the historical record of real GDP per person in the United States.

Economic growth
Increases in per capita real GDP measured by its rate of change per year.

Problems in Definition

Our definition of economic growth says nothing about the *distribution* of output and income. A nation might grow very rapidly in terms of increases in per capita real GDP, while its poor people remain poor or become even poorer. Therefore, in assessing the economic growth record of any nation, we must be careful to pinpoint which income groups have benefited the most from such growth. How much does economic growth differ across countries?

FIGURE 3-1

Economic Growth

If there is growth between 2015 and 2037, the production possibilities curve for the entire economy will shift outward from the blue line labeled 2015 to the red line labeled 2037. The distance that it shifts represents an increase in the productive capacity of the nation.

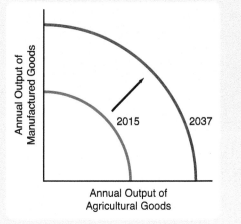

INTERNATIONAL EXAMPLE

Growth Rates around the World

Table 3-1 shows the average annual rate of growth of real GDP per person in selected countries since 1970. During this time period, the United States has been positioned about midway in the pack. Thus, even though we are one of the world's richest countries, our rate of economic growth has been in the middle range. The reason that U.S. per capita real GDP has remained higher than per capita real GDP in most other nations is that, despite the late-2000s downturn, U.S. growth has been sustained over many decades. This is something that most other countries have so far been unable to accomplish.

FOR CRITICAL THINKING

"The largest change is from zero to one." Does this statement have anything to do with relative growth rates in poorer versus richer countries?

TABLE 3-1

Per Capita Real GDP Growth Rates in Various Countries	Country	Average Annual Rate of Growth of Real GDP Per Capita, 1970–2013 (%)
	Sweden	1.6
	France	1.7
	Germany	1.7
	United States	1.8
	Canada	1.9
	Japan	2.0
	Turkey	2.0
	Brazil	2.3
	India	3.3
	Indonesia	4.3
	Malaysia	4.8
	China	7.1

Sources: World Bank, International Monetary Fund, and author's estimates.

Real standards of living can go up without any positive economic growth. This can occur if individuals are, on average, enjoying more leisure by working fewer hours but producing as much as they did before. For example, if per capita real GDP in the United States remained at $55,000 a year for a decade, we could not automatically jump to the conclusion that U.S. residents were, on average, no better off. What if, during that same 10-year period, average hours worked fell from 37 per week to 33 per week? That would mean that during the 10 years under study, individuals in the labor force were "earning" 4 more hours of leisure a week.

Nothing so extreme as this example has occurred in this country, but something similar has. Average hours worked per week fell steadily until the 1960s, when they leveled off. That means that during much of the history of this country, the increase in per capita real GDP *understated* the growth in living standards that we were experiencing because we were enjoying more and more leisure as time passed.

Go to www.econtoday.com/chap03 to get the latest figures and estimates on economic growth throughout the world.

Is Economic Growth Bad?

Some commentators on our current economic situation believe that the definition of economic growth ignores its negative effects. Some psychologists even contend that economic growth makes us worse off. They say that the more the economy grows, the more "needs" are created so that we feel worse off as we become richer. Our expectations are rising faster than reality, so we presumably always suffer from a sense of disappointment. Also, economists' measurement of economic growth does not take into account the spiritual and cultural aspects of the good life. As with all activities, both costs and benefits are associated with growth. You can see some of those listed in Table 3-2 on the bottom of the next page.

MyEconLab Real-time data

FIGURE 3-2

The Historical Record of U.S. Economic Growth

The graph traces per capita real GDP in the United States since 1900. Data are given in 2005 dollars.

Source: U.S. Department of Commerce.

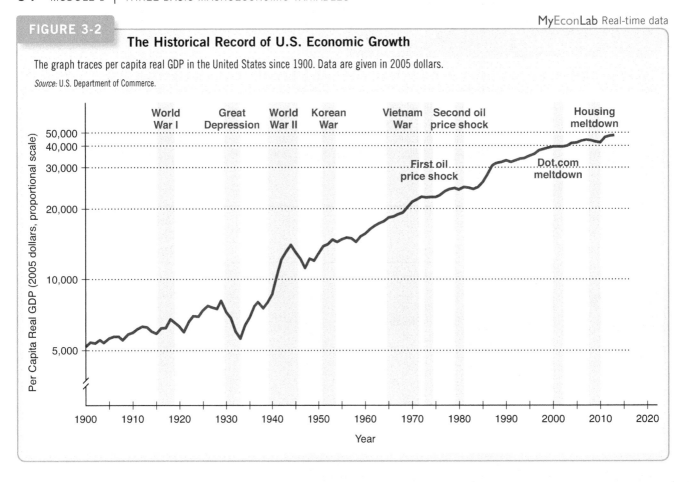

Any measure of economic growth that we use will be imperfect. Nonetheless, the measures that we do have allow us to make comparisons across countries and over time and, if used judiciously, can enable us to gain important insights. Per capita real GDP, used so often, is not always an accurate measure of economic well-being, but it is a serviceable measure of productive activity.

The Importance of Growth Rates

Notice in Table 3-1 on the previous page that the growth rates in real per capita income for most countries differ very little—generally by only a few percentage points. You might want to know why such small differences in growth rates are important. What does it matter if we grow at 3 percent rather than at 4 percent per year? The answer is that in the long run, it matters a lot.

A small difference in the rate of economic growth does not matter very much for next year or the year after. For the more distant future, however, it makes considerable difference. The power of *compounding* is impressive. Let's see what happens with three different annual rates of growth: 3 percent, 4 percent, and 5 percent. We start with

TABLE 3-2

Costs and Benefits of Economic Growth

Benefits	Costs
Reduction in illiteracy	Environmental pollution
Reduction in poverty	Breakdown of the family
Improved health	Isolation and alienation
Longer lives	Urban congestion
Political stability	

TABLE 3-3

One Dollar Compounded Annually at Different Interest Rates

Here we show the value of a dollar at the end of a specified period during which it has been compounded annually at a specified interest rate. For example, if you took $1 today and invested it at 5 percent per year, it would yield $1.05 at the end of one year. At the end of 10 years, it would equal $1.63, and at the end of 50 years, it would equal $11.50.

Number of Years	Interest Rate						
	3%	4%	5%	6%	8%	10%	20%
1	1.03	1.04	1.05	1.06	1.08	1.10	1.20
2	1.06	1.08	1.10	1.12	1.17	1.21	1.44
3	1.09	1.12	1.16	1.19	1.26	1.33	1.73
4	1.13	1.17	1.22	1.26	1.36	1.46	2.07
5	1.16	1.22	1.28	1.34	1.47	1.61	2.49
6	1.19	1.27	1.34	1.41	1.59	1.77	2.99
7	1.23	1.32	1.41	1.50	1.71	1.94	3.58
8	1.27	1.37	1.48	1.59	1.85	2.14	4.30
9	1.30	1.42	1.55	1.68	2.00	2.35	5.16
10	1.34	1.48	1.63	1.79	2.16	2.59	6.19
20	1.81	2.19	2.65	3.20	4.66	6.72	38.30
30	2.43	3.24	4.32	5.74	10.00	17.40	237.00
40	3.26	4.80	7.04	10.30	21.70	45.30	1,470.00
50	4.38	7.11	11.50	18.40	46.90	117.00	9,100.00

$1 trillion per year of U.S. GDP at some time in the past. We then compound this $1 trillion, or allow it to grow at these three different growth rates. The difference is huge. In 50 years, $1 trillion per year becomes $4.38 trillion per year if compounded at 3 percent per year. Just one percentage point more in the growth rate, 4 percent, results in a real GDP of $7.11 trillion per year in 50 years, almost double the previous amount. Two percentage points' difference in the growth rate—5 percent per year—results in a real GDP of $11.5 trillion per year in 50 years, or nearly three times as much. Obviously, very small differences in annual growth rates result in great differences in cumulative economic growth. That is why nations are concerned if the growth rate falls even a little in absolute percentage terms.

Thus, when we talk about growth rates, we are talking about compounding. In Table 3-3 above, we show how $1 compounded annually grows at different interest rates. We see in the 3 percent column that $1 in 50 years grows to $4.38. We merely multiplied $1 trillion times 4.38 to get the growth figure in our earlier example. In the 5 percent column, $1 grows to $11.50 after 50 years. Again, we multiplied $1 trillion times 11.50 to get the growth figure for 5 percent in the preceding example.

How much of a difference in your future income would result from a 1-percentage-point drop in the long-term U.S. growth rate?

EXAMPLE

Gauging the Future Impact of a 1-Percentage-Point Growth Drop

Over nearly four decades, the rate of growth in U.S. per capita real GDP has averaged close to 2 percent. Since 2008, however, the average growth rate of the nation's per capita real GDP has remained below 1 percent. If this were to become the new long-term average rate of economic growth in a dampened U.S. economy, how much lower would per capita real GDP be in future years?

Gross domestic product represents both the value of production of goods and services per year and the income generated during that year. Thus, U.S. per capita real GDP is equal to the annual inflation-adjusted income earned by an average resident during a year. This means that a permanent drop in the rate of economic growth from 2 percent to 1 percent would translate into an 18 percent dampening in that resident's income after 20 years. After 50 years, the 1-percentage-point reduction in the growth rate would cause the resident's real income to be more than 60 percent less than it would have been at the higher growth rate.

FOR CRITICAL THINKING

Why does just a 1-percentage-point reduction in the rate of economic growth make such a significant difference if it persists for many years?

Rule of 70
A rule stating that the approximate number of years required for per capita real GDP to double is equal to 70 divided by the average rate of economic growth.

THE RULE OF 70 Table 3-3 on the preceding page indicates that how quickly the level of a nation's per capita real GDP increases depends on the rate of economic growth. A formula called the **rule of 70** provides a shorthand way to calculate approximately how long it will take a country to experience a significant increase in per capita real GDP. According to the rule of 70, the approximate number of years necessary for a nation's per capita real GDP to increase by 100 percent—that is, to *double*—is equal to 70 divided by the average rate of economic growth. Thus, at an annual growth rate of 10 percent, per capita real GDP should double in about 7 years.

As you can see in Table 3-3, at a 10 percent growth rate, in 7 years per capita real GDP would rise by a factor of 1.94, which is very close to 2, or very nearly the doubling predicted by the rule of 70. At an annual growth rate of 8 percent, the rule of 70 predicts that nearly 9 years will be required for a nation's per capita real GDP to double. Table 3-3 verifies that this prediction is correct. Indeed, the table shows that after 9 years an exact doubling will occur at a growth rate of 8 percent.

The rule of 70 implies that at lower rates of economic growth, much more time must pass before per capita real GDP will double. At a 3 percent growth rate, just over 23 (70 ÷ 3) years must pass before per capita real income doubles. At a rate of growth of only 1 percent per year, 70 (70 ÷ 1) years must pass. This means that if a nation's average rate of economic growth is 1 percent instead of 3 percent, 47 more years—about two generations—must pass for per capita real GDP to double. Clearly, the rule of 70 verifies that even very slight differences in economic growth rates are important.

QUICK QUIZ See page 73 for the answers. Review concepts from this section in MyEconLab.

Economic growth can be defined as the increase in _____ _____ real GDP, measured by its rate of change per year.

The _____ of economic growth are reductions in illiteracy, poverty, and illness and increases in life spans and political stability. The _____ of economic

growth may include environmental pollution, alienation, and urban congestion.

Small percentage-point differences in growth rates lead to _____ differences in per capita real GDP over time. These differences can be seen by examining a compound interest table such as the one in Table 3-3 on page 55.

Productivity Increases: The Heart of Economic Growth

Labor productivity
Total real domestic output (real GDP) divided by the number of workers (output per worker).

Let's say that you are required to type 10 term papers and homework assignments a year. You have a digital device, but you do not know how to touch-type. You end up spending an average of two hours per typing job. The next summer, you buy a touch-typing tutorial to use on your digital device and spend a few minutes a day improving your speed. The following term, you spend only one hour per typing assignment, thereby saving 10 hours a semester. You have become more productive. This concept of productivity summarizes your ability (and everyone else's) to produce the same output with fewer inputs. Thus, **labor productivity** is normally measured by dividing total real domestic output (real GDP) by the number of workers or the number of labor hours. By definition, labor productivity increases whenever average output produced per worker (or per hour worked) during a specified time period increases.

Clearly, there is a relationship between economic growth and increases in labor productivity. If you divide all resources into just capital and labor, economic growth can be defined simply as the cumulative contribution to per capita GDP growth of three components: the rate of growth of capital, the rate of growth of labor, and the rate of growth of capital and labor productivity. If everything else remains constant, improvements in labor productivity ultimately lead to economic growth and higher living standards.

Go to www.econtoday.com/chap03 for information about the latest trends in U.S. labor productivity.

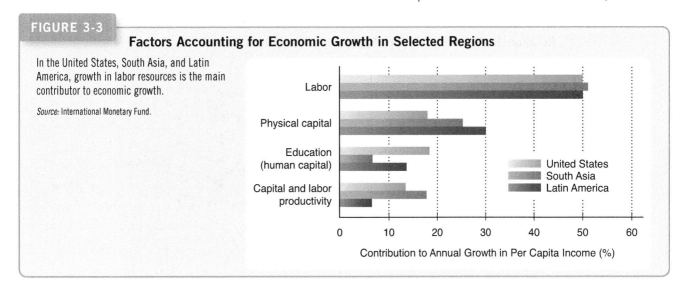

FIGURE 3-3

Factors Accounting for Economic Growth in Selected Regions

In the United States, South Asia, and Latin America, growth in labor resources is the main contributor to economic growth.

Source: International Monetary Fund.

Figure 3-3 above displays estimates of the relative contributions of the growth of labor and capital and the growth of labor and capital productivity to economic growth in the United States, nations in South Asia, and Latin American countries. The growth of labor resources, through associated increases in labor force participation, has contributed to the expansion of output that has accounted for at least half of economic growth in all three regions. Total capital is the sum of physical capital, such as tools and machines, and human capital, which is the amount of knowledge acquired from research and education.

Figure 3-3 shows the separate contributions of the growth of these forms of capital, which together have accounted for roughly a third of the growth rate of per capita incomes in the United States, South Asia, and Latin America. In these three parts of the world, growth in overall capital and labor productivity has contributed the remaining 7 to 18 percent.

Saving: A Fundamental Determinant of Economic Growth

Economic growth does not occur in a vacuum. It is not some predetermined fate of a nation. Rather, economic growth depends on certain fundamental factors. One of the most important factors that affect the rate of economic growth and hence long-term living standards is the rate of saving.

A basic proposition in economics is that if you want more tomorrow, you have to consume less today.

> *To have more consumption in the future, you have to consume less today and save the difference between your income and your consumption.*

On a national basis, this implies that higher saving rates eventually mean higher living standards in the long run, all other things held constant. Although the U.S. saving rate has recently increased, concern has been growing that we still are not saving enough. Saving is important for economic growth because without saving, we cannot have investment. If there is no investment in our capital stock, there would be much less economic growth.

The relationship between the rate of saving and per capita real GDP is shown in Figure 3-4 on the next page. Among the nations with the highest rates of saving are China, Germany, Japan, and Saudi Arabia.

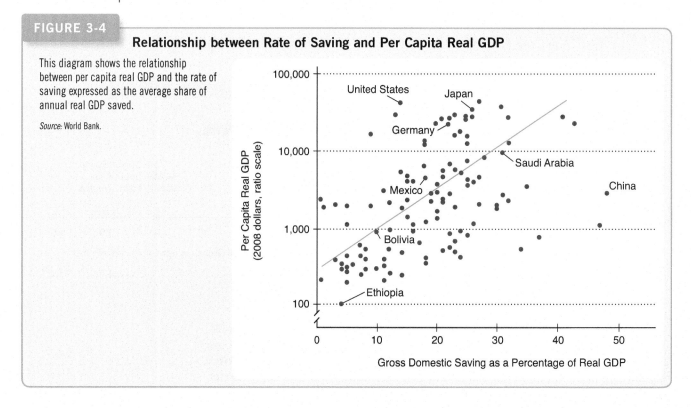

FIGURE 3-4

Relationship between Rate of Saving and Per Capita Real GDP

This diagram shows the relationship between per capita real GDP and the rate of saving expressed as the average share of annual real GDP saved.

Source: World Bank.

Economic growth is numerically equal to the rate of growth of _____ plus the rate of growth of _____ plus the rate of growth in the productivity of _____ and of _____. Improvements in labor productivity, all other things being equal, lead to greater economic growth and higher living standards.

One fundamental determinant of the rate of growth is the rate of _____. To have more consumption in the future, we have to _____ rather than consume. In general, countries that have had higher rates of _____ have had higher rates of growth in per capita real GDP.

New Growth Theory and the Determinants of Growth

A simple arithmetic definition of economic growth has already been given. The per capita growth rates of capital and labor plus the per capita growth rate of their productivity constitute the rate of economic growth. Economists have had good data on the growth of the physical capital stock in the United States as well as on the labor force. But when you add those two growth rates together, you still do not get the total economic growth rate in the United States. The difference has to be due to improvements in productivity. Economists typically labeled this "improvements in technology," and that was that. More recently, proponents of what is now called **new growth theory** argue that technology cannot simply be viewed as an outside factor without explanation. Technology must be understood in terms of what drives it. What are the forces that make productivity grow in the United States and elsewhere?

New growth theory
A theory of economic growth that examines the factors that determine why technology, research, innovation, and the like are undertaken and how they interact.

Growth in Technology

Consider some startling statistics about the growth in technology. Microprocessor speeds may increase from 4,000 megahertz to 10,000 megahertz by the year 2025. By that same year, the size of the thinnest circuit line within a transistor may decrease by 90 percent. The typical memory capacity (RAM) of digital devices will jump from 8 gigabytes, or more than 100 times the equivalent text in the Internal Revenue Code, to more than 400 gigabytes. Recent developments in phase-change memory technologies and in new techniques for storing bits of data on molecules and even individual atoms promise even greater expansions of digital memory capacities. Predictions are that computers may become as powerful as the human brain by 2030.

Technology: A Separate Factor of Production

We now recognize that technology must be viewed as a separate factor of production that is sensitive to rewards. Indeed, one of the major foundations of new growth theory is this:

> *When the rewards are greater, more technological advances will occur.*

Let's consider several aspects of technology here, the first one being research and development.

Research and Development

A certain amount of technological advance results from research and development (R&D) activities that have as their goal the development of specific new materials, new products, and new machines. How much spending a nation devotes to R&D can have an impact on its long-term economic growth. Part of how much a nation spends depends on what businesses decide is worth spending. That in turn depends on their expected rewards from successful R&D. If your company develops a new way to produce computer memory chips, how much will it be rewarded? The answer depends on what you can charge others to use the new technique.

PATENTS To protect new techniques developed through R&D, we have a system of **patents,** in which the federal government gives the patent holder the exclusive right to make, use, and sell an invention for a period of 20 years. One can argue that this special protection given to owners of patents increases expenditures on R&D and therefore adds to long-term economic growth. Figure 3-5 below shows

YOU ARE THERE

To learn about the economic implications of a change in how the U.S. legal system handles patents, take a look at **Implementing a New Patent Framework to Promote Innovation** on page 68.

Patent

A government protection that gives an inventor the exclusive right to make, use, or sell an invention for a limited period of time (currently, 20 years).

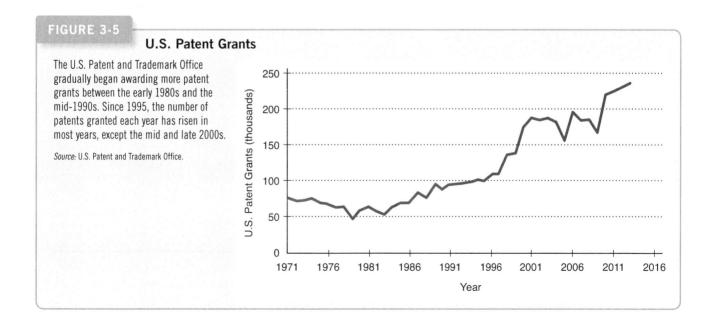

FIGURE 3-5

U.S. Patent Grants

The U.S. Patent and Trademark Office gradually began awarding more patent grants between the early 1980s and the mid-1990s. Since 1995, the number of patents granted each year has risen in most years, except the mid and late 2000s.

Source: U.S. Patent and Trademark Office.

that U.S. patent grants fell during the 1970s, increased steadily after 1982, surged following 1995, dropped in 2004 and 2005, and increased again after 2007.

POSITIVE EXTERNALITIES AND R&D Positive externalities are benefits from an activity that are enjoyed by someone besides the instigator of the activity. In the case of R&D spending, a certain amount of the benefits go to other companies that do not have to pay for them. In particular, according to economists David Coe of the International Monetary Fund and Elhanan Helpman of Harvard University, about a quarter of the global productivity gains of R&D investment in the top seven industrialized countries goes to other nations. For every 1 percent rise in the stock of R&D in the United States alone, for example, productivity in the rest of the world increases by about 0.25 percent.

One country's R&D expenditures benefit other countries because they are able to import capital goods—say, computers and telecommunications networks—from technologically advanced countries and then use them as inputs in making their own industries more efficient. In addition, countries that import high-tech goods are able to imitate the technology.

The Open Economy and Economic Growth

People who study economic growth today emphasize the importance of the openness of the economy. Free trade encourages a more rapid spread of technology and industrial ideas. Moreover, open economies may experience higher rates of economic growth because their own industries have access to a bigger market. When trade barriers are erected in the form of tariffs and the like, domestic industries become isolated from global technological progress. This occurred for many years in Communist countries and in most developing countries in Africa, Latin America, and elsewhere. Figure 3-6 below shows the relationship between economic growth and openness as measured by the level of tariff barriers.

Is China's rapid pace of economic growth threatened by a reduction in the nation's international openness?

FIGURE 3-6

The Relationship between Economic Growth and Tariff Barriers to International Trade

Nations with low tariff barriers are relatively open to international trade and have tended to have higher average annual rates of real GDP per capita growth since 1965.

Source: World Bank.

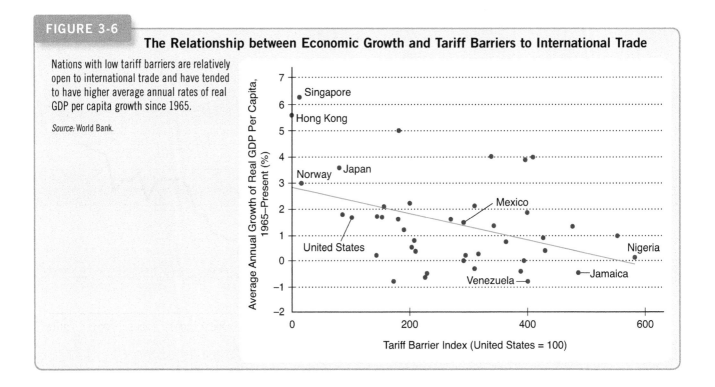

China Rethinks Its Openness to Merchandise Trade

During the latter 1990s and 2000s, China's annual rate of economic growth often exceeded 8 percent. In recent years, however, its average growth rate has dropped slightly. Some observers suggest that this growth dip has resulted from an "indigenous (home-developed) innovation" policy implemented by the nation's government. This policy gives advantages to domestic sellers of a variety of goods, including computing and telecommunications devices and office equipment. The policy thus effectively discourages imports of these items.

China's government has extended special protections to financial services, such as property-casualty and life insurance, from foreign competition. The indigenous innovation policy therefore now includes imports of services as well as physical goods. Consequently, China has a less open economy, one not so likely to grow quite as rapidly as before.

FOR CRITICAL THINKING
Why might restrictions on imports of the latest digital devices particularly threaten China's rapid pace of economic growth?

Innovation and Knowledge

We tend to think of technological progress as, say, the invention of the transistor. But invention means little by itself. **Innovation** is required. Innovation involves the transformation of something new, such as an invention, into something that benefits the economy either by lowering production costs or by providing new goods and services. Indeed, the new growth theorists believe that real wealth creation comes from innovation and that invention is but a facet of innovation.

Historically, technologies have moved relatively slowly from invention to innovation to widespread use. The dispersion of new technology remains for the most part slow and uncertain. The inventor of the transistor thought it might be used to make better hearing aids. At the time it was invented, the *New York Times*'s sole reference to it was in a small weekly column called "News of Radio." When the laser was invented, no one really knew what it could be used for. It was initially used to help in navigation, measurement, and chemical research. Today, it is used in the reproduction of music, printing, surgery, telecommunications, and optical data transmittal and storage. Tomorrow, who knows?

Typically, thousands of raw ideas emerge each year at a large firm's R&D laboratories. Only a few hundred of these ideas develop into formal proposals for new processes or products. Of these proposals, the business selects perhaps a few dozen that it deems suitable for further study to explore their feasibility. After careful scrutiny, the firm concludes that only a handful of these ideas are inventions worthy of being integrated into actual production processes or launched as novel products. The firm is fortunate if one or two ultimately become successful marketplace innovations.

How have efforts by physicists to hide objects from sight set off a search for innovations applying to a variety of markets?

Innovation
Transforming an invention into something that is useful to humans.

The Quest for Invisibility Promises Waves of Innovation

Physicists have developed ways to make objects disappear by using fabrics called *metamaterials* to deflect electromagnetic—for instance, light and magnetic—waves and thereby create artificial blind spots. Originally, the idea behind such inventive activities was to make items invisible to the human eye, thereby rendering magicians' tricks using mirrors and sleight of hand obsolete. Once physicists realized that metamaterials could effectively cancel out electromagnetic waves, however, they began to concentrate on developing potentially marketable innovations.

One possible innovation is elimination of cell phone static by making buildings disappear to wireless signals. Another is the potential for dramatic improvements in magnetic resonance images (MRIs) used to diagnose physical ailments. Finally, deflection of electromagnetic waves offers promise in canceling out waves of water, such as tsunamis that otherwise might damage offshore oil platforms. Thus, the pursuit of invisibility may produce several innovations.

FOR CRITICAL THINKING
So far, does invisibility research appear to have yielded inventions or innovations? Explain.

The Importance of Ideas and Knowledge

Economist Paul Romer has added at least one other important factor that determines the rate of economic growth. He contends that production and manufacturing knowledge is just as important as the other determinants and perhaps even more so. He considers knowledge a factor of production that, like capital, has to be paid for by forgoing current consumption. Economies must therefore invest in knowledge just as they invest in machines. Because past investment in capital may make it more profitable to acquire more knowledge, there may be an investment-knowledge cycle in which investment spurs knowledge and knowledge spurs investment.

A once-and-for-all increase in a country's rate of investment may permanently raise that country's growth rate. (According to traditional theory, a once-and-for-all increase in the rate of saving and therefore in the rate of investment simply leads to a new steady-state standard of living, not one that continues to increase.)

Another way of looking at knowledge is that it is a store of ideas. According to Romer, ideas are what drive economic growth. In fact, we have become an idea economy. Consider Apple, Inc. A relatively small percentage of that company's labor force is involved in actually building products. Rather, a majority of Apple's employees are attempting to discover new ideas that can be translated into computer code that can then be turned into products. The major conclusion that Romer and other new growth theorists draw is this:

Economic growth can continue as long as we keep coming up with new ideas.

The Importance of Human Capital

Knowledge, ideas, and productivity are all tied together. One of the threads is the quality of the labor force. Increases in the productivity of the labor force are a function of increases in human capital, the fourth factor of production. Recall that human capital consists of the knowledge and skills that people in the workforce acquire through education, on-the-job training, and self-teaching. To increase your own human capital, you have to invest by forgoing income-earning activities while you attend school. Society also has to invest in the form of teachers and education.

According to the new growth theorists, human capital is becoming nearly as important as physical capital, particularly when trying to explain international differences in living standards. It is therefore not surprising that one of the most effective ways that developing countries can become developed is by investing in secondary schooling.

One can argue that policy changes that increase human capital will lead to more technological improvements. One of the reasons that concerned citizens, policymakers, and politicians are looking for a change in the U.S. schooling system is that our educational system seems to be falling behind those of other countries. This lag is greatest in science and mathematics—precisely the areas required for developing better technology.

How have periodic drains of human capital affected economic growth in Ireland?

INTERNATIONAL EXAMPLE

Ireland Experiences Yet Another Big "Brain Drain"

It is common to refer to an emigration of many of a nation's most skilled residents to other countries as a "brain drain." During the past two centuries, Ireland has experienced several brain drains. Most well known was the departure of about a million Irish residents in response to the great potato famine of the mid-nineteenth century. About a century later, an economic meltdown induced tens of thousands of Irish residents to move to Britain. A similar population shift took place in the late 1980s, when about 120,000 Irish residents left for England.

Following a major business downturn in Ireland in 2008, yet another emigration wave began. During the past couple of years, about 1,000 people per week have departed from Ireland's shores. Current forecasts suggest that this latest population shift away from Ireland eventually will total at least 150,000 people, including many of that nation's best-educated professionals. In response to this latest Irish brain drain, many economists have reduced substantially their estimates for Ireland's long-term rate of economic growth.

FOR CRITICAL THINKING

Can you think of any policy actions, short of explicit limits on emigration, that a nation's government might implement in an effort to slow or even halt a brain drain?

QUICK QUIZ See page 73 for the answers. Review concepts from this section in MyEconLab.

_____ _____ theory argues that the greater the rewards, the more rapid the pace of technology. And greater rewards spur research and development.

The openness of a nation's economy to international _____ seems to correlate with its rate of economic growth.

Invention and innovation are not the same thing. _____ are useless until _____ transforms them into goods and services that people find valuable.

According to _____ _____ theory, economic growth can continue as long as we keep coming up with new ideas.

Increases in _____ capital can lead to greater rates of economic growth. These come about by increased education, on-the-job training, and self-teaching.

Immigration, Property Rights, and Growth

New theories of economic growth have also shed light on two additional factors that play important roles in influencing a nation's rate of growth of per capita real GDP: immigration and property rights.

Population and Immigration as They Affect Economic Growth

There are several ways to view population growth as it affects economic growth. On the one hand, population growth can result in a larger labor force and increases in human capital, which contribute to economic growth. On the other hand, population growth can be seen as a drain on the economy because for any given amount of GDP, more population means lower per capita GDP. According to Harvard economist Michael Kremer, the first of these effects is historically more important. His conclusion is that population growth drives technological progress, which then increases economic growth. The theory is simple: If there are 50 percent more people in the United States, there will be 50 percent more geniuses. And with 50 percent more people, the rewards for creativity are commensurately greater. Otherwise stated, the larger the potential market, the greater the incentive to become ingenious.

A larger market also provides an incentive for well-trained people to immigrate, which undoubtedly helps explain why the United States attracts a disproportionate number of top scientists from around the globe.

Does immigration help spur economic growth? Yes, according to the late economist Julian Simon, who pointed out that "every time our system allows in one more immigrant, on average, the economic welfare of American citizens goes up. . . . Additional immigrants, both the legal and the illegal, raise the standard of living of U.S. natives and have little or no negative impact on any occupational or income class." He further argued that immigrants do not displace natives from jobs but rather create jobs through their purchases and by starting new businesses. Immigrants' earning and spending simply expand the economy.

Not all researchers agree with Simon, and few studies have tested the theories he and Kremer have advanced. This area is currently the focus of much research.

WHAT IF... **the government halted inflows of immigrants possessing scientific training?**

Economists have found that the influx of scientifically trained immigrants contributes to about one-third of the annual flow of new inventions that obtain U.S. patents. This means that if the already-constrained inflow of immigrants with academic backgrounds in math and science were halted, the number of inventions per year likely would drop to about two-thirds of its current number. Thus, further limits on immigration of foreign scientists would substantially reduce innovative activity in the United States.

Property Rights and Entrepreneurship

If you were in a country where bank accounts and businesses were periodically expropriated by the government, how willing would you be to leave your financial assets in a savings account or to invest in a business? Certainly, you would be less willing than if such actions never occurred. In general, the more securely private property rights are assigned, the more capital accumulation there will be. People will be willing to invest their savings in endeavors that will increase their wealth in future years. This requires that property rights in their wealth be sanctioned and enforced by the government. In fact, some economic historians have attempted to show that it was the development of well-defined private property rights and legal structures that allowed Western Europe to increase its growth rate after many centuries of stagnation. The ability and certainty with which they can reap the gains from investing also determine the extent to which business owners in other countries will invest capital in developing countries. The threat of loss of property rights that hangs over some developing nations undoubtedly stands in the way of foreign investments that would allow these nations to develop more rapidly.

The legal structure of a nation is closely tied to the degree with which its citizens use their own entrepreneurial skills. We identified entrepreneurship as the fifth factor of production. Entrepreneurs are the risk takers who seek out new ways to do things and create new products. To the extent that entrepreneurs are allowed to capture the rewards from their entrepreneurial activities, they will seek to engage in those activities. In countries where such rewards cannot be captured because of a lack of property rights, there will be less entrepreneurship. Typically, this results in fewer investments and a lower rate of growth.

QUICK QUIZ   See page 73 for the answers. Review concepts from this section in MyEconLab.

While some economists argue that population growth reduces _____ growth, others contend that the opposite is true. The latter economists consequently believe that immigration should be encouraged rather than discouraged.	Well-defined and protected _____ rights are important for fostering entrepreneurship. In the absence of well-defined _____ rights, individuals have less incentive to take risks, and economic growth rates suffer.

Economic Development

Development economics
The study of factors that contribute to the economic growth of a country.

How did developed countries travel paths of growth from extreme poverty to relative riches? That is the essential issue of **development economics,** which is the study of why some countries grow and develop and others do not and of policies that might help developing economies get richer. It is not enough simply to say that people in different countries are different and that is why some countries are rich and some countries are poor. Economists do not deny that different cultures have different work ethics, but they are unwilling to accept such a pat and fatalistic answer.

Look at any world map. About four-fifths of the countries you will see on the map are considered relatively poor. The goal of economists who study development is to help the more than 4 billion people today with low living standards join the more than 2 billion people who have at least moderately high living standards.

Putting World Poverty into Perspective

Most U.S. residents cannot even begin to understand the reality of poverty in the world today. At least one-half, if not two-thirds, of the world's population lives at subsistence level, with just enough to eat for survival. Indeed, the World Bank estimates that nearly 20 percent of the world's people live on less than $1.50 per day. The official poverty line in the United States is above the annual income of at least half the human beings on the planet. This is not to say that we should ignore domestic problems with the poor and homeless simply because they are living better than many people elsewhere in the world. Rather, it is necessary for us to maintain an appropriate perspective on what are considered problems for this country relative to what are considered problems elsewhere.

The Relationship between Population Growth and Economic Development

The world's population is growing at the rate of about 2 people a second. That amounts to 172,800 a day or 63.1 million a year. Today, there are more than 6.8 billion people on earth. By 2050, according to the United Nations, the world's population will be close to leveling off at around 9 billion. Panel (a) of Figure 3-7 on the following page shows population growth. Panel (b) emphasizes an implication of panel (a), which is that almost all the growth in population is occurring in developing nations. Many developed countries are expected to lose population over the next several decades.

Ever since the Reverend Thomas Robert Malthus wrote *An Essay on the Principle of Population* in 1798, excessive population growth has been a concern. Modern-day Malthusians are able to generate great enthusiasm for the concept that population growth is bad. Over and over, media pundits and a number of scientists tell us that rapid population growth threatens economic development and the quality of life.

MALTHUS WAS PROVED WRONG Malthus predicted that population would outstrip food supplies. This prediction has never been supported by the facts, according to economist Nicholas Eberstadt of the American Enterprise Institute for Public Policy Research. As the world's population has grown, so has the world's food stock, measured by calories per person. Furthermore, the price of food, corrected for inflation, has generally been falling for more than a century. That means that the amount of food has been expanding faster than the increase in demand caused by increased population.

GROWTH LEADS TO SMALLER FAMILIES Furthermore, economists have found that as nations become richer, average family size declines. Otherwise stated, the more economic development occurs, the slower the population growth rate becomes. This has certainly been true in Western Europe and in the former Soviet Union, where populations in some countries are actually declining. Predictions of birthrates in developing countries have often turned out to be overstated if those countries experience rapid economic growth. This was the case in Chile, Hong Kong, Mexico, and Taiwan.

Recent research on population and economic development has revealed that social and economic modernization has been accompanied by a decline in childbearing significant enough that it might be called a fertility revolution. Modernization reduces infant mortality, which in turn reduces the incentive for couples to have many children to make sure that a certain number survive to adulthood. Modernization also lowers the demand for children for a variety of reasons, not the least being that couples in more developed countries do not need to rely on their children to take care of them in old age.

The Stages of Development: Agriculture to Industry to Services

If we analyze the development of modern rich nations, we find that they went through three stages. First is the agricultural stage, when most of the population is involved in agriculture. Then comes the manufacturing stage, when much of the population becomes involved in the industrialized sector of the economy. And finally there is a shift toward services. That is exactly what happened in the United States: The so-called tertiary, or service, sector of the economy continues to grow, whereas the manufacturing sector (and its share of employment) is declining in relative importance.

FIGURE 3-7

Expected Growth in World Population by 2050

Panel (a) displays the percentages of the world's population residing in the various continents by 2050 and shows projected population growth for these continents and for selected nations. It indicates that Asia and Africa are expected to gain the most in population by the year 2050.

Panel (b) indicates that population will increase in developing countries before beginning to level off around 2050, whereas industrially advanced nations will grow very little in population in the first half of this century.

Source: United Nations.

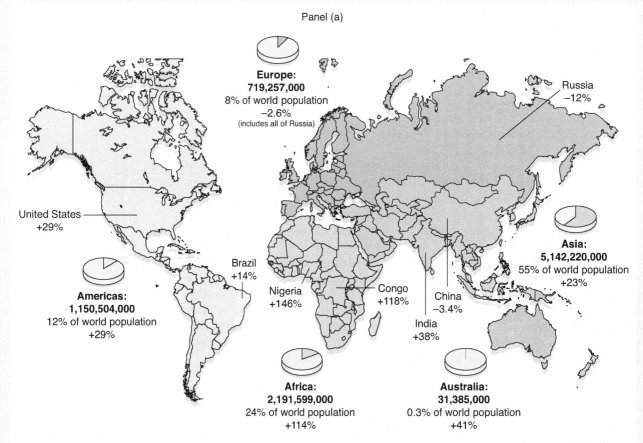

Panel (a)

Europe:
719,257,000
8% of world population
−2.6%
(includes all of Russia)

Russia
−12%

United States
+29%

Asia:
5,142,220,000
55% of world population
+23%

Brazil
+14%

Nigeria
+146%

Congo
+118%

China
−3.4%

India
+38%

Americas:
1,150,504,000
12% of world population
+29%

Africa:
2,191,599,000
24% of world population
+114%

Australia:
31,385,000
0.3% of world population
+41%

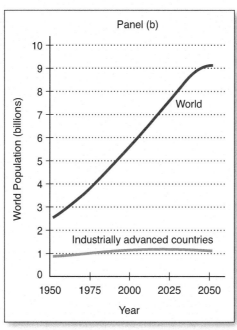

Panel (b)

World

Industrially advanced countries

World Population (billions)

Year

Of particular significance, however, is the requirement for early specialization in a nation's comparative advantage. The doctrine of comparative advantage is particularly appropriate for the developing countries of the world. If trading is allowed among nations, a country is best off if it produces what it has a comparative advantage in producing and imports the rest. This means that many developing countries should continue to specialize in agricultural production or in labor-intensive manufactured goods.

Keys to Economic Development

According to one theory of development, a country must have a large natural resource base in order to develop. This theory goes on to assert that much of the world is running out of natural resources, thereby limiting economic growth and development. Only the narrowest definition of a natural resource, however, could lead to such an opinion. In broader terms, a natural resource is something occurring in nature that we can use for our own purposes. As emphasized by new growth theory, natural resources therefore include human capital—education and experience. Also, natural resources change over time. Several hundred years ago, for example, they did not include hydroelectric power— no one knew that such a natural resource existed or how to bring it into existence.

Natural resources by themselves are not a prerequisite for or a guarantee of economic development, as demonstrated by Japan's extensive development despite a lack of domestic oil resources and by Brazil's slow pace of development in spite of a vast array of natural resources. Resources must be transformed into something usable for either investment or consumption.

Economists have found that four factors seem to be highly related to the pace of economic development:

1. *Establishing a system of property rights.* As noted earlier, if you were in a country where bank accounts and businesses were periodically expropriated by the government, you would be reluctant to leave some of your wealth in a savings account or to invest in a business. Expropriation of private property rarely takes place in developed countries. It has occurred in numerous developing countries, however. For example, private property has been nationalized in Venezuela and in Cuba. Economists have found that other things being equal, the more secure private property rights are, the more private capital accumulation and economic growth there will be.

2. *Developing an educated population.* Both theoretically and empirically, we know that a more educated workforce aids economic development because it allows individuals to build on the ideas of others. Thus, developing countries can advance more rapidly if they increase investments in education. Or, stated in the negative, economic development is difficult to sustain if a nation allows a sizable portion of its population to remain uneducated. Education allows impoverished young people to acquire skills that enable them to avoid poverty as adults.

3. *Letting "creative destruction" run its course.* The twentieth-century Harvard economist Joseph Schumpeter championed the concept of "creative destruction," through which new businesses ultimately create new jobs and economic growth after first destroying old jobs, old companies, and old industries. Such change is painful and costly, but it is necessary for economic advancement. Nowhere is this more important than in developing countries, where the principle is often ignored. Many governments in developing nations have had a history of supporting current companies and industries by discouraging new technologies and new companies from entering the marketplace. The process of creative destruction has not been allowed to work its magic in these countries.

4. *Limiting protectionism.* Open economies experience faster economic development than economies closed to international trade. Trade encourages people and businesses to discover ways to specialize so that they can become more productive and earn higher incomes. Increased productivity and subsequent increases in economic growth are the results. Thus, having fewer trade barriers promotes faster economic development.

Go to www.econtoday.com/chap03 to contemplate whether there may be a relationship between inequality and a nation's growth and to visit the home page of the World Bank's Thematic Group on Inequality, Poverty, and Socioeconomic Performance.

Go to www.econtoday.com/chap03 to link to a World Trade Organization explanation of how free trade promotes greater economic growth and higher employment.

QUICK QUIZ   See page 73 for the answers. Review concepts from this section in MyEconLab.

Although many people believe that population growth hinders economic development, there is little evidence to support that notion. What is clear is that economic development tends to lead to a reduction in the rate of _____ growth.

Historically, there are three stages of economic development: the _____ stage, the _____ stage, and the _____-_____ stage, when a large part of the workforce is employed in providing services.

Although one theory of economic development holds that a sizable natural resource base is the key to a nation's

development, this fails to account for the importance of the human element: The _____ _____ must be capable of using a country's natural resources.

Fundamental factors contributing to the pace of economic development are a well-defined system of _____ _____, training and _____, allowing new generations of companies and industries to _____ older generations, and promoting an open economy by allowing _____ _____.

YOU ARE THERE
Implementing a New Patent Framework to Promote Innovation

Senator Patrick Leahy looks on as President Barack Obama signs into law the America Invents Act, a law Leahy had authored with the aim of boosting the rate of U.S. innovation via an overhaul of the nation's patent system. Under the prior law governing patents, property rights to the returns from invention were determined on a "first-to-invent" basis. This meant that if two individuals or companies happened to invent similar products or processes at about the same time, they had to prove in court whose invention was first. Over the years, this requirement had touched off thousands of court fights among patent holders.

The legislation drawn up by Leahy and approved by Congress and the president has established a "first-to-file" rule for patents. Now the property rights associated with any invention are automatically assigned to

the first individual or firm to apply for a patent for that invention. Leahy's expectation is that patent holders who once directed financial resources toward funding court battles now will use them to transform more inventions into market innovations. Speeding along the innovation process, Leahy anticipates, will help to fuel economic growth.

Critical Thinking Questions

1. Why are inventions alone insufficient to help boost economic growth?
2. What role do you think that markets perform in determining whether inventions of new products or processes translate into longer-lasting innovations?

ISSUES & APPLICATIONS

CONCEPTS APPLIED

▶ Saving Rate

▶ Economic Growth

▶ Investment

Does a Household Shift to Thrift Signal a Growth Recovery?

A nation's saving rate is fundamental to its economic growth. Higher saving today can be channeled to current investment in capital goods, which people can use to produce more goods and services for future consumption.

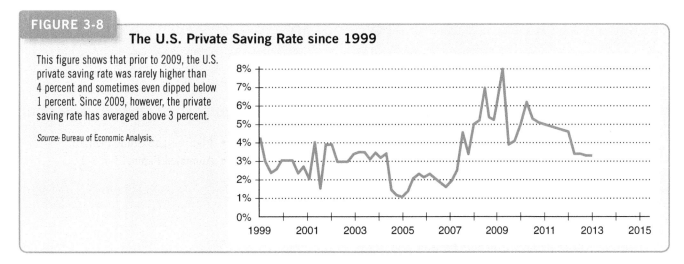

FIGURE 3-8

The U.S. Private Saving Rate since 1999

This figure shows that prior to 2009, the U.S. private saving rate was rarely higher than 4 percent and sometimes even dipped below 1 percent. Since 2009, however, the private saving rate has averaged above 3 percent.

Source: Bureau of Economic Analysis.

A Higher Private Saving Rate in the United States

Figure 3-8 above indicates that during the 2000s, the U.S. *private* saving rate—annual saving as a percentage of disposable personal income—averaged only about 2.5 percent per year. This low private saving rate helped to explain the dampened growth rate of about 1 percent during subsequent years.

Figure 3-8 shows that the private saving rate has averaged above 3 percent since 2009. This fact has generated greater optimism for some economists that U.S. economic growth might begin to recover.

A Still Low—Actually, Negative—*Overall* National Saving Rate

Bringing government actions into the story complicates the picture. Between 2000 and 2008, the government borrowed an average of $264 billion per year, so flows of public saving were *negative*. This implied an average public saving rate, relative to disposable personal income, of about −2.4 percent. Adding the private saving rate for 2000–2008 of +2.5 percent suggests that over this interval the national saving rate was about 0.1 percent. Overall, therefore, the national saving rate between 2000 and 2008 was nearly zero.

Since 2009, government borrowing has ballooned to about $1,300 billion per year, yielding a public saving rate, in relation to disposable personal income, equal to approx-

imately −11 percent. Adding this negative public saving rate to the private saving rate of about 3 percent yields an overall national saving rate of −8 percent. The fact that the national saving rate in the United States has become highly *negative* since 2009 implies that U.S. economic growth prospects actually have diminished.

For Critical Thinking

1. Why does borrowing constitute negative saving?
2. Given that a negative flow of annual national saving implies that residents of the United States are net borrowers, who must be funding this borrowing each year?

Web Resources

1. For the latest data on U.S. private saving, go to www.econtoday.com/chap03.
2. To see when the overall U.S. national saving rate first became negative, go to www.econtoday.com/chap03.

> ### MyEconLab
> For more questions on this chapter's Issues & Applications, go to MyEconLab. In the Study Plan for this chapter, select Section N: News.

MyEconLab

WHAT YOU SHOULD KNOW		WHERE TO GO TO PRACTICE
Economic Growth The rate of economic growth is the annual rate of change in per capita real GDP. This measure of the rate of growth of a nation's economy takes into account both its growth in overall production of goods and services and the growth rate of its population. It is an average measure that does not account for possible changes in the distribution of income or various welfare costs or benefits.	economic growth, 52 Key Figures Figure 3-1, 52 Figure 3-2, 54	• MyEconLab Study Plan 3.1 • Animated Figures 3-1, 3-2
Why Economic Growth Rates Are Important Economic growth compounds over time. Thus, over long intervals, relatively small differences in the rate of economic growth can accumulate to produce large disparities in per capita incomes.	rule of 70, 56	• MyEconLab Study Plan 3.1
Why Productivity Increases Are Crucial for Maintaining Economic Growth Productivity growth is a fundamental factor influencing near-term changes in economic growth. Higher productivity growth unambiguously contributes to greater annual increases in a nation's per capita real GDP.	labor productivity, 56	• MyEconLab Study Plan 3.2
The Key Determinants of Economic Growth The fundamental factors contributing to economic growth are growth in a nation's pool of labor, growth of its capital stock, and growth in the productivity of its capital and labor. A key determinant of capital accumulation is a nation's saving rate. Higher saving rates contribute to greater investment and hence increased capital accumulation and economic growth.		• MyEconLab Study Plan 3.3
New Growth Theory This theory examines why individuals and businesses conduct research into inventing and developing new technologies and how this innovation process interacts with the rate of economic growth. A key implication of the theory is that ideas and knowledge are crucial elements of the growth process.	new growth theory, 58 patent, 59 innovation, 61 Key Figures Figure 3-5, 59 Figure 3-6, 60	• MyEconLab Study Plan 3.4 • Animated Figures 3-5, 3-6

MyEconLab *continued*

WHAT YOU SHOULD KNOW ─────────────────── ───────────────── WHERE TO GO TO PRACTICE

Fundamental Factors That Contribute to a
Nation's Economic Development Key features shared by nations that attain higher levels of economic development are protection of
property rights, significant opportunities for
their residents to obtain training and education, policies that permit new companies
and industries to replace older ones, and the
avoidance of protectionist barriers that hinder
international trade.

development economics,
64

Key Figure
Figure 3-7, 66

- MyEconLab Study Plans 3.5, 3.6
- Animated Figure 3-7

Log in to MyEconLab, take a chapter test, and get a personalized Study Plan that tells you which concepts you understand and
which ones you need to review. From there, MyEconLab will give you further practice, tutorials, animations, videos,
and guided solutions. For more information, visit www.myeconlab.com

PROBLEMS

*All problems are assignable in MyEconLab; exercises that
update with real-time data are marked with* 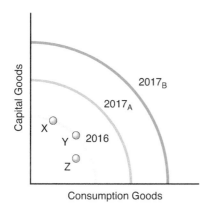 *. Answers to
odd-numbered problems appear at the back of the book.*

3-1. The graph below shows a production possibilities
curve for 2016 and two potential production possibilities curves for 2017, denoted 2017_A and
2017_B. (See page 52.)

  a. Which of the labeled points corresponds to maximum feasible 2016 production that is more likely
  to be associated with the curve denoted 2017_A?

  b. Which of the labeled points corresponds to
  maximum feasible 2016 production that is
  more likely to be associated with the curve
  denoted 2017_B?

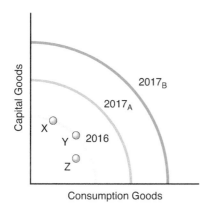

3-2. A nation's capital goods wear out over time, so a
portion of its capital goods become unusable every
year. Last year, its residents decided to produce no
capital goods. It has experienced no growth in its

population or in the amounts of other productive
resources during the past year. In addition, the
nation's technology and resource productivity
have remained unchanged during the past year.
Will the nation's economic growth rate for the
current year be negative, zero, or positive? (See
page 56.)

3-3. In the situation described in Problem 3-2, suppose
that vocational training during the past year
enable the people of this nation to repair all capital
goods so that they continue to function
as well as new. All other factors are unchanged,
however. In light of this single change to the
conditions faced in this nation, will the nation's
economic growth rate for the current year be
negative, zero, or positive? (See page 56.)

3-4. Consider the following data. What is the per
capita real GDP in each of these countries? (See
page 53.)

Country	Population (millions)	Real GDP ($ billions)
A	10	55
B	20	60
C	5	70

3-5. Suppose that during the next 10 years, real GDP
triples and population doubles in each of the
nations in Problem 3-4. What will per capita real
GDP be in each country after 10 years have
passed? (See pages 52–54.)

3-6. Consider the following table displaying annual growth rates for nations X, Y, and Z, each of which entered 2013 with real per capita GDP equal to $20,000 (see pages 52–54.)

	Annual Growth Rate (%)			
Country	2013	2014	2015	2016
X	7	1	3	4
Y	4	5	7	9
Z	5	5	3	2

a. Which nation most likely experienced a sizable earthquake in late 2013 that destroyed a significant portion of its stock of capital goods, but was followed by speedy investments in rebuilding the nation's capital stock? What is this nation's per capita real GDP at the end of 2016, rounded to the nearest dollar?

b. Which nation most likely adopted policies in 2013 that encouraged a gradual shift in production from capital goods to consumption goods? What is this nation's per capita real GDP at the end of 2016, rounded to the nearest dollar?

c. Which nation most likely adopted policies in 2013 that encouraged a quick shift in production from consumption goods to capital goods? What is this nation's per capita real GDP at the end of 2016, rounded to the nearest dollar?

3-7. Per capita real GDP grows at a rate of 3 percent in country F and at a rate of 6 percent in country G. Both begin with equal levels of per capita real GDP. Use Table 3-3 on page 55 to determine how much higher per capita real GDP will be in country G after 20 years. How much higher will real GDP be in country G after 40 years? (See page 55.)

3-8. Per capita real GDP in country L is three times as high as in country M. The economic growth rate in country M, however, is 8 percent, while country L's economy grows at a rate of 5 percent. Use Table 3-3 on page 55 to determine approximately how many years will pass before per capita real GDP in country M surpasses per capita real GDP in country L. (See page 55.)

3-9. Per capita real GDP in country S is only half as great as per capita real GDP in country T. Country T's rate of economic growth is 4 percent. The government of country S, however, enacts policies that achieve a growth rate of 20 percent. Use Table 3-3 on page 55 to determine how long country S must maintain this growth rate before its per capita real GDP surpasses that of country T. (See page 55.)

3-10. Since the early 1990s, the average rate of growth of per capita real GDP in Mozambique has been 3 percent per year, as compared with a growth rate of 8 percent in China. Refer to Table 3-3 on page 55. If a typical resident of each of these nations begins this year with a per capita real GDP of $3,000 per year, about how many more dollars' worth of real GDP per capita would the person in China be earning 10 years from now than the individual in Mozambique? (See page 55.)

3-11. On the basis of the information in Problem 3-10 and reference to Table 3-3 on page 55, about how many more dollars' worth of real GDP per capita would the person in China be earning 50 years from now than the individual in Mozambique? (See page 55.)

3-12. In 2014, a nation's population was 10 million. Its nominal GDP was $40 billion, and its price index was 100. In 2015, its population had increased to 12 million, its nominal GDP had risen to $57.6 billion, and its price index had increased to 120. What was this nation's economic growth rate during the year? (See page 55.)

3-13. Between the start of 2014 and the start of 2015, a country's economic growth rate was 4 percent. Its population did not change during the year, nor did its price level. What was the rate of increase of the country's nominal GDP during this one-year interval? (See page 55.)

3-14. In 2014, a nation's population was 10 million, its real GDP was $1.21 billion, and its GDP deflator had a value of 121. By 2015, its population had increased to 12 million, its real GDP had risen to $1.5 billion, and its GDP deflator had a value of 125. What was the percentage change in per capita real GDP between 2014 and 2015? (See page 55.)

3-15. A nation's per capita real GDP was $2,000 in 2013, and the nation's population was 5 million in that year. Between 2013 and 2014, the inflation rate in this country was 5 percent, and the nation's annual rate of economic growth was 10 percent. Its population remained unchanged. What was per capita real GDP in 2014? What was the *level* of real GDP in 2014? (See page 55.)

3-16. Brazil has a population of about 200 million, with about 145 million over the age of 15. Of these, an estimated 25 percent, or 35 million people, are functionally illiterate. The typical literate individual reads only about two nonacademic books per year, which is less than half the number read by the typical literate U.S. or European resident. Answer the following questions solely from the perspective of new growth theory (see page 58):

a. Discuss the implications of Brazil's literacy and reading rates for its growth prospects in light of the key tenets of new growth theory.

b. What types of policies might Brazil implement to improve its growth prospects? Explain.

ECONOMICS ON THE NET

Multifactor Productivity and Its Growth Growth in productivity is a key factor determining a nation's overall economic growth.

Title: Bureau of Labor Statistics: Multifactor Productivity Trends

Navigation: Use the link at www.econtoday.com/chap03 to visit the multifactor productivity home page of the Bureau of Labor Statistics.

Application Read the summary, and answer the following questions.

1. What does multifactor productivity measure? Based on your reading of this chapter, how does multifactor productivity relate to the determination of economic growth?

2. Click on *Multifactor Productivity Trends in Manufacturing.* According to these data, which industries have exhibited the greatest productivity growth in recent years?

For Group Study and Analysis Divide the class into three groups to examine multifactor productivity data for the private business sector, the private nonfarm business sector, and the manufacturing sector. Have each group identify periods when multifactor productivity growth was particularly fast or slow. Then compare notes. Does it appear to make a big difference which sector one looks at when evaluating periods of greatest and least growth in multifactor productivity?

ANSWERS TO QUICK QUIZZES

p. 56: (i) per capita; (ii) benefits . . . costs; (iii) large

p. 58: (i) capital . . . labor . . . capital . . . labor; (ii) saving . . . save . . . saving

p. 63: (i) New growth; (ii) trade; (iii) Inventions . . . innovation; (iv) new growth; (v) human

p. 64: (i) economic; (ii) property . . . property

p. 68: (i) population; (ii) agricultural . . . manufacturing . . . service-sector; (iii) working population; (iv) property rights . . . education . . . replace . . . international trade

ADDITIONAL READING:

What Determines How Fast Economies Grow?

Taken from *Macroeconomics*, Fourth Edition, by R. Glenn Hubbard and Anthony Patrick O'Brien

What Determines How Fast Economies Grow?

LEARNING OBJECTIVE
Use the economic growth model to explain why growth rates differ across countries.

To explain changes in economic growth rates over time within countries and differences in growth rates among countries, we need to develop an *economic growth model.* An **economic growth model** explains growth rates in real GDP per capita over the long run. The average person can buy more goods and services only if the average worker produces more goods and services. Recall that **labor productivity** is the quantity of goods and services that can be produced by one worker or by one hour of work. Because of the importance of labor productivity in explaining economic growth, the economic growth model focuses on the causes of long-run increases in labor productivity.

Economic growth model
A model that explains growth rates in real GDP per capita over the long run.

Labor productivity
The quantity of goods and services that can be produced by one worker or by one hour of work.

How can a country's workers become more productive? Economists believe two key factors determine labor productivity: the quantity of capital per hour worked and the level of technology. Therefore, the economic growth model focuses on technological change and changes over time in the quantity of capital available to workers in explaining changes in real GDP per capita. Recall that **technological change** is a change in the quantity of output firms can produce using a given quantity of inputs.

There are three main sources of technological change:

Technological change
A change in the quantity of output a firm can produce using a given quantity of inputs.

- *Better machinery and equipment.* Beginning with the steam engine during the Industrial Revolution, the invention of new machinery has been an important source of rising labor productivity. Today, continuing improvements in computers, factory machine tools, electric generators, and many other machines contribute to increases in labor productivity.

- *Increases in human capital.* Capital refers to *physical capital*, including computers, factory buildings, machine tools, warehouses, and trucks. The more physical capital workers have available, the more output they can produce. **Human capital** is the accumulated knowledge and skills that workers acquire from education and training or from their life experiences. As workers increase their human capital through education or on-the-job training, their productivity also increases. The more educated workers are, the greater is their human capital.

Human capital
The accumulated knowledge and skills that workers acquire from education and training or from their life experiences.

- *Better means of organizing and managing production.* Labor productivity increases if managers can do a better job of organizing production. For example, the *just-in-time system*, first developed by Toyota Motor Corporation, involves assembling goods from parts that arrive at the factory at exactly the time they are needed. With this system, Toyota needs fewer workers to store and keep track of parts in the factory, so the quantity of goods produced per hour worked increases.

Note that technological change is *not* the same thing as more physical capital. New capital can embody technological change, as when a faster computer chip is embodied in a new computer. But simply adding more capital that is the same as existing capital is not technological change. To summarize, we can say that a country's standard of living will be higher the more capital workers have available on their jobs, the better the capital, the more human capital workers have, and the better the job business managers do in organizing production.

The Per-Worker Production Function

The economic growth model explains increases in real GDP per capita over time as resulting from increases in just two factors: the quantity of physical capital available to workers and technological change. Often when analyzing economic growth, we look at increases in real GDP *per hour worked* and increases in capital *per hour worked*. We use measures of GDP per hour and capital per hour rather than per person so we can analyze changes in the underlying ability of an economy to produce more goods with a given amount of labor without having to worry about changes in the fraction of the

Per-worker production function
The relationship between real GDP per hour worked and capital per hour worked, holding the level of technology constant.

population working or in the length of the workday. We can illustrate the economic growth model using the **per-worker production function**, which is the relationship between real GDP per hour worked and capital per hour worked, *holding the level of technology constant*. Figure 3A-1 shows the per-worker production function as a graph. In the figure, we measure capital per hour worked along the horizontal axis and real GDP per hour worked along the vertical axis. Letting K stand for capital, L stand for labor, and Y stand for real GDP, real GDP per hour worked is Y/L, and capital per hour worked is K/L. The curve represents the production function. Notice that we do not explicitly show technological change in the figure. We assume that as we move along the production function, the level of technology remains constant. As we will see, we can illustrate technological change using this graph by *shifting up* the curve representing the production function.

The figure shows that increases in the quantity of capital per hour worked result in movements up the per-worker production function, increasing the quantity of output each worker produces. When *holding technology constant*, however, equal increases in the amount of capital per hour worked lead to *diminishing* increases in output per hour worked. For example, increasing capital per hour worked from $20,000 to $30,000 increases real GDP per hour worked from $200 to $350, an increase of $150. Another $10,000 increase in capital per hour worked, from $30,000 to $40,000, increases real GDP per hour worked from $350 to $475, an increase of only $125. Each additional $10,000 increase in capital per hour worked results in progressively smaller increases in real GDP per hour worked. In fact, at very high levels of capital per hour worked, further increases in capital per hour worked will not result in any increase in real GDP per hour worked. This effect results from the *law of diminishing returns*, which states that as we add more of one input—in this case, capital—to a fixed quantity of another input—in this case, labor—output increases by smaller additional amounts.

Why are there diminishing returns to capital? Consider a simple example in which you own a copy store. At first you have 10 employees but only 1 copy machine, so each of your workers is able to produce relatively few copies per day. When you buy a second copy machine, your employees will be able to produce more copies. Adding additional copy machines will continue to increase your output—but by increasingly smaller amounts. For example, adding a twentieth copy machine to the 19 you already

FIGURE 3A-1

The Per-Worker Production Function

The per-worker production function shows the relationship between capital per hour worked and real GDP per hour worked, holding technology constant. Increases in capital per hour worked increase output per hour worked but at a diminishing rate. For example, an increase in capital per hour worked from $20,000 to $30,000 increases real GDP per hour worked from $200 to $350. An increase in capital per hour worked from $30,000 to $40,000 increases real GDP per hour worked only from $350 to $475. Each additional $10,000 increase in capital per hour worked results in a progressively smaller increase in output per hour worked.

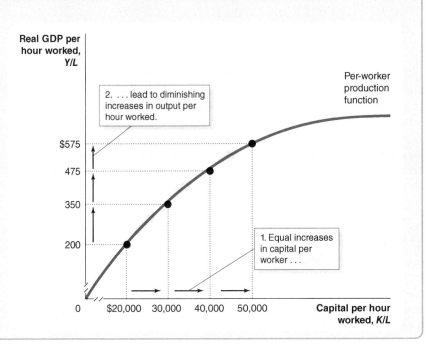

have will not increase the copies each worker is able to make by nearly as much as adding a second copy machine did. Eventually, adding additional copying machines will not increase your output at all.

Which Is More Important for Economic Growth: More Capital or Technological Change?

Technological change helps economies avoid diminishing returns to capital. Let's consider two simple examples of the effects of technological change. First, suppose you have 10 copy machines in your copy store. Each copy machine can produce 10 copies per minute. You don't believe that adding an eleventh machine identical to the 10 you already have will significantly increase the number of copies your employees can produce in a day. Then you find out that a new copy machine has become available that produces 20 copies per minute. If you replace your existing machines with the new machines, the productivity of your workers will increase. The replacement of existing capital with more productive capital is an example of technological change.

Or suppose you realize that the layout of your store could be improved. Maybe the paper for the machines is on shelves at the back of the store, which requires your workers to spend time walking back and forth whenever the machines run out of paper. By placing the paper closer to the copy machines, you can improve the productivity of your workers. Reorganizing how production takes place so as to increase output is also an example of technological change.

Technological Change: The Key to Sustaining Economic Growth

Figure 3A-2 shows the effect of technological change on the per-worker production function. Technological change shifts up the per-worker production function and allows an economy to produce more real GDP per hour worked with the same quantity

FIGURE 3A-2

Technological Change Increases Output per Hour Worked

Technological change shifts up the production function and allows more output per hour worked with the same amount of capital per hour worked. For example, along Production function$_1$ with $50,000 in capital per hour worked, the economy can produce $575 in real GDP per hour worked. However, an increase in technology that shifts the economy to Production function$_2$ makes it possible to produce $675 in real GDP per hour worked with the same level of capital per hour worked.

Technological change causes the per-worker production function to shift up.

of capital per hour worked. For example, if the current level of technology puts the economy on production function$_1$, then when capital per hour worked is $50,000, real GDP per hour worked is $575. Technological change that shifts the economy to production function$_2$ makes it possible to produce $675 in goods and services per hour worked with the same level of capital per hour worked. Further increases in technology that shift the economy to higher production functions result in further increases in real GDP per hour worked. Because of diminishing returns to capital, continuing increases in real GDP per hour worked can be sustained only if there is technological change. Remember that a country will experience increases in its standard of living only if it experiences increases in real GDP per hour worked. Therefore, we can draw the following important conclusion: *In the long run, a country will experience an increasing standard of living only if it experiences continuing technological change.*

MAKING THE CONNECTION

What Explains the Economic Failure of the Soviet Union?

The fall of the Berlin Wall in 1989 symbolized the failure of Communism.

The economic growth model can help explain one of the most striking events of the twentieth century: the economic collapse of the Soviet Union. The Soviet Union was formed from the old Russian Empire following the Communist revolution of 1917. Under Communism, the Soviet Union was a centrally planned economy where the government owned nearly every business and made all production and pricing decisions. In 1960, Nikita Khrushchev, the leader of the Soviet Union, addressed the United Nations in New York City. He declared to the United States and the other democracies, "We will bury you. Your grandchildren will live under Communism."

Many people at the time took Khrushchev's boast seriously. Capital per hour worked grew rapidly in the Soviet Union from 1950 through the 1980s. At first, these increases in capital per hour worked also produced rapid increases in real GDP per hour worked. Rapid increases in real GDP per hour worked during the 1950s caused some economists in the United States to predict incorrectly that the Soviet Union would someday surpass the United States economically. In fact, diminishing returns to capital meant that the additional factories the Soviet Union was building resulted in smaller and smaller increases in real GDP per hour worked.

The Soviet Union did experience some technological change—but at a rate much slower than in the United States and other high-income countries. Why did the Soviet Union fail the crucial requirement for growth: implementing new technologies? The key reason is that in a centrally planned economy, the people managing most businesses are government employees and not entrepreneurs or independent businesspeople, as is the case in market economies. Soviet managers had little incentive to adopt new ways of doing things. Their pay depended on producing the quantity of output specified in the government's economic plan, not on discovering new, better, and lower-cost ways to produce goods. In addition, these managers did not have to worry about competition from either domestic or foreign firms.

Entrepreneurs and managers of firms in the United States, by contrast, are under intense competitive pressure from other firms. They must constantly search for better ways of producing the goods and services they sell. Developing and using new technologies is an important way to gain a competitive edge and higher profits. The drive for profit provides an incentive for technological change that centrally planned economies are unable to duplicate. In market economies, decisions about which investments to make and which technologies to adopt are made by entrepreneurs and managers who have their own money on the line. Nothing concentrates the mind like having your own funds at risk.

In hindsight, it is clear that a centrally planned economy, such as the Soviet Union's, could not, over the long run, grow faster than a market economy. The Soviet Union collapsed in 1991, and contemporary Russia now has a more market-oriented system, although the government continues to play a much larger role in the economy than does the government in the United States.

SOLVED PROBLEM 3A.1

USING THE ECONOMIC GROWTH MODEL TO ANALYZE THE FAILURE OF THE SOVIET ECONOMY

Use the economic growth model and the information in the Making the Connection on page 80 to analyze the economic problems the Soviet Union encountered.

Solving the Problem

Step 1: **Review the chapter material.** This problem is about using the economic growth model to explain the failure of the Soviet economy, so you may want to review the Making the Connection on page 80

Step 2: **Draw a graph like Figure 3A-1 on page 78 to illustrate the economic problems of the Soviet Union.** For simplicity, assume that the Soviet Union experienced no technological change.

The Soviet Union experienced rapid increases in capital per hour worked from 1950 through the 1980s, but its failure to implement new technology meant that output per hour worked grew at a slower and slower rate.

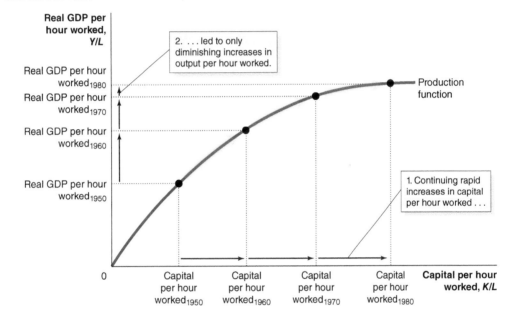

Extra Credit: The Soviet Union hoped to raise the standard of living of its citizens above that enjoyed in the United States and other high-income countries. Its strategy was to make continuous increases in the quantity of capital available to its workers. The economic growth model helps us understand the flaws in this policy for achieving economic growth

Module 2

Basic Macroeconomic Models

Real GDP and the Price Level in the Long Run

4

LEARNING OBJECTIVES

After reading this chapter, you should be able to:

▶ Understand the concept of long-run aggregate supply

▶ Describe the effect of economic growth on the long-run aggregate supply curve

▶ Explain why the aggregate demand curve slopes downward and list key factors that cause this curve to shift

▶ Discuss the meaning of long-run equilibrium for the economy as a whole

▶ Evaluate why economic growth can cause deflation

▶ Evaluate likely reasons for persistent inflation in recent decades

MyEconLab helps you master each objective and study more efficiently. See end of chapter for details.

Economic growth has trended steadily downward during the past four decades in nations with northern borders that lie within the Arctic Circle, such as Canada, Russia, and the United States. Nevertheless, estimates indicate that if underutilized and untapped Arctic and near-Arctic resources were fully exploited, substantial long-term improvements in these nations' economic growth rates would occur. How could increased use of resources within Arctic regions, as well as in other areas, contribute to the aggregate production of goods and services? What would be additional economywide effects of increased resource exploitation, such as impacts on the average level of prices? In this chapter, you will contemplate the answers to these questions.

Output Growth and the Long-Run Aggregate Supply Curve

At any point in time, the economy can be inside or on the PPC but never outside it. Along the PPC, a country's resources are fully employed in the production of goods and services, and the sum total of the inflation-adjusted value of all final goods and services produced is the nation's real GDP. Economists refer to the total of all planned production for the entire economy as the **aggregate supply** of real output.

The Long-Run Aggregate Supply Curve

Put yourself in a world in which nothing has been changing, year in and year out. The price level has not changed. Technology has not changed. The prices of inputs that firms must purchase have not changed. Labor productivity has not changed. All resources are fully employed, so the economy operates on its production possibilities curve, such as the one depicted in panel (a) of Figure 4-1 below. This is a world that is fully adjusted and in which people have all the information they are ever going to have about that world. The **long-run aggregate supply curve** (*LRAS*) in this world is some amount of real GDP—say, $15 trillion of real GDP—which is the value of the flow of production of final goods and services measured in **base-year dollars.**

We can represent long-run aggregate supply by a vertical line at $15 trillion of real GDP. This is what you see in panel (b) of the figure below. That curve, labeled *LRAS*, is a vertical line determined by technology and **endowments,** or resources that exist in our economy. It is the full-information and full-adjustment level of real output of goods and services. It is the level of real GDP that will continue being produced year after year, forever, if nothing changes.

Aggregate supply
The total of all planned production for the economy.

Long-run aggregate supply curve
A vertical line representing the real output of goods and services after full adjustment has occurred. It can also be viewed as representing the real GDP of the economy under conditions of full employment—the full-employment level of real GDP.

Base-year dollars
The value of a current sum expressed in terms of prices in a base year.

Endowments
The various resources in an economy, including both physical resources and such human resources as ingenuity and management skills.

FIGURE 4-1

The Production Possibilities Curve and the Economy's Long-Run Aggregate Supply Curve

At a point in time, a nation's base of resources and its technological capabilities define the position of its production possibilities curve (PPC), as shown in panel (a). This defines the real GDP that the nation can produce when resources are fully employed, which determines the position of the long-run aggregate supply curve (*LRAS*) displayed in panel (b). Because people have complete information and input prices adjust fully in the long run, the *LRAS* is vertical.

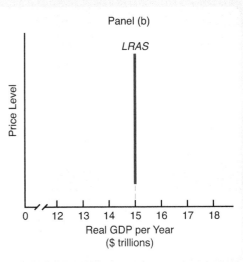

THE *LRAS* CURVE AND FULL-EMPLOYMENT REAL GDP Another way of viewing the *LRAS* is to think of it as the full-employment level of real GDP. When the economy reaches full employment along its production possibilities curve, no further adjustments will occur unless a change occurs in the other variables that we are assuming to be stable.

Some economists suggest that the *LRAS* occurs at the level of real GDP consistent with the natural rate of unemployment, the unemployment rate that occurs in an economy with full adjustment in the long run. As we discussed in Chapter 1, many economists like to think of the natural rate of unemployment as consisting of frictional and structural unemployment.

WHY THE *LRAS* CURVE IS VERTICAL To understand why the *LRAS* is vertical, think about the long run. To an economist examining the economy as a whole, the long run is a sufficiently long period that all factors of production and prices, including wages and other input prices, can change.

A change in the level of prices of goods and services has no effect on real GDP per year in the long run, because higher prices will be accompanied by comparable changes in input prices. Suppliers will therefore have no incentive to increase or decrease their production of goods and services. Remember that in the long run, everybody has full information, and there is full adjustment to price level changes. (Of, course, this is not necessarily true in the short run, as we shall discuss in Chapter 5.)

Go to www.econtoday.com/chap04 to find out how fast wages are adjusting. Under "Latest Numbers," click on "Employment Cost Index."

Economic Growth and Long-Run Aggregate Supply

In Chapter 3, you learned about the determinants of growth in per capita real GDP: the annual growth rate of labor, the rate of year-to-year capital accumulation, and the rate of growth of the productivity of labor and capital. As time goes by, population gradually increases, and labor force participation rates may even rise. The capital stock typically grows as businesses add such capital equipment as new information-technology hardware. Furthermore, technology improves. Thus, the economy's production possibilities increase, and as a consequence, the production possibilities curve shifts outward, as shown in panel (a) of Figure 4-2 below.

The result is economic growth: Aggregate real GDP and per capita real GDP increase. This means that in a growing economy such as ours, the *LRAS* will shift outward to the right, as in panel (b) below. We have drawn the *LRAS* for the year 2015 to the right of our original *LRAS* of $14.3 trillion of real GDP. We assume that between

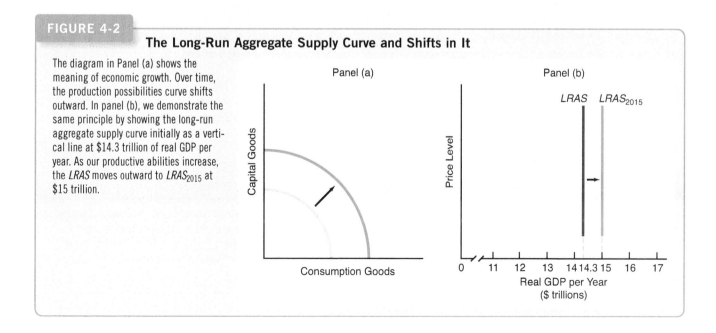

FIGURE 4-2

The Long-Run Aggregate Supply Curve and Shifts in It

The diagram in Panel (a) shows the meaning of economic growth. Over time, the production possibilities curve shifts outward. In panel (b), we demonstrate the same principle by showing the long-run aggregate supply curve initially as a vertical line at $14.3 trillion of real GDP per year. As our productive abilities increase, the *LRAS* moves outward to *LRAS*₂₀₁₅ at $15 trillion.

Panel (a)

Capital Goods

Consumption Goods

Panel (b)

LRAS   LRAS₂₀₁₅

Price Level

0   11   12   13   14 14.3 15   16   17

Real GDP per Year
($ trillions)

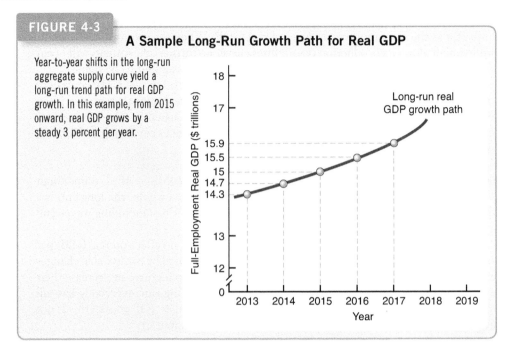

FIGURE 4-3

A Sample Long-Run Growth Path for Real GDP

Year-to-year shifts in the long-run aggregate supply curve yield a long-run trend path for real GDP growth. In this example, from 2015 onward, real GDP grows by a steady 3 percent per year.

YOU ARE THERE

To contemplate how a country's long-run trend path for real GDP could slope *downward*, take a look at **A Nation Confronts a Leftward-Shifting *LRAS* Curve** on page 98.

now and 2015, real GDP increases to $15 trillion, to give us the position of the $LRAS_{2015}$ curve. Thus, it is to the right of today's *LRAS* curve.

We may conclude that in a growing economy, the *LRAS* shifts ever farther to the right over time. If the *LRAS* happened to shift rightward at a constant pace, real GDP would increase at a steady annual rate. As shown in Figure 4-3, this means that real GDP would increase along a long-run, or *trend*, path that is an upward-sloping line. Thus, if the *LRAS* shifts rightward from $14.3 trillion to $15 trillion between now and 2015 and then increases at a steady 3 percent annual rate every year thereafter, in 2016 long-run real GDP will equal $15.5 trillion, in 2017 it will equal $15.9 trillion, and so on.

How much less is the U.S. long-run aggregate supply shifting to the right each year as a consequence of dampened economic growth?

POLICY EXAMPLE

Shrinking Rightward Shifts in the U.S. *LRAS* Curve

Between 2000 and 2007, U.S. real GDP grew at an average annual rate of 2.6 percent. As a consequence, U.S. long-run aggregate supply increased by an average of nearly $300 billion per year. Since 2007, U.S. real GDP grew on average at a much slower pace of about 0.5 percent per year. During this interval, the nation's long-run aggregate supply rose by an average of less than $70 billion per year. Thus, the average annual

amount by which the U.S. long-run aggregate supply curve is shifting rightward is now considerably reduced.

FOR CRITICAL THINKING
Is the U.S. production possibilities curve shifting outward more or less rapidly today than it was a decade ago? Explain your answer.

QUICK QUIZ   See page 103 for the answers. Review concepts from this section in MyEconLab.

The **long-run aggregate supply curve,** *LRAS,* is a _____ line determined by amounts of available resources such as labor and capital and by technology and resource productivity. The position of the *LRAS* gives the full-information and full-adjustment level of real GDP per year.

The _____ rate of unemployment occurs at the long-run level of real GDP per year given by the position of the *LRAS*.

If labor or capital increases from year to year or if the productivity of either of these resources rises from one year to the next, the *LRAS* shifts _____. In a growing economy, therefore, real GDP per year gradually _____ over time.

Total Expenditures and Aggregate Demand

In equilibrium, individuals, businesses, and governments purchase all the goods and services produced, valued in trillions of real dollars. As explained in Chapters 1 and 2, GDP is the dollar value of total expenditures on domestically produced final goods and services. Because all expenditures are made by individuals, firms, or governments, the total value of these expenditures must be what these market participants decide it shall be.

The decisions of individuals, managers of firms, and government officials determine the annual dollar value of total expenditures. You can certainly see this in your role as an individual. You decide what the total dollar amount of your expenditures will be in a year. You decide how much you want to spend and how much you want to save. Thus, if we want to know what determines the total value of GDP, the answer is clear: the spending decisions of individuals like you, firms, and local, state, and national governments. In an open economy, we must also include foreign individuals, firms, and governments (foreign residents, for short) that decide to spend their money income in the United States.

Simply stating that the dollar value of total expenditures in this country depends on what individuals, firms, governments, and foreign residents decide to do really doesn't tell us much, though. Two important issues remain:

1. What determines the total amount that individuals, firms, governments, and foreign residents want to spend?

2. What determines the equilibrium price level and the rate of inflation (or deflation)?

The *LRAS* tells us only about the economy's long-run real GDP. To answer these additional questions, we must consider another important concept. This is **aggregate demand,** which is the total of all *planned* real expenditures in the economy.

Aggregate demand
The total of all planned expenditures in the entire economy.

The Aggregate Demand Curve

The **aggregate demand curve,** *AD*, gives the various quantities of all final commodities demanded at various price levels, all other things held constant. Recall the components of GDP that you studied in Chapter 2: consumption spending, investment expenditures, government purchases, and net foreign demand for domestic production. They are all components of aggregate demand. Throughout this chapter and the next, whenever you see the aggregate demand curve, realize that it is a shorthand way of talking about the components of GDP that are measured by government statisticians when they calculate total economic activity each year. In Chapter 6, you will look more closely at the relationship between these components and, in particular, at how consumption spending depends on income.

Aggregate demand curve
A curve showing planned purchase rates for all final goods and services in the economy at various price levels, all other things held constant.

The aggregate demand curve gives the total amount, measured in base-year dollars, of *real* domestic final goods and services that will be purchased at each price level—everything produced for final use by households, businesses, the government, and foreign (non-U.S.) residents. It includes iPads, socks, shoes, medical and legal services, digital devices, and millions of other goods and services that people buy each year.

A graphical representation of the aggregate demand curve is seen in Figure 4-4 on the facing page. On the horizontal axis, real GDP is measured. For our measure of the price level, we use the GDP price deflator on the vertical axis. The aggregate demand curve is labeled *AD*. If the GDP deflator is 110, aggregate quantity demanded is $15 trillion per year (point *A*). At the price level 115, it is $14 trillion per year (point *B*). At the price level 120, it is $13 trillion per year (point *C*). The higher the price level, the lower the total real amount of final goods and services demanded in the economy, everything else remaining constant, as shown by the arrow along *AD* in Figure 4-4. Conversely, the lower the price level, the higher the total real GDP demanded by the economy, everything else staying constant.

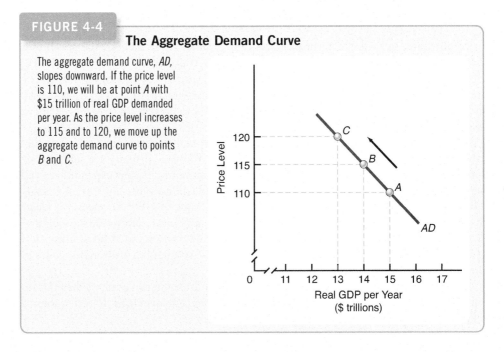

FIGURE 4-4

The Aggregate Demand Curve

The aggregate demand curve, *AD*, slopes downward. If the price level is 110, we will be at point *A* with $15 trillion of real GDP demanded per year. As the price level increases to 115 and to 120, we move up the aggregate demand curve to points *B* and *C*.

Let's take the year 2013. Estimates based on U.S. Department of Commerce preliminary statistics reveal the following information:

- Nominal GDP was estimated to be $16,344.7 billion.

- The price level as measured by the GDP deflator was about 117.9 (base year is 2005, for which the index equals 100).

- Real GDP was approximately $13,858.5 billion in 2005 dollars.

What can we say about 2013? Given the dollar cost of buying goods and services and all of the other factors that go into spending decisions by individuals, firms, governments, and foreign residents, the total amount of planned spending on final goods and services by firms, individuals, governments, and foreign residents was $13,858.5 billion in 2013 (in terms of 2005 dollars).

What Happens When the Price Level Rises?

What if the price level in the economy rose to 160 tomorrow? What would happen to the amount of real goods and services that individuals, firms, governments, and foreigners wish to purchase in the United States? We know that when the price of one good or service rises, the quantity of it demanded will fall. But here we are talking about the *price level*—the average price of *all* goods and services in the economy.

The answer is still that the total quantities of real goods and services demanded would fall, but the reasons are different. When the price of one good or service goes up, the consumer substitutes other goods and services. For the entire economy, when the price level goes up, the consumer doesn't simply substitute one good for another, for now we are dealing with the demand for *all* goods and services in the nation. There are *economywide* reasons that cause the aggregate demand curve to slope downward. They involve at least three distinct forces: the *real-balance effect*, the *interest rate effect*, and the *open economy effect*.

THE REAL-BALANCE EFFECT A rise in the price level will have an effect on spending. Individuals, firms, governments, and foreign residents carry out transactions using money, a portion of which consists of currency and coins that you have in your pocket (or stashed away) right now. Because people use money to purchase goods and services, the amount of money that people have influences the amount of goods and services they want to buy. For example, if you find a $100 bill on the sidewalk, the amount of money you have increases. Given your now greater level of money, or cash, balances—currency in this case—you will almost surely increase your spending on goods and services. Similarly, if your pocket is picked while you are at the mall, your desired spending would be affected. For instance, if your wallet had $150 in it when it was stolen, the reduction in your cash balances—in this case, currency—would no doubt cause you to reduce your planned expenditures. You would ultimately buy fewer goods and services.

This response is sometimes called the **real-balance effect** (or *wealth effect*) because it relates to the real value of your cash balances. While your *nominal* cash balances may remain the same, any change in the price level will cause a change in the *real* value of those cash balances—hence the real-balance effect on total planned expenditures.

When you think of the real-balance effect, just think of what happens to your real wealth if you have, say, a $100 bill hidden under your mattress. If the price level increases by 5 percent, the purchasing power of that $100 bill drops by 5 percent, so you have become less wealthy. You will reduce your purchases of all goods and services by some small amount.

THE INTEREST RATE EFFECT There is a more subtle but equally important effect on your desire to spend. A higher price level leaves people with too few money balances. Hence, they try to borrow more (or lend less) to replenish their real money holdings. This drives up interest rates. Higher interest rates raise borrowing costs for consumers and businesses. They will borrow less and consequently spend less. The fact that a higher price level pushes up interest rates and thereby reduces borrowing and spending is known as the **interest rate effect.**

Higher interest rates make it more costly for people to finance purchases of houses and cars. Higher interest rates also make it less profitable for firms to install new equipment and to erect new office buildings. Whether we are talking about individuals or firms, a rise in the price level will cause higher interest rates, which in turn reduce the amount of goods and services that people are willing to purchase. Therefore, an increase in the price level will tend to reduce total planned expenditures. (The opposite occurs if the price level declines.)

THE OPEN ECONOMY EFFECT: THE SUBSTITUTION OF FOREIGN GOODS Recall from Chapter 2 that GDP includes net exports—the difference between exports and imports. In an open economy, we buy imports from other countries and ultimately pay for them through the foreign exchange market. The same is true for foreign residents who purchase our goods (exports). Given any set of exchange rates between the U.S. dollar and other currencies, an increase in the price level in the United States makes U.S. goods more expensive relative to foreign goods. Foreign residents have downward-sloping demand curves for U.S. goods. When the relative price of U.S. goods goes up, foreign residents buy fewer U.S. goods and more of their own. At home, relatively cheaper prices for foreign goods cause U.S. residents to want to buy more foreign goods instead of domestically produced goods. Thus, when the domestic price level rises, the result is a fall in exports and a rise in imports. That means that a price level increase tends to reduce net exports, thereby reducing the amount of real goods and services purchased in the United States. This is known as the **open economy effect.**

What Happens When the Price Level Falls?

What about the reverse? Suppose now that the GDP deflator falls to 100 from an initial level of 120. You should be able to trace the three effects on desired purchases of goods and services. Specifically, how do the real-balance, interest rate, and open economy effects cause people to want to buy more? You should come to the conclusion that the lower the price level, the greater the total planned spending on goods and services.

Real-balance effect
The change in expenditures resulting from a change in the real value of money balances when the price level changes, all other things held constant; also called the *wealth effect.*

Interest rate effect
One of the reasons that the aggregate demand curve slopes downward: Higher price levels increase the interest rate, which in turn causes businesses and consumers to reduce desired spending due to the higher cost of borrowing.

Open economy effect
One of the reasons that the aggregate demand curve slopes downward: Higher price levels result in foreign residents desiring to buy fewer U.S.-made goods, while U.S. residents now desire more foreign-made goods, thereby reducing net exports. This is equivalent to a reduction in the amount of real goods and services purchased in the United States.

The aggregate demand curve, *AD*, shows the quantity of aggregate output that will be demanded at alternative price levels. It is downward sloping, just like the demand curve for individual goods. The higher the price level, the lower the real amount of total planned expenditures, and vice versa.

Demand for All Goods and Services versus Demand for a Single Good or Service

Even though the aggregate demand curve, *AD*, in Figure 4-4 on page 90 looks similar to the one for individual demand, *D*, for a single good or service, the two are not the same. When we derive the aggregate demand curve, we are looking at the entire economic system. The aggregate demand curve, *AD*, differs from an individual demand curve, *D*, because we are looking at total planned expenditures on *all* goods and services when we construct *AD*.

Shifts in the Aggregate Demand Curve

Any time a nonprice determinant of demand changes, the demand curve will shift inward to the left or outward to the right. The same analysis holds for the aggregate demand curve, except we are now talking about the non-price-level determinants of aggregate demand. So, when we ask the question, "What determines the position of the aggregate demand curve?" the fundamental proposition is as follows:

> *Any non-price-level change that increases aggregate spending (on domestic goods) shifts* **AD** *to the right. Any non-price-level change that decreases aggregate spending (on domestic goods) shifts* **AD** *to the left.*

The list of potential determinants of the position of the aggregate demand curve is long. Some of the most important "curve shifters" for aggregate demand are presented in Table 4-1 below.

TABLE 4-1

Determinants of Aggregate Demand

Aggregate demand consists of the demand for domestically produced consumption goods, investment goods, government purchases, and net exports. Consequently, any change in total planned spending on any one of these components of real GDP will cause a change in aggregate demand. Some possibilities are listed here.

Changes That Cause an Increase in Aggregate Demand	Changes That Cause a Decrease in Aggregate Demand
An increase in the amount of money in circulation	A decrease in the amount of money in circulation
Increased security about jobs and future income	Decreased security about jobs and future income
Improvements in economic conditions in other countries	Declines in economic conditions in other countries
A reduction in real interest rates (nominal interest rates corrected for inflation) not due to price level changes	A rise in real interest rates (nominal interest rates corrected for inflation) not due to price level changes
Tax decreases	Tax increases
A drop in the foreign exchange value of the dollar	A rise in the foreign exchange value of the dollar

How can economists track the extent to which changes in security about jobs and future incomes affect aggregate demand?

POLICY EXAMPLE

The Consumer Confidence Index and Aggregate Demand

An independent economic research organization called The Conference Board tracks an indicator of U.S. consumer sentiment called the Consumer Confidence Index (CCI). The CCI is intended to measure the degree of security that U.S. households have about their future employment and income status, as revealed by a range of data on their spending and saving activities.

Because consumer spending typically accounts for at least two-thirds of total U.S. planned expenditures, variations in the CCI normally indicate changes in U.S. aggregate demand. For instance, during a 6-month interval between late 2007 and early 2008, the CCI lost nearly half of its value. Then U.S. aggregate demand, which had been rising at about $300 billion per year during the 5 years preceding 2008, suddenly *decreased* by more than $300 billion between 2008 and 2009. Thus, a significant reduction in household security about the future, as revealed by the CCI, is associated with a leftward shift in the aggregate demand curve.

FOR CRITICAL THINKING

What would be the predicted effect on the position of the aggregate demand curve of a substantial increase in the Consumer Confidence Index?

QUICK QUIZ See page 103 for the answers. Review concepts from this section in MyEconLab.

Aggregate demand is the total of all planned _____ in the economy, and **aggregate supply** is the total of all planned _____ in the economy. The aggregate demand curve shows the various quantities of total planned _____ on final goods and services at various price levels; it is downward sloping.

There are three reasons why the aggregate demand curve is downward sloping. They are the _____-_____ effect, the _____ _____ effect, and the _____ _____ effect.

The _____-_____ effect occurs because price level changes alter the real value of cash balances, thereby causing people to desire to spend more or less, depending on whether the price level decreases or increases.

The _____ _____ effect is caused by interest rate changes that mimic price level changes. At higher interest rates, people seek to buy _____ houses and cars, and at lower interest rates, they seek to buy _____.

The **open economy effect** occurs because of a shift away from expenditures on _____ goods and a shift toward expenditures on _____ goods when the domestic price level increases.

Long-Run Equilibrium and the Price Level

Equilibrium occurs where the demand and supply curves intersect. The same is true for the economy as a whole, as shown in Figure 4-5 on the facing page: The equilibrium price level occurs at the point where the aggregate demand curve *(AD)* crosses the long-run aggregate supply curve *(LRAS)*. At this equilibrium price level of 120, the total of all planned real expenditures for the entire economy is equal to actual real GDP produced by firms after all adjustments have taken place. Thus, the equilibrium depicted in Figure 4-5 is the economy's *long-run equilibrium*.

The Long-Run Equilibrium Price Level

Note in Figure 4-5 that if the price level were to increase to 140, actual real GDP would exceed total planned real expenditures. Inventories of unsold goods would begin to accumulate, and firms would stand ready to offer more services than people wish to purchase. As a result, the price level would tend to fall.

In contrast, if the price level were 100, then total planned real expenditures by individuals, businesses, and the government would exceed actual real GDP. Inventories of unsold goods would begin to be depleted. The price level would rise toward 120, and higher prices would encourage firms to expand production and replenish inventories of goods available for sale.

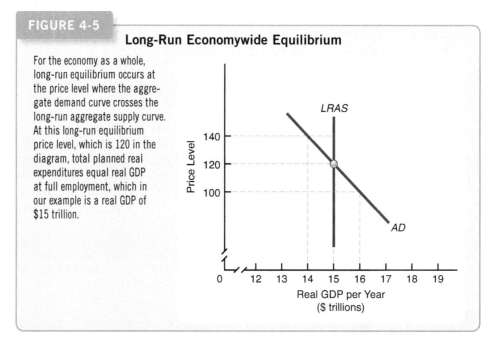

FIGURE 4-5

Long-Run Economywide Equilibrium

For the economy as a whole, long-run equilibrium occurs at the price level where the aggregate demand curve crosses the long-run aggregate supply curve. At this long-run equilibrium price level, which is 120 in the diagram, total planned real expenditures equal real GDP at full employment, which in our example is a real GDP of $15 trillion.

The Effects of Economic Growth on the Price Level

We now have a basic theory of how real GDP and the price level are determined in the long run when all of a nation's resources can change over time and all input prices can adjust fully to changes in the overall level of prices of goods and services that firms produce. Let's begin by evaluating the effects of economic growth on the nation's price level.

ECONOMIC GROWTH AND SECULAR DEFLATION Take a look at panel (a) of Figure 4-6 below, which shows what happens, other things being equal, when the *LRAS* shifts rightward over time. If the economy were to grow steadily during, say, a 4-year interval, the long-run aggregate supply schedule would shift to the right, from $LRAS_1$ to $LRAS_2$.

FIGURE 4-6

Secular Deflation versus Long-Run Price Stability in a Growing Economy

Panel (a) illustrates what happens when economic growth occurs without a corresponding increase in aggregate demand. The result is a decline in the price level over time, known as *secular deflation*. Panel (b) shows that, in principle, secular deflation can be eliminated if the aggregate demand curve shifts rightward at the same pace that the long-run aggregate supply curve shifts to the right.

In panel (a), this results in a downward movement along the aggregate demand schedule. The equilibrium price level falls, from 120 to 80.

Thus, if all factors that affect total planned real expenditures are unchanged, so that the aggregate demand curve does not noticeably move during the 10-year period of real GDP growth, the growing economy in the example would experience deflation. This is known as **secular deflation,** or a persistently declining price level resulting from economic growth in the presence of relatively unchanged aggregate demand.

Secular deflation
A persistent decline in prices resulting from economic growth in the presence of stable aggregate demand.

SECULAR DEFLATION IN THE UNITED STATES In the United States, between 1872 and 1894, the price of bricks fell by 50 percent, the price of sugar by 67 percent, the price of wheat by 69 percent, the price of nails by 70 percent, and the price of copper by nearly 75 percent. Founders of a late-nineteenth-century political movement called *populism* offered a proposal for ending deflation: They wanted the government to issue new money backed by silver. As noted in Table 4-1 on page 92, an increase in the quantity of money in circulation causes the aggregate demand curve to shift to the right. It is clear from panel (b) of Figure 4-6 on the previous page that the increase in the quantity of money would indeed have pushed the price level back upward, because the *AD* curve would shift from AD_1 to AD_2.

Go to www.econtoday.com/chap04 to learn about how the price level has changed during recent years. Then click on "Gross Domestic Product and Components" (for GDP deflators) or "Consumer Price Indexes."

Nevertheless, money growth remained low for several more years. Not until the early twentieth century would the United States put an end to secular deflation, namely, by creating a new monetary system.

Causes of Inflation

Of course, so far during your lifetime, deflation has not been a problem in the United States. Instead, what you have experienced is inflation. Figure 4-7 below shows annual U.S. inflation rates for the past few decades. Clearly, inflation rates have been variable. The other obvious fact, however, is that inflation rates have been consistently *positive.* The price level in the United States has *risen* almost every year. For today's United States, secular deflation has not been a big political issue. If anything, it is secular *inflation* that has plagued the nation.

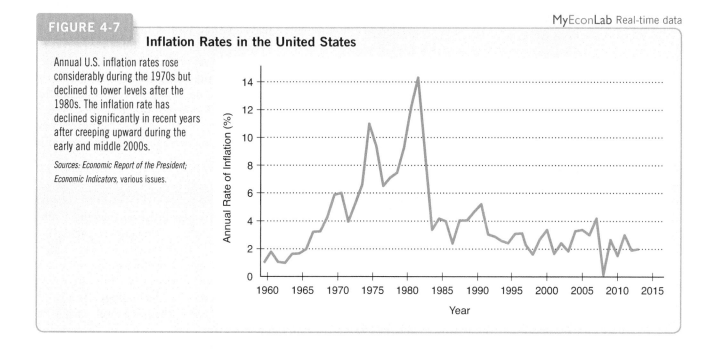

FIGURE 4-7

MyEconLab Real-time data

Inflation Rates in the United States

Annual U.S. inflation rates rose considerably during the 1970s but declined to lower levels after the 1980s. The inflation rate has declined significantly in recent years after creeping upward during the early and middle 2000s.

Sources: Economic Report of the President; Economic Indicators, various issues.

FIGURE 4-8

Explaining Persistent Inflation

As shown in panel (a), it is possible for a decline in long-run aggregate supply to cause a rise in the price level. Long-run aggregate supply *increases* in a growing economy, however, so this cannot explain the observation of persistent U.S. inflation. Panel (b) provides the actual explanation of persistent inflation in the United States and most other nations today, which is that increases in aggregate demand push up the long-run equilibrium price level. Thus, it is possible to explain persistent inflation if the aggregate demand curve shifts rightward at a faster pace than the long-run aggregate supply curve.

Supply-Side Inflation?

What causes such persistent inflation? The model of aggregate demand and long-run aggregate supply provides two possible explanations for inflation. One potential rationale is depicted in panel (a) of Figure 4-8 above. This panel shows a rise in the price level caused by a *decline in long-run aggregate supply*. Hence, one possible reason for persistent inflation would be continual reductions in economywide production.

A leftward shift in the aggregate supply schedule could be caused by several factors, such as reductions in labor force participation, higher marginal tax rates on wages, or the provision of government benefits that give households incentives *not* to supply labor services to firms. Tax rates and government benefits have increased during recent decades, but so has the U.S. population. The significant overall rise in real GDP that has taken place during the past few decades tells us that population growth and productivity gains undoubtedly have dominated other factors. In fact, the aggregate supply schedule has actually shifted *rightward*, not leftward, over time. Consequently, this supply-side explanation for persistent inflation *cannot* be the correct explanation.

Demand-Side Inflation

This leaves only one other explanation for the persistent inflation that the United States has experienced in recent decades. This explanation is depicted in panel (b) of Figure 4-8 above. If aggregate demand increases for a given level of long-run aggregate supply, the price level must increase. The reason is that at an initial price level such as 120, people desire to purchase more goods and services than firms are willing and able to produce, given currently available resources and technology. As a result, the rise in aggregate demand leads only to a general rise in the price level, such as the increase to a value of 140, depicted in the figure.

FIGURE 4-9

Real GDP and the Price Level in the United States, 1970 to the Present

This figure shows the points where aggregate demand and aggregate supply have intersected each year from 1970 to the present. The United States has experienced economic growth over this period, but not without inflation.

Sources: Economic Report of the President; Economic Indicators, various issues; author's estimates.

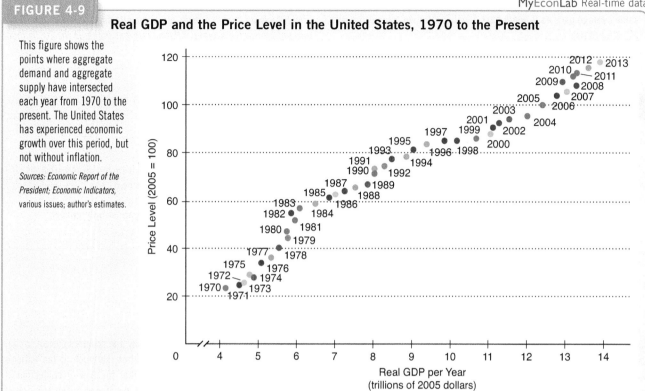

WHAT IF... **there was a sustained increase in the amount of money in circulation intended to generate a rise in the nation's real GDP per year?**

A sustained increase in the quantity of money in circulation would cause persistent rightward shifts in the aggregate demand curve. Because the long-run aggregate supply curve is vertical at the annual real output level after full adjustment has taken place, increases in aggregate demand cannot influence the equilibrium level of *real* GDP

per year. What a sustained increase in the amount of money in circulation *can* do is bring about persistently higher values of the equilibrium price level. Thus, this monetary policy action would generate only sustained inflation and would fail in its objective to raise long-run annual real GDP.

From a long-run perspective, we are left with only one possibility: Persistent inflation in a growing economy is possible only if the aggregate demand curve shifts rightward over time at a faster pace than the rightward progression of the long-run aggregate supply curve. Thus, in contrast to the experience of people who lived in the latter portion of the nineteenth century, when aggregate demand grew too slowly relative to aggregate supply to maintain price stability, your grandparents, parents, and you have lived in times when aggregate demand has grown too *speedily*. The result has been a continual upward drift in the price level, or long-term inflation.

Figure 4-9 above shows that U.S. real GDP has grown in most years since 1970. Nevertheless, this growth has been accompanied by a higher price level every single year.

Has aggregate supply growth dropped below growth in aggregate demand?

EXAMPLE

Will Slowed Growth of Potential U.S. Real GDP Fuel Inflation?

To measure the pace of growth of long-run aggregate supply, economists estimate the rate of growth of *potential real GDP*, which is a measure of how fast the long-run aggregate supply curve shifts outward. Most economists conclude that U.S. potential real GDP growth rose from about 3.5 percent in the 1940s to above 4 percent in the 1960s.

Between the 1970s and 1990s, however, this growth rate dropped to nearly 3 percent. During the 2000s, it fell even further, to between 2 and 2.5 percent. By the early 2010s, potential real GDP growth was between 1 and 1.5 percent. Thus, the position of the U.S. long-run aggregate supply curve now is shifting rightward at the slowest pace in more than 80 years. If aggregate demand continues growing at the same average pace as in years past, the U.S. inflation rate necessarily will tend to rise.

FOR CRITICAL THINKING

Could the lower growth of long-run aggregate supply in the 2000s help account for why the average inflation rate was higher in the 2000s than in the 1990s? Explain.

QUICK QUIZ   See page 103 for the answers. Review concepts from this section in MyEconLab.

When the economy is in long-run equilibrium, the price level adjusts to equate total planned real _____ by individuals, businesses, the government, and foreign (non-U.S.) residents with total planned _____ by firms.

Economic growth causes the long-run aggregate supply schedule to shift _____ over time. If the position of the aggregate demand curve does not change, the long-run

equilibrium price level tends to _____, and there is **secular deflation.**

Because the U.S. economy has grown in recent decades, the persistent inflation during those years has been caused by the aggregate demand curve shifting _____ at a faster pace than the long-run aggregate supply curve.

YOU ARE THERE
A Nation Confronts a Leftward-Shifting *LRAS* Curve

Goncalo Pascoal, chief economist at Millennium BCP, the largest bank in Portugal, sees little to cheer about when he examines the nation's economic performance. In the years since 2007, Portugal's real GDP has been *shrinking* at an average pace of 1 percent per year. Thus, the nation's long-run aggregate supply curve has been exhibiting a sustained leftward shift.

Pascoal does not have to look far for the causes of this shrinkage. In cities such as Felgueiras, once a thriving center of shoe production, empty factories with mostly broken windows line the streets. Throughout the nation, many textile and clothing facilities lie vacant. Over the years, these and other Portuguese manufacturing resources began wearing out. Instead of preventing obsolescence from reducing the nation's stock of productive capital goods, the countries' residents directed many available

resources to consumption goods. Eventually, the country's overall capital stock began to shrink. Now, Pascoal realizes, so much of the nation's capital stock is depleted and unusable that the flow of production of goods and services has declined with each passing year. This is why real GDP is steadily dropping, yielding leftward shifts in Portugal's long-run aggregate supply curve.

Critical Thinking Questions

1. In what direction is Portugal's production possibilities curve shifting over time?

2. What type of inflation might Portugal experience during the coming years?

ISSUES & APPLICATIONS

Will Arctic Assets Unfreeze Long-Run Aggregate Supply?

CONCEPTS APPLIED

▶ Aggregate Supply

▶ Long-Run Aggregate Supply Curve

▶ Endowments

Some economists have begun factoring into their long-run aggregate supply evaluations the underutilized and untapped resource endowments near and within the Arctic Circle. Bringing those resources into broader use, these economists suggest, could do much to generate speedier rightward shifts of the long-run aggregate supply curves of the United States and other northern nations.

Lands with Unexploited Resource Endowments

The Arctic, the global region north of 66.33 degrees latitude, contains only slightly more than 4 percent of the earth's surface area. Nevertheless, nearby regions stretching southward to 45 degrees latitude encompass another 11 percent of the earth's surface and an additional 25 percent of its land mass. Wide swaths of these lands contain significant endowments of as-yet unexploited resources, including minerals, oil, and natural gas.

Three key explanations can be offered for the meager utilization of Arctic and near-Arctic resources. First, the region is not particularly hospitable to people, who must adapt to long summer days and winter nights and to lengthy periods of extreme cold. Second, large tracts of land are covered with thick permafrost and with heavy sheets of ice, or glaciers. Third, much of the land near and within the Arctic is publicly owned. Governments have fewer incentives than private individuals and businesses to extract productive resources from these lands. Indeed, failure to place Arctic and near-Arctic resources in private hands has done more to consign them to an economic deep freeze than the cold air above them.

Could Unfreezing Arctic Endowments Heat Up Aggregate Supply Growth?

The volume of untapped Arctic oil is thought to be sufficiently large to provide the *entire world's* requirements for about half a year, and today's technology could fuel *global* natural gas requirements for an estimated 2 years. If all estimated Arctic oil could be extracted, it would last the world at least 3 years, and all of the region's likely natural gas reserves would be enough for about 25 years. Mineral endowments are less certain, but most geologists suspect

that unexploited Arctic and near-Arctic lands contain vast amounts of metal ores.

Of course, making most Arctic resources accessible to private producers would *gradually* add to annual flows of resources that residents of northern nations such as the United States could use to produce goods and services. Estimates indicate that drawing on these endowments would boost annual U.S. real GDP growth by an appreciable fraction of a percentage point. Thus, reducing government ownership of these underutilized and untapped endowments would contribute to higher economic growth.

For Critical Thinking

1. Why do you suppose that firms in Arctic nations are already developing specialized tanker ships and platforms for use in privately accessible Arctic areas?
2. What are possible opportunity costs of opening Arctic lands to private extraction of as-yet unavailable resource endowments?

Web Resources

1. For a summary of current data about likely Arctic oil and natural gas endowments, go to www.econtoday.com/chap04.
2. To learn about economic issues faced in extracting metal ores in the Arctic, go to www.econtoday.com/chap04.

MyEconLab

For more questions on this chapter's Issues & Applications, go to MyEconLab. In the Study Plan for this chapter, select Section N: News.

MyEconLab

Here is what you should know after reading this chapter. MyEconLab will help you identify what you know, and where to go when you need to practice.

WHAT YOU SHOULD KNOW

Long-Run Aggregate Supply The long-run aggregate supply curve is vertical at the amount of real GDP that firms plan to produce when they have full information and when complete adjustment of input prices to any changes in output prices has taken place.

aggregate supply, 86
long-run aggregate supply curve, 86
base-year dollars, 86
endowments, 86

Key Figure
Figure 4-1, 86

WHERE TO GO TO PRACTICE

- MyEconLab Study Plan 4.1
- Animated Figure 4-1

WHAT YOU SHOULD KNOW		WHERE TO GO TO PRACTICE
Economic Growth and the Long-Run Aggregate Supply Curve The production possibilities curve shifts rightward when the economy grows, and so does the nation's long-run aggregate supply curve. In a growing economy, the changes in full-employment real GDP defined by the shifting long-run aggregate supply curve define the nation's long-run, or trend, growth path.	Key Figures Figure 4-2, 87 Figure 4-3, 88	• MyEconLab Study Plan 4.1 • Animated Figures 4-2, 4-3
Why the Aggregate Demand Curve Slopes Downward and Factors That Cause It to Shift The real-balance effect occurs when a rise in the price level reduces the real value of cash balances, which induces people to cut back on planned spending. Higher interest rates typically accompany increases in the price level, and this interest rate effect induces people to cut back on borrowing and spending. Finally, a rise in the price level at home causes domestic goods to be more expensive relative to foreign goods, so there is a fall in exports and a rise in imports, both of which cause domestic planned expenditures to fall. These three factors together account for the downward slope of the aggregate demand curve, which shifts if there is any other change in total planned real expenditures at any given price level.	aggregate demand, 89 aggregate demand curve, 89 real-balance effect, 91 interest rate effect, 91 open economy effect, 91 Key Figure Figure 4-4, 90	• MyEconLab Study Plans 4.2, 4.3 • Animated Figure 4-4
Long-Run Equilibrium for the Economy In a long-run economywide equilibrium, the price level adjusts until total planned real expenditures equal actual real GDP. Thus, the long-run equilibrium price level is determined at the point where the aggregate demand curve intersects the long-run aggregate supply curve.	Key Figure Figure 4-5, 94	• MyEconLab Study Plan 4.4 • Animated Figure 4-5
Why Economic Growth Can Cause Deflation If the aggregate demand curve is stationary during a period of economic growth, the long-run aggregate supply curve shifts rightward along the aggregate demand curve. The long-run equilibrium price level falls, so there is secular deflation.	secular deflation, 95 Key Figure Figure 4-6, 94	• MyEconLab Study Plan 4.4 • Animated Figure 4-6
Likely Reasons for Recent Persistent Inflation Inflation can result from a fall in long-run aggregate supply, but in a growing economy, long-run aggregate supply generally rises. Thus, a much more likely cause of persistent inflation is a pace of aggregate demand growth that exceeds the pace at which long-run aggregate supply increases.	Key Figures Figure 4-7, 95 Figure 4-8, 96	• MyEconLab Study Plan 4.5 • Animated Figures 4-7, 4-8

PROBLEMS

All problems are assignable in MyEconLab. Answers to odd-numbered problems appear at the back of the book.

4-1. Many economists view the natural rate of unemployment as the level observed when real GDP is given by the position of the long-run aggregate supply curve. How can there be positive unemployment in this situation? (See page 86.)

4-2. Suppose that the long-run aggregate supply curve is positioned at a real GDP level of $15 trillion in base-year dollars, and the long-run equilibrium price level (in index number form) is 115. What is the full-employment level of *nominal* GDP? (See page 94.)

4-3. Continuing from Problem 4-2, suppose that the full-employment level of *nominal* GDP in the following year rises to $17.7 trillion. The long-run equilibrium price level, however, remains unchanged. By how much (in real dollars) has the long-run aggregate supply curve shifted to the right in the following year? By how much, if any, has the aggregate demand curve shifted to the right? (Hint: The equilibrium price level can stay the same only if *LRAS* and *AD* shift rightward by the same amount (See page 94.)

4-4. Suppose that the position of a nation's long-run aggregate supply curve has not changed, but its long-run equilibrium price level has increased. Which of the following factors might account for this event? (See page 94.)

   a. A rise in the value of the domestic currency relative to other world currencies

   b. An increase in the quantity of money in circulation

   c. An increase in the labor force participation rate

   d. A decrease in taxes

   e. A rise in real incomes of countries that are key trading partners of this nation

   f. Increased long-run economic growth

4-5. Identify the combined shifts in long-run aggregate supply and aggregate demand that could explain the following simultaneous occurrences. (See page 94).

   a. An increase in equilibrium real GDP and an increase in the equilibrium price level

   b. A decrease in equilibrium real GDP with no change in the equilibrium price level

   c. An increase in equilibrium real GDP with no change in the equilibrium price level

   d. A decrease in equilibrium real GDP and a decrease in the equilibrium price level

4-6. Suppose that during the past 3 years, equilibrium real GDP in a country rose steadily, from $450 billion to $500 billion, but even though the position of its aggregate demand curve remained unchanged, its equilibrium price level steadily declined, from 110 to 103. What could have accounted for these outcomes, and what is the term for the change in the price level experienced by this country? (See page 94.)

4-7. Suppose that during a given year, the quantity of U.S. real GDP that can be produced in the long run rises from $14.9 trillion to $15.0 trillion, measured in base-year dollars. During the year, no change occurs in the various factors that influence aggregate demand. What will happen to the U.S. long-run equilibrium price level during this particular year? (See page 94.)

4-8. Assume that the position of a nation's aggregate demand curve has not changed, but the long-run equilibrium price level has declined. Other things being equal, which of the following factors might account for this event? (See page 94.)

   a. An increase in labor productivity

   b. A decrease in the capital stock

   c. A decrease in the quantity of money in circulation

   d. The discovery of new mineral resources used to produce various goods

   e. A technological improvement

4-9. Suppose that there is a sudden rise in the price level. What will happen to economywide planned spending on purchases of goods and services? Why? (See page 90.)

4-10. Assume that the economy is in long-run equilibrium with complete information and that input prices adjust rapidly to changes in the prices of goods and services. If there is a rise in the price level induced by an increase in aggregate demand, what happens to real GDP? (See page 94.)

4-11. Consider the diagram below when answering the questions that follow. (See page 94.)

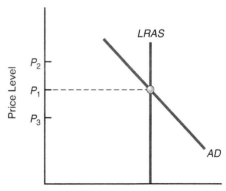

Real GDP per Year (base-year dollars)

a. Suppose that the current price level is P_2. Explain why the price level will decline toward P_1.

b. Suppose that the current price level is P_3. Explain why the price level will rise toward P_1.

4-12. Explain whether each of the following events would cause a movement along or a shift in the position of the *LRAS* curve, other things being equal. In each case, explain the direction of the movement along the curve or shift in its position. (See page 87.)

a. Last year, businesses invested in new capital equipment, so this year the nation's capital stock is higher than it was last year.

b. There has been an 8 percent increase in the quantity of money in circulation that has shifted the *AD* curve.

c. A hurricane of unprecedented strength has damaged oil rigs, factories, and ports all along the nation's coast.

d. Inflation has occurred during the past year as a result of rightward shifts of the *AD* curve.

4-13. Explain whether each of the following events would cause a movement along or a shift in the position of the *AD* curve, other things being equal. In each case, explain the direction of the movement along the curve or shift in its position. (See page 92.)

a. Deflation has occurred during the past year.

b. Real GDP levels of all the nation's major trading partners have declined.

c. There has been a decline in the foreign exchange value of the nation's currency.

d. The price level has increased this year.

4-14. This year, a nation's long-run equilibrium real GDP and price level both increased. Which of the following combinations of factors might simultaneously account for *both* occurrences? (See page 94.)

a. An isolated earthquake at the beginning of the year destroyed part of the nation's capital stock, and the nation's government significantly reduced its purchases of goods and services.

b. There was a technological improvement at the end of the previous year, and the quantity of money in circulation rose significantly during the year.

c. Labor productivity increased throughout the year, and consumers significantly increased their total planned purchases of goods and services.

d. The capital stock increased somewhat during the year, and the quantity of money in circulation declined considerably.

4-15. Explain how, if at all, each of the following events would affect equilibrium real GDP and the long-run equilibrium price level. (See page 94.)

a. A reduction in the quantity of money in circulation

b. An income tax rebate (the return of previously paid taxes) from the government to households, which they can apply only to purchases of goods and services

c. A technological improvement

d. A decrease in the value of the home currency in terms of the currencies of other nations

4-16. For each question, suppose that the economy *begins* at the long-run equilibrium point *A* in the diagram below. Identify which of the other points on the diagram—points *B*, *C*, *D*, or *E*—could represent a *new* long-run equilibrium after the described events take place and move the economy away from point *A*. (See page 94.)

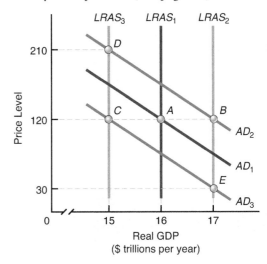

a. Significant productivity improvements occur, and the quantity of money in circulation increases.

b. No new capital investment takes place, and a fraction of the existing capital stock depreciates and becomes unusable. At the same time, the government imposes a large tax increase on the nation's households.

c. More efficient techniques for producing goods and services are adopted throughout the economy at the same time that the government reduces its spending on goods and services.

4-17. In Ciudad Barrios, El Salvador, the latest payments from relatives working in the United States have finally arrived. When the credit unions open for business, up to 150 people are already waiting in line. After receiving the funds their relatives have transmitted to these institutions, customers go off to outdoor markets to stock up on food or clothing or to appliance stores to purchase new stereos or televisions. Similar scenes occur throughout the developing world, as each year migrants working in higher-income, developed nations send around $200 billion of their earnings back to their relatives in less developed nations.

Evidence indicates that the relatives, such as those in Ciudad Barrios, typically spend nearly all of the funds on current consumption. (See page 94.)

a. Based on the information supplied, are developing countries' income inflows transmitted by migrant workers primarily affecting their economies' long-run aggregate supply curves or aggregate demand curves?

b. How are equilibrium price levels in nations that are recipients of large inflows of funds from migrants likely to be affected? Explain your reasoning.

ECONOMICS ON THE NET

Wages, Productivity, and Aggregate Supply How much firms pay their employees and the productivity of those employees influence firms' total planned production, so changes in these factors affect the position of the aggregate supply curve. This application gives you the opportunity to examine recent trends in measures of the overall wages and productivity of workers.

Title: Bureau of Labor Statistics: Economy at a Glance

Navigation: Use the link at www.econtoday.com/chap04 to visit the Bureau of Labor Statistics (BLS) Web site.

Application Perform the indicated operations, and answer the following questions.

1. In the "Pay and Benefits" popup menu, click on *Employment Costs.* Choose *Employment Cost Index.* What are the recent trends in wages and salaries and in benefits? In the long run, how should these trends be related to movements in the overall price level?

2. Back up to the home page, and in the "Productivity" popup menu, click on *Labor Productivity and Costs* and then on *PDF* next to "LPC News Releases: Productivity and Costs." How has labor productivity behaved recently? What does this imply for the long-run aggregate supply curve?

3. Back up to the home page, and now in the "Employment" popup menu, click on *National Employment* and then on *PDF* next to "Current CES Economic News Release: Employment Situation Summary." Does it appear that the U.S. economy is currently in a long-run growth equilibrium?

For Group Study and Analysis

1. Divide the class into aggregate demand and long-run aggregate supply groups. Have each group search the Internet for data on factors that influence its assigned curve. For which factors do data appear to be most readily available? For which factors are data more sparse or more subject to measurement problems?

2. The BLS home page displays a map of the United States. Assign regions of the nation to different groups, and have each group develop a short report about current and future prospects for economic growth within its assigned region. What similarities exist across regions? What regional differences are there?

ANSWERS TO QUICK QUIZZES

p. 88: (i) vertical; (ii) natural; (iii) rightward . . . increases

p. 93: (i) expenditures . . . production . . . spending; (ii) real-balance . . . interest rate . . . open economy;

(iii) real-balance; (iv) interest rate . . . fewer . . . more; (v) domestic . . . foreign

p. 98: (i) expenditures . . . production; (ii) rightward . . . decline; (iii) rightward

5

Classical and Keynesian Macro Analyses

Many Wall Street observers refer to it as the "fear index." Its true name is the *VIX index*, and it has become the most commonly used gauge of volatility in U.S. financial markets. Prior to and during the severe 2008–2009 recession, the VIX index increased substantially, reflecting significant variability of the value of financial claims traded in financial markets as well as volatility in real interest rates. How can major disturbances in financial markets sometimes translate into reductions in real GDP and even decreases in the price level? To understand the answer, you must learn about determination of the equilibrium price level in the short run, which is a fundamental topic of this chapter.

the price of a bottle containing 6.5 ounces of Coca-Cola remained unchanged at 5 cents from 1886 to 1959? The prices of many other goods and services changed at least slightly during that 73-year period, and since then the prices of most items, including Coca-Cola, have generally moved in an upward direction. Nevertheless, prices of final goods and services have not always adjusted immediately in response to changes in aggregate demand. Consequently, one approach to understanding the determination of real GDP and the price level emphasizes *incomplete* adjustment in the prices of many goods and services. The simplest version of this approach was first developed by a twentieth-century economist named John Maynard Keynes (pronounced like *canes*). It assumes that in the short run, prices of most goods and services are nearly as rigid as the price of Coca-Cola from 1886 to 1959. Although the modern version of the Keynesian approach allows for greater flexibility of prices in the short run, incomplete price adjustment still remains a key feature of the modern Keynesian approach.

The Keynesian approach does not retain the long-run assumption, which you encountered in Chapter 10, of fully adjusting prices. Economists who preceded Keynes employed this assumption in creating an approach to understanding variations in real GDP and the price level that Keynes called the *classical model*. Like Keynes, we shall begin our study of variations in real GDP and the price level by considering the earlier, classical approach.

The Classical Model

The classical model, which traces its origins to the 1770s, was the first systematic attempt to explain the determinants of the price level and the national levels of real GDP, employment, consumption, saving, and investment. Classical economists—Adam Smith, J. B. Say, David Ricardo, John Stuart Mill, Thomas Malthus, A. C. Pigou, and others—wrote from the 1770s to the 1930s. They assumed, among other things, that all wages and prices were flexible and that competitive markets existed throughout the economy.

Say's Law

Every time you produce something for which you receive income, you generate the income necessary to make expenditures on other goods and services. That means that an economy producing $15 trillion of real GDP, measured in base-year dollars (the value of current goods and services expressed in terms of prices in a base year), simultaneously produces the income with which these goods and services can be purchased. As an accounting identity, *actual* aggregate output always equals *actual* aggregate income. Classical economists took this accounting identity one step further by arguing that total national supply creates its own national demand. They asserted what has become known as **Say's law:**

> **Supply creates its own demand. Hence, it follows that** desired *expenditures will* **equal** actual *expenditures.*

THE IMPLICATION OF SAY'S LAW What does Say's law really mean? It states that the very process of producing specific goods (supply) is proof that other goods are desired (demand). People produce more goods than they want for their own use only if they seek to trade them for other goods. Someone offers to supply something only because he or she has a demand for something else.

The implication of this, according to Say, is that no general glut, or overproduction, is possible in a market economy. From this reasoning, it seems to follow that full employment of labor and other resources would be the normal state of affairs in such an economy.

Say acknowledged that an oversupply of some goods might occur in particular markets. He argued that such surpluses would simply cause prices to fall, thereby decreasing production as the economy adjusted. The opposite would occur in markets in which shortages temporarily appeared.

Say's law
A dictum of economist J. B. Say that supply creates its own demand. Producing goods and services generates the means and the willingness to purchase other goods and services.

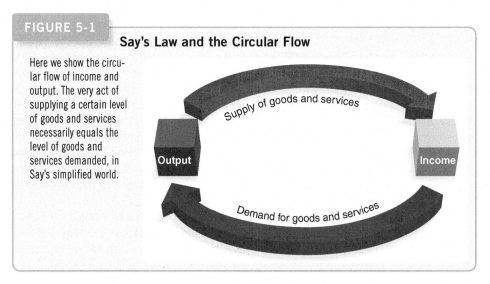

FIGURE 5-1

Say's Law and the Circular Flow

Here we show the circular flow of income and output. The very act of supplying a certain level of goods and services necessarily equals the level of goods and services demanded, in Say's simplified world.

Output

Supply of goods and services

Income

Demand for goods and services

SAY'S LAW IN A MODERN ECONOMY All this seems reasonable enough in a simple barter economy in which households produce most of the goods they want and trade for the rest. This is shown in Figure 5-1 above, where there is a simple circular flow. But what about a more sophisticated economy in which people work for others and money is used instead of barter? Can these complications create the possibility of unemployment? And does the fact that laborers receive money income, some of which can be saved, lead to unemployment? No, said the classical economists to these last two questions. They based their reasoning on a number of key assumptions.

Assumptions of the Classical Model

The classical model makes four major assumptions:

1. *Pure competition exists.* No single buyer or seller of a commodity or an input can affect its price.

2. *Wages and prices are flexible.* The assumption of pure competition leads to the notion that prices, wages and interest rates are free to move to whatever level supply and demand dictate (as the economy adjusts). Although no *individual* buyer can set a price, the community of buyers or sellers can cause prices to rise or to fall to an equilibrium level.

3. *People are motivated by self-interest.* Businesses want to maximize their profits, and households want to maximize their economic well-being.

4. *People cannot be fooled by money illusion.* Buyers and sellers react to changes in relative prices. That is to say, they do not suffer from **money illusion.** For example, workers will not be fooled into thinking that doubling their wages makes them better off if the price level has also doubled during the same time period.

Money illusion
Reacting to changes in money prices rather than relative prices. If a worker whose wages double when the price level also doubles thinks he or she is better off, that worker is suffering from money illusion.

The classical economists concluded, after taking account of the four major assumptions, that the role of government in the economy should be minimal. They assumed that pure competition prevails, all prices and wages are flexible, and people are self-interested and do not experience money illusion. If so, they argued, then any problems in the macroeconomy will be temporary. The market will correct itself.

Equilibrium in the Credit Market

When income is saved, it is not reflected in product demand. It is a type of *leakage* from the circular flow of income and output because saving withdraws funds from the income stream. Therefore, total planned consumption spending *can* fall short of total current real GDP. In such a situation, it appears that supply does not necessarily create its own demand.

FIGURE 5-2

Equating Desired Saving and Desired Investment in the Classical Model

The schedule showing planned investment is labeled "Desired investment." The desired saving curve is shown as an upward-sloping supply curve of saving. The equilibrating force here is, of course, the interest rate. At higher interest rates, people desire to save more. But at higher interest rates, businesses wish to engage in less investment because it is less profitable to invest. In this model, at an interest rate of 5 percent, planned investment just equals planned saving, which is $2 trillion per year.

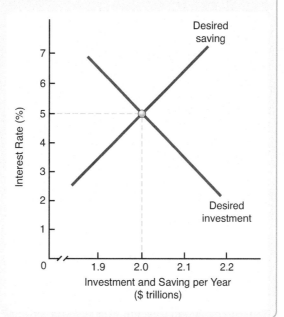

THE RELATIONSHIP BETWEEN SAVING AND INVESTMENT The classical economists did not believe that the complicating factor of saving in the circular flow model of income and output was a problem. They contended that each dollar saved would be invested by businesses so that the leakage of saving would be matched by the injection of business investment. *Investment* here refers only to additions to the nation's capital stock. The classical economists believed that businesses as a group would intend to invest as much as households wanted to save.

THE EQUILIBRIUM INTEREST RATE Equilibrium between the saving plans of consumers and the investment plans of businesses comes about, in the classical model, through the working of the credit market. In the credit market, the *price* of credit is the interest rate. At equilibrium, the price of credit—the interest rate—ensures that the amount of credit demanded equals the amount of credit supplied. Planned investment just equals planned saving, so there is no reason to be concerned about the leakage of saving. This fact is illustrated graphically in Figure 5-2 above.

In the figure, the vertical axis measures the rate of interest in percentage terms, and the horizontal axis measures flows of desired saving and desired investment per unit time period. The desired saving curve is really a supply curve of saving. It shows that people wish to save more at higher interest rates than at lower interest rates.

In contrast, the higher the rate of interest, the less profitable it is to invest and the lower is the level of desired investment. Thus, the desired investment curve slopes downward. In this simplified model, the equilibrium rate of interest is 5 percent, and the equilibrium quantity of saving and investment is $2 trillion per year.

Equilibrium in the Labor Market

Now consider the labor market. If an excess quantity of labor is supplied at a particular wage level, the wage level must be above equilibrium. By accepting lower wages, unemployed workers will quickly be put back to work. We show equilibrium in the labor market in Figure 5-3 on the facing page.

Go to www.econtoday.com/chap05 to link to Federal Reserve data on U.S. interest rates.

Go to www.econtoday.com/chap05 to find out the latest U.S. saving rate from the Bureau of Economic Analysis. Select "Personal saving as a percentage of disposable personal income."

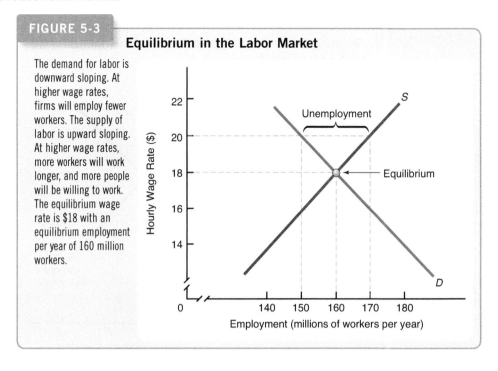

FIGURE 5-3

Equilibrium in the Labor Market

The demand for labor is downward sloping. At higher wage rates, firms will employ fewer workers. The supply of labor is upward sloping. At higher wage rates, more workers will work longer, and more people will be willing to work. The equilibrium wage rate is $18 with an equilibrium employment per year of 160 million workers.

Assume that equilibrium exists at $18 per hour and 160 million workers employed. If the wage rate were $20 per hour, there would be unemployment—170 million workers would want to work, but businesses would want to hire only 150 million. In the classical model, this unemployment is eliminated rather rapidly by wage rates dropping back to $18 per hour, as seen in Figure 5-3 above.

THE RELATIONSHIP BETWEEN EMPLOYMENT AND REAL GDP Employment is not to be regarded simply as some isolated figure that government statisticians estimate. Rather, the level of employment in an economy determines its real GDP (output), other things held constant. A hypothetical relationship between input (number of employees) and the value of output (real GDP per year) is shown in Table 5-1 below. The row that has 160 million workers per year as the labor input is highlighted. That might be considered a hypothetical level of full employment, and it is related to a rate of real GDP, in base-year dollars, of $15 trillion per year.

Classical Theory, Vertical Aggregate Supply, and the Price Level

In the classical model, unemployment greater than the natural unemployment rate is impossible. Say's law, coupled with flexible interest rates, prices, and wages, would always tend to keep workers fully employed so that the aggregate supply curve, as

TABLE 5-1

The Relationship between Employment and Real GDP

Other things being equal, an increase in the quantity of labor input increases real GDP. In this example, if 160 million workers are employed, real GDP is $15 trillion in base-year dollars.

Labor Input per Year (millions of workers)	Real GDP per Year ($ trillions)
150	12
154	13
158	14
160	15
164	16
166	17

FIGURE 5-4

Classical Theory and Increases in Aggregate Demand

The classical theorists believed that Say's law and flexible interest rates, prices, and wages would always lead to full employment at real GDP of $15 trillion, in base-year dollars, along the vertical aggregate supply curve, *LRAS*. With aggregate demand AD_1, the price level is 120. An increase in aggregate demand shifts AD_1 to AD_2. At price level 120, the quantity of real GDP demanded per year would be $15.5 trillion at point *A* on AD_2. But $15.5 trillion in real GDP per year is greater than real GDP at full employment. Prices rise, and the economy quickly moves from E_1 to E_2, at the higher price level of 130.

shown in Figure 5-4 above, is vertical at the real GDP of $15 trillion, in base-year dollars. We have labeled the supply curve *LRAS*, which is the long-run aggregate supply curve introduced in Chapter 4. It was defined there as the real GDP that would be produced in an economy with full information and full adjustment of wages and prices year in and year out. *LRAS* therefore corresponds to the long-run rate of unemployment.

In the classical model, this happens to be the *only* aggregate supply curve. The classical economists made little distinction between the long run and the short run. Prices adjust so fast that the economy is essentially always on or quickly moving toward *LRAS*. Furthermore, because the labor market adjusts rapidly, real GDP is always at, or soon to be at, full employment. Full employment does not mean zero unemployment because there is always some frictional and structural unemployment (discussed in Chapter 1), which yields the natural rate of unemployment.

EFFECT OF AN INCREASE IN AGGREGATE DEMAND IN THE CLASSICAL MODEL In this model, any change in aggregate demand will quickly cause a change in the price level. Consider starting at E_1, at price level 120, in Figure 5-4. If aggregate demand shifts to AD_2, the economy will tend toward point *A*, but because this is beyond full-employment real GDP, prices will rise, and the economy will find itself back on the vertical *LRAS* at point E_2 at a higher price level, 130. The price level will increase as a result of the increase in *AD* because employers will end up bidding up wages for workers, as well as bidding up the prices of other inputs.

The level of real GDP per year clearly does not depend on the level of aggregate demand. Hence, we say that in the classical model, the equilibrium level of real GDP per year is completely *supply determined*. Changes in aggregate demand affect only the price level, not real GDP.

EFFECT OF A DECREASE IN AGGREGATE DEMAND IN THE CLASSICAL MODEL The effect of a decrease in aggregate demand in the classical model is the converse of the analysis just presented for an increase in aggregate demand. You can simply reverse AD_2 and AD_1 in Figure 5-4 above. To help you see how this analysis works, consider the flowchart in Figure 5-5 on the next page.

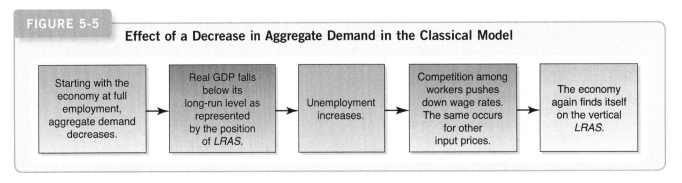

FIGURE 5-5

Effect of a Decrease in Aggregate Demand in the Classical Model

Starting with the economy at full employment, aggregate demand decreases. → Real GDP falls below its long-run level as represented by the position of *LRAS*. → Unemployment increases. → Competition among workers pushes down wage rates. The same occurs for other input prices. → The economy again finds itself on the vertical *LRAS*.

QUICK QUIZ   See page 124 for the answers. Review concepts from this section in MyEconLab.

Say's law states that _____ creates its own _____ and therefore *desired* expenditures will equal *actual* expenditures.

The classical model assumes that (1) _____ _____ exists, (2) _____ and _____ are completely flexible, (3) individuals are motivated by _____-_____, and (4) they cannot be fooled by _____ _____.

When saving is introduced into the model, equilibrium occurs in the credit market through changes in the interest rate such that desired _____ equals desired _____ at the equilibrium rate of interest.

In the labor market, full employment occurs at a _____ _____ at which quantity demanded equals quantity supplied. That particular level of employment is associated with the full-employment level of real GDP per year.

In the classical model, because *LRAS* is _____, the equilibrium level of real GDP is supply determined. Any changes in aggregate demand simply change the _____ _____.

Keynesian Economics and the Keynesian Short-Run Aggregate Supply Curve

The classical economists' world was one of fully utilized resources. There would be no unused capacity and no unemployment. But then in the 1930s, Europe and the United States entered a period of economic decline that seemingly could not be explained by the classical model. John Maynard Keynes developed an explanation that has since become known as the Keynesian model. Keynes and his followers argued that prices, especially the price of labor (wages), were inflexible downward due to the existence of unions and long-term contracts between businesses and workers. That meant that prices were "sticky." Keynes contended that in such a world, which has large amounts of excess capacity and unemployment, an increase in aggregate demand will not raise the price level, and a decrease in aggregate demand will not cause firms to lower prices.

Demand-Determined Real GDP

This situation is depicted in Figure 5-6 on the next page. For simplicity, Figure 5-6 does not show the point where the economy reaches capacity, and that is why the *short-run aggregate supply curve* (to be discussed later) never starts to slope upward and is simply the horizontal line labeled *SRAS*. Moreover, we don't show *LRAS* in Figure 5-6 either. It would be a vertical line at the level of real GDP per year that is consistent with full employment. If we start out in equilibrium with aggregate demand at AD_1, the equilibrium level of real GDP per year, measured in base-year dollars, is $15 trillion at point E_1, and the equilibrium price level is 120. If there is a rise in aggregate demand, so that the aggregate demand curve shifts outward to the right to AD_2, the equilibrium price level at point E_2 will not change. Only the equilibrium level of real GDP per year will increase, to $15.5 trillion. Conversely, if there is a fall in aggregate demand that shifts the aggregate demand curve to AD_3, the equilibrium price level will again remain at 120 at point E_3, but the equilibrium level of real GDP per year will fall to $14.5 trillion.

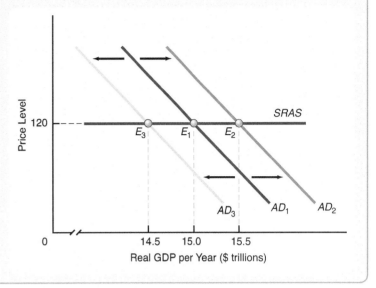

FIGURE 5-6

Demand-Determined Equilibrium Real GDP at Less Than Full Employment

Keynes assumed that prices will not fall when aggregate demand falls and that there is excess capacity, so prices will not rise when aggregate demand increases. Thus, the short-run aggregate supply curve is simply a horizontal line at the given price level, 120, represented by *SRAS*. An aggregate demand shock that increases aggregate demand to AD_2 will increase the equilibrium level of real GDP per year to $15.5 trillion. An aggregate demand shock that decreases aggregate demand to AD_3 will decrease the equilibrium level of real GDP to $14.5 trillion. The equilibrium price level will not change.

Under such circumstances, the equilibrium level of real GDP per year is completely *demand determined.*

The Keynesian Short-Run Aggregate Supply Curve

The horizontal short-run aggregate supply curve represented in Figure 5-6 above is often called the **Keynesian short-run aggregate supply curve.** According to Keynes, unions and long-term contracts are real-world factors that explain the inflexibility of *nominal* wage rates. Such stickiness of wages makes *involuntary* unemployment of labor a distinct possibility, because leftward movements along the Keynesian short-run aggregate supply curve reduce real production and, hence, employment. The classical assumption of everlasting full employment no longer holds.

Have U.S. nominal wages remained too high to reduce unemployment?

Keynesian short-run aggregate supply curve
The horizontal portion of the aggregate supply curve in which there is excessive unemployment and unused capacity in the economy.

EXAMPLE

Have Inflation-Adjusted U.S. Wages Been "Too High"?

Unemployment occurs when a surplus exists in the labor market—that is, when the quantity of labor supplied by workers at the current inflation-adjusted, or *real*, wage rate exceeds the quantity of labor that firms demand at that real wage rate. Other things being equal, a labor surplus will begin to disappear only if the inflation-adjusted wage rate drops toward that market clearing wage rate.

Since 2008, inflation-adjusted wages in the United States have declined by about 0.2 percent per year. Many economists contend that this low rate of decrease explains why unemployment has declined only from 14.3 million at the end of 2008 to just about 12.5 million today. Because

the U.S. inflation rate has remained very low, they argue, nominal wages would have to drop at a faster pace to push down the labor market surplus more rapidly and thereby bring about a quicker decline in U.S. unemployment. Thus, they conclude that nominal wages have been too inflexible to reduce the nation's unemployment level significantly.

FOR CRITICAL THINKING
In principle, if nominal wages were to remain "too high," could a sustained increase in the inflation rate significantly reduce labor unemployment? Explain.

Data from the 1930s offer evidence of a nearly horizontal aggregate supply curve. Between 1934 and 1940, the GDP deflator stayed in a range from about 8.3 to less than 9.0, implying that the price level changed by no more than 8 percent. Yet the level of real GDP measured in 2005 dollars varied between nearly $0.7 trillion and close to $1.1 trillion, or by more than 50 percent. Thus, between 1934 and 1940, the U.S. short-run aggregate supply curve was almost flat.

FIGURE 5-7

Real GDP Determination with Fixed versus Flexible Prices

In panel (a), the price level index is fixed at 120. An increase in aggregate demand from AD_1 to AD_2 moves the equilibrium level of real GDP from $15 trillion per year to $16 trillion per year in base-year dollars. In panel

(b), $SRAS$ is upward sloping. The same shift in aggregate demand yields an equilibrium level of real GDP of only $15.5 trillion per year and a higher price level index at 130.

Panel (a)
Keynesian Model

Panel (b)
Modern Keynesian Analysis

Output Determination Using Aggregate Demand and Aggregate Supply: Fixed versus Changing Price Levels in the Short Run

The underlying assumption of the simplified Keynesian model is that the relevant range of the short-run aggregate supply schedule ($SRAS$) is horizontal, as depicted in panel (a) of Figure 5-7 above. There you see that short-run aggregate supply is fixed at price level 120. If aggregate demand is AD_1, then the equilibrium level of real GDP, in base-year dollars, is $15 trillion per year. If aggregate demand increases to AD_2, then the equilibrium level of real GDP increases to $16 trillion per year.

As discussed in Chapter 4, the price level has drifted upward during recent decades. Hence, prices are not totally sticky. Modern Keynesian analysis recognizes that *some*—but not complete—price adjustment takes place in the short run. Panel (b) of Figure 5-7 above displays a more general **short-run aggregate supply curve** ($SRAS$). This curve represents the relationship between the price level and real GDP with incomplete price adjustment and in the absence of complete information in the short run. Allowing for partial price adjustment implies that $SRAS$ slopes upward, and its slope is steeper after it crosses long-run aggregate supply, $LRAS$. This is because higher and higher prices are required to induce firms to raise their production of goods and services to levels that temporarily exceed full-employment real GDP.

With partial price adjustment in the short run, if aggregate demand is AD_1, then the equilibrium level of real GDP in panel (b) is also $15 trillion per year, at a price level of 120, too. An increase in aggregate demand to AD_2 such as occurred in panel (a) produces a different short-run equilibrium, however. Equilibrium real GDP increases to $15.5 trillion per year, which is less than in panel (a) because an increase in the price level to 130 causes planned purchases of goods and services to decline.

In the modern Keynesian short run, when the price level rises partially, real GDP can be expanded beyond the level consistent with its long-run growth path, discussed in Chapter 4, for a variety of reasons:

Short-run aggregate supply curve
The relationship between total planned economywide production and the price level in the short run, all other things held constant. If prices adjust incompletely in the short run, the curve is positively sloped.

1. In the short run, most labor contracts implicitly or explicitly call for flexibility in hours of work at the given wage rate. Therefore, firms can use existing workers more intensively in a variety of ways: They can get workers to work harder, to work more hours per day, and to work more days per week. Workers can also be switched from *uncounted* production, such as maintenance, to *counted* production, which generates counted production of goods and services. The distinction between counted and uncounted is what is measured in the marketplace, particularly by government statisticians and accountants. If a worker cleans a machine, there is no measured output. But if that worker is put on the production line and helps increase the number of units produced each day, measured output will go up. That worker's production has then been counted.

2. Existing capital equipment can be used more intensively. Machines can be worked more hours per day. Some can be made to operate faster. Maintenance can be delayed.

3. Finally, if wage rates are held constant, a higher price level leads to increased profits from additional production, which induces firms to hire more workers. The duration of unemployment falls, and thus the unemployment rate falls. And people who were previously not in the labor force (homemakers and younger or older workers) can be induced to enter it.

All these adjustments cause real GDP to rise as the price level increases.

Shifts in the Aggregate Supply Curve

Just as non-price-level factors can cause a shift in the aggregate demand curve, there are non-price-level factors that can cause a shift in the aggregate supply curve. The analysis here is more complicated than the analysis for the non-price-level determinants for aggregate demand, for here we are dealing with both the short run and the long run—*SRAS* and *LRAS*. Still, anything other than the price level that affects the production of final goods and services will shift aggregate supply curves.

Shifts in Both Short- and Long-Run Aggregate Supply

There is a core class of events that cause a shift in both the short-run aggregate supply curve and the long-run aggregate supply curve. These include any change in our endowments of the factors of production. Any change in factors of production—labor, capital, or technology—that influence economic growth will shift *SRAS* and *LRAS*. Look at Figure 5-8 on the facing page. Initially, the two curves are $SRAS_1$ and $LRAS_1$. Now consider a situation in which large amounts of irreplaceable resources are lost *permanently* in a major oil spill and fire. This shifts $LRAS_1$ to $LRAS_2$ at $14.5 trillion of real GDP, measured in base-year dollars. $SRAS_1$ also shifts leftward horizontally to $SRAS_2$.

Shifts in *SRAS* Only

Some events, particularly those that are short-lived, will temporarily shift *SRAS* but not *LRAS*. One of the most obvious is a change in production input prices, particularly those caused by external events that are not expected to last forever. Consider a major hurricane that temporarily shuts down a significant portion of U.S. oil production. Oil is an important input in many production activities. The resulting drop in oil production would cause at least a temporary increase in the price of this input. In this case, the long-run aggregate supply curve would remain at $LRAS_1$ in Figure 5-8.

The short-run aggregate supply curve *alone* would shift from $SRAS_1$ to $SRAS_2$, reflecting the increase in input prices—the higher price of oil. This is because the rise in the costs of production at each level of real GDP per year would require a higher price level to cover those increased costs.

FIGURE 5-8

Shifts in Long-Run and Short-Run Aggregate Supply

Initially, the two aggregate supply curves are $SRAS_1$ and $LRAS_1$. An event that permanently reduces reserves of a key productive resource such as oil shifts $LRAS_1$ to $LRAS_2$ at $14.5 trillion of real GDP, in base-year dollars, and also shifts $SRAS_1$ horizontally leftward to $SRAS_2$. If, instead, a temporary increase in an input price occurred, $LRAS_1$ would remain unchanged, and only the short-run aggregate supply curve would shift, from $SRAS_1$ to $SRAS_2$.

How can a single insect species generate an aggregate supply shock?

INTERNATIONAL EXAMPLE

Australia's Short-Run Aggregate Supply Hit by a Locust Plague

Recently, Australia has experienced its worst plague of locusts in half of a century. The 3-inch-long insects, ferocious eaters that forage in massive swarms, have ravaged large portions of the nation's crops. Included among the damaged crops are cereal grains, such as rice, wheat, and barley, which are important inputs for many food products. Also heavily damaged by the insects are feed crops that are key inputs in livestock production. The resulting decreases in market supplies of these fundamental inputs have pushed up a wide array of input prices. The result has been a decrease in short-run aggregate supply. Thus, the plague of locusts has shifted Australia's short-run aggregate supply curve leftward.

FOR CRITICAL THINKING

Why would a plague of locusts, which rarely lasts more than two or three crop seasons, fail to generate a leftward shift of the long-run aggregate supply curve?

We summarize the possible determinants of aggregate supply in Table 5-2 on the next page. These determinants will cause a shift in the short-run or the long-run aggregate supply curve or both, depending on whether they are temporary or permanent.

QUICK QUIZ   See page 124 for the answers. Review concepts from this section in MyEconLab.

If we assume that the economy is operating on a horizontal short-run aggregate supply curve, the equilibrium level of real GDP per year is completely _____ determined.

The horizontal short-run aggregate supply curve has been called the **Keynesian short-run aggregate supply curve** because Keynes believed that many prices, especially wages, would not be _____ even when aggregate demand decreased.

In modern Keynesian theory, the **short-run aggregate supply curve, SRAS,** shows the relationship between the price level and real GDP without full adjustment or full information. It is upward sloping because it allows for only _____ price adjustment in the short run.

Real GDP can be expanded in the short run because firms can use existing workers and capital equipment more _____. Also, in the short run, when input prices are fixed, a higher price level means _____ profits, which induce firms to hire more workers.

Any change in factors influencing long-run output, such as labor, capital, or technology, will shift both *SRAS* and *LRAS*. A temporary change in input prices, however, will shift only _____.

Table 5-2		
Determinants of Aggregate Supply The determinants listed here can affect short-run or long-run aggregate supply (or both), depending on whether they are temporary or permanent.	**Changes That Cause an Increase in Aggregate Supply**	**Changes That Cause a Decrease in Aggregate Supply**
	Discoveries of new raw materials	Depletion of raw materials
	Increased competition	Decreased competition
	A reduction in international trade barriers	An increase in international trade barriers
	Fewer regulatory impediments to business	More regulatory impediments to business
	An increase in the supply of labor	A decrease in labor supplied
	Increased training and education	Decreased training and education
	A decrease in marginal tax rates	An increase in marginal tax rates
	A reduction in input prices	An increase in input prices

Consequences of Changes in Aggregate Demand

We now have a basic model to apply when evaluating short-run adjustments of the equilibrium price level and equilibrium real GDP when there are shocks to the economy. Whenever there is a shift in the aggregate demand or short-run aggregate supply curves, the short-run equilibrium price level or real GDP level (or both) may change. These shifts are called **aggregate demand shocks** on the demand side and **aggregate supply shocks** on the supply side.

Aggregate demand shock
Any event that causes the aggregate demand curve to shift inward or outward.

Aggregate supply shock
Any event that causes the aggregate supply curve to shift inward or outward.

When Aggregate Demand Falls While Aggregate Supply Is Stable

Now we can show what happens in the short run when aggregate supply remains stable but aggregate demand falls. The short-run outcome will be a rise in the unemployment rate. In Figure 5-9 below, you see that with AD_1, both long-run and short-run

FIGURE 5-9	

The Short-Run Effects of Stable Aggregate Supply and a Decrease in Aggregate Demand: The Recessionary Gap

If the economy is at equilibrium at E_1, with price level 120 and real GDP per year of $15 trillion, a shift inward of the aggregate demand curve to AD_2 will lead to a new short-run equilibrium at E_2. The equilibrium price level will fall to 115, and the short-run equilibrium level of real GDP per year will fall to $14.8 trillion. There will be a recessionary gap of $200 billion.

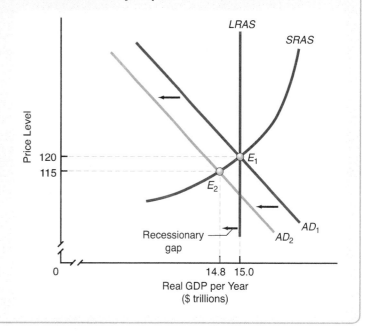

FIGURE 5-10

The Effects of Stable Aggregate Supply with an Increase in Aggregate Demand: The Inflationary Gap

The economy is at equilibrium at E_1. An increase in aggregate demand to AD_2 leads to a new short-run equilibrium at E_2, with the price level rising from 120 to 125 and equilibrium real GDP per year rising from \$15 trillion to \$15.2 trillion. The difference, \$200 billion, is called the inflationary gap.

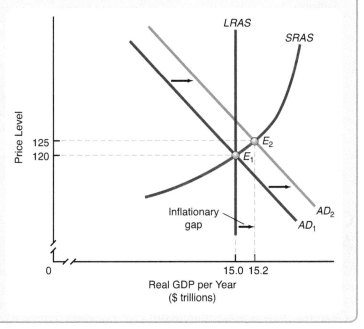

equilibrium are at \$15 trillion (in base-year dollars) of real GDP per year (because *SRAS* and *LRAS* also intersect AD_1 at that level of real GDP). The long-run equilibrium price level is 120. A reduction in aggregate demand shifts the aggregate demand curve to AD_2. The new intersection with *SRAS* is at \$14.8 trillion per year, which is less than the long-run equilibrium level of real GDP. The difference between \$15 trillion and \$14.8 trillion is called a **recessionary gap,** defined as the difference between the short-run equilibrium level of real GDP and real GDP if the economy were operating at full employment on its *LRAS*.

In effect, at E_2, the economy is in short-run equilibrium at less than full employment. With too many unemployed inputs, input prices will begin to fall. Eventually, *SRAS* will have to shift vertically downward.

Recessionary gap
The gap that exists whenever equilibrium real GDP per year is less than full-employment real GDP as shown by the position of the long-run aggregate supply curve.

Short-Run Effects When Aggregate Demand Increases

We can reverse the situation and have aggregate demand increase to AD_2, as is shown in Figure 5-10 above. The initial equilibrium conditions are exactly the same as in Figure 5-9 on the facing page. The move to AD_2 increases the short-run equilibrium from E_1 to E_2 such that the economy is operating at \$15.2 trillion of real GDP per year, which exceeds *LRAS*. This is a condition of an overheated economy, typically called an **inflationary gap.**

At E_2 in Figure 5-10, the economy is at a short-run equilibrium that is beyond full employment. In the short run, more can be squeezed out of the economy than occurs in the long-run, full-information, full-adjustment situation. Firms will be operating beyond long-run capacity. Inputs will be working too hard. Input prices will begin to rise. That will eventually cause *SRAS* to shift vertically upward.

Inflationary gap
The gap that exists whenever equilibrium real GDP per year is greater than full-employment real GDP as shown by the position of the long-run aggregate supply curve.

YOU ARE THERE

To contemplate cost-push and demand-pull inflation from the perspective of a business manager, take a look at **Worried about Shocks to Aggregate Supply—and Demand** on page 119.

Explaining Short-Run Variations in Inflation

In Chapter 4, we noted that in a growing economy, the explanation for persistent inflation is that aggregate demand increases over time at a faster pace than the full-employment level of real GDP. Short-run variations in inflation, however, can arise as a result of both demand *and* supply factors.

Demand-Pull versus Cost-Push Inflation

Figure 5-10 on the previous page presents a demand-side theory explaining a short-run jump in prices, sometimes called *demand-pull inflation*. Whenever the general level of prices rises in the short run because of increases in aggregate demand, we say that the economy is experiencing **demand-pull inflation**—inflation caused by increases in aggregate demand.

An alternative explanation for increases in the price level comes from the supply side. Look at Figure 5-11 below. The initial equilibrium conditions are the same as in Figure 5-10. Now, however, there is a leftward shift in the short-run aggregate supply curve, from $SRAS_1$ to $SRAS_2$. Equilibrium shifts from E_1 to E_2. The price level increases from 120 to 125, while the equilibrium level of real GDP per year decreases from $15 trillion to $14.8 trillion. Persistent decreases in aggregate supply causes what is called **cost-push inflation.**

As the example of cost-push inflation shows, if the economy is initially in equilibrium on its *LRAS*, a decrease in *SRAS* will lead to a rise in the price level. Thus, any abrupt change in one of the factors that determine aggregate supply will alter the equilibrium level of real GDP per year and the equilibrium price level. If the economy is for some reason operating to the left of its *LRAS*, an increase in *SRAS* will lead to a simultaneous *increase* in the equilibrium level of real GDP per year and a *decrease* in the price level. You should be able to show this in a graph similar to Figure 5-11.

Demand-pull inflation
Inflation caused by increases in aggregate demand not matched by increases in aggregate supply.

Cost-push inflation
Inflation caused by decreases in short-run aggregate supply.

Aggregate Demand and Supply in an Open Economy

In many of the international examples in the early chapters of this book, we had to translate foreign currencies into dollars when the open economy was discussed. We used the exchange rate, or the dollar price of other currencies. In Chapter 10, you also learned that the open economy effect was one of the reasons why the aggregate demand curve slopes downward. When the domestic price level rises, U.S. residents want to buy cheaper-priced foreign goods. The opposite occurs when the U.S. domestic price level falls. Currently, the foreign sector of the U.S. economy constitutes more than 15 percent of all economic activities.

FIGURE 5-11

Cost-Push Inflation

If aggregate demand remains stable but $SRAS_1$ shifts to $SRAS_2$, equilibrium changes from E_1 to E_2. The price level rises from 120 to 125. If there are continual decreases in aggregate supply of this nature, the situation is called cost-push inflation.

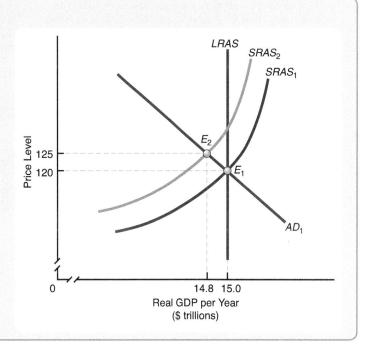

Go to www.econtoday.com/chap05 for Federal Reserve Bank of New York data showing how the dollar's value is changing relative to other currencies.

HOW A STRONGER DOLLAR AFFECTS AGGREGATE SUPPLY Assume that the dollar becomes stronger in international foreign exchange markets. If last year the dollar could buy 50 *rupees*, the Indian currency, but this year it buys 60 rupees, the dollar has become stronger. To the extent that U.S. companies import physical inputs and labor services from India, a stronger dollar can lead to lower input prices.

For instance, if a U.S. firm purchases 5 million rupees' worth of labor services per year from an Indian company, then before the strengthening of the dollar, that company paid $100,000 per year for those labor services. After the dollar's strengthening, however, the U.S. firm's Indian-labor-input expense drops to $83,333. This U.S. firm's cost reduction generated by the dollar's strengthening, as well as similar reductions in foreign-input expenses at other U.S. firms, will induce those firms to produce more final goods and services per year at any given price level.

Thus, a general strengthening of the dollar against the rupee and other world currencies will lead the short-run aggregate supply curve to shift outward to the right, as shown in panel (a) of Figure 5-12 below. In that simplified model, equilibrium real GDP would rise, and the price level would decline. Employment would also tend to increase.

HOW A STRONGER DOLLAR AFFECTS AGGREGATE DEMAND A stronger dollar has another effect that we must consider. Foreign residents will find that U.S.-made goods are now more expensive, expressed in their own currency. Suppose that as a result of the dollar's strengthening, the dollar, which previously could buy 0.80 euro, can now buy 0.85 euro. Before the dollar strengthened, a U.S.-produced $10 downloadable music album cost a French resident 8.00 euros at the exchange rate of 0.80 euro per $1. After the dollar strengthens and the exchange rate changes to 0.85 euro per $1, that same $10 digital album will cost 8.50 euros. Conversely, U.S. residents will find that the stronger dollar makes imported goods less expensive. The result for U.S. residents is fewer exports and more imports, or lower net exports (exports minus imports). If net exports fall,

FIGURE 5-12

The Two Effects of a Stronger Dollar

When the dollar increases in value in the international currency market, there are two effects. The first is lower prices for imported inputs, causing a shift in the short-run aggregate supply schedule outward and to the right, from $SRAS_1$ to $SRAS_2$ in panel (a). Equilibrium tends to move from E_1 to E_2 at a lower price level and a higher equilibrium real GDP per year. Second, a stronger dollar can also affect the aggregate demand curve

because it will lead to lower net exports and cause AD_1 to shift inward to AD_2 in panel (b). Due to this effect, equilibrium will move from E_1 to E_2 at a lower price level and a lower equilibrium real GDP per year. On balance, the combined effects of the decrease in aggregate demand and increase in aggregate supply will be to push down the price level, but real GDP may rise or fall.

Panel (a)

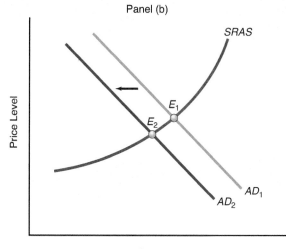

Panel (b)

employment in export industries will fall: This is represented in panel (b) of Figure 5-12 on the previous page. After the dollar becomes stronger, the aggregate demand curve shifts inward from AD_1 to AD_2. The result is a tendency for equilibrium real GDP and the price level to fall and for unemployment to increase.

THE NET EFFECTS ON INFLATION AND REAL GDP We have learned, then, that a stronger dollar *simultaneously* leads to an increase in *SRAS* and a decrease in *AD*. In such situations, the equilibrium price level definitely falls. A stronger dollar contributes to deflation.

The effect of a stronger dollar on real GDP depends on which curve—*AD* or *SRAS*—shifts more. If the aggregate demand curve shifts more than the short-run aggregate supply curve, equilibrium real GDP will decline. Conversely, if the aggregate supply curve shifts more than the aggregate demand curve, equilibrium real GDP will rise.

You should be able to redo this entire analysis for a weaker dollar.

WHAT IF... a nation's government tries to head off a recession by pushing down the exchange value of the country's currency?

On the one hand, reducing the exchange value of the currency would make the nation's export goods less expensive in foreign currencies, thereby boosting foreign spending on home exports and, hence, domestic aggregate demand. On the other hand, the fall in the foreign value of the nation's currency would cause home-currency prices of inputs that home firms import from abroad to increase. This would induce the country's firms to cut back on production of final goods and services at any given price level. The result would be a reduction in aggregate supply, which would reinforce any economic downturn already under way. On net, therefore, pushing down the exchange value of the home currency might not necessarily help to head off an economic downturn.

QUICK QUIZ See page 124 for the answers. Review concepts from this section in MyEconLab.

_____-run equilibrium occurs at the intersection of the aggregate demand curve, *AD*, and the short-run aggregate supply curve, *SRAS*. _____-run equilibrium occurs at the intersection of *AD* and the long-run aggregate supply curve, *LRAS*. Any unanticipated shifts in aggregate demand or supply are called aggregate demand _____ or aggregate supply _____.

When aggregate demand decreases while aggregate supply is stable, a _____ gap can occur, defined as the difference between how much the economy could be producing if it were operating on its *LRAS* and the equilibrium level of real GDP. An increase in aggregate demand leads to an _____ gap.

With stable aggregate supply, an abrupt outward shift in *AD* may lead to what is called _____-_____ inflation. With stable aggregate demand, an abrupt shift inward in *SRAS* may lead to what is called _____-_____ inflation.

A _____ dollar will reduce the cost of imported inputs, thereby causing *SRAS* to shift outward to the right. At the same time, a _____ dollar will also lead to lower net exports, causing the aggregate demand curve to shift inward. The equilibrium price level definitely falls, but the net effect on equilibrium real GDP depends on which shift is larger.

YOU ARE THERE
Worried about Shocks to Aggregate Supply—and Demand

Vincent Hartnett, Jr., president of Penske Logistics, is confused. Federal Reserve officials have been expressing concerns about a perceived threat of "deflation." In Hartnett's view, cost-push sources of *inflationary* pressures abound. Hartnett has watched his firm's health care costs jump, including a 9 percent increase within the past year. Fuel costs continue to escalate, and market wages required to retain workers have risen. In response to these cost increases, his firm and others throughout the nation are producing fewer goods and services at any given price level. The implication, at least as far as Hartnett can discern, is that inflation is likely to increase, and he continues to see a steady upward creep in the annual U.S. inflation rate in monthly government reports.

The fact that Fed officials keep fretting about a potential decline in the price level has made Hartnett concerned that the Fed may unexpectedly increase the quantity of money in circulation to try to raise aggregate demand. Such an action, Hartnett worries, would essentially produce an aggregate demand shock that would lead to a higher rate of inflation.

Critical Thinking Questions

1. How would "cost-push pressures" that Hartnett perceives raise the price level?

2. Why would an unexpected increase in the quantity of money generate inflation?

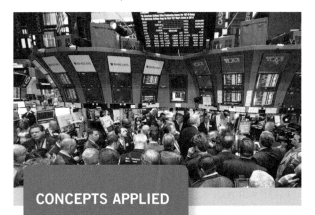

ISSUES & APPLICATIONS

Gauging Financial Sources of Aggregate Demand Shocks

CONCEPTS APPLIED

▶ Aggregate Demand Shock

▶ Short-Run Aggregate Supply Curve

▶ Recessionary Gap

During a period spanning about 2 weeks in the summer of 2011, the average value of shares of corporate ownership traded in the U.S. stock market dropped by more than 15 percent. About $2 trillion of household wealth effectively ceased to exist. In response, total planned expenditures began to decline at any given price level. Financial-market shocks generated a negative aggregate demand shock.

Tracking Financial Shocks: The VIX Index

To gauge the size of financial shocks, many observers use a measure of financial-market volatility called the *VIX index*. This measure, displayed in Figure 5-13 below for the period since 1990, is intended to indicate variability that people interacting in financial markets anticipate in the near future.

As you can see, significant jumps in the VIX index can occur because of unusual events, such as the Persian Gulf War, the September 11, 2001 ("9/11") terrorist attacks, and the Iraq War. Usually, however, large changes in the VIX index result from shocks that occur solely within financial markets.

MyEconLab Real-time data

FIGURE 5-13

The VIX Index of Financial-Market Volatility since 1990

The VIX index measure of anticipated financial volatility has exhibited substantial jumps during wars and in response to major events affecting U.S. financial markets.

Source: U.S. Department of Commerce.

Examples include a default by a major financial firm called Long-Term Capital Management in 1998, substantial accounting scandals in 2002, and the massive credit crisis and associated financial panic in 2008. In addition, jumps in the VIX index in 2010 and 2011 were caused by worries about the inability of the Greek government to honor its debts and then broader concerns about debts of other European governments as well as the U.S. government. During this latter situation in the summer of 2011, U.S. residents briefly lost almost $2 trillion of financial wealth, and real interest rates began to rise, resulting in a temporary decrease in aggregate demand.

From Financial Shocks to Aggregate Demand Shocks

Also shown in Figure 5-13 on the previous page are shaded intervals of U.S. recessions. The most recent recession is clearly related to a substantial increase in the VIX index. Indeed, the VIX index began rising prior to the onset of the 2008–2009 recession and reached its highest peak in the midst of the business downturn.

In the case of this recent recession, financial shocks were so great that a significant, prolonged reduction in aggregate demand occurred. This decrease in aggregate demand generated a upward movement along the short-run aggregate supply curve, a recessionary gap, and a significant decline in U.S. real GDP.

For Critical Thinking

1. Why do you suppose that the U.S. price level decreased over a 12-month interval during the 2008–2009 recession?
2. On the basis of Figure 5-13, are jumps in the VIX index always associated with reductions in aggregate demand that induce recessions?

Web Resources

1. Learn about the VIX index at www.econtoday.com/chap05.
2. For a discussion of the rise in the VIX index as stock share prices declined and real interest rates rose in the summer of 2011, go to www.econtoday.com/chap05.

MyEconLab

For more questions on this chapter's Issues & Applications, go to MyEconLab. In the Study Plan for this chapter, select Section N: News.

MyEconLab

Here is what you should know after reading this chapter. MyEconLab will help you identify what you know, and where to go when you need to practice.

WHAT YOU SHOULD KNOW		WHERE TO GO TO PRACTICE
Central Assumptions of the Classical Model The classical model makes four key assumptions: (1) pure competition prevails, so no individual buyer or seller of a good or service or of a factor of production can affect its price, (2) wages and prices are completely flexible, (3) people are motivated by self-interest, and (4) buyers and sellers do not experience money illusion, meaning that they respond only to changes in relative prices.	Say's law, 105 money illusion, 106	• MyEconLab Study Plan 5.1
Short-Run Determination of Equilibrium Real GDP and the Price Level in the Classical Model Under the four assumptions of the classical model, the short-run aggregate supply curve is vertical at full-employment real GDP and thus corresponds to the long-run aggregate supply curve. Variations in the position of the aggregate demand curve along the classical aggregate supply curve generate changes in the equilibrium price level.	Key Figures Figure 5-2, 107 Figure 5-3, 108 Figure 5-4, 109 Figure 5-5, 110	• MyEconLab Study Plan 5.1 • Animated Figures 5-2, 5-3, 5-4, 5-5

MyEconLab *continued*

Circumstances under Which the Short-Run Aggregate Supply Curve May Be Horizontal or Upward Sloping If product prices and wages and other input prices are "sticky," the short-run aggregate supply schedule can be horizontal over much of its range. This is the Keynesian short-run aggregate supply curve. More generally, however, to the extent that there is incomplete adjustment of prices in the short run, the short-run aggregate supply curve slopes upward.

Keynesian short-run aggregate supply curve, 111
short-run aggregate supply curve, 112

Key Figures
Figure 5-6, 111
Figure 5-7, 112

- MyEconLab Study Plans 5.2, 5.3
- Animated Figures 5-6, 5-7

Factors That Induce Shifts in the Short-Run and Long-Run Aggregate Supply Curves Both the long-run aggregate supply curve and the short-run aggregate supply curve shift in response to changes in the availability of labor or capital or to changes in technology and productivity. A widespread temporary change in the prices of factors of production, however, can cause a shift in the short-run aggregate supply curve without affecting the long-run aggregate supply curve.

Key Table
Table 5-2, 115

Key Figure
Figure 5-8, 114

- MyEconLab Study Plan 5.4
- Animated Figure 5-8

Effects of Aggregate Demand and Supply Shocks on Equilibrium Real GDP in the Short Run An aggregate demand shock that causes the aggregate demand curve to shift leftward pushes equilibrium real GDP below the level of full-employment real GDP in the short run, so there is a recessionary gap. An aggregate demand shock that induces a rightward shift in the aggregate demand curve results in an inflationary gap, in which short-run equilibrium real GDP exceeds full-employment real GDP.

aggregate demand shock, 115
aggregate supply shock, 115
recessionary gap, 116
inflationary gap, 116

Key Figures
Figure 5-9, 115
Figure 5-10, 116

- MyEconLab Study Plan 5.5
- Animated Figures 5-9, 5-10

Causes of Short-Run Variations in the Inflation Rate Demand-pull inflation occurs when the aggregate demand curve shifts rightward along an upward-sloping short-run aggregate supply curve. Cost-push inflation occurs when the short-run aggregate supply curve shifts leftward along the aggregate demand curve. A strengthening of the dollar shifts the short-run aggregate supply curve rightward and the aggregate demand curve leftward, which causes inflation but has uncertain effects on real GDP.

demand-pull inflation, 117
cost-push inflation, 117

Key Figure
Figure 5-11, 117

- MyEconLab Study Plan 5.6
- Animated Figure 5-11

Log in to MyEconLab, take a chapter test, and get a personalized Study Plan that tells you which concepts you understand and which ones you need to review. From there, MyEconLab will give you further practice, tutorials, animations, videos, and guided solutions. For more information, visit www.myeconlab.com

PROBLEMS

All problems are assignable in MyEconLab. Answers to odd-numbered problems appear at the back of the book.

5-1. Consider a country whose economic structure matches the assumptions of the classical model. After reading a recent best-seller documenting a growing population of low-income elderly people who were ill prepared for retirement, most residents of this country decide to increase their saving at any given interest rate. Explain whether or how this could affect the following (see page 107):

   a. The current equilibrium interest rate

   b. Current equilibrium real GDP

   c. Current equilibrium employment

   d. Current equilibrium investment

   e. Future equilibrium real GDP (see Chapter 3)

5-2. Consider a country with an economic structure consistent with the assumptions of the classical model. Suppose that businesses in this nation suddenly anticipate higher future profitability from investments they undertake today. Explain whether or how this could affect the following (see page 107):

   a. The current equilibrium interest rate

   b. Current equilibrium real GDP

   c. Current equilibrium employment

   d. Current equilibrium saving

   e. Future equilibrium real GDP (see Chapter 3)

5-3. "There is *absolutely no distinction* between the classical model and the model of long-run equilibrium discussed in Chapter 4." Is this statement true or false? Support your answer. (See page 109.)

5-4. Suppose that the Keynesian short-run aggregate supply curve is applicable for a nation's economy. Use appropriate diagrams to assist in answering the following questions (see page 111):

   a. What are two factors that can cause the nation's real GDP to increase in the short run?

   b. What are two factors that can cause the nation's real GDP to increase in the long run?

5-5. What determines how much real GDP responds to changes in the price level along the short-run aggregate supply curve? (See page 111.)

5-6. Suppose that there is a temporary, but significant, increase in oil prices in an economy with an upward-sloping *SRAS* curve. If policymakers wish to prevent the equilibrium price level from changing in response to the oil price increase, should they increase or decrease the quantity of money in circulation? Why? (See page 117.)

5-7. As in Problem 5-6, suppose that there is a temporary, but significant, increase in oil prices in an economy with an upward-sloping *SRAS* curve. In this case, however, suppose that policymakers wish to prevent equilibrium real GDP from changing in response to the oil price increase. Should they increase or decrease the quantity of money in circulation? Why? (See page 115.)

5-8. Based on your answers to Problems 5-6 and 5-7, can policymakers stabilize *both* the price level *and* real GDP simultaneously in response to a short-lived but sudden rise in oil prices? Explain briefly. (See pages 115–117.)

5-9. Between early 2005 and late 2007, total planned expenditures by U.S. households substantially increased in response to an increase in the quantity of money in circulation. Explain, from a short-run Keynesian perspective, the predicted effects of this event on the equilibrium U.S. price level and equilibrium U.S. real GDP. Be sure to discuss the spending gap that the Keynesian model indicates would result in the short run. (See page 116.)

5-10. Between early 2008 and the beginning of 2009, a gradual stock-market downturn and plummeting home prices generated a substantial reduction in U.S. household wealth that induced most U.S. residents to reduce their planned real spending at any given price level. Explain, from a short-run Keynesian perspective, the predicted effects of this event on the equilibrium U.S. price level and equilibrium U.S. real GDP. Be sure to discuss the spending gap that the Keynesian model indicates would result in the short run. (See page 115.)

5-11. For each question that follows, suppose that the economy *begins* at point *A*. Identify which of the other points on the diagram—point *B*, *C*, *D*, or *E*—could represent a *new* short-run equilibrium after the described events take place and move the economy away from point *A*. Briefly explain your answers. (See pages 115–117.)

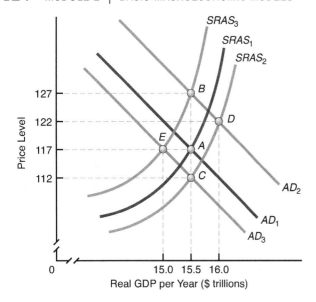

a. Most workers in this nation's economy are union members, and unions have successfully negotiated large wage boosts. At the same time, economic conditions suddenly worsen abroad, reducing real GDP and disposable income in other nations of the world.

b. A major hurricane has caused short-term halts in production at many firms and created major bottlenecks in the distribution of goods and services that had been produced prior to the storm. At the same time, the nation's central bank has significantly pushed up the rate of growth of the nation's money supply.

c. A strengthening of the value of this nation's currency in terms of other countries' currencies affects both the *SRAS* curve and the *AD* curve.

5-12. Consider an open economy in which the aggregate supply curve slopes upward in the short run. Firms in this nation do not import raw materials or any other productive inputs from abroad, but foreign residents purchase many of the nation's goods and services. What is the most likely short-run effect on this nation's economy if there is a significant downturn in economic activity in other nations around the world? (See page 118.)

ECONOMICS ON THE NET

Money, the Price Level, and Real GDP The classical and Keynesian theories have differing predictions about how changes in the money supply should affect the price level and real GDP. Here you get to look at data on growth in the money supply, the price level, and real GDP.

Title: Federal Reserve Bank of St. Louis Monetary Trends

Navigation: Use the link at **www.econtoday.com/chap05** to visit the Federal Reserve Bank of St. Louis. Click on *Gross Domestic Product and M2*.

Application Read the article; then answer these questions.

1. Classical theory indicates that, *ceteris paribus*, changes in the price level should be closely related to changes in aggregate demand induced by variations in the quantity of money. Click on *Gross Domestic Product and M2*, and take a look at the charts labeled "Gross Domestic Product Price Index" and "M2." (M2 is a measure of the quantity of money in circulation.) Are annual percentage changes in these variables closely related?

2. Keynesian theory predicts that, *ceteris paribus*, changes in GDP and the quantity of money should be directly related. Take a look at the charts labeled "Real Gross Domestic Product" and "M2." Are annual percentage changes in these variables closely related?

For Group Study and Analysis Both classical and Keynesian theories of relationships among real GDP, the price level, and the quantity of money hinge on specific assumptions. Have class groups search through the FRED database (accessible at **www.econtoday.com/chap05**) to evaluate factors that provide support for either theory's predictions. Which approach appears to receive greater support from recent data? Does this necessarily imply that this is the "true theory"? Why or why not?

ANSWERS TO QUICK QUIZZES

p. 110: (i) supply . . . demand; (ii) pure competition . . . wages . . . prices . . . self-interest . . . money illusion; (iii) saving . . . investment; (iv) wage rate; (v) vertical . . . price level

p. 114: (i) demand; (ii) reduced; (iii) partial; (iv) intensively . . . higher; (v) *SRAS*

p. 119: (i) Short . . . Long . . . shocks . . . shocks; (ii) recessionary . . . inflationary; (iii) demand-pull . . . cost-push; (iv) stronger . . . stronger

ADDITIONAL READING:

A Dynamic Aggregate Demand and Aggregate Supply Model

Taken from *Macroeconomics*, Fourth Edition, by R. Glenn Hubbard and Anthony Patrick O'Brien

A Dynamic Aggregate Demand and Aggregate Supply Model

LEARNING OBJECTIVE

Use the dynamic aggregate demand and aggregate supply model to analyze macroeconomic conditions.

The basic aggregate demand and aggregate supply model used so far in this chapter provides important insights into how short-run macroeconomic equilibrium is determined. Unfortunately, the model also provides some misleading results. For instance, it incorrectly predicts that a recession caused by the aggregate demand curve shifting to the left will cause the price level to fall, which has not happened for an entire year since the 1930s. The difficulty with the basic model arises from the following two assumptions we made: (1) The economy does not experience continuing inflation, and (2) the economy does not experience long-run growth. We can develop a more useful aggregate demand and aggregate supply model by dropping these assumptions. The result will be a model that takes into account that the economy is not static, with an unchanging level of potential real GDP and no continuing inflation, but dynamic, with potential real GDP that grows over time and inflation that continues every year. We can create a *dynamic aggregate demand and aggregate supply model* by making changes to the basic model that incorporate the following important macroeconomic facts:

- Potential real GDP increases continually, shifting the long-run aggregate supply curve to the right.

- During most years, the aggregate demand curve shifts to the right.

- Except during periods when workers and firms expect high rates of inflation, the short-run aggregate supply curve shifts to the right.

Figure 5A-1 illustrates how incorporating these macroeconomic facts changes the basic aggregate demand and aggregate supply model. We start with $SRAS_1$ and AD_1 intersecting at point A, at a price level of 100 and real GDP of $14.0 trillion. Because this intersection occurs at a point on $LRAS_1$, we know the economy is in long-run equilibrium. The long-run aggregate supply curve shifts to the right, from $LRAS_1$ to $LRAS_2$. This shift occurs because during the year, potential real GDP increases as the U.S. labor force and the U.S. capital stock increase and technological progress occurs. The short-run aggregate supply curve shifts from $SRAS_1$ to $SRAS_2$. This shift occurs because the same variables that cause the long-run aggregate supply curve to shift to the right will also increase the quantity of goods and services that firms are willing to supply in the short run. Finally, the aggregate demand curve shifts to the right, from AD_1 to AD_2. The aggregate demand curve shifts for several reasons: As the population grows and incomes rise, consumption will increase over time. As the economy grows, firms will expand capacity, and new firms will be formed, increasing investment. An expanding population and an expanding economy require increased government services, such as more police officers and teachers, so government purchases will increase.

The new equilibrium in Figure 5A-1 occurs at point B, where AD_2 intersects $SRAS_2$ on $LRAS_2$. In the new equilibrium, the price level remains at 100, while real GDP increases to $14.3 trillion. Notice that there has been no inflation because the price level is unchanged, at 100. There has been no inflation because aggregate demand and aggregate supply shifted to the right by exactly as much as long-run aggregate supply. We would not expect this to be the typical situation for two reasons. First, the *SRAS* curve is also affected by workers' and firms' expectations of future changes in the price level and by supply shocks. These variables can partially or completely offset the normal tendency of the *SRAS* curve to shift to the right over the course of a year. Second, we know that consumers, firms, and the government may cut back on expenditures. This reduced spending will result in the aggregate demand curve shifting to the right less than it normally would or, possibly, shifting to the left. In fact, as we will see shortly, *changes in the price level and in real GDP in the short run are determined by shifts in the SRAS and AD curves.*

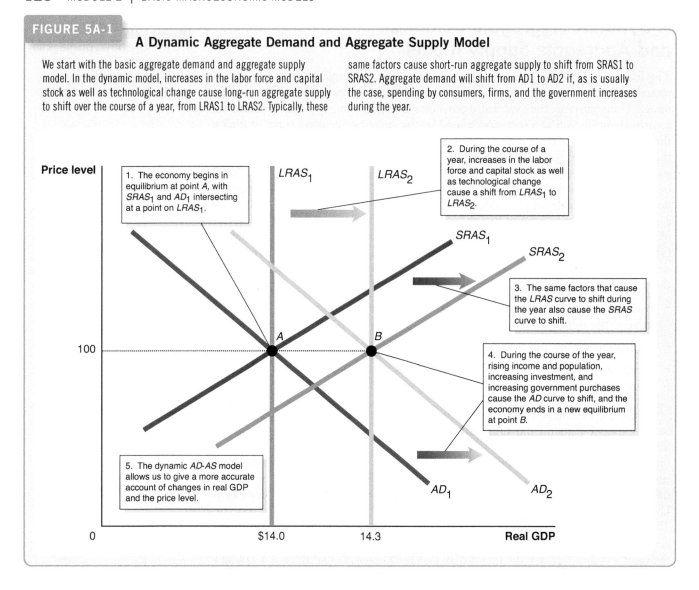

FIGURE 5A-1

A Dynamic Aggregate Demand and Aggregate Supply Model

We start with the basic aggregate demand and aggregate supply model. In the dynamic model, increases in the labor force and capital stock as well as technological change cause long-run aggregate supply to shift over the course of a year, from LRAS1 to LRAS2. Typically, these same factors cause short-run aggregate supply to shift from SRAS1 to SRAS2. Aggregate demand will shift from AD1 to AD2 if, as is usually the case, spending by consumers, firms, and the government increases during the year.

1. The economy begins in equilibrium at point *A*, with *SRAS₁* and *AD₁* intersecting at a point on *LRAS₁*.

2. During the course of a year, increases in the labor force and capital stock as well as technological change cause a shift from *LRAS₁* to *LRAS₂*.

3. The same factors that cause the *LRAS* curve to shift during the year also cause the *SRAS* curve to shift.

4. During the course of the year, rising income and population, increasing investment, and increasing government purchases cause the *AD* curve to shift, and the economy ends in a new equilibrium at point *B*.

5. The dynamic *AD-AS* model allows us to give a more accurate account of changes in real GDP and the price level.

What Is the Usual Cause of Inflation?

The dynamic aggregate demand and aggregate supply model provides a more accurate explanation than the basic model of the source of most inflation. If total spending in the economy grows faster than total production, prices rise. Figure 5A-2 illustrates this point by showing that if the *AD* curve shifts to the right by more than the *LRAS* curve, inflation results because equilibrium occurs at a higher price level, point B. In the new equilibrium, the *SRAS* curve has shifted to the right by less than the *LRAS* curve because the anticipated increase in prices offsets some of the technological change and increases in the labor force and capital stock that occur during the year. Although inflation generally results from total spending growing faster than total production, a shift to the left of the short-run aggregate supply curve can also cause an increase in the price level, as we saw earlier, in the discussion of supply shocks.

As we saw in Figure 5A-1, if aggregate demand increases by the same amount as short-run and long-run aggregate supply, the price level will not change. In this case, the economy experiences economic growth without inflation.

FIGURE 5A-2

Using Dynamic Aggregate Demand and Aggregate Supply to Understand Inflation

The most common cause of inflation is total spending increasing faster than total production.
1. The economy begins at point A, with real GDP of $14.0 trillion and a price level of 100. An increase in full-employment real GDP from $14.0 trillion to $14.3 trillion causes long-run aggregate supply to shift from LRAS1 to LRAS2. Aggregate demand shifts from AD1 to AD2.
2. Because AD shifts to the right by more than the LRAS curve, the price level in the new equilibrium rises from 100 to 104.

The Recession of 2007–2009

We can use the dynamic aggregate demand and aggregate supply model to analyze the recession of 2007–2009. The recession began in December 2007, with the end of the economic expansion that had begun in November 2001. Several factors combined to bring on the recession:

- *The end of the housing bubble.* Spending on residential construction increased rapidly from 2002 to 2005, before declining more than 60 percent between the end of 2005 and the beginning of 2010. The increase in spending on housing was partly the result of actions the Federal Reserve had taken to lower interest rates during and after the recession of 2001. As interest rates on mortgage loans declined, more consumers began to buy new homes. But by 2005, it was clear that a speculative bubble was partly responsible for the rapidly rising prices of both newly built and existing homes. A bubble occurs when people become less concerned with the underlying value of an asset— either a physical asset, such as a house, or a financial asset, such as a stock— and focus instead on expectations of the price of the asset increasing. In some areas of the country, such as California, Arizona, and Florida, many homes were purchased by investors who intended to resell them for higher prices than they paid for them and did not intend to live in them. Some popular television programs explored ways that people could "flip" houses by buying and quickly reselling them. Speculative bubbles eventually end, and the housing bubble started to deflate in 2006. Both new home sales and housing prices began to decline. The growth of aggregate demand slowed as spending on residential construction—a component of investment spending—fell.

- *The financial crisis.* Problems in the housing market were bad news for workers and firms involved with residential construction. In addition, falling housing prices led to an increased number of borrowers defaulting on their mortgage loans. These defaults caused banks and some other financial institutions to suffer heavy losses. Beginning in the spring of 2008, the U.S. Department of the Treasury and the Federal Reserve intervened to save several large financial institutions from bankruptcy. We can note that the financial crisis led to a "credit crunch" that made it difficult for many households and firms to obtain the loans they needed to finance their spending. This drying up of credit contributed to declines in consumption spending and investment spending.

- *The rapid increase in oil prices during 2008.* Oil prices, which had been as low as $34 per barrel in 2004, had risen to $140 per barrel by mid-2008. The increase in the price of oil appeared to be caused by increased demand in rapidly growing economies, particularly India and China, and by the difficulty in developing new supplies of oil in the short run. With the deepening of the recession, worldwide demand for oil declined, and oil prices fell to about $40 per barrel in early 2009. As we have seen in this chapter, rising oil prices can result in a supply shock that causes the short-run aggregate supply curve to shift to the left. Although rising oil prices contributed to the severity of the recession, they had less impact than some economists had predicted. The U.S. economy appears to have become less vulnerable to increases in oil prices. Increases in the price of oil during the 1970s and early 1980s led many firms to switch to less-oil-dependent production processes. For example, FedEx and other firms used more fuel-efficient jets and trucks. As a result, the U.S. economy was consuming almost 60 percent less oil per dollar of GDP than it had in the mid-1970s. During 2008, oil price increases did not shift the short-run aggregate supply curve as far to the left as similar increases had 30 years earlier.

Figure 5A-3 illustrates the beginning of the recession by showing the economy's short-run macroeconomic equilibrium in 2007 and 2008. In the figure, short-run equilibrium for 2007 occurs where AD_{2007} intersects $SRAS_{2007}$ at real GDP of $13.21 trillion and a price level of 106.2. Real GDP in 2007 was slightly above potential real GDP of $13.20 trillion, shown by $LRAS_{2007}$. During 2008, aggregate demand shifted to the right, from AD_{2007} to AD_{2008}. Aggregate demand increased by less than potential GDP because of the negative effects of the bursting of the housing bubble and the financial crisis on consumption spending and investment spending. The supply shock from higher oil prices caused short-run aggregate supply to shift to the left, from $SRAS_{2007}$ to $SRAS_{2008}$. Shortrun equilibrium for 2008 occurred at real GDP of $13.16 trillion and a price level of 108.6. A large gap opened between short-run equilibrium real GDP and potential GDP. Not surprisingly, unemployment rose from 4.6 percent in 2007 to 5.8 percent in 2008. The price level increased only from 106.2 to 108.6, so the inflation rate was a low 2.3 percent.

The recession persisted into 2009, as potential real GDP increased to $13.78 trillion, while real GDP fell to $12.70 trillion. This increased gap between real GDP and potential GDP caused the unemployment rate to soar to 9.3 percent—the highest unemployment rate since the recession of 1981–1982 and the second highest since the Great Depression of the 1930s. Although the recession ended in June 2009, real GDP grew only slowly during 2010 and 2011, leaving the unemployment rate above 9 percent.

The severity of the recession of 2007–2009 resulted in some of the most dramatic changes in government economic policy since the Great Depression.

FIGURE 5A-3

The Beginning of the Recession of 2007–2009

Between 2007 and 2008, the AD curve shifted to the right, but not by nearly enough to offset the shift to the right of the LRAS curve, which represented the increase in potential real GDP from $13.20 trillion to $13.51 trillion. Because of a sharp increase in oil prices, shortrun aggregate supply shifted to the left, from SRAS2007 to SRAS2008. Real GDP decreased from $13.21 trillion in 2007 to $13.16 trillion in 2008, which was far below the potential real GDP, shown by LRAS2008. As a result, the unemployment rate rose from 4.6 percent in 2007 to 5.8 percent in 2008. Because the increase in aggregate demand was small, the price level increased only from 106.2 in 2007 to 108.6 in 2008, so the inflation rate for 2008 was only 2.3 percent.

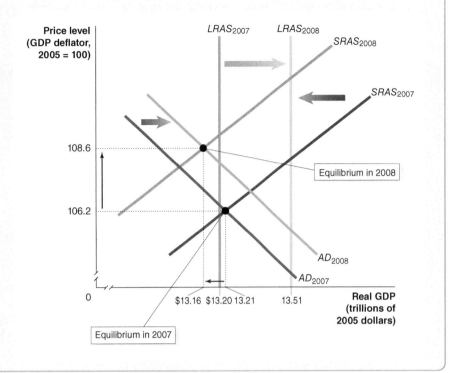

SOLVED PROBLEM 5A.1

SHOWING THE OIL SHOCK OF 1974–1975 ON A DYNAMIC AGGREGATE DEMAND AND AGGREGATE SUPPLY GRAPH

The 1974–1975 recession clearly illustrates how a supply shock affects the economy. Following the Arab–Israeli War of 1973, the Organization of the Petroleum Exporting Countries (OPEC) increased the price of a barrel of oil from less than $3 to more than $10. Use this information and the statistics in the following table to draw a dynamic aggregate demand and aggregate supply graph showing macroeconomic equilibrium for 1974 and 1975. Assume that the aggregate demand curve did not shift between 1974 and 1975. Provide a brief explanation of your graph.

	ACTUAL REAL GDP	POTENTIAL REAL GDP	PRICE LEVEL
1974	$4.89 trillion	$4.92 trillion	30.7
1975	$4.88 trillion	$5.09 trillion	33.6

Data from U.S. Bureau of Economic Analysis; and Congressional Budget Office.

Solving the Problem

Step 1: **Review the chapter material.** This problem is about using the dynamic aggregate demand and aggregate supply model, so you may want to review the section "A Dynamic Aggregate Demand and Aggregate Supply Model."

Step 2: **Use the information in the table to draw the graph.** You need to draw five curves: SRAS and *LRAS* for both 1974 and 1975 and *AD*, which is the same for both years. You know that the two *LRAS* curves will be vertical lines at the values given for potential GDP in the table. Because of the large supply shock, you know that the *SRAS* curve shifted to the left. You are instructed to assume that the AD curve did not shift. Your graph should look like this:

Step 3: **Explain your graph.** $LRAS_{1974}$ and $LRAS_{1975}$ are at the levels of potential real GDP for each year. Macroeconomic equilibrium for 1974 occurs where the AD curve intersects the $SRAS_{1974}$ curve, with real GDP of $4.89 trillion and a price level of 30.7. Macroeconomic equilibrium for 1975 occurs where the AD curve intersects the $SRAS_{1975}$ curve, with real GDP of $4.88 trillion and a price level of 33.6.

Extra Credit: As a result of the supply shock, the economy moved from an equilibrium output just below potential GDP in 1974 (the recession actually began right at the end of 1973) to an equilibrium well below potential GDP in 1975. With real GDP in 1975 about 4.1 percent below its potential level, the unemployment rate soared from 5.6 percent in 1974 to 8.5 percent in 1975.

6

Consumption, Real GDP, and the Multiplier

Since the early 2000s, *planned real investment spending*—intended inflation-adjusted expenditures on new buildings and equipment and changes in business inventories—has increased in most of the world's nations. As a percentage of global real GDP, however, planned real investment spending in the world's developed countries, including the United States, has declined. In contrast, planned real investment spending as a percentage of global real GDP has been rising in *emerging-economy nations*—that is, countries with economies that are transitioning from a less developed to a developed status. How do changes in planned real investment spending affect a country's equilibrium annual flow of real GDP? In this chapter, you will learn the answer.

the share of real GDP allocated to real consumption spending by households is about 60 percent in Germany, 66 percent in the United Kingdom, and 70 percent in the United States, but less than 41 percent in China? In all of the world's nations, inflation-adjusted consumption spending on domestically produced final goods and services is a significant component of real GDP. In this chapter, you will learn how an understanding of households' real consumption spending can assist in evaluating fluctuations in any country's real GDP.

Some Simplifying Assumptions in a Keynesian Model

Continuing in the Keynesian tradition, we will assume that the short-run aggregate supply curve within the current range of real GDP is horizontal. That is, we assume that it is similar to Figure 5-6 on page 111. Thus, the equilibrium level of real GDP is demand determined. This is why Keynes wished to examine the elements of desired aggregate expenditures. Because of the Keynesian assumption of inflexible prices, inflation is not a concern in this analysis. Hence, real values are identical to nominal values.

To simplify the income determination model that follows, a number of assumptions are made:

1. Businesses pay no indirect taxes (for example, sales taxes).

2. Businesses distribute all of their profits to shareholders.

3. There is no depreciation (capital consumption allowance), so gross private domestic investment equals net investment.

4. The economy is closed—that is, there is no foreign trade.

Given all these simplifying assumptions, **real disposable income,** or after-tax real income, will be equal to real GDP minus net taxes—taxes paid less transfer payments received.

Real disposable income
Real GDP minus net taxes, or after-tax real income.

Another Look at Definitions and Relationships

You can do only two things with a dollar of disposable income: Consume it or save it. If you consume it, it is gone forever. If you save the entire dollar, however, you will be able to consume it (and perhaps more if it earns interest) at some future time. That is the distinction between **consumption** and **saving.** Consumption is the act of using income for the purchase of consumption goods. **Consumption goods** are goods purchased by households for immediate satisfaction. (These also include services.) Consumption goods are such things as food and movies. By definition, whatever you do not consume you save and can consume at some time in the future.

Consumption
Spending on new goods and services to be used up out of a household's current income. Whatever is not consumed is saved. Consumption includes such things as buying food and going to a concert.

Saving
The act of not consuming all of one's current income. Whatever is not consumed out of spendable income is, by definition, saved. *Saving* is an action measured over time (a flow), whereas *savings* are a stock, an accumulation resulting from the act of saving in the past.

STOCKS AND FLOWS: THE DIFFERENCE BETWEEN SAVING AND SAVINGS It is important to distinguish between *saving* and *savings*. *Saving* is an action that occurs at a particular rate—for example, $40 per week or $2,080 per year. This rate is a flow. It is expressed per unit of time, usually a year. Implicitly, then, when we talk about saving, we talk about a *flow*, or rate, of saving. *Savings*, by contrast, are a *stock* concept, measured at a certain point or instant in time. Your current *savings* are the result of past *saving*. You may currently have *savings* of $8,000 that are the result of four years' *saving* at a rate of $2,000 per year. Consumption is also a flow concept. You consume from after-tax income at a certain rate per week, per month, or per year.

Consumption goods
Goods bought by households to use up, such as food and movies.

RELATING INCOME TO SAVING AND CONSUMPTION A dollar of take-home income can be allocated either to consumption or to saving. Realizing this, we can see the relationship among saving, consumption, and disposable income from the following expression:

$$\text{Consumption} + \text{saving} \equiv \text{disposable income}$$

This is called an *accounting identity*, meaning that it has to hold true at every moment in time. (To indicate that the relationship is always true, we use the $\equiv$ symbol.)

From this relationship, we can derive the following definition of saving:

$$\text{Saving} \equiv \text{disposable income} - \text{consumption}$$

Hence, saving is the amount of disposable income that is not spent to purchase consumption goods.

Investment

Investment
Spending on items such as machines and buildings, which can be used to produce goods and services in the future. (It also includes changes in business inventories.) The investment part of real GDP is the portion that will be used in the process of producing goods *in the future*.

Capital goods
Producer durables; nonconsumable goods that firms use to make other goods.

Investment is also a flow concept. As noted in Chapter 2, *investment* as used in economics differs from the common use of the term. In common speech, it is often used to describe putting funds into the stock market or real estate. In economic analysis, investment is defined to include expenditures on new machines and buildings—**capital goods**—that are expected to yield a future stream of income. This is called *fixed investment*. We also include changes in business inventories in our definition. This we call *inventory investment*.

QUICK QUIZ See page 161 for the answers. Review concepts from this section in MyEconLab.

If we assume that we are operating on a _____ short-run aggregate supply curve, the equilibrium level of real GDP per year is completely demand determined.

_____ is a flow, something that occurs over time. It equals disposable income minus consumption.

_____ are a stock. They are the accumulation resulting from saving.

_____ is also a flow. It includes expenditures on new machines, buildings, and equipment and changes in business inventories.

Determinants of Planned Consumption and Planned Saving

In the classical model discussed in Chapter 5 on pages 105–110, the supply of saving was determined by the rate of interest. Specifically, the higher the rate of interest, the more people wanted to save and consequently the less people wanted to consume.

In contrast, according to Keynes, the interest rate is *not* the most important determinant of an individual's real saving and consumption decisions. In his view, the flow of income, not the interest rate, is the main determinant of consumption and saving.

How Income Flows Can Influence Consumption and Saving

When a person decides how much to consume and save today, Keynes reasoned, that individual must take into account both current and anticipated future incomes. After all, a higher income this year enables an individual *both* to purchase more final goods and services *and* to increase the flow of saving during the current year. Furthermore, a person's anticipation about the *future* flow of income likely influences how much of *current* income is allocated to consumption and how much to saving.

The Life-Cycle Theory of Consumption

The most realistic and detailed theory of consumption, often called the **life-cycle theory of consumption,** considers how a person varies consumption and saving as income ebbs and flows during the course of an entire life span. This theory predicts that when an individual anticipates a higher income in the future, the individual will tend to consume more and save less in the current period than would have been the case otherwise. In contrast, when a person expects the flow of income to drop in the future, the individual responds in the present by allocating less of current income to consumption and more to saving.

Life-cycle theory of consumption
A theory in which a person bases decisions about current consumption and saving on both current income and anticipated future income.

The Permanent Income Hypothesis

In a related theory, called the **permanent income hypothesis,** the income level that matters for a person's decision about current consumption and saving is *permanent income*, or expected average lifetime income. The permanent income hypothesis suggests that people increase their flow of consumption only if their anticipated average lifetime income rises. Thus, if a person's flow of income temporarily rises without an increase in average lifetime income, the individual responds by saving the extra income and leaving consumption unchanged.

Permanent income hypothesis
A theory of consumption in which an individual determines current consumption based on anticipated average lifetime income.

The Keynesian Theory of Consumption and Saving

Keynes recognized that expectations about future income could affect current consumption and saving decisions. For purposes of developing a basic theory of consumption and saving, however, Keynes focused solely on the relationship between current income and current consumption and saving. Thus:

> *Keynes argued that real consumption and saving decisions depend primarily on a household's current real disposable income.*

The relationship between planned real consumption expenditures of households and their current level of real disposable income has been called the **consumption function.** It shows how much all households plan to consume per year at each level of real disposable income per year. Columns (1) and (2) of Table 6-1 on the following page illustrate a consumption function for a hypothetical household.

We see from Table 6-1 that as real disposable income rises, planned consumption also rises, but by a smaller amount, as Keynes suggested. Planned saving also increases with disposable income. Notice, however, that below an income of $60,000, the planned saving of this hypothetical household is actually negative. The further that income drops below that level, the more the household engages in **dissaving,** either by going into debt or by using up some of its existing wealth.

YOU ARE THERE

To consider a real-world application of the basic consumption and saving functions, read **Evaluating the Effects of Declining Real Disposable Income** on page 155.

Consumption function
The relationship between amount consumed and disposable income. A consumption function tells us how much people plan to consume at various levels of disposable income.

Dissaving
Negative saving; a situation in which spending exceeds income. Dissaving can occur when a household is able to borrow or use up existing assets.

Graphing the Numbers

We now graph the consumption and saving relationships presented in Table 6-1. In the upper part of Figure 6-1 on page 139, the vertical axis measures the level of planned real consumption per year, and the horizontal axis measures the level of real disposable income per year. In the lower part of the figure, the horizontal axis is again real disposable income per year, but now the vertical axis is planned real saving per year. All of these are on a dollars-per-year basis, which emphasizes the point that we are measuring flows, not stocks.

CONSUMPTION AND SAVING FUNCTIONS As you can see, we have taken income-consumption and income-saving combinations *A* through *K* and plotted them. In the upper part of

Real Consumption and Saving Schedules: A Hypothetical Case

Column 1 presents real disposable income from zero up to $120,000 per year. Column 2 indicates planned real consumption per year. Column 3 presents planned real saving per year. At levels of real disposable income below $60,000, planned real saving is negative. In column 4, we see the average propensity to consume, which is merely planned consumption divided by disposable income. Column 5 lists average propensity to save, which is planned saving divided by disposable income. Column 6 is the marginal propensity to consume, which shows the proportion of *additional* income that will be consumed. Finally, column 7 shows the proportion of *additional* income that will be saved, or the marginal propensity to save. (Δ represents "change in.")

Combination	(1) Real Disposable Income per Year (Y_d)	(2) Planned Real Consumption per Year (C)	(3) Planned Real Saving per Year ($S \equiv Y_d - C$) (1) − (2)	(4) Average Propensity to Consume ($APC \equiv C/Y_d$) (2) ÷ (1)	(5) Average Propensity to Save ($APS \equiv S/Y_d$) (3) ÷ (1)	(6) Marginal Propensity to Consume ($MPC \equiv \Delta C/\Delta Y_d$)	(7) Marginal Propensity to Save ($MPS \equiv \Delta S/\Delta Y_d$)
A	$ 0	$ 12,000	$−12,000	–	–	–	–
B	12,000	21,600	−9,600	1.8	−0.8	0.8	0.2
C	24,000	31,200	−7,200	1.3	−0.3	0.8	0.2
D	36,000	40,800	−4,800	1.133	−0.133	0.8	0.2
E	48,000	50,400	−2,400	1.05	−0.05	0.8	0.2
F	60,000	60,000	0	1.0	0.0	0.8	0.2
G	72,000	69,600	2,400	0.967	0.033	0.8	0.2
H	84,000	79,200	4,800	0.943	0.057	0.8	0.2
I	96,000	88,800	7,200	0.925	0.075	0.8	0.2
J	108,000	98,400	9,600	0.911	0.089	0.8	0.2
K	120,000	108,000	12,000	0.9	0.1	0.8	0.2

Figure 6-1 on the facing page, the result is called the *consumption function*. In the lower part, the result is called the *saving function*.

Mathematically, the saving function is the *complement* of the consumption function because consumption plus saving always equals disposable income. What is not consumed is, by definition, saved. The difference between actual disposable income and the planned rate of consumption per year *must* be the planned rate of saving per year.

THE 45-DEGREE REFERENCE LINE How can we find the rate of saving or dissaving in the upper part of Figure 6-1? We begin by drawing a line that is equidistant from both the horizontal and the vertical axes. This line is 45 degrees from either axis and is often called the **45-degree reference line.** At every point on the 45-degree reference line, a vertical line drawn to the income axis is the same distance from the origin as a horizontal line drawn to the consumption axis. Thus, at point *F*, where the consumption function intersects the 45-degree line, real disposable income equals planned real consumption.

Point *F* is sometimes called the *break-even income point* because there is neither positive nor negative real saving. This can be seen in the lower part of Figure 6-1 as well. The planned annual rate of real saving at a real disposable income level of $60,000 is indeed zero.

45-degree reference line
The line along which planned real expenditures equal real GDP per year.

Dissaving and Autonomous Consumption

To the left of point *F* in either part of Figure 6-1, this hypothetical family engages in dissaving, either by going into debt or by consuming existing assets. The rate of real saving or dissaving in the upper part of the figure can be found by measuring the

FIGURE 6-1

The Consumption and Saving Functions

If we plot the combinations of real disposable income and planned real consumption from columns 1 and 2 in Table 6-1 on the facing page, we get the consumption function.

At every point on the 45-degree line, a vertical line drawn to the income axis is the same distance from the origin as a horizontal line drawn to the consumption axis. Where the consumption function crosses the 45-degree line at *F*, we know that planned real consumption equals real disposable income and there is zero saving. The vertical distance between the 45-degree line and the consumption function measures the rate of real saving or dissaving at any given income level.

If we plot the relationship between column 1 (real disposable income) and column 3 (planned real saving) from Table 6-1 on the facing page, we arrive at the saving function shown in the lower part of this diagram. It is the complement of the consumption function presented above it.

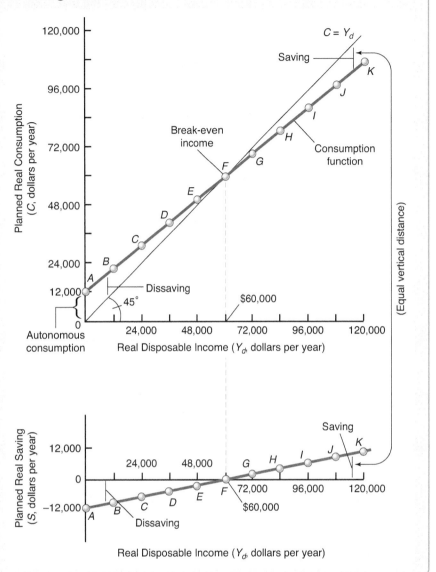

vertical distance between the 45-degree line and the consumption function. This simply tells us that if our hypothetical household sees its real disposable income fall to less than $60,000, it will not limit its consumption to this amount. It will instead go into debt or consume existing assets in some way to compensate for part of the lost income.

AUTONOMOUS CONSUMPTION Now look at the point on the diagram where real disposable income is zero but planned consumption is $12,000. This amount of real planned consumption, which does not depend at all on actual real disposable income, is called **autonomous consumption.** The autonomous consumption of $12,000 is *independent* of disposable income. That means that no matter how low the level of real income of our hypothetical household falls, the household will always attempt to consume at least $12,000 per year. (We are, of course, assuming here that the household's real disposable income does not equal zero year in and year out. There is certainly a limit to how long our hypothetical household could finance autonomous consumption without any income.)

Autonomous consumption
The part of consumption that is independent of (does not depend on) the level of disposable income. Changes in autonomous consumption shift the consumption function.

The $12,000 of yearly consumption is determined by things other than the level of income. We don't need to specify what determines autonomous consumption. We merely state that it exists and that in our example it is $12,000 per year.

THE MEANING OF AUTONOMOUS SPENDING Just remember that the word *autonomous* means "existing independently." In our model, autonomous consumption exists independently of the hypothetical household's level of real disposable income. (Later we will review some of the determinants of consumption other than real disposable income.)

There are many possible types of autonomous expenditures. Hypothetically, we can assume that investment is autonomous—independent of income. We can assume that government expenditures are autonomous. We will do just that at various times in our discussions to simplify our analysis of income determination.

Average Propensity to Consume and to Save

Average propensity to consume (APC)
Real consumption divided by real disposable income. For any given level of real income, the proportion of total real disposable income that is consumed.

Average propensity to save (APS)
Real saving divided by real disposable income. For any given level of real income, the proportion of total real disposable income that is saved.

Let's now go back to Table 6-1 on page 138, and this time let's look at columns 4 and 5: **average propensity to consume (APC)** and **average propensity to save (APS)**. They are defined as follows:

$$APC \equiv \frac{\text{real consumption}}{\text{real disposable income}}$$

$$APS \equiv \frac{\text{real saving}}{\text{real disposable income}}$$

Notice from column 4 in Table 6-1 that for this hypothetical household, the average propensity to consume decreases as real disposable income increases. This decrease simply means that the fraction of the household's real disposable income going to consumption falls as income rises. Column 5 shows that the average propensity to save, which at first is negative, finally hits zero at an income level of $60,000 and then becomes positive. In this example, the APS reaches a value of 0.1 at income level $120,000. This means that the household saves 10 percent of a $120,000 income.

It's quite easy for you to figure out your own average propensity to consume or to save. Just divide the value of what you consumed by your total real disposable income for the year, and the result will be your personal APC at your current level of income. Also, divide your real saving during the year by your real disposable income to calculate your own APS.

Marginal Propensity to Consume and to Save

Marginal propensity to consume (MPC)
The ratio of the change in consumption to the change in disposable income. A marginal propensity to consume of 0.8 tells us that an additional $100 in take-home pay will lead to an additional $80 consumed.

Marginal propensity to save (MPS)
The ratio of the change in saving to the change in disposable income. A marginal propensity to save of 0.2 indicates that out of an additional $100 in take-home pay, $20 will be saved. Whatever is not saved is consumed. The marginal propensity to save plus the marginal propensity to consume must always equal 1, by definition.

Now we go to the last two columns in Table 6-1 on page 138: **marginal propensity to consume (MPC)** and **marginal propensity to save (MPS).** The term *marginal* refers to a small incremental or decremental change (represented by the Greek letter delta, Δ, in Table 6-1). The marginal propensity to consume, then, is defined as

$$MPC \equiv \frac{\text{change in real consumption}}{\text{change in real disposable income}}$$

The marginal propensity to save is defined similarly as

$$MPS \equiv \frac{\text{change in real saving}}{\text{change in real disposable income}}$$

MARGINAL VERSUS AVERAGE PROPENSITIES What do MPC and MPS tell you? They tell you what percentage of a given increase or decrease in real income will go toward consumption and saving, respectively. The emphasis here is on the word *change*.

The marginal propensity to consume indicates how much you will change your planned real consumption if there is a change in your actual real disposable income.

If your marginal propensity to consume is 0.8, that does *not* mean that you consume 80 percent of *all* disposable income. The percentage of your total real disposable income that you consume is given by the average propensity to consume, or APC. As Table 6-1 on page 138 indicates, the APC is not equal to 0.8 anywhere in its column. Instead, an MPC of 0.8 means that you will consume 80 percent of any *increase* in your disposable income. Hence, the MPC cannot be less than zero or greater than one. It follows that households increase their planned real consumption by between 0 and 100 percent of any increase in real disposable income that they receive.

DISTINGUISHING THE MPC FROM THE APC Consider a simple example in which we show the difference between the average propensity to consume and the marginal propensity to consume. Assume that your consumption behavior is exactly the same as our hypothetical household's behavior depicted in Table 6-1. You have an annual real disposable income of $108,000. Your planned consumption rate, then, from column 2 of Table 6-1 is $98,400. So your average propensity to consume is $98,400/$108,000 = 0.911. Now suppose that at the end of the year, your boss gives you an after-tax bonus of $12,000.

What would you do with that additional $12,000 in real disposable income? According to the table, you would consume $9,600 of it and save $2,400. In that case, your *marginal* propensity to consume would be $9,600/$12,000 = 0.8 and your marginal propensity to save would be $2,400/$12,000 = 0.2. What would happen to your *average* propensity to consume? To find out, we add $9,600 to $98,400 of planned consumption, which gives us a new consumption rate of $108,000. The average propensity to consume is then $108,000 divided by the new higher salary of $120,000. Your APC drops from 0.911 to 0.9.

In contrast, your MPC remains, in our simplified example, 0.8 all the time. Look at column 6 in Table 6-1. The MPC is 0.8 at every level of income. (Therefore, the MPS is always equal to 0.2 at every level of income.) The constancy of MPC reflects the assumption that the amount that you are willing to consume out of additional income will remain the same in percentage terms no matter what level of real disposable income is your starting point.

Some Relationships

Consumption plus saving must equal income. Both your total real disposable income and the change in total real disposable income are either consumed or saved. The sums of the proportions of either measure that are consumed and saved must equal 1, or 100 percent. This allows us to make the following statements:

$$\text{APC} + \text{APS} \equiv 1 \; (= 100 \text{ percent of total income})$$

$$\text{MPC} + \text{MPS} \equiv 1 \; (= 100 \text{ percent of the } \textit{change} \text{ in income})$$

The average propensities as well as the marginal propensities to consume and save must total 1, or 100 percent. Check the two statements by adding the figures in columns 4 and 5 for each level of real disposable income in Table 6-1 on page 138. Do the same for columns 6 and 7.

Causes of Shifts in the Consumption Function

A change in any other relevant economic variable besides real disposable income will cause the consumption function to shift. The number of such nonincome determinants of the position of the consumption function is almost unlimited. Real household **net wealth** is one determinant of the position of the consumption function. An increase in the real net wealth of the average household will cause the consumption function to shift upward. A decrease in real net wealth will cause it to shift downward. So far we have been talking about the consumption function of an individual or a household. Now let's move on to the national economy.

Net wealth
The stock of assets owned by a person, household, firm, or nation (net of any debts owed). For a household, net wealth can consist of a house, cars, personal belongings, stocks, bonds, bank accounts, and cash (minus any debts owed).

Why did real consumption expenditures of U.S. households decline between 2008 and 2009 and then fail to bounce back quickly in subsequent years?

EXAMPLE

Lower Household Wealth and Subdued Growth in Consumption

Between 2007 and 2009, two key components of real household wealth—inflation-adjusted wealth in housing and in corporate stocks—declined substantially. During that interval, aggregate real wealth in housing dropped by about 25 percent, and at one point real household wealth held in stocks fell by more than 50 percent. These wealth reductions shifted the U.S. consumption function downward. Real disposable income also fell. Consequently, there was also a leftward movement along the now lower consumption function that contributed to a further drop in real household consumption between 2008 and 2009.

Inflation-adjusted household disposable income has increased each year since 2009. Nevertheless, real housing wealth held by households

has declined by another 10 percentage points. Inflation-adjusted household wealth in corporate stocks has recovered considerably but has remained between 10 percent and 20 percent lower than the peak it had reached in 2008. As a result, the U.S. consumption function has remained at a lower position than in 2007, which has dampened growth in real consumption spending during the following years.

FOR CRITICAL THINKING

Why do both *movements along and any shifts in the consumption function ultimately* jointly *determine observed changes in desired total real consumption spending?*

QUICK QUIZ   See page 161 for the answers. Review concepts from this section in MyEconLab.

The **consumption function** shows the relationship between planned rates of real consumption and real _____ _____ per year. The saving function is the complement of the consumption function because real saving plus real _____ must equal real disposable income.

The _____ propensity to consume is equal to real consumption divided by real disposable income. The _____ propensity to save is equal to real saving divided by real disposable income.

The _____ propensity to consume is equal to the change in planned real consumption divided by the change

in real disposable income. The _____ propensity to save is equal to the change in planned real saving divided by the change in real disposable income.

Any change in real disposable income will cause the planned rate of consumption to change. This is represented by a _____ _____ the consumption function. Any change in a nonincome determinant of consumption will cause a _____ _____ the consumption function.

Determinants of Investment

Investment, you will remember, consists of expenditures on new buildings and equipment and changes in business inventories. Historically, real gross private domestic investment in the United States has been extremely volatile over the years, relative to real consumption. If we were to look at net private domestic investment (investment after depreciation has been deducted), we would see that in the depths of the Great Depression and at the peak of the World War II effort, the figure was negative. In other words, we were eating away at our capital stock—we weren't even maintaining it by fully replacing depreciated equipment.

If we compare real investment expenditures historically with real consumption expenditures, we find that the latter are less variable over time than the former. Why is this so? One possible reason is that the real investment decisions of businesses are based on highly variable, subjective estimates of how the economic future looks.

The Planned Investment Function

Consider that at all times, businesses perceive an array of investment opportunities. These investment opportunities have rates of return ranging from zero to very high, with the number (or dollar value) of all such projects increasing if the rate of return rises.

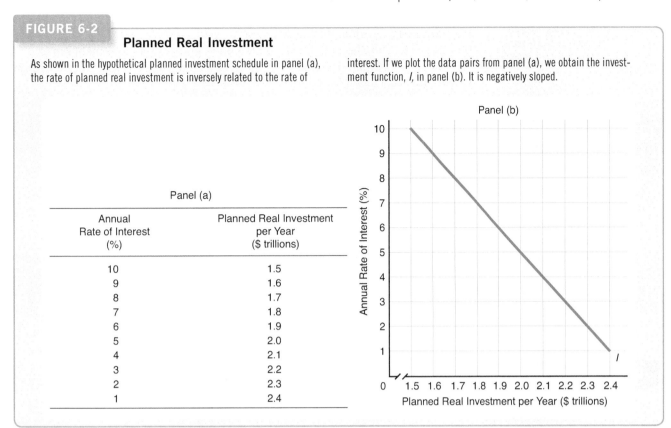

FIGURE 6-2

Planned Real Investment

As shown in the hypothetical planned investment schedule in panel (a), the rate of planned real investment is inversely related to the rate of interest. If we plot the data pairs from panel (a), we obtain the investment function, *I*, in panel (b). It is negatively sloped.

Panel (a)

Annual Rate of Interest (%)	Planned Real Investment per Year ($ trillions)
10	1.5
9	1.6
8	1.7
7	1.8
6	1.9
5	2.0
4	2.1
3	2.2
2	2.3
1	2.4

Because a project is profitable only if its rate of return exceeds the opportunity cost of the investment—the rate of interest—it follows that as the interest rate falls, planned investment spending increases, and vice versa. Even if firms use retained earnings (internal financing) to fund an investment, the lower the market rate of interest, the smaller the *opportunity cost* of using those retained earnings.

Thus, it does not matter in our analysis whether the firm must seek financing from external sources or can obtain such financing by using retained earnings. Whatever the method of financing, as the interest rate falls, more investment opportunities will be profitable, and planned investment will be higher.

It should be no surprise, therefore, that the investment function is represented as an inverse relationship between the rate of interest and the value of planned real investment. In Figure 6-2 above, a hypothetical investment schedule is given in panel (a) and plotted in panel (b). We see from this schedule that if, for example, the rate of interest is 5 percent, the dollar value of planned investment will be $2 trillion per year. Notice that planned investment is also given on a per-year basis, showing that it represents a flow, not a stock. (The stock counterpart of investment is the stock of capital in the economy measured in inflation-adjusted dollars at a point in time.)

What Causes the Investment Function to Shift?

Because planned real investment is assumed to be a function of the rate of interest, any non-interest-rate variable that changes can have the potential of shifting the investment function. One of those variables is the expectations of businesses. If higher profits are expected, more machines and bigger plants will be planned for the future. More investment will be undertaken because of the expectation of higher profits. In this case, the investment function, *I*, in panel (b) of Figure 6-2, would shift outward to the right, meaning that more investment would be desired at all rates of interest.

Any change in productive technology can potentially shift the investment function. A positive change in productive technology would stimulate demand for additional

Go to economic data provided by the Federal Reserve Bank of St. Louis via the link at www.econtoday.com/chap06 to see how U.S. real private investment has varied in recent years.

capital goods and shift *I* outward to the right. Changes in business taxes can also shift the investment schedule. If they increase, we predict a leftward shift in the planned investment function because higher taxes imply a lower (after-tax) rate of return.

How has a technological change in the display of films led to a significant upswing in investment spending by movie-theater chains?

EXAMPLE

Adding a Third Dimension Requires New Investment Spending

Of the approximately 40,000 movie screens in the United States, fewer than 8,000 utilize the digital technology required for projection of three-dimensional (3D) movies. Converting a typical multiscreen theater from a projection system using celluloid film reels to a system with digital screens and projectors requires an expenditure of about $70,000. Major movie-theater chains such as AMC Entertainment, Inc., Cinemark Holdings, Inc., and Regal Entertainment Group are in the midst of investing in new projection systems for more than 1,000 theaters. Hence, putting the latest 3D movie-projection technology into place is requiring an aggregate investment expenditure of about $70 million.

FOR CRITICAL THINKING
Will the movie-theater chains' total investment in 3D projection systems generate a movement along or a shift in the planned investment function for the United States?

QUICK QUIZ

See page 161 for the answers. Review concepts from this section in MyEconLab.

The planned investment schedule shows the relationship between real investment and the _____ _____; it slopes _____.

The non-interest-rate determinants of planned investment are _____, innovation and technological changes, and _____ _____.

Any change in the non-interest-rate determinants of planned investment will cause a _____ _____ the planned investment function so that at each and every rate of interest a different amount of planned investment will be made.

Determining Equilibrium Real GDP

We are interested in determining the equilibrium level of real GDP per year. But when we examined the consumption function earlier in this chapter, it related planned real consumption expenditures to the level of real disposable income per year. We have already shown where adjustments must be made to GDP in order to get real disposable income (see Table 2-2 on page 39). Real disposable income turns out to be less than real GDP because real net taxes (real taxes minus real government transfer payments) are usually about 14 to 21 percent of GDP. A representative average is about 18 percent, so disposable income, on average, has in recent years been around 82 percent of GDP.

Consumption as a Function of Real GDP

To simplify our model, assume that real disposable income, Y_d, differs from real GDP by the same absolute amount every year. Therefore, we can relatively easily substitute real GDP for real disposable income in the consumption function.

We can now plot any consumption function on a diagram in which the horizontal axis is no longer real disposable income but rather real GDP, as in Figure 6-3 on the facing page. Notice that there is an autonomous part of real consumption that is so labeled. The difference between this graph and the graphs presented earlier in this chapter is the change in the horizontal axis from real disposable income to real GDP per year. For the rest of this chapter, assume that the MPC out of real GDP equals 0.8, so that 20 percent of changes in real disposable income is saved. Of an additional after-tax $100 earned, an additional $80 will be consumed.

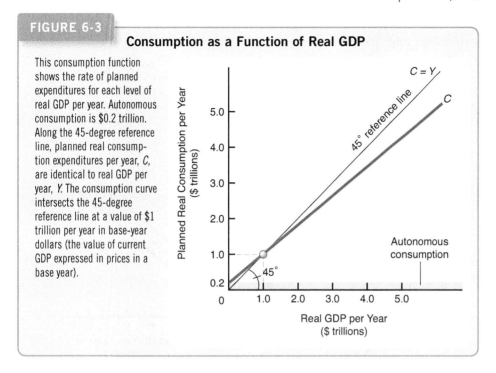

FIGURE 6-3

Consumption as a Function of Real GDP

This consumption function shows the rate of planned expenditures for each level of real GDP per year. Autonomous consumption is $0.2 trillion. Along the 45-degree reference line, planned real consumption expenditures per year, *C*, are identical to real GDP per year, *Y*. The consumption curve intersects the 45-degree reference line at a value of $1 trillion per year in base-year dollars (the value of current GDP expressed in prices in a base year).

The 45-Degree Reference Line

As in the earlier graphs, Figure 6-3 above shows a 45-degree reference line. The 45-degree line bisects the quadrant into two equal spaces. Thus, along the 45-degree reference line, planned real consumption expenditures, *C*, equal real GDP per year, *Y*. One can see, then, that at any point where the consumption function intersects the 45-degree reference line, planned real consumption expenditures will be exactly equal to real GDP per year, or *C = Y*. Note that in this graph, because we are looking only at planned real consumption on the vertical axis, the 45-degree reference line is where planned real consumption, *C*, is always equal to real GDP per year, *Y*. Later, when we add real investment, government spending, and net exports to the graph, *all* planned real expenditures will be labeled along the vertical axis. In any event, real consumption and real GDP are equal at $1 trillion per year. That is where the consumption curve, *C*, intersects the 45-degree reference line. At that GDP level, all real GDP is consumed.

Adding the Investment Function

Another component of private aggregate demand is, of course, real investment spending, *I*. We have already looked at the planned investment function, which related real investment, which includes changes in inventories of final products, to the rate of interest.

PLANNED INVESTMENT AND THE INTEREST RATE In panel (a) of Figure 6-4 on the following page, you see that at an interest rate of 5 percent, the rate of real investment is $2 trillion per year. The $2 trillion of real investment per year is *autonomous* with respect to real GDP—that is, it is independent of real GDP.

In other words, given that we have a determinant investment level of $2 trillion at a 5 percent rate of interest, we can treat this level of real investment as constant, regardless of the level of GDP. This is shown in panel (b) of Figure 6-4. The vertical distance of real investment spending is $2 trillion. Businesses plan on investing a particular amount—$2 trillion per year—and will do so no matter what the level of real GDP.

COMBINING PLANNED INVESTMENT AND CONSUMPTION How do we add this amount of real investment spending to our consumption function? We simply add a line above the *C*

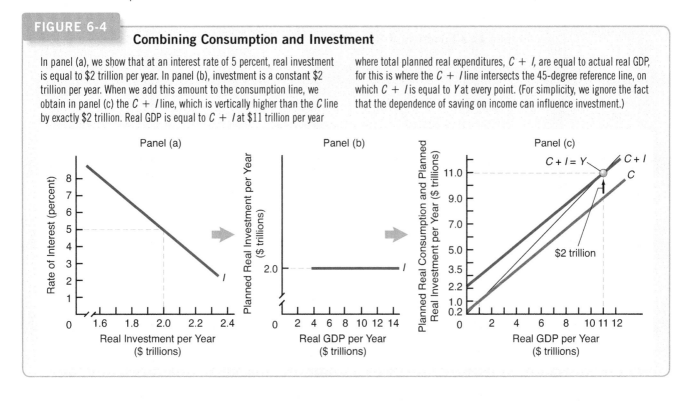

FIGURE 6-4

Combining Consumption and Investment

In panel (a), we show that at an interest rate of 5 percent, real investment is equal to $2 trillion per year. In panel (b), investment is a constant $2 trillion per year. When we add this amount to the consumption line, we obtain in panel (c) the $C + I$ line, which is vertically higher than the C line by exactly $2 trillion. Real GDP is equal to $C + I$ at $11 trillion per year where total planned real expenditures, $C + I$, are equal to actual real GDP, for this is where the $C + I$ line intersects the 45-degree reference line, on which $C + I$ is equal to Y at every point. (For simplicity, we ignore the fact that the dependence of saving on income can influence investment.)

line that we drew in Figure 6-3 on the previous page that is higher by the vertical distance equal to $2 trillion of autonomous real investment spending. This is shown by the arrow in panel (c) of Figure 6-4 above.

Our new line, now labeled $C + I$, is called the *consumption plus investment line*. In our simple economy without real government expenditures and net exports, the $C + I$ curve represents total planned real expenditures as they relate to different levels of real GDP per year. Because the 45-degree reference line shows all the points where planned real expenditures (now $C + I$) equal real GDP, we label it $C + I = Y$. Thus, in equilibrium, the sum of consumption spending (C) and investment spending (I) equals real GDP (Y), which is $11 trillion per year. Equilibrium occurs when total planned real expenditures equal real GDP (given that any amount of production of goods and services in this model in the short run can occur without a change in the price level).

Saving and Investment: Planned versus Actual

Figure 6-5 on the facing page shows the planned investment curve as a horizontal line at $2 trillion per year in base-year dollars. Real investment is completely autonomous in this simplified model—it does not depend on real GDP.

The planned saving curve is represented by S. Because in our model whatever is not consumed is, by definition, saved, the planned saving schedule is the complement of the planned consumption schedule, represented by the C line in Figure 6-3 on the previous page. For better exposition, we look at only a part of the saving and investment schedules—annual levels of real GDP between $9 trillion and $13 trillion.

Why does equilibrium have to occur at the intersection of the planned saving and planned investment schedules? If we are at E in Figure 6-5, planned saving equals planned investment. All anticipations are validated by reality. There is no tendency for businesses to alter the rate of production or the level of employment because they are neither increasing nor decreasing their inventories in an unplanned way.

UNPLANNED CHANGES IN BUSINESS INVENTORIES If real GDP is $13 trillion instead of $11 trillion, planned investment, as usual, is $2 trillion per year. It is exceeded, however, by planned saving, which is $2.4 trillion per year. The additional $0.4 trillion

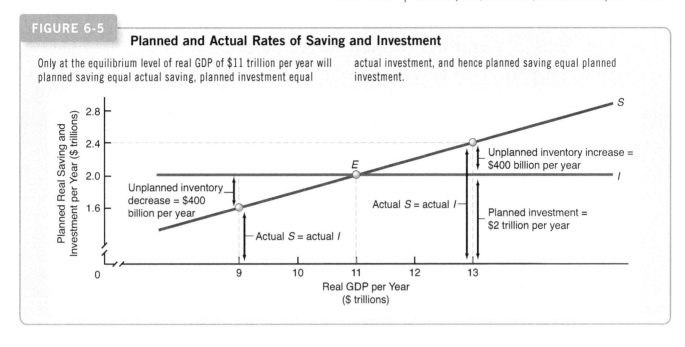

FIGURE 6-5

Planned and Actual Rates of Saving and Investment

Only at the equilibrium level of real GDP of $11 trillion per year will planned saving equal actual saving, planned investment equal actual investment, and hence planned saving equal planned investment.

($400 billion) in saving by households over and above planned investment represents less consumption spending and will translate into unsold goods that accumulate as unplanned business inventory investment. Thus, consumers will *actually* purchase fewer goods and services than businesses had *anticipated*. This will leave firms with unsold products, and their inventories will begin to rise above the levels they had planned.

Unplanned business inventories will now rise at the rate of $400 billion per year, or $2.4 trillion in actual investment (including inventories) minus $2 trillion in planned investment by firms that had not anticipated an inventory buildup. But this situation cannot continue for long. Businesses will respond to the unplanned increase in inventories by cutting back production of goods and services and reducing employment, and we will move toward a lower level of real GDP.

Naturally, the adjustment process works in reverse if real GDP is less than the equilibrium level. For instance, if real GDP is $9 trillion per year, an unintended inventory decrease of $0.4 trillion ultimately brings about an increase in real GDP toward the equilibrium level of $11 trillion.

Every time the saving rate planned by households differs from the investment rate planned by businesses, there will be a shrinkage or an expansion in the circular flow of income and output (introduced in Chapter 2) in the form of unplanned inventory changes. Real GDP and employment will change until unplanned inventory changes are again zero—that is, until we have attained the equilibrium level of real GDP.

QUICK QUIZ See page 161 for the answers. Review concepts from this section in MyEconLab.

We assume that the consumption function has an _____ part that is independent of the level of real GDP per year. It is labeled "_____ consumption."

For simplicity, we assume that real investment is _____ with respect to real GDP and therefore unaffected by the level of real GDP per year.

The _____ level of real GDP can be found where planned saving equals planned investment.

Whenever planned saving exceeds planned investment, there will be unplanned inventory _____, and real GDP will fall as producers cut production of goods and services. Whenever planned saving is less than planned investment, there will be unplanned inventory _____, and real GDP will rise as producers increase production of goods and services.

Keynesian Equilibrium with Government and the Foreign Sector Added

To this point, we have ignored the role of government in our model. We have also left out the foreign sector of the economy. Let's think about what happens when we also consider these as elements of the model.

Government

To add real government spending, G, to our macroeconomic model, we assume that the level of resource-using government purchases of goods and services (federal, state, and local), *not* including transfer payments, is determined by the political process. In other words, G will be considered autonomous, just like real investment (and a certain relatively small component of real consumption). In the United States, resource-using federal government expenditures account for almost 25 percent of real GDP.

The other side of the coin, of course, is that there are real taxes, which are used to pay for much of government spending. We will simplify our model greatly by assuming that there is a constant **lump-sum tax** of $2.3 trillion a year to finance $2.3 trillion of government spending. This lump-sum tax will reduce disposable income by the same amount. We show this below in Table 6-2 (column 2) below, where we give the numbers for a complete model.

Lump-sum tax
A tax that does not depend on income. An example is a $1,000 tax that every household must pay, irrespective of its economic situation.

The Foreign Sector

For years, the media have focused attention on the nation's foreign trade deficit. We have been buying merchandise and services from foreign residents—real imports—the value of which exceeds the value of the real exports we have been selling to them. The difference between real exports and real imports is *real net exports*, which we will label X in our graphs. The level of real exports depends on

TABLE 6-2

The Determination of Equilibrium Real GDP with Government and Net Exports Added
Figures are trillions of dollars.

(1) Real GDP	(2) Real Taxes	(3) Real Disposable Income	(4) Planned Real Consumption	(5) Planned Real Saving	(6) Planned Real Investment	(7) Real Government Spending	(8) Real Net Exports (exports minus imports)	(9) Total Planned Real Expenditures (4)+(6)+(7)+(8)	(10) Unplanned Inventory Changes	(11) Direction of Change in Real GDP
9.0	2.3	6.7	6.7	0.0	2.0	2.3	−0.8	10.2	−1.2	Increase
10.0	2.3	7.7	7.5	0.2	2.0	2.3	−0.8	11.0	−1.0	Increase
11.0	2.3	8.7	8.3	0.4	2.0	2.3	−0.8	11.8	−0.8	Increase
12.0	2.3	9.7	9.1	0.6	2.0	2.3	−0.8	12.6	−0.6	Increase
13.0	2.3	10.7	9.9	0.8	2.0	2.3	−0.8	13.4	−0.4	Increase
14.0	2.3	11.7	10.7	1.0	2.0	2.3	−0.8	14.2	−0.2	Increase
15.0	2.3	12.7	11.5	1.2	2.0	2.3	−0.8	15.0	0	Neither (equilibrium)
16.0	2.3	13.7	12.3	1.4	2.0	2.3	−0.8	15.8	+0.2	Decrease
17.0	2.3	14.7	13.1	1.6	2.0	2.3	−0.8	16.6	+0.4	Decrease

international economic conditions, especially in the countries that buy our products. Real imports depend on economic conditions here at home. For simplicity, assume that real imports exceed real exports (real net exports, X, is negative) and furthermore that the level of real net exports is autonomous—independent of real national income. Assume a level of X of –$0.8 trillion per year, as shown in column 8 of Table 6-2 on the facing page.

Determining the Equilibrium Level of GDP per Year

We are now in a position to determine the equilibrium level of real GDP per year under the continuing assumptions that the price level is unchanging; that investment, government, and the foreign sector are autonomous; and that planned consumption expenditures are determined by the level of real GDP. As can be seen in Table 6-2, total planned real expenditures of $15 trillion per year equal real GDP of $15 trillion per year, and this is where we reach equilibrium.

Remember that equilibrium *always* occurs when total planned real expenditures equal real GDP. Now look at Figure 6-6 below, which shows the equilibrium level of real GDP. There are two curves, one showing the consumption function, which is the exact duplicate of the one shown in Figure 6-3 on page 145, and the other being the $C + I + G + X$ curve, which intersects the 45-degree reference line (representing equilibrium) at $15 trillion per year.

Whenever total planned real expenditures differ from real GDP, there are unplanned inventory changes. When total planned real expenditures are greater than real GDP, inventory levels drop in an unplanned manner. To get inventories back up, firms seek to expand their production of goods and services, which increases real GDP. Real GDP rises toward its equilibrium level. Whenever total planned real expenditures are less than real GDP, the opposite occurs. There are unplanned inventory increases, causing firms to cut back on their production of goods and services in an effort to push inventories back down to planned levels. The result is a drop in real GDP toward the equilibrium level.

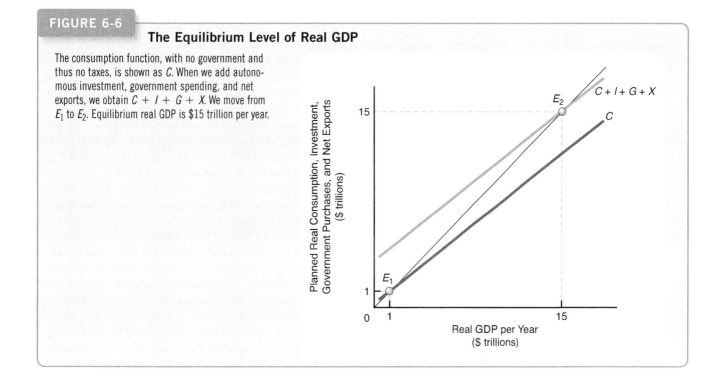

FIGURE 6-6

The Equilibrium Level of Real GDP

The consumption function, with no government and thus no taxes, is shown as C. When we add autonomous investment, government spending, and net exports, we obtain $C + I + G + X$. We move from E_1 to E_2. Equilibrium real GDP is $15 trillion per year.

When we add autonomous investment, *I*, and autonomous government spending, *G*, to the consumption function, we obtain the *C* + *I* + *G* curve, which represents total _____ _____ for a closed economy. In an open economy, we add the foreign sector, which consists of exports minus imports, or net exports, *X*. Total planned expenditures are thus represented by the *C* + *I* + *G* + *X* curve.

Equilibrium real GDP can be found by locating the intersection of the total planned real expenditures curve with the _____-_____ reference line. At that level of real GDP per year, planned real consumption plus

planned real investment plus real government expenditures plus real net exports will equal real GDP.

Whenever total planned real expenditures exceed real GDP, there will be unplanned _____ in inventories. Production of goods and services will increase, and a higher level of equilibrium real GDP will prevail. Whenever total planned real expenditures are less than real GDP, there will be unplanned _____ in inventories. Production of goods and services will decrease, and equilibrium real GDP will decrease.

The Multiplier

Look again at panel (c) of Figure 6-4 on page 146. Assume for the moment that the only real expenditures included in real GDP are real consumption expenditures. Where would the equilibrium level of real GDP be in this case? It would be where the consumption function (*C*) intersects the 45-degree reference line, which is at $1 trillion per year. Now we add the autonomous amount of planned real investment, $2 trillion, and then determine what the new equilibrium level of real GDP will be. It turns out to be $11 trillion per year. Adding $2 trillion per year of investment spending increased equilibrium real GDP by *five* times that amount, or by $10 trillion per year.

The Multiplier Effect

Multiplier
The ratio of the change in the equilibrium level of real GDP to the change in autonomous real expenditures. The number by which a change in autonomous real investment or autonomous real consumption, for example, is multiplied to get the change in equilibrium real GDP.

What is operating here is the multiplier effect of changes in autonomous spending. The **multiplier** is the number by which a permanent change in autonomous real investment or autonomous real consumption is multiplied to get the change in the equilibrium level of real GDP. Any permanent increases in autonomous real investment or in any autonomous component of consumption will cause an even larger increase in real GDP. Any permanent decreases in autonomous real spending will cause even larger decreases in real GDP per year. To understand why this multiple expansion (or contraction) in equilibrium real GDP occurs, let's look at a simple numerical example.

We'll use the same figures we used for the marginal propensity to consume and to save. MPC will equal 0.8, or $\frac{4}{5}$, and MPS will equal 0.2, or $\frac{1}{5}$. Now let's run an experiment and say that businesses decide to increase planned real investment permanently by $100 billion a year. We see in Table 6-3 on the facing page that during what we'll call the first round in column 1, investment is increased by $100 billion. This also means an increase in real GDP of $100 billion, because the spending by one group represents income for another, shown in column 2. Column 3 gives the resultant increase in consumption by households that received this additional $100 billion in income. This rise in consumption spending is found by multiplying the MPC by the increase in real GDP. Because the MPC equals 0.8, real consumption expenditures during the first round will increase by $80 billion.

But that's not the end of the story. This additional household consumption is also spending, and it will provide $80 billion of additional income for other individuals. Thus, during the second round, we see an increase in real GDP of $80 billion. Now, out of this increased real GDP, what will be the resultant increase in consumption expenditures? It will be 0.8 times $80 billion, or $64 billion. We continue these induced expenditure rounds and find that an initial increase in autonomous investment expenditures of $100 billion will eventually cause the equilibrium level of real GDP to increase by $500 billion. A permanent $100 billion increase in autonomous real investment spending has induced an additional $400 billion increase in real consumption

TABLE 6-3

The Multiplier Process

We trace the effects of a *permanent* $100 billion increase in autonomous real investment spending on real GDP per year. If we assume a marginal propensity to consume of 0.8, such an increase will eventually elicit a $500 billion increase in equilibrium real GDP per year.

(1) Round	(2) Annual Increase in Real GDP ($ billions)	(3) Annual Increase in Planned Real Consumption ($ billions)	(4) Annual Increase in Planned Real Saving ($ billions)
Assumption: MPC = 0.8, or $\frac{4}{5}$			
1 ($100 billion per year increase in I)	100.00 →	80.000	20.000
2	80.00 ← →	64.000	16.000
3	64.00 ← →	51.200	12.800
4	51.20 ← →	40.960	10.240
5	40.96 ← →	32.768	8.192
.	.	.	.
.	.	.	.
.	.	.	.
All later rounds	163.84	131.072	32.768
Totals (C + I + X)	500.00	400.000	100.000

spending, for a total increase in real GDP of $500 billion. In other words, equilibrium real GDP will change by an amount equal to five times the change in real investment.

The Multiplier Formula

It turns out that the autonomous spending multiplier is equal to 1 divided by the marginal propensity to save. In our example, the MPC was 0.8, or $\frac{4}{5}$. Therefore, because MPC + MPS = 1, the MPS was equal to 0.2, or $\frac{1}{5}$. When we divide 1 by $\frac{1}{5}$, we get 5. That was our multiplier. A $100 billion increase in real planned investment led to a $500 billion increase in the equilibrium level of real GDP. Our multiplier will always be the following:

$$\text{Multiplier} \equiv \frac{1}{1 - \text{MPC}} \equiv \frac{1}{\text{MPS}}$$

You can always figure out the multiplier if you know either the MPC or the MPS. Let's consider an example. If MPS = 0.25 or $\frac{1}{4}$,

$$\text{Multiplier} = \frac{1}{\frac{1}{4}} = 4$$

Because MPC + MPS = 1, it follows that MPS = 1 − MPC. Hence, we can always figure out the multiplier if we are given the marginal propensity to consume. In this example, if the marginal propensity to consume is given as 0.75 or $\frac{3}{4}$,

$$\text{Multiplier} = \frac{1}{1 - \frac{3}{4}} = \frac{1}{\frac{1}{4}} = 4$$

By taking a few numerical examples, you can demonstrate to yourself an important property of the multiplier:

The smaller the marginal propensity to save, the larger the multiplier.

Otherwise stated:

The larger the marginal propensity to consume, the larger the multiplier.

Demonstrate this to yourself by computing the multiplier when the marginal propensity to save equals $\frac{3}{4}$, $\frac{1}{2}$, and $\frac{1}{4}$. What happens to the multiplier as the MPS gets smaller?

When you have the multiplier, the following formula will then give you the change in equilibrium real GDP due to a permanent change in autonomous spending:

$$\text{Change in equilibrium real GDP} =$$
$$\text{multiplier} \times \text{change in autonomous spending}$$

The multiplier, as noted earlier, works for a permanent increase or a permanent decrease in autonomous spending per year. In our earlier example, if the autonomous component of real consumption had fallen permanently by $100 billion, the reduction in equilibrium real GDP would have been $500 billion per year.

Significance of the Multiplier

Depending on the size of the multiplier, it is possible that a relatively small change in planned investment or in autonomous consumption can trigger a much larger change in equilibrium real GDP per year. In essence, the multiplier magnifies the fluctuations in yearly equilibrium real GDP initiated by changes in autonomous spending.

As was just noted, the larger the marginal propensity to consume, the larger the multiplier. If the marginal propensity to consume is $\frac{1}{2}$, the multiplier is 2. In that case, a $1 billion decrease in (autonomous) real investment will elicit a $2 billion decrease in equilibrium real GDP per year. Conversely, if the marginal propensity to consume is $\frac{9}{10}$, the multiplier will be 10. That same $1 billion decrease in planned real investment expenditures with a multiplier of 10 will lead to a $10 billion decrease in equilibrium real GDP per year.

WHAT IF... the government seeks a larger multiplier effect by funding private spending on certain items rather than buying those items directly?

Whether the government gives private firms or households funds to purchase particular goods or purchases those same goods itself, the resulting increase in total autonomous expenditures is the same. The overall theoretical multiplier effect on equilibrium real GDP would be the same as well. Hence, providing a grant of public funds for private purchase of the same items the government alternatively would have bought with the same funds will not enlarge the overall theoretical multiplier effect.

How a Change in Real Autonomous Spending Affects Real GDP When the Price Level Can Change

So far, our examination of how changes in real autonomous spending affect equilibrium real GDP has considered a situation in which the price level remains unchanged. Thus, our analysis has only indicated how much the aggregate demand curve shifts in response to a change in investment, government spending, net exports, or lump-sum taxes.

Of course, when we take into account the aggregate supply curve, we must also consider responses of the equilibrium price level to a multiplier-induced change in aggregate demand. We do so in Figure 6-7 on the facing page. The intersection of AD_1 and $SRAS$ is at a price level of 120 with equilibrium real GDP of $15 trillion per year. An increase in autonomous spending shifts the aggregate demand curve outward to the right to AD_2. If the price level remained at 120, the short-run equilibrium level of real GDP would increase to $15.5 trillion per year because, for the $100 billion increase in autonomous spending, the multiplier would be 5, as it was in Table 6-3 on the previous page.

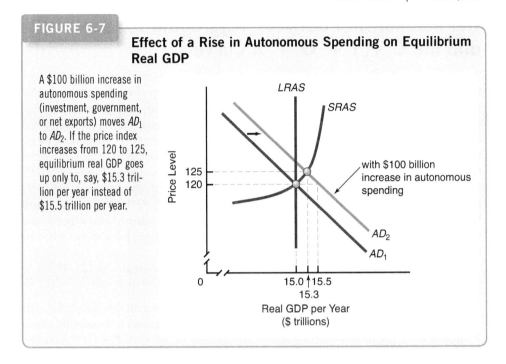

FIGURE 6-7

Effect of a Rise in Autonomous Spending on Equilibrium Real GDP

A $100 billion increase in autonomous spending (investment, government, or net exports) moves AD_1 to AD_2. If the price index increases from 120 to 125, equilibrium real GDP goes up only to, say, $15.3 trillion per year instead of $15.5 trillion per year.

The price level does not stay fixed, however, because ordinarily the *SRAS* curve is positively sloped. In this diagram, the new short-run equilibrium level of real GDP is hypothetically $15.3 trillion. The ultimate effect on real GDP is smaller than the multiplier effect on nominal income because part of the additional income is used to pay higher prices. Not all is spent on additional goods and services, as is the case when the price level is fixed.

If the economy is at an equilibrium level of real GDP that is greater than *LRAS*, the implications for the eventual effect on real GDP are even more severe. Look again at Figure 6-7 above. The *SRAS* curve starts to slope upward more dramatically after $15 trillion of real GDP per year. Therefore, any increase in aggregate demand will lead to a proportionally greater increase in the price level and a smaller increase in equilibrium real GDP per year. The ultimate effect on real GDP of any increase in autonomous spending will be relatively small because most of the changes will be in the price level. Moreover, any increase in the short-run equilibrium level of real GDP will tend to be temporary because the economy is temporarily above *LRAS*—the strain on its productive capacity will raise the price level.

How much is the initial multiplier effect of a rise in real autonomous spending on real GDP in China offset by the resulting short-run adjustment in China's price level?

INTERNATIONAL EXAMPLE

The Effect of Higher Autonomous Spending on China's Real GDP

Most estimates indicate that the marginal propensity to consume in China is approximately 0.50. If we ignore a rise in the price level generated by a boost in aggregate demand that results from an increase in real autonomous spending, the value of the multiplier would be about 2. [This is so because $1/(1 - \text{MPC}) = 1/(1 - 0.5) = 1/0.5 = 2$.] Economists at the Hong Kong Monetary Authority have estimated, though, that the short-run effect of an initial rise in real autonomous spending on China's real GDP is actually much smaller—about 1.1. Therefore, once the effect on real GDP

of an upward price level adjustment is taken into account, the estimated result from a one-unit increase in real autonomous expenditures is only a 1.1-unit increase in China's annual real GDP.

FOR CRITICAL THINKING

By about how much would China's equilibrium real GDP change if the nation's net export spending declined by 1 trillion yuan (the Chinese currency unit)?

The Relationship between Aggregate Demand and the C + I + G + X Curve

A relationship clearly exists between the aggregate demand curves that you studied in Chapters 4 and 5 and the $C + I + G + X$ curve developed in this chapter. After all, aggregate demand consists of consumption, investment, and government purchases, plus the foreign sector of our economy. There is a major difference, however, between the aggregate demand curve, *AD*, and the $C + I + G + X$ curve: The latter is drawn with the price level held constant, whereas the former is drawn, by definition, with the price level changing. To derive the aggregate demand curve from the $C + I + G + X$ curve, we must now allow the price level to change. Look at the upper part of Figure 6-8 below. Here we see the $C + I + G + X$ curve at a price level equal to 100, and at $15 trillion of real GDP per year, planned real expenditures exactly equal real GDP. This gives us point *A* in the lower graph, for it shows what real GDP would be at a price level of 100.

Now let's assume that in the upper graph, the price level increases to 125. What are the effects?

1. A higher price level can decrease the purchasing power of any cash that people hold (the real-balance effect). This is a decrease in real wealth, and it causes consumption expenditures, *C*, to fall, thereby putting downward pressure on the $C + I + G + X$ curve.

FIGURE 6-8

The Relationship between *AD* and the C + I + G + X Curve

In the upper graph, the $C + I + G + X$ curve at a price level equal to 100 intersects the 45-degree reference line at E_1, or $15 trillion of real GDP per year. That gives us point *A* (price level = 100; real GDP = $15 trillion) in the lower graph. When the price level increases to 125, the $C + I + G + X$ curve shifts downward, and the new level of real GDP at which planned real expenditures equal real GDP is at E_2 at $13 trillion per year. This gives us point *B* in the lower graph. Connecting points *A* and *B*, we obtain the aggregate demand curve.

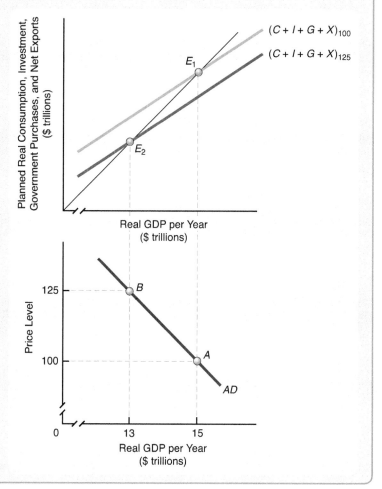

2. Because individuals attempt to borrow more to replenish their real cash balances, interest rates will rise, which will make it more costly for people to buy houses and cars (the interest rate effect). Higher interest rates also make it less profitable to install new equipment and to erect new buildings. Therefore, the rise in the price level indirectly causes a reduction in total planned spending on goods and services.

3. In an open economy, our higher price level causes foreign spending on our goods to fall (the open economy effect). Simultaneously, it increases our demand for others' goods. If the foreign exchange price of the dollar stays constant for a while, there will be an increase in imports and a decrease in exports, thereby reducing the size of X, again putting downward pressure on the $C + I + G + X$ curve.

The result is that a new $C + I + G + X$ curve at a price level equal to 125 generates an equilibrium at E_2 at $13 trillion of real GDP per year. This gives us point B in the lower part of Figure 6-8 on the facing page. When we connect points A and B, we obtain the aggregate demand curve, AD.

QUICK QUIZ See page 161 for the answers. Review concepts from this section in MyEconLab.

Any change in autonomous spending shifts the expenditure curve and causes a _____ effect on equilibrium real GDP per year.

The **multiplier** is equal to 1 divided by the _____ propensity to _____.

The smaller the marginal propensity to _____, the larger the **multiplier.** Otherwise stated, the larger the

marginal propensity to _____, the larger the **multiplier**.

The $C + I + G + X$ curve is drawn with the price level held constant, whereas the AD curve allows the price level to _____. Each different price level generates a new $C + I + G + X$ curve.

YOU ARE THERE
Evaluating the Effects of Declining Real Disposable Income

Mark Vitner, an economist with Wells Fargo Bank, examines the latest monthly economic data. U.S. real disposable personal income fell by 0.3 percent during the month, the first such decline since the 2008–2009 economic downturn. Vitner notes that other data display patterns consistent with the theory of consumption and saving. Because households consume and save out of real disposable income, real consumption spending and real saving both dipped during the month.

Vitner returns a call to a financial news reporter seeking his comments on the implications of these declines. "Everything that we see in these numbers tells us that household budgets are extremely tight and getting tighter," he states. "Consumers are having to pull out all the stops in order to try to maintain their standard of living." This dreary

assessment is the best that Vitner can offer. After all, a key measure of households' living standards is real consumption spending, which in turn derives from real disposable income. If real disposable income continues to fall, persistent downward pressure will be exerted on real consumption spending—and, hence, on estimated standards of living—of U.S. households.

Critical Thinking Questions

1. Is Vitner contemplating a shift of or movement along the consumption function?

2. Did a shift of or movement along the *saving* function occur?

ISSUES & APPLICATIONS

A Global Reversal in Planned Investment Spending

CONCEPTS APPLIED

▶ Planned Investment Spending

▶ Multiplier

▶ Planned Investment Function

In years past, countries that experienced the largest upward shifts in their planned investment functions over time were developed countries, including European nations, Japan, and the United States. Recently, however, relatively larger upward shifts in planned investment functions have occurred among *emerging-economy nations*, such as China, India, South Korea, and Singapore.

Groups of Nations Trading Places in Planned Investment

Figure 6-9 below displays real investment spending as a percentage of global real GDP since the mid-1990s for developed versus emerging nations. The figure shows that in recent years, *decreases* in planned investment expenditures as a percentage of global real GDP have occurred in highly developed countries. In contrast, planned investment spending as a percentage of global real GDP has been *rising* for nations with emerging economies.

Global real GDP has increased every year except for a brief dip during 2009. Consequently, planned real investment has risen in all nations in most years. What Figure 6-9

depicts, therefore, is a shift toward relatively greater increases in planned investment in emerging nations compared with developed countries.

Higher Real Investment Yields Faster-Growing Real GDP

Within any nation's economy, variations in planned real investment spending operate through the multiplier to bring about changes in equilibrium real GDP. Thus, a country that experiences a larger upward shift in its planned investment function than another nation will, if both countries' multipliers have close to the same values, observe a greater increase in its equilibrium real GDP.

FIGURE 6-9

Real Investment Spending as a Percentage of Global Real GDP in Two Groups of Nations since 1995

Since the early 2000s, developed countries have experienced a decrease in planned investment expenditures as a percentage of global real GDP, whereas nations with emerging economies have observed an increase in planned investment spending as a percentage of global real GDP.

Sources: International Monetary Fund; author's estimates.

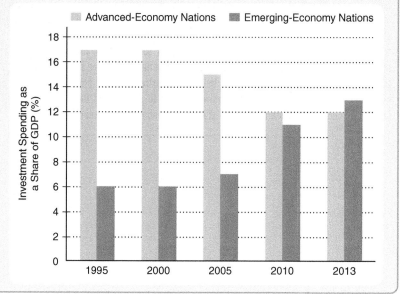

This relatively larger increase in investment spending helps to explain why countries such as China, India, South Korea, and Singapore are *emerging* from a status of less developed toward eventual classification among developed nations. Relatively higher planned real investment expenditures in these nations are, through multiplier effects, boosting real GDP per year. Thus, flows of real GDP are expanding faster in these emerging-economy countries than in developed ones.

For Critical Thinking

1. If interest rates, or opportunity costs of investment, happened to be the same in both developed countries and emerging-economy nations, what could account for faster upward shifts in the latter group's planned investment functions?
2. Are stocks of productive capital currently growing at a faster pace in developed countries or in emerging-economy nations? Explain.

Web Resources

1. To track real investment spending as a percentage of real GDP in recent years for individual nations, go to www .econtoday.com/chap06.
2. For links to economic data for both developed countries and emerging-economy nations, go to www.econtoday.com/chap06.

MyEconLab

For more questions on this chapter's Issues & Applications, go to MyEconLab. In the Study Plan for this chapter, select Section N: News.

MyEconLab

Here is what you should know after reading this chapter. MyEconLab will help you identify what you know, and where to go when you need to practice.

WHAT YOU SHOULD KNOW		WHERE TO GO TO PRACTICE
The Difference between Saving and Savings and the Relationship between Saving and Consumption Saving is a flow over time, whereas savings are a stock of resources at a point in time. Thus, the portion of your disposable income that you do not consume during a week, a month, or a year is an addition to your stock of savings. By definition, saving during a year plus consumption during that year must equal total disposable (after-tax) income earned that year.	real disposable income, 135 consumption, 135 saving, 135 consumption goods, 135 investment, 136 capital goods, 136	• MyEconLab Study Plan 6.1
Key Determinants of Consumption and Saving in the Keynesian Model In the Keynesian model, as real disposable income increases, so do real consumption expenditures. The portion of consumption unrelated to disposable income is autonomous consumption. The ratio of saving to disposable income is the average propensity to save (APS), and the ratio of consumption to disposable income is the average propensity to consume (APC). A change in saving divided by the corresponding change in disposable income is the marginal propensity to save (MPS), and a change in consumption divided by the corresponding change in disposable income is the marginal propensity to consume (MPC).	life-cycle theory of consumption, 137 permanent income hypothesis, 137 consumption function, 137 dissaving, 137 45-degree reference line, 138 autonomous consumption, 139 average propensity to consume (APC), 140 average propensity to save (APS), 140 marginal propensity to consume (MPC), 140 marginal propensity to save (MPS), 140 net wealth, 141	• MyEconLab Study Plan 6.2 • Animated Figure 6-1

(continued)

MyEconLab *continued*

WHAT YOU SHOULD KNOW		WHERE TO GO TO PRACTICE
	Key Figure Figure 6-1, 139	
Key Determinants of Planned Investment Planned investment varies inversely with the interest rate, so the investment schedule slopes downward. Changes in business expectations, productive technology, or business taxes cause the investment schedule to shift.		• MyEconLab Study Plan 6.3
How Equilibrium Real GDP Is Established in the Keynesian Model In equilibrium, total planned real consumption, investment, government, and net export expenditures equal real GDP, so $C + I + G + X = Y$. This occurs at the point where the $C + I + G + X$ curve crosses the 45-degree reference line. In a world without government spending and taxes, equilibrium also occurs when planned saving is equal to planned investment, and there is no tendency for business inventories to expand or contract.	lump-sum tax, 148 Key Figures Figure 6-5, 147 Figure 6-6, 149	• MyEconLab Study Plans 6.4, 6.5 • Animated Figures 6-5, 6-6
Why Autonomous Changes in Total Planned Real Expenditures Have a Multiplier Effect on Equilibrium Real GDP Any increase in autonomous expenditures causes a direct rise in real GDP. The resulting increase in disposable income in turn stimulates increased consumption by an amount equal to the marginal propensity to consume multiplied by the rise in disposable income that results. As consumption increases, so does real GDP, which induces a further increase in consumption spending. The ultimate expansion of real GDP is equal to the multiplier, $1/(1 - MPC)$, or $1/MPS$, times the increase in autonomous expenditures.	multiplier, 150 Key Table Table 6-3, 151	• MyEconLab Study Plans 6.6, 6.7 • Animated Table 6-3
The Relationship between Total Planned Expenditures and the Aggregate Demand Curve An increase in the price level induces households and businesses to cut back on spending. Thus, the $C + I + G + X$ curve shifts downward following a rise in the price level, so that equilibrium real GDP falls. This yields the downward-sloping aggregate demand curve.	Key Figures Figure 6-7, 153 Figure 6-8, 154	• MyEconLab Study Plan 6.8 • Animated Figures 6-7, 6-8

Log in to MyEconLab, take a chapter test, and get a personalized Study Plan that tells you which concepts you understand and which ones you need to review. From there, MyEconLab will give you further practice, tutorials, animations, videos, and guided solutions. For more information, visit www.myeconlab.com

PROBLEMS

All problems are assignable in MyEconLab. Answers to odd-numbered problems appear at the back of the book.

6-1. Classify each of the following as either a stock or a flow. (See page 135.)

   a. Myung Park earns $850 per week.

   b. Time Warner purchases $100 million in new telecomunications equipment this month.

   c. Sally Schmidt has $1,000 in a savings account at a credit union.

   d. XYZ, Inc., produces 200 units of output per week.

   e. Giorgio Giannelli owns three private jets.

   f. Apple's production declines by 750 digital devices per month.

   g. Russia owes $25 billion to the International Monetary Fund.

6-2. Consider the table below when answering the following questions. For this hypothetical economy, the marginal propensity to save is constant at all levels of real GDP, and investment spending is autonomous. There is no government. (See pages 137–147.)

Real GDP	Consumption	Saving	Investment
$ 2,000	$2,200	$_____	$400
4,000	4,000	_____	_____
6,000	_____	_____	_____
8,000	_____	_____	_____
10,000	_____	_____	_____
12,000	_____	_____	_____

   a. Complete the table. What is the marginal propensity to save? What is the marginal propensity to consume?

   b. Draw a graph of the consumption function. Then add the investment function to obtain $C + I$.

   c. Under the graph of $C + I$, draw another graph showing the saving and investment curves. Note that the $C + I$ curve crosses the 45-degree reference line in the upper graph at the same level of real GDP where the saving and investment curves cross in the lower graph. (If not, redraw your graphs.) What is this level of real GDP?

   d. What is the numerical value of the multiplier?

   e. What is equilibrium real GDP without investment? What is the multiplier effect from the inclusion of investment?

   f. What is the average propensity to consume at equilibrium real GDP?

   g. If autonomous investment declines from $400 to $200, what happens to equilibrium real GDP?

6-3. Consider the table below when answering the following questions. For this economy, the marginal propensity to consume is constant at all levels of real GDP, and investment spending is autonomous. Equilibrium real GDP is equal to $8,000. There is no government. (See pages 137–147.)

Real GDP	Consumption	Saving	Investment
$ 2,000	$ 2,000	_____	_____
4,000	3,600	_____	_____
6,000	5,200	_____	_____
8,000	6,800	_____	_____
10,000	8,400	_____	_____
12,000	10,000	_____	_____

   a. Complete the table. What is the marginal propensity to consume? What is the marginal propensity to save?

   b. Draw a graph of the consumption function. Then add the investment function to obtain $C + I$.

   c. Under the graph of $C + I$, draw another graph showing the saving and investment curves. Does the $C + I$ curve cross the 45-degree reference line in the upper graph at the same level of real GDP where the saving and investment curves cross in the lower graph, at the equilibrium real GDP of $8,000? (If not, redraw your graphs.)

   d. What is the average propensity to save at equilibrium real GDP?

   e. If autonomous consumption were to rise by $100, what would happen to equilibrium real GDP?

6-4. Calculate the multiplier for the following cases. (See page 151.)

   a. MPS = 0.25

   b. MPC = $\frac{5}{6}$

   c. MPS = 0.125

   d. MPC = $\frac{6}{7}$

6-5. Given each of the following values for the multiplier, calculate both the MPC and the MPS. (See page 151.)

   a. 20

   b. 10

   c. 8

   d. 5

6-6. The marginal propensity to consume is equal to 0.80. An increase in household wealth causes autonomous consumption to rise by $10 billion. By how much will equilibrium real GDP increase at the current price level, other things being equal? (See page 151.)

6-7. Assume that the multiplier in a country is equal to 4 and that autonomous real consumption spending is $1 trillion. If current real GDP is $15 trillion, what is the current value of real consumption spending? (See page 151.)

6-8. The multiplier in a country is equal to 5, and households pay no taxes. At the current equilibrium real GDP of $14 trillion, total real consumption spending by households is $12 trillion. What is real autonomous consumption in this country? (See page 151.)

6-9. At an initial point on the aggregate demand curve, the price level is 125, and real GDP is $15 trillion. When the price level falls to a value of 120, total autonomous expenditures increase by $250 billion. The marginal propensity to consume is 0.75. What is the level of real GDP at the new point on the aggregate demand curve? (See pages 154–155.)

6-10. At an initial point on the aggregate demand curve, the price level is 100, and real GDP is $15 trillion. After the price level rises to 110, however, there is an upward movement along the aggregate demand curve, and real GDP declines to $14 trillion. If total planned spending declined by $200 billion in response to the increase in the price level, what is the marginal propensity to consume in this economy? (See pages 154–155.)

6-11. In an economy in which the multiplier has a value of 3, the price level has decreased from 115 to 110. As a consequence, there has been a movement along the aggregate demand curve from $15 trillion in real GDP to $15.9 trillion in real GDP. (See pages 154–155.)

a. What is the marginal propensity to save?

b. What was the amount of the change in planned expenditures generated by the decline in the price level?

6-12. Consider the diagram below, which applies to a nation with no government spending, taxes, and net exports. Use the information in the diagram to answer the following questions, and explain your answers. (See pages 137–147.)

a. What is the marginal propensity to save?

b. What is the present level of planned investment spending for the present period?

c. What is the equilibrium level of real GDP for the present period?

d. What is the equilibrium level of saving for the present period?

e. If planned investment spending for the present period increases by $25 billion, what will be the resulting *change* in equilibrium real GDP? What will be the new equilibrium level of real GDP if other things, including the price level, remain unchanged?

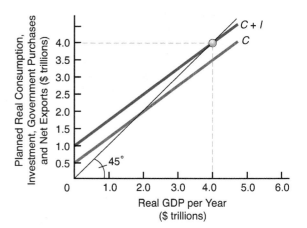

ECONOMICS ON THE NET

The Relationship between Consumption and Real GDP?
According to the basic consumption function we considered in this chapter, consumption rises at a fixed rate when both disposable income and real GDP increase. Your task here is to evaluate how reasonable this assumption is and to determine the relative extent to which variations in consumption appear to be related to variations in real GDP.

Title: Gross Domestic Product and Components

Navigation: Use the link at **www.econtoday.com/chap06** to visit the Federal Reserve Bank of St. Louis's Web page on *National Income and Product Accounts*. Then click on *Personal Income and Outlays*.

Application

1. Scan down the list, and click on *Real Personal Consumption Expenditures*. Then click on "Download Data." Write down consumption expenditures for the past eight quarters. Now back up to *National Income and Product*

Accounts, click on *Gross GDP/GNP* and then *Real Gross Domestic Product, 1 Decimal,* click on "Download Data," and write down GDP for the past eight quarters. Use these data to calculate implied values for the marginal propensity to consume, assuming that taxes do not vary with income. Is there any problem with this assumption?

2. Back up to *National Income and Product Accounts.* Select "Price Indexes & Deflators." Now click on *Gross Domestic Product: Implicit Price Deflator.* Scan

through the data since the mid-1960s. In what years did the largest variations in GDP take place? What component or components of GDP appear to have accounted for these large movements?

For Group Study and Analysis Assign groups to use the FRED database to try to determine the best measure of aggregate U.S. disposable income for the past eight quarters. Reconvene as a class, and discuss each group's approach to this issue.

ANSWERS TO QUICK QUIZZES

p. 136: (i) horizontal; (ii) Saving . . . Savings; (iii) Investment

p. 142: (i) disposable income . . . consumption; (ii) average . . . average; (iii) marginal . . . marginal; (iv) movement along . . . shift in

p. 144: (i) interest rate . . . downward; (ii) expectations . . . business taxes; (iii) shift in

p. 147: (i) autonomous . . . autonomous; (ii) autonomous; (iii) equilibrium; (iv) increases . . . decreases

p. 150: (i) planned expenditures; (ii) 45-degree; (iii) decreases . . . increases

p. 155: (i) multiplier; (ii) marginal . . . save; (iii) save . . . consume; (iv) change

APPENDIX A

The Keynesian Model and the Multiplier

We can see the multiplier effect more clearly if we look at Figure A-1 below, in which we see only a small section of the graphs that we used in Chapter 6. We start with equilibrium real GDP of $14.5 trillion per year. This equilibrium occurs with total planned real expenditures represented by $C + I + G + X$. The $C + I + G + X$ curve intersects the 45-degree reference line at $14.5 trillion per year. Now we increase real investment, I, by $100 billion. This increase in investment shifts the entire $C + I + G + X$ curve vertically to $C + I' + G + X$. The vertical shift represents that $100 billion increase in autonomous investment. With the higher level of planned expenditures per year, we are no longer in equilibrium at E. Inventories are falling. Production of goods and services will increase as firms try to replenish their inventories.

Eventually, real GDP will catch up with total planned expenditures. The new equilibrium level of real GDP is established at E' at the intersection of the new $C + I' + G + X$ curve and the 45-degree reference line, along which $C + I + G + X = Y$ (total planned expenditures equal real GDP). The new equilibrium level of real GDP is $15 trillion per year. Thus, the increase in equilibrium real GDP is equal to five times the permanent increase in planned investment spending.

FIGURE A-1

Graphing the Multiplier

We can translate Table 6-3 on page 151 into graphic form by looking at each successive round of additional spending induced by an autonomous increase in planned investment of $100 billion. The total planned expenditures curve shifts from $C + I + G + X$, with its associated equilibrium level of real GDP of $14.5 trillion, to a new curve labeled $C + I' + G + X$. The new equilibrium level of real GDP is $15 trillion. Equilibrium is again established.

Savings, Investment, and the Financial System

7

LEARNING OBJECTIVES

After reading this chapter, you should be able to:

▶ Explain how firms raise the funds they need to operate and expand

▶ Discuss the role of the financial system in facilitating long-run economic growth

▶ Understand the concept of present value and the information contained on a firm's income statement and balance sheet

MyEconLab helps you master each objective and study more efficiently. See end of chapter ack of flows of payments across a country's borders.

In this chapter, we look at firms: how they are organized, how they raise funds, and the information they provide to investors. As we have discussed in earlier chapters, firms in a market system are responsible for organizing the factors of production to produce goods and services. Firms are the vehicles entrepreneurs use to earn profits. To succeed, entrepreneurs must meet consumers' wants by producing new or better goods and services or by finding ways of producing existing goods and services at a lower cost so they can be sold at a lower price. Entrepreneurs also need access to sufficient funds, and they must be able to efficiently organize production. As the typical firm in many industries has become larger over the past 100 years, the task of efficiently organizing production has become more difficult. In the final section of this chapter, we look at problems of corporate governance that have occurred in recent years. We also look at the steps firms and the government have taken to avoid similar problems in the future.

How Firms Raise Funds

Owners and managers of firms try to earn a profit. To earn a profit, a firm must raise funds to pay for its operations, including paying its employees and buying or renting computers and other machinery and equipment. Indeed, a central challenge for anyone running a firm, whether that person is a sole proprietor or a top manager of a large corporation, is raising the funds needed to operate and expand the business. Suppose you decide to open an online social networking site, using $100,000 you have saved in a bank.

You use the $100,000 to rent a building for your firm, to buy computers, and to pay other start-up expenses. Your firm is a great success, and you decide to expand by moving to a larger building and buying more computers. As the owner of a small business, you can raise the funds for this expansion in three ways:

1. If you are making a profit, you could reinvest the profits back into your firm. Profits that are reinvested in a firm rather than taken out of a firm and paid to the firm's owners are *retained earnings*.

2. You could raise funds by recruiting additional owners to invest in the firm. This arrangement would increase the firm's *financial capital*.

3. Finally, you could borrow the funds from relatives, friends, or a bank.

   The managers of a large public firm have some additional ways to raise funds, as we will see in the next section.

Sources of External Funds

Unless firms rely on retained earnings, they have to raise the *external funds* they need from others who have funds available to invest. It is the role of an economy's *financial system* to transfer funds from savers to borrowers—directly through financial markets or indirectly through financial intermediaries such as banks.

Most firms raise external funds in two ways. The first way relies on financial intermediaries such as banks and is called **indirect finance**. If you put $1,000 in a checking account or a savings account, or if you put money in a $1,000 certificate of deposit (CD), the bank will loan most of those funds to borrowers. The bank will combine your funds with those of other depositors and, for example, make a $100,000 loan to a local business. Small businesses rely heavily on bank loans as their primary source of external funds.

A second way for firms to acquire external funds is through *financial markets*. Raising funds in these markets, such as the New York Stock Exchange on Wall Street in New York, is called **direct finance**. Direct finance usually takes the form of the borrower selling the lender a *financial security*. A financial security is a document—sometimes in electronic form—that states the terms under which the funds have passed from the buyer of the security (who is lending funds) to the borrower. *Bonds* and *stocks* are the two main types of financial securities. Typically, only large corporations are able to sell bonds and stocks on financial markets. Investors are generally unwilling to buy securities issued by small and medium-sized firms because the investors lack sufficient information on the financial health of smaller firms.

BONDS Bonds are financial securities that represent promises to repay a fixed amount of funds. When General Electric (GE) sells a bond to raise funds, it promises to pay the purchaser of the bond an interest payment each year for the term of the bond, as well as a final payment of the amount of the loan, or the *principal*, at the end of the term. GE may need to raise many millions of dollars to build a factory, but each

---

Indirect finance
A flow of funds from savers to borrowers through financial intermediaries such as banks. Intermediaries raise funds from savers to lend to firms (and other borrowers).

Direct finance
A flow of funds from savers to firms through financial markets, such as the New York Stock Exchange.

Bond
A financial security that represents a promise to repay a fixed amount of funds.

individual bond has a principal, or face value, of $1,000, which is the amount each bond purchaser is lending GE. So, GE must sell many bonds to raise all the funds it needs. Suppose GE promises it will pay interest of $60 per year to anyone who buys one of its bonds. The interest payments on a bond are referred to as **coupon payments.** The **interest rate** is the cost of borrowing funds, usually expressed as a percentage of the amount borrowed. If we express the coupon as a percentage of the face value of the bond, we find the interest rate on the bond, called the coupon rate. In this case, the interest rate is:

Coupon payment
An interest payment on a bond.

Interest rate
The cost of borrowing funds, usually expressed as a percentage of the amount borrowed.

$$\frac{\$60}{\$1,000} = 0.06, \text{ or } 6\%.$$

Many bonds that corporations issue have terms, or *maturities*, of 30 years. In this example, if you bought a bond from GE, GE would pay you $60 per year for 30 years, and at the end of the thirtieth year, GE would repay the $1,000 principal to you.

The interest rate that a borrower selling a bond has to pay depends on how likely bond buyers—investors—think that the bond seller is to default, or not make the promised coupon or principal payments. The higher the *default risk* on a bond, the higher the interest rate. For example, investors see the federal government as being very unlikely to default on its bonds, so federal government bonds pay a lower interest rate than do bonds of a firm such as GE. In turn, GE pays a lower interest rate on its bonds than does a corporation that investors believe is not as likely to make its bond payments.

MAKING THE CONNECTION

The Rating Game: Is the U.S. Treasury Likely to Default on Its Bonds?

Federal regulations require that before they can sell bonds to investors, firms and governments must first have bonds rated by one of the credit rating agencies. The three largest rating agencies are Moody's Investors Service, Standard & Poor's Corporation, and Fitch Ratings. These private firms rate bonds by giving them letter grades—AAA or Aaa being the highest—that reflect the probability that the firm or government will be able to make the payments on the bond. The following table shows the ratings:

	Moody's Investors Service	Standard & Poor's (S&P)	Fitch Ratings	Meaning of the Ratings
Investment-grade bonds	Aaa	AAA	AAA	Highest credit quality
	Aa	AA	AA	Very high credit quality
	A	A	A	High credit quality
	Baa	BBB	BBB	Good credit quality
Non-investment-grade bonds	Ba	BB	BB	Speculative
	B	B	B	Highly speculative
	Caa	CCC	CCC	Substantial default risk
	Ca	CC	CC	Very high levels of default risk
				Exceptionally high levels of default risk
	C	C	C	Default
	—	D	D	

Note: The entries in the "Meaning of the Ratings" column are slightly modified from those that Fitch uses. The other two rating agencies have similar descriptions. For each rating from Aa to Caa, Moody's adds a numerical modifier of 1, 2, or 3. The rating Aa1 is higher than the rating Aa2, and the rating Aa2 is higher than the rating Aa3. Similarly, Standard & Poor's and Fitch Ratings add a plus (+) or minus (−) sign. The rating AA+ is higher than the rating AA, and the rating AA is higher than the rating AA−.

Source: *Money, Banking, and the Financial System* 1st edition by R. Glenn Hubbard and Anthony P. O'Brien. Copyright © 2012 by Pearson Education, Inc. Reprinted and Electronically reproduced by permission of Pearson Education, Inc., Upper Saddle River, New Jersey.

Investors can use the ratings in deciding how much risk they are willing to take on when buying a bond. Generally, the lower the rating, the higher the interest rate an investor will receive, but also the higher the risk that the issuer of the bond will default.

The ratings agencies charge firms and governments—rather than investors—for their services. This arrangement raises the question of whether rating agencies face a conflict of interest. Because firms issuing bonds can choose which of the agencies to hire to rate their bonds, the agencies may have an incentive to give higher ratings than might be justified in order to keep the firms' business. During the housing boom of the mid-2000s, some financial firms issued *mortgage-backed bonds*. These bonds were similar to regular corporate bonds except that the interest payments came from mortgage loans people had taken out to buy houses. The money from those mortgage payments was passed along to investors who had bought the mortgage-backed bonds. The rating agencies gave many of these bonds AAA ratings, even though when housing prices began to decline in 2006, the issuers of many of these bonds defaulted on them. Some economists and policymakers believe the rating agencies provided the high ratings primarily to ensure that the firms that issued them would continue to hire them.

Standard & Poor's (S&P) became involved in another controversy in August 2011, when it downgraded U.S. Treasury bonds from AAA to AA+. This was the first time since the rating agencies had begun rating Treasury bonds that any of them had given Treasury bonds less than a AAA rating. The reason for the rating downgrade was the state of the federal government's budget deficit. Whenever the federal government runs a budget deficit, the Treasury must borrow an amount equal to the deficit by issuing bonds. In 2011, the federal government was spending much more than it was collecting in taxes, resulting in a large budget deficit. The budget deficit reflected the lower tax receipts and increased government spending resulting from the 2007–2009 economic recession. But forecasts from the U.S. Congressional Budget Office indicated that even after the effects of the recession had disappeared, large budget deficits would remain because spending on Social Security, Medicare, Medicaid, and other government programs were expected to increase faster than tax revenues. When prolonged negotiations between President Barack Obama and Congress failed to make much of a dent in the problem, S&P announced the rating downgrade. In the days following the announcement, interest rates on Treasury bonds actually fell rather than rising, as might have been expected if investors had believed that a default was possible.

So, is it likely that the U.S. Treasury will default on its bonds? S&P argued that while a default is still unlikely, the continuing large deficits increased the chance that someday the Treasury might not make the interest payments on its bonds. Like the Ghost of Christmas Yet to Come in Charles Dickens's *A Christmas Carol,* S&P was giving a warning of something that might happen rather than something that necessarily must happen.

Based on Tom Lauricella, Matt Phillips and Serena Ng, "Markets Brace for Downgrade's Toll," Wall Street Journal, August 8, 2011; and Andrew Ross Sorkin, "S.E.C. Urges Changes to Ratings-Agency Rules," New York Times, August, 29, 2010.

Stock
A financial security that represents partial ownership of a firm.

STOCKS When you buy a newly issued bond from a firm, you are lending funds to that firm. When you buy **stock** issued by a firm, you are actually buying part ownership of the firm. When a corporation sells stock, it is doing the same thing the owner of a small business does when she takes on a partner: The firm is increasing its financial capital by bringing additional owners into the firm. Any individual shareholder usually owns only a small fraction of the total shares of stock issued by a corporation.

Dividends
Payments by a corporation to its shareholders.

A shareholder is entitled to a share of the corporation's profits, if there are any. Corporations generally keep some of their profits—known as retained earnings—to finance future expansion. The remaining profits are paid to shareholders as **dividends**. Investors hope that a firm will earn economic profits by using its retained earnings to grow, causing the firm's share price to rise, and providing a *capital gain* for investors. If a corporation is unable to make a profit, it usually does not pay a dividend. Under the law, corporations must make payments on any debt they have before making payments to their owners. That is, a corporation must make promised payments to bondholders before it can make any dividend payments to shareholders. In addition, when firms sell stock, they acquire from investors an open-ended commitment of funds to the firm.

Unlike bonds, stocks do not have a maturity date, so the firm is not obliged to return the investor's funds at any particular date.

Stock and Bond Markets Provide Capital—and Information

The original purchasers of stocks and bonds may resell them to other investors. In fact, most of the buying and selling of stocks and bonds that takes place each day involves investors reselling existing stocks and bonds to each other rather than corporations selling new stocks and bonds to investors. The buyers and sellers of stocks and bonds together make up the *stock and bond markets*. There is no single place where stocks and bonds are bought and sold. Some trading of stocks and bonds takes place in buildings known as *exchanges*, such as the New York Stock Exchange or the Tokyo Stock Exchange. In the United States, the stocks and bonds of the largest corporations are traded on the New York Stock Exchange. The development of computer technology has spread the trading of stocks and bonds outside exchanges to *securities dealers* linked by computers. These dealers comprise the *over-the-counter market*. The stocks of many computer and other high-technology firms—including Apple, Google, and Microsoft—are traded in the most important of the over-the-counter markets, the *National Association of Securities Dealers Automated Quotations* system, which is referred to by its acronym, NASDAQ.

Shares of stock represent claims on the profits of the firms that issue them. Therefore, as the fortunes of the firms change and they earn more or less profit, the prices of the stock the firms have issued should also change. Similarly, bonds represent claims to receive coupon payments and one final payment of principal. Therefore, a particular bond that was issued in the past may have its price go up or down, depending on whether the coupon payments being offered on newly issued bonds are higher or lower than on existing bonds. If you hold a bond with a coupon of $40 per year, and newly issued bonds have coupons of $50 per year, the price of your bond will fall because it is less attractive to investors. The price of a bond will also be affected by changes in default risk, or the investors' perceptions of the issuing firm's ability to make the coupon payments. For example, if investors begin to believe that a firm may soon go out of business and stop making coupon payments to its bondholders, the price of the firm's bonds will fall to very low levels.

Changes in the value of a firm's stocks and bonds offer important information for a firm's managers, as well as for investors. An increase in the stock price means that investors are more optimistic about the firm's profit prospects, and the firm's managers might want to expand the firm's operations as a result. By contrast, a decrease in the firm's stock price indicates that investors are less optimistic about the firm's profit prospects, so management may want to shrink the firm's operations. Likewise, changes in the value of the firm's bonds imply changes in the cost of external funds to finance the firm's investment in research and development or in new factories. A higher bond price indicates a lower cost of new external funds, while a lower bond price indicates a higher cost of new external funds.

DON'T LET THIS HAPPEN TO YOU!

When Google Shares Change Hands, Google Doesn't Get the Money

Google is a popular investment, with investors buying and selling shares often as their views about the value of the firm shift. That's great for Google, right? Think of all that money flowing into Google's coffers as shares change hands and the stock price goes up. *Wrong*. Google raises funds in a primary market, but shares change hands in a secondary market. Those trades don't put money into Google's hands, but they do give important information to the firm's managers. Let's see why.

Primary markets are those in which newly issued claims are sold to initial buyers by the issuer. Businesses can raise funds in a primary financial market in two ways—by borrowing (selling bonds) or by selling shares of stock—which result in different types of claims on the borrowing firm's future income. Although you may hear about the stock market fluctuations every day in news updates, bonds actually account for more of the funds raised by borrowers. The total value of bonds in the United States is typically about twice the value of stocks.

In *secondary markets*, stocks and bonds that have already been issued are sold by one investor to another. If Google sells shares to the public, it is turning to a primary market for new funds. Once Google shares are issued, investors trade the shares in the secondary market. Google does not receive any new funds when Google shares are traded on secondary markets. The initial seller of a stock or bond raises funds from a lender only in the primary market. Secondary markets convey information to firms' managers and to investors by determining the price of stocks and bonds. For example, a major increase in Google's stock price conveys the market's good feelings about the firm, and the firm may decide to raise funds to expand. So, secondary markets are valuable sources of information for corporations that are considering raising funds.

Primary and secondary markets are both important, but they play different roles. As an investor, you principally trade stocks and bonds in a secondary market. As a corporate manager, you may help decide how to raise new funds to expand the firm where you work.

Why Do Stock Prices Fluctuate So Much?

The performance of the U.S. stock market is often measured using *stock market indexes*. Stock market indexes are averages of stock prices with the value of the index set equal to 100 in a particular year, called the *base year*. Because the stock indexes are intended to show movements in prices from one year to the next, rather than the actual dollar values of the underlying stocks, the year chosen for the base year is unimportant. Figure 7-1 shows movements from January 1995 to September 2011 in the three most widely followed stock indexes:

- The Dow Jones Industrial Average, which is an index of the stock prices of 30 large U.S. corporations.

- The S&P 500, which is an index prepared by Standard & Poor's Corporation and includes the stock prices of 500 large U.S. firms.

- The NASDAQ Composite Index, which includes the stock prices of the more than 4,000 firms whose shares are traded in the NASDAQ stock market. NAS-DAQ is an "over-the-counter" market, meaning that buying and selling on NAS-DAQ is carried out between dealers who are linked together by computer. The listings on NASDAQ are dominated by high-tech firms such as Apple, Microsoft, and Google.

As we have seen, ownership of a firm's stock represents a claim on the firm's profits. So, the larger the firm's profits are, the higher its stock price will be. When the overall economy is expanding, incomes, employment, and spending will all increase, as will corporate profits. When the economy is in a recession, incomes, employment, and spending will fall, as will corporate profits. We would expect that stock prices will rise when the economy is expanding and fall when the economy is in recession. We see this pattern reflected in the three stock market indexes in Figure 7-1. All three indexes follow a roughly similar pattern: Increases in stock prices during the economic expansion of the late 1990s, declines after the "dot-com crash" of 2000 and the recession of 2001, increases from late 2001 to late 2007, declines as the U.S. economy entered a recession at the end of 2007, and then increases beginning in early 2009.

The stock prices of many early Internet companies soared in the late 1990s, as some analysts made what turned out to be overly optimistic predictions about how rapidly online retailing would grow. In 2000, when investors came to believe that many dot-

FIGURE 7-1

Movements in Stock Market Indexes, January 1995 to September 2011

The performance of the U.S. stock market is often measured by market indexes, which are averages of stock prices. The three most important indexes are the Dow Jones Industrial Average, the S&P 500, and the NASDAQ. During the period from 1995 to 2011, the three indexes followed similar patterns, rising when the U.S. economy was expanding and falling when the economy was in recession.

(a) Dow Jones Industrial Average   (b) S&P 500   (c) NASDAQ

MAKING THE CONNECTION

Following Abercrombie & Fitch's Stock Price in the Financial Pages

If you read the online stock listings on the *Wall Street Journal's web site* or on another site, you will notice that the listings pack into a small space a lot of information about what happened to stocks during the previous day's trading. The figure on the next page reproduces a small portion of the listings from the *Wall Street Journal* from August 9, 2011, for stocks listed on the New York Stock Exchange. The listings provide information on the buying and selling of the stock of five firms during the previous day. Let's focus on the highlighted listing for Abercrombie & Fitch, the clothing store, and examine the information in each column:

- The first column gives the name of the company.
- The second column gives the firm's "ticker" symbol (ANF), which you may have seen scrolling along the bottom of the screen on cable financial news channels.
- The third column (Open) gives the price (in dollars) of the stock at the time that trading began, which is 9:30 A.M. on the New York Stock Exchange. Abercrombie & Fitch opened for trading at a price of $67.85.
- The fourth column (High) and the fifth column (Low) give the highest price and the lowest price the stock sold for during the day.
- The sixth column (Close) gives the price the stock sold for the last time it was traded before the close of trading (4:00 P.M.), which in this case was $61.05.
- The seventh column (Net Chg) gives the amount by which the closing price changed from the closing price the day before. In this case, the price of Abercrombie & Fitch's stock had fallen by $9.25 per share from its closing price the day before. Changes in Abercrombie & Fitch's stock price give the firm's managers a signal that they may want to expand or contract the firm's operations.
- The eighth column (%Chg) gives the change in the price in percentage terms rather than in dollar terms.

- The ninth column (Vol) gives the number of shares of stock traded on the previous day.
- The tenth column (52 Week High) and the eleventh column (52 Week Low) give the highest price the stock has sold for and the lowest price the stock has sold for during the previous year. These numbers tell how *volatile* the stock price is—that is, how much it fluctuates over the course of the year. In this case, Abercrombie's stock had been quite volatile, rising as high as $78.25 per share and falling as low as $33.97 per share. These large fluctuations in price are an indication of how risky investing in the stock market can be.
- The twelfth column (Div) gives the dividend, expressed in dollars. In this case, 0.70 means that Abercrombie paid a dividend of $0.70 per share.
- The thirteenth column (Yield) gives the *dividend yield,* which is calculated by dividing the dividend by the *closing price* of the stock—that is, the price at which Abercrombie's stock last sold before the close of trading on the previous day.
- The fourteenth column (PE) gives the *P-E ratio* (or *price–earnings ratio*), which is calculated by dividing the price of the firm's stock by its earnings per share. (Remember that because firms retain some earnings, earnings per share is not necessarily the same as dividends per share.) Abercrombie's P-E ratio was 37, meaning that its price per share was 37 times its earnings per share. So, you would have to pay $37 to buy $1 of Abercrombie & Fitch's earnings.
- The final column (Year-To-Date %Chg) gives the percentage change in the price of the stock from the beginning of the year to the previous day. In this case, the price of Abercrombie's stock had fallen by 5.9 percent since the beginning of 2011.

	Symbol	Open	High	Low	Close	Net Chg	%Chg	Vol	52 Week High	52 Week Low	Div	Yield	PE	Year-To-Date %Chg
ABB ADS	ABB	20.60	20.89	19.59	19.59	-2.00	-9.26	7,134,463	27.58	18.53	0.64	3.3	16	-12.7
ABBOTT LABORATORIES	ABT	49.30	50.13	47.56	48.06	-2.17	-4.32	18,398,789	54.24	45.07	1.92	4.0	17	0.3
ABERCROMBIE & FITCH CO.	ANF	67.85	68.93	58.84	61.05	-9.25	-13.16	6,891,113	78.25	33.97	0.70	1.15	37	-5.9
ABITIBIBOWATER	ABH	16.11	16.18	15.58	15.72	-0.96	-5.76	1,703,003	30.54	15.58	...	...	...	-33.6
ABM INDUSTRIES	ABM	19.79	20.72	17.29	17.29	-3.34	-16.19	1,762,427	27.14	17.29	0.56	3.2	16	-34.26

Source: "Abercrombie and Fitch Stock History" from The Wall Street Journal. Copyright © 2011 by Dow Jones & Company, Inc. Reproduced with permission of Dow Jones & Company, Inc.

coms would never be profitable, their stock prices crashed. Because the NASDAQ is dominated by high-tech stocks, it experienced greater swings during the dot-com boom and bust of the late 1990s and early 2000s than did the other two indexes. The sharp declines in all three indexes beginning in late 2007 reflected the severity of the recession that began in December of that year. The severity of the recession was due in part to problems with financial firms.

Saving, Investment, and the Financial System

The process of economic growth depends on the ability of firms to expand their operations, buy additional equipment, train workers, and adopt new technologies. Firms can finance some of these activities from *retained earnings*, which are profits that are reinvested in the firm rather than paid to the firm's owners. For many firms, retained earnings are not sufficient to finance the rapid expansion required in economies experiencing high rates of economic growth. Firms can acquire funds from households, either directly through financial markets—such as the stock and bond markets—or indirectly through financial intermediaries—such as banks. Financial markets and financial intermediaries together comprise the **financial system.** Without a well-functioning financial system, economic growth is impossible because firms will be unable to expand and adopt new technologies. As we noted earlier, no country without a well-developed financial system has been able to sustain high levels of economic growth.

Financial system
The system of financial markets and financial intermediaries through which firms acquire funds from households.

An Overview of the Financial System

The financial system channels funds from savers to borrowers and channels returns on the borrowed funds back to savers. In **financial markets**, such as the stock market or the bond market, firms raise funds by selling financial securities directly to savers. A *financial security* is a document—sometimes in electronic form—that states the terms under which funds pass from the buyer of the security—who is providing funds—to the seller. *Stocks* are financial securities that represent partial ownership of a firm. If you buy one share of stock in General Electric, you become one of millions of owners of that firm. *Bonds* are financial securities that represent promises to repay a fixed amount of funds. When General Electric sells a bond, the firm promises to pay the purchaser of the bond an interest payment each year for the term of the bond, as well as a final payment of the amount of the loan.

Financial markets
Markets where financial securities, such as stocks and bonds, are bought and sold.

Financial intermediaries, such as banks, mutual funds, pension funds, and insurance companies, act as go-betweens for borrowers and lenders. In effect, financial intermediaries borrow funds from savers and lend them to borrowers. When you deposit funds in your checking account, you are lending your funds to the bank. The bank may lend your funds (together with the funds of other savers) to an entrepreneur who wants to start a business. Suppose Lena wants to open a laundry. Rather than you lending money directly to Lena's Laundry, the bank acts as a go-between for you and Lena. Intermediaries pool the funds of many small savers to lend to many individual borrowers. The intermediaries pay interest to savers in exchange for the use of savers' funds and earn a profit by lending money to borrowers and charging borrowers a higher rate of interest on the loans. For example, a bank might pay you as a depositor a 3 percent rate of interest, while it lends the money to Lena's Laundry at a 6 percent rate of interest.

Financial intermediaries
Firms, such as banks, mutual funds, pension funds, and insurance companies, that borrow funds from savers and lend them to borrowers.

Banks, mutual funds, pension funds, and insurance companies also make investments in stocks and bonds on behalf of savers. For example, *mutual funds* sell shares to savers and then use the funds to buy a portfolio of stocks, bonds, mortgages, and other financial securities. Large mutual fund companies, such as Fidelity, Vanguard, and Dreyfus, offer many stock and bond funds. Some funds hold a wide range of stocks or bonds; others specialize in securities issued by a particular industry or sector, such as technology; and others invest as index funds in fixed market baskets of securities, such as shares of the

Standard & Poor's 500 firms. Over the past 30 years, the role of mutual funds in the financial system has increased dramatically. Today, competition among hundreds of mutual fund firms gives investors thousands of funds from which to choose.

In addition to matching households that have excess funds with firms that want to borrow funds, the financial system provides three key services for savers and borrowers: risk sharing, liquidity, and information. *Risk* is the chance that the value of a financial security will change relative to what you expect. For example, you may buy a share of stock in Google at a price of $450, only to have the price fall to $100. Most individual savers are not gamblers and seek a steady return on their savings rather than erratic swings between high and low earnings. The financial system provides risk sharing by allowing savers to spread their money among many financial investments. For example, you can divide your money among a bank certificate of deposit, individual bonds, and a mutual fund.

Liquidity is the ease with which a financial security can be exchanged for money. The financial system provides the service of liquidity by providing savers with markets in which they can sell their holdings of financial securities. For example, savers can easily sell their holdings of the stocks and bonds issued by large corporations on the major stock and bond markets.

A third service that the financial system provides savers is the collection and communication of *information*, or facts about borrowers and expectations about returns on financial securities. For example, Lena's Laundry may want to borrow $10,000 from you. Finding out what Lena intends to do with the funds and how likely she is to pay you back may be costly and time-consuming. By depositing $10,000 in the bank, you are, in effect, allowing the bank to gather this information for you. Because banks specialize in gathering information on borrowers, they are able to do it faster and at a lower cost than can individual savers. The financial system plays an important role in communicating information. If you read a news story announcing that an automobile firm has invented a car with an engine that runs on water, how would you determine the effect of that discovery on the firm's profits? Financial markets do the job for you by incorporating information into the prices of stocks, bonds, and other financial securities. In this example, the expectation of higher future profits would boost the prices of the automobile firm's stock and bonds.

The Macroeconomics of Saving and Investment

As we have seen, the funds available to firms through the financial system come from saving. When firms use funds to purchase machinery, factories, and office buildings, they are engaging in investment. In this section, we explore the macroeconomics of saving and investment. A key point we will develop is that *the total value of saving in the economy must equal the total value of investment. National income accounting* refers to the methods the Bureau of Economic Analysis uses to keep track of total production and total income in the economy. We can use some relationships from national income accounting to understand why total saving must equal total investment.

We begin with the relationship between GDP (Y) and its components, consumption (C), investment (I), government purchases (G), and net exports (NX):

$$Y = C + I + G + NX.$$

Remember that GDP is a measure of both total production in the economy and total income.

In an *open economy*, there is interaction with other economies in terms of both trading of goods and services and borrowing and lending. All economies today are open economies, although they vary significantly in the extent of their openness. In a *closed economy*, there is no trading or borrowing and lending with other economies. For simplicity, we will develop the relationship between saving and investment for a closed economy. This allows us to focus on the most important points in a simpler framework. We will consider the case of an open economy.

In a closed economy, net exports are zero, so we can rewrite the relationship between GDP and its components as

$$Y = C + I + G.$$

If we rearrange this relationship, we have an expression for investment in terms of the other variables:

$$I = Y - C - G.$$

This expression tells us that in a closed economy, investment spending is equal to total income minus consumption spending and minus government purchases.

We can also derive an expression for total saving. *Private saving* is equal to what households retain of their income after purchasing goods and services (C) and paying taxes (T). Households receive income for supplying the factors of production to firms. This portion of household income is equal to Y. Households also receive income from government in the form of *transfer payments* (TR). Recall that transfer payments include Social Security payments and unemployment insurance payments. We can write an expression for private saving ($S_{Private}$):

$$S_{Private} = Y + TR - C - T.$$

The government also engages in saving. *Public saving* (S_{Public}) equals the amount of tax revenue the government retains after paying for government purchases and making transfer payments to households:

$$S_{Public} = T - G - TR.$$

So, total saving in the economy (S) is equal to the sum of private saving and public saving:

$$S = S_{Private} + S_{Public},$$

or:

$$S = (Y + TR - C - T) + (T - G - TR),$$

or:

$$S = Y - C - G.$$

The right side of this expression is identical to the expression we derived earlier for investment spending. So, we can conclude that total saving must equal total investment:

$$S = I.$$

When the government spends the same amount that it collects in taxes, there is a *balanced budget*. When the government spends more than it collects in taxes, there is a *budget deficit*. In the case of a deficit, T is less than $G + TR$, which means that public saving is negative. Negative saving is also known as *dissaving*. How can public saving be negative? When the federal government runs a budget deficit, the U.S. Department of the Treasury sells Treasury bonds to borrow the money necessary to fund the gap between taxes and spending. In this case, rather than adding to the total amount of saving available to be borrowed for investment spending, the government is subtracting from it. (Notice that if households borrow more than they save, the total amount of saving will also fall.) With less saving, investment must also be lower. We can conclude that, holding constant all other factors, there is a lower level of investment spending in the economy when there is a budget deficit than when there is a balanced budget.

When the government spends less than it collects in taxes, there is a *budget surplus*. A budget surplus increases public saving and the total level of saving in the economy. A higher level of saving results in a higher level of investment spending. Therefore, holding constant all other factors, there is a higher level of investment spending in the economy when there is a budget surplus than when there is a balanced budget.

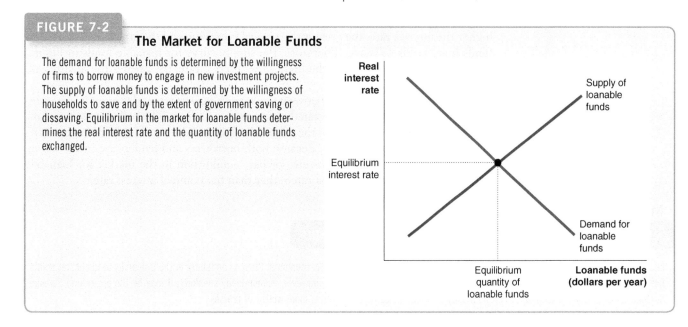

FIGURE 7-2

The Market for Loanable Funds

The demand for loanable funds is determined by the willingness of firms to borrow money to engage in new investment projects. The supply of loanable funds is determined by the willingness of households to save and by the extent of government saving or dissaving. Equilibrium in the market for loanable funds determines the real interest rate and the quantity of loanable funds exchanged.

The U.S. federal government has experienced dramatic swings in the state of its budget over the past 20 years. In 1992, the federal budget deficit was $297.4 billion. The federal budget had a surplus of $189.5 billion in 2000, but a dramatic decline in taxes and increase in government spending resulting from the recession of 2007–2009 led to record deficits of $1.4 trillion in 2009 and $1.5 trillion in 2010.

The Market for Loanable Funds

We have seen that the value of total saving must equal the value of total investment, but we have not yet discussed how this equality is actually brought about in the financial system. We can think of the financial system as being composed of many markets through which funds flow from lenders to borrowers: the market for certificates of deposit at banks, the market for stocks, the market for bonds, the market for mutual fund shares, and so on. For simplicity, we can combine these markets into a single market for *loanable funds*. In the model of the **market for loanable funds**, the interaction of borrowers and lenders determines the market interest rate and the quantity of loanable funds exchanged. Firms can also borrow from savers in other countries. For the remainder of this chapter, we will assume that there are no interactions between households and firms in the United States and those in other countries.

Market for loanable funds
The interaction of borrowers and lenders that determines the market interest rate and the quantity of loanable funds exchanged.

DEMAND AND SUPPLY IN THE LOANABLE FUNDS MARKET The demand for loanable funds is determined by the willingness of firms to borrow money to engage in new investment projects, such as building new factories or carrying out research and development of new products. In determining whether to borrow funds, firms compare the return they expect to make on an investment with the interest rate they must pay to borrow the necessary funds. For example, if Home Depot is considering opening several new stores and expects to earn a return of 15 percent on its investment, the investment will be profitable if Home Depot can borrow the funds at an interest rate of 10 percent but will not be profitable if the interest rate is 20 percent. In Figure 7-2, the demand for loanable funds is downward sloping because the lower the interest rate, the more investment projects firms can profitably undertake, and the greater the quantity of loanable funds they will demand.

The supply of loanable funds is determined by the willingness of households to save and by the extent of government saving or dissaving. When households save, they reduce the amount of goods and services they can consume and enjoy today. The willingness of households to save rather than consume their incomes today will be determined in part by the interest rate they receive when they lend their savings. The higher the interest rate, the greater the reward for saving and the larger the amount of funds households will save. Therefore, the supply curve for loanable funds in Figure 7-2 is upward sloping because the higher the interest rate, the greater the quantity of saving supplied.

We discussed the distinction between the *nominal interest rate* and the *real interest rate*. The nominal interest rate is the stated interest rate on a loan. The real interest rate corrects the nominal interest rate for the effect of inflation and is equal to the nominal interest rate minus the inflation rate. Because both borrowers and lenders are interested in the real interest rate they will receive or pay, equilibrium in the market for loanable funds determines the real interest rate rather than the nominal interest rate.

MAKING THE CONNECTION

Ebenezer Scrooge: Accidental Promoter of Economic Growth?

Ebenezer Scrooge's name has become synonymous with miserliness. Before his reform at the end of Charles Dickens's *A Christmas Carol*, Scrooge is extraordinarily reluctant to spend money. Although he earns a substantial income, he lives in a cold, dark house that he refuses to heat or light adequately, and he eats a meager diet of gruel because he refuses to buy more expensive food. Throughout most of the book, Dickens portrays Scrooge's behavior in an unfavorable way. Only at the end of the book, when the reformed Scrooge begins to spend lavishly on himself and others, does Dickens praise his behavior.

Who was better for economic growth: Scrooge the saver or Scrooge the spender?

As economist Steven Landsburg of the University of Rochester points out, however, economically speaking, it may be the pre-reform Scrooge who is more worthy of praise:

> In this whole world, there is nobody more generous than the miser—the man who could deplete the world's resources but chooses not to. The only difference between miserliness and philanthropy is that the philanthropist serves a favored few while the miser spreads his largess far and wide.

We can extend Landsburg's discussion to consider whether the actions of the pre-reform Scrooge or the actions of the post-reform Scrooge are more helpful to economic growth. Pre-reform Scrooge spends very little, investing most of his income in the financial markets. These funds became available for firms to borrow to build new factories and to carry out research and development. Post-reform Scrooge spends much more—and saves much less. Funds that he had previously saved are now spent on food for Bob Cratchit's family and on "making merry" at Christmas. In other words, the actions of post-reform Scrooge contribute to more consumption goods being produced and fewer investment goods. We can conclude that Scrooge's reform caused economic growth to slow down—if only by a little. The larger point is, of course, that savers provide the funds that are indispensable for the investment spending that economic growth requires, and the only way to save is to not consume.

From "What I Like About Scrooge," *Slate*, December 9, 2004.

EXPLAINING MOVEMENTS IN SAVING, INVESTMENT, AND INTEREST RATES Equilibrium in the market for loanable funds determines the quantity of loanable funds that will flow from lenders to borrowers each period. It also determines the real interest rate that lenders will receive and that borrowers must pay. We draw the demand curve for loanable funds by holding constant all factors, other than the interest rate, that affect the willingness of borrowers to demand funds. We draw the supply curve by holding constant all factors, other than the interest rate, that affect the willingness of lenders to supply funds. A shift in either the demand curve or the supply curve will change the equilibrium interest rate and the equilibrium quantity of loanable funds.

If, for example, the profitability of new investment increases due to technological change, firms will increase their demand for loanable funds. Figure 7-3 shows the effect of an increase in demand in the market for loanable funds. An increase in demand in the market for loanable funds shifts the demand curve to the right. In the new equi-

FIGURE 7-3

An Increase in the Demand for Loanable Funds

An increase in the demand for loanable funds increases the equilibrium interest rate from i_1 to i_2, and it increases the equilibrium quantity of loanable funds from L_1 to L_2. As a result, saving and investment both increase.

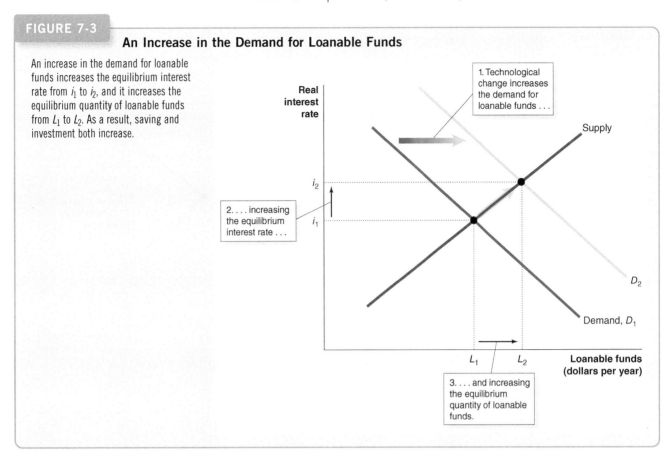

librium, the interest rate increases from i_1 to i_2, and the equilibrium quantity of loanable funds increases from L_1 to L_2. Notice that an increase in the quantity of loanable funds means that both the quantity of saving by households and the quantity of investment by firms have increased. Increasing investment increases the capital stock and the quantity of capital per hour worked, helping to increase economic growth.

We can also use the market for loanable funds to examine the effect of a government budget deficit. Putting aside the effects of foreign saving recall that if the government begins running a budget deficit, it reduces the total amount of saving in the economy. Suppose the government increases spending, which results in a budget deficit. We illustrate the effects of the budget deficit in Figure 7-4 by shifting the supply of loanable funds to the left. In the new equilibrium, the interest rate is higher, and the equilibrium quantity of loanable funds is lower. Running a deficit has reduced the level of total saving in the economy and, by increasing the interest rate, has also reduced the level of investment spending by firms. By borrowing to finance its budget deficit, the government will have *crowded out* some firms that would otherwise have been able to borrow to finance investment. **Crowding out** refers to a decline in investment spending as a result of an increase in government purchases. In Figure 7-4, the decline in investment spending due to crowding out is shown by the movement from L_1 to L_2 on the demand for loanable funds curve. Lower investment spending means that the capital stock and the quantity of capital per hour worked will not increase as much.

A government budget surplus has the opposite effect of a deficit: A budget surplus increases the total amount of saving in the economy, shifting the supply of loanable funds to the right. In the new equilibrium, the interest rate will be lower, and the quantity of loanable funds will be higher. We can conclude that a budget surplus increases the level of saving and investment.

Crowding out
A decline in private expenditures as a result of an increase in government purchases.

FIGURE 7-4

The Effect of a Budget Deficit on the Market for Loanable Funds

When the government begins running a budget deficit, the supply of loanable funds shifts to the left. The equilibrium interest rate increases from i_1 to i_2, and the equilibrium quantity of loanable funds falls from L_1 to L_2. As a result, saving and investment both decline.

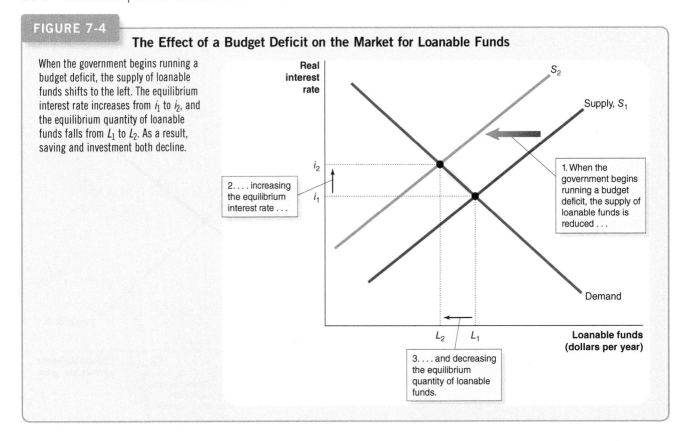

In practice, however, the effect of government budget deficits and surpluses on the equilibrium interest rate is relatively small. (This finding reflects in part the importance of global saving in determining the interest rate.) For example, a recent study found that increasing government borrowing by an amount equal to 1 percent of GDP would increase the equilibrium real interest rate by only about 0.003 percentage point. However, this small effect on interest rates does not imply that we can ignore the effect of deficits on economic growth. Paying off government debt in the future may require higher taxes, which can depress economic growth. In 2011, many economists and policymakers were concerned that the large deficits projected for future years might be an obstacle to growth.

APPENDIX B

Tools to Analyze Firms' Financial Information

As we saw in the chapter, modern business firms are not just "black boxes" transforming inputs into output. Most business revenues and profits are earned by large corporations. Unlike founder-dominated firms, the typical large corporation is run by managers who generally do not own a controlling interest in the firm. Large firms raise funds from outside investors, and outside investors seek information on firms and the assurance that the managers of firms will act in the interests of the investors.

This chapter shows how corporations raise funds by issuing stocks and bonds. This appendix provides more detail to support that discussion. We begin by analyzing *present value* as a key concept in determining the prices of financial securities. We then provide greater information on *financial statements* issued by corporations, using Google as an example.

Using Present Value to Make Investment Decisions

Firms raise funds by selling equity (stock) and debt (bonds and loans) to investors and lenders. If you own shares of stock or a bond, you will receive payments in the form of dividends or coupons over a number of years. Most people value funds they already have more highly than funds they will receive some time in the future. For example, you would probably not trade $1,000 you already have for $1,000 you will not receive for one year. The longer you have to wait to receive a payment, the less value it will have for you. One thousand dollars you will not receive for two years is worth less to you than $1,000 you will receive after one year. The value you give today to money you will receive in the future is called the future payment's **present value**. The present value of $1,000 you will receive in one year will be less than $1,000.

Why is this true? Why is the $1,000 you will not receive for one year less valuable to you than the $1,000 you already have? The most important reason is that if you have $1,000 today, you can use that $1,000 today. You can buy goods and services with the money and receive enjoyment from them. The $1,000 you receive in one year does not have direct use to you now.

Also, prices will likely rise during the year you are waiting to receive your $1,000. So, when you finally do receive the $1,000 in one year, you will not be able to buy as much with it as you could with $1,000 today. Finally, there is some risk that you will not receive the $1,000 in one year. The risk may be very great if an unreliable friend borrows $1,000 from you and vaguely promises to pay you back in one year. The risk may be very small if you lend money to the federal government by buying a U.S. Treasury bond. In either case, though, there is at least some risk that you will not receive the funds promised.

When someone lends money, the lender expects to be paid back both the amount of the loan and some additional interest. Say that you decide that you are willing to lend your $1,000 today if you are paid back $1,100 one year from now. In this case, you

Present value
The value in today's dollars of funds to be paid or received in the future.

are charging $\$100/\$1,000 = 0.10$, or 10 percent interest on the funds you have loaned. Economists would say that you value $\$1,000$ today as equivalent to the $\$1,100$ to be received one year in the future.

Notice that $\$1,100$ can be written as $\$1,000\,(1 + 0.10)$. That is, the value of money received in the future is equal to the value of money in the present multiplied by 1 plus the interest rate, with the interest rate expressed as a decimal. Or:

$$\$1,100 = \$1,000(1 + 0.10).$$

Notice, also, that if we divide both sides by $(1 + 0.10)$, we can rewrite this formula as:

$$\$1,000 = \frac{\$1,100}{(1 + 0.10)}.$$

The rewritten formula states that the present value is equal to the future value to be received in one year divided by 1 plus the interest rate. This formula is important because you can use it to convert any amount to be received in one year into its present value. Writing the formula generally, we have:

$$\text{Present value} = \frac{\text{Future value}_1}{(1 + i)}.$$

The present value of funds to be received in one year—Future value$_1$—can be calculated by dividing the amount of those funds to be received by 1 plus the interest rate. With an interest rate of 10 percent, the present value of $\$1,000,000$ to be received one year from now is:

$$\frac{\$1,000,000}{(1 + 0.10)} = \$909,090.91.$$

This method is a useful way of calculating the value today of funds that will be received in one year. But financial securities such as stocks and bonds involve promises to pay funds over many years. Therefore, it would be even more useful if we could expand this formula to calculate the present value of funds to be received more than one year in the future.

This expansion is easy to do. Go back to the original example, where we assumed you were willing to loan out your $\$1,000$ for one year, provided that you received 10 percent interest. Suppose you are asked to lend the funds for two years and that you are promised 10 percent interest per year for each year of the loan. That is, you are lending $\$1,000$, which at 10 percent interest will grow to $\$1,100$ after one year, and you are agreeing to loan that $\$1,100$ out for a second year at 10 percent interest. So, after two years, you will be paid back $\$1,100\,(1 + 0.10)$, or $\$1,210$. Or:

$$\$1,210 = \$1,000(1 + 0.10)(1 + 0.10),$$

or:

$$\$1,210 = \$1,000(1 + 0.10)^2.$$

This formula can also be rewritten as:

$$\$1,000 = \frac{\$1,210}{(1 + 0.10)^2}.$$

To put this formula in words, the $\$1,210$ you receive two years from now has a present value equal to $\$1,210$ divided by the quantity 1 plus the interest rate squared. If you agree to lend out your $\$1,000$ for three years at 10 percent interest, you will receive:

$$\$1,331 = \$1,000(1 + 0.10)^3.$$

Notice, again, that:

$$\$1,000 = \frac{\$1,331}{(1 + 0.10)^3}.$$

You can probably see a pattern here. We can generalize the concept to say that the present value of funds to be received n years in the future—whether n is 1, 20, or 85 does not matter—equals the amount of the funds to be received divided by the quantity 1 plus the interest rate raised to the nth power. For instance, with an interest rate of 10 percent, the value of $\$1,000,000$ to be received 25 years in the future is:

$$\text{Present value} = \frac{\$1,000,000}{(1 + 0.10)^{25}} = \$92,296.$$

Or, more generally:

$$\text{Present value} = \frac{\text{Future value}_n}{(1 + i)^n}$$

where Future value$_n$ represents funds that will be received in n years.

SOLVED PROBLEM 6A.1

HOW TO RECEIVE YOUR CONTEST WINNINGS

Suppose you win a contest and are given the choice of the following prizes:

Prize 1: $\$50,000$ to be received right away, with four additional payments of $\$50,000$ to be received each year for the next four years

Prize 2: $\$175,000$ to be received right away

Explain which prize you would choose and the basis for your decision.

Solving the Problem

Step 1: This problem involves applying the concept of present value, so you may want to review the section "Using Present Value to Make Investment Decisions," which begins on page 177.

Step 2: Unless you need cash immediately, you should choose the prize with the highest present value.

Step 3: Prize 2 consists of one payment of $\$175,000$ received right away, so its present value is $\$175,000$. Prize 1 consists of five payments spread out over time. To find the present value of the prize, we must find the present value of each of these payments and add them together. To calculate present value, we must use an interest rate. Let's assume an interest rate of 10 percent. In that case, the present value of Prize 1 is:

$$\$50,000 + \frac{\$50,000}{(1 + 0.10)} + \frac{\$50,000}{(1 + 0.10)^2} + \frac{\$50,000}{(1 + 0.10)^3} + \frac{\$50,000}{(1 + 0.10)^4} =$$

$$\$50,000 + \$45,454.55 + \$41,322.31 + \$37,565.74 + \$34,150.67 = \$208,493.$$

Step 4: Prize 1 has the greater present value, so you should choose it rather than Prize 2.

Using Present Value to Calculate Bond Prices

Anyone who buys a financial asset, such as shares of stock or a bond, is really buying a promise to receive certain payments—dividends in the case of shares of stock or coupons in the case of a bond. The price investors are willing to pay for a financial asset should be equal to the value of the payments they will receive as a result of owning the asset. Because most of the coupon or dividend payments will be received in the future, it is their present value that matters. Put another way, we have the following important idea: *The price of a financial asset should be equal to the present value of the payments to be received from owning that asset.*

Let's consider an example. Suppose that in 1982, General Electric issued a bond with an $80 coupon that will mature in 2012. It is now 2010, and that bond has been bought and sold by investors many times. You are considering buying it. If you buy the bond, you will receive two years of coupon payments plus a final payment of the bond's principal, or face value, of $1,000. Suppose, once again, that you need an interest rate of 10 percent to invest your funds. If the bond has a coupon of $80, the present value of the payments you receive from owning the bond—and, therefore, the present value of the bond—will be:

$$\text{Present value} = \frac{\$80}{(1 + 0.10)} + \frac{\$80}{(1 + 0.10)^2} + \frac{\$1,000}{(1 + 0.10)^2} = \$965.29.$$

That is, the present value of the bond will equal the present value of the three payments you will receive during the two years you own the bond. You should, therefore, be willing to pay $965.29 to own this bond and have the right to receive these payments from GE. This process of calculating present values of future payments is used to determine bond prices, with one qualification: The relevant interest rate used by investors in the bond market to calculate the present value and, therefore, the price of an existing bond is usually the coupon rate on comparable newly issued bonds. Therefore, the general formula for the price of a bond is:

$$\text{Bond price} = \frac{\text{Coupon}_1}{(1 + i)} + \frac{\text{Coupon}_2}{(1 + i)^2} + \ldots + \frac{\text{Coupon}_n}{(1 + i)^n} + \frac{\text{Face value}}{(1 + i)^n},$$

where Coupon_1 is the coupon payment to be received after one year, Coupon_2 is the coupon payment to be received after two years, up to Coupon_n, which is the coupon payment received in the year the bond matures. The ellipsis takes the place of the coupon payments—if any—received between the second year and the year when the bond matures. Face value is the amount that will be received when the bond matures. The interest rate on comparable newly issued bonds is i.

Using Present Value to Calculate Stock Prices

When you own a firm's stock, you are legally entitled to your share of the firm's profits. Remember that the profits a firm pays out to its shareholders are referred to as *dividends*. The price of a share of stock should be equal to the present value of the dividends investors expect to receive as a result of owning that stock. Therefore, the general formula for the price of a stock is:

$$\text{Stock price} = \frac{\text{Dividend}_1}{(1 + i)} + \frac{\text{Dividend}_2}{(1 + i)^2} + \ldots$$

Notice that this formula looks very similar to the one we used to calculate the price of a bond, with a couple important differences. First, unlike a bond, stock has no maturity date, so we have to calculate the present value of an infinite number of dividend payments. At first, it may seem that the stock's price must be infinite as well, but remember that dollars you don't receive for many years are worth very little today. For instance, a dividend payment of $10 that will be received 40 years in the future is worth only a little more than $0.20 today at a 10 percent interest rate. The second difference between the stock price formula and the bond price formula is that whereas the coupon payments you receive from owning the bond are known with certainty—they are written on the bond and cannot be changed—you don't know for sure what the dividend payments from owning a stock will be. How large a dividend payment you will receive depends on how profitable the company will be in the future.

Although it is possible to forecast the future profitability of a company, this cannot be done with perfect accuracy. To emphasize this point, some economists rewrite the basic stock price formula by adding a superscript *e* to each dividend term to emphasize that these are *expected* dividend payments. Because the future profitability of companies is often very difficult to forecast, it is not surprising that differences of opinion exist over what the price of a particular stock should be. Some investors will be very optimistic about the future profitability of a company and will, therefore, believe that the company's stock should have a high price. Other investors might be very pessimistic and believe that the company's stock should have a low price.

A Simple Formula for Calculating Stock Prices

It is possible to simplify the formula for determining the price of a stock, if we assume that dividends will grow at a constant rate:

$$\text{Stock price} = \frac{\text{Dividend}}{(i - \text{Growth rate})}.$$

In this equation, Dividend is the dividend expected to be received one year from now, and Growth rate is the rate at which those dividends are expected to grow. If a company pays a dividend of $1 per share to be received one year from now and Growth rate is 10 percent, the company is expected to pay a dividend of $1.10 the following year, $1.21 the year after that, and so on.

Now suppose that IBM will pay a dividend of $5 per share at the end of year, the consensus of investors is that these dividends will increase at a rate of 5 percent per year for the indefinite future, and the interest rate is 10 percent. Then the price of IBM's stock should be:

$$\text{Stock price} = \frac{\$5.00}{(0.10 - 0.05)} = \$100.00.$$

Particularly during the years 1999 and 2000, there was much discussion of whether the high prices of many Internet stocks—such as the stock of Amazon.com—were justified, given that many of these companies had not made any profit yet and so had not paid any dividends. Is there any way that a rational investor would pay a high price for the stock of a company currently not earning profits? The formula for determining stock prices shows that it is possible, provided that the investor's assumptions are optimistic enough! For example, during 1999, one stock analyst predicted that Amazon.com would soon be earning $10 per share of stock. That is, Amazon.com's total earnings divided by the number of shares of its stock outstanding would be $10. Suppose Amazon.com pays out that $10 in dividends and that the $10 will grow rapidly over the years, by, say, 7 percent per year. Then our formula indicates that the price of Amazon.com stock should be:

$$\text{Stock price} = \frac{\$10.00}{(0.10 - 0.07)} = \$333.33.$$

If you are sufficiently optimistic about the future prospects of a company, a high stock price can be justified even if the company is not currently earning a profit. But investors in growth stocks must be careful. Suppose investors believe that growth prospects for Amazon are only 4 percent per year instead of 7 percent because the firm turns out not to be as profitable as initially believed. Then our formula indicates that the price of Amazon.com stock should be:

$$\text{Stock price} = \frac{\$10.00}{(0.10 - 0.04)} = \$166.67.$$

This price is only half the price determined assuming a more optimistic growth rate. Hence investors use information about a firm's profitability and growth prospects to determine what the firm is worth.

Module 3

Fiscal Policy

Fiscal Policy

8

MyEconLab helps you master each objective and study more efficiently. See end of chapter for details.

In the midst of the sharp economic downturn of 2008–2009, Congress passed the American Recovery and Reinvestment Act (ARRA). The ARRA was meant to stimulate total planned expenditures via hundreds of billions of dollars of additional government spending. Hence, the media have tended to refer to the law as the "Stimulus Act." A large portion of the federal funds authorized by the ARRA went to state governments for spending at local levels. In fact, however, most estimates indicate that states used no more than 5 percent of the total ARRA funds they received to purchase final goods and services. What did the U.S. government hope to accomplish by adding hundreds of billions in additional spending to its budget? Why were so few of the funds distributed to state governments actually spent on goods and services? You will find out in this chapter.

DID YOU KNOW THAT... the U.S. government's American Recovery and Reinvestment Act of 2009 entailed a greater overall expenditure of funds than the eight-year-long Iraqi conflict? Military and other U.S. government spending related to the war effort in Iraq totaled $709 billion, or about 4.7 percent of the value of a typical year's output of goods and services. The 2009 "Stimulus Act," which was intended to boost economic activity and reduce the unemployment rate, authorized $862 billion in spending, or about 5.7 percent of the value of annual U.S. production. In this chapter, you will learn how variations in government spending and taxation affect both real GDP and the price level.

Discretionary Fiscal Policy

Fiscal policy
The discretionary changing of government expenditures or taxes to achieve national economic goals, such as high employment with price stability.

The making of deliberate, discretionary changes in federal government expenditures or taxes (or both) to achieve certain national economic goals is the realm of **fiscal policy.** Some national goals are high employment (low unemployment), price stability, and economic growth. Fiscal policy can be thought of as a deliberate attempt to cause the economy to move to full employment and price stability more quickly than it otherwise might.

Fiscal policy has typically been associated with the economic theories of John Maynard Keynes and what is now called *traditional* Keynesian analysis. Recall from Chapter 5 that Keynes's explanation of the Great Depression was that there was insufficient aggregate demand. Because he believed that wages and prices were "sticky downward," he argued that the classical economists' picture of an economy moving automatically and quickly toward full employment was inaccurate. To Keynes and his followers, government had to step in to increase aggregate demand. Expansionary fiscal policy initiated by the federal government was the preferred way to ward off recessions and depressions.

Changes in Government Spending

In Chapter 5, we looked at the recessionary gap and the inflationary gap (see Figures 5-9 and 5-10 on pages 117 and 118). The recessionary gap was defined as the amount by which the current level of real GDP falls short of the economy's *potential* production if it were operating on its *LRAS* curve. The inflationary gap was defined as the amount by which the short-run equilibrium level of real GDP exceeds the long-run equilibrium level as given by *LRAS*. Let us examine fiscal policy first in the context of a recessionary gap.

WHEN THERE IS A RECESSIONARY GAP The government, along with firms, individuals, and foreign residents, is one of the spending entities in the economy. When the government spends more, all other things held constant, the dollar value of total spending initially must rise. Look at panel (a) of Figure 8-1 on the facing page. We begin by assuming that some negative shock in the near past has left the economy at point E_1, which is a short-run equilibrium in which AD_1 intersects $SRAS$ at $14.5 trillion of real GDP per year. There is a recessionary gap of $500 billion of real GDP per year—the difference between $LRAS$ (the economy's long-run potential) and the short-run equilibrium level of real GDP per year.

When the government decides to spend more (expansionary fiscal policy), the aggregate demand curve shifts to the right to AD_2. Here we assume that the government knows exactly how much more to spend so that AD_2 intersects $SRAS$ at $15 trillion, or at $LRAS$. Because of the upward-sloping $SRAS$, the price level rises from 120 to 130 as real GDP goes to $15 trillion per year.

Did U.S. government purchases of old cars induce enough private spending on new vehicles to contribute to higher real GDP?

FIGURE 8-1

Expansionary and Contractionary Fiscal Policy: Changes in Government Spending

If there is a recessionary gap and short-run equilibrium is at E_1, in panel (a), fiscal policy can presumably increase aggregate demand to AD_2. The new equilibrium is at E_2 at higher real GDP per year and a higher price level. In panel (b), the economy is at short-run equilibrium at E_1, which is at a higher real GDP than the *LRAS*. To reduce this inflationary gap, fiscal policy can be used to decrease aggregate demand from AD_1 to AD_2. Eventually, equilibrium will fall to E_2, which is on the *LRAS*.

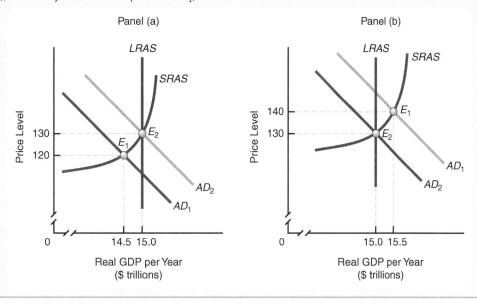

POLICY EXAMPLE

Net Real GDP Effect of "Cash-for-Clunkers" Spending: Zero

In 2009, the U.S. government offered $3,500 to $4,500 to people who surrendered used cars and bought new vehicles. Policymakers who promoted this "Cash-for-Clunkers" program at a $2.8 billion expense for taxpayers argued that it had two desirable effects. One was the removal of high-pollution vehicles from roads. The other was that consumers bought 450,000 new vehicles, which generated $12.6 billion in private expenditures that otherwise would not have taken place.

Adam Copeland and James Kahn, economists at the Federal Reserve Bank of Kansas City, have determined that many people delayed buying new vehicles until the Cash-for-Clunkers subsidies were available. Even more people bought vehicles earlier than originally planned. This meant that consumers responded to the program by shifting the *timing* of purchases of new vehicles they *already* intended to buy. Copeland and Kahn concluded that the real GDP impact of the program was zero. Hence, it was not a particularly effective fiscal policy program.

FOR CRITICAL THINKING

Why might any temporary government subsidy program mainly end up affecting the timing of spending instead of actually boosting overall planned expenditures?

WHEN THERE IS AN INFLATIONARY GAP The entire process shown above in panel (a) of Figure 8-1 can be reversed, as shown in panel (b). There, we assume that a recent shock has left the economy at point E_1, at which an inflationary gap exists at the intersection of *SRAS* and AD_1. Real GDP cannot be sustained at $15.5 trillion indefinitely, because this exceeds long-run aggregate supply, which in real terms is $15 trillion. If the government recognizes this and reduces its spending (pursues a contractionary fiscal policy), this action reduces aggregate demand from AD_1 to AD_2. Equilibrium will fall to E_2 on the *LRAS*, where real GDP per year is $15 trillion. The price level will fall from 140 to 130.

Changes in Taxes

The spending decisions of firms, individuals, and other countries' residents depend on the taxes levied on them. Individuals in their role as consumers look to their disposable (after-tax) income when determining their desired rates of consumption. Firms look at their after-tax

FIGURE 8-2

Expansionary and Contractionary Fiscal Policy: Changes in Taxes

In panel (a), the economy is initially at E_1, where real GDP is less than long-run equilibrium real GDP. Expansionary fiscal policy via a tax reduction can move aggregate demand to AD_2 so that the new equilibrium is at E_2 at a higher price level. Real GDP is now consistent with *LRAS*, which eliminates the recessionary gap. In panel (b), with an inflationary gap (in this case of $500 billion), taxes are increased. AD_1 moves to AD_2. The economy moves from E_1 to E_2, and real GDP is now at $15 trillion per year, the long-run equilibrium level.

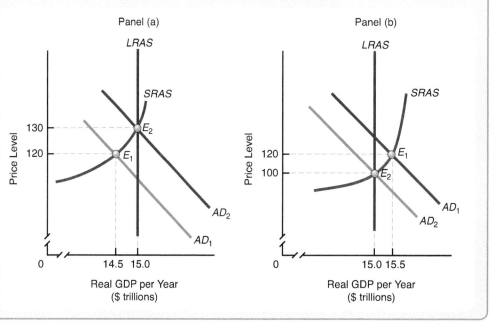

profits when deciding on the levels of investment per year to undertake. Foreign residents look at the tax-inclusive cost of goods when deciding whether to buy in the United States or elsewhere. Therefore, holding all other things constant, an increase in taxes causes a reduction in aggregate demand because it reduces consumption, investment, or net exports.

WHEN THE CURRENT SHORT-RUN EQUILIBRIUM IS TO THE LEFT OF *LRAS* Look at panel (a) in Figure 8-2. AD_1 intersects *SRAS* at E_1, with real GDP at $14.5 trillion, less than the *LRAS* of $15 trillion. In this situation, a decrease in taxes shifts the aggregate demand curve outward to the right. At AD_2, equilibrium is established at E_2, with the price level at 130 and equilibrium real GDP at $15 trillion per year.

WHEN THE CURRENT SHORT-RUN EQUILIBRIUM IS TO THE RIGHT OF *LRAS* Assume that aggregate demand is AD_1 in panel (b) of Figure 8-2 above. It intersects *SRAS* at E_1, which yields real GDP greater than *LRAS*. In this situation, an increase in taxes shifts the aggregate demand curve inward to the left. For argument's sake, assume that it intersects *SRAS* at E_2, or exactly where *LRAS* intersects AD_2. In this situation, the level of real GDP falls from $15.5 trillion per year to $15 trillion per year. The price level falls from 120 to 100.

Fiscal policy is defined as making discretionary changes in government _____ or _____ to achieve such national goals as high employment or reduced inflation.

To address a situation in which there is a _____ gap and the economy is operating at less than long-run aggregate supply (*LRAS*), the government can _____ its spending. This policy action shifts the aggregate demand curve to the right, causing the equilibrium level of real GDP per year to increase.

To address a situation in which there is an _____ gap, the government can _____ its spending and cause the aggregate demand curve to shift to the left, which reduces the equilibrium level of real GDP per year.

Changes in taxes can have similar effects on the equilibrium rate of real GDP and the price level. If there is an inflationary gap, an _____ in taxes can lead to a decrease in the equilibrium level of real GDP per year. In contrast, if there is a recessionary gap, a _____ in taxes can increase equilibrium real GDP per year.

Possible Offsets to Fiscal Policy

Fiscal policy does not operate in a vacuum. Important questions must be answered: If government spending rises by, say, $300 billion, how is the spending financed, and by whom? If taxes are increased, what does the government do with the taxes? What will happen if individuals anticipate higher *future* taxes because the government is spending more today without raising current taxes? These questions involve *offsets* to the effects of current fiscal policy. We consider them in detail here.

Indirect Crowding Out

Let's take the first example of fiscal policy in this chapter—an increase in government expenditures. If government expenditures rise and taxes are held constant, something has to give. Our government does not simply take goods and services when it wants them. It has to pay for them. When it pays for them and does not simultaneously collect the same amount in taxes, it must borrow. That means that an increase in government spending without raising taxes creates additional government borrowing from the private sector (or from other countries' residents).

INDUCED INTEREST RATE CHANGES If the government attempts to borrow in excess of $1 trillion more per year from the private sector, as it has since 2009, it will have to offer a higher interest rate to lure the additional funds from savers. This is the interest rate effect of expansionary fiscal policy financed by borrowing from the public. Consequently, when the federal government finances increased spending by additional borrowing, it will push interest rates up. When interest rates go up, firms' borrowing costs rise, which induces them to cut back on planned investment spending. Borrowing costs also increase for households, who reduce planned expenditures on cars and homes.

Thus, a rise in government spending, holding taxes constant (that is, deficit spending), tends to crowd out private spending, dampening the positive effect of increased government spending on aggregate demand. This is called the **crowding-out effect.** In the extreme case, the crowding out may be complete, with the increased government spending having no net effect on aggregate demand. The final result is simply more government spending and less private investment and consumption. Figure 8-3 below shows how the crowding-out effect occurs.

Crowding-out effect
The tendency of expansionary fiscal policy to cause a decrease in planned investment or planned consumption in the private sector. This decrease normally results from the rise in interest rates.

THE FIRM'S INVESTMENT DECISION To understand the crowding-out effect better, consider a firm that is contemplating borrowing $100,000 to expand its business. Suppose that the interest rate is 5 percent. The interest payments on the debt will be 5 percent times $100,000, or $5,000 per year ($417 per month). A rise in the interest rate to 8 percent will push the payments to 8 percent of $100,000, or $8,000 per year ($667 per month). The extra $250 per month in interest expenses will discourage some firms from making the investment. Consumers face similar decisions when they purchase

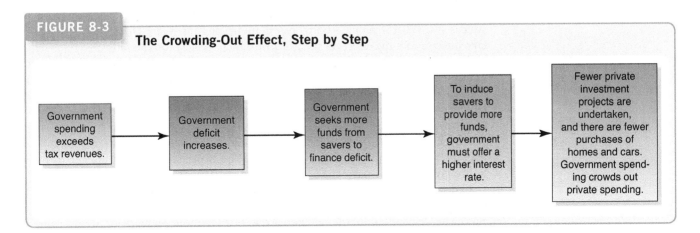

FIGURE 8-3

The Crowding-Out Effect, Step by Step

Government spending exceeds tax revenues. → Government deficit increases. → Government seeks more funds from savers to finance deficit. → To induce savers to provide more funds, government must offer a higher interest rate. → Fewer private investment projects are undertaken, and there are fewer purchases of homes and cars. Government spending crowds out private spending.

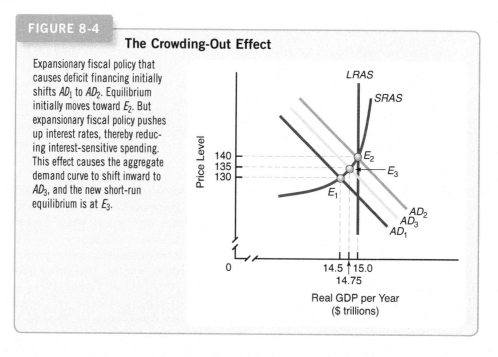

FIGURE 8-4

The Crowding-Out Effect

Expansionary fiscal policy that causes deficit financing initially shifts AD_1 to AD_2. Equilibrium initially moves toward E_2. But expansionary fiscal policy pushes up interest rates, thereby reducing interest-sensitive spending. This effect causes the aggregate demand curve to shift inward to AD_3, and the new short-run equilibrium is at E_3.

houses and cars. An increase in the interest rate causes their monthly payments to go up, thereby discouraging some of them from purchasing cars and houses.

GRAPHICAL ANALYSIS You see in Figure 8-4 above that the economy is in a situation in which, at point E_1, equilibrium real GDP is below the long-run level consistent with the position of the *LRAS* curve. But suppose that government expansionary fiscal policy in the form of increased government spending (without increasing current taxes) attempts to shift aggregate demand from AD_1 to AD_2. In the absence of the crowding-out effect, real GDP would increase to $15 trillion per year, and the price level would rise to 140 (point E_2). With the (partial) crowding-out effect, however, as investment and consumption decline, partly offsetting the rise in government spending, the aggregate demand curve shifts inward to the left to AD_3.

The new short-run equilibrium is now at E_3, with real GDP of $14.75 trillion per year at a price level of 135. In other words, crowding out dilutes the effect of expansionary fiscal policy, and a recessionary gap remains.

Planning for the Future: The Ricardian Equivalence Theorem

Economists have often implicitly assumed that people look at changes in taxes or changes in government spending only in the present. What if people actually think about the size of *future* tax payments? Does this have an effect on how they react to an increase in government spending with no current tax increases? Some economists believe that the answer is yes. What if people's horizons extend beyond this year? Don't we then have to take into account the effects of today's government policies on the future?

Consider an example. The government wants to reduce taxes by $200 billion today, as it did in 2008 and 2009 via tax "rebate" programs. Assume that government spending remains constant. Assume further that the government initially has a balanced budget. Thus, the only way for the government to pay for this $200 billion tax cut is to borrow $200 billion today. The public will owe $200 billion plus interest later. Realizing that a $200 billion tax cut today is mathematically equivalent to $200 billion plus interest later, people may wish to save the proceeds from the tax cut to meet future tax liabilities—payment of interest and repayment of debt.

Consequently, a tax cut may not affect total planned expenditures. A reduction in taxes without a reduction in government spending may therefore have no impact on aggregate demand. Similarly, an increase in taxes without an increase in government spending may not have a large (negative) impact on aggregate demand.

Suppose that a decrease in taxes shifts the aggregate demand curve from AD_1 to AD_2 in Figure 8-4 on the facing page. If consumers partly compensate for a higher future tax liability by saving more, the aggregate demand curve shifts leftward, to a position such as AD_3. In the extreme case in which individuals fully take into account their increased tax liabilities, the aggregate demand curve shifts all the way back to AD_1, so that there is no effect on the economy. This is known as the **Ricardian equivalence theorem,** after the nineteenth-century economist David Ricardo, who first developed the argument publicly.

According to the Ricardian equivalence theorem, it does not matter how government expenditures are financed—by taxes or by borrowing. Is the theorem correct? Research indicates that Ricardian equivalence effects likely exist but has not provided much compelling evidence about their magnitudes.

Ricardian equivalence theorem
The proposition that an increase in the government budget deficit has no effect on aggregate demand.

Restrained Consumption Effects of Temporary Tax Changes

Recall from Chapter 6 (page 137) that a person's consumption and saving decisions realistically depend on *both* current income *and* anticipated future income. On the basis of this fact, the theory of consumption known as the *permanent income hypothesis* proposes that an individual's current flow of consumption depends on the individual's permanent, or anticipated lifetime, income.

Sometimes, the government seeks to provide a short-term "stimulus" to economic activity through temporary tax cuts that last no longer than a year or two or by rebating lump-sum amounts back to taxpayers. According to the permanent income hypothesis, such short-term tax policies at best have minimal effects on total consumption spending. The reason is that *temporary* tax cuts or one-time tax rebates fail to raise the recipients' *permanent* incomes. Even after receiving such a temporary tax cut or rebate, therefore, people usually do not respond with significant changes in their consumption. Instead of spending the tax cut or rebate, they typically save most of the funds or use the funds to make payments on outstanding debts.

Thus, temporary tax cuts or rebates tend to have restrained effects on aggregate consumption, as the U.S. government has discovered when it has provided temporary tax rebates. For instance, one-time federal tax rebates totaling at least $200 billion in 2008 and again in 2009 boosted real disposable income temporarily in each year but had no perceptible effects on flows of real consumption spending.

Direct Expenditure Offsets

Government has a distinct comparative advantage over the private sector in certain activities such as diplomacy and national defense. Otherwise stated, certain resource-using activities in which the government engages do not compete with the private sector. In contrast, some of what government does, such as public education, competes directly with the private sector. When government competes with the private sector, **direct expenditure offsets** to fiscal policy may occur. For example, if the government starts providing milk at no charge to students who are already purchasing milk, there is a direct expenditure offset. Direct household spending on milk decreases, but government spending on milk increases.

Normally, the impact of an increase in government spending on aggregate demand is analyzed by implicitly assuming that government spending is *not* a substitute for private spending. This is clearly the case for a cruise missile. Whenever government spending is a substitute for private spending, however, a rise in government spending causes a direct reduction in private spending to offset it.

Direct expenditure offsets
Actions on the part of the private sector in spending income that offset government fiscal policy actions. Any increase in government spending in an area that competes with the private sector will have some direct expenditure offset.

THE EXTREME CASE In the extreme case, the direct expenditure offset is dollar for dollar, so we merely end up with a relabeling of spending from private to public. Assume that you have decided to spend $100 on groceries. Upon your arrival at the checkout counter, you find a U.S. Department of Agriculture official. She announces that she will pay for your groceries—but only the ones in the cart. Here increased government spending is $100. You leave the store in bliss. But just as you are deciding how to spend the $100, an Internal Revenue Service agent appears. He announces that as a result of the current budgetary crisis, your taxes are going to rise by $100. You have to pay on the spot. Increases in taxes have now been $100. We have a balanced-budget increase in government spending. In this scenario, *total* spending does not change. We simply end up with higher government spending, which directly offsets exactly an equal reduction in consumption. Aggregate demand and GDP are unchanged. Otherwise stated, if there is a full direct expenditure offset, the government spending multiplier is zero.

THE LESS EXTREME CASE Much government spending has a private-sector substitute. When government expenditures increase, private spending tends to decline somewhat (but generally not dollar for dollar), thereby mitigating the upward impact on total aggregate demand. To the extent that there are some direct expenditure offsets to expansionary fiscal policy, predicted changes in aggregate demand will be lessened. Consequently, real GDP and the price level will be less affected.

WHAT IF... the federal government seeks to boost real GDP by funding health care expenditures that people had already planned to undertake on their own?

In recent years, the U.S. government has shifted a larger share of discretionary expenditures toward construction of more public hospitals and clinics. A number of politicians have suggested that such federal health care spending adds to total planned expenditures in today's dampened economy. In many instances, however, private health care companies had originally planned to expand their facilities in response to an increasing demand for health care by an aging U.S.

population. When the federal government funded construction of competing hospitals and clinics, the private firms' intended capital investments were no longer economically viable. Thus, public health care facilities were built, and private facilities were not constructed after all. Direct fiscal offsets occurred, and, on net, total planned expenditures did not change.

The Supply-Side Effects of Changes in Taxes

We have talked about changing taxes and changing government spending, the traditional tools of fiscal policy. Let's now consider the possibility of changing *marginal* tax rates.

ALTERING MARGINAL TAX RATES The marginal tax rate is the rate applied to the last, or highest, bracket of taxable income. In our federal tax system, higher marginal tax rates are applied as income rises. In that sense, the United States has a progressive federal individual income tax system. Expansionary fiscal policy could involve reducing marginal tax rates. Advocates of such changes argue that lower tax rates will lead to an increase in productivity. They contend that individuals will work harder and longer, save more, and invest more and that increased productivity will lead to more economic growth, which will lead to higher real GDP. The government, by applying lower marginal tax rates, will not necessarily lose tax revenues, for the lower marginal tax rates will be applied to a growing tax base because of economic growth—after all, tax revenues are the product of a tax rate times a tax base.

The relationship between tax rates and tax revenues is sometimes called the *Laffer curve*, named after economist Arthur Laffer, who explained the relationship to some journalists and politicians in 1974. It is reproduced in Figure 8-5 on the facing page. On the vertical axis are tax revenues, and on the horizontal axis is the marginal tax rate. As you can see, total tax revenues initially rise but then eventually fall as the tax rate continues to increase after reaching some unspecified tax-revenue-maximizing rate at the top of the curve.

Supply-side economics
The suggestion that creating incentives for individuals and firms to increase productivity will cause the aggregate supply curve to shift outward.

SUPPLY-SIDE ECONOMICS People who support the notion that reducing tax rates does not necessarily lead to reduced tax revenues are called supply-side economists. **Supply-side economics** involves changing the tax structure to create incentives to increase productivity. Due to a shift in the aggregate supply curve to the right, there can be greater real GDP without upward pressure on the price level.

Consider the supply-side effects of changes in marginal tax rates on labor. An increase in tax rates reduces the opportunity cost of leisure, thereby inducing individuals to reduce their work effort and to consume more leisure. But an increase in tax rates

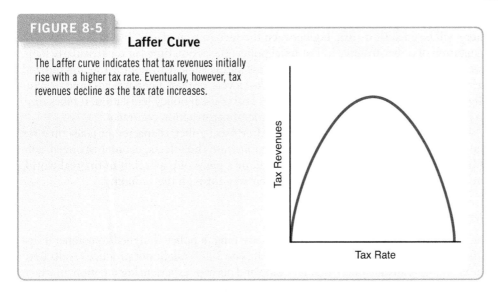

FIGURE 8-5

Laffer Curve

The Laffer curve indicates that tax revenues initially rise with a higher tax rate. Eventually, however, tax revenues decline as the tax rate increases.

will also reduce spendable income, thereby shifting the demand curve for leisure inward to the left, which tends to increase work effort. The outcome of these two effects on the choice of leisure (and thus work) depends on which of them is stronger. Supply-side economists argue that the first effect often dominates: Increases in marginal tax rates cause people to work less, and decreases in marginal tax rates induce workers to work more.

QUICK QUIZ   See page 202 for the answers. Review concepts from this section in MyEconLab.

Indirect crowding out occurs because of an interest rate effect in which the government's efforts to finance its deficit spending cause interest rates to _____, thereby crowding out private investment and spending, particularly on cars and houses. This is called the **crowding-out effect.**

_____ _____ _____ occur when government spending competes with the private sector and is increased. A direct crowding-out effect may occur.

The _____ _____ theorem holds that an increase in the government budget deficit has no effect on aggregate demand because individuals anticipate that their future taxes will increase and therefore save more today to pay for them.

Changes in marginal tax rates may cause _____-_____ effects if a reduction in marginal tax rates induces enough additional work, saving, and investing. Government tax receipts can actually increase. This is called _____-_____ economics.

Discretionary Fiscal Policy in Practice: Coping with Time Lags

We can discuss fiscal policy in a relatively precise way. We draw graphs with aggregate demand and supply curves to show what we are doing. We could in principle estimate the offsets that we just discussed. Even if we were able to measure all of these offsets exactly, however, would-be fiscal policymakers still face a problem: The conduct of fiscal policy involves a variety of time lags.

Policy Time Lags

Policymakers must take time lags into account. Not only is it difficult to measure economic variables, but it also takes time to collect and assimilate such data. Consequently, policymakers must contend with the **recognition time lag,** the months that may elapse before national economic problems can be identified.

Recognition time lag
The time required to gather information about the current state of the economy.

After an economic problem is recognized, a solution must be formulated. Thus, there will be an **action time lag** between the recognition of a problem and the implementation of policy to solve it. For fiscal policy, the action time lag is particularly long. Such policy must be approved by Congress and is subject to political wrangling and infighting. The action time lag can easily last a year or two. Then it takes time to actually implement the policy. After Congress enacts fiscal policy legislation, it takes time to decide such matters as who gets new federal construction contracts.

Finally, there is the **effect time lag:** After fiscal policy is enacted, it takes time for the policy to affect the economy. To demonstrate the effects, economists need only shift curves on a chalkboard, a whiteboard, or a piece of paper, but in the real world, such effects take quite a while to work their way through the economy.

Problems Posed by Time Lags

Because the various fiscal policy time lags are long, a policy designed to combat a significant recession such as the recession of the late 2000s might not produce results until the economy is already out of that recession and perhaps experiencing inflation, in which case the fiscal policy action would worsen the situation. Or a fiscal policy designed to eliminate inflation might not produce effects until the economy is in a recession. In that case, too, fiscal policy would make the economic problem worse rather than better.

Furthermore, because fiscal policy time lags tend to be *variable* (each lasting anywhere from one to three years), policymakers have a difficult time fine-tuning the economy. Clearly, fiscal policy is more guesswork than science.

YOU ARE THERE

To consider a specific example of how time lags can slow the economic effects of fiscal policy, take a look at **Why a Federal Stimulus Project Took Time to Provide Stimulus** on page 197.

Automatic Stabilizers

Not all changes in taxes (or in tax rates) or in government spending (including government transfers) constitute discretionary fiscal policy. There are several types of automatic (or nondiscretionary) fiscal policies. Such policies do not require new legislation on the part of Congress. Specific automatic fiscal policies—called **automatic, or built-in, stabilizers**—include the tax system itself, unemployment compensation, and income transfer payments.

The Tax System as an Automatic Stabilizer

You know that if you work less, you are paid less, and therefore you pay fewer taxes. The amount of taxes that our government collects falls automatically during a recession. Basically, as observed in the U.S. economy during the severe recession of the late 2000s, incomes and profits fall when business activity slows down, and the government's tax revenues drop, too. Some economists consider this an automatic tax cut, which therefore may stimulate aggregate demand. It thereby may reduce the extent of any negative economic fluctuation.

The progressive nature of the federal personal and corporate income tax systems magnifies any automatic stabilization effect that might exist. If your hours of work are reduced because of a recession, you still pay some federal personal income taxes. But because of our progressive system, you may drop into a lower tax bracket, thereby paying a lower marginal tax rate. As a result, your disposable income falls by a smaller percentage than your before-tax income falls.

Unemployment Compensation and Income Transfer Payments

Like our tax system, unemployment compensation payments stabilize aggregate demand. Throughout the course of business fluctuations, unemployment compensation reduces *changes* in people's disposable income. When business activity drops, most laid-off workers automatically become eligible for unemployment compensation from their state governments. Their disposable income therefore remains positive, although at a lower level than when they were employed. During boom periods, there is less

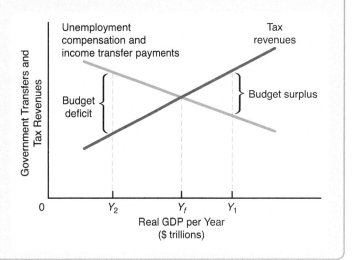

FIGURE 8-6

Automatic Stabilizers

Here we assume that as real GDP rises, tax revenues rise and government transfers fall, other things remaining constant. Thus, as the economy expands from Y_f to Y_1, a budget surplus automatically arises. As the economy contracts from Y_f to Y_2, a budget deficit automatically arises. Such automatic changes tend to drive the economy back toward its full-employment real GDP.

unemployment, and consequently fewer unemployment payments are made to the labor force. Less purchasing power is being added to the economy because fewer unemployment checks are paid out. In contrast, during recessions the opposite is true.

Income transfer payments act similarly as an automatic stabilizer. When a recession occurs, more people become eligible for income transfer payments, such as Supplemental Security Income and Temporary Assistance to Needy Families. Therefore, those people do not experience as dramatic a drop in disposable income as they otherwise would have.

Stabilizing Impact

The key stabilizing impact of our tax system, unemployment compensation, and income transfer payments is their ability to mitigate changes in disposable income, consumption, and the equilibrium level of real GDP. If disposable income is prevented from falling as much as it otherwise would during a recession, the downturn will be moderated. In contrast, if disposable income is prevented from rising as rapidly as it otherwise would during a boom, the boom is less likely to get out of hand. The progressive income tax and unemployment compensation thus provide automatic stabilization to the economy. We present the argument graphically in Figure 8-6 above.

Does the current state of the business cycle influence the effects of fiscal policy actions on real GDP?

Do Fiscal Policy Effects Vary as Real GDP Rises or Falls?

Alan Auerbach and Yuriy Gorodnichenko of the University of California at Berkeley have recently estimated the impacts of discretionary fiscal policy actions on U.S. real GDP. They found that increases in government *non*-defense spending have similar effects on real GDP during either business contractions or expansions. The effects are relatively small, with each $1 increase in *non*-defense expenditures estimated to boost real GDP by not much more than $1.10.

In contrast, Auerbach and Gorodnichenko's estimates indicate that changes in government *defense* spending consistently have larger ultimate real GDP effects during recessions than during business expansions. During a recession, each $1 increase in defense spending boosts

real GDP by more than $3.50, whereas during an expansion, the resulting increase in real GDP is less than $1.20. Thus, if the effect lag associated with a rise in defense spending is the same during either a recession or an expansion, the "bang for the buck" from an increase in defense spending per unit of time is much greater during a recession.

FOR CRITICAL THINKING

Why might boosting defense spending have a larger impact on real GDP than increasing non-defense spending? (Hint: Which form of spending is least likely to be subject to direct fiscal offsets?)

What Do We Really Know about Fiscal Policy?

There are two ways of looking at fiscal policy. One prevails during normal times and the other during abnormal times.

Fiscal Policy during Normal Times

Go to www.econtoday.com/chap08 to learn about expanding spending and budget deficits of the U.S. government.

During normal times (without "excessive" unemployment, inflation, or unusual problems in the national economy), we know that due to the recognition time lag and the modest size of any fiscal policy action that Congress will actually take, discretionary fiscal policy is probably not very effective. Congress ends up doing too little too late to help in a minor recession. Moreover, fiscal policy that generates repeated tax changes (as has happened) creates uncertainty, which may do more harm than good. To the extent that fiscal policy has any effect during normal times, it probably achieves this by way of automatic stabilizers rather than by way of discretionary policy.

Fiscal Policy during Abnormal Times

During abnormal times, fiscal policy may be effective. Consider some classic examples: the Great Depression and war periods.

THE GREAT DEPRESSION When there is a catastrophic drop in real GDP, as there was during the Great Depression, fiscal policy may be able to stimulate aggregate demand. Because so many people have few assets left and thus are income-constrained during such periods, government spending is a way to get income into their hands—income that they are likely to spend immediately.

WARTIME Wars are in fact reserved for governments. War expenditures are not good substitutes for private expenditures—they have little or no direct expenditure offsets. Consequently, war spending as part of expansionary fiscal policy usually has noteworthy effects, such as occurred while we were waging World War II, when real GDP increased dramatically (though much of the output of new goods and services was expended for military uses).

The "Soothing" Effect of Keynesian Fiscal Policy

One view of traditional Keynesian fiscal policy does not call for it to be used on a regular basis but nevertheless sees it as potentially useful. As you have learned in this chapter, many problems are associated with attempting to use fiscal policy. But if we should encounter a severe downturn, fiscal policy is available. Knowing this may reassure consumers and investors. Thus, the availability of fiscal policy may induce more buoyant and stable expectations of the future, thereby smoothing investment spending.

QUICK QUIZ See page 202 for the answers. Review concepts from this section in MyEconLab.

Time lags of various sorts reduce the effectiveness of fiscal policy. These include the _____ time lag, the _____ time lag, and the _____ time lag.

Two _____, or built-in, stabilizers are the progressive income tax and unemployment compensation.

Built-in stabilizers automatically tend to _____ changes in disposable income resulting from changes in overall business activity.

Although discretionary fiscal policy may not necessarily be a useful policy tool in normal times because of time lags, it may work well during _____ times, such as depressions and wartimes. In addition, the existence of fiscal policy may have a soothing effect on consumers and investors.

YOU ARE THERE
Why a Federal Stimulus Project Took Time to Provide Stimulus

Shenetta Coleman directs the Detroit agency charged with spending the city's share of $5 billion that the American Recovery and Reinvestment Act (ARRA) authorized to fund insulation of private homes. Hoping to help stimulate the struggling local economy, Coleman immediately placed a want ad for contractors to install insulation in drafty Detroit homes. Soon, 46 firms responded. When Coleman wanted to start home weatherizing projects, however, she learned that she had not met the federal government's requirements for placing her ad. The ad failed to specify wages that firms would have to pay their employees, rules governing other labor standards, legally permissible forms for contract bids, and special rules for preserving historic homes.

Thus, Coleman had to start the process all over again. Two years after her initial efforts to speed government spending on weatherizing Detroit homes, only about half of the houses she had targeted had new insulation. Thus, her efforts "stimulated" the Detroit economy at a much slower pace than she had anticipated when the ARRA funds first became available.

Critical Thinking Questions

1. What policy time lag did Detroit experience in implementing the ARRA?
2. Did another policy time lag likely follow the above lag? Explain.

ISSUES & APPLICATIONS

CONCEPTS APPLIED

▶ Fiscal Policy

▶ Direct Expenditure Offsets

▶ Effect Time Lag

How Federal "Stimulus" Was Swallowed Up by States

Although the federal government directly spent some funds authorized by the American Recovery and Reinvestment Act (ARRA) of 2009, it turned many of those funds over to state governments to spend locally. The bulk of these funds contributed very little to raising the flow of total expenditures, however.

Paying Off State Debts Instead of Boosting Expenditures

Figure 8-7 on the following page displays two sets of data. One is the cumulative quantity of grants of discretionary funds transmitted from the federal government to state governments since late 2008. The other is the net amount of borrowing by state governments.

As grants of federal funds to state governments accumulated after 2008, the net borrowing of state governments declined. Many state governments were heavily in debt at the end of 2008, with borrowings in excess of $160 billion. For these states, the receipt of discretionary federal grants beginning in 2009 was a godsend, because it allowed them to start paying off a number of existing debts.

Debt Repayments Are Not Immediate Flows of Spending

The funds intended by the federal government to enter the nation's flow of income and expenditures did not reach that flow. States sent them to creditors.

Rather than direct the federal funds to *additional* spending, therefore, the state governments used the bulk of ARRA federal grants to pay off part of debts generated by spending projects completed in prior years. Most estimates indicate that of the federal "stimulus" funds given to state governments, less than 5 percent were directed toward *new* spending within the nation's flow of income and expenditures. Thus, a 95 percent direct fiscal offset resulted. Instead of providing an immediate boost in state infrastructure spending on roads, bridges, and the like, nearly all of the federal funds transmitted to state governments for spending instead were saved.

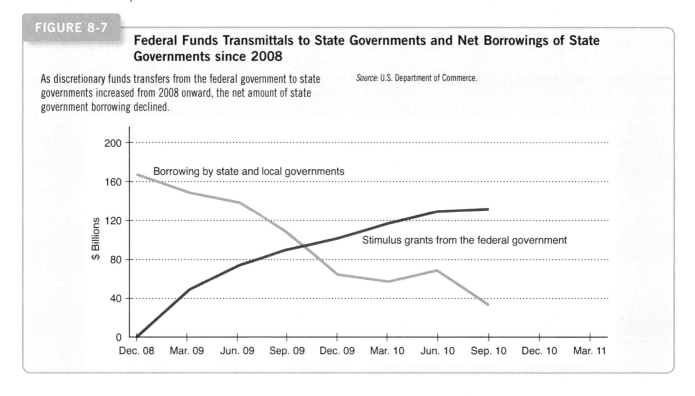

FIGURE 8-7

Federal Funds Transmittals to State Governments and Net Borrowings of State Governments since 2008

As discretionary funds transfers from the federal government to state governments increased from 2008 onward, the net amount of state government borrowing declined.

Source: U.S. Department of Commerce.

For Critical Thinking

1. Why might federal spending on roads, waterways, or national security be less subject to direct expenditure offsets than spending on health care or education?
2. What might account for the fact that estimates of effect time lags for fiscal policy often differ considerably across different types of government expenditures?

Web Resources

1. Take a look at the U.S. government's official Web site for tracking the use of ARRA funds at www.econtoday.com/chap08.

2. For further discussion of why directing so many federal ARRA funds to the states failed to produce very much fiscal stimulus to the U.S. economy, go to www.econtoday.com/chap08.

MyEconLab

For more questions on this chapter's Issues & Applications, go to MyEconLab. In the Study Plan for this chapter, select Section N: News.

MyEconLab

Here is what you should know after reading this chapter. MyEconLab will help you identify what you know, and where to go when you need to practice.

--- WHAT YOU SHOULD KNOW ---

The Effects of Discretionary Fiscal Policies Using Traditional Keynesian Analysis In short-run Keynesian analysis, an increase in government spending or tax decrease shifts the aggregate demand curve outward and thereby closes a recessionary gap in which current real GDP is less than the long-run level of real GDP. Likewise, a reduction in government spending or a tax increase shifts the aggregate demand curve inward and closes an inflationary gap in which current real GDP exceeds the long-run level of real GDP.

fiscal policy, 186

Key Figures
Figure 8-1, 187
Figure 8-2, 188

--- WHERE TO GO TO PRACTICE ---

- MyEconLab Study Plan 8.1
- Animated Figures 8-1, 8-2

MyEconLab *continued*

WHAT YOU SHOULD KNOW
WHERE TO GO TO PRACTICE

How Indirect Crowding Out and Direct Expenditure Offsets Can Reduce the Effectiveness of Fiscal Policy Actions Indirect crowding out occurs when the government must borrow from the private sector because government spending exceeds tax revenues. To obtain the necessary funds, the government must offer a higher interest rate, thereby driving up market interest rates. This reduces, or crowds out, interest-sensitive private spending. Increased government spending may also substitute directly for private expenditures and thereby offset the increase in total planned expenditures that the government had intended to bring about.

crowding-out effect, 189
direct expenditure offsets, 191
supply-side economics, 192

Key Figures
Figure 8-3, 189
Figure 8-4, 190
Figure 8-5, 193

- MyEconLab Study Plan 8.2
- Animated Figures 8-3, 8-4, 8-5

The Ricardian Equivalence Theorem This proposition states that when the government cuts taxes and borrows to finance the tax reduction, people realize that in the future the government will have to raise taxes to repay the loan. This induces them to save the proceeds of the tax cut to meet their future tax liabilities. Thus, a tax cut fails to induce an increase in aggregate consumption spending and consequently has no effect on total planned expenditures and aggregate demand.

Ricardian equivalence theorem, 191

Key Figure
Figure 8-4, 190

- MyEconLab Study Plan 8.2
- Animated Figure 8-4

Fiscal Policy Time Lags and the Effectiveness of Fiscal "Fine-Tuning" Efforts to use fiscal policy to bring about changes in aggregate demand are complicated by policy time lags. One of these is the recognition time lag, which is the time required to collect information about the economy's current situation. Another is the action time lag, the period between recognition of a problem and implementation of a policy intended to address it. Finally, there is the effect time lag, which is the interval between the implementation of a policy and its having an effect on the economy.

recognition time lag, 193
action time lag, 194
effect time lag, 194

- MyEconLab Study Plan 8.3

Automatic Stabilizers Income taxes diminish automatically when economic activity drops, and unemployment compensation and income transfer payments increase. Thus, when there is a decline in real GDP, the automatic reduction in income tax collections and increases in unemployment compensation and income transfer payments tend to minimize the reduction in total planned expenditures that would otherwise have resulted.

automatic, or built-in, stabilizers, 194

Key Figure
Figure 8-6, 195

- MyEconLab Study Plans 8.4, 8.5
- Animated Figure 8-6

Log in to MyEconLab, take a chapter test, and get a personalized Study Plan that tells you which concepts you understand and which ones you need to review. From there, MyEconLab will give you further practice, tutorials, animations, videos, and guided solutions. For more information, visit www.myeconlab.com

PROBLEMS

All problems are assignable in MyEconLab. Answers to odd-numbered problems appear at the back of the book.

8-1. Suppose that Congress and the president decide that the nation's economic performance is weakening and that the government should "do something" about the situation. They make no tax changes but do enact new laws increasing government spending on a variety of programs. (See page 187.)

   a. Prior to the congressional and presidential action, careful studies by government economists indicated that the direct multiplier effect of a rise in government expenditures on equilibrium real GDP per year is equal to 3. In the 12 months since the increase in government spending, however, it has become clear that the actual ultimate effect on real GDP will be less than half of that amount. What factors might account for this?

   b. Another year and a half elapses following passage of the government spending boost. The government has undertaken no additional policy actions, nor have there been any other events of significance. Nevertheless, by the end of the second year, real GDP has returned to its original level, and the price level has increased sharply. Provide a possible explanation for this outcome.

8-2. Suppose that Congress enacts a significant tax cut with the expectation that this action will stimulate aggregate demand and push up real GDP in the short run. In fact, however, neither real GDP nor the price level changes significantly as a result of the tax cut. What might account for this outcome? (See pages 190–191)

8-3. Explain how time lags in discretionary fiscal policy making could thwart the efforts of Congress and the president to stabilize real GDP in the face of an economic downturn. Is it possible that these time lags could actually cause discretionary fiscal policy to *destabilize* real GDP?

8-4. Determine whether each of the following is an example of a situation in which a direct expenditure offset to fiscal policy occurs. (See page 191.)

   a. In an effort to help rejuvenate the nation's railroad system, a new government agency buys unused track, locomotives, and passenger and freight cars, many of which private companies would otherwise have purchased and put into regular use.

   b. The government increases its expenditures without raising taxes. To cover the resulting budget deficit, it borrows more funds from the private sector, thereby pushing up the market interest rate and discouraging private planned investment spending.

   c. The government finances the construction of a classical music museum that otherwise would never have received private funding.

8-5. Determine whether each of the following is an example of a situation in which there is indirect crowding out resulting from an expansionary fiscal policy action. (See pages 189–190.)

   a. The government provides a subsidy to help keep an existing firm operating, even though a group of investors otherwise would have provided a cash infusion that would have kept the company in business.

   b. The government reduces its taxes without decreasing its expenditures. To cover the resulting budget deficit, it borrows more funds from the private sector, thereby pushing up the market interest rate and discouraging private planned investment spending.

   c. Government expenditures fund construction of a high-rise office building on a plot of land where a private company otherwise would have constructed an essentially identical building.

8-6. The U.S. government is in the midst of spending more than $1 billion on seven buildings containing more than 100,000 square feet of space to be used for study of infectious diseases. Prior to the government's decision to construct these buildings, a few universities had been planning to build essentially the same facilities using privately obtained funds. After construction on the government buildings began, however, the universities dropped their plans. Evaluate whether the government's $1 billion expenditure is actually likely to push U.S. real GDP above the level it would have reached in the absence of the government's construction spree. (See page 191.)

8-7. Determine whether each of the following is an example of a discretionary fiscal policy action. (See page 191.)

   a. A recession occurs, and government-funded unemployment compensation is paid to laid-off workers.

   b. Congress votes to fund a new jobs program designed to put unemployed workers to work.

   c. The Federal Reserve decides to reduce the quantity of money in circulation in an effort to slow inflation.

d. Under powers authorized by an act of Congress, the president decides to authorize an emergency release of funds for spending programs intended to head off economic crises.

8-8. Determine whether each of the following is an example of an automatic fiscal stabilizer. (See pages 194–195.)

   a. A federal agency must extend loans to businesses whenever an economic downturn begins.

   b. As the economy heats up, the resulting increase in equilibrium real GDP per year immediately results in higher income tax payments, which dampen consumption spending somewhat.

   c. As the economy starts to recover from a severe recession and more people go back to work, government-funded unemployment compensation payments begin to decline.

   d. To stem an overheated economy, the president, using special powers granted by Congress, authorizes emergency impoundment of funds that Congress had previously authorized for spending on government programs.

8-9. Consider the diagram below, in which the current short-run equilibrium is at point A, and answer the questions that follow. (See pages 187–188.)

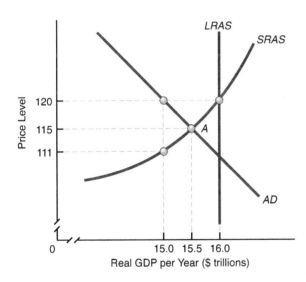

   a. What type of gap exists at point A?

   b. If the marginal propensity to save equals 0.20, what change in government spending financed by borrowing from the private sector could eliminate the gap identified in part (a)? Explain.

8-10. Consider the diagram in the next column, in which the current short-run equilibrium is at point A, and answer the questions that follow. (See pages 187–188.)

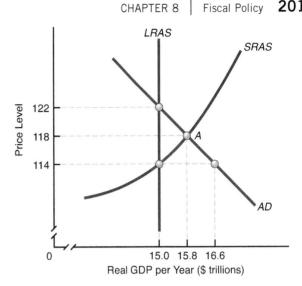

   a. What type of gap exists at point A?

   b. If the marginal propensity to consume equals 0.75, what change in government spending financed by borrowing from the private sector could eliminate the gap identified in part (a)? Explain.

8-11. Currently, a government's budget is balanced. The marginal propensity to consume is 0.80. The government has determined that each additional $10 billion it borrows to finance a budget deficit pushes up the market interest rate by 0.1 percentage point. It has also determined that every 0.1-percentage-point change in the market interest rate generates a change in planned investment expenditures equal to $2 billion. Finally, the government knows that to close a recessionary gap and take into account the resulting change in the price level, it must generate a net rightward shift in the aggregate demand curve equal to $200 billion. Assuming that there are no direct expenditure offsets to fiscal policy, how much should the government increase its expenditures? (See pages 189–190. Hint: How much private investment spending will each $10 billion increase in government spending crowd out?)

8-12. A government is currently operating with an annual budget deficit of $40 billion. The government has determined that every $10 billion reduction in the amount it borrows each year would reduce the market interest rate by 0.1 percentage point. Furthermore, it has determined that every 0.1-percentage-point change in the market interest rate generates a change in planned investment expenditures in the opposite direction equal to $5 billion. The marginal propensity to consume is 0.75. Finally, the government knows that to eliminate an inflationary gap and take into account the resulting change in the price level, it must generate a net leftward shift in the aggregate demand curve equal to $40 billion. Assuming that there are no direct expenditure offsets to fiscal policy, how much should the government increase taxes? (See pages 189–190. Hint: How much new private investment spending is induced by each $10 billion decrease in government spending?)

8-13. Assume that the Ricardian equivalence theorem is not relevant. Explain why an income-tax-rate cut should affect short-run equilibrium real GDP. (See pages 192–193.)

8-14. Suppose that Congress enacts a lump-sum tax cut of $750 billion. The marginal propensity to consume is equal to 0.75. Assuming that Ricardian equivalence holds true, what is the effect on equilibrium real GDP? On saving? (See page XXX.)

8-15. In May and June of 2008, the federal government issued one-time tax rebates—checks returning a small portion of taxes previously paid—to millions

of U.S residents, and U.S. real disposable income temporarily jumped by nearly $500 billion. Household real consumption spending did not increase in response to the short-lived increase in real disposable income. Explain how the logic of the permanent income hypothesis might help to account for this apparent non-relationship between real consumption and real disposable income in the late spring of 2008. (See page 191.)

8-16. It is late 2017, and the U.S. economy is showing signs of slipping into a potentially deep recession. Government policymakers are searching for income-tax-policy changes that will bring about a significant and lasting boost to real consumption spending. According to the logic of the permanent income hypothesis, should the proposed income-tax-policy changes involve tax increases or tax reductions, and should the policy changes be short-lived or long-lasting? (See page 191.)

ECONOMICS ON THE NET

Federal Government Spending and Taxation A quick way to keep up with the federal government's spending and taxation is by examining federal budget data at the White House Internet address.

Title: Historical Tables: Budget of the United States Government

Navigation: Use the link at **www.econtoday.com/chap08** to visit the Office of Management and Budget. Select the most recent budget. Then click on *Historical Tables.*

Application After the document downloads, perform the indicated operations and answer the questions.

1. Go to section 2, "Composition of Federal Government Receipts." Take a look at Table 2.2, "Percentage Composition of Receipts by Source." Before World War II, what was the key source of revenues of the federal government? What has been the key revenue source since World War II?

2. Now scan down the document to Table 2.3, "Receipts by Source as Percentages of GDP." Have any government revenue sources declined as a percentage of GDP? Which ones have noticeably risen in recent years?

For Group Study and Analysis Split into four groups, and have each group examine section 3, "Federal Government Outlays by Function," and in particular Table 3-1, "Outlays by Superfunction and Function." Assign groups to the following functions: national defense, health, income security, and Social Security. Have each group prepare a brief report concerning recent and long-term trends in government spending on each function. Which functions have been capturing growing shares of government spending in recent years? Which have been receiving declining shares of total spending?

ANSWERS TO QUICK QUIZZES

p. 188: (i) expenditures . . . taxes; (ii) recessionary . . . increase; (iii) inflationary . . . decrease; (iv) increase . . . decrease

p. 193: (i) increase; (ii) Direct expenditure offsets; (iii) Ricardian equivalence; (iv) supply-side . . . supply-side

p. 196: (i) recognition . . . action . . . effect; (ii) automatic; (iii) moderate; (iv) abnormal

APPENDIX C

Fiscal Policy: A Keynesian Perspective

The traditional Keynesian approach to fiscal policy differs in three ways from that presented in Chapter 7. First, it emphasizes the underpinnings of the components of aggregate demand. Second, it assumes that government expenditures are not substitutes for private expenditures and that current taxes are the only taxes taken into account by consumers and firms. Third, the traditional Keynesian approach focuses on the short run and so assumes that as a first approximation, the price level is constant.

Changes in Government Spending

Figure C-1 below measures real GDP along the horizontal axis and total planned real expenditures (aggregate demand) along the vertical axis. The components of aggregate demand are real consumption (C), investment (I), government spending (G), and net exports (X). The height of the schedule labeled $C + I + G + X$ shows total planned real expenditures (aggregate demand) as a function of real GDP. This schedule slopes upward because consumption depends positively on real GDP. Everywhere along the 45-degree reference line, planned real spending equals real GDP.

At the point Y^*, where the $C + I + G + X$ line intersects the 45-degree line, planned real spending is consistent with real GDP per year. At any income less than Y^*, spending exceeds real GDP, and so real GDP and thus real spending will tend to rise. At any level of real GDP greater than Y^*, planned spending is less than real GDP, and so real GDP and thus spending will tend to decline. Given the determinants of C, I, G, and X, total real spending (aggregate demand) will be Y^*.

FIGURE C-1

The Impact of Higher Government Spending on Aggregate Demand

Government spending increases, causing $C + I + G + X$ to move to $C + I + G' + X$. Equilibrium real GDP per year increases to Y^{**}.

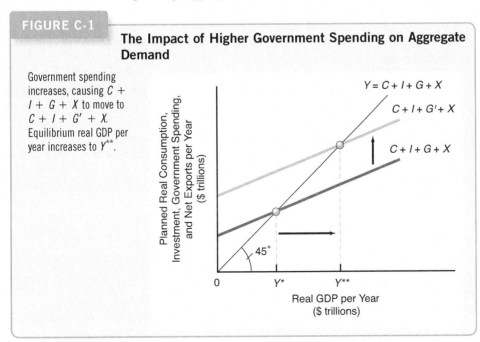

203

The Keynesian approach assumes that changes in government spending cause no direct offsets in either consumption or investment spending because G is not a substitute for C, I, or X. Hence, a rise in government spending from G to G' causes the $C + I + G + X$ line to shift upward by the full amount of the rise in government spending, yielding the line $C + I + G' + X$. The rise in real government spending causes real GDP to rise, which in turn causes consumption spending to rise, which further increases real GDP. Ultimately, aggregate demand rises to the level Y^{**}, where spending again equals real GDP. A key conclusion of the traditional Keynesian analysis is that total spending rises by *more* than the original rise in government spending because consumption spending depends positively on real GDP.

Changes in Taxes

According to the Keynesian approach, changes in current taxes affect aggregate demand by changing the amount of real disposable (after-tax) income available to consumers. A rise in taxes reduces disposable income and thus reduces real consumption; conversely, a tax cut raises disposable income and thus causes a rise in consumption spending. The effects of a tax increase are shown in Figure C-2 below. Higher taxes cause consumption spending to decline from C to C', causing total spending to shift downward to $C' + I + G + X$. In general, the decline in consumption will be less than the increase in taxes because people will also reduce their saving to help pay the higher taxes.

The Balanced-Budget Multiplier

One interesting implication of the Keynesian approach concerns the impact of a balanced-budget change in government real spending. Suppose that the government increases spending by $1 billion and pays for it by raising current taxes by $1 billion. Such a policy is called a *balanced-budget increase in real spending*. Because the higher spending tends to push aggregate demand *up* by *more* than $1 billion while the higher taxes tend to push aggregate demand *down* by *less* than $1 billion, a most remarkable thing happens: A balanced-budget increase in G causes total spending to rise by *exactly* the amount of the rise in G—in this case, $1 billion. We say that the *balanced-budget multiplier* is equal to 1. Similarly, a balanced-budget reduction in government spending will cause total spending to fall by exactly the amount of the government spending cut.

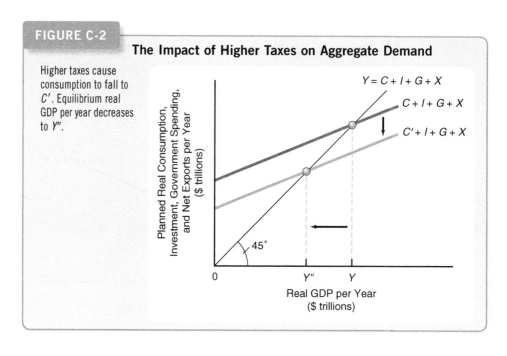

FIGURE C-2

The Impact of Higher Taxes on Aggregate Demand

Higher taxes cause consumption to fall to C'. Equilibrium real GDP per year decreases to Y''.

The Fixed Price Level Assumption

The final key feature of the traditional Keynesian approach is that it typically assumes that as a first approximation, the price level is fixed. Recall that nominal GDP equals the price level multiplied by real GDP. If the price level is fixed, an increase in government spending that causes nominal GDP to rise will show up exclusively as a rise in *real* GDP. This will in turn be accompanied by a decline in the unemployment rate because the additional real GDP can be produced only if additional factors of production, such as labor, are utilized.

PROBLEMS

All problems are assignable in MyEconLab. *Answers to odd-numbered problems appear at the back of the book.*

C-1. Assume that equilibrium real GDP is $15.2 trillion and full-employment equilibrium (*FE*) is $15.55 trillion. The marginal propensity to save is $\frac{1}{7}$. Answer the questions using the data in the following graph. (See pages 203–204.)

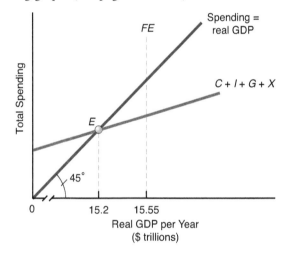

a. What is the marginal propensity to consume?

b. By how much must new investment or government spending increase to bring the economy up to full employment?

c. By how much must government cut personal taxes to stimulate the economy to the full-employment equilibrium?

C-2. Assume that MPC = $\frac{4}{5}$ when answering the following questions. (See pages 203–204.)

a. If government expenditures rise by $2 billion, by how much will the aggregate expenditure curve shift upward? By how much will equilibrium real GDP per year change?

b. If taxes increase by $2 billion, by how much will the aggregate expenditure curve shift downward? By how much will equilibrium real GDP per year change?

C-3. Assume that MPC = $\frac{4}{5}$ when answering the following questions (See pages 203–204.)

a. If government expenditures rise by $1 billion, by how much will the aggregate expenditure curve shift upward?

b. If taxes rise by $1 billion, by how much will the aggregate expenditure curve shift downward?

c. If both taxes and government expenditures rise by $1 billion, by how much will the aggregate expenditure curve shift? What will happen to the equilibrium level of real GDP?

d. How does your response to the second question in part (c) change if MPC = $\frac{3}{4}$? If MPC = $\frac{1}{2}$?

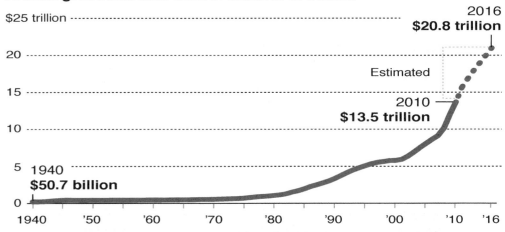

Rising deficit threatens U.S. credit rating

Standard & Poor's warned that it could downgrade the United States' sterling debt rating if the White House and Congress fail to reach a deal to control the massive federal deficit, which is feeding the nation's debt. Here is a look at growth of the debt in recent decades.

Annual gross national debt in trillions of dollars

2016
$20.8 trillion

Estimated

2010
$13.5 trillion

1940
$50.7 billion

9 Deficit Spending and the Public Debt

In recent years, the federal government's total expenditures—the sum of discretionary spending and nondiscretionary expenditures on programs such as Social Security and Medicare—have been considerably greater than receipts. Indeed, total federal spending is now so high that discretionary spending eats up nearly all of the borrowed funds. Every discretionary federal spending program, including those for developing green technologies or finding cures for cancer and other diseases, has been financed almost fully with borrowed funds. Because its nondiscretionary discretionary spending has exceeded its tax revenues, the federal government has had to borrow more than $1 trillion per year to pay for its discretionary expenditures. In this chapter, you will contemplate the economic implications of this federal borrowing.

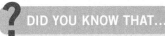
even though the government projected for two decades that 2020 would be the year in which tax collections to fund the Social Security program would fall below beneficiary payments, the actual year was 2011? The federal government is making up the difference by allocating a portion of regular government spending to payments to Social Security beneficiaries. Nevertheless, the federal government's tax revenues are already insufficient to cover all of its other expenditures—that is, the rest of the government's budget also is in deficit. Consequently, the federal government is borrowing from domestic and foreign residents, firms, and governments to finance a portion of the Social Security program's payments. Some elderly and disabled U.S. residents are receiving Social Security benefits from funds that the federal government has borrowed and must repay in future years.

Every year since 2001, the U.S. government has spent more than it collected in taxes. The government anticipates that it will continue to spend more than it receives indefinitely. Should you be worried about this? The answer, as you will see in this chapter, is both yes and no. First, let's examine what the government does when it spends more than it receives.

Public Deficits and Debts: Flows versus Stocks

A **government budget deficit** exists if the government spends more than it receives in taxes during a given period of time. The government has to finance this shortfall somehow. Barring any resort to money creation (the subject matter of Chapters 10 and 11), the U.S. Treasury sells IOUs on behalf of the U.S. government, in the form of securities that are normally called bonds. In effect, the federal government asks U.S. and foreign households, businesses, and governments to lend funds to the government to cover its deficit. For example, if the federal government spends $1 trillion more than it receives in revenues, the Treasury will obtain that $1 trillion by selling $1 trillion of new Treasury bonds. Those who buy the Treasury bonds (lend funds to the U.S. government) will receive interest payments over the life of the bond plus eventual repayment of the entire amount lent. In return, the U.S. Treasury receives immediate purchasing power. In the process, it also adds to its indebtedness to bondholders.

Government budget deficit
An excess of government spending over government revenues during a given period of time.

Distinguishing between Deficits and Debts

You have already learned about flows. GDP, for instance, is a flow because it is a dollar measure of the total amount of final goods and services produced within a given period of time, such as a year.

The federal deficit is also a flow. Suppose that the current federal deficit is $1.5 trillion. Consequently, the federal government is currently spending at a rate of $1.5 trillion *per year* more than it is collecting in taxes and other revenues.

Of course, governments do not always spend more each year than the revenues they receive. If a government spends an amount exactly equal to the revenues it collects during a given period, then during this interval the government operates with a **balanced budget.** If a government spends less than the revenues it receives during a given period, then during this interval it experiences a **government budget surplus.**

Balanced budget
A situation in which the government's spending is exactly equal to the total taxes and other revenues it collects during a given period of time.

Government budget surplus
An excess of government revenues over government spending during a given period of time.

The Public Debt

You have also learned about stocks, which are measured at a point in time. Stocks change between points in time as a result of flows. The amount of unemployment, for example, is a stock. It is the total number of people looking for work but unable to find it at a given point in time. Suppose that the stock of unemployed workers at the beginning of the month is 12.8 million and that at the end of the month the stock of unemployed workers has increased to 13.0 million. This means that during the month, assuming an unchanged labor force, there was a net flow of 0.2 million individuals away from the state of being employed into the state of being out of work but seeking employment.

Public debt
The total value of all outstanding federal government securities.

Likewise, the total accumulated **public debt** is a stock measured at a given point in time, and it changes from one time to another as a result of government budget deficits or surpluses. For instance, on December 31, 2011, one measure of the public debt was about $10.1 trillion. During 2012, the federal government operated at a deficit of about $1.3 trillion. As a consequence, on December 31, 2012, this measure of the public debt had increased to about $11.4 trillion.

Government Finance: Spending More Than Tax Collections

Go to www.econtoday.com/chap09 to learn more about the activities of the Congressional Budget Office, which reports to the legislative branch of the U.S. government about the current state of the federal government's spending and receipts.

Following four consecutive years—1998 through 2001—of official budget surpluses, the federal government began to experience budget deficits once more beginning in 2002. Since then, government spending has increased considerably, and tax revenues have failed to keep pace. Consequently, the federal government has operated with a deficit. Indeed, since 2009 the federal budget deficit has widened dramatically—to inflation-adjusted levels not seen since World War II.

The Historical Record of Federal Budget Deficits

Figure 9-1 below charts inflation-adjusted expenditures and revenues of the federal government since 1940. The *real* annual budget deficit is the arithmetic difference between real expenditures and real revenues during years in which the government's spending has exceeded its revenues. As you can see, this nation has experienced numerous years of federal budget deficits. Indeed, the annual budget surpluses of 1998 through 2001 were somewhat out of the ordinary. The 1998 budget surplus was the first since 1968, when the government briefly operated with a surplus. Before the 1998–2001 budget surpluses, the U.S. government had not experienced back-to-back annual surpluses since the 1950s.

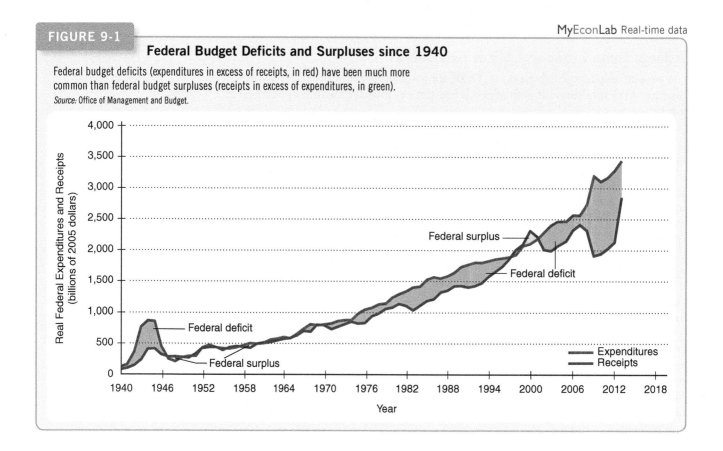

FIGURE 9-1

MyEconLab Real-time data

Federal Budget Deficits and Surpluses since 1940

Federal budget deficits (expenditures in excess of receipts, in red) have been much more common than federal budget surpluses (receipts in excess of expenditures, in green).
Source: Office of Management and Budget.

MyEconLab Real-time data

FIGURE 9-2

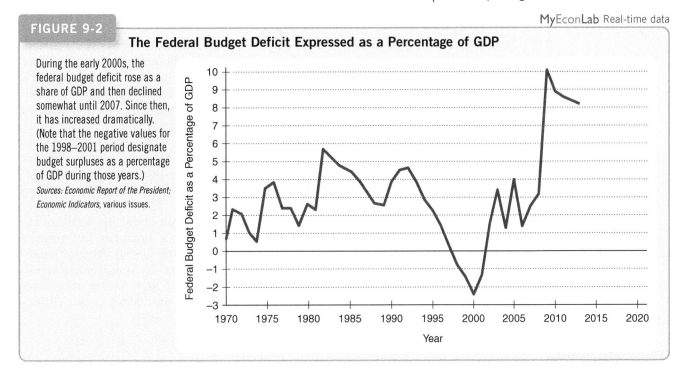

The Federal Budget Deficit Expressed as a Percentage of GDP

During the early 2000s, the federal budget deficit rose as a share of GDP and then declined somewhat until 2007. Since then, it has increased dramatically. (Note that the negative values for the 1998–2001 period designate budget surpluses as a percentage of GDP during those years.)

Sources: Economic Report of the President; Economic Indicators, various issues.

Indeed, since 1940 the U.S. government has operated with an annual budget surplus for a total of only 13 years. In all other years, it has collected insufficient taxes and other revenues to fund its spending. Every year this has occurred, the federal government has borrowed to finance its additional expenditures.

Even though Figure 9-1 on the facing page accounts for inflation, it does not give a clear picture of the size of the federal government's deficits or surpluses in relation to overall economic activity in the United States. Figure 9-2 above provides a clearer view of the size of government deficits or surpluses relative to the size of the U.S. economy by expressing them as percentages of GDP. As you can see, the federal budget deficit rose to nearly 6 percent of GDP in the early 1980s. It then fell back, increased once again during the late 1980s and early 1990s, and then declined steadily into the budget surplus years of 1998–2001. Since 2001, the government budget deficit has increased to nearly 4 percent of GDP, dropped back below 3 percent of GDP, and then risen rapidly, to more than 8 percent of GDP.

Why do you suppose some nations complain that the U.S. government performs "cosmetic surgery" on its reports about public deficits and debts?

INTERNATIONAL EXAMPLE

Cosmetic Enhancement of the U.S. Deficits and Debts?

The official U.S. government deficit and net public debt may be huge, but the reality is even worse. Most other countries' reports combine figures for *all* governments—that is, national, state or provincial, and municipal governments. U.S. reports, in contrast, typically provide only data on the *federal* government's annual budget deficit and net public debt. The U.S. federal government's budget deficit per year as a percentage of the nation's annual GDP is close to 8.2 percent.

If U.S. statistical reports were altered to include state and municipal budget deficits, about 2 more percentage points would be added. Thus, the resulting *aggregate* national government budget deficit,

inclusive of *all* government entities in the United States, would rise as a percentage of U.S. annual GDP to more than 10.2 percent. In addition, if the net public indebtedness of U.S. states and municipalities were included, the aggregate net debt of all U.S. government entities would rise from more than 77 percent of GDP per year to about 80 percent of GDP per year.

FOR CRITICAL THINKING

Why might differences in the reporting of national debt and deficit levels complicate governments' abilities to finance these debts and deficits?

The Resurgence of Federal Government Deficits

Why has the government's budget slipped from a surplus equal to nearly 2.5 percent of GDP into a deficit of more than 8 percent of GDP? The answer is that the government has been spending much more than its revenues. Spending has increased at a faster pace since the early 2000s—particularly in light of the ongoing bailout of financial institutions and a sharp rise in discretionary fiscal expenditures—than during any other decade since World War II.

The more complex answer also considers government revenues. In 2001, Congress and the executive branch slightly reduced income tax rates, and in 2003 they also cut federal capital gains tax rates and estate tax tates. Because tax rates were reduced toward the end of a recession when real income growth was relatively low, government tax revenues were stagnant for a time.

When economic activity began to expand into the middle of the first decade of this century, tax revenues started rising at a pace closer to the rapid rate of growth of government spending. Then, later in that decade, economic activity dropped significantly. Thus, annual tax collections declined at the same time that annual federal expenditures increased. As long as this situation persists, the U.S. government will operate with massive budget deficits such as those observed in the late 2000s and early 2010s.

QUICK QUIZ   See page 224 for the answers. Review concepts from this section in MyEconLab.

Whenever the federal government spends more than it receives during a given year, it operates with a _____ _____. If federal government spending exactly equals government revenues, then the government experiences a _____ _____. If the federal government collects more revenues than it spends, then it operates with a _____ _____.

The federal budget deficit is a flow, whereas accumulated budget deficits represent a _____, called the **public debt.**

The federal budget deficit expressed as a percentage of GDP rose to around 6 percent in the early 1980s. Between 1998 and 2001, the federal government experienced a budget _____, but since then its budget has once more been in _____. Currently, the budget _____ is more than 8 of GDP.

Evaluating the Rising Public Debt

Gross public debt
All federal government debt irrespective of who owns it.

Net public debt
Gross public debt minus all government interagency borrowing.

All federal public debt, taken together, is called the **gross public debt.** We arrive at the **net public debt** when we subtract from the gross public debt the portion that is held by government agencies (in essence, what the federal government owes to itself). For instance, if the Social Security Administration holds U.S. Treasury bonds, the U.S. Treasury makes debt payments to another agency of the government. On net, therefore, the U.S. government owes these payments to itself.

The net public debt increases whenever the federal government experiences a budget deficit. That is, the net public debt increases when government outlays are greater than total government receipts.

Accumulation of the Net Public Debt

Table 9-1 on the facing page displays, for various years since 1940, real values, in base-year 2005 dollars, of the federal budget deficit, the total and per capita net public debt (the amount owed on the net public debt by a typical individual), and the net interest cost of the public debt in total and as a percentage of GDP. It shows that the level of the real net public debt and the real net public debt per capita grew following the early 1980s and rose again very dramatically after 2007. Thus, the real, inflation-adjusted amount that a typical individual owes to holders of the net public debt has varied considerably over time.

TABLE 9-1

The Federal Deficit, Our Public Debt, and the Interest We Pay on It

The inflation-adjusted net public debt in column 3 is defined as total federal debt *excluding* all loans between federal government agencies. Per capita net public debt shown in column 4 is obtained by dividing the net public debt by the population.

(1) Year	(2) Federal Budget Deficit (billions of 2005 dollars)	(3) Net Public Debt (billions of 2005 dollars)	(4) Per Capita Net Public Debt (2005 dollars)	(5) Net Interest Costs (billions of 2005 dollars)	(6) Net Interest as a Percentage of GDP
1940	8.9	97.3	736.2	2.1	0.9
1945	492.9	2,150.7	15,372.8	28.3	1.45
1950	21.1	1,490.7	9,788.0	32.7	1.68
1955	18.0	1,360.8	8,202.8	29.4	1.23
1960	1.6	1,253.5	6,937.0	36.5	1.37
1965	7.9	1,287.7	6,627.5	42.3	1.26
1970	11.5	1,169.1	5,700.1	59.1	1.47
1975	134.1	1,180.0	5,463.1	69.3	1.52
1980	154.3	1,482.6	6,564.3	109.7	1.92
1985	344.1	2,430.0	10,247.4	209.7	3.22
1990	306.5	3,337.4	13,349.4	243.1	3.23
1995	201.2	4,421.6	16,585.2	284.7	3.24
2000	−267.1	3,853.1	13,644.1	252.0	2.34
2005	318.3	4,592.2	15,480.8	184.0	1.38
2010	1,165.3	8,125.1	29,814.3	176.8	1.35
2011	1,146.4	8,934.5	29,902.1	202.9	1.52
2012	1,189.5	10,379.5	33,309.6	201.5	1.63
2013	1,194.2	11,304.0	36,026.6	221.6	1.52

Sources: U.S. Department of the Treasury; Office of Management and Budget. *Note:* Data for 2013 are estimates.

The net public debt levels reported in Table 9-1 do not provide a basis of comparison with the overall size of the U.S. economy. Figure 9-3 below does this by displaying the net public debt as a percentage of GDP. We see that after World War II, this ratio fell steadily until the early 1970s (except for a small rise in the late 1950s) and

MyEconLab Real-time data

FIGURE 9-3

The Official Net U.S. Public Debt as a Percentage of GDP

During World War II, the officially reported net public debt grew dramatically. After the war, it fell until the 1970s, started rising in the 1980s, and then declined once more in the 1990s. Recently, it has increased significantly.

Source: U.S. Department of the Treasury.

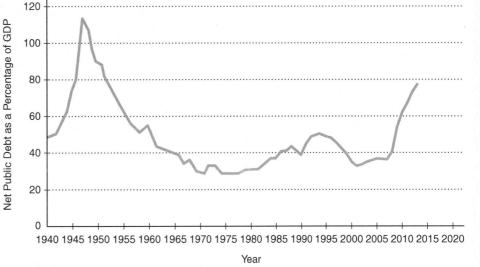

then leveled off until the 1980s. After that, the ratio of the net public debt to GDP more or less continued to rise to around 50 percent of GDP, before dropping slightly in the late 1990s. The ratio has been rising once again since 2001 and has jumped dramatically since 2007.

Annual Interest Payments on the Public Debt

Columns 5 and 6 of Table 9-1 show an important consequence of the net public debt. This is the interest that the government must pay to those who hold the bonds it has issued to finance past budget deficits. Those interest payments started rising dramatically around 1975 and then declined into the middle of the first decade of this century. Deficits have recently been higher. Interest payments expressed as a percentage of GDP will rise in the years to come.

If U.S. residents were the sole owners of the government's debts, the interest payments on the net public debt would go only to U.S. residents. In this situation, we would owe the debt to ourselves, with most people being taxed so that the government could pay interest to others (or to ourselves). During the 1970s, however, the share of the net public debt owned by foreign individuals, businesses, and governments started to rise, reaching 20 percent in 1978. From there it declined until the late 1980s, when it began to rise rapidly. Today, foreign residents, businesses, and governments hold more than 50 percent of the net public debt. Thus, we do not owe the debt just to ourselves.

Burdens of the Public Debt

Do current budget deficits and the accumulating public debt create social burdens? One perspective on this question considers possible burdens on future generations. Another focuses on transfers from U.S. residents to residents of other nations.

HOW TODAY'S BUDGET DEFICITS MIGHT BURDEN FUTURE GENERATIONS If the federal government wishes to purchase goods and services valued at $300 billion, it can finance this expenditure either by raising taxes by $300 billion or by selling $300 billion in bonds. Many economists maintain that the second option, deficit spending, would lead to a higher level of national consumption and a lower level of national saving than the first option.

The reason, say these economists, is that if people are taxed, they will have to forgo private consumption now as society substitutes government goods for private goods. If the government does not raise taxes but instead sells bonds to finance the $300 billion in expenditures, the public's disposable income remains the same. Members of the public have merely shifted their allocations of assets to include $300 billion in additional government bonds. There are two possible circumstances that could cause people to treat government borrowing differently than they treat taxes. One is that people will fail to realize that their liabilities (in the form of higher future taxes due to increased interest payments on the public debt) have *also* increased by $300 billion. Another is that people will believe that they can consume the governmentally provided goods without forgoing any private consumption because the bill for the government goods will be paid by *future* taxpayers.

THE CROWDING-OUT EFFECT But if full employment exists, and society raises its present consumption by adding consumption of government-provided goods to the original quantity of privately provided goods, then something must be *crowded out*. In a closed economy, investment expenditures on capital goods must decline. As you learned in Chapter 7, the mechanism by which investment is crowded out is an increase in the interest rate. Deficit spending increases the total demand for credit but leaves the total supply of credit unaltered. The rise in interest rates causes a reduction in the growth of investment and capital formation, which in turn slows the growth of productivity and improvement in society's living standard.

This perspective suggests that deficit spending can impose a burden on future generations in two ways. First, unless the deficit spending is allocated to purchases that lead to long-term increases in real GDP, future generations will have to be taxed at a higher rate. That is, only by imposing higher taxes on future generations will the government be able to retire the higher public debt resulting from the present generation's consumption of governmentally provided goods. Second, the increased level of spending by the present generation crowds out investment and reduces the growth of capital goods, leaving future generations with a smaller capital stock and thereby reducing their wealth.

PAYING OFF THE PUBLIC DEBT IN THE FUTURE Suppose that after several more years of running substantial deficits financed by selling bonds to U.S. residents, the public debt becomes so large that each adult person's implicit share of the net public debt liability is $60,000. Suppose further that the government chooses (or is forced) to pay off the debt at that time. Will that generation be burdened with our government's overspending? Assume that all of the debt is owed to ourselves.

To learn about the agency that manages the public debt, go to www.econtoday.com/chap09.

It is true that every adult will have to come up with $60,000 in taxes to pay off the debt, but then the government will use these funds to pay off the bondholders. Sometimes the bondholders and taxpayers will be the same people. Thus, *some* people will be burdened because they owe $60,000 and own less than $60,000 in government bonds. Others, however, will receive more than $60,000 for the bonds they own. Nevertheless, as a generation within society, they could—if all government debt were issued within the nation's borders—pay and receive about the same amount of funds.

Of course, there could be a burden on some low-income adults who will find it difficult or impossible to obtain $60,000 to pay off the tax liability. Still, nothing says that taxes to pay off the debt must be assessed equally. Indeed, it seems likely that a special tax would be levied, based on the ability to pay.

OUR DEBT TO FOREIGN RESIDENTS So far we have been assuming that we owe all of the public debt to ourselves. But, as we saw earlier, that is not the case. What about the more than 50 percent owned by foreign residents?

It is true that if foreign residents buy U.S. government bonds, we do not owe that debt to ourselves. Thus, when debts held by foreign residents come due, future U.S. residents will be taxed to repay these debts plus accumulated interest. Portions of the incomes of future U.S. residents will then be transferred abroad. In this way, a potential burden on future generations may result.

But this transfer of income from U.S. residents to residents of other nations will not necessarily be a burden. It is important to realize that if the rate of return on projects that the government funds by operating with deficits exceeds the interest rate paid to foreign residents, both foreign residents and future U.S. residents will be better off. If funds obtained by selling bonds to foreign residents are expended on wasteful projects, however, a burden will be placed on future generations.

We can apply the same reasoning to the problem of current investment and capital creation being crowded out by current deficits. If deficits lead to slower growth rates, future generations will be poorer. But if the government expenditures are really investments, and if the rate of return on such public investments exceeds the interest rate paid on the bonds, both present and future generations will be economically better off.

QUICK QUIZ See page 224 for the answers. Review concepts from this section in MyEconLab.

When we subtract the funds that government agencies borrow from each other from the _____ public debt, we obtain the _____ public debt.

The public debt may impose a burden on _____ generations if they have to be taxed at higher rates to pay for the _____ generation's increased consumption of governmentally provided goods. In addition, there may be a burden if the debt leads to crowding out of current

investment, resulting in _____ capital formation and hence a _____ economic growth rate.

If foreign residents hold a significant part of our public debt, then we no longer "owe it to ourselves." If the rate of return on the borrowed funds is _____ than the interest to be paid to foreign residents, future generations can be made better off by government borrowing. Future generations will be worse off, however, if the opposite is true.

FIGURE 9-4

The Related U.S. Deficits

The United States exported more than it imported until the mid-1970s. Then it started experiencing large trade deficits, as shown in this diagram. The federal budget has been in deficit most years since the 1960s.

The question is, has the federal budget deficit created the trade deficit?

Sources: Economic Report of the President; Economic Indicators, various issues; author's estimates.

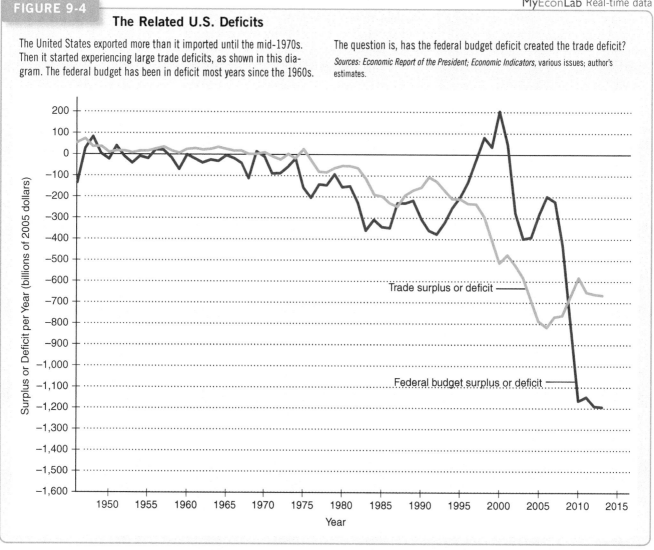

Federal Budget Deficits in an Open Economy

Many economists believe that it is no accident that foreign residents hold such a large portion of the U.S. public debt. Their reasoning suggests that a U.S. trade deficit—a situation in which the value of U.S. imports of goods and services exceeds the value of its exports—will often accompany a government budget deficit.

Trade Deficits and Government Budget Deficits

Figure 9-4 above shows U.S. trade deficits and surpluses compared with federal budget deficits and surpluses. In the mid-1970s, imports of goods and services began to consistently exceed exports of those items on an annual basis in the United States. At the same time, the federal budget deficit rose dramatically. Both deficits increased once again in the early 2000s. Then, during the economic turmoil of the late 2000s, the budget deficit exploded while the trade deficit shrank somewhat.

Overall, however, it appears that larger trade deficits tend to accompany larger government budget deficits.

Why the Two Deficits Tend to Be Related

Intuitively, there is a reason why we would expect federal budget deficits to be associated with trade deficits. You might call this the unpleasant arithmetic of trade and budget deficits.

Suppose that, initially, the government's budget is balanced; government expenditures are matched by an equal amount of tax collections and other government revenues. Now assume that the federal government begins to operate with a budget deficit. It increases its spending, collects fewer taxes, or both. Assume further that domestic consumption and domestic investment do not decrease relative to GDP. Where, then, do the funds come from to finance the government's budget deficit? A portion of these funds must come from abroad. That is to say, dollar holders abroad ultimately will purchase newly created government bonds.

Of course, foreign dollar holders will choose to hold the new U.S. government bonds only if there is an economic inducement to do so, such as an increase in U.S. interest rates. Given that private domestic spending and other factors are unchanged, interest rates will indeed rise whenever there is an increase in deficits financed by increased borrowing.

When foreign dollar holders purchase the new U.S. government bonds, they will have fewer dollars to spend on U.S. items, including U.S. export goods. Hence, when our nation's government operates with a budget deficit, we should expect to see foreign dollar holders spending more on U.S. government bonds and less on U.S.-produced goods and services. As a consequence of the U.S. government deficit, therefore, we should generally anticipate a decline in U.S. exports relative to U.S. imports, or a higher U.S. trade deficit.

Growing U.S. Government Deficits: Implications for U.S. Economic Performance

We have seen that one consequence of higher U.S. government budget deficits tends to be higher international trade deficits. Higher budget deficits, such as the much higher deficits of recent years (especially during the recession of the late 2000s), are also likely to have broader consequences for the economy.

For more information about the role of the Office of Management and Budget in the government's budgeting process, go to www.econtoday.com/chap09.

The Macroeconomic Consequences of Budget Deficits

When evaluating additional macroeconomic effects of government deficits, two important points must be kept well in mind. First, given the level of government expenditures, the main alternative to the deficit is higher taxes. Therefore, the effects of a deficit should be compared to the effects of higher taxes, not to zero. Second, it is important to distinguish between the effects of deficits when full employment exists and the effects when substantial unemployment exists.

SHORT-RUN MACROECONOMIC EFFECTS OF HIGHER BUDGET DEFICITS How do increased government budget deficits affect the economy in the short run? The answer depends on the initial state of the economy. Recall from Chapter 8 that higher government spending and lower taxes that generate budget deficits typically add to total planned expenditures, even after taking into account direct and indirect expenditure offsets. When there is a recessionary gap, the increase in aggregate demand can eliminate the recessionary gap and push the economy toward its full-employment real GDP level. In the presence of a short-run recessionary gap, therefore, government deficit spending can influence both real GDP and employment.

If the economy is at the full-employment level of real GDP, however, increased total planned expenditures and higher aggregate demand generated by a larger government budget deficit create an inflationary gap. Although greater deficit spending temporarily raises equilibrium real GDP above the full-employment level, the price level also increases.

LONG-RUN MACROECONOMIC EFFECTS OF HIGHER BUDGET DEFICITS In a long-run macroeconomic equilibrium, the economy has fully adjusted to changes in all factors. These factors include changes in government spending and taxes and, consequently, the government budget deficit. Although increasing the government budget deficit raises aggregate demand, in the long run equilibrium real GDP remains at its full-employment level. Further increases in the government deficit via higher government expenditures or tax cuts can only be inflationary. They have no effect on equilibrium real GDP, which remains at the full-employment level in the long run.

The fact that long-run equilibrium real GDP is unaffected in the face of increased government deficits has an important implication:

> *In the long run, higher government budget deficits have no effect on equilibrium real GDP per year. Ultimately, therefore, government spending in excess of government receipts simply redistributes a larger share of real GDP per year to government-provided goods and services.*

Thus, if the government operates with higher deficits over an extended period, the ultimate result is a shrinkage in the share of privately provided goods and services. By continually spending more than it collects in taxes and other revenue sources, the government takes up a larger portion of economic activity.

QUICK QUIZ See page 224 for the answers. Review concepts from this section in MyEconLab.

To obtain the dollars required to purchase newly issued U.S. government bonds, foreign residents must sell _____ goods and services in the United States than U.S. residents sell abroad. Thus, U.S. imports must _____ U.S. exports. For this reason, the federal budget deficit and the international trade _____ tend to be related.

Higher government deficits arise from increased government spending or tax cuts, which raise aggregate demand. Thus, larger government budget deficits can raise real GDP in a _____ gap situation. If the economy is

already at the full-employment level of real GDP, however, higher government deficits can only temporarily push equilibrium real GDP _____ the full-employment level.

In the long run, higher government budget deficits cause the equilibrium price level to rise but fail to raise equilibrium real GDP above the full-employment level. Thus, the long-run effect of increased government deficits is simply a redistribution of real GDP per year from _____ provided goods and services to _____-provided goods and services.

How Could the Government Reduce All of Its Red Ink?

There have been many suggestions about how to reduce the government deficit. One way to reduce the deficit is to increase tax collections.

INCREASING TAXES FOR EVERYONE From an arithmetic point of view, a federal budget deficit can be wiped out by simply increasing the amount of taxes collected. Let's see what this would require. Projections for 2013 are instructive. The Office of Management and Budget estimated the 2013 federal budget deficit at about $1 trillion. To have prevented this deficit from occurring by raising taxes, in 2013 the government would have had to collect more than $8,000 in additional taxes from *every worker* in the United States. Needless to say, reality is such that we will never see annual federal budget deficits wiped out by simple tax increases.

YOU ARE THERE

To consider some "easy" cuts that the government could make to its budget deficit, read **A Long List of Ways to Cut the Federal Budget Deficit** on page 219.

WHAT IF... the government imposed a one-time tax to pay off all of the net public debt?

The net public debt is nearly $13 trillion and rising, while nominal GDP exceeds $15 trillion. If the government confiscated about three-fourths of all income generated by production in a single year, it could repay the outstanding net public debt. To avoid creating more debt during that year, however, the government also would have to

seize almost $3 trillion to fund its continued spending. Thus, to eliminate the net public debt within a single year, the government would have to confiscate at least 100 percent of all income generated during that year. In theory, this could be done, but only at the expense of impoverishing the nation's residents for 12 months.

TAXING THE RICH Some people suggest that the way to eliminate the deficit is to raise taxes on the rich. What does it mean to tax the rich more? If you talk about taxing "millionaires," you are referring to those who pay taxes on more than $1 million in income per year. There are fewer than 100,000 of them. Even if you were to double the taxes they now pay, the reduction in the deficit would be relatively trivial. Changing marginal tax rates at the upper end will produce similarly unimpressive results. The Internal Revenue Service (IRS) has determined that an increase in the top marginal tax rate from 35 percent to 45 percent would raise, at best, only about $35 billion in additional taxes. (This assumes that people do not figure out a way to avoid the higher tax rate.) Extra revenues of $35 billion per year represent only about 3 percent of the estimated 2013 federal budget deficit.

The reality is that the data do not support the notion that tax increases can completely *eliminate* deficits. Although eliminating a deficit in this way is possible arithmetically, politically just the opposite has occurred. When more tax revenues have been collected, Congress has usually responded by increasing government spending.

Could taxing more of the incomes of people earning in excess of $1 million per year eliminate the federal government's current annual deficit?

POLICY EXAMPLE

Could a 100 Percent Tax on "Millionaires" Eliminate the Deficit?

Some have claimed that raising income tax rates for "millionaires and billionaires" could eliminate the federal deficit. To contemplate this suggestion, consider Figure 9-5 below, and imagine a 100 percent income tax rate on all people earning more than $1 million per year.

The last bar displayed in the figure indicates that in a typical year, the sum of *all* incomes earned by these high-income individuals is less than $1 trillion. Since 2008, however, the average federal deficit has exceeded $1 trillion per year. Thus, even if the federal government were

to *confiscate* each year *all* of the earnings of people with incomes exceeding $1 million per year—thereby ending their incentives to earn incomes—this action could not cover the government's annual deficit.

FOR CRITICAL THINKING

Why do you think that most economists suggest that ending deficits without cutting spending would require the government to raise tax rates on middle-income earners?

FIGURE 9-5

Distribution of Total Taxable Income Based on Annual Taxpayer Earnings

This figure shows that the largest amount of total annual taxable income—more than $1.3 trillion per year—goes to people who earn between $100,000 and $200,000 per year. The total income received by individuals who earn more than $1 million per year—indicated by

the last bar on the right-hand side of the figure—typically is less than $1 trillion.

Source: Internal Revenue Service.

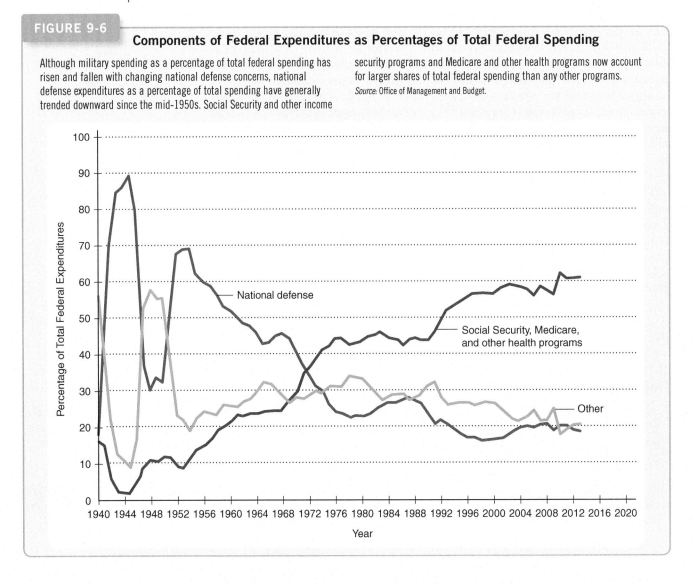

FIGURE 9-6

Components of Federal Expenditures as Percentages of Total Federal Spending

Although military spending as a percentage of total federal spending has risen and fallen with changing national defense concerns, national defense expenditures as a percentage of total spending have generally trended downward since the mid-1950s. Social Security and other income security programs and Medicare and other health programs now account for larger shares of total federal spending than any other programs.

Source: Office of Management and Budget.

REDUCING EXPENDITURES Reducing expenditures is another way to decrease the federal budget deficit. Figure 9-6 above shows various components of government spending as a percentage of total expenditures. There you see that military spending (national defense) as a share of total federal expenditures has risen slightly in some recent years, though it remains much lower than in most previous years.

During the period from the conclusion of World War II until 1972, military spending was the most important aspect of the federal budget. Figure 9-6 shows that it no longer is, even taking into account the war on terrorism that began in late 2001. **Entitlements,** which are legislated federal government payments that anyone who qualifies is entitled to receive, are now the most important component of the federal budget. These include payments for Social Security and other income security programs and for Medicare and other health programs such as Medicaid. Entitlements are consequently often called **noncontrollable expenditures,** or nondiscretionary expenditures unrelated to national defense that automatically change without any direct action by Congress.

IS IT TIME TO BEGIN WHITTLING AWAY AT ENTITLEMENTS? In 1960, spending on entitlements represented about 20 percent of the total federal budget. Today, entitlement expenditures make up more than 60 percent of total federal spending. Consider Social Security, Medicare, and Medicaid. In constant 2005 dollars, in 2013 Social Security, Medicare, and Medicaid represented about $2,200 billion of estimated federal expenditures. (This calculation excludes military and international payments and interest on the government debt.)

Entitlements
Guaranteed benefits under a government program such as Social Security, Medicare, or Medicaid.

Noncontrollable expenditures
Government spending that changes automatically without action by Congress.

Entitlement payments for Social Security, Medicare, and Medicaid now exceed all other domestic spending. Entitlements are growing faster than any other part of the federal government budget. During the past two decades, real spending on entitlements (adjusted for inflation) grew between 7 and 8 percent per year, while the economy grew less than 3 percent per year. Social Security payments are growing in real terms at about 6 percent per year, but Medicare and Medicaid are growing at double-digit rates. The passage of Medicare prescription drug benefits in 2003 and the new federal health care legislation in 2010 simply added to the already rapid growth of these health care entitlements.

Many people believe that entitlement programs are "necessary" federal expenditures. Interest on the public debt must be paid, but Congress can change just about every other federal expenditure labeled "necessary." The federal budget deficit is not expected to drop in the near future because entitlement programs are not likely to be reduced. Governments have trouble cutting government benefit programs once they are established. One must conclude that containing federal budget deficits is likely to prove a difficult task.

By how much does an accurate accounting of entitlement promises by the U.S. government increase its measured indebtedness?

POLICY EXAMPLE

Federal Indebtedness Is *Much* Higher Than the Net Public Debt

The U.S. government's *official* net public debt has been ballooning in recent years, but its *actual* indebtedness has increased even more rapidly. Every year, Congress borrows and spends more than contributions to Social Security payments made to these beneficiaries. Thus, instead of saving these funds to finance payments to future Social Security beneficiaries, every year Congress uses the funds for other purposes. Congress likewise has promised Medicare and Medicaid benefits to future beneficiaries but has not set aside funds to pay for those benefits.

Laurence Kotlikoff of Boston University has calculated the current dollar value of all amounts the U.S. government has promised to provide to future Social Security, Medicare, and Medicaid recipients. Kotlikoff estimates that the total value of these currently *unfunded* promises amounts to more than $200 trillion. This amount, which is twelve times greater than a typical year's entire flow of national income, is almost *sixteen times* larger than the official value of today's net public debt.

FOR CRITICAL THINKING

How could the federal government try to reduce its entitlement indebtedness?

QUICK QUIZ See page 224 for the answers. Review concepts from this section in MyEconLab.

One way to reduce federal budget _____ is to increase taxes. Proposals to reduce deficits by raising taxes on the highest-income individuals will not appreciably reduce budget deficits, however.	Another way to decrease federal budget _____ is to cut back on government spending, particularly on _____, defined as benefits guaranteed under government programs such as Social Security and Medicare.

YOU ARE THERE

A Long List of Ways to Cut the Federal Budget Deficit

Gene Dodaro, head of the Government Accountability Office (GAO), issues a report listing separately funded programs with "duplicative" objectives. Among these are:

- 100 programs related to highway and rail transportation
- 82 programs to improve teacher quality
- 80 programs to help low-income people with transportation
- 80 programs to promote economic development
- 57 programs to help U.S. residents become more financially literate
- 52 programs to promote entrepreneurship
- 47 programs to assist with job training

Eliminating the duplicative programs, Dodaro and the GAO report, would permit the federal government to cut about $200 billion per year from its annual deficit.

After reporting to Congress, Dodaro returns to his office. He and others at the GAO have accomplished their task. But only Congress can make budget cuts.

Critical Thinking Questions

1. By what percentage could a $1 trillion annual deficit be reduced if Congress were to enact the spending cuts identified by Dodaro and the GAO?

2. How much less would be added to the net public debt every year if duplicative programs were eliminated?

Rising deficit threatens U.S. credit rating

Standard & Poor's warned that it could downgrade the United States' sterling debt rating if the White House and Congress fail to reach a deal to control the massive federal deficit, which is feeding the nation's debt. Here is a look at growth of the debt in recent decades.

Annual gross national debt in trillions of dollars

$25 trillion

2016
$20.8 trillion

20

Estimated

15

2010
$13.5 trillion

10

5 1940
$50.7 billion

'90   '00   '10   '16

ISSUES & APPLICATIONS

Borrowing Total Discretionary Spending—And More

CONCEPTS APPLIED

▶ Government Budget Deficit

▶ Entitlements

▶ Noncontrollable Expenditures

Since 2008, higher federal budget deficits have had three causes: lower tax revenues, higher discretionary spending, and greater entitlement expenditures. Tax revenues have dropped so much that in some recent years, the government has borrowed to fund *all* discretionary spending.

The Share of Tax Revenues Going to Discretionary Spending

Figure 9-6 on page 218 shows that the share of total federal spending on entitlements has increased during the past 20 years. How has this trend affected the government's ability to fund its *discretionary* spending? Figure 9-7 below displays the percentage of tax revenues available to apply toward discretionary spending—that is, after paying for

entitlement expenditures—since the early 1990s. During the late 1990s, this percentage rose above 100 percent, meaning that the federal government officially operated with surpluses and paid down some of its outstanding debts.

After the late 1990s, however, the percentage of tax revenues available to cover discretionary spending after paying entitlements steadily declined. Since the late 2000s, this percentage has dropped substantially.

FIGURE 9-7

The Percentage of Federal Tax Receipts Available for Federal Discretionary Spending

The share of federal tax revenues available for discretionary spending after paying for entitlement expenditures declined after the late 1990s and has fallen considerably since the mid-2000s. Indeed, during some recent years the percentage of federal tax receipts allocated to discretionary spending has even dropped to or below zero. Within these intervals, the federal government has had to borrow funds to finance all of its discretionary spending plus part of its noncontrollable expenditures on entitlements.

Source: Congressional Budget Office.

Y-axis: Percentage of Tax Revenues Available to Cover Discretionary Spending (%); X-axis: Year (1993–2015)

Indeed, during periods in which the percentage of tax revenues available to allocate to discretionary spending has been zero or negative, the federal government's tax revenues have been insufficient to pay for *any* of its discretionary spending. During these intervals, *all* discretionary spending has been financed with borrowed funds.

Borrowing in Part to Cover Entitlement Spending

When the share of federal tax revenues allocated to discretionary spending is below zero, the government borrows *more* than the amount of its discretionary spending. During these intervals, the government borrows funds to help pay some of its noncontrollable expenditures on entitlements as well as to cover its discretionary spending.

For Critical Thinking

1. What would be true of entitlement spending if the percentage of taxes allocated to discretionary spending rose to 100 percent and the federal budget was balanced? (Hint: Under a balanced budget, tax revenues equal the sum of discretionary and nondiscretionary expenditures.)
2. How would entitlement spending be funded if tax revenues just covered discretionary spending and there was a government budget deficit?

Web Resources

1. To review recent trends in federal discretionary and entitlement expenditures, go to www.econtoday.com/chap09.
2. For projections of federal entitlement expenditures for the first half of this century, go to www.econtoday.com/chap09.

MyEconLab

For more questions on this chapter's
Issues & Applications, go to MyEconLab.
In the Study Plan for this chapter,
select Section N: News.

MyEconLab

Here is what you should know after reading this chapter. MyEconLab will help you identify what you know, and where to go when you need to practice.

WHAT YOU SHOULD KNOW		WHERE TO GO TO PRACTICE
Federal Government Budget Deficits A budget deficit occurs whenever the flow of government expenditures exceeds the flow of government revenues during a period of time. If government expenditures are less than government revenues during a given interval, a budget surplus occurs. The government operates with a balanced budget during a specific period if its expenditures equal its revenues. The deficit recently has risen to more than 8 percent of GDP.	government budget deficit, 207 balanced budget, 207 government budget surplus, 207 public debt, 208 **Key Figures** Figure 9-1, 208 Figure 9-2, 209	• MyEconLab Study Plans 9.1, 9.2 • Animated Figures 9-1, 9-2
The Public Debt The federal budget deficit is a flow, whereas accumulated budget deficits are a stock, called the public debt. The gross public debt is the stock of total government bonds, and the net public debt is the difference between the gross public debt and the amount of government agencies' holdings of government bonds. In recent years, the net public debt as a share of GDP has exceeded 70 percent of GDP.	gross public debt, 210 net public debt, 210 **Key Figure** Figure 9-3, 211	• MyEconLab Study Plan 9.3 • Figure 9-3

MyEconLab *continued*

WHAT YOU SHOULD KNOW

How the Public Debt Might Prove a Burden to Future Generations People taxed at a higher rate must forgo private consumption as society substitutes government goods for private goods. Any current crowding out of investment as a consequence of additional debt accumulation can reduce capital formation and future economic growth. Furthermore, if capital invested by foreign residents who purchase some of the U.S. public debt has not been productively used, future generations will be worse off.

Key Figure
Figure 9-4, 214

WHERE TO GO TO PRACTICE

- MyEconLab Study Plans 9.3, 9.4
- Animated Figure 9-4

The Macroeconomic Effects of Government Budget Deficits Higher government deficits contribute to a rise in total planned expenditures and aggregate demand. If there is a short-run recessionary gap, higher government deficits can thereby push equilibrium real GDP toward the full-employment level. If the economy is already at the full-employment level of real GDP, however, then a higher deficit creates a short-run inflationary gap.

- MyEconLab Study Plan 9.5

Possible Ways to Reduce the Government Budget Deficit Suggested ways to reduce the deficit are to increase taxes, particularly on the rich, and to reduce expenditures, particularly on entitlements, defined as guaranteed benefits under government programs such as Social Security and Medicare.

entitlements, 218
noncontrollable
    expenditures, 218

Key Figure
Figure 9-6, 218

- MyEconLab Study Plan 9.5
- Animated Figure 9-6

Log in to MyEconLab, take a chapter test, and get a personalized Study Plan that tells you which concepts you understand and which ones you need to review. From there, MyEconLab will give you further practice, tutorials, animations, videos, and guided solutions. For more information, visit www.myeconlab.com

PROBLEMS

All problems are assignable in MyEconLab; exercises that update with real-time data are marked with 🌐. Answers to odd-numbered problems appear at the back of the book.

9-1. In 2015, government spending is $4.3 trillion, and taxes collected are $3.9 trillion. What is the federal government deficit in that year? (See page 208.)

9-2. Suppose that the Office of Management and Budget provides the estimates of federal budget receipts, federal budget spending, and GDP at the right, all expressed in billions of dollars. Calculate the implied

estimates of the federal budget deficit as a percentage of GDP for each year. (See pages 208–209.)

Year	Federal Budget Receipts	Federal Budget Spending	GDP
2015	3,829.8	4,382.6	15,573.2
2016	3,892.4	4,441.6	16,316.0
2017	3,964.2	4,529.3	16,852.1
2018	4,013.5	4,600.1	17,454.4

9-3. It may be argued that the effects of a higher public debt are the same as the effects of a higher deficit. Why? (See pages 208–210.)

9-4. What happens to the net public debt if the federal government operates next year with the following (see page 208):

    a. A budget deficit?

    b. A balanced budget?

    c. A budget surplus?

9-5. What is the relationship between the gross public debt and the net public debt? (See page 210.)

9-6. Explain how each of the following will affect the net public debt, other things being equal. (See page 208.)

    a. Previously, the government operated with a balanced budget, but recently there has been a sudden increase in federal tax collections.

    b. The government had been operating with a very small annual budget deficit until three hurricanes hit the Atlantic Coast, and now government spending has risen substantially.

    c. The Government National Mortgage Association, a federal government agency that purchases certain types of home mortgages, buys U.S. Treasury bonds from another government agency.

9-7. Explain in your own words why there is likely to be a relationship between federal budget deficits and U.S. international trade deficits. (See page 214.)

9-8. Suppose that the share of U.S. GDP going to domestic consumption remains constant. Initially, the federal government was operating with a balanced budget, but this year it has increased its spending well above its collections of taxes and other sources of revenues. To fund its deficit spending, the government has issued bonds. So far, very few foreign residents have shown any interest in purchasing the bonds. (See page 212.)

    a. What must happen to induce foreign residents to buy the bonds?

    b. If foreign residents desire to purchase the bonds, what is the most important source of dollars to buy them?

9-9. Suppose that the economy is experiencing the short-run equilibrium position depicted at point *A* in the diagram near the top of the next column. Then the government raises its spending and thereby runs a budget deficit in an effort to boost equilibrium real GDP to its long-run equilibrium level of $15 trillion (in base-year dollars). Explain the effects of an increase in the government deficit on equilibrium real GDP and the equilibrium price level. In addition, given that many taxes and

government benefits vary with real GDP, discuss what change we might expect to see in the budget deficit as a result of the effects on equilibrium real GDP. (See pages 215–216.)

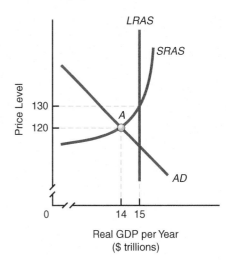

9-10. Suppose that the economy is experiencing the short-run equilibrium position depicted at point *B* in the diagram below. Explain the short-run effects of an increase in the government deficit on equilibrium real GDP and the equilibrium price level. What will be the long-run effects? (See pages 215–216.)

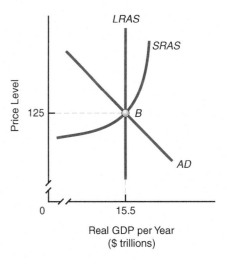

9-11. To eliminate the deficit (and halt the growth of the net public debt), a politician suggests that "we should tax the rich." The politician makes a simple arithmetic calculation in which he applies a higher tax rate to the total income reported by "the rich" in a previous year. He says that the government could thereby solve the deficit problem by taxing "the rich." What is the major fallacy in such a claim? (See page 217.)

9-12. Refer back to Problem 9-11. If the politician defines "the rich" as people with annual taxable incomes exceeding $1 million per year, what is another difficulty with the politician's reasoning, given that "the rich" rarely earn a combined taxable income exceeding $1 trillion, yet the federal deficit has regularly exceeded $1 trillion in recent years? (See page 217.)

9-13. In each of the past few years, the federal government has regularly borrowed funds to pay for at least one-third of expenditures that tax revenues were insufficient to cover. More than 60 percent of all federal expenditures now go for entitlement spending. What does this fact imply about how the government is paying for most of its discretionary expenditures? (See page 220.)

ECONOMICS ON THE NET

The Public Debt By examining the federal government's budget data, its current estimates of the public debt can be determined.

Title: Historical Tables: Budget of the United States Government

Navigation: Use the link at **www.econtoday.com/chap09** to visit the Office of Management and Budget. Select the most recent budget. Then select *Historical Tables*.

Application After the document downloads, perform each of the indicated operations and answer the following questions.

1. In the Table of Contents in the left-hand margin of the Historical Tables, click on Table 7.1, "Federal Debt at the End of the Year, 1940–2015." In light of the discussion in this chapter, which column shows the net public debt? What is the conceptual difference between the gross public debt and the net public debt? Last year, what was the dollar difference between these two amounts?

2. Table 7.1 includes estimates of the gross and net public debt over the next several years. Suppose that these estimates turn out to be accurate. Calculate how much the net public debt would increase on average each year. What are possible ways that the government could prevent these predicted increases from occurring?

For Group Study and Analysis Divide into two groups, and have each group take one side in answering the question, "Is the public debt a burden or a blessing?" Have each group develop rationales for supporting its position. Then reconvene the entire class, and discuss the relative merits of the alternative positions and rationales.

ANSWERS TO QUICK QUIZZES

p. 210: (i) budget deficit . . . balanced budget . . . budget surplus; (ii) stock; (iii) surplus . . . deficit . . . deficit

p. 213: (i) gross . . . net; (ii) future . . . current . . . less . . . lower; (iii) higher

p. 216: (i) more . . . exceed . . . deficit; (ii) recessionary . . . above; (iii) privately . . . government

p. 219: (i) deficits; (ii) deficits . . . entitlements

Module 4

Monetary Policy

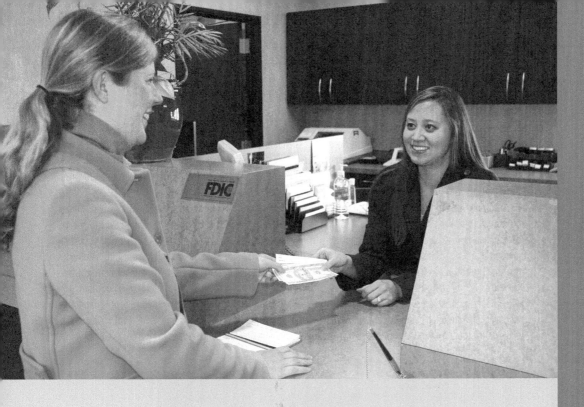

Money, Banking, and Central Banking

10

LEARNING OBJECTIVES

After reading this chapter, you should be able to:

▶ Define the fundamental functions of money and identify key properties that any good that functions as money must possess

▶ Explain official definitions of the quantity of money in circulation

▶ Understand why financial intermediaries such as banks exist

▶ Describe the basic structure and functions of the Federal Reserve System

▶ Determine the maximum potential extent that the money supply will change following a Federal Reserve monetary policy action

▶ Explain the essential features of federal deposit insurance

MyEconLab helps you master each objective and study more efficiently. See end of chapter for details.

During the early 2000s, bank managers across the United States sought to boost total deposits at their institutions, both by inducing existing customers to increase their deposits and by attracting new depositors. In the early 2010s, their efforts paid off: Total deposits at U.S. banks had increased by about 10 percent. Since then, however, banks generally have reversed course. Most banks have halted their efforts to gain more deposits, and a few even have begun actively discouraging increases in funds held on deposit with their institutions. What accounts for this abrupt change in course on the part of U.S. banks? In this chapter, you will find out.

? DID YOU KNOW THAT... since 2009, U.S. consumers' use of currency and coins to make payments has, for the first time since the 1970s, increased relative to other means of making payments? In other words, consumers now are buying more items with cash. As a consequence, the public's desired holdings of currency and coins have risen even as they have boosted their holdings of funds on deposit with banks. The Federal Reserve includes currency and coins and deposits in its measure of the quantity of money in circulation. Thus, this increase in the public's holdings of cash and deposits has translated into substantial recent growth in these measures of the quantity of money.

Traditionally, the primary task of the Federal Reserve System has been to regulate the quantity of money in circulation in the U.S. economy—that is, to conduct *monetary policy*. Money has been important to society for thousands of years. In the fourth century BC, Aristotle claimed that everything had to "be accessed in money, for this enables men always to exchange their services, and so makes society possible." Money is indeed a part of our everyday existence. Nevertheless, we have to be careful when we talk about money. Often we hear a person say, "I wish I had more money," instead of "I wish I had more wealth," thereby confusing the concepts of money and wealth. Economists use the term **money** to mean anything that people generally accept in exchange for goods and services. Table 10-1 below provides a list of some items that various civilizations have used as money. The best way to understand how these items served this purpose is to examine the functions of money.

Money
Any medium that is universally accepted in an economy both by sellers of goods and services as payment for those goods and services and by creditors as payment for debts.

The Functions of Money

Money traditionally has four functions. The one that most people are familiar with is money's function as a *medium of exchange*. Money also serves as a *unit of accounting*, a *store of value* or *purchasing power*, and a *standard of deferred payment*. Anything that serves these four functions is money. Anything that could serve these four functions could be considered money.

Money as a Medium of Exchange

When we say that money serves as a **medium of exchange,** we mean that sellers will accept it as payment in market transactions. Without some generally accepted medium of exchange, we would have to resort to *barter*. In fact, before money was used, transactions took place by means of barter. **Barter** is simply a direct exchange of goods for goods. In a barter economy, the shoemaker who wants to obtain a dozen water glasses must seek out a glassmaker who at exactly the same time is interested in obtaining a pair of shoes. For this to occur, there has to be a high likelihood of a *double coincidence of wants* for each specific item to be exchanged. If there isn't, the shoemaker

Medium of exchange
Any item that sellers will accept as payment.

Barter
The direct exchange of goods and services for other goods and services without the use of money.

TABLE 10-1

Types of Money

This is a partial list of items that have been used as money. Native Americans used *wampum*, beads made from shells. Fijians used whale teeth. The early colonists in North America used tobacco. And cigarettes were used in post–World War II Germany and in Poland during the breakdown of Communist rule in the late 1980s.

Boar tusk	Goats	Rice
Boats	Gold	Round stones with centers removed
Cigarettes	Horses	Rum
Copper	Iron	Salt
Corn	Molasses	Silver
Cows	Polished beads (wampum)	Tobacco
Feathers	Pots	Tortoise shells
Glass	Red woodpecker scalps	Whale teeth

Source: Adapted from MONEY, BANKING, and FINANCIAL MARKETS, Third Edition, by Roger Miller and David VanHoose. Copyright © 2007 by Cengage Learning, Inc..

must go through several trades in order to obtain the desired dozen glasses—perhaps first trading shoes for jewelry, then jewelry for some pots and pans, and then the pots and pans for the desired glasses.

Money facilitates exchange by reducing the transaction costs associated with means-of-payment uncertainty. That is, the existence of money means that individuals no longer have to hold a diverse collection of goods as an exchange inventory. As a medium of exchange, money allows individuals to specialize in producing those goods for which they have a comparative advantage and to receive money payments for their labor. Money payments can then be exchanged for the fruits of other people's labor. The use of money as a medium of exchange permits more specialization and the inherent economic efficiencies that come with it (and hence greater economic growth).

Money as a Unit of Accounting

A **unit of accounting** is a way of placing a specific price on economic goods and services. It is the common denominator, the commonly recognized measure of value. The dollar is the unit of accounting in the United States. It is the yardstick that allows individuals easily to compare the relative value of goods and services. Accountants at the U.S. Department of Commerce use dollar prices to measure national income and domestic product, a business uses dollar prices to calculate profits and losses, and a typical household budgets regularly anticipated expenses using dollar prices as its unit of accounting.

Another way of describing money as a unit of accounting is to say that it serves as a *standard of value* that allows people to compare the relative worth of various goods and services. This allows for comparison shopping, for example.

Unit of accounting
A measure by which prices are expressed; the common denominator of the price system; a central property of money.

Money as a Store of Value

One of the most important functions of money is that it serves as a **store of value** or purchasing power. The money you have today can be set aside to purchase things later on. If you have $1,000 in your checking account, you can choose to spend it today on goods and services, spend it tomorrow, or spend it a month from now. In this way, money provides a way to transfer value (wealth) into the future.

Store of value
The ability to hold value over time; a necessary property of money.

Money as a Standard of Deferred Payment

The fourth function of the monetary unit is as a **standard of deferred payment.** This function involves the use of money both as a medium of exchange and as a unit of accounting. Debts are typically stated in terms of a unit of accounting, and they are paid with a monetary medium of exchange. That is to say, a debt is specified in a dollar amount and paid in currency (or by debit card or check). A corporate bond, for example, has a face value—the dollar value stated on it, which is to be paid upon maturity. The periodic interest payments on that corporate bond are specified and paid in dollars, and when the bond comes due (at maturity), the corporation pays the face value in dollars to the holder of the bond.

Standard of deferred payment
A property of an item that makes it desirable for use as a means of settling debts maturing in the future; an essential property of money.

Properties of Money

Money is an asset—something of value—that accounts for part of personal wealth. Wealth in the form of money can be exchanged for other assets, goods, or services. Although money is not the only form of wealth that can be exchanged for goods and services, it is the most widely and readily accepted one.

Money—The Most Liquid Asset

Money's attribute as the most readily tradable asset is called **liquidity.** We say that an asset is *liquid* when it can easily be acquired or disposed of without high transaction costs and with relative certainty as to its value. Money is by definition the most

Liquidity
The degree to which an asset can be acquired or disposed of without much danger of any intervening loss in *nominal* value and with small transaction costs. Money is the most liquid asset.

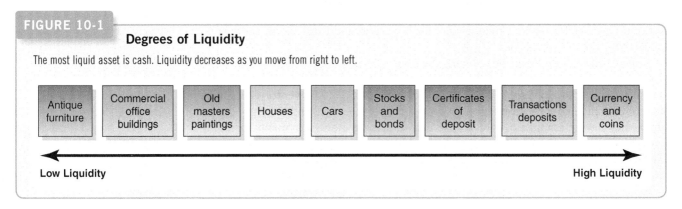

FIGURE 10-1

Degrees of Liquidity

The most liquid asset is cash. Liquidity decreases as you move from right to left.

| Antique furniture | Commercial office buildings | Old masters paintings | Houses | Cars | Stocks and bonds | Certificates of deposit | Transactions deposits | Currency and coins |

Low Liquidity ← → **High Liquidity**

liquid asset. People can easily convert money to other asset forms. Therefore, most individuals hold at least a part of their wealth in the form of the most liquid of assets, money. You can see how assets rank in liquidity relative to one another in Figure 10-1 above.

When we hold money, however, we incur a cost for this advantage of liquidity. Because cash in your pocket and many checking or debit account balances do not earn interest, that cost is the interest yield that could have been obtained had the asset been held in another form—for example, in the form of stocks and bonds.

The cost of holding money (its opportunity cost) is measured by the alternative interest yield obtainable by holding some other asset.

Monetary Standards, or What Backs Money

In the past, many different monetary standards have existed. For example, commodity money, which is a physical good that may be valued for other uses it provides, has been used (see Table 10-1 on page 228). The main forms of commodity money were gold and silver. Today, though, most people throughout the world accept coins, paper currency, and balances held on deposit as **transactions deposits** (debitable and checkable accounts with banks and other financial institutions) in exchange for items sold, including labor services.

But these forms of money raise a question: Why are we willing to accept as payment something that has no intrinsic value? After all, you could not sell checks or debit cards to very many producers for use as a raw material in manufacturing. The reason is that payments in the modern world arise from a **fiduciary monetary system.** This concept refers to the fact that the value of the payments rests on the public's confidence that such payments can be exchanged for goods and services. *Fiduciary* comes from the Latin *fiducia*, which means "trust" or "confidence." In our fiduciary monetary system, there is no legal requirement for money, in the form of currency or transactions deposits, to be convertible to a fixed quantity of gold, silver, or some other precious commodity. The bills are just pieces of paper. Coins have a value stamped on them that today is usually greater than the market value of the metal in them. Nevertheless, currency and transactions deposits are money because of their acceptability and predictability of value.

ACCEPTABILITY Transactions deposits and currency are money because they are accepted in exchange for goods and services. They are accepted because people have confidence that these items can later be exchanged for other goods and services. This confidence is based on the knowledge that such exchanges have occurred in the past without problems.

PREDICTABILITY OF VALUE Money retains its usefulness even if its purchasing power is declining year in and year out, as during periods of inflation, if it still retains the characteristic of predictability of value. If you anticipate that the inflation rate is

Transactions deposits
Checkable and debitable account balances in commercial banks and other types of financial institutions, such as credit unions and savings banks. Any accounts in financial institutions from which you can easily transmit debit-card and check payments without many restrictions.

Fiduciary monetary system
A system in which money is issued by the government and its value is based uniquely on the public's faith that the currency represents command over goods and services and will be accepted in payment for debts.

going to be around 3 percent during the next year, you know that any dollar you receive a year from now will have a purchasing power equal to 3 percent less than that same dollar today. Thus, you will not necessarily refuse to accept money in exchange simply because you know that its value will decline by the rate of inflation during the next year.

YOU ARE THERE

To learn about how private currencies are circulating widely in Brazil, read **Why a Currency Displaying a Giant Rodent Circulates in Brazil** on page 248.

QUICK QUIZ See page 253 for the. Review concepts from this section in MyEconLab.

Money is defined by its functions, which are as a _____ of _____, _____ of _____, _____ of _____, and _____ of _____ _____.

Money is a highly _____ asset because it can be disposed of with low transaction costs and with relative certainty as to its value.

Modern nations have _____ monetary systems—national currencies are not convertible into a fixed quantity of a commodity such as gold or silver.

Money is accepted in exchange for goods and services because people have confidence that it can later be exchanged for other goods and services. In addition, money has _____ value.

Defining Money

Money is important. Changes in the total **money supply**—the amount of money in circulation—and changes in the rate at which the money supply increases or decreases affect important economic variables, such as the rate of inflation, interest rates, and (at least in the short run) employment and the level of real GDP. Economists have struggled to reach agreement about how to define and measure money, however. There are two basic approaches: the **transactions approach,** which stresses the role of money as a medium of exchange, and the **liquidity approach,** which stresses the role of money as a temporary store of value.

The Transactions Approach to Measuring Money: M1

Using the transactions approach to measuring money, the money supply consists of currency, transactions deposits, and traveler's checks not issued by banks. One key designation of the money supply, including currency, transactions deposits, and traveler's checks not issued by banks, is **M1.** The various elements of M1 for a typical year are presented in panel (a) of Figure 10-2 on the following page.

CURRENCY The largest component of U.S. currency is paper bills called Federal Reserve notes, which are designed and printed by the U.S. Bureau of Engraving and Printing. U.S. currency also consists of coins minted by the U.S. Treasury. Federal Reserve banks (to be discussed shortly) issue paper notes and coins throughout the U.S. banking system.

TRANSACTIONS DEPOSITS Individuals transfer ownership of deposits in financial institutions by using debit cards and checks. Hence, debitable and checkable transactions deposits are normally acceptable as a medium of exchange. The **depository institutions** that offer transactions deposits are numerous and include commercial banks and almost all **thrift institutions**—savings banks, savings and loan associations (S&Ls), and credit unions.

TRAVELER'S CHECKS **Traveler's checks** are paid for by the purchaser at the time of transfer. The total quantity of traveler's checks outstanding issued by institutions other than banks is part of the M1 money supply. American Express and other institutions issue traveler's checks.

Money supply
The amount of money in circulation.

Transactions approach
A method of measuring the money supply by looking at money as a medium of exchange.

Liquidity approach
A method of measuring the money supply by looking at money as a temporary store of value.

M1
The money supply, measured as the total value of currency plus transactions deposits plus traveler's checks not issued by banks.

Depository institutions
Financial institutions that accept deposits from savers and lend funds from those deposits out at interest.

Thrift institutions
Financial institutions that receive most of their funds from the savings of the public. They include savings banks, savings and loan associations, and credit unions.

Traveler's checks
Financial instruments obtained from a bank or a nonbanking organization and signed during purchase that can be used in payment upon a second signature by the purchaser.

MyEconLab Real-time data

FIGURE 10-2

Composition of the U.S. M1 and M2 Money Supply, 2013

Panel (a) shows estimates of the M1 money supply, of which the largest component (over 52 percent) is transactions deposits. M2 consists of M1 plus three other components, the most important of which is savings deposits at all depository institutions.

Sources: *Federal Reserve Bulletin; Economic Indicators,* various issues; author's estimates.

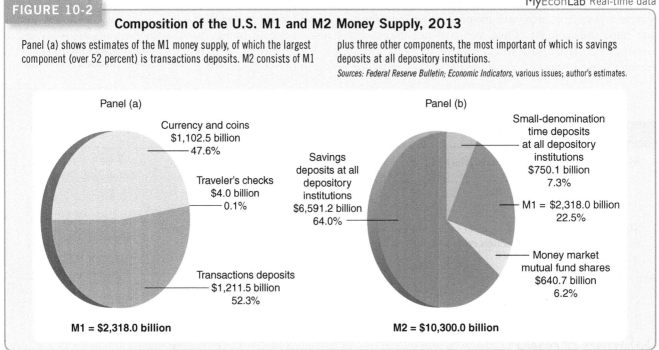

Panel (a)

Currency and coins
$1,102.5 billion
47.6%

Traveler's checks
$4.0 billion
0.1%

Transactions deposits
$1,211.5 billion
52.3%

M1 = $2,318.0 billion

Panel (b)

Savings deposits at all depository institutions
$6,591.2 billion
64.0%

Small-denomination time deposits at all depository institutions
$750.1 billion
7.3%

M1 = $2,318.0 billion
22.5%

Money market mutual fund shares
$640.7 billion
6.2%

M2 = $10,300.0 billion

The Liquidity Approach to Measuring Money: M2

The liquidity approach to defining and measuring the U.S. money supply views money as a temporary store of value and so includes all of M1 *plus* several other highly liquid assets. Panel (b) of Figure 10-2 above shows the components of **M2**—money as a temporary store of value. These components include the following:

M2
M1 plus (1) savings deposits at all depository institutions, (2) small-denomination time deposits, and (3) balances in retail money market mutual funds.

1. *Savings deposits.* Total *savings deposits*—deposits with no set maturities—are the largest component of the M2 money supply.

2. *Small-denomination time deposits.* With a *time deposit*, the funds must be left in a financial institution for a given period before they can be withdrawn without penalty. To be included in the M2 definition of the money supply, time deposits must be less than $100,000—hence, the designation *small-denomination time deposits.*

3. *Money market mutual fund balances.* Many individuals keep part of their assets in the form of shares in *money market mutual funds*—highly liquid funds that investment companies obtain from the public. All money market mutual fund balances except those held by large institutions (which typically use them more like large time deposits) are included in M2 because they are very liquid.

When all of these assets are added together, the result is M2, as shown in panel (b) of Figure 10-2.

For Federal Reserve data concerning the latest trends in the monetary aggregates, go to **www.econtoday.com/chap10** and click on "Money Stock Measures—H.6" under Money Stock and Reserve Balances.

OTHER MONEY SUPPLY DEFINITIONS Economists and other researchers have come up with additional definitions of money. Some businesspeople and policymakers prefer a monetary aggregate known as *MZM*. The MZM aggregate is the so-called money-at-zero-maturity money stock. Obtaining MZM entails adding to M1 those deposits without set maturities, such as savings deposits, that are included in M2. MZM includes *all* money market funds but excludes all deposits with fixed maturities, such as small-denomination time deposits.

QUICK QUIZ See page 253 for the answers. Review concepts from this section in MyEconLab.

The **money supply** can be defined in a variety of ways, depending on whether we use the transactions approach or the liquidity approach. Using the _____ approach, the money supply consists of currency, **transactions deposits,** and traveler's checks. This is called _____.

_____ deposits are any deposits in financial institutions from which the deposit owner can transfer funds using a debit card or checks.

When we add savings deposits, small-denomination time deposits, and retail money market mutual fund balances to _____, we obtain the measure known as _____.

Financial Intermediation and Banks

Most nations, including the United States, have a banking system that encompasses two types of institutions. One type consists of privately owned profit-seeking institutions, such as commercial banks and thrift institutions. The other type of institution is a **central bank,** which typically serves as a banker's bank and as a bank for the national treasury or finance ministry.

Central bank
A banker's bank, usually an official institution that also serves as a bank for a nation's government treasury. Central banks normally regulate commercial banks.

Direct versus Indirect Financing

When individuals choose to hold some of their savings in new bonds issued by a corporation, their purchases of the bonds are in effect direct loans to the business. This is an example of *direct finance*, in which people lend funds directly to a business. Business financing is not always direct. Individuals might choose instead to hold a time deposit at a bank. The bank may then lend to the same company. In this way, the same people can provide *indirect finance* to a business. The bank makes this possible by *intermediating* the financing of the company.

Financial Intermediation

Banks and other financial institutions are all in the same business—transferring funds from savers to investors. This process is known as **financial intermediation,** and its participants, such as banks and savings institutions, are **financial intermediaries.** The process of financial intermediation is illustrated in Figure 10-3 on the following page.

Financial intermediation
The process by which financial institutions accept savings from businesses, households, and governments and lend the savings to other businesses, households, and governments.

ASYMMETRIC INFORMATION, ADVERSE SELECTION, AND MORAL HAZARD Why might people wish to direct their funds through a bank instead of lending them directly to a business? One important reason is **asymmetric information**—the fact that the business may have better knowledge of its own current and future prospects than potential lenders do. For instance, the business may know that it intends to use borrowed funds for projects with a high risk of failure that would make repaying the loan difficult.

This potential for borrowers to use the borrowed funds in high-risk projects is known as **adverse selection.** Alternatively, a business that had intended to undertake low-risk projects may change management after receiving a loan, and the new managers may use the borrowed funds in riskier ways. The possibility that a borrower might engage in behavior that increases risk after borrowing funds is called **moral hazard.**

To minimize the possibility that a business might fail to repay a loan, people thinking about lending funds directly to the business must study the business carefully before making the loan, and they must continue to monitor its performance afterward. Alternatively, they can choose to avoid the trouble by holding deposits with financial intermediaries, which then specialize in evaluating the creditworthiness of business borrowers and in keeping tabs on their progress until loans are repaid. Thus, adverse selection and moral hazard both help explain why people use financial intermediaries.

Financial intermediaries
Institutions that transfer funds between ultimate lenders (savers) and ultimate borrowers.

Asymmetric information
Information possessed by one party in a financial transaction but not by the other party.

Adverse selection
The tendency for high-risk projects and clients to be overrepresented among borrowers.

Moral hazard
The possibility that a borrower might engage in riskier behavior after a loan has been obtained.

FIGURE 10-3

The Process of Financial Intermediation

The process of financial interme-diation is depicted here. Note that ultimate lenders and ultimate borrowers are the same economic units—households, businesses, and governments—but not necessarily the same individuals. Whereas individual households can be net lenders or borrowers, households as an economic unit typically are net lenders. Specific businesses or governments similarly can be net lenders or borrowers. As economic units, both are net borrowers.

Ultimate Lenders
- Households
- Businesses
- Governments

Financial Intermediaries
- Commercial banks
- S&Ls
- Savings banks
- Credit unions
- Insurance companies
- Mutual funds
- Pension funds
- Governments

Ultimate Borrowers
- Households
- Businesses
- Governments

LARGER SCALE AND LOWER MANAGEMENT COSTS Another important reason that financial intermediaries exist is that they make it possible for many people to pool their funds, thereby increasing the size, or *scale*, of the total amount of savings managed by an intermediary. This centralization of management reduces costs and risks below the levels savers would incur if all were to manage their savings alone.

Pension fund companies, which are institutions that specialize in managing funds that individuals save for retirement, owe their existence largely to their abilities to provide such cost savings to individual savers. Likewise, *investment companies*, which are institu-tions that manage portfolios of financial instruments called mutual funds on behalf of shareholders, also exist largely because of cost savings from their greater scale of operations. In addition, *government-sponsored financial institutions*, such as the Federal National Mortgage Association, seek to reduce overall lending costs by pooling large volumes of funds from investors in order to buy groups of mortgage loans.

Liabilities
Amounts owed; the legal claims against a business or household by nonowners.

FINANCIAL INSTITUTION LIABILITIES AND ASSETS Every financial intermediary has its own sources of funds, which are **liabilities** of that institution. When you place $100 in your

TABLE 10-2

Financial Intermediaries and Their Assets and Liabilities

Financial Intermediary	Assets	Liabilities
Commercial banks, savings and loan associations, savings banks, and credit unions	Car loans and other consumer debt, business loans, government securities, home mortgages	Transactions deposits, savings deposits, various other time deposits
Insurance companies	Mortgages, stocks, bonds, real estate	Insurance contracts, annuities, pension plans
Pension and retirement funds	Stocks, bonds, mortgages, time deposits	Pension plans
Money market mutual funds	Short-term credit instruments such as large-denomination certificates of deposit, Treasury bills, and high-grade commercial paper	Fund shares with limited checking privileges
Government-sponsored financial institutions	Home mortgages	Mortgage-backed securities issued to investors

transactions deposit at a bank, the bank creates a liability—it owes you $100—in exchange for the funds deposited. A commercial bank gets its funds from transactions and savings accounts, and an insurance company gets its funds from insurance policy premiums.

Each financial intermediary has a different primary use of its **assets.** For example, a credit union usually makes small consumer loans, whereas a savings bank makes mainly mortgage loans. Table 10-2 on the bottom of the facing page lists the assets and liabilities of typical financial intermediaries. Be aware, though, that the distinctions between different types of financial institutions are becoming more and more blurred. As laws and regulations change, there will be less need to make any distinction. All may ultimately be treated simply as financial intermediaries.

How are online firms pooling funds to assist small-business entrepreneurs in obtaining loans when banks have rejected their requests?

Assets
Amounts owned; all items to which a business or household holds legal claim.

EXAMPLE

Going Online for Credit When Bank Loans Dry Up

Today, a growing number of entrepreneurs who fail to receive loans from banks instead obtain credit from Internet-based companies such as Lending Club and Prosper Marketplace. These firms provide online forums for entrepreneurs to post detailed business plans along with the specific amounts of credit desired to try to achieve success. Individual savers can assess these plans and, if they wish, commit some of their own funds to help fund entrepreneurs' projects.

In exchange for service fees, the online firms pool these individual funding commitments into larger loan packages. For example, if an entrepreneur requests $15,000 in credit and 150 savers provide an average amount of $100 each, the online company collects the savers' funds and extends a loan to the entrepreneur. In this way, firms such as Lending Club and Prosper Marketplace act as financial intermediaries.

FOR CRITICAL THINKING
Why do you suppose that default rates on loans arranged by online firms tend to be substantially higher than default rates on bank loans?

Transmitting Payments via Debit-Card Transactions

Since 2006, the dollar volume of payments transmitted using debit cards has exceeded the value of checking transactions. To see how a debit-card transaction clears, take a look at Figure 10-4 on the next page. Suppose that Bank of America has provided a debit card to a college student named Jill Jones, who in turn uses the card to purchase $200 worth of clothing from Macy's, which has an account at Citibank. The debit-card transaction generates an electronic record, which the debit-card system transmits to Citibank.

The debit-card system also automatically uses the electronic record to determine the bank that issued the debit card used to purchase the clothing. It transmits this information to Bank of America. Then Bank of America verifies that Jill Jones is an account holder, deducts $200 from her transactions deposit account, and transmits these funds electronically, via the debit-card system, to Citibank. Finally, Citibank credits $200 to Macy's transactions deposit account, and payment for the clothing purchase is complete.

How can food-cart and farmers' market vendors accept debit cards today?

EXAMPLE

Vendors Use Smartphones to Process Debit-Card Purchases

A company called Square makes it possible for small retailers on the move, such as mobile food-cart and farmers' market vendors, to accept card payments. Square distributes plastic card-reading devices at no charge to owners of such businesses. The retailers can attach them to smartphones and thereby transform the devices into payment terminals. After a payment card is swiped through the device, the smartphone transmits payment information for Square to process, at a fee, to complete a purchase. In this way, Square enables sellers to move wherever buyers are located while broadening the means of payment that sellers can accept.

FOR CRITICAL THINKING
In what sense is a payment order sent using a smartphone economically indistinguishable from a payment order made via a check?

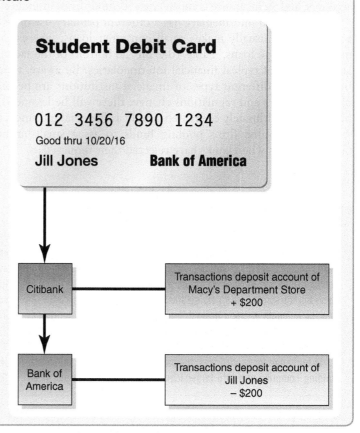

FIGURE 10-4

How a Debit-Card Transaction Clears

A college student named Jill Jones uses a debit card issued by Bank of America to purchase clothing valued at $200 from Macy's, which has an account with Citibank. The debit-card transaction creates an electronic record that is transmitted to Citibank. The debit-card system forwards this record to Bank of America, which deducts $200 from Jill Jones's transactions deposit account. Then the debit-card system transmits the $200 payment to Citibank, which credits the $200 to Macy's account.

Student Debit Card

012 3456 7890 1234

Good thru 10/20/16

Jill Jones   Bank of America

Citibank → Transactions deposit account of Macy's Department Store + $200

Bank of America → Transactions deposit account of Jill Jones − $200

QUICK QUIZ See page 253 for the answers. Review concepts from this section in MyEconLab.

_____ intermediaries, including depository institutions such as commercial banks and savings institutions, insurance companies, mutual funds, and pension funds, transfer funds from ultimate lenders (savers) to ultimate borrowers.

Financial intermediaries specialize in tackling problems of _____ information. They address the _____

_____ problem by carefully reviewing the creditworthiness of loan applicants, and they deal with the _____ _____ problem by monitoring borrowers after they receive loans. Many financial intermediaries also take advantage of cost reductions arising from the centralized management of funds pooled from the savings of many individuals.

The Federal Reserve System: The U.S. Central Bank

The Federal Reserve System, which serves as the nation's central bank, is one of the key banking institutions in the United States. It is partly a creature of government and partly privately directed.

The Federal Reserve System

The Fed
The Federal Reserve System; the central bank of the United States.

The Federal Reserve System, also known simply as **the Fed,** is the most important regulatory agency in the U.S. monetary system and is usually considered the monetary authority. The Fed was established by the Federal Reserve Act, signed on December 13, 1913, by President Woodrow Wilson.

FIGURE 10-5

Organization of the Federal Reserve System

The 12 Federal Reserve district banks are headed by 12 separate presidents. The main authority of the Fed resides with the Board of Governors of the Federal Reserve System, whose seven members are appointed for 14-year terms by the president of the United States and confirmed by the Senate. Open market operations are carried out through the Federal Open

Market Committee (FOMC), consisting of the seven members of the Board of Governors plus five presidents of the district banks (always including the president of the New York bank, with the others rotating).

Source: Board of Governors of the Federal Reserve System, *The Federal Reserve System: Purposes and Functions,* 7th ed. (Washington, D.C., 1984), p. 5.

Board of Governors (7 appointed members)
- Sets reserve requirements and approves discount rates as part of monetary policy
- Supervises and regulates member banks and bank holding companies
- Establishes and administers protective regulations in consumer finance
- Oversees Federal Reserve banks

Exercises general supervision →

Federal Reserve Banks (12 districts)
- Propose discount rates
- Hold reserve balances for depository institutions and lend to them at the discount window
- Furnish currency
- Collect and clear checks and transfer funds for depository institutions
- Handle U.S. government debt and cash balances

Advise

Compose

- Consumer Advisory Council
- Federal Advisory Council
- Thrift Institutions Advisory Council

Federal Open Market Committee (Board of Governors and 5 reserve bank presidents)
- Directs open market operations—buying and selling existing U.S. government securities, the primary instruments of monetary policy

ORGANIZATION OF THE FEDERAL RESERVE SYSTEM Figure 10-5 above shows how the Federal Reserve System is organized. It is managed by the Board of Governors, composed of seven full-time members appointed by the U.S. president with the approval of the Senate. The chair of the Board of Governors is the leading official of the Board of Governors and of the Federal Reserve System. Since 2006, Ben Bernanke has held this position.

The 12 Federal Reserve district banks have a total of 25 branches. The boundaries of the 12 Federal Reserve districts and the cities in which Federal Reserve banks are located are shown in Figure 10-6 on the following page. The Federal Open Market Committee (FOMC) determines the future growth of the money supply and other important variables. This committee is composed of the members of the Board of Governors, the president of the New York Federal Reserve Bank, and presidents of four other Federal Reserve banks, rotated periodically. The chair of the Board of Governors also chairs the FOMC.

DEPOSITORY INSTITUTIONS Depository institutions—all financial institutions that accept deposits—comprise our monetary system consisting of nearly 6,500 commercial banks, 1,100 savings and loan associations and savings banks, and about 8,000 credit unions. All depository institutions may purchase services from the Federal Reserve System on an equal basis. Also, almost all depository institutions are required to keep a certain percentage of their deposits in reserve at the Federal Reserve district banks or as vault cash. This percentage depends on the bank's volume of business.

FIGURE 10-6

The Federal Reserve System

The Federal Reserve System is divided into 12 districts, each served by one of the Federal Reserve district banks, located in the cities indicated. The Board of Governors meets in Washington, D.C.

Source: Board of Governors of the Federal Reserve System.

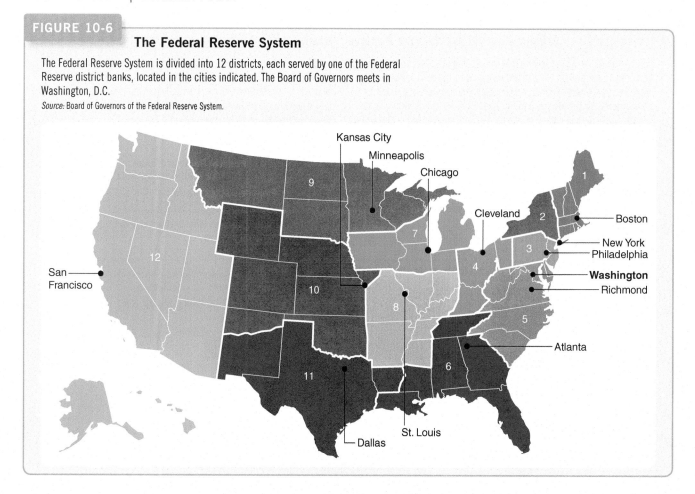

Functions of the Federal Reserve System

The Federal Reserve performs several functions:

1. ***The Fed supplies the economy with fiduciary currency.*** The Federal Reserve banks supply the economy with paper currency called Federal Reserve notes. Even though all Federal Reserve notes are printed at the Bureau of Engraving and Printing in Washington, D.C., each note is assigned a code indicating which of the 12 Federal Reserve banks first introduced the note into circulation. Moreover, each of these notes is an obligation (liability) of the Federal Reserve System, *not* the U.S. Treasury.

2. ***The Fed holds depository institutions' reserves and provides payment-clearing systems.*** The 12 Federal Reserve district banks hold the reserves (other than vault cash) of depository institutions. Depository institutions are required by law to keep a certain percentage of their transactions deposits as reserves. Even if they weren't required to do so by law, they would still wish to keep some reserves on which they can draw funds as needed for expected and unexpected transactions. The Federal Reserve System also operates systems for transmitting and clearing payments among depository institutions' reserve accounts. Federal Reserve banks all offer check-clearing services and electronic payments transfer services to commercial banks, savings institutions, and credit unions.

3. ***The Fed acts as the government's fiscal agent.*** The Federal Reserve is the primary banker and fiscal agent for the federal government. Consequently, the U.S. Treasury has a transactions account with the Federal Reserve, which helps the government collect certain tax revenues and aids in the purchase and sale of government securities.

4. ***The Fed supervises depository institutions.*** The Fed (along with the Comptroller of the Currency, the Federal Deposit Insurance Corporation, the Office of Thrift

Supervision in the Treasury Department, and the National Credit Union Administration) is a supervisor and regulator of depository institutions.

5. *The Fed conducts monetary policy.* Perhaps the Fed's most important task is to regulate the nation's money supply. To understand how the Fed manages the money supply, we must examine more closely its reserve-holding function and the way in which depository institutions aid in expansion and contraction of the money supply. We will do this later in this chapter.

6. *The Fed intervenes in foreign currency markets.* Sometimes the Fed attempts to keep the value of the dollar from changing. It does this by buying and selling U.S. dollars in foreign exchange markets. You will read more about this important topic in Chapter 12.

7. *The Fed acts as the "lender of last resort."* From time to time, an individual bank that is otherwise in good financial condition may be temporarily low on cash and other liquid assets. Such an institution is said to be illiquid. A key justification for the formation of the Federal Reserve System was that the Fed would stand ready to prevent temporarily illiquid banks from failing by serving as the financial system's **lender of last resort.** In this capacity, the Fed stands ready to lend to any temporarily illiquid but otherwise financially healthy banking institution. In this way, the Fed seeks to prevent illiquidity at a few banks from leading to a general loss of depositors' confidence in the overall soundness of the banking system.

What institutions, to the surprise of many U.S. residents, were among the largest recipients of Fed lender-of-last-resort loans at the height of the financial panic of the late 2000s?

Lender of last resort
The Federal Reserve's role as an institution that is willing and able to lend to a temporarily illiquid bank that is otherwise in good financial condition to prevent the bank's illiquid position from leading to a general loss of confidence in that bank or in others.

POLICY EXAMPLE

The Fed Becomes a Lender of Last Resort for Foreign Banks

During the financial meltdown that stretched across several months in the late 2000s, the Federal Reserve extended more than $3 trillion in emergency loans to financial institutions that it judged to be illiquid but otherwise financially healthy. What the Fed did not reveal until years later, however, was that emergency loans totaling hundreds of billions of dollars went to private financial institutions based outside the United States. The Fed also extended more than $600 billion in additional credit to a number of central banks around the globe. Thus,

in the midst of the financial panic of 2008 and 2009, the Fed became a key lender of last resort for many financial institutions located outside the United States.

FOR CRITICAL THINKING

How do you suppose the fact that foreign banks owed substantial funds to U.S. banks influenced the Federal Reserve's decision to lend to these institutions?

QUICK QUIZ   See page 253 for the answers. Review concepts from this section in MyEconLab.

The central bank in the United States is the _____ _____ _____, which was established on December 13, 1913.

There are 12 Federal Reserve district banks, with 25 branches. The Federal Reserve System is managed by the _____ of _____ in Washington, D.C. The Fed interacts with almost all depository institutions in the United States, most of which must keep a certain percentage of their transactions deposits on reserve with the Fed. The Fed serves as the chief regulatory agency for all

depository institutions that have Federal Reserve System membership.

The functions of the Federal Reserve System are to supply fiduciary _____, provide payment-clearing services, hold depository institution _____, act as the government's fiscal agent, supervise depository institutions, regulate the supply of money, intervene in foreign currency markets, and act as the _____ of _____ _____.

Fractional Reserve Banking, the Federal Reserve, and the Money Supply

As early as 1000 B.C., uncoined gold and silver were being used as money in Mesopotamia. Goldsmiths weighed and assessed the purity of those metals. Later they started issuing paper notes indicating that the bearers held gold or silver of given weights and purity on deposit with the goldsmith. These notes could be transferred in exchange for goods and became the first paper currency. The gold and silver on deposit with the goldsmiths were the first bank deposits. Eventually, goldsmiths realized that inflows of gold and silver for deposit always exceeded the average amount of gold and silver withdrawn at any given time—often by a predictable ratio.

These goldsmiths started making loans by issuing to borrowers paper notes that exceeded in value the amount of gold and silver the goldsmiths actually kept on hand. They charged interest on these loans. This constituted the earliest form of what is now called **fractional reserve banking.** We know that goldsmiths operated this way in Delphi, Didyma, and Olympia in Greece as early as the seventh century B.C. In Athens, fractional reserve banking was well developed by the sixth century B.C.

Depository Institution Reserves

In a fractional reserve banking system, banks do not keep sufficient funds on hand to cover 100 percent of their depositors' accounts. And the funds held by depository institutions in the United States are not kept in gold and silver, as they were with the early goldsmiths. Instead, the funds are held as **reserves** in the form of cash in banks' vaults and deposits that banks hold on deposit with Federal Reserve district banks.

The fraction of deposits that banks hold as reserves is called the **reserve ratio.** There are two determinants of the size of this ratio. One is the quantity of reserves that the Federal Reserve requires banks to hold, which are called *required reserves*. The other determinant of the reserve ratio is whatever additional amount of reserves that banks voluntarily hold, known as *excess reserves*.

To show the relationship between reserves and deposits at an individual bank, let's examine the **balance sheet,** or statement of assets owned and liabilities (amounts owed to others), for a particular depository institution. Balance Sheet 10-1 below displays a balance sheet for a depository institution called Typical Bank. Liabilities for this institution consist solely of $1 million in transactions deposits. Assets consist of $100,000 in reserves and $900,000 in loans to customers. Total assets of $1 million equal total liabilities of $1 million. Because Typical Bank has $100,000 of reserves and $1 million of transactions deposits, its reserve ratio is 10 percent. Thus, Typical Bank is part of a system of fractional reserve banking, in which it holds only 10 percent of its deposits as reserves.

Fractional reserve banking
A system in which depository institutions hold reserves that are less than the amount of total deposits.

Reserves
In the U.S. Federal Reserve System, deposits held by Federal Reserve district banks for depository institutions, plus depository institutions' vault cash.

Reserve ratio
The fraction of transactions deposits that banks hold as reserves.

Balance sheet
A statement of the assets and liabilities of any business entity, including financial institutions and the Federal Reserve System. Assets are what is owned; liabilities are what is owed.

BALANCE SHEET 10-1

Typical Bank	Assets		Liabilities	
	Reserves	$100,000	Transactions deposits	$1,000,000
	Loans	$900,000		
	Total	$1,000,000	Total	$1,000,000

Fractional Reserve Banking and Money Expansion

Under fractional reserve banking, the Federal Reserve can add to the quantity of money in circulation by bringing about an expansion of deposits within the banking system. To understand how the Fed can create money within the banking system, we must look at how depository institutions respond to Fed actions that increase reserves in the entire system.

Let's consider the effect of a Fed **open market operation,** which is a Fed purchase or sale of existing U.S. government securities in the open market—the private secondary market in which people exchange securities that have not yet matured. Assume that the Fed engaged in an *open market purchase* by buying a $100,000 U.S. government security from a bond dealer. The Fed does this by electronically transferring $100,000 to the bond dealer's transactions deposit account at Bank 1. Thus, as shown in Balance Sheet 10-2 below, Bank 1's transactions deposit liabilities increase by $100,000.

Let's suppose that the reserve ratio for Bank 1 and all other depository institutions is 10 percent. As shown in Balance Sheet 10-2, therefore, Bank 1 responds to this $100,000 increase in transactions deposits by adding 10 percent of this amount, or $10,000, to its reserves. The bank allocates the remaining $90,000 of additional deposits to new loans, so its loans increase by $90,000.

Open market operations
The purchase and sale of existing U.S. government securities (such as bonds) in the open private market by the Federal Reserve System.

BALANCE SHEET 10-2

Bank 1	Assets		Liabilities	
	Reserves	+$10,000	Transactions deposits	+$100,000
	Loans	+$90,000		
	Total	+$100,000	Total	+$100,000

EFFECT ON THE MONEY SUPPLY At this point, the Fed's purchase of a $100,000 U.S. government security from a bond dealer has increased the money supply immediately by $100,000. This occurs because transactions deposits held by the public—bond dealers are part of the public—are part of the money supply. Hence, the addition of $100,000 to deposits with Bank 1, with no corresponding deposit reduction elsewhere in the banking system, raises the money supply by $100,000. (If another member of the public, instead of the Fed, had purchased the bond, that person's transactions deposit would have been reduced by $100,000, so there would have been no change in the money supply.)

The process of money creation does not stop here. The borrower who receives the $90,000 loan from Bank 1 will spend these funds, which will then be deposited in other banks. In this instance, suppose that the $90,000 spent by Bank 1's borrower is deposited in a transactions deposit account at Bank 2. At this bank, as shown in Balance Sheet 10-3 below, transactions deposits and hence the money supply increase by $90,000. Bank 2 adds 10 percent of these deposits, or $9,000, to its reserves. It uses the remaining $81,000 of new deposits to add $81,000 to its loans.

BALANCE SHEET 10-3

Bank 2	Assets		Liabilities	
	Reserves	+$9,000	Transactions deposits	+$90,000
	Loans	+$81,000		
	Total	+$90,000	Total	+$90,000

CONTINUATION OF THE DEPOSIT CREATION PROCESS Look at Bank 3's account in Balance Sheet 10-4 on the following page. Assume that the borrower receiving the $81,000 loan from Bank 2 spends these funds, which then are deposited in an account at Bank 3.

Transactions deposits and the money supply increase by $81,000. Reserves of Bank 3 rise by 10 percent of this amount, or $8,100. Bank 3 uses the rest of the newly deposited funds, or $72,900, to increase its loans.

BALANCE SHEET 10-4

Bank 3

	Assets		Liabilities	
Reserves		+$8,100	Transactions deposits	+$81,000
Loans		+$72,900		
Total		+$81,000	Total	+$81,000

This process continues to Banks 4, 5, 6, and so forth. Each bank obtains smaller and smaller increases in deposits because banks hold 10 percent of new deposits as reserves. Thus, each succeeding depository institution makes correspondingly smaller loans. Table 10-3 below shows new deposits, reserves, and loans for the remaining depository institutions.

EFFECT ON TOTAL DEPOSITS AND THE MONEY SUPPLY In this example, deposits and the money supply increased initially by the $100,000 that the Fed paid the bond dealer in exchange for a U.S. government security. Deposits and the money supply were further increased by a $90,000 deposit in Bank 2, and they were again increased by an $81,000 deposit in Bank 3. Eventually, total deposits and the money supply increase by $1 million, as shown in Table 10-3. This $1 million expansion of deposits and the money supply consists of the original $100,000 created by the Fed, plus an extra $900,000 generated by deposit-creating bank loans. The deposit creation process is portrayed graphically in Figure 10-7 on the facing page.

You should be able to work through the foregoing example to show the reverse process when there is a *decrease* in reserves because the Fed engages in an *open market sale* by selling a $100,000 U.S. government security. The result is a multiple contraction of deposits and, therefore, of the total money supply in circulation.

The Money Multiplier

In the example just given, a $100,000 increase in reserves generated by the Fed's purchase of a security yielded a $1 million increase in transactions deposits and, hence, the money supply. Thus, deposits and the money supply increased by a multiple of

TABLE 10-3

Maximum Money Creation with 10 Percent Reserve Ratio

This table shows the maximum new loans that banks can make, given the Fed's electronic transfer of $100,000 to a transactions deposit account at Bank 1. The reserve ratio is 10 percent.

Bank	New Deposits	New Reserves	Maximum New Loans
1	$100,000 (from Fed)	$10,000	$90,000
2	90,000	9,000	81,000
3	81,000	8,100	72,900
4	72,900	7,290	65,610
.	.	.	.
.	.	.	.
.	.	.	.
All other banks	656,100	65,610	590,490
Totals	$1,000,000	$100,000	$900,000

FIGURE 10-7

The Multiple Expansion in the Money Supply Due to $100,000 in New Reserves When the Reserve Ratio Is 10 Percent

The banks are all aligned in decreasing order of new deposits created. Bank 1 receives the $100,000 in new reserves and lends out $90,000. Bank 2 receives the $90,000 and lends out $81,000. The process continues through Banks 3 to 19 and then the rest of the banking system. Ultimately, assuming no leakages into currency, the $100,000 of new reserves results in an increase in the money supply of $1 million, or 10 times the new reserves, because the reserve ratio is 10 percent.

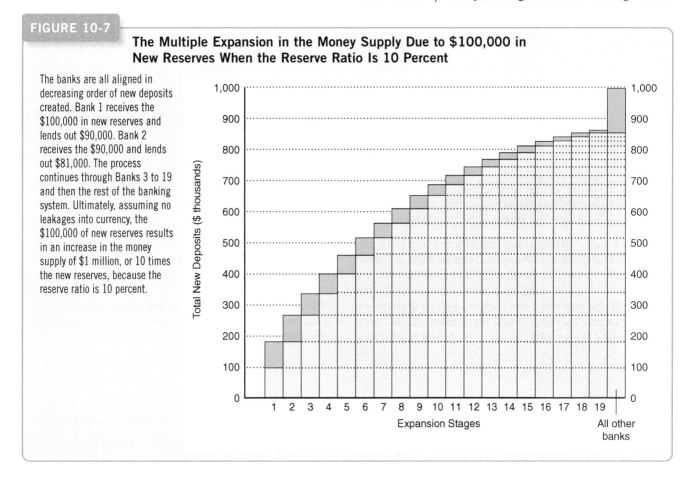

10 times the initial $100,000 increase in overall reserves. Conversely, a $100,000 decrease in reserves generated by a Fed sale of a security will yield a decrease in total deposits of $1 million—that is, a multiple of 10 times the initial $100,000 decrease in overall reserves.

We can now make a generalization about the extent to which the total money supply will change when the banking system's reserves are increased or decreased. The **money multiplier** gives the change in the money supply due to a change in reserves. In our example, the value of the money multiplier is 10.

Money multiplier
A number that, when multiplied by a change in reserves in the banking system, yields the resulting change in the money supply.

POTENTIAL VERSUS ACTUAL MONEY MULTIPLIERS If we assume, as in our example, that all loan proceeds are deposited with banks, we obtain the **potential money multiplier**—the *maximum* possible value of the money multiplier:

$$\text{Potential money multiplier} = \frac{1}{\text{reserve ratio}}$$

Potential money multiplier
The reciprocal of the reserve ratio, assuming no leakages into currency. It is equal to 1 divided by the reserve ratio.

That is, the potential money multiplier is equal to 1 divided by the fraction of transactions deposits that banks hold as reserves. In our example, the reserve ratio was 10 percent, or 0.10 expressed as a decimal fraction. Thus, in the example the value of the potential money multiplier was equal to 1 divided by 0.10, which equals 10.

What happens if the entire amount of a loan from a depository institution is not redeposited? When borrowers want to hold a portion of their loans as currency outside the banking system, these funds cannot be held by banks as reserves from which to make loans. The greater the amount of cash leakage, the smaller the *actual* money multiplier. Typically, borrowers do hold a portion of loan proceeds as currency, so the actual money multiplier usually is smaller than the potential money multiplier.

REAL-WORLD MONEY MULTIPLIERS The potential money multiplier is rarely attained for the banking system as a whole. Furthermore, each definition of the money supply, M1 or M2, will yield a different actual money multiplier.

In most years, the actual M1 multiplier has been in a range between 1.5 and 2.0. The actual M2 multiplier showed an upward trend until recently, rising from 6.5 in the 1960s to over 12 in the mid-2000s. Since then, however, it has dropped to about 6.

What was the ultimate effect of a steady stream of increases in the required reserve ratio for China's banking system?

INTERNATIONAL POLICY EXAMPLE

Seeking to Slash the Money Multiplier in China

Most central banks only rarely change required reserve ratios for bank deposits. The Federal Reserve, for instance, last changed the required reserve ratio in 1990. Nevertheless, China's central bank, the People's Bank of China, raised its required reserve ratio a number of times during the early 2010s, including more than a dozen increases during a single two-year interval. The cumulative effect of these increases was that the average required reserve ratio exceeded 20 percent—nearly twice its initial value.

As a result, the potential and actual money multipliers for China's banking system fell to approximately 50 percent of their original levels.

FOR CRITICAL THINKING
If the People's Bank of China increases bank reserves by 100 billion yuan, by how many fewer yuan will China's quantity of money now potentially expand? (Hint: What is the new money multiplier?)

QUICK QUIZ
See page 253 for the answers. Review concepts from this section in MyEconLab.

_____ of depository institutions consist of their vault cash and deposits that they hold with _____ _____ district banks.

The fraction of transactions deposit liabilities that depository institutions hold as reserves is the _____ _____.

The _____ _____ _____ is equal to 1 divided by the reserve ratio.

Federal Deposit Insurance

As you have seen, fractional reserve banking enables the Federal Reserve to use an open market purchase (or sale) of U.S. government bonds to generate an expansion (or contraction) of deposits. The change in the money supply is a multiple of the open market purchase (or sale). Another effect of fractional reserve banking is to make depository institutions somewhat fragile. After all, the institutions have only a fraction of reserves on hand to honor their depositors' requests for withdrawals.

If many depositors simultaneously rush to their bank to withdraw all of their transactions and time deposits—a phenomenon called a **bank run**—the bank would be unable to satisfy their requests. The result would be the failure of that depository institution. Widespread bank runs could lead to the failure of many institutions.

Bank run
Attempt by many of a bank's depositors to convert transactions and time deposits into currency out of fear that the bank's liabilities may exceed its assets.

Seeking to Limit Bank Failures with Deposit Insurance

When businesses fail, they create hardships for creditors, owners, and customers. But when a depository institution fails, an even greater hardship results, because many individuals and businesses depend on the safety and security of banks. As Figure 10-8 on the facing page shows, during the 1920s an average of about 600 banks failed each year. In the early 1930s, during the Great Depression, that average soared to nearly 3,000 failures each year.

FIGURE 10-8

Bank Failures

A tremendous number of banks failed prior to the creation of federal deposit insurance in 1933. Thereafter, bank failures were few until the mid-1980s. Annual failure rates jumped again in the early and late 2000s.

Source: Federal Deposit Insurance Corporation.

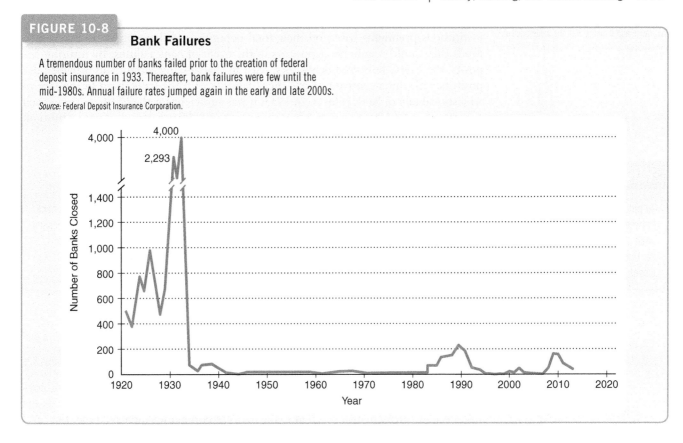

In 1933, at the height of these bank failures, the **Federal Deposit Insurance Corporation (FDIC)** was founded to insure the funds of depositors and remove the reason for ruinous runs on banks. In 1934, federal deposit insurance was extended to deposits in savings and loan associations and mutual savings banks, and in 1971 it was offered for deposits in credit unions.

As can be seen in Figure 10-8 above, bank failure rates dropped dramatically after passage of the early federal legislation. The long period from 1935 until the 1980s was relatively quiet. From World War II to 1984, fewer than nine banks failed per year. From 1995 until 2008, failures again averaged about nine per year. Since 2009, however, more than 400 banks have failed, and hundreds more are still in danger of failing. We will examine the reasons for this shortly. But first we need to understand how deposit insurance works.

Federal Deposit Insurance Corporation (FDIC)

A government agency that insures the deposits held in banks and most other depository institutions. All U.S. banks are insured this way.

The Rationale for Deposit Insurance

Consider the following scenario. A bank begins to look shaky. Its assets do not seem sufficient to cover its liabilities. If the bank has no deposit insurance, depositors in this bank (and any banks associated with it) will all want to withdraw their funds from the bank at the same time. Their concern is that this shaky bank will not have enough assets to return their deposits to them in the form of currency.

Indeed, this is what happens in a bank failure when insurance doesn't exist. Just as when a regular business fails, the creditors of the bank may not all get paid, or if they do, they will get paid less than 100 percent of what they are owed. Depositors are creditors of a bank because their funds are on loan to the bank. As explained earlier, however, banks do not hold 100 percent of their depositors' funds as cash. Instead, banks lend out most of their deposit funds to borrowers. Consequently, all depositors cannot withdraw all their funds simultaneously. Hence, the intent of the legislation enacted in the 1930s was to assure depositors that they could have their deposits converted into cash when they wished, no matter how serious the financial situation of the bank.

To keep up with the latest issues in deposit insurance and banking with the assistance of the FDIC, go to www.econtoday.com/chap10.

Federal deposit insurance provided this assurance. The FDIC charged depository institutions premiums based on their total deposits, and these premiums went into funds that would reimburse depositors in the event of bank failures. By insuring deposits, the FDIC bolstered depositors' trust in the banking system and provided depositors with the incentive to leave their deposits with the bank, even in the face of widespread talk of bank failures. In 1933, it was sufficient for the FDIC to cover each account up to $2,500. The current maximum is $250,000 per depositor per institution.

WHAT IF... the costs of bank failures exceeded the funds on hand at the Federal Deposit Insurance Corporation?

To put this issue into context, so many costly bank failures occurred between 2008 and 2010 that the FDIC's reserve fund did run out of cash. At that point, the FDIC borrowed from the U.S. Treasury to continue paying the costs of protecting banks' depositors from losses. The FDIC raised more deposit insurance premiums from banks. Ultimately, the FDIC raised sufficient premiums to pay back the Treasury and to replenish its reserve fund gradually. If expenses of bank failures were to rise above the FDIC's reserves at some future date, the FDIC undoubtedly would borrow from the U.S. Treasury once again.

How Deposit Insurance Causes Increased Risk Taking by Bank Managers

Until the 1990s, all insured depository institutions paid the same small fee for coverage. The fee that they paid was completely unrelated to how risky their assets were. A depository institution that made loans to companies such as Apple, Inc., and Google, Inc. paid the same deposit insurance premium as another depository institution that made loans (at higher interest rates) to the governments of developing countries that were teetering on the brink of financial collapse.

Although deposit insurance premiums for a while were adjusted somewhat in response to the riskiness of a depository institution's assets, they never reflected all of the relative risk. Indeed, between the late 1990s and the late 2000s, very few depository institutions paid *any* deposit insurance premiums. This lack of correlation between risk and premiums can be considered a fundamental flaw in the deposit insurance scheme. Because bank managers do not have to pay higher insurance premiums when they make riskier loans, they have an incentive to invest in more assets of higher yield, and therefore necessarily higher risk, than they would if there were no deposit insurance.

ARTIFICIALLY LOW INSURANCE PREMIUMS The problem with the insurance scheme is that the premium rate is artificially low. Depository institution managers are able to obtain deposits at less than full cost (because depositors will accept a lower interest payment on insured deposits). Consequently, managers can increase their profits by using insured deposits to purchase higher-yield, higher-risk assets. The gains to risk taking accrue to the managers and stockholders of the depository institutions. The losses go to the deposit insurer (and, as we will see, ultimately to taxpayers).

A REGULATORY SOLUTION To combat these flaws in the financial industry and in the deposit insurance system, a vast regulatory apparatus oversees depository institutions. The FDIC and other federal deposit insurance agencies possess regulatory powers to offset the risk-taking temptations to depository institution managers.

These regulatory powers include the ability to require higher capital investment, to regulate, examine, and supervise bank affairs, and to enforce regulatory decisions. Higher capital requirements were imposed in the early 1990s and then adjusted somewhat beginning in 2000, but the recent jump in bank failures reveals that basic flaws remain.

Deposit Insurance, Adverse Selection, and Moral Hazard

As a deposit insurer, the FDIC effectively acts as a government-run insurance company. This means that the FDIC's operations expose the federal government to the same kinds of asymmetric information problems that other financial intermediaries face.

ADVERSE SELECTION IN DEPOSIT INSURANCE One of these problems is *adverse selection*, which is often a problem when insurance is involved because people or firms that are relatively poor risks are sometimes able to disguise that fact from insurers. It is instructive to examine the way this works with the deposit insurance provided by the FDIC. Deposit insurance shields depositors from the potential adverse effects of risky decisions and so makes depositors willing to accept riskier investment strategies by their banks. Clearly, protection of depositors from risks encourages more high-flying, risk-loving entrepreneurs to become managers of banks.

Moreover, because depositors have so little incentive to monitor the activities of insured banks, it is also likely that the insurance actually encourages outright crooks— embezzlers and con artists—to enter the industry. The consequences for the FDIC— and for taxpayers—are larger losses.

MORAL HAZARD IN DEPOSIT INSURANCE Moral hazard is also an important phenomenon in the presence of insurance contracts, such as the deposit insurance provided by the FDIC. Insured depositors know that they will not suffer losses if their bank fails. Hence, they have little incentive to monitor their bank's investment activities or to punish their bank by withdrawing their funds if the bank assumes too much risk. This means that insured banks have incentives to take on more risks than they otherwise would.

Can Deposit Insurance Be Reformed?

Since 2005, Congress has sought to reform federal deposit insurance. These efforts are still under way.

A REFORM EFFORT THAT CAME TOO LATE The Federal Deposit Insurance Reform Act of 2005 aimed to reform federal deposit insurance. On the one hand, this legislation expanded deposit insurance coverage and potentially added to the system's moral hazard problems. It increased deposit insurance coverage for Individual Retirement Accounts (IRAs) offered by depository institutions from $100,000 to $250,000 and authorized the FDIC to periodically adjust the insurance limit on all deposits to reflect inflation.

On the other hand, the act provided the FDIC with improved tools for addressing moral hazard risks. The law changed a rule that had prevented the FDIC from charging deposit insurance premiums if total insurance funds exceeded 1.25 percent of all insured deposits. This limit had enabled practically all U.S. depository institutions to avoid paying deposit insurance premiums for about a decade. Now the FDIC can adjust deposit insurance premiums at any time.

A NEW STRUCTURAL REFORM IN PROGRESS During the banking troubles of the late 2000s, Congress sought to increase the public's confidence in depository institutions by extending coverage to virtually all liabilities in the banking system. Although this move succeeded in boosting trust in banks, it also expanded the scope of deposit insurance. To reflect this fact, in late 2010 the FDIC altered the structure for deposit insurance premiums. The FDIC now assesses premium rates on banks' total liabilities—that is, the banks' deposits plus their borrowings from other sources.

The FDIC also raised its premium rates. Because the base for assessing premiums and the premium rates are both higher, the FDIC is now collecting premiums and adding to its reserve fund at a faster pace. Nevertheless, most economists agree that, on net, the FDIC's exposure to moral hazard risks has increased considerably in recent years.

QUICK QUIZ   See page 253 for the answers. Review concepts from this section in MyEconLab.

To limit the fallout from systemwide failures and bank runs, Congress created the _____ _____ _____ _____ in 1933. Since the advent of federal deposit insurance, there have been no true bank runs at federally insured banks.

Federal insurance of bank deposits insulates depositors from risks, so depositors are _____ concerned about riskier investment strategies by depository institutions. Thus, bank managers have an incentive to invest in _____ assets to make _____ rates of return.

On the one hand, the Federal Deposit Insurance Reform Act of 2005 expanded the _____ hazard risks associated with deposit insurance by increasing limits for insured retirement deposits and indexing limits for other deposits to inflation. On the other hand, the law granted the FDIC greater discretion to assess risk-based deposit insurance _____ intended to restrain _____ hazard risks.

YOU ARE THERE
Why a Currency Displaying a Giant Rodent Circulates in Brazil

What induces firms in Silva Jardim, Brazil, to accept a private regional money called the *capivari*—named for the capybara, a pig-sized rodent common in a local river—in payment for goods and services? Roseanne Augusto, the manager of a hardware store, offers a simple answer: "It brings customers through the door."

The *capivari* that Augusto accepts at her store is one of 63 circulating private currencies in Brazil. Each currency's value is based on Brazil's official currency, the *real* (with multiple units called *reais*). In Silva Jardim, a local bank holds, on deposit, an amount of *reais* equal to the number of *capivaris* placed into circulation. Merchants such as Augusto's retail establishment offer price discounts to customers who pay with the private *capivaris* instead of the official *reais*. Consequently, people who use the *capivari* add "discount coupon" to the currency's function as a

medium of exchange. Indeed, for Silva Jardim consumers, this discount is the only advantage of the *capivari* over the government's *real*. For sellers, Augusto's statement above sums up the key advantage: Consumers are willing to use the currency to buy enough items to raise sales by more than the discounts offered by the sellers when they accept the currency.

Critical Thinking Questions

1. If price tags in Augusto's retail store display prices in terms of *capivaris*, what function does the currency fulfill?

2. When Silva Jardim residents set *capivari* notes aside today for possible use a few weeks from now, what function does the currency fulfill?

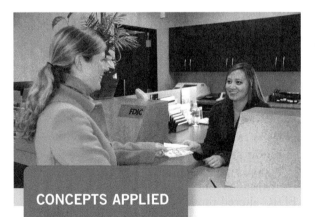

CONCEPTS APPLIED
▶ Balance Sheet
▶ Net Worth
▶ Fractional Reserve Banking

ISSUES & APPLICATIONS

Bankers Are Not Sure That They Want More Deposits

Between the early 1960s and late 2000s, bankers sought to raise and lend out more deposit funds. Today, however, a number of banks have stopped trying to attract more deposits. A few are even actively discouraging deposits by charging customers fees if they deposit "too many" funds. Why have bankers' views about the desirability of increased deposits shifted so dramatically in recent years?

Low Returns on Lending

One key reason that banks have soured on deposits is that earnings they can anticipate from lending deposit funds are now very low. In today's dampened U.S. economy, many fewer households and firms are seeking credit than in years past. As a consequence, banks have been competing with one another for a dwindling set of borrowers, and they have bid market interest rates on bank loans downward.

Thus, existing deposits are now yielding lower returns for banks. This fact gives them less incentive to seek out more deposits from current or new customers.

Higher Deposit Insurance Premiums

Even as banks' returns from lending deposit funds have dropped, the costs they must pay for deposits have increased. Since 2006, the premium rate that banks must pay the Federal Deposit Insurance Corporation has jumped from close to zero to more than $0.30 per $100 of insured deposits—the highest rate since the FDIC's establishment in 1933.

The net result? Some banks have begun actively discouraging customers from substantially increasing their deposits. Recently, for instance, the Bank of New York Mellon began *charging* large depositors for the privilege of holding federally insured deposits. The bank now charges an annual interest fee of 0.13 percent to customers with deposit accounts of $50 million or more. Unless market loan rates rise and deposit insurance premiums fall, it appears likely that other banks will follow suit. Some banking experts speculate that eventually banks might begin charging interest fees to customers with small deposits.

For Critical Thinking

1. Why do you suppose that the market clearing interest rates on bank savings and time deposits have fallen as the interest rates on bank loans have dropped?
2. If interest rates earned by banks on their assets fell close to zero, why might all bank customers have to pay interest fees on deposits they hold with banks?

Web Resources

1. To take a look at the latest statistics on the status and performance of U.S. commercial banks, go to www.econtoday.com/chap10.
2. For a look at historical U.S. commercial banking data, go to www.econtoday.com/chap10.

MyEconLab

For more questions on this chapter's Issues & Applications, go to MyEconLab. In the Study Plan for this chapter, select Section N: News.

MyEconLab

Here is what you should know after reading this chapter. MyEconLab will help you identify what you know, and where to go when you need to practice.

WHAT YOU SHOULD KNOW

The Key Functions and Properties of Money Money is a medium of exchange that people use to make payments for goods, services, and financial assets. It is also a unit of accounting for quoting prices in terms of money values. In addition, money is a store of value, so people can hold money for future use in exchange. Finally, money is a standard of deferred payment, enabling lenders to make loans and buyers to repay those loans with money. A good will function as money only if people are widely willing to accept the good in exchange for other goods and services. People will use money only if its value is relatively predictable.

money, 228
medium of exchange, 228
barter, 228
unit of accounting, 229
store of value, 229
standard of deferred payment, 229
liquidity, 229
transactions deposits, 230
fiduciary monetary system, 230

Key Figure
Figure 10-1, 230

WHERE TO GO TO PRACTICE

- MyEconLab Study Plans 10.1, 10.2
- Animated Figure 10-1

MyEconLab *continued*

Official Definitions of the Quantity of Money in Circulation The narrow definition of the quantity of money in circulation, called M1, includes only currency, transactions deposits, and traveler's checks. A broader definition, called M2, is equal to M1 plus savings deposits, small-denomination time deposits, and noninstitutional holdings of money market mutual fund balances.

money supply, 231
transactions approach, 231
liquidity approach, 231
M1, 231
depository institutions, 231
thrift institutions, 231
traveler's checks, 231
M2, 232

- MyEconLab Study Plan 10.3

Why Financial Intermediaries Such as Banks Exist Financial intermediaries help reduce problems stemming from the existence of asymmetric information. Adverse selection arises when uncreditworthy individuals and firms seek loans, Moral hazard problems exist when an individual or business that has been granted credit begins to engage in riskier practices. Financial intermediaries may also permit savers to benefit from economies of scale, which is the ability to reduce the costs and risks of managing funds by pooling funds and spreading costs and risks across many savers.

central bank, 233
financial intermediation, 233
financial intermediaries, 233
asymmetric information, 233
adverse selection, 233
moral hazard, 233
liabilities, 234
assets, 235

Key Figures
Figure 10-3, 234
Figure 10-4, 236

- MyEconLab Study Plan 10.4
- Animated Figures 10.3, 10.4

The Basic Structure and Functions of the Federal Reserve System The Federal Reserve System consists of 12 district banks overseen by the Board of Governors. The Fed's main functions are supplying fiduciary currency, holding banks' reserves and clearing payments, acting as the goverment's fiscal agent, supervising banks, regulating the money supply, intervening in foreign exchange markets, and acting as a lender of last resort.

The Fed, 236
lender of last resort, 239

Key Figure
Figure 10-6, 238

- MyEconLab Study Plan 10.5
- Animated Figure 10-6

The Maximum Potential Change in the Money Supply Following a Federal Reserve Monetary Policy Action When a bond dealer deposits funds received from the Fed in payment for a security following a Fed open market purchase, there is an increase in the total deposits in the banking system. The money supply increases by the amount of the initial deposit. The bank receiving this deposit can lend out funds in excess of those it holds as reserves, which will generate a rise in deposits at another bank. The maximum potential change in deposits throughout the banking system equals the amount of reserves injected (or withdrawn) by the Fed times the potential money multiplier, which is 1 divided by the reserve ratio.

fractional reserve banking, 240
reserves, 240
reserve ratio, 240
balance sheet, 240
open market operations, 241
money multiplier, 243
potential money multiplier, 243

Key Table
Table 10-3, 242

Key Figure
Figure 10-7, 243

- MyEconLab Study Plan 10.6
- Animated Table 10-3
- Animated Figure 10-7

MyEconLab

Log in to MyEconLab, take a chapter test, and get a personalized Study Plan that tells you which concepts you understand and which ones you need to review. From there, MyEconLab will give you further practice, tutorials, animations, videos, and guided solutions. For more information, visit www.myeconlab.com

PROBLEMS

All problems are assignable in MyEconLab; *exercises that update with real-time data are marked with* 🌐. *Answers to odd-numbered problems appear at the back of the book.*

10-1. Until 1946, residents of the island of Yap used large doughnut-shaped stones as financial assets. Although prices of goods and services were not quoted in terms of the stones, the stones were often used in exchange for particularly large purchases, such as livestock. To make the transaction, several individuals would insert a large stick through a stone's center and carry it to its new owner. A stone was difficult for any one person to steal, so an owner typically would lean it against the side of his or her home as a sign to others of accumulated purchasing power that would hold value for later use in exchange. Loans would often be repaid using the stones. In what ways did these stones function as money? (See pages 228–230.)

10-2. During the late 1970s, prices quoted in terms of the Israeli currency, the shekel, rose so fast that grocery stores listed their prices in terms of the U.S. dollar and provided customers with dollar-shekel conversion tables that they updated daily. Although people continued to buy goods and services and make loans using shekels, many Israeli citizens converted shekels to dollars to avoid a reduction in their wealth due to inflation. In what way did the U.S. dollar function as money in Israel during this period? (See pages 228–230.)

10-3. During the 1945–1946 Hungarian hyperinflation, when the rate of inflation reached 41.9 *quadrillion* percent per month, the Hungarian government discovered that the real value of its tax receipts was falling dramatically. To keep real tax revenues more stable, it created a good called a "tax pengö,"

in which all bank deposits were denominated for purposes of taxation. Nevertheless, payments for goods and services were made only in terms of the regular Hungarian currency, whose value tended to fall rapidly even though the value of a tax pengö remained stable. Prices were also quoted only in terms of the regular currency. Lenders, however, began denominating loan payments in terms of tax pengös. In what ways did the tax pengö function as money in Hungary in 1945 and 1946? (See pages 228–230.)

10-4. Considering the following data (expressed in billions of U.S. dollars), calculate M1 and M2. (See pages 231–232.)

Currency	1,050
Savings deposits	5,500
Small-denomination time deposits	1,000
Traveler's checks outside banks and thrifts	10
Total money market mutual funds	800
Institution-only money market mutual funds	1,800
Transactions deposits	1,140

10-5. Considering the following data (expressed in billions of U.S. dollars), calculate M1 and M2. (See pages 231–232.)

Transactions deposits	1,025
Savings deposits	3,300
Small-denomination time deposits	1,450
Money market deposit accounts	1,950
Noninstitution money market mutual funds	1,900
Traveler's checks outside banks and thrifts	25
Currency	1,050
Institution-only money market mutual funds	1,250

10-6. Identify whether each of the following amounts is counted in M1 only, M2 only, both M1 and M2, or neither. (See pages 231–232.)

  a. $50 billion in U.S. Treasury bills

  b. $15 billion in small-denomination time deposits

  c. $5 billion in traveler's checks not issued by a bank

  d. $20 billion in money market deposit accounts

10-7. Identify whether each of the following items is counted in M1 only, M2 only, both M1 and M2, or neither. (See pages 231–232.)

  a. A $1,000 balance in a transactions deposit at a mutual savings bank

  b. A $100,000 time deposit in a New York bank

  c. A $10,000 time deposit an elderly widow holds at her credit union

  d. A $50 traveler's check not issued by a bank

  e. A $50,000 savings deposit

10-8. Match each of the rationales for financial intermediation listed below with at least one of the following financial intermediaries: insurance company, pension fund, savings bank. Explain your choices. (See pages 233–234.)

  a. Adverse selection

  b. Moral hazard

  c. Lower management costs generated by larger scale

10-9. Identify whether each of the following events poses an adverse selection problem or a moral hazard problem in financial markets. (See pages 233–234.)

  a. A manager of a savings and loan association responds to reports of a likely increase in federal deposit insurance coverage. She directs loan officers to extend mortgage loans to less creditworthy borrowers.

  b. A loan applicant does not mention that a legal judgment in his divorce case will require him to make alimony payments to his ex-wife.

  c. An individual who was recently approved for a loan to start a new business decides to use some of the funds to take a Hawaiian vacation.

10-10. In what sense is currency a liability of the Federal Reserve System? (See page 238.)

10-11. In what respects is the Fed like a private banking institution? In what respects is it more like a government agency? (See pages 236–239.)

10-12. Take a look at the map of the locations of the Federal Reserve districts and their headquarters in Figure 10-6 on page 238. Today, the U.S. population is centered just west of the Mississippi River—that is, about half of the population is either to the west or the east of a line running roughly just west of this river. Can you reconcile the current locations of Fed districts and banks with this fact? Why do you suppose the Fed has its current geographic structure? (See page 238.)

10-13. Draw an empty bank balance sheet, with the heading "Assets" on the left and the heading "Liabilities" on the right. Then place the following items on the proper side of the balance sheet (see page 240):

  a. Loans to a private company

  b. Borrowings from a Federal Reserve district bank

  c. Deposits with a Federal Reserve district bank

  d. U.S. Treasury bills

  e. Vault cash

  f. Transactions deposits

10-14. Draw an empty bank balance sheet, with the heading "Assets" on the left and the heading "Liabilities" on the right. Then place the following items on the proper side of the balance sheet. (see page 240.)

  a. Borrowings from another bank in the interbank loans market

  b. Deposits this bank holds in an account with another private bank

  c. U.S. Treasury bonds

  d. Small-denomination time deposits

  e. Mortgage loans to household customers

  f. Money market deposit accounts

10-15. The reserve ratio is 11 percent. What is the value of the potential money multiplier? (See page 243.)

10-16. The Federal Reserve purchases $1 million in U.S. Treasury bonds from a bond dealer, and the dealer's bank credits the dealer's account. The reserve ratio is 15 percent. Assuming that no currency leakage occurs, how much will the bank lend to its customers following the Fed's purchase? (See pages 241–242.)

10-17. Suppose that the value of the potential money multiplier is equal to 4. What is the reserve ratio? (See page 243.)

10-18. Consider a world in which there is no currency and depository institutions issue only transactions deposits. The reserve ratio is 20 percent. The central bank sells $1 billion in government securities. What ultimately happens to the money supply? (See page 243.)

10-19. Assume a 1 percent reserve ratio and no currency leakages. What is the potential money multiplier? How will total deposits in the banking system ultimately change if the Federal Reserve purchases $5 million in U.S. government securities? (See page 243.)

ECONOMICS ON THE NET

What's Happened to the Money Supply? Deposits at banks and other financial institutions make up a portion of the U.S. money supply. This exercise gives you the chance to see how changes in these deposits influence the Fed's measures of money.

Title: FRED (Federal Reserve Economic Data)

Navigation: Go to www.econtoday.com/chap10 to visit the Web page of the Federal Reserve Bank of St. Louis.

Application

1. Select the data series for *Demand Deposits at Commercial Banks (Bil. of $; M)*, either seasonally adjusted or not. Scan through the data. Do you notice any recent trend? (Hint: Compare the growth in the figures before 1993 with their growth after 1993.) In addition, take a look at the data series for currency and for other transactions deposits. Do you observe similar recent trends in these series?

2. Back up, and click on *M1 Money Stock (Bil. of $; M)*, again either seasonally adjusted or not. Does it show any change in pattern beginning around 1993?

For Group Study and Analysis FRED contains considerable financial data series. Assign individual members or groups of the class the task of examining data on assets included in M1, M2, and MZM. Have each student or group look for big swings in the data. Then ask the groups to report to the class as a whole. When did clear changes occur in various categories of the monetary aggregates? Were there times when people appeared to shift funds from one aggregate to another? Are there any other noticeable patterns that may have had something to do with economic events during various periods?

ANSWERS TO QUICK QUIZZES

p. 231: (i) medium of exchange . . . unit of accounting . . . store of value . . . standard of deferred payment; (ii) liquid; (iii) fiduciary; (iv) predictable

p. 233: (i) transactions . . . M1; (ii) Transactions; (iii) M1 . . . M2

p. 236: (i) Financial; (ii) asymmetric . . . adverse selection . . . moral hazard

p. 239: (i) Federal Reserve System; (ii) Board . . . Governors; (iii) currency . . . reserves . . . lender of last resort

p. 244: (i) Reserves . . . Federal Reserve; (ii) reserve ratio; (iii) potential money multiplier

p. 248: (i) Federal Deposit Insurance Corporation; (ii) less . . . riskier . . . higher; (iii) moral . . . premiums . . . moral

11

Domestic and International Dimensions of Monetary Policy

S ince 2008, the Fed has provided a number of "credit programs" through which it transmitted funds directly to individual financial institutions. In addition, the Fed bought bad debts from selected institutions, and it even purchased securities issued by nonfinancial firms, such as General Electric and McDonald's. The fundamental aims of this new Fed *credit policy* included making banks and firms more liquid and preventing insolvencies of selected institutions. Another objective was to keep borrowing costs low for all households and firms in order to stimulate borrowing that would fuel increases in total planned expenditures and aggregate demand. At various times between 2008 and 2010, though, the Fed failed to make sure that its monetary policy actions supported this latter credit policy goal. To understand how this policy breakdown occurred, you first must learn about the implementation of monetary policy, a key topic of this chapter.

during a couple of brief intervals within the past few years, Apple had more cash on hand than did the U.S. Treasury? For instance, at one point, the U.S. Treasury held just over $73 billion in accounts from which federal government checks could be written, whereas Apple's accounts contained more than $76 billion. Of course, one reason for this situation has been that the federal government's tax collections have been lower than in prior years, leading to reduced Treasury cash balances. In addition, Apple has maintained unusually large stockpiles of funds in checkable accounts. Indeed, total cash balances across all U.S. nonfinancial companies have recently totaled in excess of $1.8 trillion, or about 7 percent of all businesses' assets, which is the highest percentage since the early 1960s.

Most economists agree that a major reason U.S. companies are holding so much cash is that the rate of interest—the opportunity cost of holding money instead of an interest-bearing asset—has been very low. In this chapter, you will learn about determinants of how much money people desire to hold—that is, about their *demand for money.*

The Demand for Money

In the previous chapter, we saw how the Federal Reserve's open market operations can increase or decrease the money supply. Our focus was on the effects of the Fed's actions on the banking system. In this chapter, we widen our discussion to see how Fed monetary policy actions have an impact on the broader economy by influencing market interest rates. First, though, you must understand the factors that determine how much money people desire to hold—in other words, you must understand the demand for money.

All of us engage in a flow of transactions. We buy and sell things all of our lives. But because we use money—dollars—as our medium of exchange, all *flows* of nonbarter transactions involve a *stock* of money. We can restate this as follows:

To use money, one must hold money.

Given that everybody must hold money, we can now talk about the *demand* to hold it. People do not demand to hold money just to look at pictures of past leaders. They hold it to be able to use it to buy goods and services.

The Demand for Money: What People Wish to Hold

People have certain motivations that cause them to want to hold **money balances.** Individuals and firms could try to do without non-interest-bearing money balances. But life is inconvenient without a ready supply of money balances. Thus, the public has a demand for money, motivated by several factors.

Money balances
Synonymous with money, money stock, money holdings.

THE TRANSACTIONS DEMAND The main reason people hold money is that money can be used to purchase goods and services. People are paid at specific intervals (once a week, once a month, and the like), but they wish to make purchases more or less continuously. To free themselves from having to buy goods and services only on payday, people find it beneficial to hold money. The benefit they receive is convenience: They willingly forgo interest earnings in order to avoid the inconvenience of cashing in nonmoney assets such as bonds every time they wish to make a purchase. Thus, people hold money to make regular, *expected* expenditures under the **transactions demand.** As nominal GDP (see page 40 in Chapter 2) rises, people will want to hold more money because they will be making more transactions.

Transactions demand
Holding money as a medium of exchange to make payments. The level varies directly with nominal GDP.

THE PRECAUTIONARY DEMAND The transactions demand involves money held to make *expected* expenditures. People also hold money for the **precautionary demand** to make *unexpected* purchases or to meet emergencies. When people hold money for the precautionary demand, they incur a cost in forgone interest earnings that they balance against the benefit of having cash on hand. The higher the rate of interest, the lower the precautionary money balances people wish to hold.

Precautionary demand
Holding money to meet unplanned expenditures and emergencies.

Asset demand
Holding money as a store of value instead of other assets such as corporate bonds and stocks.

THE ASSET DEMAND Remember that one of the functions of money is to serve as a store of value. People can hold money balances as a store of value, or they can hold bonds or stocks or other interest-earning assets. The desire to hold money as a store of value leads to the **asset demand** for money. People choose to hold money rather than other assets for two reasons: its liquidity and the lack of risk.

The disadvantage of holding money balances as an asset, of course, is the interest earnings forgone. Each individual or business decides how much money to hold as an asset by looking at the opportunity cost of holding money. The higher the interest rate—which is the opportunity cost of holding money—the lower the money balances people will want to hold as assets. Conversely, the lower the interest rate offered on alternative assets, the higher the money balances people will want to hold as assets.

The Demand for Money Curve

Assume for simplicity's sake that the amount of money demanded for transactions purposes is proportionate to income. That leaves the precautionary and asset demands for money, both determined by the opportunity cost of holding money. If we assume that the interest rate represents the cost of holding money balances, we can graph the relationship between the interest rate and the quantity of money demanded.

In Figure 11-1 below, the demand for money curve shows a familiar downward slope. The horizontal axis measures the quantity of money demanded, and the vertical axis is the interest rate. The rate of interest is the cost of holding money. At a higher interest rate, a lower quantity of money is demanded, and vice versa.

To see this, imagine two scenarios. In the first one, you can earn 20 percent a year if you put your funds into purchases of U.S. government securities. In the other scenario, you can earn 1 percent if you put your funds into purchases of U.S. government securities. If you have $1,000 average cash balances in a non-interest-bearing checking account, in the first scenario over a one-year period, your opportunity cost would be 20 percent of $1,000, or $200. In the second scenario, the opportunity cost that you would incur would be 1 percent of $1,000, or $10. Under which scenario would you hold more funds in your checking account instead of securities?

QUICK QUIZ See page 277 for the answers. Review concepts from this section in MyEconLab.

To use money, people must hold money. Therefore, they have a _____ for money balances.

The determinants of the demand for money balances are the _____ demand, the _____ demand, and the _____ demand.

Holding money carries an _____ cost—the interest income forgone. Hence, the demand for money curve showing the relationship between the quantity of money balances demanded and the interest rate slopes _____.

FIGURE 11-1

The Demand for Money Curve

If we use the interest rate as a proxy for the opportunity cost of holding money balances, the demand for money curve, M_d, is downward sloping, similar to other demand curves

How the Fed Influences Interest Rates

When the Fed takes actions that alter the rate of growth of the money supply, it is seeking to influence investment, consumption, and total aggregate expenditures. In taking these monetary policy actions, the Fed in principle has four tools at its disposal: open market operations, changes in the reserve ratio, changes in the interest rates paid on reserves, and discount rate changes. The first two tools were introduced in Chapter 10. The discount rate and interest rates paid on reserves will be discussed later in this chapter. Let's consider the effects of open market operations, the tool that the Fed regularly employs on a day-to-day basis.

Open Market Operations

As we saw in the previous chapter, the Fed changes the amount of reserves in the banking system by its purchases and sales of government bonds issued by the U.S. Treasury. To understand how these actions by the Fed influence the market interest rate, we start out in an equilibrium in which all individuals, including the holders of bonds, are satisfied with the current situation. There is some equilibrium level of interest rate (and bond prices). Now, if the Fed wants to conduct open market operations, it must somehow induce individuals, businesses, and foreign residents to hold more or fewer U.S. Treasury bonds. The inducement must take the form of making people better off. So, if the Fed wants to buy bonds, it will have to offer to buy them at a higher price than exists in the marketplace. If the Fed wants to sell bonds, it will have to offer them at a lower price than exists in the marketplace. Thus, an open market operation must cause a change in the price of bonds.

Go to www.econtoday.com/chap11 to learn about the Federal Reserve's current policy regarding open market operations. Scan down the page, and select the "Minutes" for the most recent date.

GRAPHING THE SALE OF BONDS The Fed sells some of the bonds it has on hand. This is shown in panel (a) of Figure 11-2 below. Notice that the supply of bonds in the private market is shown here as a vertical line with respect to price. The demand for bonds is downward sloping. If the Fed offers more bonds it owns for sale, the supply curve shifts from S_1 to S_2. People will not be willing to buy the extra bonds at the initial equilibrium bond price, P_1. They will be satisfied holding the additional bonds at the new equilibrium price, P_2.

THE FED'S PURCHASE OF BONDS The opposite occurs when the Fed purchases bonds. You can view this purchase of bonds as a reduction in the stock of bonds available for

---

FIGURE 11-2

Determining the Price of Bonds

In panel (a), the Fed offers more bonds for sale. The price drops from P_1 to P_2. In panel (b), the Fed purchases bonds. This is the equivalent of a reduction in the supply of bonds available for private investors to hold. The price of bonds must rise from P_1 to P_3 to clear the market.

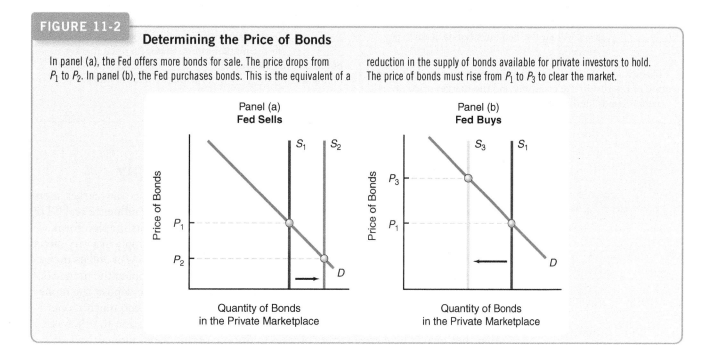

private investors to hold. In panel (b) of Figure 11-2 on the previous page, the original supply curve is S_1. The new supply curve of outstanding bonds will end up being S_3 because of the Fed's purchases of bonds. To get people to give up these bonds, the Fed must offer them a more attractive price. The price will rise from to P_1 to P_3.

Relationship between the Price of Existing Bonds and the Rate of Interest

The price of existing bonds and the rate of interest are inversely related. Assume that the average yield on bonds is 5 percent. You decide to purchase a bond. A local corporation agrees to sell you a bond that will pay you $50 a year forever. What is the price you are willing to pay for the bond? It is $1,000. Why? Because $50 divided by $1,000 equals 5 percent, which is as good as the best return you can earn elsewhere. You purchase the bond. The next year something happens in the economy, and you can now obtain bonds that have effective yields of 10 percent. (In other words, the prevailing interest rate in the economy is now 10 percent.) What will happen to the market price of the existing bond that you own, the one you purchased the year before? It will fall.

If you try to sell the bond for $1,000, you will discover that no investors will buy it from you. Why should they when they can obtain the same $50-a-year yield from someone else by paying only $500? Indeed, unless you offer your bond for sale at a price that is no higher than $500, no buyers will be forthcoming. Hence, an increase in the prevailing interest rate in the economy has caused the market value of your existing bond to fall.

The important point to be understood is this:

The market price of existing bonds (and all fixed-income assets) is inversely related to the rate of interest prevailing in the economy.

As a consequence of the inverse relationship between the price of existing bonds and the interest rate, the Fed is able to influence the interest rate by engaging in open market operations. A Fed open market sale that reduces the equilibrium price of bonds brings about an increase in the interest rate. A Fed open market purchase that boosts the equilibrium price of bonds generates a decrease in the interest rate.

QUICK QUIZ   See page 277 for the answers. Review concepts from this section in MyEconLab.

When the Fed sells bonds, it must offer them at a _____ price. When the Fed buys bonds, it must pay a _____ price.

There is an _____ relationship between the prevailing rate of interest in the economy and the market price of *existing* bonds (and all fixed-income assets).

A Federal Reserve open market sale generates a _____ in the price of *existing* bonds and an _____ in the market interest rate. An open market purchase brings about an _____ in the price of *existing* bonds and a _____ in the market rate of interest.

Effects of an Increase in the Money Supply

Now that we've seen how the Fed's monetary policy actions influence the market interest rate, we can ask a broader question: How does monetary policy influence real GDP and the price level? To understand how monetary policy works in its simplest form, we are going to run an experiment in which you increase the money supply in a very direct way. Assume that the government has given you hundreds of millions of dollars in just-printed bills. You then fly around the country in a helicopter, dropping the money out of the window. People pick it up and put it in their pockets. Some deposit the money in their transactions deposit accounts. As a result, they now have too much money—not in the sense that they want to throw it away but rather in relation to other assets that they own. There are a variety of ways to dispose of this "new" money.

Direct Effect

The simplest thing that people can do when they have excess money balances is to go out and spend them on goods and services. Here they have a direct impact on aggregate demand. Aggregate demand rises because with an increase in the money supply, at any given price level people now want to purchase more output of real goods and services.

Indirect Effect

Not everybody will necessarily spend the newfound money on goods and services. Some people may wish to deposit a portion or all of those excess money balances in banks. The recipient banks now discover that they have higher reserves than they wish to hold. As you learned in Chapter 10, one thing that banks can do to get higher-interest-earning assets is to lend out the excess reserves. But banks cannot induce people to borrow more funds than they were borrowing before unless the banks lower the interest rate that they charge on loans. This lower interest rate encourages people to take out those loans. Businesses will therefore engage in new investment with the funds loaned. Individuals will engage in more consumption of durable goods such as housing, autos, and home entertainment centers. Either way, the increased loans generate a rise in aggregate demand. More people will be involved in more spending—even those who did not pick up any of the money that was originally dropped out of your helicopter.

What happens if the market interest rate on bonds falls close to zero, as has occurred in recent years? In that case, monetary policy traditionally must rely on the direct effect of a change in bank reserves and, through the money multiplier effect, the quantity of money in circulation. Monetary policy cannot depend on the indirect effect of an interest rate that is already at zero. A policy action in which the Federal Reserve conducts open market purchases to increase bank reserves without seeking to alter the interest rate, which is already zero, is called **quantitative easing.**

Quantitative easing
Federal Reserve open market purchases intended to generate an increase in bank reserves at a nearly zero interest rate.

Graphing the Effects of an Expansionary Monetary Policy

To consider the effects of an expansionary monetary policy on real GDP and the price level, look at Figure 11-3 below. We start out in a situation in which the economy is operating at less than full employment. You see a recessionary gap in the figure, which is

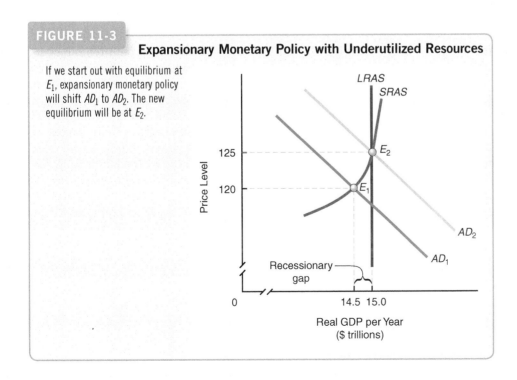

FIGURE 11-3

Expansionary Monetary Policy with Underutilized Resources

If we start out with equilibrium at E_1, expansionary monetary policy will shift AD_1 to AD_2. The new equilibrium will be at E_2.

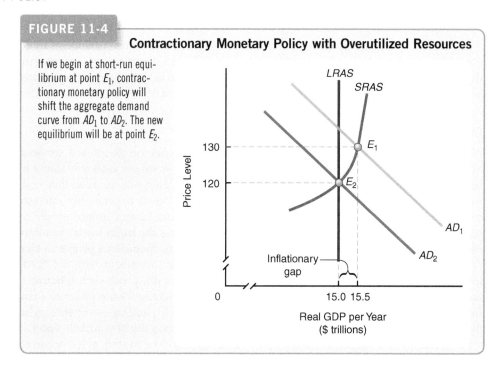

FIGURE 11-4

Contractionary Monetary Policy with Overutilized Resources

If we begin at short-run equilibrium at point E_1, contractionary monetary policy will shift the aggregate demand curve from AD_1 to AD_2. The new equilibrium will be at point E_2.

measured as the horizontal difference between the long-run aggregate supply curve, *LRAS*, and the current equilibrium. Short-run equilibrium is at E_1, with a price level of 120 and real GDP of $14.5 trillion. The *LRAS* curve is at $15 trillion. Assume now that the Fed increases the money supply. Because of the direct and indirect effects of this increase in the money supply, aggregate demand shifts outward to the right to AD_2. The new equilibrium is at an output rate of $15 trillion of real GDP per year and a price level of 125. Here expansionary monetary policy can move the economy toward its *LRAS* curve sooner than otherwise.

Graphing the Effects of Contractionary Monetary Policy

Assume that there is an inflationary gap as shown in Figure 11-4 above. There you see that the short-run aggregate supply curve, *SRAS*, intersects aggregate demand, AD_1, at E_1. This is to the right of the *LRAS* of real GDP per year of $15 trillion. Contractionary monetary policy can eliminate this inflationary gap. Because of both the direct and indirect effects of monetary policy, the aggregate demand curve shifts inward from AD_1 to AD_2. Equilibrium is now at E_2, which is at a lower price level, 120. Equilibrium real GDP has now fallen from $15.5 trillion to $15 trillion.

Note that contractionary monetary policy involves a reduction in the money supply, with a consequent decline in the price level (deflation). In the real world, contractionary monetary policy more commonly involves reducing the *rate of growth* of the money supply, thereby reducing the rate of increase in the price level (inflation). Similarly, real-world expansionary monetary policy typically involves increasing the rate of growth of the money supply.

QUICK QUIZ See page 277 for the answers. Review concepts from this section in MyEconLab.

The _____ effect of an increase in the money supply arises because people desire to spend more on real goods and services when they have excess money balances.

The _____ effect of an increase in the money supply works through a _____ in the interest rate, which

encourages businesses to make new investments with the funds loaned to them. Individuals will also engage in more consumption (on consumer durables) because of _____ interest rates.

Open Economy Transmission of Monetary Policy

So far we have discussed monetary policy in a closed economy. When we move to an open economy, with international trade and the international purchases and sales of all assets including dollars and other currencies, monetary policy becomes more complex. Consider first the effect of monetary policy on exports.

Go to www.econtoday.com/chap11 for links to central banks around the globe, provided by the Bank for International Settlements.

The Net Export Effect of Contractionary Monetary Policy

To see how a change in monetary policy can affect net exports, suppose that the Federal Reserve implements a contractionary policy that boosts the market interest rate. The higher U.S. interest rate, in turn, tends to attract foreign investment in U.S. financial assets, such as U.S. government securities.

If more residents of foreign countries decide that they want to purchase U.S. government securities or other U.S. assets, they first have to obtain U.S. dollars. As a consequence, the demand for dollars goes up in foreign exchange markets. The international price of the dollar therefore rises. This is called an *appreciation* of the dollar, and it tends to reduce net exports because it makes our exports more expensive in terms of foreign currency and imports cheaper in terms of dollars. Foreign residents demand fewer of our goods and services, and we demand more of theirs.

This reasoning implies that when contractionary monetary policy increases the U.S. interest rate at the current price level, there will be a negative net export effect because foreign residents will want more U.S. financial instruments. Hence, they will demand additional dollars, thereby causing the international price of the dollar to rise. This makes our exports more expensive for the rest of the world, which then demands a smaller quantity of our exports. It also means that foreign goods and services are less expensive in the United States, so we therefore demand more imports. We come up with this conclusion:

Contractionary monetary policy causes interest rates to rise. Such a rise will induce international inflows of funds, thereby raising the international value of the dollar and making U.S. goods less attractive abroad. The net export effect of contractionary monetary policy will be in the same direction as the monetary policy effect, thereby amplifying the effect of such policy.

The Net Export Effect of Expansionary Monetary Policy

Now assume that the economy is experiencing a recession and the Federal Reserve wants to pursue an expansionary monetary policy. In so doing, it will cause interest rates to fall in the short run, as discussed earlier. Declining interest rates will cause funds to flow out of the United States. The demand for dollars will decrease, and their international price will go down. Foreign goods will now look more expensive to U.S. residents, and imports will fall. Foreign residents will desire more of our exports, and exports will rise. The result will be an increase in net exports. Again, the international consequences reinforce the domestic consequences of monetary policy, in this case by stimulating the economy.

On a broader level, the Fed's ability to control the rate of growth of the money supply may be hampered as U.S. money markets become less isolated. With the push of a computer button, billions of dollars can change hands halfway around the world. If the Fed reduces the growth of the money supply, individuals and firms in the United States can obtain dollars from other sources. People in the United States who want more liquidity can obtain their dollars from foreign residents. Indeed, as world markets become increasingly integrated, U.S. residents, who can already hold U.S. bank accounts denominated in foreign currencies, more regularly conduct transactions using other nations' currencies.

QUICK QUIZ   See page 277 for the answers. Review concepts from this section in MyEconLab.

Monetary policy in an open economy has repercussions for net _____.

If contractionary monetary policy raises U.S. interest rates, there is a _____ net export effect because foreign residents will demand _____ U.S. financial instruments, thereby demanding _____ dollars and hence causing the international price of the dollar to rise.

This makes our exports more expensive for the rest of the world.

When expansionary monetary policy causes interest rates to fall, foreign residents will want _____ U.S. financial instruments. The resulting _____ in the demand for dollars will reduce the dollar's value in foreign exchange markets, leading to an _____ in net exports.

Monetary Policy and Inflation

Most media discussions of inflation focus on the short run. The price index can fluctuate in the short run because of events such as oil price shocks, labor union strikes, or discoveries of large amounts of new natural resources. In the long run, however, empirical studies show that excessive growth in the money supply results in inflation.

If the supply of money rises relative to the demand for money, people have more money balances than desired. They adjust their mix of assets to reduce money balances in favor of other items. This ultimately causes their spending on goods and services to increase. The result is a rise in the price level, or inflation.

The Equation of Exchange and the Quantity Theory

A simple way to show the relationship between changes in the quantity of money in circulation and the price level is through the **equation of exchange,** developed by Irving Fisher (note that $\equiv$ refers to an identity or truism):

$$M_s V \equiv PY$$

where M_s = actual money balances held by the nonbanking public
  V = **income velocity of money,** which is the number of times, on average per year, each monetary unit is spent on final goods and services
  P = price level or price index
  Y = real GDP per year

Equation of exchange
The formula indicating that the number of monetary units (M_s) times the number of times each unit is spent on final goods and services (V) is identical to the price level (P) times real GDP (Y).

Income velocity of money (V)
The number of times per year a dollar is spent on final goods and services; identically equal to nominal GDP divided by the money supply.

Consider a numerical example involving the entire economy. Assume that in this economy, the total money supply, M_s, is $10 trillion; real GDP, Y, is $15 trillion (in base-year dollars); and the price level, P, is 1.3333 (133.33 in index number terms). Using the equation of exchange,

$$M_s V \equiv PY$$
$$\$10 \text{ trillion} \times V \equiv 1.3333 \times \$15 \text{ trillion}$$
$$\$10 \text{ trillion} \times V \equiv \$20 \text{ trillion}$$
$$V \equiv 2.0$$

Thus, each dollar is spent an average of 2 times per year.

THE EQUATION OF EXCHANGE AS AN IDENTITY The equation of exchange must always be true—it is an *accounting identity*. The equation of exchange states that the total amount of funds spent on final output, $M_s V$, is equal to the total amount of funds *received* for final output, PY. Thus, a given flow of funds can be viewed from either the buyers' side or the producers' side. The value of goods purchased is equal to the value of goods sold.

If Y represents real GDP and P is the price level, PY equals the dollar value of national output of goods and services or *nominal* GDP. Thus,

$$M_s V \equiv PY \equiv \text{nominal GDP}$$

THE QUANTITY THEORY OF MONEY AND PRICES If we now make some assumptions about different variables in the equation of exchange, we come up with the simplified theory of

FIGURE 11-5

The Relationship between Money Supply Growth Rates and Rates of Inflation

If we plot rates of inflation and rates of monetary growth for different countries, we come up with a scatter diagram that reveals an obvious direct relationship. If you were to draw a line through the "average" of the points in this figure, it would be upward sloping, showing that an increase in the rate of growth of the money supply leads to an increase in the rate of inflation.

Sources: International Monetary Fund and national central banks. Data are for latest available periods.

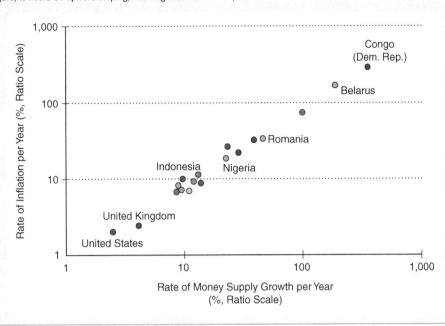

why the price level changes, called the **quantity theory of money and prices.** If we assume that the velocity of money, V, is constant and that real GDP, Y, is also constant, the simple equation of exchange tells us that a change in the money supply can lead only to an equiproportional change in the price level. Continue with our numerical example. Y is $15 trillion. V equals 2.0. If the money supply increases by 20 percent, to $12 trillion, the only thing that can happen is that the price level, P, has to go up from 1.3333 to 1.6. In other words, the price level must also increase by 20 percent. Otherwise the equation is no longer in balance. An increase in the money supply of 20 percent results in a rise in the price level (inflation) of 20 percent.

EMPIRICAL VERIFICATION There is considerable evidence of the empirical validity of the relationship between monetary growth and high rates of inflation. Figure 11-5 above tracks the correspondence between money supply growth and the rates of inflation in various countries around the world.

Why did Iran recently decide to make each unit of its money 10,000 times smaller?

Quantity theory of money and prices
The hypothesis that changes in the money supply lead to equiproportional changes in the price level.

YOU ARE THERE

To contemplate how the quantity theory of money and prices operates in a multiplayer online game, take a look at **Applying the Quantity Theory of Money and Prices to a Universe of Star Systems** on page 271.

INTERNATIONAL POLICY EXAMPLE

Iran Removes Four Zeros from Each Unit of Its Currency

In recent years, the annual inflation rate reported by Iran's government has ranged from about 15 percent to just over 20 percent. These high inflation rates followed on the heels of double-digit-percentage rates of growth in the quantity of *rials*—Iran's currency—in circulation. So many rials circulated and the average price level rose so high that the currency note most widely used in trade was the 100,000-rial note (worth less than $10).

To save Iranian residents the complication of keeping careful track of the extra zeros in their currency notes and posted prices, the Central Bank of the Iranian Republic took the step of dividing the value of every unit of its currency by 10,000. To implement this change, the central bank announced the formal removal of four zeros from every currency note. It also gradually introduced into circulation a new currency, called the *parsi*, defined as equal to 10,000 rials, and began gradually removing rials from circulation.

FOR CRITICAL THINKING

Even after the new parsi notes replace the old rial notes, will the inflation rate change if the rate of growth of Iran's money supply stays the same?

The _____ of _____ states that the expenditures by some people will equal income receipts by others, or $M_sV \equiv PY$ (money supply times velocity equals nominal GDP).

Viewed as an accounting identity, the equation of exchange is always _____, because the amount of funds _____ on final output of goods and services must equal the total amount of funds _____ for final output.

The quantity theory of money and prices states that a change in the _____ _____ will bring about a proportional change in the _____ _____.

Monetary Policy in Action: The Transmission Mechanism

Earlier in this chapter, we talked about the direct and indirect effects of monetary policy. The direct effect is simply that an increase in the money supply causes people to have excess money balances. To get rid of these excess money balances, people increase their expenditures. The indirect effect, depicted in Figure 11-6 below, as the interest-rate-based money transmission mechanism, occurs because some people have decided to purchase interest-bearing assets with their excess money balances. This causes the price of such assets—bonds—to go up. Because of the inverse relationship between the price of existing bonds and the interest rate, the interest rate in the economy falls. This lower interest rate induces people and businesses to spend more than they otherwise would have spent.

An Interest-Rate-Based Transmission Mechanism

The indirect, interest-rate-based transmission mechanism can be seen explicitly in Figure 11-7 on the facing page. In panel (a), you see that an increase in the money supply reduces the interest rate. The economywide demand curve for money is labeled M_d in panel (a). At first, the money supply is at M_s, a vertical line determined by the Federal Reserve. The equilibrium interest rate is r_1. This occurs where the money supply curve intersects the money demand curve.

Now assume that the Fed increases the money supply, say, via open market operations. This will shift the money supply curve outward to the right to M_s'. People find themselves with too much cash (liquidity). They buy bonds. When they buy bonds, they bid up the prices of bonds, thereby lowering the interest rate. The interest rate falls to r_2, where the new money supply curve M_s' intersects the money demand curve M_d. This reduction in the interest rate from r_1 to r_2 has an effect on planned investment, as can be seen in panel (b). Planned investment per year increases from I_1 to I_2. An increase in investment will increase aggregate demand, as shown in panel (c). Aggregate demand increases from AD_1 to AD_2. Equilibrium in the economy increases from real GDP per year of \$14.5 trillion, which is not on the $LRAS$, to equilibrium real GDP per year of \$15 trillion, which is on the $LRAS$.

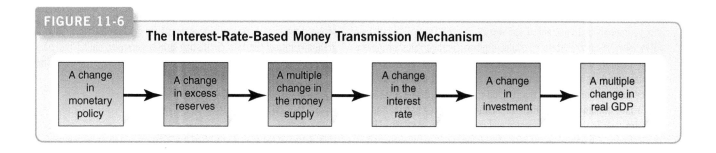

FIGURE 11-6

The Interest-Rate-Based Money Transmission Mechanism

A change in monetary policy → A change in excess reserves → A multiple change in the money supply → A change in the interest rate → A change in investment → A multiple change in real GDP

Adding Monetary Policy to the Aggregate Demand–Aggregate Supply Model

In panel (a), we show a demand for money function, M_d. It slopes downward to show that at lower rates of interest, a larger quantity of money will be demanded. The money supply is given initially as M_s, so the equilibrium rate of interest will be r_1. At this rate of interest, we see from the planned investment schedule given in panel (b) that the quantity of

planned investment demanded per year will be I_1. After the shift in the money supply to M_s', the resulting increase in investment from I_1 to I_2 shifts the aggregate demand curve in panel (c) outward from AD_1 to AD_2. Equilibrium moves from E_1 to E_2, at real GDP of $15 trillion per year.

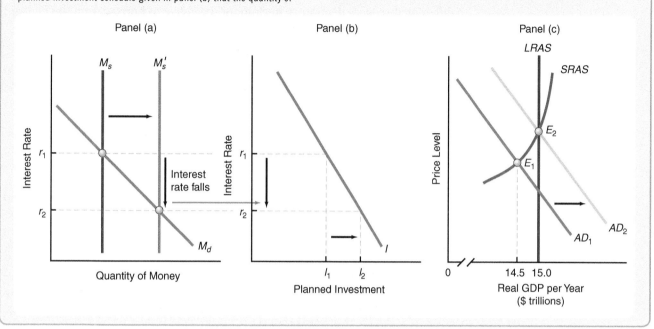

Targeting the Federal Funds Rate

As we have seen, the Fed can influence interest rates only by actively entering the market for federal government securities (usually Treasury bills). So, if the Fed wants to raise "the" interest rate, it essentially must engage in contractionary open market operations. That is to say, it must sell more Treasury securities than it buys, thereby reducing total reserves in the banking system and, hence, the money supply. This tends to boost the rate of interest. Conversely, when the Fed wants to decrease "the" rate of interest, it engages in expansionary open market operations, thereby increasing reserves and the money supply. But what interest rate is the Fed attempting to change?

In reality, more than one interest rate matters for Fed policymaking. Three interest rates are particularly relevant.

1. *The Federal Funds Rate.* In normal times, depository institutions wishing to borrow funds rarely seek to borrow directly from the Fed. In years past, this was because the Fed would not lend them all they wanted to borrow. Instead, the Fed encouraged banks to obtain funds in the **federal funds market** when they wanted to expand their reserves. The federal funds market is an interbank market in reserves where one bank borrows the excess reserves—resources held voluntarily over and above required reserves—of another. The generic term *federal funds market* refers to the borrowing or lending of reserve funds that are usually repaid within the same 24-hour period.

Depository institutions that borrow in the federal funds market pay an interest rate called the **federal funds rate.** Because the federal funds rate is a ready measure of the cost that banks must incur to raise funds, the Federal Reserve often uses it as a yardstick by which to measure the effects of its policies. Consequently, the federal funds rate is closely watched as an indicator of the Fed's intentions.

Federal funds market
A private market (made up mostly of banks) in which banks can borrow reserves from other banks that want to lend them. Federal funds are usually lent for overnight use.

Federal funds rate
The interest rate that depository institutions pay to borrow reserves in the interbank federal funds market.

Discount rate
The interest rate that the Federal Reserve charges for reserves that it lends to depository institutions. It is sometimes referred to as the *rediscount rate* or, in Canada and England, as the *bank rate*.

2. *The Discount Rate.* When the Fed does lend reserves directly to depository institutions, the rate of interest that it charges is called the **discount rate.** When depository institutions borrow reserves from the Fed at this rate, they are said to be borrowing through the Fed's "discount window." Borrowing from the Fed increases reserves and thereby expands the money supply, other things being equal.

Since 2003, the differential between the discount rate and the federal funds rate has ranged from 0.25 percentage point to 1.0 percentage point. An increase in this differential reduces depository institutions' incentive to borrow from the Fed and thereby generates a reduction in discount window borrowings.

3. *The Interest Rate on Reserves.* In October 2008, Congress granted the Fed authority to pay interest on both required reserves and excess reserves of depository institutions. Initially, the Fed paid different rates of interest on required and excess reserves, but since late 2008 the Fed has paid the same interest rate on both categories of reserves.

Varying the interest rate on reserves alters the incentives that banks face when deciding whether to hold any additional reserves they obtain as excess reserves or to lend those reserves out to other banks in the federal funds market. If the Fed raises the interest rate on reserves and thereby reduces the differential between the federal funds rate and the interest rate on reserves, banks have less incentive to lend reserves in the federal funds market. Thus, it is not surprising that excess reserves in the U.S. banking system now amount to more than $1.5 trillion, as discussed in more detail later in this chapter.

ESTABLISHING THE FED POLICY STRATEGY The policy decisions that determine open market operations by which the Fed pursues its announced objective for the federal funds rate are made by the Federal Open Market Committee (FOMC). Every six to eight weeks, the voting members of the FOMC—the seven Fed board governors and five regional bank presidents—determine the Fed's general strategy of open market operations.

FOMC Directive
A document that summarizes the Federal Open Market Committee's general policy strategy, establishes near-term objectives for the federal funds rate, and specifies target ranges for money supply growth.

The FOMC outlines its strategy in a document called the **FOMC Directive.** This document lays out the FOMC's general economic objectives, establishes short-term federal funds rate objectives, and specifies target ranges for money supply growth. After each meeting, the FOMC issues a brief statement to the media, which then publish stories about the Fed's action or inaction and what it is likely to mean for the economy. Typically, these stories have headlines such as "Fed Cuts Key Interest Rate," "Fed Acts to Push Up Interest Rates," or "Fed Decides to Leave Interest Rates Alone."

Trading Desk
An office at the Federal Reserve Bank of New York charged with implementing monetary policy strategies developed by the Federal Open Market Committee.

THE TRADING DESK The FOMC leaves the task of implementing the Directive to officials who manage an office at the Federal Reserve Bank of New York known as the **Trading Desk.** The media spend little time considering how the Fed's Trading Desk conducts its activities, taking for granted that the Fed can implement the policy action that it has announced to the public. The Trading Desk's open market operations typically are confined within a one-hour interval each weekday morning.

The Taylor Rule

Taylor rule
An equation that specifies a federal funds rate target based on an estimated long-run real interest rate, the current deviation of the actual inflation rate from the Federal Reserve's inflation objective, and the gap between actual real GDP per year and a measure of potential real GDP per year.

In 1990, John Taylor of Stanford University suggested a relatively simple equation that the Fed might use for the purpose of selecting a federal funds rate target. This equation would direct the Fed to set the federal funds rate target based on an estimated long-run real interest rate (see page 15 in Chapter 1), the current deviation of the actual inflation rate from the Fed's inflation objective, and the proportionate gap between actual real GDP per year and a measure of potential real GDP per year. Taylor and other economists have applied his equation, which has become known as the **Taylor rule,** to actual Fed policy choices. They have concluded that the Taylor rule's recommendations for federal funds rate target values come close to the actual targets the Fed has selected over time.

FIGURE 11-8

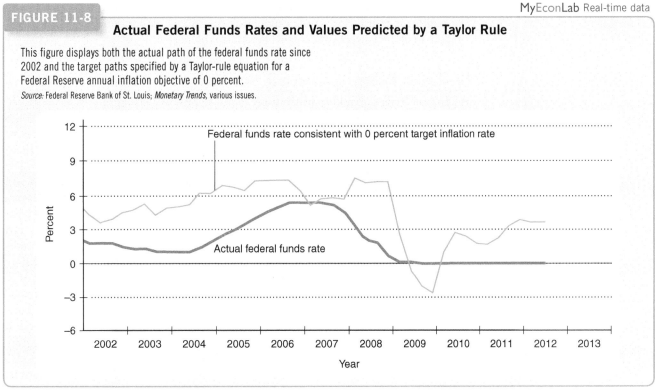

Actual Federal Funds Rates and Values Predicted by a Taylor Rule

This figure displays both the actual path of the federal funds rate since 2002 and the target paths specified by a Taylor-rule equation for a Federal Reserve annual inflation objective of 0 percent.

Source: Federal Reserve Bank of St. Louis; *Monetary Trends*, various issues.

PLOTTING THE TAYLOR RULE ON A GRAPH The Federal Reserve Bank of St. Louis now regularly tracks target levels for the federal funds rate predicted by a basic Taylor-rule equation. Figure 11-8 above displays paths of both the actual federal funds rate (the orange line) and the Taylor-rule recommendation if the Fed's inflation objective (the green line) is 0 percent inflation.

ASSESSING THE STANCE OF FED POLICY WITH THE TAYLOR RULE Suppose that the actual federal funds rate is *below* the rate implied by a 0 percent inflation goal. In this situation, the Taylor rule implies that the Fed's policymaking is expansionary. As a consequence, the actual inflation rate will rise above 0 percent. Thus, during the 2003–2005 interval, the actual federal funds rate was well below the level consistent with a 0 percent inflation rate. This implies that Fed policymaking was very expansionary during this period, sufficiently so as to be expected to yield a long-run inflation rate substantially in excess of 0 percent per year. The Taylor-rule graph implies that in late 2006, the Fed's policy stance became much more contractionary, with the actual federal funds rate above the level consistent with 0 percent inflation. Then, the graph suggests, Fed policymaking became expansionary once more beginning in late 2007.

Until the early 2000s, the actual federal funds rate remained relatively close to the Taylor-rule predictions over time. Since 2003, the Fed has failed to set its federal funds rate target in a manner consistent with the Taylor rule.

Credit Policy at Today's Fed

Federal Reserve policymakers continue to announce and to try to achieve a target value for the federal funds rate. Since the financial meltdown of the late 2000s, however, the Fed has pursued a new approach to policymaking, called **credit policy,** under which it directly extends credit to specific banks, other financial intermediaries, and even nonfinancial companies. When Fed officials initiated this new policy approach in

Credit policy
Federal Reserve policymaking involving direct lending to financial and nonfinancial firms.

2008, they indicated their intention to make it a temporary undertaking. In reality, the Fed continues to use credit policy alongside traditional monetary policy and appears unlikely to end its direct extensions of credit in the near future.

The Credit Policy Approach in Practice

When hundreds of banking institutions found themselves struggling to avoid severe illiquidity and bankruptcy in 2008, the Fed introduced a number of programs through which it provided credit directly to these institutions. The Fed auctioned funds to banking institutions and also bought many debt securities held by a number of these institutions.

In addition, the Fed purchased some of the debts of auto finance companies and then later allowed the companies to obtain bank charters so that they could receive direct loans from the Fed's discount window. The Fed even provided short-term emergency financing arrangements for nonfinancial firms such as Caterpillar, Inc. and Toyota. Even though the Fed had engaged in none of these varied forms of credit policy activities prior to 2008, *today more than $1 trillion, or 40 percent, of the Fed's asset holdings relate to its conduct of credit policy.*

In recent years, the Fed has slowed its extension of credit to institutions and firms. Nevertheless, many of the debts that it purchased from banks and other firms have long *maturities*—periods of time before full repayments are due. This situation is quite different from the situation prior to 2008, when only a small portion of the Fed's assets had lengthy maturities.

Furthermore, a number of the debts the Fed has purchased from private institutions are based on mortgage obligations of dubious value. Consequently, the Fed faces considerable risk that at least some of the debts will never be fully repaid. This state of affairs is also quite different from the situation in preceding years, when the bulk of the Fed's assets, about 80 percent of which were U.S. government securities, offered very low risks of loss.

How the Fed Finances the Credit It Extends

In an important sense, the Fed's credit policy results in its activities more closely resembling those of a private bank than a central bank. Like a private banking institution, the Fed extends credit by lending out funds that it obtains from depositors. Unlike private banks, however, the Fed collects the bulk of its deposits from banking institutions instead of from households and firms. These deposits consist of the reserve deposits that banks hold with Federal Reserve banks.

To engage in its active and substantial credit policy, the Fed must induce private banks to maintain substantial reserve deposits with the Federal Reserve banks. A key inducement is the interest rate the Fed pays on reserves. Even though the Fed has paid a very low interest rate of about 0.25 percent on reserve deposits since 2008, throughout most this period, the market clearing federal funds rate has been even lower. Thus, banks have earned more by setting funds aside in reserve deposit accounts at Federal Reserve banks than by lending to other banks in the federal funds market. This means that the Fed essentially has paid banks a per-unit *subsidy* to keep hundreds of billions of dollars on deposit with the Fed.

All such funds held at Federal Reserve banks do not remain idle, though. Just as private banks can use the deposits of households and firms to fund loans and purchases of securities, the Fed can use the reserve deposits of private banks to fund its own lending and securities-buying activities. Since 2008, reserve deposits at Federal Reserve banks have risen from less than $50 billion to more than $1.5 *trillion*. These funds have financed the Fed's credit policy—lending to domestic and foreign banks, nonfinancial companies, and central banks and buying risky, longer-term mortgage obligations.

How has payment of interest on banks' *excess* reserves constituted a subsidy?

POLICY EXAMPLE

Interest on Excess Reserves as a Subsidy

To induce banks to hold the more than $1.5 trillion in funds desired by the Fed to finance its credit policy, in 2008 the Fed began paying interest on excess as well as required reserves. Receipt of these interest payments gave banks an incentive to borrow funds from other sources (at a lower interest rate) to hold on reserve at the Fed. These sources of funds were the government-sponsored housing finance institutions—the Federal National Mortgage Association (FNMA) and the Federal Home Loan Mortgage Corporation (FHLMC).

Banks thereby borrow from FNMA and FHLMC to add to their excess reserves holdings with the Fed at a slightly higher interest rate. In this way, the Fed effectively pays interest on reserves that banks split with FNMA and FHLMC. As a result, the Fed's policy of paying interest on excess reserves effectively grants an estimated $1 billion per year in subsidies to banks and to these two government-sponsored housing finance institutions.

FOR CRITICAL THINKING
How does interest on excess reserves reduce bank lending to households and firms?

Arguments in Favor of the Fed's Credit Policy

Three arguments support the Federal Reserve's credit policy:

1. *Giving Banks Time to Recover from the Financial Meltdown.* The original rationale for initiating the credit policy was to address the deteriorating condition of the U.S. banking industry that began in 2007. As more and more banks weakened during 2008 and 2009, the Fed created an array of lending programs aimed at countering the fact that institutions were less willing to lend to one another in private markets. These new Fed lending programs made banks much more liquid than they would have been otherwise, which ensured their ability to withstand bank runs. The Fed's lending programs also succeeded in keeping many otherwise insolvent banks—those for which the value of assets dropped below the value of liabilities—afloat until they could become more economically viable. A few large institutions ultimately could not continue as stand-alone banks, and hundreds of smaller community banks failed. Nevertheless, the programs provided "breathing space" until other financial institutions could acquire those banks and their lower-valued assets.

2. *Making Financial Markets and Institutions More Liquid and Solvent.* The Fed's purchases of debt securities also helped make financial markets and institutions more liquid and solvent. At the height of the financial crisis, the Fed's purchases of debt securities from companies such as Ford Motor Company and Harley & Davidson, Inc. ensured that these otherwise profitable and solvent firms remained liquid. The Fed's later purchases of mortgage-obligation debt securities removed many high-risk assets from banks' balance sheets and thereby improved the banks' longer-term solvency prospects.

3. *Contributing to International Financial Liquidity.* Finally, the credit extended by the Fed to foreign private banks and central banks enabled these institutions to maintain holdings of U.S. dollars. This credit policy action helped ensure liquidity in international financial markets.

Thus, the Fed's credit policy activities did much to help prevent banks, firms, and financial markets from becoming illiquid, which undoubtedly forestalled possible bank runs in 2008 and 2009. Its credit policy actions also prevented a number of bank failures.

Arguments Against the Fed's Credit Policy

Critics of the Fed's credit policy have offered three arguments against it.

1. *Providing an Incentive for Institutions to Operate Less Efficiently.* Critics point out that the Fed is capable of creating as much liquidity as desired via open market purchases. These critics worry that the Fed encourages institutions to which it directs credit to operate with less attention to minimizing operating costs than they would otherwise.

2. *Reducing Incentives to Screen and Monitor in Order to Limit Asymmetric Information Problems.* Critics of the Fed argue that preventing insolvencies via this credit policy interferes with the functions of private institutions and markets in identifying and addressing asymmetric information problems (see Chapter 10). If banks know the Fed will bail them out, critics suggest, banks will do poorer jobs of screening and monitoring borrowers. Hence, in the longer term, the Fed's credit policy could broaden the scope of asymmetric information problems.

3. *Making Monetary Policy Less Effective.* Critics suggest that the Fed has pursued its credit policy so vigorously that its performance in the realm of monetary policy has worsened. They point out that while the Fed was providing credit to many individual institutions and firms, difficulties in predicting how these actions would affect the money supply contributed to substantial swings in monetary aggregates. In fact, although quantitative-easing policies when the interest rate was near zero raised bank reserves by more than $1.5 trillion, the Fed's credit policies induced banks to hold those reserves idle at Federal Reserve banks. Thus, the reserve ratio increased, and the money multiplier fell. On net, therefore, the money supply failed to grow very much in response to the Fed's quantitative easing. Indeed, over some intervals the money supply even declined.

WHAT IF... the Fed responded to a future financial meltdown by buying up *all* bad debts?

In principle, the Fed possesses authority to buy IOUs from anyone in the event of an emergency. If the Fed were to respond to a future financial meltdown by buying up *all* bad debts, its actions technically would prevent *any* failures from occurring and effectively "bail out" the entire U.S. financial system. Purchasing all bad debts would increase the Fed's assets considerably. Because the Fed's total assets equal its total liabilities, the Fed's liabilities, including reserves of banks, would also increase by a significant amount. The result would be a multiplier effect on the money supply. Consequently, the quantity of money in circulation would rise substantially, which likely would contribute to higher annual inflation rates.

QUICK QUIZ See page 277 for the answers. Review concepts from this section in MyEconLab.

At present, the policy strategy of the Federal Open Market Committee (FOMC) focuses on aiming for a target value of the _____ _____ rate, which the FOMC seeks to achieve via _____ _____ _____ that alter the supply of reserves to the banking system.

The FOMC outlines the Fed's general monetary policy strategy in the FOMC _____, which it transmits to the Trading Desk of the Federal Reserve Bank of _____ _____ for implementation.

Since 2008, the Fed has implemented _____ policy, under which it has extended _____ directly to selected financial institutions and has purchased debt securities that have lost much of their market value.

Advantages of the Fed's _____ policy are that it has provided institutions with more liquidity, has helped to limit the number of bank _____, and has provided more dollars for use in international markets. Disadvantages include reduced incentives for banks to minimize operating costs and to screen and to _____ borrowers and potential conflicts of _____ policy with the Fed's monetary policy responsibilities.

YOU ARE THERE
Applying the Quantity Theory of Money and Prices to a Universe of Star Systems

Eyjolfur Gudmundsson is the central banker for a universe of 7,000 star systems traversed by more than 300,000 starship pilots. The stars and pilots are located in cyberspace, scattered among hundreds of thousands of computers worldwide.

Gudmundsson determines the supply of money used in exchange by players ("starship pilots") who participate in a multiplayer Internet-based game called Eve Online. Gudmundsson has learned that when Eve Online's general level of prices—tabulated from a consumer price index based on game items such as asteroid-mining gear and laser guns—begins to tick upward, a policy response is required. In Eve Online's economy, Gudmundsson has determined, reducing the inflation rate requires decreasing the rate of growth of the quantity of money in circulation. He brings about a lower money growth rate by reducing the amount of new game currency transmitted to players whenever they succeed in certain tasks required to move to different levels within the game. In this way, Gudmundsson conducts monetary policy based on the quantity theory of money and prices.

Critical Thinking Questions

1. How would Gudmundsson respond if Eve Online's economy experiences deflation?

2. If Eve Online's real GDP and income velocity of money remain unchanged, what determines the rate of inflation experienced by its "starship pilots"?

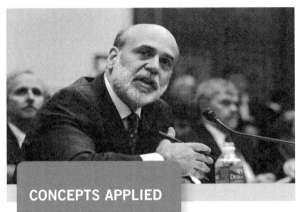

ISSUES & APPLICATIONS

While Credit Policy Gives, Monetary Policy Takes Away

CONCEPTS APPLIED

▶ Credit Policy

▶ Federal Funds Rate

▶ Money Balances

Since the Fed began implementing credit policy alongside traditional monetary policy in 2008, it has struggled to coordinate these two forms of policymaking. A consequence has been greater variability in the money supply and in the real interest rate.

Increased Money Supply Variability during the Recession

Panel (a) of Figure 11-9 on the following page shows the M2 measure of the money supply since 2001. As you can see, aside from some intermittent and very brief dips, the money supply generally rose at a steady pace until 2008.

When the Fed first began its credit policy programs in 2008, the M2 measure of aggregate money balances dipped and did not grow for several months. Throughout the rest of 2008, M2 grew rapidly. Then M2 steadily *decreased* during the middle part of 2009 before very slightly increasing during 2010.

Thus, just as the economic downturn began in 2008, the Fed allowed money supply growth to drop. Moreover, just as a recovery began in 2009 and 2010, the Fed again allowed the money supply to decline. Both actions reduced aggregate demand.

A "Low" Nominal Federal Funds Rate but a Volatile Real Rate

Panel (b) displays the nominal federal funds rate and the estimated real federal funds rate—the nominal rate minus the estimated expected inflation rate. Until 2008, the nominal and estimated real values of the federal funds rate moved in tandem.

During 2008, the Fed acted to keep the nominal federal funds rate very close to zero. Through its credit policy programs, the Fed extended loans to selected institutions at very low nominal rates of interest. After the Fed allowed money growth to falter in 2008, a significant decrease in inflation occurred. (Indeed, there was a short period of deflation.) As a consequence, although the nominal federal funds rate remained close to zero after 2008, the estimated real federal funds rate rose in 2008, and again during 2009 and 2010 following the second dip in money growth during 2009.

FIGURE 11-9

M2 and Nominal and Estimated Real Federal Funds Rates since 2001

Panel (a) shows that M2 generally increased until 2008. Its level dropped early that year and again during 2009. As indicated in panel (b), even though the nominal federal funds rate has been very low since 2008, the real federal funds rate increased in 2008 and again during 2009 and 2010 following the declines in M2.

Source: Board of Governors of the Federal Reserve System.

(a)

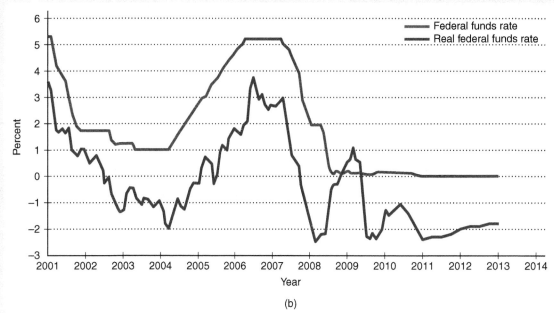

(b)

The Fed sought to support its credit policy with a near-zero nominal interest rate after 2008, but volatility in aggregate money balances contributed to variable real interest rates. Higher real interest rates raised real borrowing costs in 2009 and again in 2010 even as the Fed perceived that its credit policy was helping to keep borrowing costs low. Thus, the Fed failed to implement a consistently counter-recessionary monetary policy in conjunction with its credit policy.

For Critical Thinking

1. Why did decreases in inflation follow the drops in the money supply?
2. How does deflation raise real interest expenses for borrowers?

Web Resources

1. Take a look at recent values of M2 at www.econtoday.com/chap11.
2. Track the nominal federal funds rate at www.econtoday.com/chap11.

MyEconLab

For more questions on this chapter's Issues & Applications, go to MyEconLab. In the Study Plan for this chapter, select Section N: News.

MyEconLab

Here is what you should know after reading this chapter. MyEconLab will help you identify what you know, and where to go when you need to practice.

WHAT YOU SHOULD KNOW		WHERE TO GO TO PRACTICE
Key Factors That Influence the Quantity of Money That People Desire to Hold People desire to hold more money to make transactions when nominal GDP increases. In addition, money is a store of value that people may hold alongside bonds, stocks, and other interest-earning assets. The opportunity cost of holding money as an asset is the interest rate, so the quantity of money demanded declines as the market interest rate increases.	money balances, 255 transactions demand, 255 precautionary demand, 255 asset demand, 256 Key Figure Figure 11-1, 256	• MyEconLab Study Plan 11.1
How the Federal Reserve's Open Market Operations Influence Market Interest Rates When the Fed sells U.S. government bonds, it must offer them for sale at a lower price to induce buyers to purchase the bonds. The market price of existing bonds and the prevailing interest rate in the economy are inversely related, so the market interest rate rises when the Fed sells bonds.	Key Figure Figure 11-2, 257	• MyEconLab Study Plan 11.2 • Animated Figure 11-2
How Expansionary and Contractionary Monetary Policies Affect Equilibrium Real GDP and the Price Level in the Short Run An expansionary monetary policy action increases the money supply and causes a decrease in market interest rates. The aggregate demand curve shifts rightward, which can eliminate a short-run recessionary gap in real GDP. In contrast, a contractionary monetary policy action reduces the money supply and causes an increase in market interest rates. This results in a leftward shift in the aggregate demand curve, which can eliminate a short-run inflationary gap.	quantitative easing 259 Key Figures Figure 11-3, 259 Figure 11-4, 260	• MyEconLab Study Plan 11.3 • Animated Figures 11-3, 11-4

MyEconLab *continued*

The Equation of Exchange and the Quantity Theory of Money and Prices The equation of exchange states that the quantity of money times the average number of times a unit of money is used in exchange—the income velocity of money—must equal the price level times real GDP. The quantity theory of money and prices assumes that the income velocity of money is constant and real GDP is relatively stable. Thus, a rise in the quantity of money leads to an equiproportional increase in the price level.

equation of exchange, 262
income velocity of money (V), 262
quantity theory of money and prices, 263

- MyEconLab Study Plan 11.3

The Interest-Rate-Based Transmission Mechanism of Monetary Policy The interest-rate-based approach to the monetary policy transmission mechanism operates through effects of monetary policy actions on market interest rates, which bring about changes in desired investment and thereby affect equilibrium real GDP via the multiplier effect. At present, the Fed uses an interest rate target, which is the federal funds rate. Some economists favor selecting the federal funds rate target using a Taylor rule, which specifies an equation for the federal funds rate target based on an estimated long-run real interest rate, the current deviation of actual inflation from the Fed's inflation goal, and the gap between actual real GDP and a measure of potential real GDP.

federal funds market, 265
federal funds rate, 265
discount rate, 266
FOMC Directive, 266
Trading Desk, 266
Taylor rule, 266

Key Figures
Figure 11-6, 264
Figure 11-7, 265
Figure 11-8, 267

- MyEconLab Study Plans 11.3, 11.4, 11.5
- Animated Figures 11-6, 11-7, 11-8

The Use of Credit Policy by Today's Fed Since the late 2000s, the Federal Reserve has used credit policy, which involves direct lending to financial and nonfinancial firms. Today, more than $1.5 trillion, or 40 percent, of the Fed's asset holdings are related to the conduct of credit policy. The Fed's payment of an interest subsidy on reserves provides banks with an incentive to hold the reserves the Fed requires to obtain the funds that it lends. Arguments favoring the Fed credit policy are that it has helped banks recover from the financial meltdown, has contributed to liquidity and solvency of financial markets and institutions, and has made global financial markets more liquid. Arguments against the policy are that it contributes to lower efficiency of the banking system, has reduced bank incentives to screen and monitor in order to reduce asymmetric information problems, and has reduced the effectiveness of monetary policy.

credit policy, 267

- MyEconLab Study Plans 11.5, 11.6, 11.7

Log in to MyEconLab, take a chapter test, and get a personalized Study Plan that tells you which concepts you understand and which ones you need to review. From there, MyEconLab will give you further practice, tutorials, animations, videos, and guided solutions. For more information, visit www.myeconlab.com

PROBLEMS

All problems are assignable in MyEconLab; exercises that update with real-time data are marked with 🌐. Answers to odd-numbered problems appear at the back of the book.

11-1. Let's denote the price of a nonmaturing bond (called a *consol*) as P_b. The equation that indicates this price is $P_b = I/r$, where I is the annual net income the bond generates and r is the nominal market interest rate. (See pages 257–258.)

   a. Suppose that a bond promises the holder $500 per year forever. If the nominal market interest rate is 5 percent, what is the bond's current price?

   b. What happens to the bond's price if the market interest rate rises to 10 percent?

11-2. On the basis of Problem 11-1, imagine that initially the market interest rate is 5 percent and at this interest rate you have decided to hold half of your financial wealth as bonds and half as holdings of non-interest-bearing money. You notice that the market interest rate is starting to rise, however, and you become convinced that it will ultimately rise to 10 percent. (See pages 255–258.)

   a. In what direction do you expect the value of your bond holdings to go when the interest rate rises?

   b. If you wish to prevent the value of your financial wealth from declining in the future, how should you adjust the way you split your wealth between bonds and money? What does this imply about the demand for money?

11-3. You learned in Chapter 5 that if there is an inflationary gap in the short run, then in the long run a new equilibrium arises when input prices and expectations adjust upward, causing the short-run aggregate supply curve to shift upward and to the left and pushing equilibrium real GDP per year back to its long-run value. In this chapter, however, you learned that the Federal Reserve can eliminate an inflationary gap in the short run by undertaking a policy action that reduces aggregate demand. (See page 260.)

   a. Propose one monetary policy action that could eliminate an inflationary gap in the short run.

   b. In what way might society gain if the Fed implements the policy you have proposed instead of simply permitting long-run adjustments to take place?

11-4. You learned in Chapter 5 that if a recessionary gap occurs in the short run, then in the long run a new equilibrium arises when input prices and expectations adjust downward, causing the short-run aggregate supply curve to shift downward and

to the right and pushing equilibrium real GDP per year back to its long-run value. In this chapter, you learned that the Federal Reserve can eliminate a recessionary gap in the short run by undertaking a policy action that increases aggregate demand. (See page 260.)

   a. Propose one monetary policy action that could eliminate the recessionary gap in the short run.

   b. In what way might society gain if the Fed implements the policy you have proposed instead of simply permitting long-run adjustments to take place?

11-5. Suppose that the economy currently is in long-run equilibrium. Explain the short- and long-run adjustments that will take place in an aggregate demand–aggregate supply diagram if the Fed expands the quantity of money in circulation. (See page 260.)

11-6. Explain why the net export effect of a contractionary monetary policy reinforces the usual impact that monetary policy has on equilibrium real GDP per year in the short run. (See page 261.)

11-7. Suppose that, initially, the U.S. economy was in an aggregate demand–aggregate supply equilibrium at point *A* along the aggregate demand curve *AD* in the diagram below. Now, however, the value of the U.S. dollar suddenly appreciates relative to foreign currencies. This appreciation happens to have no measurable effects on either the short-run or the long-run aggregate supply curve in the United States. It does, however, influence U.S. aggregate demand. (See page 261.)

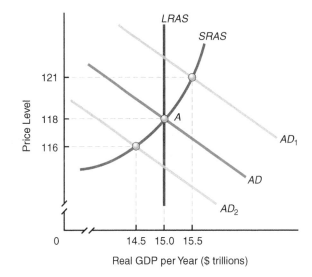

a. Explain in your own words how the dollar appreciation will affect net export expenditures in the United States.

b. Of the alternative aggregate demand curves depicted in the figure—AD_1 versus AD_2—which could represent the aggregate demand effect of the U.S. dollar's appreciation? What effects does the appreciation have on real GDP and the price level?

c. What policy action might the Federal Reserve take to prevent the dollar's appreciation from affecting equilibrium real GDP in the short run?

11-8. Suppose that the quantity of money in circulation is fixed but the income velocity of money doubles. If real GDP remains at its long-run potential level, what happens to the equilibrium price level? (See page 262.)

11-9. Suppose that following adjustment to the events in Problem 11-8, the Fed cuts the money supply in half. How does the price level now compare with its value before the income velocity and the money supply changed? (See page 262.)

11-10. Consider the following data: The money supply is $1 trillion, the price level equals 2, and real GDP is $5 trillion in base-year dollars. What is the income velocity of money? (See page 262.)

11-11. Consider the data in Problem 11-10. Suppose that the money supply increases by $100 billion and real GDP and the income velocity remain unchanged. (See pages 262–263.)

a. According to the quantity theory of money and prices, what is the new equilibrium price level after full adjustment to the increase in the money supply?

b. What is the percentage increase in the money supply?

c. What is the percentage change in the price level?

d. How do the percentage changes in the money supply and price level compare?

11-12. Assuming that the Fed judges inflation to be the most significant problem in the economy and that it wishes to employ all of its policy instruments except interest on reserves, what should the Fed do with its three policy tools? (See page 265.)

11-13. Suppose that the Fed implements each of the policy changes you discussed in Problem 11-12.

Now explain how the net export effect resulting from these monetary policy actions will reinforce their effects that operate through interest rate changes. (See page 261.)

11-14. Imagine working at the Trading Desk at the New York Fed. Explain whether you would conduct open market purchases or sales in response to each of the following events. Justify your recommendation. (See page 261.)

a. The latest FOMC Directive calls for an increase in the target value of the federal funds rate.

b. For a reason unrelated to monetary policy, the Fed's Board of Governors has decided to raise the differential between the discount rate and the federal funds rate. Nevertheless, the FOMC Directive calls for maintaining the present federal funds rate target.

11-15. To implement a credit policy intended to expand liquidity of the banking system, the Fed desires to increase its assets by lending to a substantial number of banks. How might the Fed adjust the interest rate that it pays banks on reserves in order to induce them to hold the reserves required for funding this credit policy action? What will happen to the Fed's liabilities if it implements this policy action? (See pages 267–270.)

11-16. Suppose that to finance its credit policy, the Fed pays an annual interest rate of 0.25 percent on bank reserves. During the course of the current year, banks hold $1 trillion in reserves. What is the total amount of interest the Fed pays banks during the year? (See pages 267–270.)

11-17. During an interval between mid-2010 and early 2011, the Federal Reserve embarked on a policy it termed "quantitative easing." Total reserves in the banking system increased. Hence, the Federal Reserve's liabilities to banks increased, and at the same time its assets rose as it purchased more assets—many of which were securities with private market values that had dropped considerably. The money multiplier declined, so the net increase in the money supply was negligible. Indeed, during a portion of the period, the money supply actually declined before rising near its previous value. Evaluate whether the Fed's "quantitative easing" was a monetary policy or credit policy action. (See pages 259 and 267–270.)

ECONOMICS ON THE NET

The Fed's Policy Report to Congress Congress requires the Fed to make periodic reports on its recent activities. In this application, you will study recent reports to learn about what factors affect Fed decisions.

Title: Monetary Policy Report to the Congress

Navigation: Go to www.econtoday.com/chap11 to view the Federal Reserve's Monetary Policy Report to the Congress (formerly called the Humphrey-Hawkins Report).

Application Read the report; then answer the following questions.

1. According to the report, what economic events were most important in shaping recent monetary policy?
2. Based on the report, what are the Fed's current monetary policy goals?

For Group Study and Analysis Divide the class into "domestic" and "foreign" groups. Have each group read the past four monetary policy reports and then explain to the class how domestic and foreign factors, respectively, appear to have influenced recent Fed monetary policy decisions. Which of the two types of factors seems to have mattered most during the past year?

ANSWERS TO QUICK QUIZZES

p. 256: (i) demand; (ii) transactions . . . precautionary . . . asset; (iii) opportunity . . . downward

p. 258: (i) lower . . . higher; (ii) inverse; (iii) decrease . . . increase . . . increase . . . decrease

p. 260: (i) direct; (ii) indirect . . . reduction . . . lower

p. 262: (i) exports; (ii) negative . . . more . . . more; (iii) fewer . . . decrease . . . increase

p. 264: (i) equation . . . exchange; (ii) true . . . spent . . . received; (iii) money supply . . . price level

p. 270: (i) federal funds . . . open market operations; (ii) Directive . . . New York; (iii) credit . . . loans; (iv) credit . . . failures . . . monitor . . . credit

Monetary Policy:
A Keynesian Perspective

According to the traditional Keynesian approach to monetary policy, changes in the money supply can affect the level of aggregate demand only through their effect on interest rates. Moreover, interest rate changes act on aggregate demand solely by changing the level of real planned investment spending. Finally, the traditional Keynesian approach argues that there are plausible circumstances under which monetary policy may have little or no effect on interest rates and thus on aggregate demand.

Figure D-1 below measures real GDP per year along the horizontal axis and total planned expenditures (aggregate demand) along the vertical axis. The components of aggregate demand are real consumption (C), investment (I), government spending (G), and net exports (X). The height of the schedule labeled $C + I + G + X$ shows total real planned expenditures (aggregate demand) as a function of real GDP per year. This schedule slopes upward because consumption depends positively on real GDP. All along the line labeled $Y = C + I + G + X$, real planned spending equals real GDP per year. At point Y^*, where the $C + I + G + X$ line intersects this 45-degree reference line, real planned spending is consistent with real GDP.

At any real GDP level less than Y^*, spending exceeds real GDP, so real GDP and thus spending will tend to rise. At any level of real GDP greater than Y^*, real planned spending is less than real GDP, so real GDP and thus spending will tend to decline. Given the determinants of $C, I, G,$ and X, total spending (aggregate demand) will be Y^*.

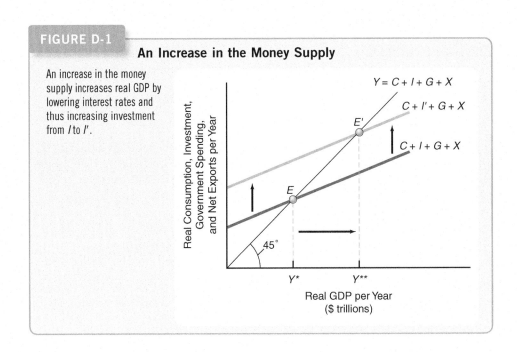

FIGURE D-1

An Increase in the Money Supply

An increase in the money supply increases real GDP by lowering interest rates and thus increasing investment from I to I'.

Increasing the Money Supply

According to the Keynesian approach, an increase in the money supply pushes interest rates down. This induces firms to increase the level of investment spending from I to I'. As a result, the $C + I + G + X$ line shifts upward in Figure D-1 on the facing page by the full amount of the rise in investment spending, thus yielding the line $C + I' + G + X$. The rise in investment spending causes real GDP to rise, which in turn causes real consumption spending to rise, further increasing real GDP. Ultimately, aggregate demand rises to Y^{**}, where spending again equals real GDP. A key conclusion of the Keynesian analysis is that total spending rises by *more* than the original rise in investment spending because consumption spending depends positively on real GDP.

Decreasing the Money Supply

Not surprisingly, contractionary monetary policy works in exactly the reverse manner. A reduction in the money supply pushes interest rates up. Firms respond by reducing their investment spending, and this pushes real GDP downward. Consumers react to the lower real GDP by scaling back on their real consumption spending, which further depresses real GDP. Thus, the ultimate decline in real GDP is larger than the initial drop in investment spending. Indeed, because the change in real GDP is a multiple of the change in investment, Keynesians note that changes in investment spending (similar to changes in government spending) have a *multiplier* effect on the economy.

Arguments Against Monetary Policy

It might be thought that this multiplier effect would make monetary policy a potent tool in the Keynesian arsenal, particularly when it comes to getting the economy out of a recession. In fact, however, many traditional Keynesians argue that monetary policy is likely to be relatively ineffective as a recession fighter.

According to their line of reasoning, although monetary policy has the potential to reduce interest rates, changes in the money supply have little *actual* impact on interest rates. Instead, during recessions, people try to build up as much as they can in liquid assets to protect themselves from risks of unemployment and other losses of income. When the monetary authorities increase the money supply, individuals are willing to allow most of it to accumulate in their bank accounts. This desire for increased liquidity thus prevents interest rates from falling very much, which in turn means that there will be almost no change in investment spending and thus little change in aggregate demand.

PROBLEMS

All problems are assignable in MyEconLab. *Answers to odd-numbered problems appear at the back of the book.*

D-1. Suppose that each 0.1-percentage-point decrease in the equilibrium interest rate induces a $10 billion increase in real planned investment spending by businesses. In addition, the investment multiplier is equal to 5, and the money multiplier is equal to 4. Furthermore, every $20 billion increase in the money supply brings about a 0.1-percentage-point reduction in the equilibrium interest rate. Use this information to answer the following

questions under the assumption that all other things are equal. (See page 278–279.)

a. How much must real planned investment increase if the Federal Reserve desires to bring about a $100 billion increase in equilibrium real GDP?

b. How much must the money supply change for the Fed to induce the change in real planned investment calculated in part (a)?

c. What dollar amount of open market operations must the Fed undertake to bring about the money supply change calculated in part (b)?

D-2. Suppose that each 0.1-percentage-point increase in the equilibrium interest rate induces a $5 billion decrease in real planned investment spending by businesses. In addition, the investment multiplier is equal to 4, and the money multiplier is equal to 3. Furthermore, every $9 billion decrease in the money supply brings about a 0.1-percentage-point increase in the equilibrium interest rate. Use this information to answer the following questions under the assumption that all other things are equal. (See pages 278–279.)

  a. How much must real planned investment decrease if the Federal Reserve desires to bring about an $80 billion decrease in equilibrium real GDP?

  b. How much must the money supply change for the Fed to induce the change in real planned investment calculated in part (a)?

  c. What dollar amount of open market operations must the Fed undertake to bring about the money supply change calculated in part (b)?

D-3. Assume that the following conditions exist (see pages 278–279):

  a. All banks are fully loaned up—there are no excess reserves, and desired excess reserves are always zero.

  b. The money multiplier is 3.

  c. The planned investment schedule is such that at a 6 percent rate of interest, investment is $1,200 billion; at 5 percent, investment is $1,225 billion.

  d. The investment multiplier is 3.

  e. The initial equilibrium level of real GDP is $12 trillion.

  f. The equilibrium rate of interest is 6 percent.

Now the Fed engages in expansionary monetary policy. It buys $1 billion worth of bonds, which increases the money supply, which in turn lowers the market rate of interest by 1 percentage point. Determine how much the money supply must have increased, and then trace out the numerical consequences of the associated reduction in interest rates on all the other variables mentioned.

D-4. Assume that the following conditions exist (see pages 278–279):

  a. All banks are fully loaned up—there are no excess reserves, and desired excess reserves are always zero.

  b. The money multiplier is 4.

  c. The planned investment schedule is such that at a 4 percent rate of interest, investment is $1,400 billion. At 5 percent, investment is $1,380 billion.

  d. The investment multiplier is 5.

  e. The initial equilibrium level of real GDP is $13 trillion.

  f. The equilibrium rate of interest is 4 percent.

Now the Fed engages in contractionary monetary policy. It sells $2 billion worth of bonds, which reduces the money supply, which in turn raises the market rate of interest by 1 percentage point. Determine how much the money supply must have decreased, and then trace out the numerical consequences of the associated increase in interest rates on all the other variables mentioned.

Module 5

International Economics

Exchange Rates and the Balance of Payments

12

Every few months, a U.S. media story reports on the substantial gap between U.S. imports of physical goods from China and U.S. exports of goods to China. Typically, media commentators follow up with complaints that U.S. residents are thoughtlessly paying prices for Chinese imports that effectively transfer a portion of U.S. residents' incomes to people in China. Does every dollar that you pay for a Chinese-manufactured item translate into an income transfer from the United States to China? Before you can answer this question, you must learn how economists use an accounting system called the *balance of payments* to track flows of spending on goods and services exported from and imported into the United States.

the annual dollar value of trading in *foreign exchange markets*—markets in which people buy and sell national currencies, such as the U.S. dollar, European euro, Japanese yen, or Chinese yuan—exceeds $4 trillion? Thus, the total value of exchanges of the world's currencies during a given year amounts to more than one-fourth of the value of exchanges for all goods and services produced per year in the United States. By the time you have completed this chapter, you will understand why people desire to obtain so many currencies of other nations in foreign exchange markets scattered around the globe. First, however, you must learn how we keep track of flows of payments across a country's borders.

The Balance of Payments and International Capital Movements

Balance of trade
The difference between exports and imports of physical goods.

Balance of payments
A system of accounts that measures transactions of goods, services, income, and financial assets between domestic households, businesses, and governments and residents of the rest of the world during a specific time period.

Governments typically keep track of each year's economic activities by calculating the gross domestic product—the total of expenditures on all newly domestic-produced final goods and services—and its components. A summary information system has also been developed for international trade. It covers the balance of trade and the balance of payments. The **balance of trade** refers specifically to exports and imports of physical goods, or merchandise. When international trade is in balance, the value of exports equals the value of imports. When the value of imports exceeds the value of exports, we are running a deficit in the balance of trade. When the value of exports exceeds the value of imports, we are running a surplus.

The **balance of payments** is a more general concept that expresses the total of all economic transactions between a nation and the rest of the world, usually for a period of one year. Each country's balance of payments summarizes information about that country's exports and imports of services as well as physical goods, earnings by domestic residents on assets located abroad, earnings on domestic assets owned by residents of foreign nations, international capital movements, and official transactions by central banks and governments. In essence, then, the balance of payments is a record of all the transactions between households, firms, and the government of one country and the rest of the world. Any transaction that leads to a *payment* by a country's residents (or government) is a deficit item, identified by a negative sign (−) when the actual numbers are given for the items listed in the second column of Table 12-1 on the facing page. Any transaction that leads to a *receipt* by a country's residents (or government) is a surplus item and is identified by a plus sign (+) when actual numbers are considered. Table 12-1 provides a list of the surplus and deficit items on international accounts.

Accounting Identities

Accounting identities
Values that are equivalent by definition.

Accounting identities—definitions of equivalent values—exist for financial institutions and other businesses. We begin with simple accounting identities that must hold for families and then go on to describe international accounting identities.

If a family unit is spending more than its current income, the family unit must necessarily be doing one of the following:

1. Reducing its money holdings or selling stocks, bonds, or other assets

2. Borrowing

3. Receiving gifts from friends or relatives

4. Receiving public transfers from a government, which obtained the funds by taxing others (a transfer is a payment, in money or in goods or services, made without receiving goods or services in return)

We can use this information to derive an identity: If a family unit is currently spending more than it is earning, it must draw on previously acquired wealth, borrow, or receive either private or public aid. Similarly, an identity exists for a family unit that is

TABLE 12-1

Surplus (+) and Deficit (−) Items on the International Accounts	Surplus Items (+)	Deficit Items (−)
	Exports of merchandise	Imports of merchandise
	Private and governmental gifts from foreign residents	Private and governmental gifts to foreign residents
	Foreign use of domestically operated travel and transportation services	Use of foreign-operated travel and transportation services
	Foreign tourists' expenditures in this country	U.S. tourists' expenditures abroad
	Foreign military spending in this country	Military spending abroad
	Interest and dividend receipts from foreign entities	Interest and dividends paid to foreign individuals and businesses
	Sales of domestic assets to foreign residents	Purchases of foreign assets
	Funds deposited in this country by foreign residents	Funds placed in foreign depository institutions
	Sales of gold to foreign residents	Purchases of gold from foreign residents
	Sales of domestic currency to foreign residents	Purchases of foreign currency

currently spending less than it is earning: It must be increasing its money holdings or be lending and acquiring other financial assets, or it must pay taxes or bestow gifts on others. When we consider businesses and governments, each unit in each group faces its own accounting identities or constraints. Ultimately, *net* lending by households must equal *net* borrowing by businesses and governments.

DISEQUILIBRIUM Even though our individual family unit's accounts must balance, in the sense that the identity discussed previously must hold, sometimes the item that brings about the balance cannot continue indefinitely. *If family expenditures exceed family income and this situation is financed by borrowing, the household may be considered to be in disequilibrium because such a situation cannot continue indefinitely.* If such a deficit is financed by drawing on previously accumulated assets, the family may also be in disequilibrium because it cannot continue indefinitely to draw on its wealth.

Eventually, the family will find it impossible to continue that lifestyle. (Of course, if the family members are retired, they may well be in equilibrium by drawing on previously acquired assets to finance current deficits. This example illustrates that it is necessary to understand all circumstances fully before pronouncing an economic unit in disequilibrium.)

EQUILIBRIUM Individual households, businesses, and governments, as well as the entire group of all households, businesses, and governments, must eventually reach equilibrium. Certain economic adjustment mechanisms have evolved to ensure equilibrium. Deficit households must eventually increase their income or decrease their expenditures. They will find that they have to pay higher interest rates if they wish to borrow to finance their deficits. Eventually, their credit sources will dry up, and they will be forced into equilibrium. Businesses, on occasion, must lower costs or prices—or go bankrupt—to reach equilibrium.

AN ACCOUNTING IDENTITY AMONG NATIONS When people from different nations trade or interact, certain identities or constraints must also hold. People buy goods from people in other nations. They also lend to and present gifts to people in other nations. If residents of a nation interact with residents of other nations, an accounting identity ensures a balance (but not necessarily an equilibrium, as will soon become clear). Let's look at the three categories of balance of payments transactions: current account transactions, capital account transactions, and official reserve account transactions.

Current Account Transactions

Current account
A category of balance of payments transactions that measures the exchange of merchandise, the exchange of services, and unilateral transfers.

During any designated period, all payments and gifts that are related to the purchase or sale of both goods and services constitute the **current account** in international trade. Major types of current account transactions include the exchange of merchandise, the exchange of services, and unilateral transfers.

MERCHANDISE TRADE EXPORTS AND IMPORTS The largest portion of any nation's balance of payments current account is typically the importing and exporting of merchandise. During 2013, for example, as shown in lines 1 and 2 of Table 12-2 below, the United States exported an estimated $1,609.7 billion of merchandise and imported $2,404.5 billion. The balance of merchandise trade is defined as the difference between the value of merchandise exports and the value of merchandise imports. For 2013, the United States had a balance of merchandise trade deficit because the value of its merchandise imports exceeded the value of its merchandise exports. This deficit was about $794.8 billion (line 3).

SERVICE EXPORTS AND IMPORTS The balance of (merchandise) trade involves tangible items—things you can feel, touch, and see. Service exports and imports involve invisible or intangible items that are bought and sold, such as shipping, insurance, tourist expenditures, and banking services. Also, income earned by foreign residents on U.S. investments and income earned by U.S. residents on foreign investments are part of service imports and exports. As shown in lines 4 and 5 of Table 12-2, in 2013, estimated service exports were $564.6 billion, and service imports were $416.8 billion. Thus, the balance of services was about $147.8 billion in 2013 (line 6). Exports constitute receipts or inflows into the United States and are positive. Imports constitute payments abroad or outflows of money and are negative.

When we combine the balance of merchandise trade with the balance of services, we obtain a balance on goods and services equal to −$647.0 billion in 2013 (line 7).

TABLE 12-2

U.S. Balance of Payments Account, Estimated for 2013 (in billions of dollars)

Current Account

(1) Exports of merchandise goods	+1,609.7	
(2) Imports of merchandise goods	−2,404.5	
(3) Balance of merchandise trade		−794.8
(4) Exports of services	+564.6	
(5) Imports of services	−416.8	
(6) Balance of services		+147.8
(7) Balance on goods and services [(3) + (6)]		−647.0
(8) Net unilateral transfers	−159.3	
(9) Balance on current account		−806.3

Capital Account

(10) U.S. private capital going abroad	−299.2	
(11) Foreign private capital coming into the United States	+665.3*	
(12) Balance on capital account [(10) + (11)]		+366.1
(13) Balance on current account plus balance on capital account [(9) + (12)]		−440.2

Official Reserve Transactions Account

(14) Official transactions balance		+440.2
(15) Total (balance)		0

Sources: U.S. Department of Commerce, Bureau of Economic Analysis; author's estimates.

*Includes an approximately $28 billion statistical discrepancy, probably uncounted capital inflows, many of which relate to the illegal drug trade.

UNILATERAL TRANSFERS U.S. residents give gifts to relatives and others abroad, the federal government makes grants to foreign nations, foreign residents give gifts to U.S. residents, and in the past some foreign governments have granted funds to the U.S. government. In the current account, we see that net unilateral transfers—the total amount of gifts given by U.S. residents and the government minus the total amount received from abroad by U.S. residents and the government—came to an estimated −$159.3 billion in 2013 (line 8). The minus sign before the number for unilateral transfers means that U.S. residents and the U.S. government gave more to foreign residents than foreign residents gave to U.S. residents.

BALANCING THE CURRENT ACCOUNT The balance on current account tracks the value of a country's exports of goods and services (including income on investments abroad) and transfer payments (private and government) relative to the value of that country's imports of goods and services and transfer payments (private and government). In 2013, it was estimated to be −$806.3 billion (line 9).

Go to www.econtoday.com/chap12 for the latest U.S. balance of payments data from the Bureau of Economic Analysis.

If the sum of net exports of goods and services plus net unilateral transfers plus net investment income exceeds zero, a **current account surplus** *is said to exist. If this sum is negative, a* **current account deficit** *is said to exist. A current account deficit means that we are importing more goods and services than we are exporting. Such a deficit must be paid for by the export of financial assets.*

WHAT IF... all governments attempted to require their nations to have current account surpluses?

By definition, a current account surplus arises in a nation when its residents export more goods and services than they import. The only way for some nations to have current account surpluses, though, is for others to operate with current account deficits. That is, residents of some countries must import more goods and services than they export in order for other nations to be able to export more goods and services than they import. Thus, if all governments were to require that their countries have current account surpluses, their efforts would be doomed to failure.

Capital Account Transactions

In world markets, it is possible to buy and sell not only goods and services but also financial assets. These international transactions are measured in the **capital account**. Capital account transactions occur because of foreign investments—either by foreign residents investing in the United States or by U.S. residents investing in other countries. The purchase of shares of stock in British firms on the London stock market by a U.S. resident causes an outflow of funds from the United States to Britain. The construction of a Japanese automobile factory in the United States causes an inflow of funds from Japan to the United States. Any time foreign residents buy U.S. government securities, there is an inflow of funds from other countries to the United States. Any time U.S. residents buy foreign government securities, there is an outflow of funds from the United States to other countries. Loans to and from foreign residents cause outflows and inflows.

Capital account
A category of balance of payments transactions that measures flows of financial assets.

Line 10 of Table 12-2 on the facing page indicates that in 2013, the value of private capital going out of the United States was an estimated −$299.2 billion, and line 11 shows that the value of private capital coming into the United States (including a statistical discrepancy) was $665.3 billion. U.S. capital going abroad constitutes payments or outflows and is therefore negative. Foreign capital coming into the United States constitutes receipts or inflows and is therefore positive. Thus, there was a positive net capital movement of $366.1 billion into the United States (line 12). This net private flow of capital is also called the balance on capital account.

There is a relationship between the current account balance and the capital account balance, assuming no interventions by the finance ministries or central banks of nations.

In the absence of interventions by finance ministries or central banks, the current account balance and the capital account balance must sum to zero. Stated differently, the current account deficit must equal the capital account surplus when governments or central banks do not engage in foreign exchange interventions. In this situation, any nation experiencing a current account deficit, such as the United States, must also be running a capital account surplus.

This basic relationship is apparent in the United States, as you can see in Figure 12-1 below. As the figure shows, U.S. current account deficits experienced since the early 1980s have been balanced by private capital inflows and *official reserve transactions*, to which we now turn our attention.

Official Reserve Account Transactions

The third type of balance of payments transaction concerns official reserve assets, which consist of the following:

1. Foreign currencies

2. Gold

Special drawing rights (SDRs)
Reserve assets created by the International Monetary Fund for countries to use in settling international payment obligations.

3. **Special drawing rights (SDRs)**, which are reserve assets that the **International Monetary Fund** created to be used by countries to settle international payment obligations

International Monetary Fund
An agency founded to administer an international foreign exchange system and to lend to member countries that had balance of payments problems. The IMF now functions as a lender of last resort for national governments.

4. The reserve position in the International Monetary Fund

5. Financial assets held by an official agency, such as the U.S. Treasury Department

To consider how official reserve account transactions occur, look again at Table 12-2 on page 286. The surplus in the U.S. capital account was $366.1 billion. But the deficit in the U.S. current account was −$806.3 billion, so the United States had a net deficit

---

FIGURE 12-1

MyEconLab Real-time data

The Relationship between the Current Account and the Capital Account

The current account balance is the mirror image of the sum of the capital account balance and the official transactions balance. We can see this in years since 1970. When the current account balance was in surplus, the sum of the capital account balance and the official transactions balance was negative. When the current account balance was in deficit, the sum of the current account balance and the official transactions balance was positive.

Sources: International Monetary Fund; *Economic Indicators.*

on the combined accounts (line 13) of −$440.2 billion. In other words, the United States obtained less in foreign funds in all its international transactions than it used. How is this deficiency made up? By foreign central banks and governments adding to their U.S. funds, shown by the +$440.2 billion in official transactions on line 14 in Table 12-2 on page 286. There is a plus sign on line 14 because this represents an *inflow* of foreign exchange in our international transactions.

The U.S. balance of payments deficit is measured by the official transactions figure on line 14. The balance (line 15) in Table 12-2 is zero, as it must be with double-entry bookkeeping. Hence, as shown in Figure 12-1 on the facing page, the current account balance is a mirror image of the sum of the capital account balance and the official reserve transactions account.

What Affects the Distribution of Account Balances within the Balance of Payments?

A major factor affecting the distribution of account balances within any nation's balance of payments is its rate of inflation relative to that of its trading partners. Assume that the rates of inflation in the United States and in the European Monetary Union (EMU)—the nations that use the euro as their currency—are equal. Now suppose that all of a sudden, the U.S. inflation rate increases. EMU residents will find that U.S. products are becoming more expensive, and U.S. firms will export fewer of them to EMU nations. At the current dollar-euro exchange rate, U.S. residents will find EMU products relatively cheaper, and they will import more. Other things being equal, the reverse will occur if the U.S. inflation rate suddenly falls relative to that of the EMU. All other things held constant, whenever the U.S. rate of inflation exceeds that of its trading partners, we expect to see a larger deficit in the U.S. balance of merchandise trade and in the U.S. current account balance. Conversely, when the U.S. rate of inflation is less than that of its trading partners, other things being constant, we expect to see a smaller deficit in the U.S. balance of merchandise trade and in the U.S. current account balance.

Another important factor that sometimes influences account balances within a nation's balance of payments is its relative political stability. Political instability causes *capital flight*. Owners of capital in countries anticipating or experiencing political instability will often move assets to countries that are politically stable, such as the United States. Hence, the U.S. capital account balance is likely to increase whenever political instability looms in other nations in the world.

QUICK QUIZ See page 304 for the answers. Review concepts from this section in MyEconLab.

The _____ of _____ reflects the value of all transactions in international trade, including goods, services, financial assets, and gifts.

The merchandise trade balance gives us the difference between exports and imports of _____ items.

Included in the _____ account along with merchandise trade are service exports and imports relating to commerce in intangible items, such as shipping, insurance, and tourist expenditures. The _____ account also includes income earned by foreign residents on U.S. investments and income earned by U.S. residents on foreign investments.

_____ _____ involve international private gifts and federal government grants or gifts to foreign nations.

When we add the balance of merchandise trade and the balance of services and take account of net unilateral

transfers and net investment income, we come up with the balance on the _____ account, a summary statistic.

There are also _____ account transactions that relate to the buying and selling of financial assets. Foreign capital is always entering the United States, and U.S. capital is always flowing abroad. The difference is called the balance on the _____ account.

Another type of balance of payments transaction concerns the _____ _____ assets of individual countries, or what is often simply called official transactions. By standard accounting convention, official transactions are exactly equal to but opposite in sign from the sum of the current account balance and the capital account balance.

Account balances within a nation's balance of payments can be affected by its relative rate of _____ and by its _____ stability relative to other nations.

Determining Foreign Exchange Rates

Foreign exchange market
A market in which households, firms, and governments buy and sell national currencies.

Exchange rate
The price of one nation's currency in terms of the currency of another country.

When you buy foreign products, such as European pharmaceuticals, you have dollars with which to pay the European manufacturer. The European manufacturer, however, cannot pay workers in dollars. The workers are European, they live in Europe, and they must have euros to buy goods and services in nations that are members of the European Monetary Union (EMU) and use the euro as their currency. There must therefore be a way to exchange dollars for euros that the pharmaceuticals manufacturer will accept. That exchange occurs in a **foreign exchange market,** which in this case involves the exchange of euros and dollars.

The particular **exchange rate** between euros and dollars that prevails—the dollar price of the euro—depends on the current demand for and supply of euros and dollars. In a sense, then, our analysis of the exchange rate between dollars and euros will be familiar, for we have used supply and demand throughout this book. If it costs you $1.20 to buy 1 euro, that is the foreign exchange rate determined by the current demand for and supply of euros in the foreign exchange market. The European person going to the foreign exchange market would need about 0.83 euro to buy 1 dollar.

Now let's consider what determines the demand for and supply of foreign currency in the foreign exchange market. We will continue to assume that the only two regions in the world are Europe and the United States.

Demand for and Supply of Foreign Currency

You wish to purchase European-produced pharmaceuticals directly from a manufacturer located in Europe. To do so, you must have euros. You go to the foreign exchange market (or your U.S. bank). Your desire to buy the pharmaceuticals causes you to offer (supply) dollars to the foreign exchange market. Your demand for euros is equivalent to your supply of dollars to the foreign exchange market.

> *Every U.S. transaction involving the importation of foreign goods constitutes a supply of dollars and a demand for some foreign currency, and the opposite is true for export transactions.*

In this case, the import transaction constitutes a demand for euros.

In our example, we will assume that only two goods are being traded, European pharmaceuticals and U.S. tablet devices. The U.S. demand for European pharmaceuticals creates a supply of dollars and a demand for euros in the foreign exchange market. Similarly, the European demand for U.S. tablet devices creates a supply of euros and a demand for dollars in the foreign exchange market. Under a system of **flexible exchange rates,** the supply of and demand for dollars and euros in the foreign exchange market will determine the equilibrium foreign exchange rate. The equilibrium exchange rate will tell us how many euros a dollar can be exchanged for—that is, the euro price of dollars—or how many dollars a euro can be exchanged for—the dollar price of euros.

Flexible exchange rates
Exchange rates that are allowed to fluctuate in the open market in response to changes in supply and demand. Sometimes called *floating exchange rates*.

Go to www.econtoday.com/chap12 for recent data from the Federal Reserve Bank of St. Louis on the exchange value of the U.S. dollar relative to the major currencies of the world.

The Equilibrium Foreign Exchange Rate

To determine the equilibrium foreign exchange rate, we have to find out what determines the demand for and supply of foreign exchange. We will ignore for the moment any speculative aspect of buying foreign exchange. That is, we assume that there are no individuals who wish to buy euros simply because they think that their price will go up in the future.

The idea of an exchange rate is no different from the idea of paying a certain price for something you want to buy. Suppose that you have to pay about $1.50 for a cup of coffee. If the price goes up to $2.50, you will probably buy fewer cups. If the price goes down to 50 cents, you will likely buy more. In other words, the demand curve for cups of coffee, expressed in terms of dollars, slopes downward following the law of demand. The demand curve for euros slopes downward also, and we will see why.

Let's think more closely about the demand schedule for euros. If it costs you $1.10 to purchase 1 euro, that is the exchange rate between dollars and euros. If tomorrow you have to pay $1.25 for the same euro, the exchange rate would have changed. Looking at such a change, we would say that there has been an **appreciation** in the value of the euro in the foreign exchange market. But another way to view this increase in the value of the euro is to say that there has been a **depreciation** in the value of the dollar in the foreign exchange market. The dollar used to buy almost 0.91 euro, but tomorrow the dollar will be able to buy only 0.80 euro at a price of $1.25 per euro.

If the dollar price of euros rises, you will probably demand fewer euros. Why? The answer lies in the reason you and others demand euros in the first place.

APPRECIATION AND DEPRECIATION OF EUROS Recall that in our example, you and others demand euros to buy European pharmaceuticals. The demand curve for European pharmaceuticals follows the law of demand and therefore slopes downward. If it costs more U.S. dollars to buy the same quantity of European pharmaceuticals, presumably you and other U.S. residents will not buy the same quantity. Your quantity demanded will be less. We say that your demand for euros is *derived from* your demand for European pharmaceuticals. In panel (a) of Figure 12-2 on the following page, we present the hypothetical demand schedule for packages of European pharmaceuticals by a representative set of U.S. consumers during a typical week. In panel (b) of Figure 12-2, we show graphically the U.S. demand curve for European pharmaceuticals in terms of U.S. dollars taken from panel (a).

AN EXAMPLE OF DERIVED DEMAND Let us assume that the price of a package of European pharmaceuticals in Europe is 100 euros. Given that price, we can find the number of euros required to purchase 500 packages of European pharmaceuticals. That information is given in panel (c) of Figure 12-2. If purchasing one package of European pharmaceuticals requires 100 euros, 500 packages require 50,000 euros. Now we have enough information to determine the derived demand curve for euros. If 1 euro costs $1.20, a package of pharmaceuticals would cost $120 (100 euros per package × $1.20 per euro = $120 per package). At $120 per package, the representative group of U.S. consumers would, we see from panel (a) of Figure 12-2, demand 500 packages of pharmaceuticals.

From panel (c), we see that 50,000 euros would be demanded to buy the 500 packages of pharmaceuticals. We show this quantity demanded in panel (d). In panel (e), we draw the derived demand curve for euros. Now consider what happens if the price of euros goes up to $1.25. A package of European pharmaceuticals priced at 100 euros in Europe would now cost $125. From panel (a), we see that at $125 per package, 300 packages of pharmaceuticals will be imported from Europe into the United States by our representative group of U.S. consumers. From panel (c), we see that 300 packages of pharmaceuticals would require 30,000 euros to be purchased. Thus, in panels (d) and (e), we see that at a price of $1.25 per euro, the quantity demanded will be 30,000 euros.

We continue similar calculations all the way up to a price of $1.30 per euro. At that price, a package of European pharmaceuticals with a price of 100 euros in Europe would have a U.S. dollar price of $130, and our representative U.S. consumers would import only 100 packages of pharmaceuticals.

DOWNWARD-SLOPING DERIVED DEMAND As can be expected, as the price of the euro rises, the quantity demanded will fall. The only difference here from the standard demand analysis developed and used throughout this text is that the demand for euros is derived from the demand for a final product—European pharmaceuticals in our example.

SUPPLY OF EUROS Assume that European pharmaceutical manufacturers buy U.S. tablet devices. The supply of euros is a derived supply in that it is derived from the European demand for U.S. tablet devices. We could go through an example similar to the one for pharmaceuticals to come up with a supply schedule of euros in Europe. It slopes upward.

Appreciation
An increase in the exchange value of one nation's currency in terms of the currency of another nation.

Depreciation
A decrease in the exchange value of one nation's currency in terms of the currency of another nation.

YOU ARE THERE

To consider how an appreciation of Brazil's currency has affected Brazilian spending on U.S. goods and services, take a look at **An Exchange-Rate-Induced U.S. Shopping** *Bagunça* **for Brazilians** on page 300.

Panel (a)
Demand Schedule for Packages of European Pharmaceuticals in the United States per Week

Price per Package	Quantity Demanded
$130	100
125	300
120	500
115	700

Panel (b)
U.S. Demand Curve for European Pharmaceuticals

Panel (c)
Euros Required to Purchase Quantity Demanded (at *P* = 100 euros per package of pharmaceuticals)

Quantity Demanded	Euros Required
100	10,000
300	30,000
500	50,000
700	70,000

Panel (d)
Derived Demand Schedule for Euros in the United States with Which to Pay for Imports of Pharmaceuticals

Dollar Price of One Euro	Dollar Price of Pharmaceuticals	Quantity of Pharmaceuticals Demanded	Quantity of Euros Demanded per Week
$1.30	$130	100	10,000
1.25	125	300	30,000
1.20	120	500	50,000
1.15	115	700	70,000

FIGURE 12-2

Deriving the Demand for Euros

In panel (a), we show the demand schedule for European pharmaceuticals in the United States, expressed in terms of dollars per package of pharmaceuticals. In panel (b), we show the demand curve, *D*, which slopes downward. In panel (c), we show the number of euros required to purchase up to 700 packages of pharmaceuticals. If the price per package of pharmaceuticals is 100 euros, we can now find the quantity of euros needed to pay for the various quantities demanded. In panel (d), we see the derived demand for euros in the United States in order to purchase the various quantities of pharmaceuticals given in panel (a). The resultant demand curve, D_1, is shown in panel (e). This is the U.S. derived demand for euros.

Panel (e)
U.S. Derived Demand for Euros

Obviously, Europeans want dollars to purchase U.S. goods. European residents will be willing to supply more euros when the dollar price of euros goes up, because they can then buy more U.S. goods with the same quantity of euros. That is, the euro would be worth more in exchange for U.S. goods than when the dollar price for euros was lower.

FIGURE 12-3

The Supply of Euros

If the market price of a U.S.-produced tablet device is $200, then at an exchange rate of $1.20 per euro, the price of the tablet to a European consumer is 167.67 euros. If the exchange rate rises to $1.25 per euro, the European price of the tablet falls to 160 euros. This induces an increase in the quantity of tablets demanded by European consumers and consequently an increase in the quantity of euros supplied in exchange for dollars in the foreign exchange market. In contrast, if the exchange rate falls to $1.15 per euro, the European price of the tablet rises to 173.91 euros. This causes a decrease in the quantity of tablets demanded by European consumers. As a result, there is a decline in the quantity of euros supplied in exchange for dollars in the foreign exchange market. Hence, the euro supply curve slopes up.

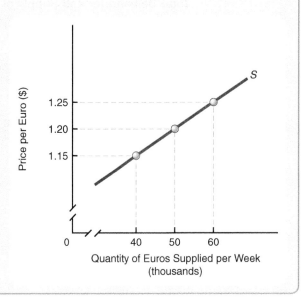

AN EXAMPLE Let's take an example. Suppose a U.S.-produced tablet device costs $200. If the exchange rate is $1.20 per euro, a European resident will have to come up with 166.67 euros ($200 ÷ $1.20 per euro = 166.67 euros) to buy one tablet. If, however, the exchange rate goes up to $1.25 per euro, a European resident must come up with only 160 euros ($200 ÷ $1.25 per euro = 160 euros) to buy a U.S. tablet. At this lower price (in euros) of U.S. tablets, Europeans will demand a larger quantity.

In other words, as the price of euros goes up in terms of dollars, the quantity of U.S. tablets demanded will go up, and hence the quantity of euros supplied will go up. Therefore, the supply schedule of euros, which is derived from the European demand for U.S. goods, will slope upward, as seen in Figure 12-3 above.

TOTAL DEMAND FOR AND SUPPLY OF EUROS Let us now look at the total demand for and supply of euros. We take all U.S. consumers of European pharmaceuticals and all European consumers of U.S. tablet devices and put their demands for and supplies of euros together into one diagram. Thus, we are showing the total demand for and total supply of euros. The horizontal axis in Figure 12-4 on the following page represents the quantity of foreign exchange—the number of euros per year. The vertical axis represents the exchange rate—the price of foreign currency (euros) expressed in dollars (per euro). The foreign currency price of $1.25 per euro means it will cost you $1.25 to buy 1 euro. At the foreign currency price of $1.20 per euro, you know that it will cost you $1.20 to buy 1 euro. The equilibrium, *E*, is again established at $1.20 for 1 euro.

In our hypothetical example, assuming that there are only representative groups of pharmaceutical consumers in the United States and tablet consumers in Europe, the equilibrium exchange rate will be set at $1.20 per euro.

This equilibrium is not established because U.S. residents like to buy euros or because Europeans like to buy dollars. Rather, the equilibrium exchange rate depends on how many tablet devices Europeans want and how many European pharmaceuticals U.S. residents want (given their respective incomes, their tastes, and, in our example, the relative prices of pharmaceuticals and tablet devices).

A SHIFT IN DEMAND Assume that a successful advertising campaign by U.S. pharmaceutical importers causes U.S. demand for European pharmaceuticals to rise. U.S. residents demand more pharmaceuticals at all prices. Their demand curve for European pharmaceuticals shifts outward to the right.

Total Demand for and Supply of Euros

The market supply curve for euros results from the total European demand for U.S. tablet devices. The demand curve, *D*, slopes downward like most demand curves, and the supply curve, *S*, slopes upward. The foreign exchange price, or the U.S. dollar price of euros, is given on the vertical axis. The number of euros is represented on the horizontal axis. If the foreign exchange rate is $1.25—that is, if it takes $1.25 to buy 1 euro—U.S. residents will demand 20 billion euros.

The equilibrium exchange rate is at the intersection of *D* and *S*, or point *E*. The equilibrium exchange rate is $1.20 per euro. At this point, 30 billion euros are both demanded and supplied each year.

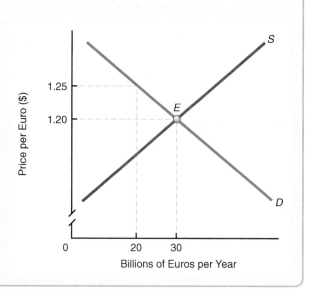

The increased demand for European pharmaceuticals can be translated into an increased demand for euros. All U.S. residents clamoring for European pharmaceuticals will supply more dollars to the foreign exchange market while demanding more euros to pay for the pharmaceuticals. Figure 12-5 below presents a new demand schedule, D_2, for euros. This demand schedule is to the right of the original demand schedule. If Europeans do not change their desire for U.S. tablet devices, the supply schedule for euros will remain stable.

A new equilibrium will be established at a higher exchange rate. In our particular example, the new equilibrium is established at an exchange rate of $1.25 per euro. It now takes $1.25 to buy 1 euro, whereas formerly it took $1.20. This will be translated into an increase in the price of European pharmaceuticals to U.S. residents and into a decrease in the price of U.S. tablet devices to Europeans. For example, a package of European pharmaceuticals priced at 100 euros that sold for $120 in the United States will now be priced at $125. Conversely, a U.S. tablet priced at $200 that previously sold for 166.67 euros will now sell for 160 euros.

A Shift in the Demand Schedule

The demand schedule for European pharmaceuticals shifts to the right, causing the derived demand schedule for euros to shift to the right also. We have shown this as a shift from D_1 to D_2. We have assumed that the supply schedule for euros has remained stable—that is, European demand for U.S. tablet devices has remained constant. The old equilibrium foreign exchange rate was $1.20 per euro.

The new equilibrium exchange rate will be E_2. It will now cost $1.25 to buy 1 euro. The higher price of euros will be translated into a higher U.S. dollar price for European pharmaceuticals and a lower euro price for U.S. tablet devices.

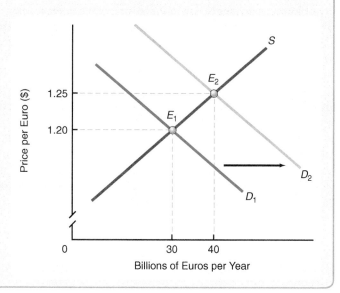

FIGURE 12-6

A Shift in the Supply of Euros

There has been a shift in the supply curve for euros. The new equilibrium will occur at E_1, meaning that $1.15, rather than $1.20, will now buy 1 euro. After the exchange rate adjustment, the annual amount of euros demanded and supplied will increase from 30 billion to 60 billion.

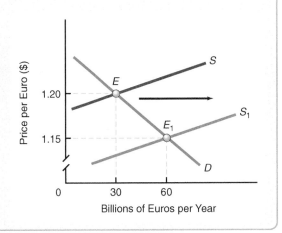

A SHIFT IN SUPPLY We just assumed that the U.S. demand for European pharmaceuticals shifted due to a successful ad campaign. The demand for euros is derived from the demand by U.S. residents for pharmaceuticals. This change in pharmaceuticals demand is translated into a shift in the demand curve for euros. As an alternative exercise, we might assume that the supply curve of euros shifts outward to the right. Such a supply shift could occur for many reasons, one of which is a relative rise in the European price level. For example, if the prices of all European-manufactured tablets went up 20 percent in euros, U.S. tablets would become relatively cheaper. That would mean that European residents would want to buy more U.S. tablets. But remember that when they want to buy more U.S. tablets, they supply more euros to the foreign exchange market.

Thus, we see in Figure 12-6 above that the supply curve of euros moves from S to S_1. In the absence of restrictions—that is, in a system of flexible exchange rates—the new equilibrium exchange rate will be $1.15 equals 1 euro. The quantity of euros demanded and supplied will increase from 30 billion per year to 60 billion per year. We say, then, that in a flexible international exchange rate system, shifts in the demand for and supply of foreign currencies will cause changes in the equilibrium foreign exchange rates. Those rates will remain in effect until world supply or demand shifts.

Which national currencies are most actively traded in global foreign exchange markets?

INTERNATIONAL EXAMPLE

The Most Traded Currencies in Foreign Exchange Markets

On a given day, the U.S. dollar is involved in more than 80 percent of trades of one currency for another in the world's foreign exchange markets. Thus, the dollar is utilized more than twice as often in exchange for other currencies as the second most commonly traded currency, the European euro. The dollar is involved in currency exchanges more than four times as often as either the Japanese yen or the British pound, the third and fourth most commonly exchanged currencies.

FOR CRITICAL THINKING

In light of the fact that the dollar valuation of all currency trades during a given year is $4 trillion, about how many U.S. dollars circulate within foreign exchange markets within a given year?

Market Determinants of Exchange Rates

The foreign exchange market is affected by many other variables in addition to changes in relative price levels, including the following:

- *Changes in real interest rates.* Suppose that the U.S. interest rate, corrected for people's expectations of inflation, increases relative to the rest of the world. Then international investors elsewhere seeking the higher returns now available in the United States will increase their demand for dollar-denominated assets, thereby increasing the demand for dollars in foreign exchange markets. An increased demand for dollars in foreign exchange markets, other things held constant, will cause the dollar to appreciate and other currencies to depreciate.

- *Changes in consumer preferences.* If Germany's citizens, for example, suddenly develop a taste for U.S.-made automobiles, this will increase the derived demand for U.S. dollars in foreign exchange markets.

- *Perceptions of economic stability.* As already mentioned, if the United States looks economically and politically more stable relative to other countries, more foreign residents will want to put their savings into U.S. assets rather than in their own domestic assets. This will increase the demand for dollars.

QUICK QUIZ   See page 304 for the answers. Review concepts from this section in MyEconLab.

The foreign _____ _____ is the rate at which one country's currency can be exchanged for another's.

The _____ for foreign exchange is a derived _____, which is derived from the demand for foreign goods and services (and financial assets). The _____ of foreign exchange is derived from foreign residents' demands for U.S. goods and services.

The demand curve of foreign exchange slopes _____, and the supply curve of foreign exchange slopes

_____. The equilibrium foreign exchange rate occurs at the intersection of the demand and supply curves for a currency.

A _____ in the demand for foreign goods will result in a shift in the _____ for foreign exchange, thereby changing the equilibrium foreign exchange rate. A shift in the supply of foreign currency will also cause a change in the equilibrium exchange rate.

The Gold Standard and the International Monetary Fund

The current system of more or less freely floating exchange rates is a relatively recent development. In the past, we have had periods of a gold standard, fixed exchange rates under the International Monetary Fund, and variants of the two.

The Gold Standard

Until the 1930s, many nations were on a gold standard. The value of their domestic currency was fixed, or *pegged*, in units of gold. Nations operating under this gold standard agreed to redeem their currencies for a fixed amount of gold at the request of any holder of that currency. Although gold was not necessarily the means of exchange for world trade, it was the unit to which all currencies under the gold standard were pegged. And because all currencies in the system were pegged to gold, exchange rates between those currencies were fixed.

Two problems plagued the gold standard, however. One was that by fixing the value of its currency in relation to the amount of gold, a nation gave up control of its domestic monetary policy. Another was that the world's commerce was at the mercy of gold discoveries. Throughout history, each time new veins of gold were found, desired domestic expenditures on goods and services increased. If production of goods and services failed to increase proportionately, inflation resulted.

298   MODULE 5 | INTERNAT   FIGURE 12-8

This figure illust
dinar exchan
by a rise
an

Bretton Woods and the International Monetary Fund

On December 27, 1945, the world's capitalist countries, which in 1944 had sent re
sentatives to meetings in Bretton Woods, New Hampshire, created a new perman
institution, the International Monetary Fund (IMF). The IMF's task was to lend
member countries for which the sum of the current account balance and the capi
account balance was negative, thereby helping them maintain an offsetting surplus i
their official reserve transactions accounts. Governments that joined the Bretto
Woods system agreed to maintain the value of their currencies within 1 percent of the
declared **par value**—the officially determined value. The United States, which owned
most of the world's gold stock, was similarly obligated to maintain gold prices within a
1 percent margin of the official rate of $35 an ounce. Except for a transitional arrange-
ment permitting a one-time adjustment of up to 10 percent in par value, members
could alter exchange rates thereafter only with the approval of the IMF.

On August 15, 1971, President Richard Nixon suspended the convertibility of the
dollar into gold. On December 18, 1971, the United States officially devalued the dollar—
that is, lowered its official value—relative to the currencies of 14 major industrial nations. Finally, on March 16, 1973, the finance ministers of the European Economic
Community (now the European Union) announced that they would let their currencies float against the dollar, something Japan had already begun doing with its yen.
Since 1973, the United States and most other trading countries have had either freely
floating exchange rates or managed ("dirty") floating exchange rates, in which their
governments or central banks intervene from time to time to try to influence world
market exchange rates.

Fixed versus Floating Exchange Rates

The United States went off the Bretton Woods system of fixed exchange rates in 1973.
As Figure 12-7 below indicates, many other nations of the world have been less willing
to permit the values of their currencies to vary in the foreign exchange markets.

Fixing the Exchange Rate

How did nations fix their exchange rates in years past? How do many countries accomplish this today? Figure 12-8 on the following page shows the market for dinars,
the currency of Bahrain. At the initial equilibrium point E_1, U.S. residents had to give
up $2.66 to obtain 1 dinar. Suppose now that there is an increase in the supply of
dinars for dollars, perhaps because Bahraini residents wish to buy more U.S. goods.

FIGURE 12-7

Current Foreign Exchange Rate Arrangements

Today, 21 percent of the member nations of the International Monetary Fund
have an independent float, and 24 percent have a managed float exchange
rate arrangement. Another 12 percent of all nations use the currencies of other
nations instead of issuing their own currencies. The remaining 43 percent of
countries have fixed exchange rates.

Source: International Monetary Fund.

Independent float 21%
No separate legal currency 12%
Managed float 24%
Fixed exchange rate 43%

A Fixed Exchange Rate

...ates how the Central Bank of Bahrain could fix the dollar-
...ge rate in the face of an increase in the supply of dinars caused
... in the demand for U.S. goods by Bahraini residents. In the absence of
...action by the Central Bank of Bahrain, the result would be a movement
from point E_1 to point E_2. The dollar value of the dinar would fall from $2.66 to
$2.00. The Central Bank of Bahrain can prevent this exchange rate change by
purchasing dinars with dollars in the foreign exchange market, thereby
increasing the demand for dinars. At the new equilibrium point, E_3, the dinar's
value remains at $2.66.

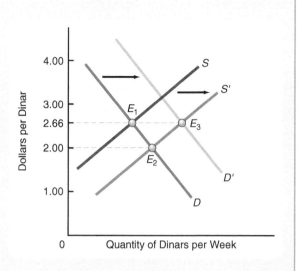

Other things being equal, the result would be a movement to point E_2 in Figure 12-8 above. The dollar value of the dinar would fall to $2.00.

To prevent a dinar depreciation from occurring, however, the Central Bank of Bahrain could increase the demand for dinars in the foreign exchange market by purchasing dinars with dollars. The Central Bank of Bahrain can do this using dollars that it has on hand as part of its *foreign exchange reserves*. All central banks hold reserves of foreign currencies. Because the U.S. dollar is a key international currency, the Central Bank of Bahrain and other central banks typically hold billions of dollars in reserve so that they can make transactions such as the one in this example.

Note that a sufficiently large purchase of dinars could, as shown in Figure 12-8, cause the demand curve to shift rightward to achieve the new equilibrium point E_3, at which the dinar's value remains at $2.66. Provided that it has enough dollar reserves on hand, the Central Bank of Bahrain could maintain—effectively fix—the exchange rate in the face of the rise in the supply of dinars.

The Central Bank of Bahrain has maintained the dollar-dinar exchange rate in this manner since 2001. This basic approach—varying the amount of the national currency demanded at any given exchange rate in foreign exchange markets when necessary—is also the way that *any* central bank seeks to keep its nation's currency value unchanged in light of changing market forces.

> *Central banks can keep exchange rates fixed as long as they have enough foreign exchange reserves to deal with potentially long-lasting changes in the demand for or supply of their nation's currency.*

Pros and Cons of a Fixed Exchange Rate

Why might a nation such as Bahrain wish to keep the value of its currency from fluctuating? One reason is that changes in the exchange rate can affect the market values of assets that are denominated in foreign currencies. This can increase the financial risks that a nation's residents face, thereby forcing them to incur costs to avoid these risks.

FOREIGN EXCHANGE RISK The possibility that variations in the market value of assets can take place due to changes in the value of a nation's currency is the **foreign exchange risk** that residents of a country face because their nation's currency value can vary. Suppose that companies in Bahrain have many loans denominated in dollars but earn nearly all their revenues in dinars from sales within Bahrain. A decline in the dollar

Foreign exchange risk
The possibility that changes in the value of a nation's currency will result in variations in the market value of assets.

value of the dinar would mean that Bahraini companies would have to allocate a larger portion of their earnings to make the same *dollar* loan payments as before. Thus, a fall in the dinar's value would increase the operating costs of these companies, thereby reducing their profitability and raising the likelihood of eventual bankruptcy.

Limiting foreign exchange risk is a classic rationale for adopting a fixed exchange rate. Nevertheless, a country's residents are not defenseless against foreign exchange risk. In what is known as a **hedge,** they can adopt strategies intended to offset the risk arising from exchange rate variations. For example, a company in Bahrain that has significant euro earnings from sales in Germany but sizable loans from U.S. investors could arrange to convert its euro earnings into dollars via special types of foreign exchange contracts called *currency swaps*. The Bahraini company could likewise avoid holdings of dinars and shield itself—*hedge*—against variations in the dinar's value.

Hedge
A financial strategy that reduces the chance of suffering losses arising from foreign exchange risk.

THE EXCHANGE RATE AS A SHOCK ABSORBER If fixing the exchange rate limits foreign exchange risk, why do so many nations allow the exchange rates to float? The answer must be that there are potential drawbacks associated with fixing exchange rates. One is that exchange rate variations can actually perform a valuable service for a nation's economy. Consider a situation in which residents of a nation speak only their own nation's language. As a result, the country's residents are very *immobile*: They cannot trade their labor skills outside their own nation's borders.

Now think about what happens if this nation chooses to fix its exchange rate. Imagine a situation in which other countries begin to sell products that are close substitutes for the products its people specialize in producing, causing a sizable drop in worldwide demand for that nation's goods. If wages and prices do not instantly and completely adjust downward, the result will be a sharp decline in production of goods and services, a falloff in national income, and higher unemployment. Contrast this situation with one which the exchange rate floats. In this case, a sizable decline in outside demand for the nation's products will cause it to experience a trade deficit, which will lead to a significant drop in the demand for that nation's currency. As a result, the nation's currency will experience a sizable depreciation, making the goods that the nation offers to sell abroad much less expensive in other countries. People abroad who continue to consume the nation's products will increase their purchases, and the nation's exports will increase. Its production will begin to recover somewhat, as will its residents' incomes. Unemployment will begin to fall.

This example illustrates how exchange rate variations can be beneficial, especially if a nation's residents are relatively immobile. It can be difficult, for example, for a Polish resident who has never studied Portuguese to move to Lisbon, even if she is highly qualified for available jobs there. If many residents of Poland face similar linguistic or cultural barriers, Poland could be better off with a floating exchange rate even if its residents must incur significant costs hedging against foreign exchange risk as a result.

How did having a separate currency and a floating exchange rate actually end up helping Poland in the early 2010s?

INTERNATIONAL POLICY EXAMPLE

Poland's Floating Exchange Rate Protects It from Euro Ills

During the 2000s, Estonia, Slovakia, and Slovenia rushed to adopt the euro as their currency, and other nations of Eastern Europe fixed their exchange rates in relation to the euro. In contrast, Poland retained its *zloty* currency and allowed its value to float in the foreign exchange market.

A European-wide economic slowdown that began during the early 2010s triggered downturns in Estonia, Slovakia, Slovenia, and other countries in Eastern Europe. When the Polish *zloty* depreciated sharply relative to the euro, Polish goods and services became cheaper for most Europeans. As a consequence, European spending on Polish merchandise exports rose sharply, and the Polish tourism industry boomed as more Europeans selected Poland as a less expensive vacation destination. By maintaining its own currency and a floating exchange rate, Poland thereby helped to insulate its economy from problems afflicting the rest of Europe. Thus, Poland was the only European Union nation to experience uninterrupted economic growth during the early 2010s.

FOR CRITICAL THINKING
Why do you suppose that the Polish unemployment rate remained stable during the early 2010s while unemployment rates elsewhere in Eastern Europe rose?

QUICK QUIZ See page 304 for the answers. Review concepts from this section in MyEconLab.

The International Monetary Fund was developed after World War II as an institution to maintain _____ exchange rates in the world. Since 1973, however, _____ exchange rates have disappeared in most major trading countries. For these nations, exchange rates are largely determined by the forces of demand and supply in global foreign exchange markets.

Central banks can fix exchange rates by buying or selling foreign _____ and thereby adding to or subtracting from their foreign exchange _____.

Although fixing the exchange rate helps protect a nation's residents from foreign exchange _____, this policy makes less mobile residents susceptible to greater volatility in income and employment.

YOU ARE THERE

An Exchange-Rate-Induced U.S. Shopping *Bagunça* for *Brazilians*

Ana Ligia Paladino has traveled 5,000 miles from her home in the southernmost part of Brazil to engage in a 10-day-long shopping spree in New York City. When Paladino emerges from her first morning of shopping at Macy's, the only words she can think of to describe her experience are, "It was a *bagunça!*"—that is, a combination of "mess" and "mayhem." During the year of her visit, Paladino is among 700,000 Brazilians to visit New York City, where Brazilians have spent more than $1.6 billion. Within the same year, Brazilians also have spent more than $2 billion in Florida. In both U.S. locations, Brazilians have outspent visitors from any other country in the world.

What has induced Paladino and so many other Brazilians to engage in spending in the United States is that the Brazilian currency, the *real*, can

now buy a great deal more U.S. goods and services than was true previously. Indeed, during the two years prior to Paladino's visit, the *real* appreciated relative to the U.S. dollar by 25 percent. Thus, during her New York shopping *bagunça*, Paladino was able to buy about 25 percent more items in the United States than she could have bought 24 months earlier.

Critical Thinking Questions

1. What happened to the U.S. dollar's value in relation to the Brazilian *real* during the preceding two years?

2. Why do you suppose that more Brazilian students are now studying at U.S. colleges and universities than was true several years ago?

ISSUES & APPLICATIONS

CONCEPTS APPLIED

▶ Balance of Payments

▶ Merchandise Trade Deficit

▶ Balance on Goods and Services

Items "Made in China" Generate Income Elsewhere

In a typical year, the value of U.S. imports from China amounts to one-sixth of total U.S. import spending recorded in the nation's balance of payments. Expenditures on merchandise imported from China make up more than 70 percent of both the U.S. merchandise trade deficit and the U.S. balance on goods and services. These facts do not imply, however, that every dollar you spend as a consumer on an item "made in China" finds its way to people in China. In fact, less than half of each dollar you spend on Chinese merchandise actually reaches someone in China.

Only Part of the Price of a Chinese Import Is Chinese Income

Consider a toy action figure manufactured in China that has a price of $15 in the United States. A substantial portion of the U.S. retail price pays for transportation of the toy within the United States, rent for the U.S. retail outlet that sells the action figure, profits for the retailer's owners, and expenses incurred in marketing the toy. The latter expenses include the wages paid to managers and employees of the U.S. firms that marketed the action figure in the United States.

Alternatively, consider the iPhone, which earns substantial profits for U.S.-based Apple. iPhones are assembled in China from components that are made by and that generate revenues for firms located outside both the United States and China. Yet when an assembled iPhone is shipped from China for a U.S. consumer to purchase, that device is classified as a Chinese export and a U.S. import.

The U.S. Content of "Made in China"

Galina Hale and Bart Hoblin of the Federal Reserve Bank of San Francisco have calculated shares of spending on U.S. imports from China that flow to Chinese producers and to U.S. firms and their workers. They find that only 45 cents of each dollar U.S. consumers pay toward the price of a typical Chinese-imported good actually makes its way to China as income.

Thus, your spending on merchandise imported from China contributes dollar-for-dollar to the U.S. merchandise trade deficit, but fewer than half of the dollars that you spend on items "made in China" ultimately flow to that nation as income. The income that your spending generates is split among people who live in China, the United States, and sometimes—as in the case of iPhones—other nations.

For Critical Thinking

1. The United States is a net exporter of services to China. What does this imply about the magnitude of the deficit in the U.S. balance on goods and services with China compared with the size of the U.S. merchandise trade deficit with China?

2. Why does a portion of Chinese residents' expenditures on goods and services exported from the United States to China likely add to the earnings of Chinese firms and those firms' managers and workers?

Web Resources

1. To view key trade balance statistics for China, go to www.econtoday.com/chap12.

2. For a look at U.S. balance of payments data, go to www.econtoday.com/chap12.

MyEconLab

For more questions on this chapter's
Issues & Applications, go to MyEconLab.
In the Study Plan for this chapter,
select Section N: News.

MyEconLab

Here is what you should know after reading this chapter. MyEconLab will help you identify what you know, and where to go when you need to practice.

WHAT YOU SHOULD KNOW		WHERE TO GO TO PRACTICE
The Balance of Trade versus the Balance of Payments The balance of trade is the difference between exports and imports of physical goods, or merchandise, during a given period. The balance of payments is a system of accounts for all transactions between a nation's residents and the residents of other countries of the world.	balance of trade, 284 balance of payments, 284 accounting identities, 284	• MyEconLab Study Plan 12.1

MyEconLab *continued*

The Key Accounts within the Balance of Payments There are three accounts within the balance of payments. The current account measures net exchanges of goods and services, transfers, and income flows across a nation's borders. The capital account measures net flows of financial assets. The official reserve transactions account tabulates exchanges of financial assets involving the home nation's and foreign nations' governments and central banks. Because each international exchange generates both an inflow and an outflow, the sum of the balances on all three accounts must equal zero.

current account, 286
capital account, 287
special drawing rights (SDRs), 288
International Monetary Fund, 288

Key Figure
Figure 12-1, 288

- MyEconLab Study Plan 12.1
- Animated Figure 12-1

Exchange Rate Determination in the Market for Foreign Exchange From the perspective of the United States, the demand for a nation's currency by U.S. residents is derived largely from the demand for imports from that nation. Likewise, the supply of a nation's currency is derived mainly from the supply of U.S. exports to that country. The equilibrium exchange rate is the rate of exchange between the dollar and the other nation's currency at which the quantity of the currency demanded is equal to the quantity supplied.

foreign exchange market, 290
exchange rate, 290
flexible exchange rates, 290
appreciation, 291
depreciation, 291

Key Figures
Figure 12-2, 292
Figure 12-3, 293
Figure 12-4, 294
Figure 12-5, 294

- MyEconLab Study Plan 12.2
- Animated Figures 12-2, 12-3, 12-4, 12-5

Factors That Can Induce Changes in Equilibrium Exchange Rates The equilibrium exchange rate changes in response to changes in the demand for or supply of another nation's currency. Changes in desired flows of exports or imports, real interest rates, tastes and preferences of consumers, and perceptions of economic stability affect the positions of the demand and supply curves in foreign exchange markets and induce variations in equilibrium exchange rates.

Key Figure
Figure 12-6, 295

- MyEconLab Study Plan 12.2
- Animated Figure 12-6

How Policymakers Can Attempt to Keep Exchange Rates Fixed If the current price of the home currency in terms of another nation's currency starts to fall below the level where the home country wants it to remain, the home country's central bank can use reserves of the other nation's currency to purchase the home currency in foreign exchange markets. This raises the demand for the home currency and thereby pushes up the currency's value in terms of the other nation's currency.

par value, 297
foreign exchange risk, 298
hedge, 299

Key Figure
Figure 12-8, 298

- MyEconLab Study Plans 12.3, 12.4
- Animated Figure 12-8

Log in to MyEconLab, take a chapter test, and get a personalized Study Plan that tells you which concepts you understand and which ones you need to review. From there, MyEconLab will give you further practice, tutorials, animations, videos, and guided solutions. For more information, visit www.myeconlab.com

PROBLEMS

All problems are assignable in MyEconLab; exercises that update with real-time data are marked with 〰. Answers to the odd-numbered problems appear at the back of the book.

12-1. Suppose that during a recent year for the United States, merchandise imports were $2 trillion, unilateral transfers were a net outflow of $0.2 trillion, service exports were $0.2 trillion, service imports were $0.1 trillion, and merchandise exports were $1.4 trillion. (See pages 286–287.)

   a. What was the merchandise trade deficit?

   b. What was the balance on goods and services?

   c. What was the current account balance?

12-2. Suppose that during a recent year for the United States, the current account balance was −0.2 trillion, the flow of U.S. private holdings of assets abroad was −$0.1 trillion, and the flow of foreign private assets held in the United States was +0.2 trillion. (See pages 287–288.)

   a. What was the balance on the capital account during the year?

   b. What was the change in official reserves during the year?

12-3. Over the course of a year, a nation tracked its foreign transactions and arrived at the following amounts:

Merchandise exports	500
Service exports	75
Net unilateral transfers	10
Domestic assets abroad (capital outflows)	−200
Foreign assets at home (capital inflows)	300
Changes in official reserves	−35
Merchandise imports	600
Service imports	50

What are this nation's balance of trade, current account balance, and capital account balance? (See pages 286–288.)

12-4. Identify whether each of the following items creates a surplus item or a deficit item in the current account of the U.S. balance of payments. (See page 284.)

   a. A Central European company sells products to a U.S. hobby-store chain.

   b. Japanese residents pay a U.S. travel company to arrange hotel stays, ground transportation, and tours of various U.S. cities, including New York, Chicago, and Orlando.

   c. A Mexican company pays a U.S. accounting firm to audit its income statements.

   d. U.S. churches and mosques send relief aid to Pakistan following a major earthquake in that nation.

   e. A U.S. microprocessor manufacturer purchases raw materials from a Canadian firm.

12-5. Explain how the following events would affect the market for the Mexican peso, assuming a floating exchange rate. (See pages 293–295.)

   a. Improvements in Mexican production technology yield superior guitars, and many musicians around the world buy these guitars.

   b. Perceptions of political instability surrounding regular elections in Mexico make international investors nervous about future business prospects in Mexico.

12-6. Explain how the following events would affect the market for South Africa's currency, the rand, assuming a floating exchange rate. (See page 294.)

   a. A rise in U.S. inflation causes many U.S. residents to seek to buy gold, which is a major South African export good, as a hedge against inflation.

   b. Major discoveries of the highest-quality diamonds ever found occur in Russia and Central Asia, causing a significant decline in purchases of South African diamonds.

12-7. Suppose that the following two events take place in the market for China's currency, the yuan: U.S. parents are more willing than before to buy action figures and other Chinese toy exports, and China's government tightens restrictions on the amount of U.S. dollar–denominated financial assets that Chinese residents may legally purchase. What happens to the dollar price of the yuan? Does the yuan appreciate or depreciate relative to the dollar? (See pages 293–295.)

12-8. On Wednesday, the exchange rate between the Japanese yen and the U.S. dollar was $0.010 per yen. On Thursday, it was $0.009. Did the dollar appreciate or depreciate against the yen? By how much, expressed as a percentage change? (See page 288.)

12-9. On Wednesday, the exchange rate between the euro and the U.S. dollar was $1.20 per euro, and the exchange rate between the Canadian dollar and the U.S. dollar was U.S. $1.05 per Canadian dollar. What is the exchange rate between the Canadian dollar and the euro? (See page 288.)

12-10. Suppose that signs of an improvement in the Japanese economy lead international investors to resume lending to the Japanese government and businesses. How would this event affect the market for the yen? How should the central bank, the Bank of Japan, respond to this event if it wants to keep the value of the yen unchanged? (See pages 297–298.)

12-11. Briefly explain the differences between a flexible exchange rate system and a fixed exchange rate system. (See pages 296–297.)

12-12. Suppose that under a gold standard, the U.S. dollar is pegged to gold at a rate of $35 per ounce and the pound sterling is pegged to gold at a rate of £17.50 per ounce. Explain how the gold standard constitutes an exchange rate arrangement between the dollar and the pound. What is the exchange rate between the U.S. dollar and the pound sterling? (See pages 296–297.)

12-13. Suppose that under the Bretton Woods system, the dollar is pegged to gold at a rate of $35 per ounce and the pound sterling is pegged to the dollar at a rate of $2 = £1. If the dollar is devalued against gold and the pegged rate is changed to

$40 per ounce, what does this imply for the exchange value of the pound in terms of dollars? (See page 297.)

12-14. Suppose that the People's Bank of China wishes to peg the rate of exchange of its currency, the yuan, in terms of the U.S. dollar. In each of the following situations, should it add to or subtract from its dollar foreign exchange reserves? Why? (See pages 297–298.)

a. U.S. parents worrying about safety begin buying fewer Chinese-made toys for their children.

b. U.S. interest rates rise relative to interest rates in China, so Chinese residents seek to purchase additional U.S. financial assets.

c. Chinese furniture manufacturers produce high-quality early American furniture and successfully export large quantities of the furniture to the United States.

ECONOMICS ON THE NET

Daily Exchange Rates It is easy to keep up with daily changes in exchange rates by using the Web site of Oanda.com. In this application, you will learn how hard it is to predict exchange rate movements, and you will get some practice thinking about what factors can cause exchange rates to change.

Title: Oanda Currency Converter

Navigation: Go to www.econtoday.com/chap12 to visit the Oanda.com's currency converter home page. Click on *Foreign Exchange 12 PM Rates*.

Application Answer the following questions.

1. Choose a currency from the many available in the drop-down menu. How many dollars does it take to purchase a unit of the currency in the spot foreign exchange market?

2. For currency you chose in Question 1, keep track of its value relative to the dollar over the course of several days. Based on your tabulations, try to predict the value of the currency at the end of the week *following* your data collections. Use any information you may have, or just do your best without any additional information. How far off did your prediction turn out to be?

For Group Study and Analysis Divide the class into groups, and assign a currency to each group. Ask the group to track the currency's value over the course of two days and to determine whether the currency's value appreciated or depreciated relative to the dollar from one day to the next. In addition, ask each group to discuss what kinds of demand or supply shifts could have caused the change that occurred during this interval.

ANSWERS TO QUICK QUIZZES

p. 289: (i) balance . . . payments; (ii) physical; (iii) current . . . current; (iv) Unilateral transfers; (v) current; (vi) capital . . . capital; (vii) official reserve; (viii) inflation . . . political

p. 296: (i) exchange rate; (ii) demand . . . demand . . . supply; (iii) downward . . . upward; (iv) shift . . . demand
p. 300: (i) fixed . . . fixed; (ii) currencies . . . reserves; (iii) risk

Answers to Odd-Numbered Problems

CHAPTER 1

1-1. a. Multiplying the fraction of people who participate in the labor force, 0.7, times the adult, non-institutionalized, nonmilitary population of 200.0 million yields a labor force of 140.0 million.

b. Subtracting the 7.5 million unemployed from the labor force of 140.0 million yields 132.5 million people who are employed.

c. Dividing the 7.5 million unemployed by the 140.0 million in the labor force and multiplying by 100 yields an unemployment rate of about 5.36 percent.

1-3. a. The labor force equals the number employed plus the number unemployed, or 156 million + 8 million = 164 million. In percentage terms, therefore, the unemployment rate is 100 times 8 million/164 million, or 4.9 percent.

b. These 60 million people are not in the labor force. The labor force participation rate is, in percentage terms, 100 times 164 million/224 million, or 73.2 percent.

1-5. a. Four of the 100 people are always continuously unemployed because they are between jobs, so the frictional unemployment rate is $(4/100) \times 100 = 4$ percent.

b. Three of the 100 people are always unemployed as a result of government regulations, so the structural unemployment rate is $(3/100) \times 100 = 3$ percent.

c. The unemployment rate is the sum of the frictional and structural rates of unemployment, or 7 percent.

1-7. The overall unemployment rate is 8 percent, and the natural rate of unemployment is 5 percent.

1-9. In 2013, the value of the price index is $\$10,000/\$10,000 \times 100 = 100$. In 2014, the value of the price index is $\$11,100/\$10,000 \times 100 = 111$.

1-11. a. 2014

b. 10 percent

c. 10 percent

d. $1,800 in 2013; $3,000 in 2017

1-13. The expected rate of inflation is equal to $100 \times [(99 - 90)/90] = 10$ percent. Hence, the real interest rate equals the difference between the 12 percent

nominal interest rate and the 10 percent anticipated inflation rate, or 2 percent.

1-15. a. The homeowner gains; the savings bank loses.

b. The tenants gain; the landlord loses.

c. The auto buyer gains; the bank loses.

d. The employer gains; the pensioner loses.

CHAPTER 2

2-1. As illustrated by the basic circular-flow diagram, the flow of the market value of final goods and services produced within a nation's borders during a given interval—that is, gross domestic product—is what generates the gross domestic income received by the nation's households during that interval, which they in turn spend in the nation's product markets. Consequently, the flows of gross domestic product and gross domestic income must be equivalent.

2-3. a. When Maria does all the work herself, only purchases of the materials in markets (magazines, texturing materials, paint brushes, and paints), which total $280 per year, count in GDP.

b. She must pay the market price of $200 for the texturing, so her contribution to annual GDP from this project, including the materials, is $480.

c. Because Maria now pays for the entire project via market transactions, her total contribution to GDP equals the sum of the $280 material purchases from part (a), $200 for the texturing from part (b), and $350 for the painting, or $830 per year.

2-5. a. GDP = $16.6 trillion; NDP = $15.3 trillion; NI = $14.5 trillion.

b. GDP in 2017 will equal $15.5 trillion.

2-7. a. Gross domestic income = $14.6 trillion; GDP = $14.6 trillion.

b. Gross private domestic investment = $2.0 trillion.

c. Personal income = $12.0 trillion; personal disposable income = $10.3 trillion.

2-9. a. Measured GDP declines.

b. Measured GDP increases.

c. Measured GDP does not change (the firearms are not newly produced).

2-11. a. The chip is an intermediate good, so its purchase in June is not included in GDP; only the final sale in November is included.

b. This is a final sale of a good that is included in GDP for the year.

c. This is a final sale of a service that is included in GDP for the year.

2-13. a. Nominal GDP for 2013 is $2,300; for 2017, nominal GDP is $2,832.

b. Real GDP for 2013 is $2,300; for 2017, real GDP is $2,229.

2-15. The price index is (2015 nominal GDP/2015 real GDP) × 100 = ($88,000/$136,000) × 100 = 64.7.

2-17. The $1 billion expended to pay for employees and equipment and the additional $1 billion paid to clean up the oil spill would be included in GDP, for a total of $2 billion added to GDP in 2015. The rise in oil reserves increases the stock of wealth but is not included in the current flow of newly produced goods and services. In addition, the welfare loss relating to the deaths of wildlife is also not measured in the marketplace and therefore is not included in GDP.

CHAPTER 3

3-1. a. Y

b. X

3-3. The nation will maintain its stock of capital goods at its current level, so its rate of economic growth will be zero.

3-5. A: $8,250 per capita; B: $4,500 per capita; C: $21,000 per capita

3-7. 1.77 times higher after 20 years; 3.16 times higher after 40 years

3-9. 5 years

3-11. In Mozambique, in 50 years the typical resident's annual real GDP per capita will equal $3,000 × 4.38 = $13,140. In China, a typical resident's real GDP per capita will equal $3,000 × 46.90 = $140,700, which is $127,560 per year greater than in Mozambique.

3-13. 4 percent

3-15. Per capita real GDP in 2014 was 10 percent higher than in 2013, or $2,200. The level of real GDP is $2,200 per person × 5 million people = $11 billion.

CHAPTER 4

4-1. The amount of unemployment would be the sum of frictional, structural, and seasonal unemployment.

4-3. The real value of the new full-employment level of nominal GDP is ($17.7 trillion/1.15) = $15.39 trillion, so the long-run aggregate supply curve has shifted rightward by $2.35 trillion, in base-year dollars.

4-5. a. A rightward shift of the *LRAS* curve coupled with a shift in the *AD* curve farther to the right

b. A leftward shift of the *LRAS* curve coupled with a leftward shift of the *AD* curve of the same magnitude

c. A rightward shift of the *LRAS* curve coupled with a rightward shift of the *AD* curve of the same magnitude

d. A leftward shift of the *LRAS* curve coupled with a shift of the *AD* curve farther to the left

4-7. This change implies a rightward shift of the long-run aggregate supply curve along the unchanged aggregate demand curve, so the long-run equilibrium price level will decline.

4-9. There are three effects. First, there is a real-balance effect, because the rise in the price level reduces real money balances, inducing people to cut back on their spending. In addition, there is an interest rate effect as a higher price level pushes up interest rates, thereby reducing the attractiveness of purchases of autos, houses, and plants and equipment. Finally, there is an open-economy effect as home residents respond to the higher price level by reducing purchases of domestically produced goods in favor of foreign-produced goods, while foreign residents cut back on their purchases of our home-produced goods. All three effects entail a reduction in purchases of goods and services, so the aggregate demand curve slopes downward.

4-11. a. At the price level P_2 above the equilibrium price level P_1, the total quantity of real goods and services that people plan to consume is less than the total quantity that is consistent with firms' production plans. One reason is that at the higher-than-equilibrium price level, real money balances are lower, which reduces real wealth and induces lower planned consumption. Another is that interest rates are higher at the higher-than-equilibrium price level, which generates a cutback in spending on consumer durables. Finally, at the higher-than-equilibrium price level P_2, people tend to cut back on purchasing domestic goods in favor of foreign-produced goods, and foreign residents reduce purchases of our domestic goods. As unsold inventories of output accumulate, the price level drops toward the equilibrium price level P_1, which ultimately causes planned consumption to rise toward equality with total production.

b. At the price level P_3 below the equilibrium price level P_1, the total quantity of real goods and services that people plan to consume exceeds the total quantity that is consistent with firms' production plans. One reason is that at the lower-than-equilibrium price level, real money balances are higher, which raises real wealth and induces higher planned consumption. Another is that interest rates are lower at the lower-than-equilibrium price level, which generates an increase in consumption spending. Finally, at the lower-than-equilibrium price level P_3, people tend to raise their purchases of domestic goods and cut back on buying foreign-produced goods, and foreign residents increase purchases of our domestic goods. As inventories of output are depleted, the price level begins to rise toward the equilibrium price level P_1, which ultimately causes planned consumption to fall toward equality with total production.

4-13. a. When the price level falls with deflation, there is a movement downward along the *AD* curve.

b. The decline in foreign real GDP levels reduces incomes of foreign residents, who cut back on their spending on our domestic exports. Thus, the domestic *AD* curve shifts leftward.

c. The fall in the foreign exchange value of the nation's currency makes our domestically produced goods and services less expensive to foreign residents, who increase their spending on our domestic exports. Thus, the domestic *AD* curve shifts rightward.

d. An increase in the price level causes a movement upward along the *AD* curve.

4-15. a. The aggregate demand curve shifts leftward along the long-run aggregate supply curve. The equilibrium price level falls, and equilibrium real GDP remains unchanged.

b. The aggregate demand curve shifts rightward along the long-run aggregate supply curve. The equilibrium price level rises, and equilibrium real GDP remains unchanged.

c. The long-run aggregate supply curve shifts rightward along the aggregate demand curve. The equilibrium price level falls, and equilibrium real GDP increases.

d. The aggregate demand curve shifts rightward along the long-run aggregate supply curve. The equilibrium price level rises, and equilibrium real GDP remains unchanged.

4-17. a. The income flows are mainly influencing relatives' consumption, so the main effect is on the aggregate demand curve.

b. A rise in aggregate demand will lead to an increase in the equilibrium price level.

CHAPTER 5

5-1. a. Because saving increases at any given interest rate, the desired saving curve shifts rightward. This causes the equilibrium interest rate to decline.

b. There is no effect on current equilibrium real GDP, because in the classical model, the vertical long-run aggregate supply curve always applies.

c. A change in the saving rate does not directly affect the demand for labor or the supply of labor in the classical model, so equilibrium employment does not change.

d. The decrease in the equilibrium interest rate generates a downward movement along the demand curve for investment. Consequently, desired investment increases.

e. The rise in current investment implies greater capital accumulation. Other things being equal, this will imply increased future production and higher equilibrium real GDP in the future.

5-3. False. In fact, an important distinction can be made. The classical model of short-run real GDP determination applies to an interval short enough that some factors of production, such as capital, are fixed. Nevertheless, the classical model implies that even in the short run the economy's short-run aggregate supply curve is the same as its long-run aggregate supply curve.

5-5. In the long run, the aggregate supply curve is vertical because all input prices adjust fully and people are fully informed in the long run. Thus, the short-run aggregate supply curve is more steeply sloped if input prices adjust more rapidly and people become more fully informed within a short-run interval.

5-7. To prevent a short-run decrease in real GDP from taking place after the temporary rise in oil prices shifts the *SRAS* curve leftward, policymakers should increase the quantity of money in circulation. This will shift the *AD* curve rightward and prevent equilibrium real GDP from declining in the short run.

5-9. An increase in total planned real expenditures by U.S. households in response to an increase in the quantity of money in circulation implies a rightward shift in the position of the aggregate demand curve along the short-run aggregate supply curve. The predicted effects are increases in both the equilibrium U.S. price level and the equilibrium U.S. real GDP. Keynesian theory indicates that a consequence would be a short-term inflationary gap between expenditures on real GDP in the short run and expenditures on real GDP that would be consistent with long-run equilibrium.

5-11. **a.** *E*: The union wage boost causes the *SRAS* curve to shift leftward, from $SRAS_1$ to $SRAS_3$. The reduction in incomes abroad causes import spending in this nation to fall, which induces a leftward shift in the *AD* curve, from AD_1 to AD_3.

b. *B*: The short-term reduction in production capabilities causes the *SRAS* curve to shift leftward, from $SRAS_1$ to $SRAS_3$, and the increase in money supply growth generates a rightward shift in the *AD* curve, from AD_1 to AD_2.

c. *C*: The strengthening of the value of this nation's currency reduces the prices of imported inputs that domestic firms utilize to produce goods and services, which causes the *SRAS* curve to shift rightward, from $SRAS_1$ to $SRAS_2$. At the same time, currency's strengthening raises the prices of exports and reduces the prices of imports, so net export spending declines, thereby inducing a leftward shift in the *AD* curve, from AD_1 to AD_3.

CHAPTER 6

6-1. **a.** Flow

   b. Flow

   c. Stock

   d. Flow

   e. Stock

   f. Flow

   g. Stock

6-3. **a.** The completed table follows (all amounts in dollars):

Real GDP	Consumption	Saving	Investment
2,000	2,000	0	1,200
4,000	3,600	400	1,200
6,000	5,200	800	1,200
8,000	6,800	1,200	1,200
10,000	8,400	1,600	1,200
12,000	10,000	2,000	1,200

$$\text{MPC} = 1{,}600/2000 = 0.8;$$
$$\text{MPS} = 400/2{,}000 = 0.2.$$

b. The graph appears at top of next column.

c. The graph appears below. Equilibrium real GDP on both graphs equals $8,000 per year.

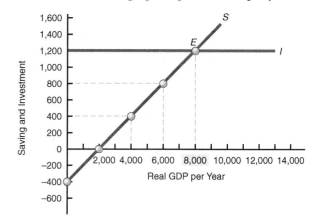

d. APS = $1,200/$8,000 = 0.15

e. The multiplier is $1/(1 - \text{MPC}) = 1/(1 - 0.8) = 1/0.2 = 5$. Thus, if autonomous consumption were to rise by $100, then equilibrium real GDP would increase by $100 times 5, or $500.

6-5. **a.** MPC = 0.95; MPS = 0.05

   b. MPC = 0.90; MPS = 0.10

   c. MPC = 0.875; MPS = 0.125

   d. MPC = 0.80; MPS = 0.20

6-7. The multiplier is $1/(1 - \text{MPC}) = 4$, so $1 - \text{MPC} = 0.25$, which implies that MPC = 0.75. Thus, when real GDP equals $15 trillion, consumption is $1 trillion + (0.75 × $15 trillion) = $12.25 trillion.

6-9. The multiplier is $1/(1 - \text{MPC}) = 1/(1 - 0.75) = 4$, so the increase in equilibrium real GDP is $250 billion × 4 = $1 trillion, and the level of real GDP at the new point on the aggregate demand curve is $16 trillion per year.

6-11. **a.** The MPS is equal to 1/3.

   b. $0.1 trillion

CHAPTER 8

8-1. a. A key factor that could help explain why the actual effect may have turned out to be lower is the crowding-out effect. Some government spending may have entailed direct expenditure offsets that reduced private expenditures on a dollar-for-dollar basis. In addition, indirect crowding out may have occurred. Because the government did not change taxes, it probably sold bonds to finance its increased expenditures, and this action likely pushed up interest rates, thereby discouraging private investment. Furthermore, the increase in government spending likely pushed up aggregate demand, which may have caused a short-run increase in the price level. This, in turn, may have induced foreign residents to reduce their expenditures on U.S. goods. It also could have reduced real money holdings sufficiently to discourage consumers from spending as much as before. On net, therefore, real GDP rose in the short run, but not by the full amount predicted by the basic multiplier effect.

b. In the long run, as the increased spending raised aggregate demand, wages and other input prices likely increased in proportion to the resulting increase in the price level. Thus, in the long run the aggregate supply schedule was vertical, and the increase in government spending induced only a rise in the price level.

8-3. Because of the recognition time lag entailed in gathering information about the economy, policymakers may be slow to respond to a downturn in real GDP. Congressional approval of policy actions to address the downturn may be delayed; hence, an action time lag may also arise. Finally, there is an effect time lag, because policy actions take time to exert their full effects on the economy. If these lags are sufficiently long, it is possible that by the time a policy to address a downturn has begun to have its effects, equilibrium real GDP per year may already be rising. If so, the policy action may push real GDP up faster than intended, thereby making real GDP less stable.

8-5. Situation *b* is an example of indirect crowding out because the reduction in private expenditures takes place indirectly in response to a change in the interest rate. In contrast, situations *a* and *c* are examples of direct expenditure offsets.

8-7. Situation *b* is an example of a discretionary fiscal policy action because this is a discretionary action by Congress. So is situation *d* because the president uses discretionary authority. Situation *c* is an example of monetary policy, not fiscal policy, and situation *a* is an example of an automatic stabilizer.

8-9. There is a recessionary gap, because at point *A*, equilibrium real GDP of $15.5 trillion is below the long-run level of $16.0 trillion. To eliminate the recessionary gap of $0.5 trillion, government spending must increase sufficiently to shift the *AD* curve rightward to a long-run equilibrium, which will entail a price level increase from 115 to 120. Hence, the spending increase must shift the *AD* curve rightward by $1 trillion, or by the multiplier, which is $1/0.20 = 5$, times the increase in spending. Government spending must rise by $200 billion, or $0.2 trillion per year.

8-11. Because the MPC is 0.80, the multiplier equals $1/(1 - \text{MPC}) = 1/0.2 = 5$. Net of indirect crowding out, therefore, total autonomous expenditures must rise by $40 billion in order to shift the aggregate demand curve rightward by $200 billion. If the government raises its spending by $50 billion, the market interest rate rises by 0.5 percentage point and thereby causes planned investment spending to fall by $10 billion, which results in a net rise in total autonomous expenditures equal to $40 billion. Consequently, to accomplish its objective, the government should increase its spending by $50 billion.

8-13. A cut in the tax rate should induce a rise in consumption and, consequently, a multiple short-run increase in equilibrium real GDP. In addition, however, a tax-rate reduction reduces the automatic-stabilizer properties of the tax system, so equilibrium real GDP would be less stable in the face of changes in autonomous spending.

8-15. According to the logic of the permanent income hypothesis, these small, one-time payments did not raise people's average lifetime disposable incomes. Instead of using the funds to increase their consumption spending, people applied them toward paying down outstanding debts or to their savings. Hence, consumption spending did not rise in response to the temporary increase in real disposable income.

APPENDIX C

C-1. a. The marginal propensity to consume is equal to $1 - \text{MPS}$, or $6/7$.

b. The required increase in equilibrium real GDP is $0.35 trillion, or $350 billion. The multiplier equals $1/(1 - \text{MPC}) = 1/\text{MPS} = 1/(1/7) = 7$. Hence, investment or government spending must increase by $50 billion to bring about a $350 billion increase in equilibrium real GDP.

c. The multiplier relevant for a tax change equals $-\text{MPC}/(1 - \text{MPC}) = -\text{MPC}/\text{MPS} = -(6/7)/(1/7) = -6$. Thus, the government would have to cut taxes by $58.33 billion to induce a rise in equilibrium real GDP equal to $350 billion.

C-3. a. The aggregate expenditures curve shifts up by $1 billion; equilibrium real GDP increases by $5 billion per year.

b. The aggregate expenditures curve shifts down by the MPC times the tax increase, or by $0.8 \times \$1$ billion = $0.8 billion; equilibrium real income falls by $4 billion per year.

c. The aggregate expenditures curve shifts upward by $(1 - \text{MPC})$ times $1 billion = $0.2 billion. Equilibrium real income rises by $1 billion.

d. No change; no change

CHAPTER 9

9-1. $0.4 trillion

9-3. A higher deficit creates a higher public debt.

9-5. The net public debt is obtained by subtracting government interagency borrowing from the gross public debt.

9-7. When foreign dollar holders hold more of our domestic government bonds issued to finance higher domestic government budget deficits, they purchase fewer of our domestic exports, so the domestic trade deficit rises, other things being equal.

9-9. As shown in the diagram below, the increase in government spending and/or tax reduction that creates the budget deficit also causes the aggregate demand curve to shift rightward, from *AD* to *AD*$_2$. Real GDP rises to its long-run equilibrium level of $15 trillion at point *B*. The equilibrium price level increases to a value of 130 at this point. As real GDP rises, the government's tax collections increase and benefit payouts fall, both of which will help ultimately reduce the deficit.

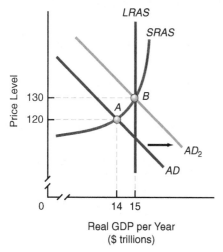

9-11. "The rich" are likely to respond to higher tax rates by reducing their activities that generate taxable income, so actual tax collections from "the rich" will not turn out to be as high as the politician suggests. In any event, as shown in Figure 9-5 on page 173, even imposing a 100 percent tax rate on the highest-income taxpayers could not raise sufficient tax revenues to eliminate the deficit.

9-13. These data indicate that tax revenues have been able to cover only about two-thirds—about 67 percent—of federal expenditures. Because more than 60 percent of all federal expenditures are entitlements, this implies that the federal government has been borrowing to pay for most discretionary spending.

CHAPTER 10

10-1. Medium of exchange; store of value; standard of deferred payment

10-3. Store of value; standard of deferred payment

10-5. M1 equals transactions deposits plus currency plus traveler's checks, or $1,025 billion + $1,050 billion + $25 billion = $2,100 billion; M2 equals M1 + savings deposits plus small-denomination time deposits plus money market deposit accounts plus retail (noninstitution) money market mutual funds, or $2,100 billion + $3,300 billion + $1,450 billion + $1,950 billion + $1,900 billion = $10,700 billion.

10-7. a. M1 and M2

b. Neither

c. M2 only

d. M1 and M2

e. M2 only

10-9. a. Moral hazard problem

b. Adverse selection problem

c. Moral hazard problem

10-11. The Fed provides banking services such as check clearing services and large-value payment services for other banks and for the U.S. Treasury, just as a private bank provides such services for its customers. Unlike a private bank, however, the Federal Reserve serves as a lender of last resort, a regulator, and a policymaker.

10-13. a. Asset

b. Liability

c. Asset

d. Asset

e. Asset

f. Liability

10-15. 9.09

10-17. 25 percent (or 0.25)

10-19. The maximum potential money multiplier is $1/0.01$ = 100, so total deposits in the banking system will increase by $5 million $\times$ 100 = $500 million.

CHAPTER 11

11-1. a. $500/0.05 = $10,000

   b. Its price falls to $500/0.10 = $5,000.

11-3. a. One possible policy action would be an open market sale of securities, which would reduce the money supply and shift the aggregate demand curve leftward. Others would be to increase the discount rate relative to the federal funds rate or to raise the required reserve ratio.

   b. In principle, the Fed's action would reduce inflation more quickly.

11-5. The short-run effect is an upward movement along the short-run aggregate supply curve generated by an increase in aggregate demand. The equilibrium price level rises, and equilibrium real GDP increases. In the long run, input prices rise, and people anticipate a higher price level, which causes the short-run aggregate supply curve to shift upward and to the left. The equilibrium price level rises once more, and equilibrium real GDP falls back to its long-run equilibrium level.

11-7. a. The dollar appreciation will raise the prices of U.S. goods and services from the perspective of foreign residents, so they will reduce their spending on U.S. exports. It will reduce the prices of foreign goods and services from the perspective of U.S. residents, so they will increase their spending on foreign imports. Thus, net export expenditures per year will decline.

   b. The fall in net export expenditures will bring about a decrease in U.S. aggregate demand, so the aggregate demand curve AD_2 will apply to this situation. In the short run, the equilibrium price level will fall from 118 to 116, and equilibrium real GDP, measured in base-year dollars, will fall from $15.0 trillion to $14.5 trillion per year.

   c. The Federal Reserve could engage in a policy action, such as open market purchases, that increases aggregate demand to its original level.

11-9. The price level remains at its original value. Because $M_sV = PY$, V has doubled, and Y is unchanged, cutting M_s in half leaves P unchanged.

11-11. a. $M_sV = PY$, so $P = M_sV/Y = ($1.1 \text{ trillion} \times 10)/$5 \text{ trillion} = 2.2$.

   b. $100 billion/$1 trillion = 0.1, or 10 percent.

   c. 0.2/2 = 0.1, or 10 percent.

   d. Both the money supply and the price level increased by 10 percent.

11-13. Any one of these contractionary actions will tend to raise interest rates, which in turn will induce international inflows of financial capital. This pushes up the value of the dollar and makes U.S. goods less attractive abroad. As a consequence, real planned total expenditures on U.S. goods decline even further.

11-15. To induce the banks to hold the reserves, the Fed would have to raise the interest rate it pays on the reserves. The increase in reserves owned by private banks would generate a rise in the Fed's liabilities equal to the expansion of the Fed's assets.

11-17. The money supply did not change, so this did not actually constitute a monetary policy action. Instead, the Fed only expanded its reserves and, hence, its liabilities, which corresponded to the increase in the Fed's holdings of privately issued assets. Consequently, the Fed's "quantitative easing" was primarily a credit policy action.

APPENDIX D

D-1. a. $20 billion increase

   b. $40 billion increase

   c. $10 billion open market purchase

D-3. Through its purchase of $1 billion in bonds, the Fed increased reserves by $1 billion. This ultimately caused a $3 billion increase in the money supply after full multiple expansion. The 1 percentage-point drop in the interest rate, from 6 percent to 5 percent, caused investment to rise by $25 billion, from $1,200 billion to $1,225 billion. An investment multiplier of 3 indicates that equilibrium real GDP rose by $75 billion, to $12,075 billion, or $12.075 trillion per year.

CHAPTER 12

12-1 a. −$0.6 trillion

   b. −$0.5 trillion

   c. −$0.7 trillion

12-3. The trade balance is merchandise exports minus merchandise imports, which equals 500 − 600 = −100, or a deficit of 100. Adding service exports of 75 and subtracting net unilateral transfers of 10 and service imports of 50 yields −100 + 75 − 10 − 50 = −85, or a current account balance of −85. The capital account balance equals the difference between capital inflows and capital outflows, or 300 − 200 = +100, or a capital account surplus of 100.

12-5. a. The increase in demand for Mexican-made guitars increases the demand for Mexican pesos, and the peso appreciates.

   b. International investors will remove some of their financial capital from Mexico. The increase in the supply of pesos in the foreign exchange market will cause the peso to depreciate.

12-7. The demand for Chinese yuan increases, and the supply of yuan decreases. The dollar-yuan exchange rate rises, so the yuan appreciates.

12-9. The Canadian dollar–euro exchange rate is found by dividing the U.S. dollar–euro exchange rate by the U.S. dollar–Canadian dollar exchange rate, or (1.45 $U.S./euro)/(0.94 $U.S./$C) = 1.54 $C/euro, or 1.54 Canadian dollars per euro.

12-11. A flexible exchange rate system allows the exchange value of a currency to be determined freely in the foreign exchange market with no intervention by the government. A fixed exchange rate pegs the value of the currency, and the authorities responsible for the value of the currency intervene in foreign exchange markets to maintain this value.

12-13. When the dollar is pegged to gold at a rate of $35 and the pound is pegged to the dollar at $2 = £1, an implicit value between gold and the pound is established at £17.50 = 1 ounce of gold. If the dollar falls in value relative to gold, yet the pound is still valued to the dollar at $2 = £1, the pound become undervalued relative to gold. The exchange rate between the dollar and the pound will have to be adjusted to 2.29 $/£.

Glossary

A

Absolute advantage The ability to produce more units of a good or service using a given quantity of labor or resource inputs. Equivalently, the ability to produce the same quantity of a good or service using fewer units of labor or resource inputs.

Accounting identities Values that are equivalent by definition.

Accounting profit Total revenues minus total explicit costs.

Action time lag The time between recognizing an economic problem and implementing policy to solve it. The action time lag is quite long for fiscal policy, which requires congressional approval.

Active (discretionary) policymaking All actions on the part of monetary and fiscal policymakers that are undertaken in response to or in anticipation of some change in the overall economy.

Ad valorem **taxation** Assessing taxes by charging a tax rate equal to a fraction of the market price of each unit purchased.

Adverse selection The tendency for high-risk projects and clients to be over-represented among borrowers.

Age-earnings cycle The regular earnings profile of an individual throughout his or her lifetime. The age-earnings cycle usually starts with a low income, builds gradually to a peak at around age 50, and then gradually curves down until it approaches zero at retirement.

Aggregate demand The total of all planned expenditures in the entire economy.

Aggregate demand curve A curve showing planned purchase rates for all final goods and services in the economy at various price levels, all other things held constant.

Aggregate demand shock Any event that causes the aggregate demand curve to shift inward or outward.

Aggregate supply The total of all planned production for the economy.

Aggregate supply shock Any event that causes the aggregate supply curve to shift inward or outward.

Aggregates Total amounts or quantities. Aggregate demand, for example, is total planned expenditures throughout a nation.

Anticipated inflation The inflation rate that we believe will occur. When it

does occur, we are in a situation of fully anticipated inflation.

Antitrust legislation Laws that restrict the formation of monopolies and regulate certain anticompetitive business practices.

Appreciation An increase in the exchange value of one nation's currency in terms of the currency of another nation.

Asset demand Holding money as a store of value instead of other assets such as corporate bonds and stocks.

Assets Amounts owned; all items to which a business or household holds legal claim.

Asymmetric information Information possessed by one party in a financial transaction but not by the other party.

Automatic, or built-in, stabilizers Special provisions of certain federal programs that cause changes in desired aggregate expenditures without the action of Congress and the president. Examples are the federal progressive tax system and unemployment compensation.

Autonomous consumption The part of consumption that is independent of (does not depend on) the level of disposable income. Changes in autonomous consumption shift the consumption function.

Average fixed costs Total fixed costs divided by the number of units produced.

Average physical product Total product divided by the variable input.

Average propensity to consume (APC) Real consumption divided by real disposable income. For any given level of real income, the proportion of total real disposable income that is consumed.

Average propensity to save (APS) Real saving divided by real disposable income. For any given level of real income, the proportion of total real disposable income that is saved.

Average tax rate The total tax payment divided by total income. It is the proportion of total income paid in taxes.

Average total costs Total costs divided by the number of units produced; sometimes called *average per-unit total costs*.

Average variable costs Total variable costs divided by the number of units produced.

B

Balance of payments A system of accounts that measures transactions of goods, services, income, and financial assets between domestic households, businesses, and governments and residents of the rest of the world during a specific time period.

Balance of trade The difference between exports and imports of physical goods.

Balance sheet A statement of the assets and liabilities of any business entity, including financial institutions and the Federal Reserve System. Assets are what is owned; liabilities are what is owed.

Balanced budget A situation in which the government's spending is exactly equal to the total taxes and other revenues it collects during a given period of time.

Bank run Attempt by many of a bank's depositors to convert transactions and time deposits into currency out of fear that the bank's liabilities may exceed its assets.

Barter The direct exchange of goods and services for other goods and services without the use of money.

Base year The year that is chosen as the point of reference for comparison of prices in other years.

Base-year dollars The value of a current sum expressed in terms of prices in a base year.

Behavioral economics An approach to the study of consumer behavior that emphasizes psychological limitations and complications that potentially interfere with rational decision making.

Bilateral monopoly A market structure consisting of a monopolist and a monopsonist.

Black market A market in which goods are traded at prices above their legal maximum prices or in which illegal goods are sold.

Bond A legal claim against a firm, usually entitling the owner of the bond to receive a fixed annual coupon payment, plus a lump-sum payment at the bond's maturity date. Bonds are issued in return for funds lent to the firm.

Bounded rationality The hypothesis that people are *nearly*, but not fully, rational, so that they cannot examine every possible choice available to them but instead use simple rules of thumb to sort among the alternatives that happen to occur to them.

Budget constraint All of the possible combinations of goods that can be purchased (at fixed prices) with a specific budget.

Bundling Offering two or more products for sale as a set.

Business fluctuations The ups and downs in business activity throughout the economy.

C

Capital account A category of balance of payments transactions that measures flows of financial assets.

Capital consumption allowance Another name for depreciation, the amount that businesses would have to put aside in order to take care of deteriorating machines and other equipment.

Capital gain A positive difference between the purchase price and the sale price of an asset. If a share of stock is bought for $5 and then sold for $15, the capital gain is $10.

Capital goods Producer durables; nonconsumable goods that firms use to make other goods.

Capital loss A negative difference between the purchase price and the sale price of an asset.

Capture hypothesis A theory of regulatory behavior that predicts that regulators will eventually be captured by special interests of the industry being regulated.

Cartel An association of producers in an industry that agree to set common prices and output quotas to prevent competition.

Central bank A banker's bank, usually an official institution that also serves as a bank for a nation's government treasury. Central banks normally regulate commercial banks.

Ceteris paribus **[KAY-ter-us PEAR-uh-bus] assumption** The assumption that nothing changes except the factor or factors being studied.

Ceteris paribus **conditions** Determinants of the relationship between price and quantity that are unchanged along a curve. Changes in these factors cause the curve to shift.

Closed shop A business enterprise in which employees must belong to the union before they can be hired and must remain in the union after they are hired.

Collective bargaining Negotiation between the management of a company and the management of a union for the purpose of reaching a mutually agreeable contract that sets wages, fringe benefits, and working conditions for all employees in all the unions involved.

Collective decision making How voters, politicians, and other interested parties act and how these actions influence nonmarket decisions.

Common property Property that is owned by everyone and therefore by no one. Air and water are examples of common property resources.

Comparative advantage The ability to produce a good or service at a lower opportunity cost than other producers.

Complements Two goods are complements when a change in the price of one causes an opposite shift in the demand for the other.

Concentration ratio The percentage of all sales contributed by the leading four or leading eight firms in an industry; sometimes called the *industry concentration ratio*.

Constant dollars Dollars expressed in terms of real purchasing power, using a particular year as the base or standard of comparison, in contrast to current dollars.

Constant returns to scale No change in long-run average costs when output increases.

Constant-cost industry An industry whose total output can be increased without an increase in long-run per-unit costs. Its long-run supply curve is horizontal.

Consumer optimum A choice of a set of goods and services that maximizes the level of satisfaction for each consumer, subject to limited income.

Consumer Price Index (CPI) A statistical measure of a weighted average of prices of a specified set of goods and services purchased by typical consumers in urban areas.

Consumer surplus The difference between the total amount that consumers would have been willing to pay for an item and the total amount that they actually pay.

Consumption Spending on new goods and services to be used up out of a household's current income. Whatever is not consumed is saved. Consumption includes such things as buying food and going to a concert.

Consumption function The relationship between amount consumed and disposable income. A consumption function tells us how much people plan to consume at various levels of disposable income.

Consumption goods Goods bought by households to use up, such as food and movies.

Contraction A business fluctuation during which the pace of national economic activity is slowing down.

Cooperative game A game in which the players explicitly cooperate to make themselves jointly better off. As applied to firms, it involves companies colluding in order to make higher than perfectly competitive rates of return.

Corporation A legal entity that may conduct business in its own name just as an individual does. The owners of a corporation, called shareholders, own shares of the firm's profits and have the protection of limited liability.

Cost-of-living adjustments (COLAs) Clauses in contracts that allow for increases in specified nominal values to take account of changes in the cost of living.

Cost-of-service regulation Regulation that allows prices to reflect only the actual average cost of production and no monopoly profits.

Cost-push inflation Inflation caused by decreases in short-run aggregate supply.

Craft unions Labor unions composed of workers who engage in a particular trade or skill, such as baking, carpentry, or plumbing.

Creative response Behavior on the part of a firm that allows it to comply with the letter of the law but violate the spirit, significantly lessening the law's effects.

Credence good A product with qualities that consumers lack the expertise to assess without assistance.

Credit policy Federal Reserve policymaking involving direct lending to financial and nonfinancial firms.

Cross price elasticity of demand (E_{xy}) The percentage change in the amount of an item demanded (holding its price constant) divided by the percentage change in the price of a related good.

Crowding-out effect The tendency of expansionary fiscal policy to cause a decrease in planned investment or planned consumption in the private sector. This decrease normally results from the rise in interest rates.

Current account A category of balance of payments transactions that measures the exchange of merchandise, the exchange of services, and unilateral transfers.

Cyclical unemployment Unemployment resulting from business recessions that occur when aggregate (total) demand is insufficient to create full employment.

D

Dead capital Any capital resource that lacks clear title of ownership.

Deadweight loss The portion of consumer surplus that no one in society is able to obtain in a situation of monopoly.

Decreasing-cost industry An industry in which an increase in output leads to a reduction in long-run per-unit costs, such that the long-run industry supply curve slopes downward.

Deflation A sustained decrease in the average of all prices of goods and services in an economy.

Demand A schedule showing how much of a good or service people will purchase at any price during a specified time period, other things being constant.

Demand curve A graphical representation of the demand schedule. It is a negatively sloped line showing the inverse relationship between the price and the quantity demanded (other things being equal).

Demand-pull inflation Inflation caused by increases in aggregate demand not matched by increases in aggregate supply.

Dependent variable A variable whose value changes according to changes in the value of one or more independent variables.

Depository institutions Financial institutions that accept deposits from savers and lend funds from those deposits out at interest.

Depreciation A decrease in the exchange value of one nation's currency in terms of the currency of another nation.

Depression An extremely severe recession.

Derived demand Input factor demand derived from demand for the final product being produced.

Development economics The study of factors that contribute to the economic growth of a country.

Diminishing marginal utility The principle that as more of any good or service is consumed, its *extra* benefit declines. Otherwise stated, increases in total utility from the consumption of a good or service become smaller and smaller as more is consumed during a given time period.

Direct expenditure offsets Actions on the part of the private sector in spending income that offset government fiscal policy actions. Any increase in government spending in an area that competes with the private sector will have some direct expenditure offset.

Direct marketing Advertising targeted at specific consumers, typically in the form of postal mailings, telephone calls, or e-mail messages.

Direct relationship A relationship between two variables that is positive, meaning that an increase in one variable is associated with an increase in the other and a decrease in one variable is associated with a decrease in the other.

Discount rate The interest rate that the Federal Reserve charges for reserves that it lends to depository institutions.

It is sometimes referred to as the *rediscount rate* or, in Canada and England, as the *bank rate*.

Discounting The method by which the present value of a future sum or a future stream of sums is obtained.

Discouraged workers Individuals who have stopped looking for a job because they are convinced that they will not find a suitable one.

Diseconomies of scale Increases in long-run average costs that occur as output increases.

Disposable personal income (DPI) Personal income after personal income taxes have been paid.

Dissaving Negative saving; a situation in which spending exceeds income. Dissaving can occur when a household is able to borrow or use up existing assets.

Distribution of income The way income is allocated among the population based on groupings of residents.

Dividends Portion of a corporation's profits paid to its owners (shareholders).

Division of labor The segregation of resources into different specific tasks. For instance, one automobile worker puts on bumpers, another doors, and so on.

Dominant strategies Strategies that always yield the highest benefit. Regardless of what other players do, a dominant strategy will yield the most benefit for the player using it.

Dumping Selling a good or a service abroad below the price charged in the home market or at a price below its cost of production.

Durable consumer goods Consumer goods that have a life span of more than three years.

Dynamic tax analysis Economic evaluation of tax rate changes that recognizes that the tax base eventually declines with ever-higher tax rates, so that tax revenues may eventually decline if the tax rate is raised sufficiently.

E

Economic freedom The rights to own private property and to exchange goods, services, and financial assets with minimal government interference.

Economic goods Goods that are scarce, for which the quantity demanded exceeds the quantity supplied at a zero price.

Economic growth Increases in per capita real GDP measured by its rate of change per year.

Economic profits Total revenues minus total opportunity costs of all inputs used, or the total of all implicit and explicit costs.

Economic rent A payment for the use of any resource over and above its opportunity cost.

Economic system A society's institutional mechanism for determining the way in which scarce resources are used to satisfy human desires.

Economics The study of how people allocate their limited resources to satisfy their unlimited wants.

Economies of scale Decreases in long-run average costs resulting from increases in output.

Effect time lag The time that elapses between the implementation of a policy and the results of that policy.

Efficiency The case in which a given level of inputs is used to produce the maximum output possible. Alternatively, the situation in which a given output is produced at minimum cost.

Effluent fee A charge to a polluter that gives the right to discharge into the air or water a certain amount of pollution; also called a *pollution tax*.

Elastic demand A demand relationship in which a given percentage change in price will result in a larger percentage change in quantity demanded.

Empirical Relying on real-world data in evaluating the usefulness of a model.

Endowments The various resources in an economy, including both physical resources and such human resources as ingenuity and management skills.

Entitlements Guaranteed benefits under a government program such as Social Security, Medicare, or Medicaid.

Entrepreneurship The component of human resources that performs the functions of raising capital; organizing, managing, and assembling other factors of production; making basic business policy decisions; and taking risks.

Equation of exchange The formula indicating that the number of monetary units (M_s) times the number of times each unit is spent on final goods and services (V) is identical to the price level (P) times real GDP (Y).

Equilibrium The situation when quantity supplied equals quantity demanded at a particular price.

Exchange rate The price of one nation's currency in terms of the currency of another country.

Excise tax A tax levied on purchases of a particular good or service.

Expansion A business fluctuation in which the pace of national economic activity is speeding up.

Expenditure approach Computing GDP by adding up the dollar value at current market prices of all final goods and services.

Experience good A product that an individual must consume before the product's quality can be established.

Explicit costs Costs that business managers must take account of because they must be paid. Examples are wages, taxes, and rent.

Externality A consequence of a diversion of a private cost (or benefit) from a social cost (or benefit). A situation in which the costs (or benefits) of an action are not fully borne (or gained) by the decision makers engaged in an activity that uses scarce resources.

F

Featherbedding Any practice that forces employers to use more labor than they would otherwise or to use existing labor in an inefficient manner.

Federal Deposit Insurance Corporation (FDIC) A government agency that insures the deposits held in banks and most other depository institutions. All U.S. banks are insured this way.

Federal funds market A private market (made up mostly of banks) in which banks can borrow reserves from other banks that want to lend them. Federal funds are usually lent for overnight use.

Federal funds rate The interest rate that depository institutions pay to borrow reserves in the interbank federal funds market.

Fiduciary monetary system A system in which money is issued by the government and its value is based uniquely on the public's faith that the currency represents command over goods and services and will be accepted in payment for debts.

Final goods and services Goods and services that are at their final stage of production and will not be transformed into yet other goods or services. For example, wheat ordinarily is not considered a final good because it is usually used to make a final good, bread.

Financial capital Funds used to purchase physical capital goods, such as buildings and equipment, and patents and trademarks.

Financial intermediaries Institutions that transfer funds between ultimate lenders (savers) and ultimate borrowers.

Financial intermediation The process by which financial institutions accept savings from businesses, households, and governments and lend the savings to other businesses, households, and governments.

Firm A business organization that employs resources to produce goods or services for profit. A firm normally owns and operates at least one "plant" or facility in order to produce.

Fiscal policy The discretionary changing of government expenditures or taxes to achieve national economic goals, such as high employment with price stability.

Fixed costs Costs that do not vary with output. Fixed costs typically include such expenses as rent on a building. These costs are fixed for a certain period of time (in the long run, though, they are variable).

Fixed investment Purchases by businesses of newly produced producer durables, or capital goods, such as production machinery and office equipment.

Flexible exchange rates Exchange rates that are allowed to fluctuate in the open market in response to changes in supply and demand. Sometimes called *floating exchange rates*.

Flow A quantity measured per unit of time; something that occurs over time, such as the income you make per week or per year or the number of individuals who are fired every month.

FOMC Directive A document that summarizes the Federal Open Market Committee's general policy strategy, establishes near-term objectives for the federal funds rate, and specifies target ranges for money supply growth.

Foreign direct investment The acquisition of more than 10 percent of the shares of ownership in a company in another nation.

Foreign exchange market A market in which households, firms, and governments buy and sell national currencies.

Foreign exchange rate The price of one currency in terms of another.

Foreign exchange risk The possibility that changes in the value of a nation's currency will result in variations in the market value of assets.

45-degree reference line The line along which planned real expenditures equal real GDP per year.

Fractional reserve banking A system in which depository institutions hold reserves that are less than the amount of total deposits.

Free-rider problem A problem that arises when individuals presume that others will pay for public goods so that, individually, they can escape paying for their portion without causing a reduction in production.

Frictional unemployment Unemployment due to the fact that workers must search for appropriate job offers. This activity takes time, and so they remain temporarily unemployed.

Full employment An arbitrary level of unemployment that corresponds to "normal" friction in the labor market. In 1986, a 6.5 percent rate of unemployment was considered full employment. Today it is somewhat higher.

G

Gains from trade The sum of consumer surplus and producer surplus.

Game theory A way of describing the various possible outcomes in any situation involving two or more interacting individuals when those individuals are aware of the interactive nature of their situation and plan accordingly. The plans made by these individuals are known as *game strategies*.

GDP deflator A price index measuring the changes in prices of all new goods and services produced in the economy.

General Agreement on Tariffs and Trade (GATT) An international agreement established in 1947 to further world trade by reducing barriers and tariffs. The GATT was replaced by the World Trade Organization in 1995.

Goods All things from which individuals derive satisfaction or happiness.

Government budget constraint The limit on government spending and transfers imposed by the fact that every dollar the government spends, transfers, or uses to repay borrowed funds must ultimately be provided by the user charges and taxes it collects.

Government budget deficit An excess of government spending over government revenues during a given period of time.

Government budget surplus An excess of government revenues over government spending during a given period of time.

Government, or political, goods Goods (and services) provided by the public sector; they can be either private or public goods.

Government-inhibited good A good that has been deemed socially undesirable through the political process. Heroin is an example.

Government-sponsored good A good that has been deemed socially desirable through the political process. Museums are an example.

Gross domestic income (GDI) The sum of all income—wages, interest, rent, and profits—paid to the four factors of production.

Gross domestic product (GDP) The total market value of all final goods and services produced during a year by factors of production located within a nation's borders.

Gross private domestic investment The creation of capital goods, such as factories and machines, that can yield production and hence consumption in the future. Also included in this definition are changes in business inventories and repairs made to machines or buildings.

Gross public debt All federal government debt irrespective of who owns it.

H

Health insurance exchanges Government agencies to which the national health care program assigns the task of assisting individuals, families, and small businesses in identifying health insurance policies to purchase.

Hedge A financial strategy that reduces the chance of suffering losses arising from foreign exchange risk.

Herfindahl-Hirschman Index (HHI) The sum of the squared percentage sales shares of all firms in an industry.

Horizontal merger The joining of firms that are producing or selling a similar product.

Human capital The accumulated training and education of workers.

I

Implicit costs Expenses that managers do not have to pay out of pocket and hence normally do not explicitly calculate, such as the opportunity cost of factors of production that are owned. Examples are owner-provided capital and owner-provided labor.

Import quota A physical supply restriction on imports of a particular good, such as sugar. Foreign exporters are unable to sell in the United States more than the quantity specified in the import quota.

Incentive structure The system of rewards and punishments individuals face with respect to their own actions.

Incentives Rewards or penalties for engaging in a particular activity.

Income approach Measuring GDP by adding up all components of national income, including wages, interest, rent, and profits.

Income elasticity of demand (E_i) The percentage change in the amount of a good demanded, holding its price constant, divided by the percentage change in income. The responsiveness of the amount of a good demanded to a change in income, holding the good's relative price constant.

Income in kind Income received in the form of goods and services, such as housing or medical care. Income in kind differs from money income, which is simply income in dollars, or general purchasing power, that can be used to buy *any* goods and services.

Income velocity of money (V) The number of times per year a dollar is spent on final goods and services; identically equal to nominal GDP divided by the money supply.

Increasing-cost industry An industry in which an increase in industry output is accompanied by an increase in long-run per-unit costs, such that the long-run industry supply curve slopes upward.

Independent variable A variable whose value is determined independently of, or outside, the equation under study.

Indifference curve A curve composed of a set of consumption alternatives, each of which yields the same total amount of satisfaction.

Indirect business taxes All business taxes except the tax on corporate profits. Indirect business taxes include sales and business property taxes.

Industrial unions Labor unions that consist of workers from a particular industry, such as automobile manufacturing or steel manufacturing.

Industry supply curve The locus of points showing the minimum prices at which given quantities will be forthcoming; also called the *market supply curve*.

Inefficient point Any point below the production possibilities curve, at which the use of resources is not generating the maximum possible output.

Inelastic demand A demand relationship in which a given percentage change in price will result in a less-than-proportionate percentage change in the quantity demanded.

Infant industry argument The contention that tariffs should be imposed to protect from import competition an industry that is trying to get started. Presumably, after the industry becomes technologically efficient, the tariff can be lifted.

Inferior goods Goods for which demand falls as income rises.

Inflation A sustained increase in the average of all prices of goods and services in an economy.

Inflationary gap The gap that exists whenever equilibrium real GDP per year is greater than full-employment real GDP as shown by the position of the long-run aggregate supply curve.

Information product An item that is produced using information-intensive inputs at a relatively high fixed cost but distributed for sale at a relatively low marginal cost.

Informational advertising Advertising that emphasizes transmitting knowledge about the features of a product.

Innovation Transforming an invention into something that is useful to humans.

Inside information Information that is not available to the general public about what is happening in a corporation.

Interactive marketing Advertising that permits a consumer to follow up directly by searching for more information and placing direct product orders.

Interest The payment for current rather than future command over resources; the cost of obtaining credit.

Interest rate effect One of the reasons that the aggregate demand curve slopes downward: Higher price levels increase the interest rate, which in turn causes businesses and consumers to reduce desired spending due to the higher cost of borrowing.

Intermediate goods Goods used up entirely in the production of final goods.

International financial crisis The rapid withdrawal of foreign investments and loans from a nation.

International Monetary Fund An agency founded to administer an international foreign exchange system and to lend to member countries that had balance of payments problems. The IMF now functions as a lender of last resort for national governments.

Inventory investment Changes in the stocks of finished goods and goods in process, as well as changes in the raw materials that businesses keep on hand. Whenever inventories are decreasing, inventory investment is negative. Whenever they are increasing, inventory investment is positive.

Inverse relationship A relationship between two variables that is negative, meaning that an increase in one variable is associated with a decrease in the other and a decrease in one variable is associated with an increase in the other.

Investment Spending on items such as machines and buildings, which can be used to produce goods and services in the future. (It also includes changes in business inventories.) The investment part of real GDP is the portion that will be used in the process of producing goods *in the future*.

J

Job leaver An individual in the labor force who quits voluntarily.

Job loser An individual in the labor force whose employment was involuntarily terminated.

Jurisdictional dispute A disagreement involving two or more unions over which should have control of a particular jurisdiction, such as a particular craft or skill or a particular firm or industry.

K

Keynesian short-run aggregate supply curve The horizontal portion of the aggregate supply curve in which there is excessive unemployment and unused capacity in the economy.

L

Labor Productive contributions of humans who work.

Labor force Individuals aged 16 years or older who either have jobs or who are looking and available for jobs; the number of employed plus the number of unemployed.

Labor force participation rate The percentage of noninstitutionalized working-age individuals who are employed or seeking employment.

Labor productivity Total real domestic output (real GDP) divided by the number of workers (output per worker).

Labor unions Worker organizations that seek to secure economic improvements for their members. They also seek to improve the safety, health, and other benefits (such as job security) of their members.

Land The natural resources that are available from nature. Land as a resource includes location, original fertility and mineral deposits, topography, climate, water, and vegetation.

Law of demand The observation that there is a negative, or inverse, relationship between the price of any good or service and the quantity demanded, holding other factors constant.

Law of diminishing marginal product The observation that after some point, successive equal-sized increases in a variable factor of production, such as labor, added to fixed factors of production will result in smaller increases in output.

Law of increasing additional cost The fact that the opportunity cost of additional units of a good generally increases as people attempt to produce more of that good. This accounts for the bowed-out shape of the production possibilities curve.

Law of supply The observation that the higher the price of a good, the more of that good sellers will make available over a specified time period, other things being equal.

Leading indicators Events that have been found to occur before changes in business activity.

Lemons problem The potential for asymmetric information to bring about a general decline in product quality in an industry.

Lender of last resort The Federal Reserve's role as an institution that is willing and able to lend to a temporarily illiquid bank that is otherwise in good financial condition to prevent the bank's illiquid position from leading to a general loss of confidence in that bank or in others.

Liabilities Amounts owed; the legal claims against a business or household by nonowners.

Life-cycle theory of consumption A theory in which a person bases decisions about current consumption and saving on both current income and anticipated future income.

Limited liability A legal concept in which the responsibility, or liability, of the owners of a corporation is limited to the value of the shares in the firm that they own.

Liquidity The degree to which an asset can be acquired or disposed of without much danger of any intervening loss in *nominal* value and with small transaction costs. Money is the most liquid asset.

Liquidity approach A method of measuring the money supply by looking at money as a temporary store of value.

Long run The time period during which all factors of production can be varied.

Long-run aggregate supply curve A vertical line representing the real output of goods and services after full adjustment has occurred. It can also be viewed as representing the real GDP of the economy under conditions of full employment—the full-employment level of real GDP.

Long-run average cost curve The locus of points representing the minimum unit cost of producing any given rate of output, given current technology and resource prices.

Long-run industry supply curve A market supply curve showing the relationship between prices and quantities after firms have been allowed the time to enter into or exit from an industry, depending on whether there have been positive or negative economic profits.

Lorenz curve A geometric representation of the distribution of income. A Lorenz curve that is perfectly straight represents complete income equality. The more bowed a Lorenz curve, the more unequally income is distributed.

Lump-sum tax A tax that does not depend on income. An example is a $1,000 tax that every household must pay, irrespective of its economic situation.

M

M1 The money supply, measured as the total value of currency plus transactions deposits plus traveler's checks not issued by banks.

M2 M1 plus (1) savings deposits at all depository institutions, (2) small-denomination time deposits, and (3) balances in retail money market mutual funds.

Macroeconomics The study of the behavior of the economy as a whole, including such economywide phenomena as changes in unemployment, the general price level, and national income.

Majority rule A collective decision-making system in which group decisions are made on the basis of more than 50 percent of the vote. In other words, whatever more than half of the electorate votes for, the entire electorate has to accept.

Marginal cost pricing A system of pricing in which the price charged is equal to the opportunity cost to society of producing one more unit of the good or service in question. The opportunity cost is the marginal cost to society.

Marginal costs The change in total costs due to a one-unit change in production rate.

Marginal factor cost (MFC) The cost of using an additional unit of an input. For example, if a firm can hire all the workers it wants at the going wage rate, the marginal factor cost of labor is that wage rate.

Marginal physical product The physical output that is due to the addition of one more unit of a variable factor of production. The change in total product occurring when a variable input is increased and all other inputs are held constant. It is also called *marginal product*.

Marginal physical product (MPP) of labor The change in output resulting from the addition of one more worker. The MPP of the worker equals the change in total output accounted for by hiring the worker, holding all other factors of production constant.

Marginal propensity to consume (MPC) The ratio of the change in consumption to the change in disposable income. A marginal propensity to consume of 0.8 tells us that an additional $100 in take-home pay will lead to an additional $80 consumed.

Marginal propensity to save (MPS) The ratio of the change in saving to the change in disposable income. A marginal propensity to save of 0.2 indicates that out of an additional $100 in take-home pay, $20 will be saved. Whatever is not saved is consumed. The marginal propensity to save plus the marginal propensity to consume must always equal 1, by definition.

Marginal revenue The change in total revenues resulting from a one-unit change in output (and sale) of the product in question.

Marginal revenue product (MRP) The marginal physical product (MPP) times marginal revenue (MR). The MRP gives the additional revenue obtained from a one-unit change in labor input.

Marginal tax rate The change in the tax payment divided by the change in income, or the percentage of *additional* dollars that must be paid in taxes. The marginal tax rate is applied to the highest tax bracket of taxable income reached.

Marginal utility The change in total utility due to a one-unit change in the quantity of a good or service consumed.

Market All of the arrangements that individuals have for exchanging with one another. Thus, for example, we can speak of the labor market, the automobile market, and the credit market.

Market clearing, or equilibrium, price The price that clears the market, at which quantity demanded equals quantity supplied; the price where the demand curve intersects the supply curve.

Market demand The demand of all consumers in the marketplace for a particular good or service. The summation at each price of the quantity demanded by each individual.

Market failure A situation in which an unrestrained market operation leads to either too few or too many resources going to a specific economic activity.

Mass marketing Advertising intended to reach as many consumers as possible, typically through television, newspaper, radio, or magazine ads.

Medium of exchange Any item that sellers will accept as payment.

Microeconomics The study of decision making undertaken by individuals (or households) and by firms.

Minimum efficient scale (MES) The lowest rate of output per unit time at which long-run average costs for a particular firm are at a minimum.

Minimum wage A wage floor, legislated by government, setting the lowest hourly rate that firms may legally pay workers.

Models, or theories Simplified representations of the real world used as the basis for predictions or explanations.

Money Any medium that is universally accepted in an economy both by sellers of goods and services as payment for those goods and services and by creditors as payment for debts.

Money balances Synonymous with money, money stock, money holdings.

Money illusion Reacting to changes in money prices rather than relative prices. If a worker whose wages double when the price level also doubles thinks he or she is better off, that worker is suffering from money illusion.

Money multiplier A number that, when multiplied by a change in reserves in the banking system, yields the resulting change in the money supply.

Money price The price expressed in today's dollars; also called the *absolute* or *nominal price*.

Money supply The amount of money in circulation.

Monopolist The single supplier of a good or service for which there is no close substitute. The monopolist therefore constitutes its entire industry.

Monopolistic competition A market situation in which a large number of firms produce similar but not identical products. Entry into the industry is relatively easy.

Monopolization The possession of monopoly power in the relevant market and the willful acquisition or maintenance of that power, as distinguished from growth or development as a consequence of a superior product, business acumen, or historical accident.

Monopoly A firm that can determine the market price of a good. In the extreme case, a monopoly is the only seller of a good or service.

Monopsonist The only buyer in a market.

Monopsonistic exploitation Paying a price for the variable input that is less than its marginal revenue product; the difference between marginal revenue product and the wage rate.

Moral hazard The possibility that a borrower might engage in riskier behavior after a loan has been obtained.

Multiplier The ratio of the change in the equilibrium level of real GDP to the change in autonomous real expenditures. The number by which a change in autonomous real investment or autonomous real consumption, for example, is multiplied to get the change in equilibrium real GDP.

N

National income (NI) The total of all factor payments to resource owners. It can be obtained from net domestic product (NDP) by subtracting indirect business taxes and transfers and adding net U.S. income earned abroad and other business income adjustments.

National income accounting A measurement system used to estimate national income and its components. One approach to measuring an economy's aggregate performance.

Natural monopoly A monopoly that arises from the peculiar production characteristics in an industry. It usually arises when there are large economies of scale relative to the industry's demand such that one firm can produce at a lower average cost than can be achieved by multiple firms.

Natural rate of unemployment The rate of unemployment that is estimated to prevail in long-run macroeconomic equilibrium, when all workers and employers have fully adjusted to any changes in the economy.

Negative market feedback A tendency for a good or service to fall out of favor with more consumers because other consumers have stopped purchasing the item.

Negative-sum game A game in which players as a group lose during the process of the game.

Net domestic product (NDP) GDP minus depreciation.

Net investment Gross private domestic investment minus an estimate of the wear and tear on the existing capital stock. Net investment therefore measures the change in the capital stock over a one-year period.

Net public debt Gross public debt minus all government interagency borrowing.

Net wealth The stock of assets owned by a person, household, firm, or nation (net of any debts owed). For a household, net wealth can consist of a house, cars, personal belongings, stocks, bonds, bank accounts, and cash (minus any debts owed).

Network effect A situation in which a consumer's willingness to purchase a good or service is influenced by how many others also buy or have bought the item.

New entrant An individual who has never held a full-time job lasting two weeks or longer but is now seeking employment.

New growth theory A theory of economic growth that examines the factors that determine why technology, research, innovation, and the like are undertaken and how they interact.

New Keynesian inflation dynamics In new Keynesian theory, the pattern of inflation exhibited by an economy with growing aggregate demand—initial sluggish adjustment of the price level in response to increased aggregate demand followed by higher inflation later.

Nominal rate of interest The market rate of interest observed in contracts expressed in today's dollars.

Nominal values The values of variables such as GDP and investment expressed in current dollars, also called *money values*; measurement in terms of the actual market prices at which goods and services are sold.

Noncontrollable expenditures Government spending that changes automatically without action by Congress.

Noncooperative game A game in which the players neither negotiate nor cooperate in any way. As applied to firms in an industry, this is the common situation in which there are relatively few firms and each has some ability to change price.

Nondurable consumer goods Consumer goods that are used up within three years.

Nonincome expense items The total of indirect business taxes and depreciation.

Nonprice rationing devices All methods used to ration scarce goods that are price-controlled. Whenever the price system is not allowed to work, nonprice rationing devices will evolve to ration the affected goods and services.

Normal goods Goods for which demand rises as income rises. Most goods are normal goods.

Normal rate of return The amount that must be paid to an investor to induce investment in a business. Also known as the *opportunity cost of capital*.

Normative economics Analysis involving value judgments about economic policies; relates to whether outcomes are good or bad. A statement of *what ought to be*.

Number line A line that can be divided into segments of equal length, each associated with a number.

O

Oligopoly A market structure in which there are very few sellers. Each seller knows that the other sellers will react to its changes in prices, quantities, and qualities.

Open economy effect One of the reasons that the aggregate demand curve slopes downward: Higher price levels result in foreign residents desiring to buy fewer U.S.-made goods, while U.S. residents now desire more foreign-made goods, thereby reducing net exports. This is equivalent to a reduction in the amount of real goods and services purchased in the United States.

Open market operations The purchase and sale of existing U.S. government securities (such as bonds) in the open private market by the Federal Reserve System.

Opportunistic behavior Actions that focus solely on short-run gains because long-run benefits of cooperation are perceived to be smaller.

Opportunity cost The highest-valued, next-best alternative that must be sacrificed to obtain something or to satisfy a want.

Opportunity cost of capital The normal rate of return, or the available return on the next-best alternative investment. Economists consider this a cost of production, and it is included in our cost examples.

Optimal quantity of pollution The level of pollution for which the marginal benefit of one additional unit of pollution abatement just equals the marginal cost of that additional unit of pollution abatement.

Origin The intersection of the *y* axis and the *x* axis in a graph.

Outsourcing A firm's employment of labor outside the country in which the firm is located.

P

Par value The officially determined value of a currency.

Partnership A business owned by two or more joint owners, or partners, who share the responsibilities and the profits of the firm and are individually liable for all the debts of the partnership.

Passive (nondiscretionary) policymaking Policymaking that is carried out in response to a rule. It is therefore not in response to an actual or potential change in overall economic activity.

Patent A government protection that gives an inventor the exclusive right to make, use, or sell an invention for a limited period of time (currently, 20 years).

Payoff matrix A matrix of outcomes, or consequences, of the strategies available to the players in a game.

Perfect competition A market structure in which the decisions of *individual* buyers and sellers have no effect on market price.

Perfectly competitive firm A firm that is such a small part of the total *industry* that it cannot affect the price of the product it sells.

Perfectly elastic demand A demand that has the characteristic that even the slightest increase in price will lead to zero quantity demanded.

Perfectly elastic supply A supply characterized by a reduction in quantity supplied to zero when there is the slightest decrease in price.

Perfectly inelastic demand A demand that exhibits zero responsiveness to price changes. No matter what the price is, the quantity demanded remains the same.

Perfectly inelastic supply A supply for which quantity supplied remains constant, no matter what happens to price.

Permanent income hypothesis A theory of consumption in which an individual determines current consumption based on anticipated average lifetime income.

Personal Consumption Expenditure (PCE) Index A statistical measure of average prices that uses annually updated weights based on surveys of consumer spending.

Personal income (PI) The amount of income that households actually receive before they pay personal income taxes.

Persuasive advertising Advertising that is intended to induce a consumer to purchase a particular product and discover a previously unknown taste for the item.

Phillips curve A curve showing the relationship between unemployment and changes in wages or prices. It was long thought to reflect a trade-off between unemployment and inflation.

Physical capital All manufactured resources, including buildings, equipment, machines, and improvements to land that are used for production.

Planning curve The long-run average cost curve.

Planning horizon The long run, during which all inputs are variable.

Plant size The physical size of the factories that a firm owns and operates to produce its output. Plant size can be defined by square footage, maximum physical capacity, and other physical measures.

Policy irrelevance proposition The conclusion that policy actions have no real effects in the short run if the policy actions are anticipated and none in the long run even if the policy actions are unanticipated.

Portfolio investment The purchase of less than 10 percent of the shares of ownership in a company in another nation.

Positive economics Analysis that is *strictly* limited to making either purely descriptive statements or scientific predictions; for example, "If A, then B." A statement of *what is*.

Positive market feedback A tendency for a good or service to come into favor with additional consumers because other consumers have chosen to buy the item.

Positive-sum game A game in which players as a group are better off at the end of the game.

Potential money multiplier The reciprocal of the reserve ratio, assuming no leakages into currency. It is equal to 1 divided by the reserve ratio.

Precautionary demand Holding money to meet unplanned expenditures and emergencies.

Present value The value of a future amount expressed in today's dollars; the most that someone would pay today to receive a certain sum at some point in the future.

Price ceiling A legal maximum price that may be charged for a particular good or service.

Price controls Government-mandated minimum or maximum prices that may be charged for goods and services.

Price differentiation Establishing different prices for similar products to reflect differences in marginal cost in providing those commodities to different groups of buyers.

Price discrimination Selling a given product at more than one price, with the price difference being unrelated to differences in marginal cost.

Price elasticity of demand (E_p) The responsiveness of the quantity demanded of a commodity to changes in its price; defined as the percentage change in quantity demanded divided by the percentage change in price.

Price elasticity of supply (E_s) The responsiveness of the quantity supplied of a commodity to a change in its price—the percentage change in quantity supplied divided by the percentage change in price.

Price floor A legal minimum price below which a good or service may not be sold. Legal minimum wages are an example.

Price index The cost of today's market basket of goods expressed as a percentage of the cost of the same market basket during a base year.

Price searcher A firm that must determine the price-output combination that maximizes profit because it faces a downward-sloping demand curve.

Price system An economic system in which relative prices are constantly changing to reflect changes in supply and demand for different commodities. The prices of those commodities are signals to everyone within the system as to what is relatively scarce and what is relatively abundant.

Price taker A perfectly competitive firm that must take the price of its product as given because the firm cannot influence its price.

Principle of rival consumption The recognition that individuals are rivals in consuming private goods because one person's consumption reduces the amount available for others to consume.

Principle of substitution The principle that consumers shift away from goods and services that become priced relatively higher in favor of goods and services that are now priced relatively lower.

Prisoners' dilemma A famous strategic game in which two prisoners have a choice between confessing and not confessing to a crime. If neither confesses, they serve a minimum sentence. If both confess, they serve a longer sentence. If one confesses and the other doesn't, the one who confesses goes free. The dominant strategy is always to confess.

Private costs Costs borne solely by the individuals who incur them. Also called *internal costs*.

Private goods Goods that can be consumed by only one individual at a time. Private goods are subject to the principle of rival consumption.

Private property rights Exclusive rights of ownership that allow the use, transfer, and exchange of property.

Producer durables, or capital goods Durable goods having an expected service life of more than three years that are used by businesses to produce other goods and services.

Producer Price Index (PPI) A statistical measure of a weighted average of prices of goods and services that firms produce and sell.

Producer surplus The difference between the total amount that producers actually receive for an item and the total amount that they would have been willing to accept for supplying that item.

Product differentiation The distinguishing of products by brand name, color, and other minor attributes. Product differentiation occurs in other than perfectly competitive markets in which products are, in theory, homogeneous, such as wheat or corn.

Production Any activity that results in the conversion of resources into products that can be used in consumption.

Production function The relationship between inputs and maximum physical output. A production function is a technological, not an economic, relationship.

Production possibilities curve (PPC) A curve representing all possible combinations of maximum outputs that could be produced, assuming a fixed amount of productive resources of a given quality.

Profit-maximizing rate of production The rate of production that maximizes total profits, or the difference between total revenues and total costs. Also, it is the rate of production at which marginal revenue equals marginal cost.

Progressive taxation A tax system in which, as income increases, a higher percentage of the additional income is paid as taxes. The marginal tax rate exceeds the average tax rate as income rises.

Property rights The rights of an owner to use and to exchange property.

Proportional rule A decision-making system in which actions are based on the proportion of the "votes" cast and are in proportion to them. In a market system, if 10 percent of the "dollar votes" are cast for blue cars, 10 percent of automobile output will be blue cars.

Proportional taxation A tax system in which, regardless of an individual's income, the tax bill comprises exactly the same proportion.

Proprietorship A business owned by one individual who makes the business decisions, receives all the profits, and is legally responsible for the debts of the firm.

Public debt The total value of all outstanding federal government securities.

Public goods Goods for which the principle of rival consumption does not apply and for which exclusion of non-paying consumers is too costly to be feasible. They can be jointly consumed by many individuals simultaneously at no additional cost and with no reduction in quality or quantity. Furthermore, no one who fails to help pay for the good can be denied the benefit of the good.

Purchasing power The value of money for buying goods and services. If your money income stays the same but the price of one good that you are buying goes up, your effective purchasing power falls.

Purchasing power parity Adjustment in exchange rate conversions that takes into account differences in the true cost of living across countries.

Q

Quantitative easing Federal Reserve open market purchases intended to generate an increase in bank reserves at a nearly zero interest rate.

Quantity theory of money and prices The hypothesis that changes in the money supply lead to equiproportional changes in the price level.

Quota subscription A nation's account with the International Monetary Fund, denominated in special drawing rights.

Quota system A government-imposed restriction on the quantity of a specific good that another country is allowed to sell in the United States. In other words, quotas are restrictions on imports. These restrictions are usually applied to one or several specific countries.

R

Random walk theory The theory that there are no predictable trends in securities prices that can be used to "get rich quick."

Rate of discount The rate of interest used to discount future sums back to present value.

Rate-of-return regulation Regulation that seeks to keep the rate of return in an industry at a competitive level by not allowing prices that would produce economic profits.

Rational expectations hypothesis A theory stating that people combine the effects of past policy changes on important economic variables with their own judgment about the future effects of current and future policy changes.

Rationality assumption The assumption that people do not intentionally make decisions that would leave them worse off.

Reaction function The manner in which one oligopolist reacts to a change in price, output, or quality made by another oligopolist in the industry.

Real disposable income Real GDP minus net taxes, or after-tax real income.

Real rate of interest The nominal rate of interest minus the anticipated rate of inflation.

Real values Measurement of economic values after adjustments have been made for changes in the average of prices between years.

Real-balance effect The change in expenditures resulting from a change in the real value of money balances when the price level changes, all other things held constant; also called the *wealth effect*.

Real-income effect The change in people's purchasing power that occurs when, other things being constant, the price of one good that they purchase changes. When that price goes up, real income, or purchasing power, falls, and when that price goes down, real income increases.

Recession A period of time during which the rate of growth of business activity is consistently less than its long-term trend or is negative.

Recessionary gap The gap that exists whenever equilibrium real GDP per year is less than full-employment real GDP as shown by the position of the long-run aggregate supply curve.

Recognition time lag The time required to gather information about the current state of the economy.

Reentrant An individual who used to work full-time but left the labor force and has now reentered it looking for a job.

Regional trade bloc A group of nations that grants members special trade privileges.

Regressive taxation A tax system in which as more dollars are earned, the percentage of tax paid on them falls. The marginal tax rate is less than the average tax rate as income rises.

Reinvestment Profits (or depreciation reserves) used to purchase new capital equipment.

Relative price The money price of one commodity divided by the money price of another commodity; the number of units of one commodity that must be sacrificed to purchase one unit of another commodity.

Relevant market A group of firms' products that are closely substitutable and available to consumers within a geographic area.

Rent control Price ceilings on rents.

Repricing, or menu, cost of inflation The cost associated with recalculating prices and printing new price lists when there is inflation.

Reserve ratio The fraction of transactions deposits that banks hold as reserves.

Reserves In the U.S. Federal Reserve System, deposits held by Federal Reserve district banks for depository institutions, plus depository institutions' vault cash.

Resources Things used to produce goods and services to satisfy people's wants.

Retained earnings Earnings that a corporation saves, or retains, for investment in other productive activities; earnings that are not distributed to stockholders.

Ricardian equivalence theorem The proposition that an increase in the government budget deficit has no effect on aggregate demand.

Right-to-work laws Laws that make it illegal to require union membership as a condition of continuing employment in a particular firm.

Rule of 70 A rule stating that the approximate number of years required for per capita real GDP to double is equal to 70 divided by the average rate of economic growth.

Rules of origin Regulations that nations in regional trade blocs establish to delineate product categories eligible for trading preferences.

S

Sales taxes Taxes assessed on the prices paid on most goods and services.

Saving The act of not consuming all of one's current income. Whatever is not consumed out of spendable income is, by definition, saved. *Saving* is an action measured over time (a flow), whereas *savings* are a stock, an accumulation resulting from the act of saving in the past.

Say's law A dictum of economist J. B. Say that supply creates its own demand. Producing goods and services generates the means and the willingness to purchase other goods and services.

Scarcity A situation in which the ingredients for producing the things that people desire are insufficient to satisfy all wants at a zero price.

Search good A product with characteristics that enable an individual to evaluate the product's quality in advance of a purchase.

Seasonal unemployment Unemployment resulting from the seasonal pattern of work in specific industries. It is usually due to seasonal fluctuations in demand or to changing weather conditions that render work difficult, if not impossible, as in the agriculture, construction, and tourist industries.

Secondary boycott A refusal to deal with companies or purchase products sold by companies that are dealing with a company being struck.

Secular deflation A persistent decline in prices resulting from economic

growth in the presence of stable aggregate demand.

Securities Stocks and bonds.

Services Mental or physical labor or assistance purchased by consumers. Examples are the assistance of physicians, lawyers, dentists, repair personnel, housecleaners, educators, retailers, and wholesalers; items purchased or used by consumers that do not have physical characteristics.

Share of stock A legal claim to a share of a corporation's future profits. If it is *common stock*, it incorporates certain voting rights regarding major policy decisions of the corporation. If it is *preferred stock*, its owners are accorded preferential treatment in the payment of dividends but do not have any voting rights.

Share-the-gains, share-the-pains theory A theory of regulatory behavior that holds that regulators must take account of the demands of three groups: legislators, who established and oversee the regulatory agency; firms in the regulated industry; and consumers of the regulated industry's products.

Short run The time period during which at least one input, such as plant size, cannot be changed.

Shortage A situation in which quantity demanded is greater than quantity supplied at a price below the market clearing price.

Short-run aggregate supply curve The relationship between total planned economywide production and the price level in the short run, all other things held constant. If prices adjust incompletely in the short run, the curve is positively sloped.

Short-run break-even price The price at which a firm's total revenues equal its total costs. At the break-even price, the firm is just making a normal rate of return on its capital investment. (It is covering its explicit and implicit costs.)

Short-run economies of operation A distinguishing characteristic of an information product arising from declining short-run average total cost as more units of the product are sold.

Short-run shutdown price The price that covers average variable costs. It occurs just below the intersection of the marginal cost curve and the average variable cost curve.

Signals Compact ways of conveying to economic decision makers information needed to make decisions. An effective signal not only conveys information but also provides the incentive to react appropriately. Economic profits and economic losses are such signals.

Slope The change in the y value divided by the corresponding change in the x

value of a curve; the "incline" of the curve.

Small menu costs Costs that deter firms from changing prices in response to demand changes–for example, the costs of renegotiating contracts or printing new price lists.

Social costs The full costs borne by society whenever a resource use occurs. Social costs can be measured by adding external costs to private, or internal, costs.

Special drawing rights (SDRs) Reserve assets created by the International Monetary Fund for countries to use in settling international payment obligations.

Specialization The organization of economic activity so that what each person (or region) consumes is not identical to what that person (or region) produces. An individual may specialize, for example, in law or medicine. A nation may specialize in the production of coffee, e-book readers, or digital cameras.

Stagflation A situation characterized by lower real GDP, lower employment, and a higher unemployment rate during the same period that the rate of inflation increases.

Standard of deferred payment A property of an item that makes it desirable for use as a means of settling debts maturing in the future; an essential property of money.

Static tax analysis Economic evaluation of the effects of tax rate changes under the assumption that there is no effect on the tax base, meaning that there is an unambiguous positive relationship between tax rates and tax revenues.

Stock The quantity of something, measured at a given point in time—for example, an inventory of goods or a bank account. Stocks are defined independently of time, although they are assessed at a point in time.

Store of value The ability to hold value over time; a necessary property of money.

Strategic dependence A situation in which one firm's actions with respect to price, quality, advertising, and related changes may be strategically countered by the reactions of one or more other firms in the industry. Such dependence can exist only when there are a limited number of major firms in an industry.

Strategy Any rule that is used to make a choice, such as "Always pick heads."

Strikebreakers Temporary or permanent workers hired by a company to replace union members who are striking.

Structural unemployment Unemployment of workers over lengthy intervals resulting from skill mismatches with position requirements of employers and from fewer jobs being offered by

employers constrained by governmental business regulations and labor market policies.

Subsidy A negative tax; a payment to a producer from the government, usually in the form of a cash grant per unit.

Substitutes Two goods are substitutes when a change in the price of one causes a shift in demand for the other in the same direction as the price change.

Substitution effect The tendency of people to substitute cheaper commodities for more expensive commodities.

Supply A schedule showing the relationship between price and quantity supplied for a specified period of time, other things being equal.

Supply curve The graphical representation of the supply schedule; a line (curve) showing the supply schedule, which generally slopes upward (has a positive slope), other things being equal.

Supply-side economics The suggestion that creating incentives for individuals and firms to increase productivity will cause the aggregate supply curve to shift outward.

Surplus A situation in which quantity supplied is greater than quantity demanded at a price above the market clearing price.

Sympathy strike A work stoppage by a union in sympathy with another union's strike or cause.

T

Tariffs Taxes on imported goods.

Tax base The value of goods, services, wealth, or incomes subject to taxation.

Tax bracket A specified interval of income to which a specific and unique marginal tax rate is applied.

Tax incidence The distribution of tax burdens among various groups in society.

Tax rate The proportion of a tax base that must be paid to a government as taxes.

Taylor rule An equation that specifies a federal funds rate target based on an estimated long-run real interest rate, the current deviation of the actual inflation rate from the Federal Reserve's inflation objective, and the gap between actual real GDP per year and a measure of potential real GDP per year.

Technology The total pool of applied knowledge concerning how goods and services can be produced.

The Fed The Federal Reserve System; the central bank of the United States.

Theory of public choice The study of collective decision making.

Third parties Parties who are not directly involved in a given activity or transaction. For example, in the

relationship between caregivers and patients, fees may be paid by third parties (insurance companies, government).

Thrift institutions Financial institutions that receive most of their funds from the savings of the public. They include savings banks, savings and loan associations, and credit unions.

Tie-in sales Purchases of one product that are permitted by the seller only if the consumer buys another good or service from the same firm.

Tit-for-tat strategic behavior In game theory, cooperation that continues as long as the other players continue to cooperate.

Total costs The sum of total fixed costs and total variable costs.

Total income The yearly amount earned by the nation's resources (factors of production). Total income therefore includes wages, rent, interest payments, and profits that are received by workers, landowners, capital owners, and entrepreneurs, respectively.

Total revenues The price per unit times the total quantity sold.

Trade deflection Moving partially assembled products into a member nation of a regional trade bloc, completing assembly, and then exporting them to other nations within the bloc, so as to benefit from preferences granted by the trade bloc.

Trade diversion Shifting existing international trade from countries outside a regional trade bloc to nations within the bloc.

Trading Desk An office at the Federal Reserve Bank of New York charged with implementing monetary policy strategies developed by the Federal Open Market Committee.

Transaction costs All of the costs associated with exchange, including the informational costs of finding out the price and quality, service record, and durability of a product, plus the cost of contracting and enforcing that contract.

Transactions approach A method of measuring the money supply by looking at money as a medium of exchange.

Transactions demand Holding money as a medium of exchange to make payments. The level varies directly with nominal GDP.

Transactions deposits Checkable and debitable account balances in commercial banks and other types of financial institutions, such as credit unions and savings banks. Any accounts in financial institutions from which you can easily transmit debit-card and check payments without many restrictions.

Transfer payments Money payments made by governments to individuals for which no services or goods are rendered in return. Examples are Social Security old-age and disability benefits and unemployment insurance benefits.

Transfers in kind Payments that are in the form of actual goods and services, such as food stamps, subsidized public housing, and medical care, and for which no goods or services are rendered in return.

Traveler's checks Financial instruments obtained from a bank or a nonbanking organization and signed during purchase that can be used in payment upon a second signature by the purchaser.

Two-sided market A market in which an intermediary firm provides services that link groups of producers and consumers.

U

Unanticipated inflation Inflation at a rate that comes as a surprise, either higher or lower than the rate anticipated.

Unemployment The total number of adults (aged 16 years or older) who are willing and able to work and who are actively looking for work but have not found a job.

Union shop A business enterprise that may hire nonunion members, conditional on their joining the union by some specified date after employment begins.

Unit elasticity of demand A demand relationship in which the quantity demanded changes exactly in proportion to the change in price.

Unit of accounting A measure by which prices are expressed; the common denominator of the price system; a central property of money.

Unit tax A constant tax assessed on each unit of a good that consumers purchase.

Unlimited liability A legal concept whereby the personal assets of the owner of a firm can be seized to pay off the firm's debts.

Util A representative unit by which utility is measured.

Utility The want-satisfying power of a good or service.

Utility analysis The analysis of consumer decision making based on utility maximization.

V

Value added The dollar value of an industry's sales minus the value of intermediate goods (for example, raw materials and parts) used in production.

Variable costs Costs that vary with the rate of production. They include wages paid to workers and purchases of materials.

Versioning Selling a product in slightly altered forms to different groups of consumers.

Vertical merger The joining of a firm with another to which it sells an output or from which it buys an input.

Voluntary exchange An act of trading, done on an elective basis, in which both parties to the trade expect to be better off after the exchange.

Voluntary import expansion (VIE) An official agreement with another country in which it agrees to import more from the United States.

Voluntary restraint agreement (VRA) An official agreement with another country that "voluntarily" restricts the quantity of its exports to the United States.

W

Wants What people would buy if their incomes were unlimited.

World Bank A multinational agency that specializes in making loans to about 100 developing nations in an effort to promote their long-term development and growth.

World Trade Organization (WTO) The successor organization to the GATT that handles trade disputes among its member nations.

X

x **axis** The horizontal axis in a graph.

Y

y **axis** The vertical axis in a graph.

Z

Zero-sum game A game in which any gains within the group are exactly offset by equal losses by the end of the game.

Index

... Interest Rate

... of inflation

... interest

... rest

Marginal versus Average Tax Rates

$$\text{Marginal tax rate} = \frac{\text{change in taxes due}}{\text{change in taxable income}}$$

$$\text{Average tax rate} = \frac{\text{total taxes due}}{\text{total taxable income}}$$

GDP—The Expenditure and Income Approaches

$$GDP = C + I + G + X$$

where C = consumption expenditures
$\quad I$ = investment expenditures
$\quad G$ = government expenditures
$\quad X$ = net exports

$$GDP = \text{wages} + \text{rent} + \text{interest} + \text{profits}$$

Say's Law

Supply creates its own demand, or *desired* aggregate expenditures will equal *actual* aggregate expenditures.

Saving, Consumption, and Investment

$$\text{Consumption} + \text{saving} = \text{disposable income}$$

$$\text{Saving} = \text{disposable income} - \text{consumption}$$

Average and Marginal Propensities

$$APC = \frac{\text{real consumption}}{\text{real disposable income}}$$

$$APS = \frac{\text{real saving}}{\text{real disposable income}}$$

$$MPC = \frac{\text{change in real consumption}}{\text{change in real disposable income}}$$

$$MPS = \frac{\text{change in real saving}}{\text{change in real disposable income}}$$

The Multiplier Formula

$$\text{Multiplier} = \frac{1}{MPS} = \frac{1}{1 - MPC}$$

$$\text{Multiplier} \times \begin{array}{c}\text{change in}\\ \text{autonomous}\\ \text{real spending}\end{array} = \begin{array}{c}\text{change in}\\ \text{equilibrium}\\ \text{real GDP}\end{array}$$

Relationship between Bond Prices and Interest Rates

The market price of existing (old) bonds is inversely related to "the" rate of interest prevailing in the economy.

Government Spending and Taxation Multipliers

$$M_g = \frac{1}{MPS}$$

$$M_t = -MPC \times \frac{1}{MPS}$$